SECOND EDITION

UNDERSTANDING BEHAVIORS FOR EFFECTIVE LEADERSHIP

Jon P. Howell

New Mexico State University
College of Business Administration and Economics

Dan L. Costley
(Deceased)

Formerly with New Mexico State University
College of Business Administration and Economics

PEARSON

Prentice
Hall

Upper Saddle River, NJ 07458

Library of Congress Cataloging-in-Publication Data

Howell, Jon P.
   Understanding behaviors for effective leadership / Jon P. Howell, Dan
L. Costley.—2nd ed.
     p. cm.
   Includes bibliographical references and index.
   ISBN 0-13-148452-4
   1. Organizational behavior. 2. Psychology, Industrial.
3. Supervision of employees. 4. Leadership. I. Title: Effective
leadership. II. Costley, Dan L. III. Title.

HD58.7.H684 2006
158.7—dc22

2004031091

Editorial Director: Jeff Shelstad
Senior Acquisition Editor: David Parker
Project Manager: Ashley Santora
Editorial Assistant: Denise Vaughn
Marketing Manager: Anke Braun
Marketing Assistant: Patrick Danzusa
Managing Editor: John Roberts
Production Editor: Renata Butera
Permissions Supervisor: Charles Morris
Manufacturing Buyer: Michelle Klein

Design Director: Marie Lange
Cover Design: Jayne Conte
Cover Illustration Photo: Jimmy Chin/
National Geographic/Getty Images, Inc.
**Composition/Full-Service Project
Management:** Interactive Composition
Corporation
Printer/Binder: R.R. Donnelley
Harrisonburg
Typeface: 10/12 Times Ten Roman

Credits and acknowledgments borrowed from other sources and reproduced, with permission, in this textbook appear on appropriate page within the text.

Microsoft® and Windows® are registered trademarks of the Microsoft Corporation in the U.S.A. and other countries. Screen shots and icons reprinted with permission from the Microsoft Corporation. This book is not sponsored or endorsed by or affiliated with the Microsoft Corporation.

Pearson Education LTD.
Pearson Education Singapore, Pte. Ltd
Pearson Education, Canada, Ltd
Pearson Education–Japan

Pearson Education Australia PTY, Limited
Pearson Education North Asia Ltd
Pearson Educación de Mexico, S.A. de C.V.
Pearson Education Malaysia, Pte. Ltd

10 9 8 7 6 5 4 3 2 1
ISBN 0-13-148452-4

To Julie, Jesse, Matt, Rachel Lee,
and for Dan

Contents

x ▐▐▐▐ Contents

Preface

In the second edition of this book we emphasize that leaders' effectiveness is determined by what they do. Leaders demonstrate their competence by setting worthwhile and challenging goals with followers, by showing confidence in followers and supporting their efforts to perform well and improve themselves, by giving recognition to followers when they do a job well, and by behaving in a fair and ethical manner. We expect our leaders to perform these and other important leadership behaviors. We may also expect leaders to be intelligent, visionary, inspirational, self-confident, and assertive, but we only perceive these personal characteristics by observing and experiencing a leader's behavior. When leaders successfully carry out these behaviors and produce favorable results for their groups and organizations, we view these leaders as effective.

We have been teaching leadership in universities and colleges for over 25 years. We became frustrated with the use of existing textbooks and articles in these classes when students became lost in the mass of leadership theories and research presented. There were simply too many theories and approaches to leadership for most undergraduates (and many MBA students) to absorb and use. By the end of the course, they usually had no idea when or if a given theory was appropriate and often latched on to an overly simplistic and poorly supported model of leadership because it was simple enough for them to understand and remember.

Just as in the first edition of this book, we have not emphasized leadership theories in this second edition. Instead, we organized the book according to a simple common-sense structure that describes current knowledge on what effective leaders really do. Most of the leadership behaviors described in the chapters that follow have been extensively researched as part of various theoretical models proposed by leadership scholars. Several chapters have been combined in this edition in order to provide a more integrated understanding of leadership behaviors and how they are effectively used. We have presented what is known about each leadership behavior without the baggage of many different theories. Although these leadership behaviors may overlap to some degree, they are widely recognized and discussed by managers and leadership experts. This structure is designed to minimize confusion, to facilitate understanding, and to provide students with some psychological closure on each leadership behavior.

Changes in the Second Edition

The second edition of *Understanding Behaviors for Effective Leadership* updates the first edition with recent research findings and developments in leadership practices. We added new chapters on leadership ethics and diversity (Chapter 12), and leadership development and organizational change (Chapter 13). These are currently hot topics among organizational leaders, and were requested by reviewers of the first edition. Other new features include material on current leadership issues (Chapter 1), leaders' influence tactics (Chapter 2), the Normative Decision-Making model of participative leadership (Chapter 3), transformational leadership and the Full Range Leadership theory (Chapter 8), leadership in different types of teams (Chapter 9), negotiation (Chapter 9), organizational fairness or justice (Chapter 10), and cross-cultural leadership (Chapter 14).

New material was also added throughout this edition in the form of:

- New examples of practicing leaders
- More cases and examples from nonbusiness organizations
- New cases that are longer and more detailed than the first edition
- New self-assessments that focus on feedback and development of aspiring leaders
- New discussion questions at the end of chapters

Extensive classic and current references are also provided throughout this edition for readers who wish to learn more about specific topics. Additional cases and case notes are also provided in the instructor's manual that accompanies this edition.

▬▬▬ Audience

This book is intended for use in any college course that focuses on effective leadership. Examples of these courses include leadership in society, leadership and motivation, nursing leadership, not-for-profit leadership, leadership in law enforcement, or leadership in education. The book is also appropriate for a first course in leadership training in business, public, educational, health care, or other organizations.

▬▬▬ Structure and Features

Part I of the book includes three chapters that introduce the concept of leadership and the approach of the book, and describe and evaluate several currently popular theories of leadership. Part II is composed of five chapters that focus on five core leadership behavior patterns that have been studied extensively in different organizational contexts. These chapters are devoted to leaders' supportive, directive, participation, reward and punishment, and charismatic behaviors. These core chapters emphasize *what effective leaders do* by describing in detail each of the core leadership behaviors. They also describe leaders' traits, skills, and sources of power associated with each behavior, as well as examples of effective and ineffective leaders carrying out the behaviors. The core chapters also describe *when leaders use each behavior* by identifying situational factors that tell effective leaders when a specific core behavior will be most effective. Part III presents three chapters addressing less-researched leadership behavior patterns that are increasingly important in the 21st century. These behaviors include leaders' boundary spanning, building social exchanges, and followership. Part IV describes the current leadership issues of ethics, diversity, leadership development, and change. It also includes a concluding chapter that integrates findings from earlier chapters and describes popular leadership styles that are combinations of the specific leadership behaviors described earlier.

This edition also emphasizes the effects of the increasing number of jobs performed by highly educated and professionally oriented employees who use computer technology or teams to perform job activities. These individuals and teams are often able to assume more responsibility with less active direction and control by their formal leaders. These emerging workforce and job structure characteristics do not eliminate the need for leadership, but they help organizations economize by reducing the number of middle managers and allowing workers and work groups more freedom to manage their own daily activities.

Examples are provided in each chapter that highlight current and historical leaders who exhibit the leadership behaviors and styles discussed. Self-assessment exercises also help the reader understand and apply concepts described in the text. Exercises and cases are also included to allow students to further understand and apply chapter material. Numerous illustrations and figures also summarize text material and provide advice on how to apply the material to real leadership situations.

▪▪▪ Instructor's Material

Instructor's Resource Center on CD-ROM: The Instructor's Resource Center, available on CD, includes presentation and classroom resources. Instructors can collect the materials, edit them to create powerful class lectures, and upload them to an online course management system. Using the Instructor's Resource Center, instructors can easily create custom presentations. Select a chapter from the table of contents to see a list of available resources or simply search by keyword. After you've found the files you'd like to use, click on each to select, and place in your export list for exporting to your computer's hard drive or other disk. The Instructor's Resource Center on CD will organize your newly created files into folders according to file type.

With the Instructor's Resource Center, you will find the following faculty supplements:

PowerPoints: A comprehensive package of text outlines and figures corresponding to the text, the PowerPoint transparencies are designed to aid the educator and supplement in-class lectures.

Instructor's Manual: The Instructor's Manual features learning objectives, lecture outlines, more complex answers to review and discussion questions, case analyses, and suggested activities for each chapter in the text. The authors have also included a sample syllabus which offers suggestions for structuring your course.

Test Item File: An improved test item file offering a variety of true or false, multiple choice, and essay questions that facilitate different classroom needs.

The PowerPoints, Instructor's Manual and Test Item File can also be downloaded from www.prenhall.com/howell

▪▪▪ Acknowledgments

During the years it took to complete the two editions of this book, numerous individuals provided valuable assistance by conducting library research, editing, and discussing with us many of the issues we wrote about. Lei Wang, Jim Weber, Jennifer Villa, Jim Paul, Michael Clugston, and Lori Paris all provided capable and generous support to our efforts. The College of Business Administration and Economics at New Mexico State University provided the library facilities and the environment that allowed us to persist on the project. Our longtime friend and colleague, Peter Dorfman, asked many thought-provoking questions about our project, and continues to participate with the senior author on various research projects that have produced findings reported in the book. Our students provided valuable input that improved the presentation of text material. Our families put up with our long hours of work over the years, provided words of encouragement, and never wavered in their confidence that we would complete the project. The many reviewers who read and commented on earlier versions of the manuscript provided the essential feedback we needed to keep the book relevant to students of leadership, as well as true to the leadership literature. These reviewers are listed below:

Jim Paul, University of Kansas
Claudia C. Cogliser, University of Oklahoma
John Barbuto, University of Nebraska, Lincoln
Melinda Blackman, California State University, Fullerton
John Chism, Truckee Meadows Community College
Samuel Felton, Strategic Management Databases–Maine
Daron Jones, FranklinCovey
Tiffany Keller, University of Richmond
Brenda LeTendre, Pittsburgh State University
Bronston T. Mayes, California State University, Fullerton
Leslie Michael, Big Bend Community College
Lyman Porter, University of California, Irvine
Josh Powers, Indiana University
Ron Riggio, Claremont McKenna College
Bruce Schooling, Point Loma Nazarene University
Betty Scott, Community College of Southern Nevada
Paula M. Short, University of Missouri, Columbia
Judy Turman, Tyler Junior College
Robert Vecchio, University of Notre Dame
Jim Weber, St. Cloud State University

CHAPTER 1

Leadership and Its Importance

Learning Objectives

After reading this chapter you should be able to do the following:

1. Define and describe the leadership process.
2. Discuss the similarity of leadership and management in organizations.
3. Describe traits leaders often possess.
4. Discuss how leadership behaviors are critical to a leader's effectiveness.
5. Describe how situational factors can affect a leader's success.
6. Describe the three key tasks leaders must carry out in order to be effective.

Leadership is a fascinating social phenomenon that occurs in all groups of people regardless of geography, culture, or nationality. Ancient Chinese and Greek leaders looked to philosophers for advice, Egyptians attributed specific godlike traits to their leader–kings, and famous writers such as Homer and Machiavelli documented shrewd and cunning strategies of successful leaders. Much of history is recorded through the lives of famous leaders. Names such as George Washington, Abraham Lincoln, Clara Barton, Mahatma Gandhi, Golda Meir, John F. Kennedy, Martin Luther King Jr., and Nelson Mandela symbolize major eras of social upheaval that have had immense repercussions. Most young people today aspire to become leaders in school, athletics, entertainment, politics, industry, the military, medicine, or some other area of endeavor. Although Bass[1] has noted that the word "leadership" did not appear in the English language until about 1300, this social phenomenon has been recognized since the beginning of recorded history. The Leadership in Action box describing Lilly Yeh demonstrates the importance of leadership in a community environment. Her leadership style will be addressed in an exercise at the end of this chapter.

▬▬▬▬▬▬▬▬▬▬▬▬▬▬▬▬▬▬▬▬▬▬▬▬▬

LEADERSHIP IN ACTION

Lilly Yeh

Lilly Yeh describes herself as a small Chinese woman, but she is having a big impact on the inner city of North Philadelphia. She directs the Village of Arts and Humanities in this small portion of Philadelphia. For the past fifteen years, Ms. Yeh and her organization have been transforming a poor and depressed inner city neighborhood into a model of urban development. Through numerous programs that focus on the arts and humanities, as well as education, community building, and urban beautification, Ms. Yeh created and leads a grassroots movement that is changing the neighborhood and the lives of thousands of people.

Lilly Yeh was born in Kueizhou, China, in 1941. In her youth, she developed a love for Chinese landscape painting and its representation of a "tranquil and luminous place." After obtaining a college degree in Taiwan, Ms. Yeh studied at the University of Pennsylvania and became an artist and teacher at Philadelphia's University of the Arts. In 1986, North Philadelphia was filled with poverty, condemned houses that were slowly being leveled, garbage, and crime. Ms. Yeh obtained a $2,500 grant from the Pennsylvania Council of the Arts and worked with some neighborhood children to convert a rubbish filled vacant lot into something beautiful. She demonstrated her first vision of urban transformation by drawing a circle in the dirt. As the curious children watched, she told them, "This is the center. This is where we begin." Her vision of the luminous place as a shared physical space has unfolded over the years.

Lilly Yeh returned to North Philadelphia for several summers and helped design and create more gardens while building allies in the local African American community. In 1989, she decided to make community development a year-round endeavor. She was inspired by a visit to Tiananmen Square, where thousands of students confronted their country's government and military to demonstrate for democratic reform. Ms. Yeh established the Village as a nonprofit corporation and began an after-school arts program, followed shortly by classes in nutrition, health care, computing, and writing, to meet the needs of local children. Other courses in sex education, HIV awareness, silk screening, and puppet shows were added. Art classes began in local schools, taught by local artists. Village members are encouraged to express themselves through theater, dance, poetry, and writing. Village classes and administrative staff are located in renovated townhouses, with sculptures, murals, and flower gardens in between. Ms. Yeh continually emphasizes the Village mission of "reconnecting people to the earth," and she collaborated to write a guidebook titled *Learning through Creating.*

Ms. Yeh is a highly active leader whose energy mobilizes those around her. One young student stated, "People feel like anything is possible when Miss Lilly is around." She has obtained volunteer assistance from numerous individuals and organizations—including AmeriCorps, the City of Philadelphia Redevelopment Authority, the Pennsylvania Horticultural Society, the Philadelphia Eagles football team, and young artists from other countries, who come to get ideas for their own country. The Village has received numerous honors from national organizations representing the arts, humanities, and urban development. It has also received grants for over $1 million in 2003 alone from different foundations, corporations, and local businesses.

Lilly Yeh places a heavy emphasis on developing people. She works with prison inmates on Friday afternoons, teaching and collaborating on sculptures, creative writing, and painting. She sees this process as helping them to reconnect with their community because they are still present in the minds and hearts of families in their neighborhoods. She helped a local unemployed drug user by asking for his assistance in creating a mosaic. He is now a Village spokesman and teacher who credits her with saving his life.

Ms. Yeh now works closely with 20–30 Village administrators and educators developing new ideas and grant proposals, and providing overall guidance for the Village. She describes community building as mostly "trench work," and she finds it truly fulfills her needs to connect with others and the earth. She is clearly a dedicated leader who effectively combines her creativity and talent in an organization that is providing life-giving service to its community.

SOURCE: Adapted from Christy West, "Lilly Yeh—Filling the niches of North Philadelphia with creativity and hope," *Orion,* January–February 2003, 72–74.

▪▪▪ Importance of Leadership

Many of us have known poor leaders who promote their own image by taking credit for work done by others, who are selfish, inconsiderate, or tyrannical with followers, or who are unfair, dishonest, and threatened by competence in other people. These factors decrease our quality of life by lowering our job and life satisfaction and our commitment to organizations, while creating high levels of conflict and stress.[2] One recent survey indicated that over 75 percent of U.S. employees are unhappy with their jobs. The primary reason given was that they were treated poorly by their boss.[3]

Some writers have argued that leadership is a romantic ideal or a convenient attribution that people use to explain why some teams or organizations succeed while others fail. The evidence is quite strong, however, that leadership is a real social process that affects important events in our lives and in organizations. Careful studies in organizations show that executive leadership can account for 45 percent of an organization's performance.[4] Hundreds of studies show that leadership makes a difference in followers' satisfaction and performance.[5–8] Leadership affects the educational climate in schools, church attendance, job stress, organizational change, and military success. Effective leadership can create shared beliefs, values, and expectations in organizations and societies and can modify followers' interpretations and understanding of issues and events. Much of history has been passed down through stories of key leaders. It is difficult to explain many major human events such as the independence of India without Mahatma Gandhi, the Roman military campaigns without Alexander the Great or Julius Caesar, the American civil rights movement without Martin Luther King Jr., Nazi Germany without Adolf Hitler, the People's Republic of China without Mao Tse Tung, the United Farm Workers without Cesar Chavez, the Jonestown massacre without Jim Jones, the Waco, Texas, disaster without David Koresh, or business debacles such as Enron without Kenneth Lay or Andrew Fastow.

A recent study of a large sample of Fortune 500 companies found charismatic leadership to be an important factor influencing the financial performance of the firm, especially when the environment was uncertain.[9] J.C. Penny hired Allen Questrom to help the company with needed changes when they faced a rapidly changing environment and poorly performing stores. In one year he implemented changes in store appearance, merchandise, and purchasing that resulted in improvements in market share and profitability.[10] One writer recently noted that about 40,000 articles and books have been published about leadership.[11] Leadership training is increasingly a topic of college and university courses and programs in organizations.

Although there are fewer managers in a world of downsized corporations, the need for leadership does not disappear. Leadership is needed not only at the top of organizations, but at all levels. Many people emerge as effective leaders of groups or teams without any formal title or office. These individuals often play key roles in team-based organizations in which decision making is decentralized and employees have a high amount of education and training. These leadership roles are somewhat different from traditional roles of formal leaders, but they are critical for effective team performance. There are also an unprecedented number of new businesses and other organizations being formed in the United States and abroad, as free enterprise becomes more common around the world. These new organizations require direction by knowledgeable leaders who are sensitive to market niches and other environmental factors that influence their organizations' survival. The need for good leadership is clearly ubiquitous because it affects almost every aspect of our lives.

▪▪▪ Defining Leadership

Should any person who exerts influence over others be considered a leader? Is the use of coercion and force to gain compliance a part of leadership? Are the processes of management and leadership the same? Numerous definitions of leadership have been offered and discussed over the years.[12–15] Recently, experts on the subject have agreed on certain core characteristics of leadership. The following definition contains these characteristics and is intended as a broad but concise explanation of the leadership process to be discussed in the chapters that follow:

Leadership is a process used by an individual to influence group members toward the achievement of group goals in which the group members view the influence as legitimate.

The core characteristics of this definition will be considered one by one.

First, leadership is a process or a reasonably systematic and continuous series of actions directed toward group goals. Leadership is not usually a single act or even a few acts performed only in certain situations. It is a pattern of behaviors that is demonstrated fairly consistently over time with specific objectives. Some writers use the term leadership to represent the individual who carries out these activities. Others define it as the properties or qualities of individuals who carry out this series of actions effectively.[16] Because it is the actions of individuals that distinguish them as leaders, most experts today focus on the series of actions or pattern of behaviors that nearly all leaders exhibit.

Second, the actions of leaders are designed to influence people to modify their behavior. Those being influenced are often referred to as followers. Followers play an important role in the leadership process for at least two reasons: without followers, no one can be a leader; and all leaders are followers at times.[17,18] Most leaders today do not have total control (absolute power) over followers' behavior. Instead, leaders typically use various behaviors to influence followers.

Third, although at times the series of actions may be carried out by more than one person, a single individual will usually be expected to fulfill the leadership role for a given group. The individual may be appointed to the role by someone outside the group (such as with most managers), he or she may be elected by the group members to serve as leader for a fixed period of time (such as the president of a sorority), or the leader may emerge informally from interaction of the members (such as the leader of a street gang). The rights and obligations vary somewhat for each of these leaders, but the pattern of behaviors they exhibit while fulfilling their leadership roles are remarkably similar.

Fourth, followers view the leader's influence as legitimate; that is, the influence is reasonable and justifiable under the circumstances. This usually means the leader utilizes noncoercive methods to convince followers to comply with requests. In modern societies, leaders often achieve compliance by rewarding or recognizing; displaying their expertise, superior knowledge, or moral rightness; emphasizing formal authority; or threatening punishment for noncompliance. When threats of punishment are used, they normally involve a material change, such as transfer to a less desirable work shift, a reduction in pay, or discontinuance of employment. In certain contexts, leaders use threats of physical punishment (coercion) and followers may view the threats as legitimate. Such is the case when a military leader has a deserter arrested and jailed. The legitimacy issue reflects accepted patterns for the group members' behavior. In street gangs or modern drug cartels, for example, violence is an accepted way of life, and followers probably consider the leader's use of violence legitimate. In most modern organizations, however, society's expectations cause leaders to refrain from threatening physical punishment as a means of influence.

Fifth, the leader's influence is directed toward group goals. The goal may be a desired level of performance such as the number of games won or the number of automobiles sold; or it may be a level of donations for a worthy charity or a percentage of market share for a given product. The leader is often involved in setting the goals for or with the group, or the leader may inherit established group goals. Business, education, and military leaders often assume leadership positions with goals set for them by higher authority. Their immediate leadership task is to develop group strategies and commitment to achieve these goals. Once achievement is assured, the leader focuses efforts on future goal setting for the group. The most important point regarding this core characteristic of leadership is that there is a goal or target that the group is seeking to achieve. The leader is there to help the group achieve this goal. Figure 1-1

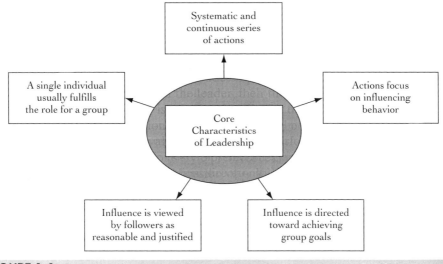

summarizes the core characteristics of the definition of leadership. The Leadership in Action box describing Martin Luther King Jr. demonstrates many of these core characteristics in this well-known civil rights leader.

Martin Luther King Jr. demonstrated effective leadership in a particularly difficult situation. He did not have an established organization with tradition and history to fall back on. He emerged in a period of turmoil and change and was thrust into a position that required pulling disparate groups into a movement with extremely difficult, unclear, and dangerous goals. His success sprung in part from important leadership characteristics such as speaking ability, high energy, and courage in the face of repeated threats and attacks. He attended to his followers by directing their activities and serving as a role model for them. His support for followers was shown through encouragement and declarations of the righteousness of their cause. He sought followers' advice on decisions about strategies and tactics. King represented their cause by working frequently with leaders outside the civil rights movement. Activities such as outlining an appealing future vision for followers, clarifying their identities, providing a historical perspective, expressing constant dissatisfaction with the status quo, and using symbolism to develop public appeal were examples of King's charismatic behaviors. Such leadership behaviors and traits are the subject of much of this book and will be discussed in detail in the following chapters. Although King was a master at many of these behaviors, the beginning of mastery is understanding. We have dedicated this book to providing an understanding of these effective leadership traits and behaviors.

▬▬▬ Leadership Effectiveness

How do we know if a leader is effective? Leadership scholars have used many different indicators to measure the effectiveness of leaders. One set of indicators addresses individual followers' behavior, such as job performance. This is a common indicator of leader effectiveness and may include objective data on followers' productivity or the amount of work completed, or it may be the results of performance ratings by supervisors or peers. Measures of followers' attitudes or perceptions are also frequently used as indicators of leadership effectiveness. Examples are followers' job satisfaction, commitment to the organization, role clarity, and motivation. These attitudes and perceptions are largely psychological and describe the most immediate effects of a leader's behavior on followers. Measures of followers' attitudes and perceptions are usually obtained via questionnaires completed by followers; they are described in more detail in Chapter 2 and throughout this book.

Another set of commonly used indicators of leadership effectiveness are group and organizational outcomes. Leaders are often considered effective when their organization's profitability or productivity is high, especially if these favorable results occur after the leader assumes his or her position following a period of poorer performance. Good researchers may also consider other factors such as market growth, competitive position, and other recently acquired resources before attributing all favorable results to the leader. Other group and organizational outcomes that are considered indicators of leadership effectiveness include market share, union membership, church attendance, games or battles won, group cohesion, and rates of employee turnover, absenteeism, or grievances filed with a union.

LEADERSHIP IN ACTION
Martin Luther King Jr.

Martin Luther King Jr. was born in 1929 in Atlanta, Georgia. He was a gifted student and earned a doctorate from Boston University in 1955. King was an eloquent speaker and studied philosophy, American democracy, Gandhi's writings on nonviolent resistance, and the teachings of Jesus Christ. He became minister of Dexter Avenue Baptist Church in Montgomery, Alabama, in 1954.

In that same year, the United States Supreme Court issued a decision on school desegregation known as *Brown v. Board of Education.* In December 1955, a well-respected black seamstress named Rosa Parks was jailed in Montgomery for refusing to give up her seat on a bus to a white person. Black leaders in Montgomery decided to make the Parks case a test of the gains made by the Supreme Court decision. They chose Martin Luther King Jr., the well-spoken young Baptist minister of a relatively affluent black congregation, to lead their boycott of the Montgomery bus system.

King gave his first speech as leader of the boycott on short notice. His charismatic presentation ignited the crowd of several thousand. Then, in 1956, he was arrested for boycott activities and received widespread publicity. When the Supreme Court declared Alabama's bus laws unconstitutional, King made the cover of *Time.* He declared the decision a victory for all Americans and enunciated a series of lessons for the "new Negro."

During the next several years, he honed his speaking skills and learned to adapt his style to match his audience while directing and participating in a variety of civil rights causes. King learned organization skills from other organizers and traveled to Africa and India to observe political action at close range. He learned when to listen, when to compromise, and when to hold his ground. He gave up his goal of being a successful minister and university professor, formed the Southern Christian Leadership Conference, and assumed his role as the premier leader of African Americans.

King's popularity culminated in his "I have a dream" speech during the August 1963 civil rights march in Washington, D.C. He described his dream as deeply rooted in American values, traditions, and freedoms, and used all the rhetorical skills he had gained. Millions viewed the speech on television, and he won the hearts of much of the nation. He was congratulated immediately afterward by President John Kennedy, named *Time*'s "Man of the Year" in 1963, and awarded the Nobel Peace Prize in 1964.

The mid-1960s were marked by violence in the United States and abroad. The assassination of President Kennedy in November 1963 was followed by numerous killings of civil rights workers and of four black girls attending a church in Birmingham, Alabama. During this period, King became more vocal about general national issues such as poverty, economic injustice, and the Vietnam War. He began to speak about a needed revolution in American values rather than more gradual changes he had earlier advocated. He was assassinated in April 1968 in Memphis, Tennessee, where he was supporting a strike by the city sanitation workers. He became a symbol for the cause of civil rights in this country.

Martin Luther King Jr. had the capabilities, insight, and leadership behavior to match the situation he was thrust into in December 1955. He bound together numerous groups in American society who shared low economic status and a common cultural experience. King addressed issues with spellbinding rhetoric while appealing to shared values, advocating nonviolence, and professing a commitment to the founding principles of American democracy. He was truly one of the great leaders of the 20th century.

The psychological effects of leaders on followers' attitudes and perceptions are often said to mediate or intervene between the leader's behavior and follower, group, or organizational outcomes. When a leader is supportive and caring toward his followers, they will likely respond with higher job satisfaction (an attitude), which may result in better attendance, fewer grievances, and a low likelihood of the followers leaving the organization. If a leader carefully explains effective work methods to followers, this often creates a clear picture (perception) in followers' minds of how to efficiently complete a work task, which can result in improved follower job performance. This process may operate more quickly with some leader behaviors than others, but a leader's behavior has its most direct and immediate effects on followers' attitudes and perceptions, which in turn influence follower or group behaviors and outcomes. This process is explained in more detail in Chapter 2 in connection with the Leadership Process Model.

▪▪▪ Leadership versus Management

Many writers have attempted to distinguish between management and leadership. From early classical writers to modern researchers, the distinction between management and leadership has often been based on viewing management as "doing things right" and viewing leadership as "doing the right things." Management is seen as a mechanical and administrative activity, while leadership involves changing and developing more effective organizations. Managers are often viewed as "organizational engineers" who apply rational problem solving, use objective technical criteria, and manipulate standardized building blocks in organizations to achieve well-known goals. Leadership, however, is viewed as the process of creating a social organism or "living enterprise" that is active, capable of changing, and responsive to the environment. Finding an environmental niche in which an organization can function and grow is a leadership role.[19,20]

Each of these views is incomplete in its description of the leadership/management role in real organizations. Each perspective emphasizes certain aspects of the leadership/management role while ignoring other interpretations. These incomplete views have inhibited our ability to understand the increasingly complex leadership/management process.

Today's complex organizations and increasingly complicated environments require a more well-rounded view of the leadership/management process. The process must include rational analysis and problem solving while also encouraging organizational growth, identification of environmental niches, and development of a mission to guide the organization in adapting to its surroundings. In modern organizations, leadership and management roles are seldom separable. At times a leader/manager may need to charge up followers, creating commitment, inspiration, growth, and adaptation. Here the individual is clearly exerting leadership. At other times, the same person must attend to mundane administrative matters, such as modifying rules and regulations, allocating resources, and assigning tasks. Here the individual is generally viewed as managing. In this book, we acknowledge that management and leadership are closely related and that the same individuals usually perform both activities. It therefore is not realistic to separate leadership activities from management activities when both are designed to influence followers to accomplish goals. The behaviors described in this book are useful for any person who attempts to influence a group of people toward achievement of group goals.

LEADERSHIP SELF-ASSESSMENT
Evaluating Leadership Traits

Objective: To help the reader think about how personal traits of leaders may help or hinder the leader's effectiveness.

Instructions: The following leader traits or personal characteristics have been the subject of research on leaders' effectiveness. Some of these traits have contributed to the successful performance of leaders, while others have been detrimental to leadership performance, although the effectiveness of a leader trait usually depends on the situation and followers involved. Place an "×" in the appropriate place depending on whether you believe the trait makes a leader more effective or less effective.

	Usually Makes Leaders	
Leadership Trait	*More Effective*	*Less Effective*
1. Persistent	_____	_____
2. Good speaking ability	_____	_____
3. Perfectionist	_____	_____
4. Sociable	_____	_____
5. Arrogant	_____	_____
6. Cooperative	_____	_____
7. Afraid of failure	_____	_____
8. Impulsive	_____	_____
9. Task oriented	_____	_____
10. Argumentative	_____	_____
11. Self-confident	_____	_____
12. Adaptable	_____	_____

Refer to the end of the chapter to compare your answers with research results on leader traits.

SOURCES: Based on R. T. Hogan, G. T. Curphy, and J. Hogan, "What do we know about leadership?: Effectiveness and personality," *American Psychologist,* 49, 493–504; and B. M. Bass, *Bass and Stogdills Handbook of Leadership,* 3rd ed. (New York: The Free Press, 1990).

▪▪▪ Traits of Leaders

For centuries, most people believed in the *Great Man theory* of leadership—that leaders are born, not made. Leaders were believed to possess some unspecified personal characteristics from birth that suited them for leadership positions. Although there is no good research to support this belief, early attempts to understand why some individuals were effective leaders focused on their personal characteristics—often called traits.

A leadership *trait* is a relatively permanent characteristic that does not change as the individual moves from situation to situation. The first published article on

TABLE 1-1 Important traits of leaders from early research

Physical or Background Traits	Personality or Ability Traits	Task or Social Traits
Activity or energy	Assertiveness	Motivation to achieve
Education	Dominance	Responsibility
Social status	Originality or creativity	Initiative
	Self-confidence	Persistence
	Administrative ability	Task orientation
	Fluency of speech	Cooperativeness
	Social perceptiveness	Sociability
	Adaptability	

leadership traits appeared in the United States in 1904 and focused on intelligence. Examples of other leadership traits that were studied include height, energy, socioeconomic status, education, age, alertness, aggressiveness, and popularity. Between 1904 and 1970, hundreds of leadership trait studies were published with apparently significant findings regarding leaders' physical and social characteristics, psychological and background traits, as well as task and ability variables. Table 1-1 summarizes findings of these and more recent trait studies. At first, the leadership trait research seemed to support the notion that effective leaders had some inherent general characteristics that enabled them to influence people toward group goals—that good leaders were born, not made. Summaries of this research, however, uncovered several problems with the findings.[21]

First, researchers did not agree on which leadership traits were most important. Second, much of the trait research distinguished leaders from nonleaders rather than effective from ineffective leaders. Third, researchers often disagreed on how to define and measure certain traits. Finally, the research findings showed little or nothing about how much of a given trait was needed for leadership effectiveness. When individuals who apparently possessed important leadership traits were selected for leadership positions, their performance was usually no more effective than leaders who did not have the traits. Based on these observations, in the 1950s, leadership traits became less popular as a topic of leadership research, and most leadership researchers changed their focus to study how leaders actually behaved.

Recently, however, there has been a renewal of interest in personal traits of leaders.[22] Though many years of research showed no one set of traits was characteristic of all effective leaders, the decrease in popularity of the trait approach among researchers may have been premature. Certain traits can help a leader to be effective in specific situations, although most important traits vary with the situation. Still, a few traits, such as fluency of speech, self-confidence, assertiveness, originality, social perceptiveness, and adaptability appear to help leaders be effective in a broad spectrum of situations. Some of these traits are contained in the *Big Five* model of personality that is currently popular. Assertiveness and sociability are important aspects of *extraversion,* which is part of the Big Five model. Originality is important in *openness to experience,* which is also included in the Big Five model. Recent research has shown these two personality dimensions to be important for effective leadership.[23]

Another look at Table 1-1 reveals that some of the so-called traits of leaders are learned abilities and skills, not inherited physical or personal characteristics a leader possesses at birth. Fluency of speech and administrative ability are obvious examples, and training programs exist to increase participants' assertiveness skills and achievement motivation. Also, during the 1950s, scholars developed a high level of interest in group dynamics. How groups perform and develop and how key roles emerge, including leadership roles, were topics from social psychology that leadership researchers began to address. These two developments helped support the trend toward the study of how leaders behave.

▪▪▪ Leadership Behaviors

During the 1950s and 1960s, researchers sought an ideal pattern of leadership behavior that would produce satisfaction and high performance among followers regardless of the leadership situation or type of followers. For some time it appeared that the ideal pattern had been found in leaders who were very considerate of their followers' personal feelings and concerns, and were very active in structuring, guiding, and monitoring followers' work activities. Several studies showed increased group cohesion, improved performance, and increased effectiveness ratings when leaders demonstrated this pattern of behavior with followers.[24–27] By the mid-1970s, however, it became clear that the notion of an ideal pattern of leadership behavior was as much a myth as the idea that a single set of personal traits would characterize all effective leaders.[28] Comparative studies using multiple samples from different organizations showed that the most effective leadership behavior pattern varied, depending on the situation and the type of followers involved.

Nearly all current leadership experts agree that effective leadership behavior depends on situational and follower characteristics. This means that a leadership behavior pattern that is effective in one situation is not necessarily effective in another situation. For a leader to be continuously effective over time and in different situations, the leader's behavior must vary with the situation. In order to vary leadership behavior correctly, the leader must be able to diagnose the situation and follower characteristics, determine the pattern of leadership behaviors that will result in high performance, and then provide the appropriate leadership behaviors. Several writers have proposed theoretical models to explain which leadership behaviors are needed in which situation. The Path-Goal Theory,[29] the Situational Leadership Theory,[30] and the Multiple Linkage Model[31] are three well-known models of this type. These models are generally known as *contingency* or *situational* leadership theories, meaning that the most effective leadership behavior depends on the situation.

A factor common to contingency models of leadership is that behaviors that make leaders effective can be learned. Thus, they depart from the original impetus for research on leadership traits, which assumed leaders were naturally gifted individuals who possessed certain "magical" traits that gave them influence over followers. ("Leaders are born, not made.") Contingency models of leadership behavior maintain that much effective leadership can be learned, and therefore leadership training can be a key factor in effective leadership. This is not to say that anyone can learn to be a Rudolph Giuliani or a Martin Luther King Jr. People learn at different rates, some learn more than others, some put forth extra effort to enhance their learning, and some

LEADERSHIP IN ACTION
Effective Leadership Behaviors

The following are specific examples of leadership behaviors that many leaders use to influence followers:

- Explaining methods and techniques for followers to use in completing tasks
- Being friendly and informative and encouraging two-way communication
- Consulting with followers to obtain information and opinions before making important decisions
- Praising followers for a job well done
- Expressing high expectations and confidence in followers' performance

These and other behaviors by the leader help followers to work efficiently, to feel they are part of a productive team in which good work is recognized, and to have confidence in their own abilities. Leaders who effectively demonstrate these behaviors are not born with the knowledge and experience needed to carry them out. They must develop this type of leadership expertise over time, usually through interaction with followers, peers, and higher-level leaders. However, certain traits and skills may assist a knowledgeable leader in providing specific leadership behaviors effectively, such as fluency of speech, self-confidence, sociability, or a desire for influence over others. Each of the major behavior patterns used by leaders will be described in detail in the following chapters.

are able to apply their learning more effectively than others. But people can learn about how effective leaders behave and how they diagnose situations. With effort, many people can learn to exhibit leadership behaviors with varying degrees of expertise. Several leadership behaviors often used by highly effective leaders are described in the Leadership in Action box titled Effective Leadership Behaviors.

It should be clear from this brief discussion that leadership behaviors differ from leadership traits or skills. Moreover, behaviors and traits or skills interact to determine a leader's effectiveness. For example, a leader who has considerable expertise at the employees' tasks, is self-confident, enjoys influencing others, and is articulate (all traits and skills), will likely enjoy assigning followers to specific tasks and explaining appropriate work methods (leadership behaviors). The leader will have the verbal and task skills to make this guidance meaningful and easily understandable. Leaders who lack several of these characteristics may be reserved, uncertain of their task or verbal skills, and unwilling to take the initiative necessary to provide this type of guidance. Another example is the leader who is naturally sociable and agreeable, and enjoys friendly and informative interactions with followers (leadership traits). This person will probably be effective involving followers in decision making (leadership behaviors).

▮▮▮ Situational Factors and Leadership

Situational factors are often extremely important to effective leadership. Some situational factors actually increase a leader's impact on followers.[32] An example is when a leader is given control over important rewards, such as bonuses, promotions, or desirable job assignments. When followers know a leader controls these rewards, they are more responsive to the leaders' efforts to influence them. Other situational factors that increase a leader's influence may be the followers' lack of experience or unclear work tasks, which often cause followers to look to the leader for guidance.

Other situational factors decrease a leader's impact on followers.[33] Specific follower characteristics are often important aspects of the leader's situation. An example is a follower who has an unusually strong desire for independence and autonomy. This type of individual may resent being told how to do a task and refuse to comply with a leader's directions even though guidance may be needed to do the task well. Another situational factor that can decrease a leader's impact is a cohesive but uncooperative work group that may conspire to make the leader look bad. These factors make followers less responsive to a leader's behavior.

Finally, certain situational factors replace or substitute for followers' needs for specific leader behaviors.[34] In these situations, other factors often provide followers with guidance, motivation, and satisfaction. Examples of these factors include:

- Redesigned job tasks that are inherently interesting and motivating
- Self-managed work teams that structure and control their members' activities
- Reward systems, such as bonus programs based on company profits, that guide and motivate follower efforts with little or no leader involvement
- Follower self-leadership, where followers are encouraged to become increasingly responsible for planning, monitoring, and controlling their own activities
- Participative goal-setting programs, where key motivating factors are the goals followers establish for themselves (often in conjunction with the leader) to guide and control task behavior

Each of these situational factors can motivate, guide, and influence employees toward higher performance and improved attitudes. They also replace the need for many leadership actions. Leaders should obviously consider implementing these types of situational factors. In the following chapters we will explain when and how leaders should adjust their behavior to make the most of these factors. The Leadership in Action box describing Margaret Thatcher demonstrates how a leader's traits and behaviors can fit the situation at one time, resulting in success for the leader. Later, when the situation changes, the leader's behavior may no longer fit, and, as with Thatcher, he or she can lose the consent of his or her followers to lead. Table 1-2 summarizes the history of research on leadership effectiveness.

The Leadership Process: Three Key Tasks

The discussion of leadership behaviors and situational factors thus far leads us to three key tasks effective leaders must carry out to fulfill their role in increasingly complex organizations. These three tasks are shown in Figure 1-2. The first task in the leadership process is *diagnosing situational and follower characteristics*. Effective leaders must carefully evaluate their followers, the tasks followers perform, and the organizations in which they work, to determine the extent to which followers need a particular leadership behavior. Diagnosing situations also requires an understanding of the followers and situational factors that may prevent certain types of leadership from being effective or that allow individuals to function on their own. Leaders need this diagnostic

LEADERSHIP IN ACTION
Margaret Thatcher

Margaret Thatcher served three terms as prime minister of Great Britain and was highly influential in changing the course of post–World War II British society. She responded to a change in British sentiment away from socialist institutions, heavy public spending, and repeated concessions to unions, and toward privatization of industry, conservative spending, and curbing union power. The daughter of a middle-class grocer and local politician, she demonstrated her intelligence, self-confidence, energy, and skills at public speaking, debating, and networking early in her career. These skills and traits helped her move successfully among the male-dominated government elite in Britain. When she became prime minister, she was so firm in her views that she became divisive—she viewed people as either on the "right side or the wrong side." She liked to direct her personnel, but also seemed to enjoy browbeating and humiliating her political opponents. She ignored criticism and preferred to make her own decisions over participation and consensus in decision making. Her exclusionary and decisive style and another shift in public sentiment resulted in her resignation in 1990 under pressure from her own party.

information so they can make informed decisions about appropriate types of leadership behavior.

If the leader's diagnosis indicates that a follower's ability, experience, and motivation are adequate to permit the follower to make all necessary task decisions, then the leader should refrain from providing task guidance and allow the follower to work independently. Attempts by the leader to provide guidance in this situation will likely be viewed as a lack of trust and may lead to follower resentment. If, on the other hand,

TABLE 1-2 History of research on leadership effectiveness

Pre-1900	Great Man theory	Great leaders are born, not made.
1904–1950	Trait theories	Effective leaders have specific inherent characteristics that make them effective leaders (such as intelligence, aggressiveness, or alertness).
1950s–1970s	Behavioral theories	Effective leaders use an ideal pattern of leader behaviors that are effective in all situations.
Late 1970s–present	Situational theories	Effective leaders must vary their behavior to fit the requirements of the situation. A corollary of situational theories is that specific leadership traits can help a leader diagnose the situation and provide the leadership behavior that is needed.

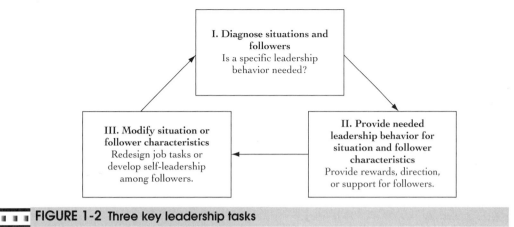

FIGURE 1-2 Three key leadership tasks

the leader's diagnosis indicates that a follower needs guidance on a specific task, then the leader must provide it or see that someone else provides it. This is the second task in the leadership process: *providing the leadership behavior needed by followers.* In this second leadership task, the leader matches leadership behaviors with situational and follower needs. Some followers deserve to be complimented for outstanding performance; others may need a sympathetic ear for a personal problem that affects their work. Providing the appropriate leadership behavior requires that the leader be familiar with the needed leadership behavior and have the necessary traits and skills to demonstrate it. The third leadership task requires the leader to be familiar with methods or programs for developing followers, and modifying their situations to make them more productive. As the effective leader diagnoses the situation and provides the needed leadership behavior, the leader is also thinking about what could be done to develop the followers or change the environmental situation to permit more independent follower action in the future. The final task in the leadership process is *developing followers or modifying their tasks or environment* to allow them to act more effectively or independently of the leader. Here the leader may actually promote self-leadership by followers. However, some followers need or prefer more direction and personal involvement with the leader than others. For these individuals, the leader can often modify the situation to make the followers more responsive to the leader's behavior. This book provides information to enable a leader to effectively carry out this leadership process.

Current Issues in Leadership

Several current leadership issues are addressed in detail in this book. These issues include leaders' ethics and fairness, diversity, leader development and change, and transformational leadership.

Ethics and Fairness

When leaders interact with followers to achieve goals, there is an implicit assumption that both parties will behave fairly and ethically. This is essential in order for them to trust one another, and trust is needed for mutual cooperation. Unethical behavior by high-level leaders in large organizations has been the topic of several scandals in recent years, and many writers and journalists have demanded more-responsible leadership. Unethical leaders do not treat everyone fairly; they often benefit themselves and inflict harm on others, including followers, customers, and investors who trusted them. By doing this, they destroy the commitment and willing cooperation of these other parties, which are needed to make their organizations survive and prosper. These scandals demonstrate that leadership plays a critical role in establishing an ethical climate in an organization. Leaders provide the role model for everyone in the organization to observe and learn from regarding ethical and fair behavior. Ethical issues in leadership are described in Chapter 13.

Diversity

Globalization is a major worldwide trend. This trend involves the movement of many people across borders who seek jobs and who become customers and recipients of services offered by organizations. The U.S. population is composed of increasing numbers of identifiable groups based on factors such as age, race, gender, national and ethnic heritage, mental and physical capabilities, or sexual orientation. Organizations increasingly conduct operations in different parts of the world, where they employ, serve, and sell to people with different cultural beliefs and practices. A major task of leaders in these organizations is to somehow integrate the diverse groups of individuals into a coordinated organizational effort to facilitate the achievement of organizational goals. This task is not easy and requires a good understanding of how culture affects us, including the operation of human bias and prejudice. Leaders must be aware of and communicate the benefits of diversity to their followers, and they must design and implement programs that promote a true appreciation of the value of diversity in organizations. These leadership issues are also described in Chapter 13.

Leadership Development

Leadership development involves increasing the ability of a leader or an aspiring leader to carry out effective leadership behaviors that enable a group or organization to work together productively. Leadership development programs typically emphasize one or more of three processes: assessment, challenge, and support. *Assessment* provides individuals with information about their strengths and weaknesses; successful development usually involves building on one's strengths and improving on weaknesses. *Challenge* causes people to see the need for new capabilities to help their followers adapt to changing organizations. *Support* provides leaders with encouragement and reassurance as they work to improve their skills and abilities to lead. All three processes are probably needed for individuals to initiate and maintain their development as leaders. Insight into one's own values can also provide a helpful basis for further development as a leader. This and other important skills are described in Chapter 14.

Leading Organizational Change

Forces for change are everywhere today. They include changes in technology, globalization, population shifts, political and social expectations, environmental concerns, and quality and ethical standards. Leaders must act as change agents to anticipate important changes that affect their organizations, to implement needed changes, and to support their followers as they adapt to these changes. Leaders are critical in any major organizational change effort, and they must demonstrate flexibility and continued learning and development while acting as role models for followers. The classic model for implementing change—unfreezing, changing, and refreezing—requires active direction by organizational leaders. Another recent model involves the leader's efforts to shape the organization's culture to encourage and facilitate continuous learning. With this approach, the leader's objective is to develop an organization that continually diagnoses current and future environmental needs, and adapts to meet those needs. Leaders structure followers' interactions around needed changes, they assure that new learning is shared, and they take responsibility for the organization and followers' welfare throughout the change. These activities in leading organizational change are described in detail in Chapter 14.

Transformational Leadership

This leadership style is currently popular in the management literature, and is thought to create extreme devotion and extraordinary effort among followers. This type of leader is highly charismatic and is typically an excellent communicator, giving inspirational speeches and describing highly desirable visions of the future. These leaders also demonstrate caring and consideration for followers as individuals. Transformational leaders are highly self-confident, they like to influence people, and they place considerable effort into making a positive impression on others. These leaders may be most suited for certain organizational situations—such as when followers are highly frustrated, stressed, or unhappy with their current situation. This leadership style is described in detail in Chapter 8.

SUMMARY

Leadership is a process an individual uses to influence group members toward the achievement of group goals in which the group members view the influence as legitimate. The processes of leadership and management are complex and interconnected, with both being focused on influencing groups of people toward the achievement of goals. Early leadership researchers focused on personal characteristics of leaders in explaining who emerged as a leader and who became an effective leader. Most later researchers, however, have emphasized leadership behavior as key to leader effectiveness. Certain

---

RESEARCH RESULTS FOR LEADERSHIP SELF-ASSESSMENT

Evaluating Leadership Traits

Items 1, 2, 4, 6, 9, 11, and 12 have usually been related to effective performance as a leader. These traits are helpful for gaining followers' support, dealing with new situations, and overcoming obstacles. Items 3, 5, 7, 8, and 10 can often decrease a leader's performance by making the leader less helpful, intolerant of mistakes, unreactive, self-centered, and unpredictable. These tendencies often eliminate followers' trust and confidence in their leader, and decrease their willingness to support and communicate important information the leader often needs.

situational or follower characteristics can increase or decrease the effectiveness of leadership behavior. Other characteristics can cause followers to perform effectively or to have positive attitudes with little or no need for a leader's influence. Nevertheless leaders have important roles to play in organizations, and effective leaders need to be aware of the three tasks in the effective leadership process: diagnosing situations to determine the need for a specific leadership behavior, providing the needed leadership behavior(s), and modifying situations and followers to increase their ability to work effectively or independently of the leader in attaining high performance and positive attitudes. Chapter 2 will describe the leadership behaviors that have been the primary focus of leadership researchers. The model of leadership to be utilized throughout this book is described in detail in Chapter 2.

KEY TERMS AND CONCEPTS IN THIS CHAPTER ▪▪▪▪▪▪▪▪

- Attitudes
- Authority
- Charismatic
- Group and organizational outcomes

- Key leadership tasks
- Leadership
- Leadership behaviors
- Leadership traits
- Perceptions

- Situational factors and leadership

REVIEW AND DISCUSSION QUESTIONS ▪▪▪▪▪▪▪

1. Identify a leader you think has had a major impact on society. What characteristics did this leader have that contributed to his or her effectiveness?
2. What are the traits you have most frequently observed in effective leaders? What could you do to develop these traits yourself?
3. What leadership behaviors have been effective in influencing your behavior toward group goals? How could you develop these behaviors?
4. What situational or task factors could increase followers' needs for certain types of behavior by the leader?
5. What situational or task factors could decrease followers' needs for certain types of behavior by the leader?

EXERCISE: LEADERS YOU HAVE OBSERVED ▪▪▪▪▪▪▪

Review the definition of leadership in this chapter. Think of at least five or six individuals you have observed who carried out the process of leadership. These people may have been leaders in school, your family, your community, in religious organizations, of sports teams, in student groups, in political groups, in service organizations, or in other situations you observed. The only requirement is that they influenced followers to achieve group goals in a reasonable or legitimate manner.

Select one of these leaders and answer the following questions:

1. What was the organizational context (type of business or organization, task, coworkers)?
2. What leadership behaviors were used to influence followers?
3. Was the leader's behavior effective or ineffective? How do you know? Why was it effective or ineffective?

Keep the list of leaders you have made for this exercise. You will use this list in later exercises that ask for specific examples of leadership behaviors and characteristics of the situation in which the leader was functioning.

▪▪▪▪▪▪ C A S E   I N C I D E N T ▪▪▪▪▪

Michael D. Eisner

Chairman and CEO of Walt Disney Productions

Michael Eisner has been the chairman and CEO of Walt Disney Productions since 1984. During the first ten years of his reign, Disney's earnings and stock price skyrocketed, and Eisner became a corporate superstar. However, starting in 1995, Disney and Eisner experienced a series of setbacks that posed serious threats to the future of the company and its CEO. Disney was faced with problems of a tumbling stock price, falling earnings, and financial losses due to the misguided acquisition of a cable company. Eisner lost credit among shareholders for several of his actions: the hiring and firing of Michael Ovitz as president of the Walt Disney Corporation; the legal war against former studio chief Jeffrey Katzenberg; and enforcement of a mandatory retirement policy that forced out Director Roy E. Disney, nephew of the late Walt Disney. Roy Disney launched a 3-month campaign with an aim to have Eisner step down from his CEO position. Eisner has played a central role in Disney's success and setbacks for the past two decades.

Eisner started his career in the entertainment industry in 1964, when he graduated with a B.A. in english literature, and theater from Denison University in Granville, Ohio. He held several administrative positions at CBS and ABC, and was involved in production of such movies and TV programs as *All My Children, One Life to Live, Happy Days, Saturday Night Fever,* and *Raiders of the Lost Ark.* In 1984, he accepted an invitation by Roy Disney to be the CEO and chairman of Walt Disney

Productions. Disney's performance was boosted immediately under the leadership of Eisner. The company thrived in multiple areas, with new theme parks opening in France and Japan, carefully implemented price increases at theme parks, popular animated movies such as *The Lion King,* and the acquisition of an independent film company (Miramax), which was then developed into a successful movie distributor. Disney's prosperity in those days was attributed to its creative culture. Eisner stated that he actively prompted this organizational culture by encouraging a loose environment in which employees felt free to speak their minds, inviting employees to weekly conferences to generate diversity of ideas and opinions, listening to their input, and constantly emphasizing that work is fun and exciting.

Eisner's leadership style, however, may not be as inclusive as he claimed. He is described as self-confident and assertive, and he relied on those personality traits in overcoming obstacles during his early years at Disney. Years of success reinforced his self-confidence and he became more authoritarian in his leadership style. Some writers claim that he made Disney the instrument of his own will. Observers say he does not delegate, focuses on the tiniest details, and often makes decisions on his own with little or no input from others. He controlled the board of directors by filling it with his personal acquaintances. His assertiveness, arrogance, and tough stand on issues proved to be costly to the Disney organization. He overcame considerable opposition on the board and insisted on hiring his friend Michael Ovitz as president of Disney with a lavish compensation package. Eisner soon realized Ovitz was not appropriate for the position, so he granted him a no-fault termination and Ovitz left with a cash and stock package valued at $90 million. Eisner also made insulting remarks in public about Katzenberg while a lawsuit was pending between Disney and Katzenberg. Weeks later, the lawsuit was settled for $250 million, instead of under $100 million as expected by many. When shareholders and the public began questioning Eisner's leadership, the Disney board awarded him a 10-year contract, which made him almost untouchable. Facing criticism from shareholders, the press, and scholars writing about corporate governance, Eisner defended his practices. He claimed that outside critics, such as law professors, lack understanding of corporate leadership. Although the Disney board has been reformed to make it more independent of the CEO and the company has improved its performance, Eisner's problems are not over. Disney's shareholders are deciding whether to continue their support for the company's CEO and chairman. ■

DISCUSSION QUESTIONS

1. How would you describe Michael Eisner's leadership at Disney? What kind of leadership behaviors did he display?
2. How could his leadership be improved?

SOURCES: Bruce Orwall and Joann S. Lublin, "For Disney's Eisner, years of corporate sparring catch up," *The Wall Street Journal Online,* March 1, 2004. online.wsj.com/article_print/0,,SB107809753438642334,00.html; Suzy Wetlaufer, Common sense and conflict—An interview with Disney's Michael Eisner, *Harvard Business Review,* January–February 2000; and R. Grover, *The Disney Touch.* Burr Ridge, IL: Irwin, 1997.

ENDNOTES ▮▮▮▮▮▮▮

1. Bass, B. (1990). *Bass & Stogdill's Handbook of Leadership.* New York: The Free Press.
2. Tepper, B. J. (2000). Consequences of abusive supervision. *Academy of Management Journal, 43,* 178–190.
3. Williams, G. (2002). Whale watching. *Entrepreneur,* June, 32.
4. Day, D. V., and Lord, R. G. (1988). Executive leadership and organizational performance: Suggestions for a new theory and methodology. *Journal of Management, 14,* 453–464.
5. Bass. *Bass & Stogdill's Handbook of Leadership.*
6. Katzell, R. A., and Guzzo, R. A. (1983). Psychological approaches to productivity improvement. *American Psychologist, 38,* 468–472.
7. Virany, B., and Tushman, M. L. (1986). Executive succession: The changing characteristics of top management teams. Paper presented at the Academy of Management Meeting, Chicago.
8. Schriesheim, C. A. and Neider, L. L. (1996). Leadership theory and development: The coming "new phase." *Organizational Behavior and Human Performance, 22,* 374–403.
9. Waldman, D. A., Ramirez, R. J., House, R. J., and Puranam, P. (2001). Does leadership matter? CEO leadership attributes and profitability under conditions of perceived environmental uncertainty. *Academy of Management Journal, 44,* 134–143.
10. Anderson, S. (2001). Can an outsider fix J. C. Penny? *Business Week,* June, 56–58.
11. Dubrin, A., Jr. (2004). *Leadership: Research Findings, Practice and Skills.* New York: Houghton Mifflin.
12. Bass. *Bass & Stogdill's Handbook of Leadership.*

13. Yukl, G. (1998). *Leadership in Organizations,* 4th ed. Upper Saddle River, NJ: Prentice Hall.
14. Zaleznik, A. (1990). The leadership gap. *Academy of Management Executive,* 4(1), 1–22.
15. Kouzes, J. M., and Posner, B. Z. (1993). *Credibility: How Leaders Gain and Lose It, Why People Demand It.* San Francisco: Jossey-Bass.
16. Jago, A. G. (1982). Leadership: Perspectives in theory and research. *Management Science,* 28(3), 315–336.
17. Yukl. *Leadership in Organizations,* 4th ed.
18. Hollander, E. P. (1993). Legitimacy, power and influence: A perspective on relational features of leadership. In M. M. Chemers and R. Ayman (Eds.), *Leadership Theory and Research.* San Diego, CA: Academic Press, 29–44.
19. Terry, L. D. (1995). The leadership-management distinction: The domination and displacement of mechanistic and organismic theories. *Leadership Quarterly,* 6(4), 515–527.
20. Bennis, W., and Nanus, B. (1985). *Leaders: The Strategies for Taking Charge.* New York: Harper and Row.
21. Bass. *Bass and Stogdill's Handbook of Leadership.*
22. Lord, R. G., DeVader, C. L., and Alliger, G. M. (1996). A meta-analysis of the relations between personality traits and leadership perceptions: An application of validity generalization procedures. *Journal of Applied Psychology,* 71(3), 402–410.
23. Judge, T. A., Bono, J. E., Ilies, R., and Gerhardt, M. W. (2002). Personality and leadership: A qualitative and quantitative review. *Journal of Applied Psychology,* 87(4), 765–780.
24. Hemphill, J. K., and Coons, A. E. (1957). Development of the leader behavior description questionnaire. In R. M. Stogdill and A. E. Coons (Eds.), *Leader Behavior: Its Description and Measurement.* Columbus, OH: Ohio State University, Bureau of Business Research.
25. Hemphill, J. K. (1955). Leadership behaviors associated with the administrative reputation of college departments. *Journal of Educational Psychology,* 46, 385–401.
26. House, R. J., and Filly, A. C. (1971). Leadership style, hierarchical influence, and the satisfaction of subordinate role expectations: A test of Likert's influence propositions. *Journal of Applied Psychology,* 55, 422–432.
27. Keller, B. T., and Andrews, J. H. M. (1963). Leader behavior of principals, staff morale, and productivity. *Alberta Journal of Educational Research,* 9, 179–191.
28. Larson, L. L., Hunt, J. G., and Osborn, R. N. (1976). The great hi-hi leader behavior myth: A lesson from Occam's razor. *Academy of Management Journal,* 19, 628–639.
29. House, R. J., and Mitchell, T. R. (1974). Path-goal theory of leadership. *Journal of Contemporary Business,* 3, 81–97.
30. Hersey, D., and Blanchard, K. (1982). *Management of Organizational Behavior,* 4th ed. Englewood Cliffs, NJ: Prentice Hall.
31. Yukl. *Leadership in Organizations,* 4th ed.
32. Howell, J. P., Dorfman, P. W., and Kerr, S. (1986). Moderator variables in leadership research. *Academy of Management Journal,* 11, 88–102.
33. Ibid.
34. Kerr, S., and Jermier, J. (1978). Substitutes for leadership: Their meaning and measurement. *Organizational Behavior and Human Performance,* 22, 374–403.

Leadership Behaviors and Processes

Learning Objectives

After reading this chapter, you should be able to do the following:

1. Describe patterns of behavior that leaders frequently exhibit.
2. Identify the effects of specific leadership behaviors on followers' psychological reactions and performance.
3. Discuss the impact of situational and follower characteristics on leader effectiveness.
4. Explain how leaders can utilize specific types of situational and follower characteristics to increase their effectiveness.
5. Describe the sources of power and influence tactics often used by leaders.
6. Describe the Leadership Process Model for influencing followers' behavior.

At one time or another leaders typically exhibit different kinds of behavior patterns to influence followers to achieve group goals. The following are examples of leadership behaviors:

- Explaining to a follower the level of performance that is expected.
- Showing respect and concern for the personal feelings of a follower.
- Asking a follower for suggestions on how to solve a problem.
- Complimenting a follower for doing outstanding work.
- Coordinating the activities of the group with those of other groups.
- Communicating displeasure when a follower's work is below acceptable levels.
- Insisting that followers comply with policies and procedures of the organization.
- Making sure that followers have adequate resources to complete assigned work.
- Communicating ideas about the future of the organization.
- Taking high personal risks to benefit the organization.
- Providing information that helps a follower perform effectively.

To positively influence followers, the leader must use these behavior patterns in an effective manner.[1,2] When leaders fail to use needed behaviors or use behaviors in an

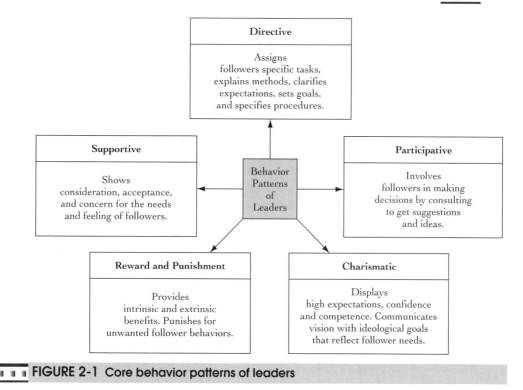

▪▪▪ **FIGURE 2-1 Core behavior patterns of leaders**

inappropriate way, followers are not influenced to achieve group goals.[3] This chapter introduces the major behavior patterns most leaders use to influence followers. Factors that may increase or decrease the effectiveness of leadership behaviors and overall impacts that leaders have on followers are also described in this chapter. Types of situational and follower characteristics that leaders must consider in selecting an appropriate behavior are identified.

Figure 2-1 presents the five core leadership behavior patterns that will be focused on in Part II of this book. The chapters in Part II will identify how and when to effectively use each of the behavior patterns.

▪▪▪ Behavior Patterns of Leaders

Each behavior pattern in Figure 2-1 is described in more detail below:

1. **Supportive Leadership Behavior:** This behavior pattern refers to the leader's role in showing concern for the comfort and well-being of followers; demonstrating a considerate, kind, and understanding attitude in dealing with followers; being friendly and informative, and encouraging open, two-way communication and follower development. Familiar terms associated with supportive leadership are consideration, relationship orientation, and concern for people leadership.

2. **Directive Leadership Behavior:** This pattern refers to the leader's behaviors in assigning followers to specific tasks, explaining the methods to be used in completing the tasks, clarifying expectations regarding quantity and quality of follower performance, setting goals for followers, planning and coordinating followers' work, and specifying rules and procedures to be followed. This behavior pattern has also been known as or is closely related to initiating structure, instrumental leadership, or task-oriented leadership.

3. **Participative Leadership Behavior:** When leaders use this approach, they involve followers in the decision-making processes. Participative leadership behaviors may include holding one-on-one meetings with individuals or groups of followers to gather input for decisions; it may involve a group decision-making effort initiated by the leader; or it may involve assigning a particular problem to a follower to resolve. Each of these options represents different degrees or types of participative leadership behavior. Participative leadership is sometimes referred to as consultative, democratic, or delegatory leadership.

4. **Leader Reward and Punishment Behavior:** With this leadership behavior, when followers provide services to the organization, the leader rewards them with tangible and intangible benefits. The rewards may be monetary or they may consist of praise. Punishments may come in the form of a reduction in pay or a notice to the follower that work needs improvement. Rewards and punishments may be provided based on follower performance (contingently) or based on the leader's whim (noncontingently). Rewards and punishments based on performance are usually the most effective.

5. **Charismatic Leadership Behavior:** This pattern of behavior involves the leader communicating a vision of the future that has ideological significance to followers (often through use of powerful imagery and metaphors), arousing follower needs that are relevant to goal accomplishment, serving as a role model, expressing high expectations and confidence in followers' capabilities, and projecting a high degree of self-confidence.

Although there are other ways to describe and classify leader behaviors, these five have been extensively researched and have been found useful in describing specific behaviors that improve leader effectiveness. These patterns of behavior are not as independent of each other as they might at first appear. For example, a specific behavior by a leader, such as providing information, may serve different leadership functions depending on the situation and therefore may be considered an aspect of more than one leadership behavior pattern. If the information is intended to show the leader's concern for followers' anxieties over possible layoffs, then it is an aspect of supportive leadership behavior. If the information is to help in a group problem solving effort, it may be part of participative leadership. If the information clarifies management expectations of follower performance, then it is directive leadership. Although the leadership behavior patterns are described as distinct from one another, they are not mutually exclusive, and a given activity may occasionally be included in more than one leadership behavior category.

Three other leadership behavior patterns are emerging as especially important in organizations in the twenty-first century. These behaviors have not been studied as extensively as the five core leadership behaviors, but they warrant attention by leaders and will be described in detail in Part III of this book. These emerging leadership behaviors include the leader's role in *boundary spanning,* which is representing the group, protecting members from outsiders, obtaining resources, and resolving conflicts among members and with other groups. *Developing exchange relationships with followers* is another emerging leadership behavior. It includes identifying and developing follower potential, delegating and helping with challenging assignments, and providing additional time for particular followers. A final behavior pattern of leaders that is becoming increasingly important is *followership.* This involves leaders building a close exchange with their own leader, being proactive in attacking problems without the leader's request, developing one's own competencies, and role modeling followership behaviors for followers. In today's complex and highly technological organizations, these behavior patterns will become critical to a leader's success.

Leaders use these behavior patterns to influence followers to accomplish group goals. At times, however, different leadership behaviors may be used to achieve the same influence objective. For example, in order to motivate followers to put forth added effort, a leader might engage in inspirational speeches (an aspect of charismatic leadership behavior) or simply offer followers a special reward for a certain level of performance. Some leaders rely heavily on a limited set of behavioral strategies. However, those leaders who use a variety of behaviors are most likely to obtain desired outcomes with followers.[4]

A leader may demonstrate all of the behavior patterns or any subset of them with any group of followers. For example, because a leader participates extensively with one group does not mean the leader should do so with all groups or with the same group in all situations. As another example, a leader may be directive in some situations and participative or supportive in others. A leader may demonstrate a combination of two or three leadership behaviors in one five-minute exchange with a group of followers. Different combinations of behaviors are called *leadership styles.* Several popular styles are described in Chapter 14. Many effective leaders demonstrate all of these behavior patterns at one time or another as required by the situation.

Figure 2-2 represents the basic elements in the leadership process to influence followers. As indicated in the figure, leadership behaviors influence followers' psychological reactions, which in turn result in followers' behavioral outcomes. Future chapters will cover these psychological reactions and behavioral outcomes in connection with each of the leadership behavior patterns.

■ ■ ■ Effects of a Leader's Behavior on Followers

A leader's behavior has its most direct impact on the *psychological reactions* of individual followers and groups of followers (see Figure 2-2). These reactions include followers' attitudes, feelings, perceptions, motivations, and expectations. More specific examples of these factors include followers' satisfaction with supervision, general job satisfaction, organizational commitment, job stress, role clarity, motivation, and group cohesion. Followers' psychological reactions are important to organizations because they indicate the quality of the work environment by demonstrating how satisfied or frustrated people are on the job. Psychological reactions indicate whether the workplace is seen as a pleasant or unpleasant place to spend one's time. A leader's behavior can produce positive or negative psychological reactions. Positive effects make the workplace more pleasant and can help individuals cope with the frustrating or unpleasant aspects of

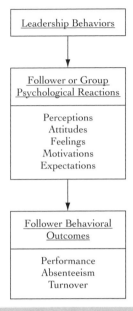

▪▪▪ **FIGURE 2-2** Leadership model for influencing follower behaviors

their jobs. In addition, leaders more easily obtain group cooperation in a pleasant work-place. Negative effects reduce satisfaction and can result in resentful and uncooperative followers.

The real objective of effective leadership is to influence followers' behaviors and outcomes. As shown in Figure 2-2, followers' behaviors and outcomes result from psychological reactions. For example, a follower who is motivated to excel (a favorable psychological reaction) exhibits high effort on the job and often performs effectively (a favorable behavioral outcome). Important outcomes include high individual and group performance; low turnover, absenteeism, lateness, and grievance rates; and high quality levels, all of which result in a productive organization.[5] To maintain high levels of productivity, it is necessary to have a stable workforce without overspending on training and recruitment; low grievance rates and high quality result in money saved from costly grievance procedures and errors. A supportive leader (who frequently shows concern and consideration for the personal welfare of followers) tends to increase followers' job satisfaction (a psychological reaction), and a high level of job satisfaction among workers typically results in lower turnover, absenteeism, and grievance rates. In this situation, the supportive leader's behavior increases employees' job satisfaction, which in turn reduces employee turnover, absenteeism, and grievances.

One purpose of Figure 2-2 is to explain the process by which leaders influence organizational outcomes. By understanding which psychological reactions are affected by a specific leadership behavior and how those reactions affect outcomes, leaders can make better choices of behaviors for specific situations. Choosing an effective behavior is critical in achieving leader effectiveness.

Figure 2-3 provides an example of the application of the leadership model from Figure 2-2 in analyzing the leadership behaviors of Eisenhower.

LEADERSHIP IN ACTION
Dwight D. Eisenhower

Dwight D. Eisenhower played a role in shaping history for almost twenty years. He was supreme commander of the Allied forces in Europe during World War II, commander of the North Atlantic Treaty Alliance, and president of the United States from 1953 to 1961.

Eisenhower's great test as a leader was as supreme commander of the Allied Expeditionary Forces in World War II. He was able to weld together a team of British and American officers unequaled for its cooperation in the annals of warfare. Eisenhower's leadership style was in dramatic contrast to the flamboyant, colorful egotists who were the other Allied leaders during World War II. Eisenhower's calm, participative style was well suited to developing the Allies into an effective military force capable of the largest amphibious invasion in history at Normandy.

Eisenhower led with the great and powerful and was challenged by leaders who were accustomed to having their own way. The issues were always critical when Eisenhower had discussions with men like Churchill, De Gaulle, Montgomery, Patton, and Bradley. They did everything they could to convince Eisenhower of their point of view, and he could not insult any of them while still maintaining their cooperation. He gave each person the opportunity to fully state his case and used great patience to hold the alliance together. Eisenhower was convinced that victory depended on making the alliance work, and he was constantly focused on that purpose.

The basic method of Eisenhower's leadership was to approach problems objectively and to convince others that he was objective. He had the ability to see issues from the other person's point of view. He was also known for getting the best out of people by adapting his leadership behaviors to their unique personalities, habits, and motivations. And no matter how bitter the disagreements over an issue, Eisenhower always maintained good interpersonal relations.

Eisenhower liked to emphasize his Kansas childhood and express amazement at his good fortune. He was known for being a modest person. He could be directive when it was necessary, tolerant to promote cooperation, and participative and conciliatory to obtain commitment to objectives. World War II was a "people's war," and Eisenhower's qualities of moderation and natural good sense appealed to the people. He was able to communicate his ordinariness in an extraordinary manner by projecting human warmth in talking with the troops.

General Eisenhower captured the imagination of the public as he led the assault on Hitler's European fortress, the invasion of Normandy, the drive through France, the battles on the German border, and the final victory over the Third Reich. Eisenhower was certainly one of the greatest generals of the twentieth century. Contributing to his greatness was his breadth of view, his unmatched strategic vision, and his ability to involve others to obtain commitment to a common purpose.

▪▪▪ Determining an Appropriate Behavior Pattern: Situational and Follower Characteristics

In addition to the leader's influence on followers' psychological reactions and behaviors, situational and follower characteristics also affect followers.[6] For example, situational characteristics such as aspects of the follower's work task—its challenge, complexity, or

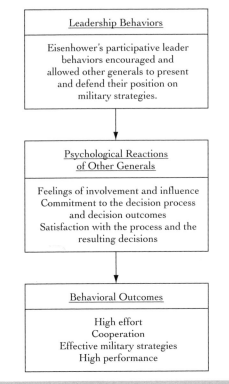

▪▪▪▪ **FIGURE 2-3 Leadership model applied to Eisenhower's leadership behavior**

danger; the follower's work group—its cohesiveness, norms, or size; and the organizations' structure—rules and procedures or overall mission—all affect followers' reactions and behaviors. Important followers' characteristics include abilities—their skills, education, and training; needs—for achievement or power, for example; and value orientation—their work ethic, culture and self-esteem. These situational and follower characteristics affect followers' attitudes, motivation, and performance.

The leader can manipulate many situational and follower characteristics to effectively influence followers. This is one reason why leaders often use a wide range of approaches in dealing with a follower problem and still obtain effective results. As alternatives, the leader may modify the follower's task to make it more interesting and challenging, or transfer an individual to a new work group the members of which are especially helpful. A leader may implement rules and procedures to decrease the danger associated with a task or see that a follower obtains additional training to help deal with task-related problems. Both the leader's behavior vis-à-vis the follower and the follower's individual and situational characteristics influence followers' reactions and behaviors. Leaders must consider their own behavior, the followers' characteristics, and the situational factors to be effective in influencing followers to achieve group goals. Any one or a combination of situation and follower characteristics can often be modified to obtain the desired effect on followers. Figure 2-4 summarizes factors that interact to influence leader effectiveness. The boxed quote by Sandy Alderson emphasizes the importance of situational factors for leadership effectiveness.

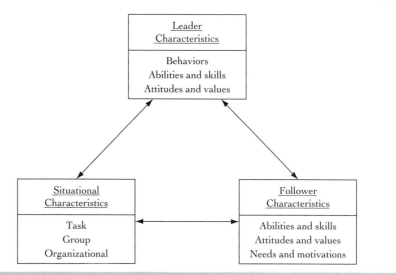

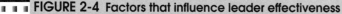

▪ ▪ ▪ **FIGURE 2-4 Factors that influence leader effectiveness**

> "Managers aren't fired because they are incompetent.
> They're fired because leadership situations change."
> Sandy Alderson, Major League Baseball
> Vice President for Operations

Situational Factors That Increase Leadership Effectiveness

Leadership enhancers are situational or follower characteristics that increase the leader's influence on followers. A highly cohesive work group is an important leadership enhancer. When cohesive groups have "strong norms in support of cooperation with management [they] can crystallize ambiguous goals and role definitions, amplify overly subtle leader provided feedback, and otherwise increase the power of weak, inconsistent leaders."[7] In a study of leadership in four large hospitals, it was found that the development of a culture with strong performance norms greatly enhanced the impact of the head nurse's directive leadership behavior.[8] Enhancers are clearly something that most leaders would like to create. Creating situational or follower characteristics that increase leader effectiveness can require the cooperation of upper-level management. Several enhancers that suit specific leadership behaviors are summarized below:

- Members of cohesive work groups with strong norms to cooperate with leaders are highly responsive to participative leadership behaviors.
- Workers on stressful, dangerous, or dissatisfying job tasks are especially appreciative of a supportive leader who shows concern for their difficulties.
- Directive leadership is needed to organize a large number of followers and prevent their working at cross purposes with one another.

Situational Factors That Decrease Leadership Effectiveness

Leadership neutralizers are situational or follower characteristics that can decrease the effectiveness of the leader's influence on followers. Spatial or geographic distance between a leader and subordinate is a typical example of a condition that decreases leadership effectiveness. Kinko's, which provides professional copying services at many widely dispersed locations nationwide, has reported the neutralizing effect of geographic distance as a major leadership problem for its regional managers. The managers are constantly frustrated because they are unable to provide enough personal direction, guidance, and support for new store managers due to the great distances involved. Telephone calls, memos, and occasional visits are just not enough. Continuous personal interaction is needed, but it is impossible with their current management structure. Other factors that can decrease the effectiveness of leaders include organizational reward systems based on seniority; union contracts or civil service policies that limit a leader's freedom in motivating followers; or a senior manager who continually countermands a leader's directions and instructions.

These factors and the leadership behaviors they neutralize are summarized below:

- A large spatial or geographic distance between leaders and followers inhibits leaders from effectively directing followers.
- Organizational reward systems based on seniority, union contracts, or civil service policies prevent leaders from adequately rewarding the best performers.
- Senior managers who countermand or modify effective directions by a lower-level manager prevent leaders from having the influence that is needed.

Although neutralizers are usually dysfunctional, they can also be used to the followers' advantage. When an incompetent manager cannot be replaced because of political factors or seniority, a neutralizer such as a large spatial distance between the manager and followers can be implemented to minimize the damage this individual may cause.

Situational Factors That Substitute for Leadership Behaviors

Another group of factors that can provide important benefits to leaders are situational and follower characteristics that *substitute* for specific leadership behaviors. Characteristics of followers, their work tasks, or the organization can provide task guidance and incentives to such an extent that they replace certain leadership behaviors. To the extent that powerful factors substitute for the need for leadership, certain types of leadership behavior may be unnecessary. The following example demonstrates two factors that substitute for directive leadership:

> Todd LaPorte, Gene Rochlin, and Karlene Roberts are three researchers studying highly stressful work such as landing jet fighters on a nuclear carrier or directing air traffic into San Francisco's main airport. They have found that in such situations, directive leadership is relatively unimportant compared to the experience and training of these workers and their closely knit work groups. These influences become particularly evident ". . . in the white heat of danger, when the whole system threatens to collapse. . . . The stress creates a need for competence among colleagues who by necessity develop close working relationships with each other." All individuals are trained extensively and daily, regardless of their position in the hierarchy, to redirect operations or to bring them to an abrupt halt. This can involve ignoring orders from managers who are removed from the front line of action.

Here the experience and continuous training of individuals along with the close working relationships with members of their work group substitute for the manager's directive leadership.[9]

Many models of leadership suggest that leadership effectiveness can be improved in one of three ways: (1) by finding a leader who is better suited to deal with the problem and challenges posed by situational and follower characteristics; (2) by coaching or training the existing leader to more effectively influence the followers and cope with the situational factors; or (3) by modifying situational or follower characteristics to increase the leader's influence and effectiveness. Situational factors can also be created that substitute for specific leadership behaviors. These factors focus on assuring that subordinates are receiving needed task guidance and incentives without assuming that the formal leader is the only supplier. Leadership scholars recently noted that:

> . . . strong leaders understand and are comfortable with the idea that effective results can be achieved when task guidance and incentives to perform emanate from sources other than themselves. When other sources are deficient, the hierarchical superior is in a position to play a dominant role; when strong incentives and guidance derive from other sources, the hierarchical superior has less opportunity, but also less need, to exert influence.[10]

Other factors that effectively substitute for specific leadership behaviors include work tasks that are intrinsically satisfying to subordinates, computer integrated manufacturing combined with networked computer systems, and the existence of a highly trained, competent, and professional workforce. Each of these factors has effectively decreased the need for certain types of leadership influence and has substituted for that influence with guidance or incentives of its own, resulting in very favorable outcomes for the organization and the people involved. These situational factors and the specific types of leadership behaviors they replace are summarized below:

- A high degree of training and experience by followers can enable them to perform well without the leader's direction and guidance.
- Work tasks that followers find intrinsically satisfying can result in positive follower attitudes and alleviate the need for a leader's supportive leadership behaviors.
- Networked computer systems and computer integrated manufacturing can make needed knowledge, information, and feedback available to followers and alleviate the need for much direction by the leader.

These situational factors substitute for leadership because (1) their purpose is to attain the same results leaders strive to attain, (2) they create situations in which followers receive guidance, motivation, and good feelings on the job from sources other than the leader, and (3) they can make certain types of leadership behavior unnecessary in achieving individual and group goals. To say that these situational factors can substitute for leadership does not mean that leadership is no longer needed. Some followers are not secure without personal leader–follower interaction. Leaders must also attend to many other activities in addition to direct task guidance and attitude improvement. For example, they create visions to inspire followers, they model desired values for followers to emulate, they obtain resources and buffer the group against

LEADERSHIP IN PERSPECTIVE
Ethics in Leadership

When leaders choose appropriate behavior patterns to help achieve group goals, they sometimes face ethical dilemmas. In these situations, the leader's choice is difficult because each alternative may have possible undesirable consequences. The following are examples of possible ethical dilemmas that confront leaders:

1. The leader's superior insists that the leader's followers work overtime to complete an important and dangerous job, when they are already exhausted from overtime work during the past week.

2. A college coach is expected to help players stay academically eligible in order to field a competitive team by providing tutors who not only instruct, but sometimes write term papers for the athletes to assure passing grades.

3. A college professor assigns a group of students to research a topic and present their findings to the class. Noncontributing members are to be reported to the professor. A group member who is a close friend of the elected leader never attends the group meetings and makes no contribution to the project, but asks the leader not to inform the instructor.

4. A very competitive employee who is having family problems asks his supervisor to make an exception to a company rule that specifies disciplinary action for too many absences. The rule has been strictly enforced in the past with other employees.

Leaders may use one or more of the major leadership behaviors to address these situations, but choosing the appropriate action involves ethical issues and consequences. Choices like these are almost never clear cut, and leaders need to carefully assess the consequences of their action in each situation. Ethical dilemmas such as these will be addressed in more detail in Chapter 12.

---

unreasonable requests, and they monitor the group environment to keep members apprised of important developments. Situational factors that substitute for specific leadership behaviors can support leadership effectiveness. For one thing, the leader does not have to be continuously present and ever-mindful of the day-to-day monitoring and control of follower activities. Thus, situational factors can give the leader more time to devote to other important matters, such as vision creation, modeling, and obtaining resources. Situational factors can also positively contribute to the leader's effectiveness in handling large numbers of followers, thus reducing managerial costs. Finally, situational factors can benefit organizations by making leadership influence consistent across organizational units. This is especially important in organizations in which leaders are frequently transferred, such as the military or multinational corporations. When situational or follower characteristics are stable sources of guidance and motivation for followers, a change in leadership is less upsetting for the unit's performance. Because situational factors that substitute for leadership can be created by leaders, they are actually an indirect form of leader influence.

▬▬ Power, Influence, and Authority

In discussions of leadership, *power* is usually considered the ability of one person to cause another person to do something. Authority is a specific type of power. An individual has *authority* if he or she has a legitimate right to require another person to do something, usually because the individual with authority holds a certain position. *Influence* is often defined as the use of power or power in action. Power and influence are clearly related, and both play a major role in the leadership process. As mentioned previously, leaders use a variety of methods to exert influence on followers—offering rewards, threatening punishment, demonstrating expertise or formal authority, and using moral persuasion. The major sources or types of power that leaders use can be classified according to whether they emanate primarily from characteristics of the individual leader, from the position the leader holds in the group or organization, or from both these sources. Table 2-1, which defines these types of power, is partially based on early work by French and Raven.[11-13]

Some writers believe that leaders rely most heavily (or exclusively) on person-based types of power. But research shows that leaders also utilize rewards, punishments, and formal authority to influence followers.[14-17] Leaders in any formal organization also use connections or networks to obtain resources that they use to encourage followers to comply with requests. The role of position-based types of influence in leadership is often underestimated.[18] This is probably because followers prefer to attribute their own compliance to the leader's referent or expert power rather than admit they were primarily influenced out of fear or a hope for personal gain. Most effective leaders use various types of power, including formal authority, to influence followers. The type of influence a leader uses also depends on the situation.[19,20]

TABLE 2-1 Types of power used by leaders

Person-Based Power

Expert power—The followers comply because they believe the leader has special knowledge about the best way to do something.

Referent power—The followers comply because they admire or identify with the leader and want to gain the leader's approval.

Position-Based Power

Legitimate power—The followers comply because they believe the leader has the right to make requests and the followers have the obligation to comply.

Position- or Person-Based Power

Reward power—The followers comply in order to obtain rewards (e.g., a raise or a compliment) from the leader.

Coercive power—The followers comply in order to avoid punishments from the leader.

Connection/Resource power—The followers comply because the leader provides needed resources or has close ties with another powerful person who can influence the followers' status.

SOURCE: Adapted from G. Yukl. *Leadership in Organizations,* 3rd Ed., Englewood Cliffs, NJ: Prentice Hall, 1994.

Influence tactics are behavioral strategies of leaders that make use of different types of power. Leaders exert influence on individuals inside and outside of their organization, including followers, peers, superiors, customers, suppliers, and so on. Table 2-2 describes several proactive influence tactics that leaders use to influence others to carry out a request. The "target" referred to in Table 2-2 is the person being influenced by the leader.

Influence attempts by a leader can have several results. *Commitment* is when the target is convinced of the value of the leader's request and exerts a high level of effort to carry out the request. *Compliance* is when the target does what the leader asks but shows little enthusiasm or effort. *Resistance* is when the target opposes the request and tries to avoid carrying it out.[21]

The leaders' proactive influence tactics that most frequently result in target commitment are rational persuasion, consultation, collaboration, and inspirational

---

TABLE 2-2 Proactive influence tactics

Rational persuasion—The leader demonstrates expert power by using logical arguments and evidence to show a proposal or request is feasible and important to achieve shared objectives.

Apprising—The leader uses expert power to explain how complying with a request or proposal will benefit the target in some way.

Inspirational appeal—The leader uses referent power while appealing to the target's values and ideals or arousing his or her emotions to obtain commitment to a proposal or request.

Consultation—The leader probably uses referent power when asking the target for ideas or suggestions to improve the proposal or requested activity that requires the target's support.

Collaboration—The leader uses connection/resource power to offer resources or assistance if the target will carry out a request or proposal.

Ingratiation—The leader uses reward power in the form of praise and flattery for the target to convince him or her to carry out a request or support a proposal.

Personal appeal—The leader uses referent power when asking the target to carry out a request or proposal as a personal favor due to their friendship.

Exchange—The leader uses reward power by offering the target something he or she wants if the target will do what the leader requests.

Coalition tactics—The leader uses connection/resource power to enlist the support of others in influencing the target to carry out a request.

Legitimating tactics—The leader uses legitimate power by referring to rules, policies, or his or her own authority to influence the target to do something.

Pressure—The leader uses coercive or legitimate power to demand, threaten, or persistently check and remind the target to carry out a request.

SOURCE: Adapted from G. Yukl and C. Chavez. Influence tactics and leader effectiveness. In G. Yukl (Ed.), *Leadership in Organizations*, 5th Ed. Upper Saddle River, NJ: Prentice Hall, 2002.

LEADERSHIP IN PERSPECTIVE
Nazi Germany

In Nazi Germany during the 1930s and early 1940s, the idea of *führer princip* required complete obedience and loyalty to leaders. This type of absolute command was believed to result in order and prosperity for those members of society who were the favored race. Others were imprisoned and many were executed. After the destruction of the Nazi war machine during World War II, the German people rejected this principle of leadership. This resulted in the current practice in many German organizations of consulting with workers about management decisions.

appeals. These tactics make extensive use of the leader's expert, referent, and connection/resource power. Ingratiation, exchange, and apprising can be effective, but they require skill and experience by the leader. These tactics rely on reward as well as expert power. Personal appeals, which rely on the leader's referent power, are effective for influencing individuals who have a friendly relationship with the leader.

Pressure and legitimating tactics do not normally result in target commitment, but they may be used to obtain compliance. Follower or peer compliance is sometimes adequate for a leader to achieve important goals. These tactics make use of the leader's legitimate or coercive power, and may cause resentment of the leader if used too often. Strong forms of pressure should probably only be used when absolutely necessary. Coalition tactics are often ineffective because they can be viewed as ganging up on the target. In this case the leader is using his or her connection power, and this tactic can be especially ineffective when the leader is trying to influence his or her boss.

When leaders use two or more tactics in combination, their influence efforts can often be highly effective. Certain combinations work better than others. Rational persuasion can be used effectively with most other influence tactics. It works especially well with consultation or apprising tactics. Rational persuasion helps clarify why a proposal is important; apprising explains the benefits to the target; and consultation involves the target in making the proposal work. Consultation and collaboration are also an effective combination. Consultation can bring out the target's suggestions and concerns; and collaboration provides the resources and assistance to address those concerns and suggestions.

Pressure tactics can undermine personal appeals or ingratiation, which rely on friendship and loyalty between the leader and target. Pressure may also erode the trust needed for consultation and collaboration to be effective. There may be times, however, when pressure is needed to influence a target whose objectives differ from the leader's.[22]

The following chapters will address behavior patterns common to most leaders, and specific types of power or influence appropriate for each situation. The Leadership in Perspective box demonstrates how leadership and power were viewed in Nazi Germany prior to World War II.

Figure 2-5 summarizes much of this chapter in a Leadership Process Model that will be used throughout this book to describe important leadership behaviors. Leadership behaviors (such as directiveness or supportiveness) are a major focus of the model in Figure 2-5. A leader selects a behavior pattern based on an assessment of situational and follower characteristics. The leader often makes use of specific power sources and influence tactics in carrying out these behaviors. Then, as noted earlier, the leader's behavior most immediately affects the psychological reactions of followers and groups of followers, such as their perceptions and attitudes. These follower reactions then affect follower behaviors and outcomes, such as absenteeism and group performance. This process is also affected by situational and follower characteristics that may neutralize, enhance, or substitute for a leader's influence or directly affect follower reactions that influence behavioral outcomes. Followers' behavioral outcomes also affect the leader's choice of leadership behavior. However, the model shows that leaders may influence followers directly through their own leadership behavior or indirectly by modifying situational or follower characteristics. Leaders are thus the primary source of influence in the Leadership Process Model, and their behavior is the focus of the remainder of this book.

■ ■ ■ ■ **FIGURE 2-5 Leadership Process Model for influencing follower behaviors**

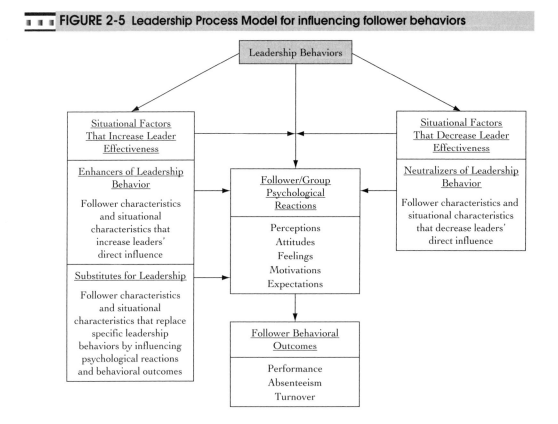

KEY TERMS AND CONCEPTS IN THIS CHAPTER

- Apprising
- Boundary spanning
- Charismatic leadership behaviors
- Coalition tactics
- Coercive power
- Collaboration
- Connection/resource power
- Consultation
- Directive leadership behaviors

- Exchange
- Expert power
- Followership
- Ingratiation
- Inspirational appeal
- Leader reward and punishment behavior
- Leadership enhancers
- Leadership neutralizers
- Leadership substitutes
- Legitimating tactics

- Participative leadership behaviors
- Personal appeal
- Pressure
- Psychological reactions
- Rational persuasion
- Referent power
- Reward power
- Supportive leadership behaviors

REVIEW AND DISCUSSION QUESTIONS

1. Give a specific example of each of the five core patterns of leadership behaviors that were exhibited by a leader you have observed.
2. Which follower or group psychological reactions are likely to be most important where you have worked or plan to work?
3. Discuss how a specific situational characteristic (task, group, or organization) has affected your reactions to a leader.
4. Discuss how one of your own characteristics (abilities, needs, or values) has affected your reactions to a leader.
5. Identify several leadership behaviors that could produce a high level of satisfaction among followers you have known. Identify leadership behaviors that could produce high follower performance.
6. Describe situational or follower characteristics you have observed that neutralized or enhanced a leader's impact on followers.
7. Analyze a situation you experienced as a leader or follower using the concepts contained in the Leadership Process Model in Figure 2-5.

LEADERSHIP: SELF-ASSESSMENT

Important Leadership Behaviors

Objective: To help the reader identify patterns of leadership behavior that may be used when leading a task group

Directions: Circle the number on the 1 to 5 scale that best indicates how you would normally behave as leader of a group that is responsible for completing some task.

	Almost Never				*Almost Always*
1. I assign specific tasks to others.	1	2	3	4	5
2. I explain methods and set goals for the group.	1	2	3	4	5
3. I explain what each group member needs to accomplish.	1	2	3	4	5
4. I show consideration and acceptance of others.	1	2	3	4	5
5. I show concern for the feelings of others.	1	2	3	4	5
6. I help develop the abilities of others to contribute to the task.	1	2	3	4	5
7. I get others involved in making decisions.	1	2	3	4	5
8. I consult others to get their ideas and suggestions.	1	2	3	4	5
9. I encourage subgroups to handle certain aspects of the group's task.	1	2	3	4	5
10. I provide others with benefits and rewards.	1	2	3	4	5
11. I punish others for undesirable behavior.	1	2	3	4	5
12. I compliment those who do a good job.	1	2	3	4	5
13. I display high expectations and confidence.	1	2	3	4	5
14. I communicate a vision for the group.	1	2	3	4	5
15. I attempt to inspire others by pointing out the importance of the group's task and their part in accomplishing it.	1	2	3	4	5

If you rated items 1, 2, and 3 highly (by giving them a rating of 4 or 5), then you normally would tend to be directive with followers. If you rated items 4, 5, and 6 highly, you tend to be supportive. High ratings on items 7, 8, and 9 indicate participative leadership. High ratings on items 10, 11, and 12 indicate a reward-and-punishment type of leadership behavior. High ratings on items 13, 14, and 15 indicate a charismatic approach with followers. These behavior patterns are important in different situations, and most effective leaders vary their behavior patterns with different situations and followers.

SOURCE: The items for this exercise are based on research instruments used in an empirical study of leadership effectiveness by P. W. Dorfman, J. P. Howell, B. G. Cotton, and U. Tate, "Leadership within the discontinuous hierarchy structure of the military: Are effective leadership behaviors similar within and across command structures," In K. E. Clark, M. B. Clark, and D. P. Campbell. *Impact of Leadership,* Greensboro, NC: Center for Creative Leadership, 1992.

▪ ▪▪▪ ▪ C A S E   I N C I D E N T ▪ ▪▪▪ ▪

Bobby Knight

Basketball Coach

Bobby Knight is a legend in the world of college basketball. He became the youngest NCAA Division I head basketball coach in the country when he was named the coach at West Point. He later became head coach at Indiana University in 1971 and created a record of success during the ensuing 29 years, including 3 NCAA championships. In 2001, Bobby Knight took the coaching position at Texas Tech, and on February 5, 2003, he achieved his 800th career victory. Knight also coached the U.S. Olympic Team in 1984, leading the first Dream Team to the Olympic championship. He has been selected as the national coach of the year four times, and in 1991, he was admitted to the Basketball Hall of Fame.

Several decades of playing and coaching experience have given Bobby Knight a unique understanding of basketball. He has extremely strong confidence in his knowledge of the game and in his capability to lead his teams to victory. He instills the belief in his players that he is the basketball expert and his way is the right way to play. He does not tolerate questioning or criticism of his approach.

Knight believes disciplined players are indispensable for a winning team. He never hesitates to yell at players when they fail to meet his expectations. At times, verbal outbursts have turned into physical abuse. Over the years, news reports emerged about Knight's violent behavior toward his players, such as grabbing a player's neck or throwing unopened soda cans at players.

Knight's temper flare-ups extend outside his team. He used insulting language toward a secretary at Indiana University when he believed the secretary mistreated two of his assistants. He is well known for throwing a chair across the basketball court to express his dissatisfaction with a referee.

In 2000, Knight's temper finally cost him his coaching job at Indiana University. A former player had filed a complaint that Knight violently grabbed him and shouted obscenities at him because the player addressed him as "Knight," instead of "Coach Knight," "Mr. Knight," or "Bob." Bobby Knight admitted in an interview with Larry King that he is troubled by "small things" (such as how his players address him) in the course of achieving "big things" (winning games). A sportswriter described Bobby Knight by saying that no one was better at the big things, but "it was the little things that always brought him down."

Bobby Knight is acclaimed as much as he is criticized. He emphasizes dedication to the game on the court, and dedication to study off the court. His players have an impressive 98 percent graduation rate. He articulates and role models passion for the game, assertiveness, self-confidence, tenacity, and a sense of responsibility. His philosophy is usually well adopted by his players and welcomed by their parents. Knight has developed a wide recruiting network for his basketball programs and helps recruit players for other sports. He also helped raise over $5 million for the library at Indiana University.

Being fired from Indiana was the biggest slump in Bobby Knight's career. He rose from this setback when he restarted his basketball coaching career at Texas Tech. He has continued his winning magic. At the same time, members of the press are watching Bobby Knight. ▪

DISCUSSION QUESTIONS

1. What type of leadership behaviors does Bobby Knight display?
2. What flaws (if any) do you see in his leadership behavior?
3. How could he improve his leadership?

ENDNOTES ▪▪▪▪▪▪▪

1. House, R. J. (1996). Path-goal theory of leadership: Lessons, legacy and a reformulated theory. *The Leadership Quarterly,* 7(3), 323–352.
2. Yukl, G. (1998). *Leadership in Organizations,* 4th ed. Upper Saddle River, NJ: Prentice Hall.
3. Huntington, A. S. (1997). A ship with no captain. *HRMagazine,* November 1997, 94–99.
4. Zaccaro, S. J., Foti, R. J., and Kenny, K. A. (1991). Self-monitoring and trait based variance in leadership: An investigation of leader flexibility across multiple group situations. *Journal of Applied Psychology,* 76, 308–315.
5. Bass, B. (1990). *Bass and Stogdill's Handbook of Leadership.* New York: The Free Press.
6. Howell, J. P., Dorfman, P. W., and Kerr, S. (1986). Moderator variables in leadership research. *Academy of Management Review,* 11(1), 88–102.
7. Howell, J. P., Bowen, D., Dorfman, P. W., Kerr, S., and Podsakoff, P. M. (1990). Substitutes for leadership: Effective alternatives for ineffective leadership. *Organizational Dynamics,* Summer 1990.
8. Sheridan, J. E., Vredenburgh, D. J., and Abelson, M. A. (1984). Contextual model of leadership influence in hospital units. *Academy of Management Journal,* 27, 57–78.
9. LaPorte, T., Rochlin, E., and Roberts, K. (1989). The secret of life at the limits: Cogs become big wheels. *Smithsonian Magazine,* July 1989.
10. Howell, Bowen, Dorfman, Kerr, and Podsakoff. Substitutes for leadership: Effective alternatives for ineffective leadership.
11. French, J. R. P., and Raven, B. (1959). The basis of social power. In D. Cartwright (Ed.), *Studies in Social Power.* Ann Arbor, MI: University of Michigan, Institute for Social Research.
12. Pfeffer, J. (1992). *Managing With Power.* Boston: Harvard Business School Press.
13. Whetten, D. A., and Cameron, K. S. (1998). *Developing Management Skills,* 4th ed. Reading, MA: Addison-Wesley.
14. Podsakoff, P. M., Todor, W. D., and Skov, R. (1982). Effects of leader contingent and noncontingent reward and punishment behaviors on subordinate performance and satisfaction. *Academy of Management Journal,* 25, 810–821.
15. Warren, D. I. (1968). Power, visibility, and conformity in formal organizations. *American Sociological Review,* 6, 951–970.
16. Podsakoff, P. M., Todor, W. D., Grover, R. A., and Huber, V. L. (1984). Situational moderators of leader reward and punishment behavior: Fact or fiction? *Organizational Behavior and Human Performance,* 34, 21–63.
17. Yukl, G., and Falbe, C. M. (1991). The importance of different power sources in downward and lateral relations. *Journal of Applied Psychology,* 76, 416–423.
18. Yukl. *Leadership in Organizations,* 4th ed.
19. Yukl and Falbe. The importance of different power sources in downward and lateral relations.
20. Kipnis, D., Schmidt, S. M., and Wilkinson D. (1980). Intra-organizational influence tactics. *Journal of Applied Psychology,* 65, 440–452.
21. Yukl, G., and Chavez, C. (2002). Influence tactics and leader effectiveness. In L. L. Neider and C. A. Schriesheim (Eds.), *Leadership.* Greenwich, CT: Information Age Publishing, 139–165.
22. Ibid.

3

Contingency Models of Leadership

Learning Objectives

After reading this chapter, you should be able to do the following:

1. Describe the concept of contingency theories of leadership.
2. Explain the two leadership styles used in Fiedler's Contingency model of leadership.
3. Use Fiedler's Contingency model to predict the leadership style that will be most effective.
4. Describe the four leadership styles of the Hersey and Blanchard Situational Leadership model.
5. Explain the relationship described by the Situational Leadership theory between leadership styles and followers' competence and commitment.
6. Describe the four leadership behaviors of the Path-Goal theory of leadership and their motivational effects.
7. Discuss the recommendations of the Path-Goal theory for effective leadership behaviors.
8. Describe the Multiple Linkage model of leadership and its recommendations for leadership behavior to improve group performance.
9. Describe the Normative Decision-Making model of participative leadership.

There are numerous theories of leadership effectiveness, and many of these theories imply that one leadership style can be effective in all situations. Examples include Blake and Mouton's 9, 9 leadership style, Ouchi's Theory Z, Bass's transformational leadership, House's charismatic leadership, and Stephen Covey's principle-centered leadership. Most of these theories recommend an approach involving extensive participation, delegation, and group involvement, or a visionary style involving inspirational rhetoric and a value-oriented mission with strong moral dimensions. Specific situational factors are seldom considered in detail in these models. When situational factors are mentioned, the leader is usually expected to make only minor adjustments in leadership behaviors. Little guidance is given in these models as to how the leader's approach should be modified under different organizational conditions or with different types of followers.

Other leadership theories incorporate aspects of the organization or characteristics of followers as key elements of the leader's effectiveness. These theories are referred to as *contingency* or *situational theories of leadership* because a leader's impact on followers depends on (is contingent on) both the leader's behavior and the characteristics of the organizational situation. An effective leader in one situation is not assumed to be effective in all situations. Effectiveness depends on the match between the leader's characteristics and behavior, and the situational and follower characteristics.[1]

These contingency theories of leadership are more realistic than the "one best style" approach because they include characteristics of leadership situations that can be vastly different. The types of followers, work tasks, resources, technology, and legal and economic environments all vary from organization to organization. Effective leaders recognize these differences and adapt their leadership behaviors to fit the situational characteristics.[2]

Five contingency theories of leadership are described in this chapter to provide a background for the remainder of this book. Two early models that have been very popular and relatively unchanged for more than twenty years are described first. The last three models that are described have evolved over the years into very sophisticated, complex, and current contingency theories of leadership. These five theories are representative of contingency models available today. Each has strengths and weaknesses that are described, and their implications for the approach taken in this book are discussed.

▮▮▮ Fiedler's Contingency Theory of Leadership

Fred Fiedler's Contingency theory of leadership is a situational theory that focuses on the match between the leader's predisposition or style and the characteristics of the situation. In the early 1950s, Fiedler noted that the style of the leader and the leader's acceptance by subordinates had a strong effect on the performance of the group. This and other observations led to the development of the Least Preferred Coworker (LPC) scale (a questionnaire), and a situational theory of leadership based on the LPC score of the leader and the "favorableness" or "control" of the situation.[3]

A leader's LPC score is determined by asking the leader to indicate characteristics of a person with whom it is most difficult to work. Thus, the LPC is a description of the leader's emotional reaction to a person who obstructs goal attainment. A low LPC score indicates that a leader would reject an unsatisfactory worker and that the leader has a high need for task accomplishment, recognition, and reward. This type of leader is described by Fiedler as "task oriented." A high LPC score reveals a more tolerant attitude toward the difficult worker and a high need by the leader for positive social interaction. This type of leader is described by Fiedler as "relationship oriented."[4-6] A medium LPC score implies a style that Fiedler calls "socioindependent." The self-assessment shows the LPC scale that Fiedler uses to measure a leader's predisposition or style.

The situational favorableness or situational control depends on: (1) the quality of leader–member relations—high-quality relations indicate high cohesiveness and

LEADERSHIP SELF-ASSESSMENT
Least Preferred Coworker (LPC) Scale

Instructions: Think of the person with whom you can work least well. This may be someone you work with now or someone you knew in the past. It does not have to be the person you like least well, but should be the person with whom you had the most difficulty in getting a job done. Describe this person as he or she appears to you, by circling a number for each scale. There are no right or wrong answers.

Pleasant	8	7	6	5	4	3	2	1	Unpleasant
Friendly	8	7	6	5	4	3	2	1	Unfriendly
Rejecting	1	2	3	4	5	6	7	8	Accepting
Helpful	8	7	6	5	4	3	2	1	Frustrating
Unenthusiastic	1	2	3	4	5	6	7	8	Enthusiastic
Tense	1	2	3	4	5	6	7	8	Relaxed
Distant	1	2	3	4	5	6	7	8	Close
Cold	1	2	3	4	5	6	7	8	Warm
Cooperative	8	7	6	5	4	3	2	1	Uncooperative
Supportive	8	7	6	5	4	3	2	1	Hostile
Boring	1	2	3	4	5	6	7	8	Interesting
Quarrelsome	1	2	3	4	5	6	7	8	Harmonious
Self-assured	8	7	6	5	4	3	2	1	Hesitant
Efficient	8	7	6	5	4	3	2	1	Inefficient
Gloomy	1	2	3	4	5	6	7	8	Cheerful
Open	8	7	6	5	4	3	2	1	Guarded

Scoring and interpretation: Your LPC score is the sum of the answers to these 16 items. According to Fiedler's Contingency model, a score greater than 76 indicates a relationship orientation, and a score of less than 62 indicates a task orientation. A score of 63 to 75 places you in the intermediate range, which indicates socioindependent leadership orientation. Relationship-oriented leaders tend to function best in situations that are moderately favorable for exercising control. Task-oriented leaders tend to function best in situations that are either highly favorable or highly unfavorable for exercising control. Socioindependent leaders tend to be more effective in situations that are highly favorable for exercising control.

SOURCE: Adapted from F. E. Fiedler, M. M. Chemers, and L. Mahar, *Improving Leadership Effectiveness.* New York: John Wiley & Sons, 1976. Reprinted by permission of Fred E. Fiedler.

support for the leader by the group members, which is a favorable situation for the leader; (2) the degree of task structure—the leader's task is highly structured when his or her task goals and procedures are clear, allowing the leader to confidently guide the group's activities, which is a favorable situation; and (3) the amount of position power—the leader's

TABLE 3-1 Fiedler's Contingency model of leadership

Octant	Situation Classification and Leader Type							
	I	*II*	*III*	*IV*	*V*	*VI*	*VII*	*VIII*
Leader–Member Relations	Good				Poor			
Task Structure	Structured		Unstructured		Structured		Unstructured	
Position Power	High	Low	High	Low	High	Low	High	Low
Recommended Leader Type	Task motivated (low LPC) Socioindependent (medium LPC)				Relationship motivated (high LPC)			Task motivated (low LPC)

administrative authority and control over rewards and punishments, which are favorable for the leader's influence attempts.[7, 8] Leadership situations are classified in this model as either high or low on each of these three characteristics—good or poor leader–member relations, high or low task structure, and high or low position power. This results in eight possible combinations (called octants) of situational control. The most favorable situation (high control) is good leader–member relations, a structured task, and strong position power. A very unfavorable situation (low control) is poor leader–member relations, an unstructured task, and weak position power. An example of a moderately favorable situation (moderate control) is poor leader–member relations, a structured task, and strong position power.

Fiedler's model predicts that task oriented leaders are expected to produce high group performance in either very favorable or very unfavorable situations. Relationship-oriented leaders will produce high group performance when the situation is only moderately favorable. Socioindependent leaders (who are midway between task oriented and relationship oriented) tend to perform best in situations that are very favorable. Table 3-1 summarizes Fiedler's situation classifications and recommended leader types.[9]

Recommendations of the Contingency Model

Fiedler and his associates believe that the LPC score reflects a stable characteristic of the leader and that a consistent leadership style results from the LPC score. They therefore suggest it is ineffective to try to change a person's leadership style.[10] Fiedler advocates that an effective leadership approach is to assess the situation and then select leaders with the appropriate style to match the situational characteristics. When choosing or changing the leader is not an option, the situation should be reengineered to match the leader's style. The favorableness of the situation is altered (engineered) by changing one or more of the three elements of situational control—leader–member relations, task structure, or position power. The *Leader Match training program* is used to teach managers how to determine their LPC score, assess their situation, and engineer the situation to better match their leadership style.[11]

How Valid and Useful Is the Model?

Fiedler's Contingency model has been examined, criticized, and defended by many writers, and detractors have called LPC "a measure in search of a meaning".[12] Fiedler has redefined the LPC several times. Some researchers find a leader's LPC to be fairly stable over time while others find the score for a leader to vary dramatically at different times. If LPC does vary for a leader, then engineering situations to fit a leader's LPC score may be like trying to hit a moving target, and may be an expensive and ineffective strategy to improve group performance. Research shows that a leader's behavior does not always directly reflect the leader's LPC score. There is also some evidence that the leader's LPC score and leader–member relations may be affected by group performance rather than the other way around.[13]

Recent reviews of much research on Fiedler's Contingency model show that both high LPC and low LPC leaders can be effective in different situations.[14] High LPC leaders are sometimes more effective in situations in which low LPC leaders are supposed to be best. The reviews also found statistical evidence that other situational factors can have important effects on a leader's performance.[15]

▪▪▪ Hersey and Blanchard's Situational Leadership Theory

Paul Hersey and Ken Blanchard developed a contingency model of leader effectiveness that recommends four possible combinations of task-oriented and relationship-oriented behavior depending on a subordinate's readiness to perform a particular task. Leadership behavior is described as consisting of two factors that are similar to those in Fiedler's model: task-oriented or directive behavior, which focuses on assuring that followers complete their work tasks efficiently and effectively, and relationship-oriented or supportive behavior, which focuses on listening, encouraging, supporting, and caring about followers' welfare. The terms directive and supportive behavior are used in current versions of this model and are therefore used in this description. These factors are represented in this theory by a two-dimensional graph with four quadrants that describe different combinations of high and low levels of directive and supportive behavior. Quadrant 1 (Telling) represents a high-directiveness, low-supportiveness style of leader behavior. Quadrant 2 (Selling) represents a high-directiveness, high-supportiveness style of leader behavior. Quadrant 3 (Participating) represents a low-directiveness, high-supportiveness leadership style. Quadrant 4 (Delegating) is characterized by a low-directiveness, low-supportiveness style of leader behavior. These four styles of leadership are said to be effective for different levels of follower readiness to perform (developmental level).[16]

The follower's developmental level reflects the stages or levels an employee might go through in learning new tasks. Level 1 is described as unable and unwilling, reflecting low follower ability and lack of confidence or commitment when trying something new. Level 2 is described as unable but willing, where the follower is low in ability, but is motivated and making an effort. Level 3 is characterized as able but unwilling, where followers have the ability to perform, the task, but are insecure or apprehensive about doing it on their own. Level 4 is described as able and willing, where followers have the ability to perform, and are confident and committed to the task. The developmental level is specific to the task. For example, an employee would be considered highly

TABLE 3-2 Hersey and Blanchard's behavioral recommendations for leaders

| | Leadership Behavior | | Leadership |
Subordinate Developmental Level	*Supportiveness*	*Directiveness*	*Style*
Low ability and low willingness	Low	High	Telling
Low ability and high willingness	High	High	Selling
High ability and low willingness	High	Low	Participating
High ability and high willingness	Low	Low	Delegating

developed if able and willing and working at a task that is liked. The same employee would be considered less developed if working at an unfamiliar task that is disliked. Table 3-2 shows the leadership behavior combinations that Hersey and Blanchard recommend for followers at different developmental levels.

Recommendations of the Situational Leadership Theory

Leaders are advised to use a telling style of leadership behavior (high direction, low support) with employees who lack the ability to complete the task without guidance (level 1 development). That is, the leader needs to set goals, organize the work, set time deadlines for completing the work, and direct and observe the performance of the employee.

Employees who still have low ability but are willing and motivated to perform the task (level 2 development) require a selling style from the leader (high direction, high support). The leader is expected to provide encouragement, listen to the subordinate's opinions, and provide feedback on the employee's performance, in addition to closely supervising the work.

For employees who have the ability, skills, and knowledge to complete the task, but are unwilling or insecure about doing it on their own (level 3 development), a participating style is recommended (low direction, high support). The leader should share ideas with employees and facilitate their decision making, but the amount of direct supervisory involvement in organizing and directing the work is reduced.

A delegating style of leadership behavior (low direction, low support) is recommended for those employees who are both able and willing to perform their assigned tasks on their own (level 4 development). The leader should entrust such employees with the implementation and completion of their projects.

How Valid and Useful Is the Model?

The research evidence for Hersey and Blanchard's Situational Leadership theory is mixed and generally weak. A recent study of senior executives in a large business organization found results that contradicted the model.[17] Another researcher studied high school teachers and found some support for the model in low-development conditions, but not for high-development level followers.[18] Other studies found follower performance and satisfaction were not significantly higher when leaders' behavior fit the model's recommendations.[19] Another study of retail employees also found little support for the model.[20] For these individuals, the delegating and telling styles produced low levels of satisfaction and commitment for both high- and low-development employees.

Supportive behaviors produced high satisfaction for all employees. These findings do not match the model's predictions. However, the participating style did fit well for highly-developed employees and the selling style fit less-developed employees.

Although the model has not been well supported by researchers, it remains widely accepted by managers and management trainers. Part of the reason for this acceptance is the ease with which the model and its behavioral recommendations are learned. The emphasis on adapting the leader's behavior to match subordinate levels of ability and willingness (development) is reasonable. The development level of the subordinate is assessed by the manager. It is likely that few employees will be completely lacking in ability, or so able and willing that they will require no supervision. This means the most common leadership style will be either a selling or participating style. It appears that the leadership process in real organizations is more complex than these simple recommendations.

▪▪▪ Path-Goal Theory of Leadership

The Path-Goal theory of leadership is a contingency theory that addresses a leader's interaction with individual followers. The theory suggests that a leader's behavior is motivating or satisfying to followers if the behavior increases the attractiveness of goals and increases followers' confidence in achieving them. The Path-Goal theory also suggests that effective leaders help followers achieve task goals and make followers' efforts satisfying and rewarding. With this model, the leader is very active in coaching, guiding, encouraging, motivating, and rewarding followers for their efforts and achievements.[21]

Four types of leadership behavior are usually included in this model—*directive, supportive, participative,* and *achievement oriented.* Directive leadership behavior is nonauthoritarian and nonpunitive guidance by the leader. The leader organizes and schedules the work and tells the followers in a nonthreatening manner what, when, and how the work is to be done. Supportive leadership behavior involves being concerned and considerate of the well-being and needs of followers. The supportive leader creates a "friendly and psychologically supportive work environment".[22] Participative leadership behavior involves encouraging subordinates to contribute to the decision-making process. Participative behaviors consist of asking followers for suggestions and opinions, and using their input when making decisions. Achievement-oriented leadership behavior includes setting challenging goals, encouraging followers to perform at high levels, and showing confidence in their ability to do so. The model states that these four leadership behaviors will result in improved follower attitudes and expectations, such as satisfaction with work, acceptance of the leader, and follower beliefs that their effort will lead to effective performance and rewards (see Table 3-3).

The Path-Goal theory predicts that situational factors will influence the effectiveness of the four types of leadership behavior as follows:

1. Nonauthoritarian and nonpunitive directive leadership behavior will increase follower satisfaction and performance when followers are engaged in unstructured or ambiguous tasks.
2. Supportive leadership behavior will increase the satisfaction of followers engaged in frustrating, stressful, or dissatisfying tasks. When supportive leadership behavior is provided primarily for followers who show high effort, it will increase the performance of those followers.

TABLE 3-3　Predicted effects of Path-Goal leadership behaviors

Leadership Behavior	*Predicted Motivational Effects*
Directive	Reduces role ambiguity Increases follower beliefs that effort will result in good performance and performance will be rewarded
Supportive	Increases self-confidence Increases the personal value of job-related effort
Participative	Reduces ambiguity Clarifies expectations Increases consistency of subordinate and organizational goals Increases involvement with and commitment to organizational goals
Achievement Oriented	Increases subordinate confidence and the personal value of goal-directed effort

3. Participative leadership behavior will increase follower satisfaction and motivation when tasks are ambiguous, nonrepetitive, and challenging. Participative leadership behavior will also increase satisfaction of nonauthoritarian followers who have a high need for independence when tasks are clearly specified in advance.

4. Achievement-oriented leadership behavior will increase follower effort and confidence in goal achievement when tasks are ambiguous, nonrepetitive, and challenging.

Recommendations of the Path-Goal Theory

The main recommendation of the Path-Goal theory is that the leader should consider the existing follower characteristics and task and organizational factors, and choose a leadership behavior that is appropriate for the situation. If the leader demonstrates the appropriate behavior, followers will be highly satisfied and accepting of the leader. They will put forth considerable effort and will utilize effective work methods to achieve their task-related goals. These effects should result in low levels of follower grievances and turnover and high levels of overall performance.

How Valid and Useful Is the Model?

Portions of the Path-Goal theory have been widely tested with varying results. One comprehensive review of research on the Path-Goal theory[23] demonstrated considerable support for some aspects of the theory. Directive leadership behavior improved the satisfaction of subordinates whose tasks were ambiguous. However, contrary to the Path-Goal theory, directive leadership improved follower performance even when followers' tasks were repetitive and unambiguous. As predicted by the theory, supportive behavior had a strong positive effect on the satisfaction and performance of followers doing highly repetitive, unambiguous, and stressful tasks. However, support also had positive effects on satisfaction, performance, and job clarity in jobs that were ambiguous and nonrepetitive. Supportive leadership behavior also improved the job clarity of lower-level employees more than that of higher-level employees. Another recent review of Path-Goal theory research supports some of these findings but not others.[24] A limited amount of research data on participative leadership behavior indicates some support for its positive effects when followers' tasks are ambiguous and nonrepetitive.[25] There is almost no published research on achievement-oriented leadership behavior.

The overall proposition of the Path-Goal theory, that the effects of leadership behavior are contingent on situational factors, is generally supported. Furthermore, although some specific predictions of the Path-Goal theory have not been supported, researchers point to faulty testing methods as the potential culprit. In response to the mixed research results and methodological problems, Bob House (the originator of the Path-Goal theory) introduced a new version of the theory.[26] The reformulated theory expands the focus from the effects of four leadership behaviors on the work satisfaction, motivation, and performance of individual subordinates, to include the effects of ten types of leadership behaviors on subordinate empowerment, satisfaction, ability, performance, and work unit performance. The revised model also includes the immediate (short-term) effects of leadership behaviors on followers as well as longer-term outcomes. Twenty-six propositions are presented relating different types of leadership behaviors and situational characteristics to individual and work unit outcomes. The theory now includes charismatic leadership as well as a broader emphasis on shared decision making, representation, and networking behaviors of managers. The newest version of the Path-Goal theory is very complex and has not been tested by research in organizations. Table 3-4 presents the ten types of leadership behaviors in the revised Path-Goal theory, as well as specific examples of each type.

TABLE 3-4 Revised Path-Goal theory leadership behaviors

General Leadership Behavior	*Specific Leadership Behaviors*
Clarifying	Clarifying performance goals, standards, and means to achieve them
	Clarifying who subordinates should respond to
	Implementing contingency rewards and punishments
Participative	Consulting with subordinates
	Incorporating subordinate opinions in decision making
Achievement oriented	Setting high goals and seeking improvement
	Emphasizing excellence and showing confidence in subordinates
	Stressing pride in work
Work facilitation	Planning, scheduling, and organizing work
	Coordinating subordinates' work
	Guiding, coaching, counseling, and giving feedback
	Eliminating roadblocks and bottlenecks
	Providing resources
	Delegating authority to subordinates
Supportive	Creating a friendly and psychologically supportive environment
	Displaying concern for subordinates' welfare
Interaction facilitation	Resolving disputes and facilitating communication
	Giving minority views a hearing
	Emphasizing collaboration and teamwork
	Encouraging close relationships among team members

(cont.)

TABLE 3-4 (cont.)

General Leadership Behavior	Specific Leadership Behaviors
Group oriented decision processes	Posing problems to the group
	Searching for mutual interests in problem solving
	Encouraging participation by all group members
	Searching for and displaying alternatives
	Delaying evaluation until all alternatives are found
	Encouraging evaluation of all alternatives
	Combining advantages of alternatives to create solutions
Representing and networking	Representing the group in a favorable way
	Communicating the importance of the group's work
	Maintaining positive relations with influential others
	Being an effective trading partner
	Keeping in touch with network members
	Participating in social functions and ceremonies
	Doing favors for others
	Showing positive regard for others
Charismatic	Articulating a vision of a better future
	Displaying a passion for the vision
	Displaying self-sacrifice in the interest of the vision
	Demonstrating self-confidence, confidence in the attainment of the vision, and determination and persistence in the interest of the vision
	Selectively arousing nonconscious motives of followers
	Taking extraordinary personal and organizational risks
	Communicating high performance expectations
	Using symbolic behaviors to emphasize values
	Providing frequent positive evaluation of followers
Shared leadership	Encouraging subordinates to behave as leaders
	Setting an example for subordinates to follow

As House stated, "all theories, no matter how good at explaining a set of phenomena, are ultimately incorrect and consequently will undergo modification over time."[27] It appears that the original Path-Goal theory has produced enough research and insight into the leadership process to produce another generation of leadership theories.

▮▮▮ Multiple Linkage Theory of Leadership

The Multiple Linkage Theory of leadership presents four broad categories of leadership behavior that are broken down into eleven mid-range behaviors, which in turn comprise numerous specific behaviors (see Table 3-5). This model, developed by Gary Yukl, proposes that the overall impact of specific leadership behaviors on work group performance is complex and is influenced by two sets of factors. One set is the immediate effects of the leader's behavior on follower effort, job knowledge, resources, organization of the work, cooperation, cohesion, and coordination with other individuals and groups. These immediate effects are called *intervening variables* in this model, and when they are improved by the leader, group performance is usually high. The second set of factors that influence the

TABLE 3-5 Leadership behaviors in Yukl's Multiple Linkage model

Broad Behavior	Mid-Range Behaviors	Specific Behaviors
Building relationships	Supporting	Being friendly Showing concern Listening to problems Giving advice and support
	Networking	Developing and maintaining positive relationships with influential others
	Managing conflict and team building	Reducing and resolving disputes Facilitating communication Encouraging teamwork and cooperation
Influencing people	Motivating	Influencing subordinates to achieve work goals Setting good behavioral examples
	Rewarding and recognizing	Providing valued rewards, praise, and recognition for performance Expressing appreciation, respect, and admiration for achievement
Making decisions	Problem solving	Identifying and analyzing problems and solutions Implementing and evaluating solutions
	Planning and organizing	Determining objectives, strategies, and actions needed to improve efficiency and productivity
	Consulting and delegating	Discussing decision options with subordinates Asking for input from subordinates Allowing subordinates some autonomy in decision making
Giving or seeking information	Monitoring	Collecting information on work progress and quality Determining opportunities, threats, and needs
	Clarifying	Providing direction Telling subordinates what, how, and when to do certain tasks
	Informing	Providing information subordinates need to do their work and to understand the importance of their work

leader's impact on group performance are *situational characteristics,* such as the formal organizational reward system, the type of work task performed by followers, the organization's policies and procedures, and the technology of the workplace. These situational factors may affect group performance, they may constrain leaders from using certain behaviors, or they may affect the type of impact the leader has on group performance.[28]

In this model, intervening variables may also be directly affected by situational characteristics. For example, the formal reward system and aspects of the tasks (situational characteristics) can affect the degree of effort subordinates will exhibit (intervening variables). Recruitment and selection procedures (situational characteristics) also affect the level of job knowledge in the subordinates' work group (intervening variable). Other organizational policies and procedures, as well as the technology of the workplace (situational characteristics), can affect how efficiently the work is organized and the adequacy of available resources (intervening variable). The Multiple Linkage model clearly allows for many sources of influence on followers.

Recommendations of the Multiple Linkage Model

The model makes two general recommendations in the form of propositions to improve group performance:

Proposition 1: In the short term, group effectiveness is determined by the degree to which the leader uses the leadership behaviors shown in Table 3-5 to correct deficiencies in the intervening variables.

Proposition 2: In the long term, group effectiveness is determined by the degree to which the leader improves situational factors.[29]

Proposition 1 of the Multiple Linkage model addresses the short-term motivational needs of subordinates. Leaders need to set challenging goals; provide direction, recognition, and support; organize the work; reduce conflict; and encourage cooperation. Proposition 2 addresses longer-term strategic actions that modify situational influences in such a way as to decrease negative effects and increase the positive effects of situational factors. For example, leaders can increase demand for the unit's products by finding new customers; upgrade the skill level of the work unit through training programs and personnel changes; and expand output by replacing old equipment, simplifying procedures, and improving sources of supplies.

How Valid and Useful Is the Model?

The model is not specific about the effects individual leadership behaviors have on the intervening variables. It also fails to specify when certain situational factors affect intervening variables or group performance, or how the situational factors influence the impacts of specific leadership behaviors. This lack of specific predictions makes it very difficult to test the model, and very few tests have been conducted.[30] However, the linkages between leadership behaviors and their impacts on followers are grounded in prior research in the field of leadership. Yukl recognizes the limitations of the model, and suggests that it is a general framework for describing the leadership process rather than a formal theory with precise predictions for effective leadership.

▮▮▮ Normative Decision-Making Theory of Participation

The Normative Decision-Making theory was initiated by Vroom and Yetton,[31] and was later revised by Vroom and Jago.[32] The model involves the degree of participation that followers should be allowed in different decision-making situations. In the current version of this model, five decision-making styles with different degrees of employee participation are identified, including *decide, consult individually, consult group, facilitate,* and *delegate:*[33]

> *Decide*—The leader makes decisions alone by using his or her expertise and information available at the time, which may include discussions with group members or others.
> *Consult individually*—The leader shares the problem with followers on an individual basis and obtains suggestions regarding problem solutions, but makes the final decision him- or herself.
> *Consult group*—The leader shares the problem with followers as a group and obtains suggestions from the group, but makes the final decision him- or herself.
> *Facilitate*—The leader and followers meet as a group. The leader helps the group define and analyze the problem, and they discuss alternative solutions. The final decision is a product of group consensus.
> *Delegate*—The leader assigns the decision problem to the group for their diagnosis, analysis, and final decision. The leader provides resources and encouragement, and is available to respond to any group requests.

The Normative Decision-Making model contends that each of these decision-making styles is appropriate in different situations. One style will be effective in certain situations and a different style will be effective in other situations. Several outcomes of the decision-making styles are addressed in this model, including decision acceptance, decision quality, decision timeliness, costs of decision making, and followers' development. These outcomes represent different dimensions of decision effectiveness:

1. *Decision acceptance.* Decision acceptance refers to the degree to which a decision is accepted and is willingly implemented by followers. Decision acceptance is especially important when successful implementation of a decision largely depends on followers. Examples of this type of decision include adopting different work shifts so as to improve resource utilization rate, having members in a team rotate work tasks, and adopting new sales targets.
2. *Decision quality.* The quality of a decision refers to the degree to which the action chosen leads to achievement of organizational goals.[34] Decision quality is important to a decision when there are a variety of alternatives and the decision outcome is significant. Examples of this type of decision include selecting a marketing strategy for a new product, and adopting a new technology in the production process.
3. *Decision timeliness.* Decision timeliness refers to the degree to which a decision has time constraints. A decision has a high degree of timeliness when it requires immediate consideration and solution. Examples of this type of decision include discounting fashion merchandise that is past the season, or selecting strategies to cope with the unexpected price war launched by a competitor.
4. *Costs of decision making.* Costs of decision making involve the efficiency of the decision process. This type of cost mainly involves time used for decision making. Higher degrees of participation require longer time periods for decision making. More hours are consumed to reach a consensus in the group decision-making style than to have a leader make the decision alone.
5. *Followers' development.* This criterion involves the degree to which the decision process provides a learning opportunity for organizational members. When using a decision style with a high degree of participation, organizational members will

be more likely to (1) develop knowledge and competence to work through problems, (2) acquire the ability to work with team members, and (3) identify with organizational goals.[35]

The Normative Decision-Making model contends that the effectiveness of a decision depends on applying a decision-making style that matches the situation. Multiple important situational factors were identified, including decision significance, importance of follower commitment to the decision, leader's expertise, likelihood of follower commitment to the decision, group support for objectives, group expertise, and team competence.[36]

Decision significance involves how significant a decision is to the success of a project or an organization. *Importance of commitment* involves how important it is for group members to be committed to the decision. *Leader's expertise* involves a leader's knowledge or expertise in relation to the problem. *Likelihood of commitment* involves the probability that the group will commit to a decision that is made by a leader alone. *Group support for objectives* involves the degree to which the group supports the organizational objectives at stake in this problem. *Group expertise* involves the group members' knowledge or expertise in relation to the problem. *Team competence* refers to the ability of group members to work together to solve a problem.

The Normative Decision-Making model matches the decision-making styles with different combinations of the previously described situational factors. It provides guidance for managers to identify properties of a situation and determine appropriate decision-making styles. The most recent edition of this model has two versions: one is for decisions in which time is a major constraint, and the other is for when the development of group members is emphasized. The latter version relies most heavily on group decision making, even though this process takes more time than the other styles. The time-driven model shown by the matrix in Figure 3-1 is used by leaders to analyze decision situations to decide which decision style to use.

Recommendations of the Normative Decision-Making Model

To use this model for a specific decision, the leader starts on the left side of the matrix in Figure 3-1, labeled "Problem Statement." Along the top of the matrix are the seven situational factors, called situational questions, to be considered. Each of these factors may be present (H for high) or absent (L for low) in a specific decision situation. To obtain the recommended decision style, the leader must first determine if the decision is significant. If it is, the leader selects H, and then answers the second situational question about the importance of gaining the groups' commitment. The leader continues answering each situational question (without crossing any horizontal lines), and eventually reaches a recommended decision style on the right side of the matrix. For some decisions, the recommended style is reached by answering only two situational questions (for example, L, L); other decisions may require answering all seven questions (for example, H, H, L, L, H, H, H). Answering the situational questions accurately requires that the leader have a good understanding of the decision problem, as well as his or her own and the group's capabilities. To help leaders use the model, a computer program was developed that allows them to quickly make complex assessments of decision situations. According to Vroom and his colleagues, when leaders use the decision styles recommended by this model, their decisions are more likely to be effective and therefore successful.

Decision Significance	Importance of Commitment	Leader Expertise	Likelihood of Commitment	Group Support	Group Expertise	Team Competence	Recommended Decision Style
H	H	H	H	—	—	—	Decide
			L	H	H	H	Delegate
						L	Consult (Group)
					L	—	Consult (Group)
				L	—	—	Consult (Group)
		L	H	H	H	H	Facilitate
						L	Consult (Individually)
					L	—	Consult (Individually)
				L	—	—	Consult (Individually)
			L	H	H	H	Facilitate
						L	Consult (Group)
					L	—	Consult (Group)
				L	—	—	Consult (Group)
	L	H	—	—	—	—	Decide
		L	—	H	H	H	Facilitate
						L	Consult (Individually)
					L	—	Consult (Individually)
				L	—	—	Consult (Individually)
L	H	—	H	—	—	—	Decide
			L			H	Delegate
				—	—	L	Facilitate
	L	—	—	—	—	—	Decide

*(Leftmost vertical label spanning the table: **Problem Statement**)*

▪ ▪ ▪ ▪ **FIGURE 3-1** The time-driven model

Instructions: The matrix operates like a funnel. You start at the left with a specific decision problem in mind. The column headings denote situational factors that may or may not be present in that problem. You progress by selecting high (H) or low (L) for each relevant situational factor. Proceed to the right, judging only those situational factors for which a judgment is called for, until you reach the recommended decision style.

SOURCE: V. H. Vroom. Leadership and the decision making process. *Organizational Dynamics,* 28(4) (2000), 82–94. Copyright © 2000 with permission from Elsevier.

How Valid and Useful Is the Model?

Overall, the Normative Decision-Making model has received considerable support.[37–40] Vroom and Jago found that decisions made using styles recommended by the model have higher success rates than those made using styles the model describes as inappropriate. Other researchers found that employees were more satisfied with supervision and work, and spent more time on productive activities, when leaders' decision-making styles are consistent with the Normative Decision-Making model. A recent study analyzed battlefield behavior of 10 commanding generals in six major battles of the American Civil War. These researchers found that the commanders who acted in accordance with the prescriptions of the Normative Decision-Making model were more often successful in their campaign than those who did not.[41] Although research results on the Normative Decision-Making model are promising, most studies were conducted on earlier versions of the model. The current version should be tested more extensively before a conclusion is reached about its validity.

TABLE 3-6 Summary of leadership behaviors, situational factors, and leadership effects in five major contingency theories of leadership

Contingency Theories	Leadership Behaviors or Predispositions	Situational Characteristics	Follower's Psychological Reactions	Follower and Group Behaviors
Fiedler's Contingency Theory	Task oriented Relationship oriented	Leader–member relations Task structure Leader's position power		High group performance
Hersey and Blanchard's Situational Leadership Theory	Task oriented/directive Relationship oriented/ supportive	Follower/ Development/ Task Relevant Maturity	Satisfaction Commitment	High follower performance
House's Path-Goal Theory	Directive Supportive Participative Achievement oriented Work facilitation (e) Interaction facilitation (e) Group oriented (e) Representative (e) Charismatic (e) Shared leadership (e)	Task structure or ambiguity Frustrating, stressful, or dissatisfying tasks Challenging tasks Low follower authori- tarianism or high need for indepen- dence	Satisfaction Motivation Acceptance of the leader Job clarity High effort	High follower performance Low levels of grievances and turnover High group performance
Yukl's Multiple Linkage Theory	Supporting Networking Managing conflict Team building Motivating Rewarding and recognizing Problem solving Planning and organizing Consulting and delegating Monitoring Clarifying Informing	Organization's reward system Follower's tasks Policies and procedures Technology of the workplace Organizational crises or major change Follower's charac- teristics Economic conditions	Job knowledge High effort Organization of the work Adequate resources Cooperation and group cohesion Role clarity Coordination with other groups	High group performance
Vroom, Yetton, and Jago's Normative Decision- Making Theory	Five decision-making styles: Decide Consult individually Consult group Facilitate Delegate	Decision significance Importance of com- mitment Leader's expertise Likelihood of com- mitment Group support for objectives Group expertise Team competence	High decision acceptance	High decision quality Decision timeliness Cost of decision making Opportunities for learning and develop- ment

▪ ▪ ▪ ▪ ▪ ▪ ▪ ▪ ▪

(e)—indicates items that are part of a recently expanded version of this model with no research support at this time.

The Normative Decision-Making model has been criticized as being overly complex.[42,43] According to one writer, the five decision-making styles described in the model can be replaced by a smaller number of styles. In addition, the model assumes that the decision-making process is a single and discrete episode, whereas complex decision making requires multiple meetings at different times with different groups of people. Finally, the model assumes leaders have the necessary skills to practice all five of the decision-making processes.[44] An important point to remember is that the Normative Decision-Making model only tells the leader which decision style he or she should use to make a decision. It does not tell the leader which decision alternative is best.

Table 3-6 provides a summary of the elements in each of the five major contingency theories of leadership described in this chapter. The reader will notice these models often share some of the same elements, although there are differences in the recommendations made to improve leaders' effectiveness. These models are compared and evaluated in the concluding section of this chapter.

SUMMARY ▪ ▪ ▪ ▪ ▪ ▪ ▪

All the contingency leadership theories presented in this chapter describe the leadership situation as a key aspect of leadership effectiveness. Some models focus on the leader's effect on individuals' attitudes and performance, and others focus on group performance. Four of the models describe specific leadership behaviors, and one model describes an aspect of the leader's personality or predisposition. All the models indicate that some type of adaptation is required between the leader and the situation. Most of the contingency theories recommend that the leader modify behavior to fit the situation. One model suggests that either the situation should be changed to fit the leader's style or the leader should be transferred to a different situation in order to be effective.

Fiedler's Contingency theory and Hersey and Blanchard's Situational Leadership theory were both proposed more than twenty-five years ago and have remained largely unchanged. Although they can be helpful, research evidence indicates that these models are too simple to provide adequate guidance for effective leadership in today's complex organizational environments. The Path-Goal theory and the Multiple Linkage theory have both evolved over several years to be more comprehensive and realistic in their description of the leader's behavior and the situational factors important to leadership effectiveness. However, the newly revised Path-Goal theory is untested and the Multiple Linkage theory is very general, with no specific recommendations about when certain leadership behaviors are most appropriate. Consequently, these models also are lacking in the amount of guidance they provide for practicing leaders. The Normative Decision-Making theory of participation has been recently revised and shows much promise as a tool to help managers involve their followers in decision making.

The approach of this book is to build on these contingency theories by describing key leadership behaviors that have been proposed and researched in conjunction with the various leadership models. In coming chapters, we describe leadership characteristics that help leaders exhibit each behavior effectively; identify sources of power for leaders that tend to facilitate these leadership behaviors; examine situational factors that increase or decrease the impact of the behaviors; and describe the effects of the behaviors on followers and their groups. We will also expand on the suggestion contained in some of the contingency models: that leaders should modify the situations facing their groups to make followers more effective with or without the leader.[45] We also describe several newer and less-researched leadership behaviors and issues, along with their implications for leadership effectiveness in organizations of the future.

The Leadership Process model described in Chapter 2 is a general way of describing the leadership behaviors detailed in this book. The model's basic structure incorporates features of several earlier contingency models.

KEY TERMS AND CONCEPTS IN THIS CHAPTER ▪▪▪▪▪▪▪

- Achievement-oriented leadership behaviors
- Consult group
- Consult individually
- Contingency theories of leadership
- Decide
- Delegate
- Directive leadership behaviors
- Facilitate

- Fiedler's Contingency theory
- Hersey and Blanchard's Situational Leadership theory
- Intervening variables
- Leader's position power
- Multiple Linkage theory
- Normative Decision-Making theory
- Participative leadership behaviors

- Path-Goal theory
- Relationship-oriented leadership behaviors
- Situational characteristics
- Situational favorableness or control
- Supportive leadership behaviors
- Task structure
- Task-oriented leadership behaviors

REVIEW AND DISCUSSION QUESTIONS ▪▪▪▪▪▪▪

1. Which of the five contingency models described in this chapter would be the most useful to you as a leader? Why?
2. Which of the elements of situational favorableness or situation control in Fiedler's Contingency theory do you think is the most important for a leader? Why?
3. According to Fiedler's Contingency theory, how does changing the situation influence the effectiveness of the leader?
4. Using the Hersey and Blanchard Situational Leadership theory, describe the four leadership styles that result from combining directive and supportive leadership behaviors.
5. How does the Hersey and Blanchard Situational Leadership theory define the developmental level of followers? How could a leader determine the developmental level of specific followers?
6. Think of a job you have had or may have in the future. Using the Path-Goal theory, identify the task and organizational factors a leader should consider. Given the factors you have identified, which of the four types of leadership behavior would be most effective?
7. How does the Multiple Linkage theory of leadership expand our understanding of the leadership process?
8. How can the Normative Decision-Making theory of participation help a manager make effective decisions?

EXERCISE: CHANGING SITUATIONAL FAVORABLENESS OR CONTROL ▪▪▪▪▪▪▪

Using the concepts in Fiedler's Contingency theory, how could a leader increase or decrease the situational favorableness or situational control by increasing or decreasing each of the three situational characteristics used in the model? Indicate specific actions a leader could take to increase and decrease each characteristic. Try to be innovative and creative in identifying possible leader actions.

1. **Quality of leader–member relations (high quality results from liking and trusting the leader)**
Leader actions to increase the quality of leader–member relations
Leader actions to decrease the quality of leader–member relations

2. **Leader's task structure (highly structured tasks can be performed using a planned set of procedures)**
   Leader actions to increase the task structure
   Leader actions to decrease the task structure
3. **Leader's position power (leader's authority and control over rewards and punishments)**
   Leader actions to increase position power
   Leader actions to decrease position power

▪ ▪ ▪▪▪ ▪ C A S E   I N C I D E N T ▪ ▪ ▪ ▪ ▪ ▪

Tough Assignment

Ted Wills has been hired as the new supervisor for the parts department of a large automobile dealership. His first day on the job, his manager, Linda Dunn, tells him, "You have a tough assignment. In the group you supervise there is an active troublemaker who has managed to keep from getting fired because he is the only employee who knows the inventory system inside and out. Three other employees follow his lead in consistently finding things to complain about, and the other four employees stay out of trouble by doing only what they are told." Linda handed the personnel files for the department employees to Ted. "The most important thing," Linda continued, "is that you change the sloppy way work is being done in the department and improve the accuracy in filling parts orders."

After hesitating a moment, Ted asked, "What was the former supervisor like?"

"Well," replied Linda, "he had semiretired on the job and let the employees do what they wanted. He was not concerned about accuracy in filling orders or maintaining the inventory. As I said before, it is a tough assignment, especially because all your employees have been with the dealership for more than five years, and most are friends with the owner."

Ted smiled, "I guess I have my work cut out for me." ▪

DISCUSSION QUESTIONS

1. What situational factors should Ted take into account before deciding on what leadership actions to take?
2. What leadership behaviors would you recommend to Ted? Why?

ENDNOTES ▪▪▪▪▪▪▪

1. House, R. J., and Aditya, R. N. (1997). The scientific study of leadership: Quo vadis? *Journal of Management,* 23(3), 409–473.
2. Wofford, J. C., and Liska, L. Z. (1993). Path-Goal theories of leadership: A meta-analysis. *Journal of Management,* 19(4), 857–876.
3. Jacobs, T. O. (1970). *Leadership and Exchange in Formal Organizations.* Alexandria, VA: Office of Naval Research.
4. Schriesheim, C. A., and Kerr, S. (1977). Theories and measures of leadership: A critical appraisal of current and future

directions. In J. G. Hunt and L. L. Larson (Eds.), *Leadership: The Cutting Edge,* 9–45. Carbondale, IL: Southern Illinois University Press.

5. Fiedler, F. E., and Garcia, J. E. (1987). *New Approaches to Effective Leadership: Cognitive Resources and Organizational Performance.* New York: John Wiley & Sons.

6. Jacobs, *Leadership and Exchange in Formal Organizations.*

7. Schriesheim and Kerr. Theories and measures of leadership: A critical appraisal of current and future directions.

8. Ayman, R., Chemers, M. M., and Fiedler, F. (1995). The contingency model of leadership effectiveness: Its levels of analysis. *The Leadership Quarterly,* 6(2), 147–167.

9. Fiedler, F. E., Chemers, M. H., and Mahar, L. (1994). *Improving Leadership Effectiveness: The Leader Match Concept,* 2nd ed. New York: John Wiley & Sons.

10. Fiedler and Garcia. *New Approaches to Effective Leadership: Cognitive Resources and Organizational Performance.*

11. Fiedler, Chemers, and Mahar. *Improving Leadership Effectiveness: The Leader Match Concept.*

12. Schriesheim and Kerr. Theories and measures of leadership: A critical appraisal of current and future directions.

13. Bass, B. M. (1990). *Bass & Stogdill's Handbook of Leadership,* 3rd ed. New York: Free Press.

14. Yukl, G. (1998). *Leadership in Organizations,* 4th ed. Upper Saddle River, NJ: Prentice Hall.

15. Schriesheim, C. A., Tepper, B. J., and Terault, L. A. (1994). Least Preferred Co-worker score, situational control, and leadership effectiveness: A meta-analysis of contingency theory model performance predictions. *Journal of Applied Psychology,* 79(4), 561–573.

16. Hersey, P., Blanchard, K. H., and Johnson, D. E. (1996). *Management of Organizational Behavior: Utilizing Human Resources,* 7th ed. Upper Saddle River, NJ: Prentice Hall; and Graeff, C. L. (1997). Evolution of situational leadership theory: A critical review. *Leadership Quarterly,* 8(2), 153–170.

17. Cairns, T. D., Hollenbeck, J., Preziosi, R. C., and Snow, W. A. (1998). Technical note: A study of Hersey and Blanchard's Situational Leadership theory. *Leadership and Organizational Development Journal,* 19(2), 113–116.

18. Vecchio, R. P. (1987). Situational leadership theory: An examination of a prescriptive theory. *Journal of Applied Psychology,* 72, 444–451.

19. Norris, W. R., and Vecchio, R. P. (1992). Situational Leadership theory: A replication. *Group and Organizational Management,* 17(3), 331–342; and Fernandez, C. F., and Vecchio, R. P. (1997). Situational Leadership theory revisited: A test of an across-job perspective. *Leadership Quarterly,* 8(1), 67–84.

20. Goodson, J. R., McGee, G. W., and Cashman, J. F. (1989). Situational Leadership theory. *Personnel Psychology,* 43, 579–597.

21. House, R. J., and Mitchell, T. R. (1974). Path-Goal theory of leadership. *Journal of Contemporary Business,* 5, 81–97.

22. Ibid.

23. Indvik, J. (1986). Path-Goal theory of leadership: A meta-analysis. In *Proceedings of the Academy of Management Meetings,* 189–192.

24. Wofford and Liska. Path-Goal theories of leadership: A meta-analysis.

25. Indvik. Path-Goal theory of leadership: A meta-analysis.

26. House, R. J. (1996). Path-Goal theory of leadership: Lessons, legacy, and a reformulated theory. *Leadership Quarterly,* in press.

27. Ibid.

28. Yukl, G. (1998). *Leadership in Organizations,* 4th ed. Upper Saddle River, NJ: Prentice Hall.

29. Ibid.

30. Yukl, *Leadership in Organizations,* 4th ed. and Dorfman, P. W., Howell, J. P., Hibino, S., Lee, J. K., and Tate, U. (1997). Leadership in western and Asian countries: Commonalties and differences in effective leadership practices. *Leadership Quarterly,* 8(3), 233–274.

31. Vroom, V. H., and Yetton, P. W. (1973). *Leadership and Decision Making.*

Pittsburgh, PA: University of Pittsburgh Press.

32. Vroom, V. H., and Jago, A. G. (1988). *The new leadership: Managing participation in organizations.* Englewood Cliffs, NJ: Prentice Hall.

33. Vroom, V. H. (2000). Leadership and the decision making process. *Organizational Dynamics,* 28, 82–94.

34. Vroom, V. H. (2003). Educating managers for decision making and leadership. *Management Decision,* 41, 968–978.

35. Vroom. Leadership and the decision making process.

36. Ibid.

37. Duncan, W. J., LaFrance, K. G., and Ginter, P. M. (2003). Leadership and decision making: A retrospective application and assessment. *The Journal of Leadership and Organizational Studies,* 9, 1–20.

38. Field, R. H. G., and House, R. J. (1990). A test of the Vroom-Yetton model using manager and subordinate reports. *Journal of Applied Psychology,* 75, 362–366.

39. Paul, R. J., and Ebadi, Y. M. (1989). Leadership decison making in a service organization: A field test of the Vroom-Yetton model. *Journal of Occupational Psychology,* 62, 201–211.

40. Vroom and Yetton. The new leadership: Managing participation in organizations.

41. Duncan, La France, and Ginter. Leadership and decision making: A retrospective application and assessment.

42. Field, R. H. G. (1979). A contingency model of leadership effectiveness. In L. Berkowitz (Ed.), *Advances in experimental social psychology,* Vol. 1. New York: Academic Press.

43. Yukl, G. (2002). *Leadership in organizations.* Upper Saddle River, NJ: Prentice Hall.

44. Crouch, A., and Yetton, P. (1987). Manager behavior, leadership style, and subordinate performance: An empirical extension of the Vroom-Yetton conflict rule. *Organizational Behavior and Human Decision Processes,* 39, 384–396.

45. Howell, J. P., and Dorfman, P. W. (1986). Leadership and substitutes for leadership among professional and non-professional workers. *Journal of Applied Behavioral Science,* 22(1), 29–46.

CHAPTER 4

Supportive Leadership Behavior

Learning Objectives

After reading this chapter, you should be able to do the following:

1. Describe supportive leadership as an effective leadership behavior.
2. Explain why supportive leadership is important for individual followers and groups.
3. Describe some of the skills, traits, and sources of power a leader needs to develop to be an effective supportive leader.
4. Discuss some of the skills needed for effective listening, which is part of supportive leadership.
5. Describe several impacts leader supportiveness has on follower psychological reactions and behaviors.
6. Identify organizational situations in which supportive leadership is especially effective.
7. Identify situations in which supportive leadership is probably not effective.
8. Discuss how leaders can modify situations to increase the effectiveness of their supportive behaviors.
9. Understand how leaders can modify followers' tasks to substitute for some supportiveness and still maintain positive follower attitudes and performance.

⊞ Examples of Effective Supportive Leadership

- Jake, our supervisor, called to pass along news of a pending organization change, which has more positive implications than most of the rumors. I appreciated his call from vacation to let me know of this glimmer of bright light in the sea of uncertainty.
- Our project manager sat down with us and took time to share how she was feeling. It was fun, and it made me feel better to think that she trusted us with her feelings. This made me want to work harder so that I'd be more supportive of her

and the team. It also made me feel lucky to be part of a team in which others can take time to share honestly.[1]

- A supervisor told her followers she knew that their clerical work was often boring and time consuming, but she appreciated their effort during a very busy day.
- A subordinate approached her supervisor and said she would not be able to make a scheduled committee meeting on Friday because she had a doctor's appointment. She asked if she could reschedule the meeting. The supervisor replied she would check with the other committee members, and if possible, set up the meeting for the first thing Monday morning.
- In describing his performance evaluation, an employee praised his supervisor for not talking down to him; he also said that by encouraging input, observations, and feedback on his own behavior, the supervisor showed respect for the subordinate as a valuable member of the department.
- A military officer showed ongoing concern and respect for subordinate differences in cultural or racial values, life styles, and mores.
- A leader made a conscious effort to encourage and provide "air time" for everyone during staff meetings, and to distribute privileges or choice task assignments equitably.[2,3]

▪▪▪ Definition, Background, and Importance of Supportive Leadership Behaviors

These are examples of effective supportive leadership behaviors. Supportive leadership involves showing concern for the status, well being, and needs of followers; demonstrating a kind, considerate, and understanding attitude regarding followers' problems; and fostering followers' professional development. Supportive leaders are friendly and informative, and they encourage open, two-way communication. They also show trust and respect for followers in a way that enhances followers' feelings of personal worth and importance. Keeping followers informed and helping them develop professionally are other marks of supportive leaders.[4,5]

Supportiveness is common in effective leaders. Its importance has been well established in industrial, military, educational, human service, and governmental organizations. Its popularity with leaders results from its importance in establishing and maintaining the well-being of followers and groups.

Supportive behaviors are effective because they satisfy people's needs to be liked and appreciated by others, to be respected as capable and valuable, and to be continually improving.[6] Supportiveness also helps keep a group together by promoting cohesion among members and keeping individuals from becoming alienated. Some organizations have the same characteristics as dysfunctional families; that is, certain members do not interact effectively, resulting in strife and unhappiness. In organizations, supportive behaviors can help promote the emotional health of individuals and groups,[7,8] and improve the leader's interactions with followers. These behaviors are summarized in Figure 4-1.

Many names have been used to describe supportive leadership behaviors. Perhaps the earliest term for leadership behaviors of this type was consideration, used by researchers at The Ohio State University during the 1950s and 1960s. At the University

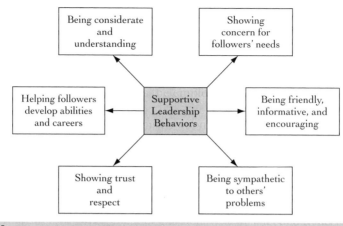

▪▪▪ **FIGURE 4-1** Types of supportive leadership behaviors

of Michigan, the term relationship-oriented behavior was used to refer to supportive leadership behaviors, and this term is still popular with consultants and used in the Situational Leadership theory described in Chapter 3.[9] Concern for people refers to a similar type of leadership behavior and is part of the Managerial Grid model used for many years in leadership training.[10] Researchers have used different methods to measure supportive leadership, and although each measurement approach is unique, they generally assess most of the previously described behaviors. The Leadership in Action box on Pat Carrigan shows how one leader used supportive leadership effectively.

▪▪▪ Ineffective Supportive Leadership

Although the impacts of supportive leadership are usually positive, the following incidents demonstrate how a leader can provide supportiveness that is ineffective because of the follower reactions it produces.

- Community mental health centers are staffed by highly trained mental health professionals—primarily psychologists and social workers. These individuals provide counseling and therapy for center clients. In their roles as caregivers, they are highly attuned to interpersonal processes, particularly those that involve manipulation of others. They deal on a daily basis with clients who feel manipulated and who manipulate others, and their job is to subtly reshape (manipulate) their clients' behavior. This process can make them very sensitive to any manipulation of their own behavior by their manager. In one such center, some managers chose to be supportive by discussing client-related problems openly in meetings and encouraging their staff to do the same. Caregivers saw this behavior as an attempt to manipulate the type of care they gave their clients. As trained professionals, they resented and resisted what they saw as interference in their caregiving activities, and they reacted very negatively to this type of supportive leadership. Managers in other centers, who were more subtle in their supportive behaviors, being friendly, informative, and approachable, for example, had more positive results.

LEADERSHIP IN ACTION

Pat Carrigan, Plant Manager for General Motors

Pat Carrigan was the first woman to manage a General Motors (GM) auto assembly plant. She obtained a doctorate in clinical psychology and worked as a teacher in the public schools before becoming a human resource specialist in industry. She started with GM as a human resource consultant and became interested in becoming a line manager. With the help of several other executives in GM, she worked out a five-year plan to prepare her to become a plant manager. She worked in various aspects of plant operations and served two years as a general plant superintendent. During this time she impressed those who worked with her as a knowledgeable and trustworthy colleague and friend.

Her performance as a plant manager at the Lakewood plant near Atlanta, Georgia, was stellar. Grievances were reduced to near zero from a very high level, and discipline incidents were reduced by 82 percent. During her tenure at the Bay City plant in Michigan, productivity increased 40 percent, major budget savings were made, and voluntary, self-managed work teams were begun.

Her supportive leadership style is founded on the principle that people are more important than things. Managers at the Bay City plant had the habit of keeping their doors closed. She made a point of keeping her door open, and the other managers learned to do likewise. She believes strongly in personal contact with all employees, and she frequently walked the plant floor talking with workers. Other writers have noted that it is her physical presence, closeness, and concern for employees that earned her their respect and trust. One United Auto Workers local president described Carrigan as not having a "phony bone in her body."

Although she is no longer a plant manager at GM, this personal, supportive approach won her the cooperation of employees. She spent time on the factory floor meeting each of the 2,000 workers in the plant, shaking their hands, showing she wanted to listen, and entering into a dialog with them. She showed employees that she wanted to know them as human beings, and they responded with cooperation, respect, and excellent performances.

- A new manager was placed in charge of the accounting and billing department of a construction company. The manager was part of a new management group brought in by the board of directors. The company was a rapidly growing, family-owned corporation, and the owners were convinced that a professional management team was needed to operate the rapidly growing enterprise. Because the new accounting manager was an unknown quantity to the accounting staff, they viewed her as having a mission to shake up the place by changing the procedures and possibly some of the accounting staff. When she encouraged them to discuss their problems with her, they felt she was trying to gather data she could use to replace them. They did not trust the motives of the new management group, and a norm developed in the department to stonewall the manager whenever she urged them to discuss their problems. All efforts by the new manager to elicit questions, show concern, and demonstrate kindness and understanding were greeted with a matter-of-fact "no problems" by the staff members. A different supportive approach in which management provided information about changes or brought in upper management to discuss their plans with the departmental staff would have been more effective.

These examples show that some leaders may use supportive leadership ineffectively, with counterproductive results. The leader must be careful how supportiveness is used and tailor the approach to the needs and concerns of the followers. The next section describes how leaders can effectively use supportive leadership behaviors to work with followers.

▪▪▪ Skills, Traits, and Sources of Power for Supportive Leadership

Supportive leaders often develop specific skills, traits, and sources of power to help them effectively support their followers. They usually develop good *communication skills,* effectively conveying their ideas and feelings, listening actively and carefully, and eliciting ideas and feelings from followers. The ability to listen to followers and understand what they are saying is a key element in showing acceptance and consideration. The supportive leader uses communication skills to be responsive to followers' task-related problems, complaints, and personal problems. The leader uses verbal and nonverbal communication to indicate how much followers are valued. Supportive leaders can suspend biases and prejudices while interacting with followers. The Leadership in Perspective: Supportive and Nonsupportive Communication box describes the difference between supportive and nonsupportive communication. The self-assessment exercise that follows it is intended to identify important listening skills for supportive leadership.

▪▪▪▪▪▪▪▪▪ ▪▪▪▪▪▪▪▪▪

LEADERSHIP IN PERSPECTIVE
Supportive and Nonsupportive Communication

Supportive communication delivers the message accurately, and supports or enhances the relationship between the parties.

Supportive and Nonsupportive Communication

Supportive	Nonsupportive
Problem oriented	Person oriented (naming)
Descriptive	Evaluative
Words and actions consistent	Incongruent words and actions
Encouraging	Puts people down
Specific	General or vague
Interactive (listening)	One-way (telling)

▪▪▪▪▪▪▪▪▪

LEADERSHIP SELF-ASSESSMENT
Effective Listening

Objective: To help the reader understand and distinguish effective and ineffective listening skills for supportive leadership

Instructions: Rank the following statements in order of importance from 1 (high) to 9 (low) for effective listening behavior by a leader.

1. _____ Empathize when someone is speaking by trying to understand the speaker's point of view.

2. _____ Ask questions to show interest and further your understanding.

3. _____ Develop arguments with a speaker's main points while he or she is speaking, to be ready to respond.

4. _____ Eliminate physical and psychological distractions when listening.

5. _____ Listen for areas of common interest and agreement.

6. _____ Decide quickly if a message is going to be dull or unimportant and terminate the conversation in order to save time.

7. _____ Actively focus your attention on concepts, ideas, attitudes, and feelings related to the speaker's message.

8. _____ Carefully evaluate the speaker's physical characteristics before comprehending the message.

9. _____ Take into account the speaker's attitudes and beliefs to help understand how the speaker feels about the message.

Interpretation: If you ranked items 1, 2, 4, 5, 7, and 9 as high, then you have a good understanding of effective listening behavior. If you ranked items 3, 6, and 8 as high, you may not be an effective listener and could have difficulty with this aspect of supportive leadership.

Interpersonal skills are closely related to communication skills, and are also basic to effective supportive leadership.[11] It is through positive, friendly interpersonal relations that the leader supports followers, cooperates with them, develops trust with them, and assists them. Leaders use their interpersonal skills to provide social support when followers are upset or under pressure. Thus, it is within the context of interpersonal relations that the leader shows appreciation and takes an interest in followers' lives. Supportive leaders use interpersonal skills to increase followers' self-confidence, and they accept and understand the diverse beliefs of followers.

Leaders who make an effort to be *sociable* often develop effective interpersonal and communication skills. A person high in sociability tends to be outgoing and expressive, and is often seen as empathetic, warm, and giving.[12,13] Sociable leaders enjoy spending time on a regular basis with each follower. They get to know followers, understand their feelings, and find out about their interests.[14] They are often described as extraverts, and they are agreeable or easy to get along with, friendly, and cooperative. They tend to maintain a pleasant and cheerful disposition, and show consideration and trust toward followers. Leaders who are low in sociability or agreeableness are somewhat withdrawn or reserved, cautious in interpersonal relations, and are often insensitive to the needs and feelings of followers. They are also moody, aloof, intolerant, and suspicious in interpersonal relations. These individuals often have difficulty showing effective supportiveness with followers. Sociable and agreeable leaders find it easier to be supportive by showing positive regard and acceptance, and are less likely to show rejection, harsh criticism, or personal insults.

Effective supportive leaders also usually develop high levels of competence and *expertise* at followers' tasks.[15] Leaders must have technical and professional competence to provide followers with training and development. In addition, to be a supportive resource in solving problems, the leader must have task-related expertise. Moreover, providing useful feedback on performance requires job-related competence. Effective support of decision making also draws on the leader's technical expertise. High levels of technical competence can also increase the leader's confidence and willingness to support followers.

Being sociable and agreeable probably comes naturally to many supportive leaders, but these tendencies also can be developed by conscious effort. The same is true for communication, interpersonal, and task skills. Leaders can obtain additional training and coaching in these areas to improve their capabilities to provide supportive leadership effectively.

Regardless of any other skills or traits, a leader's philosophy of leadership will affect the degree of supportiveness shown with followers.[16] For example, if a leader believes in a strongly autocratic and heavily directive approach in dealing with subordinates, supportive, caring, concerned, and encouraging behavior will probably not be used with followers. On the other hand, if a leader believes that people are the most important asset and enjoys helping followers develop, then highly supportive behaviors will likely be used with followers. We believe this desire to help followers develop is the most constructive approach for long-term performance and positive follower attitudes.

In addition to developing key skills, supportive leaders also work at developing three types of power sources to help them influence their followers. As leaders build their competence at followers' tasks (described previously), they increase their *expert power,* and can support followers by providing knowledge, skill, and ability through rational persuasion to assist in performing important tasks and solving problems. The more important the follower's problem, the greater the likelihood the leader will use expert power. The follower must recognize the leader's expertise and perceive the leader as a trustworthy source of advice. Effective leaders use expert power to support followers by providing needed knowledge, being available as a source of technical advice, helping individuals solve job problems, providing rational explanations of processes, and referring followers to needed sources of assistance or information.

As explained in Chapter 1, leaders whose personality, accomplishments, and integrity cause followers to admire or identify with them have *referent power.* Furthermore, when leaders have referent power, followers attribute favorable motives to the leaders, they want their leaders' approval, they respond favorably to personal and inspirational appeals, and they interpret small, apparently insignificant behaviors by leaders as supportive (such as a smile or other friendly gesture). At the same time,

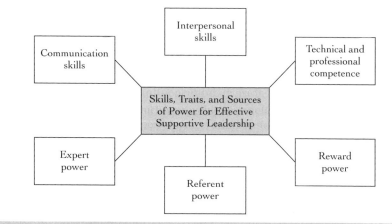

▪▪▪ **FIGURE 4-2** Skills, traits, and sources of power for effective supportive leadership

supportive behaviors increase the leader's referent power. Examples of supportive behaviors that are facilitated by referent power and also increase it include displaying respect and acceptance, providing help in problem solving, showing interest and collaborating with followers, and backing them up.

Supportive leaders also develop *reward power* to satisfy followers' needs and wants. Leaders with high reward power are often watched closely by followers, and they see the leader's supportiveness as very significant. Reward power can be used to provide needed resources, a better work schedule, a larger expense account, or advice for followers. Figure 4-2 summarizes skills, traits, and sources of power for effective supportive leadership.

▪▪▪ Facilitating and Limiting Conditions for Supportive Leadership

Leaders may be encouraged or discouraged from providing supportive leadership by organizational factors that are largely beyond their control. The style preferences of the leader's superior can encourage or discourage a leader's supportiveness.[17] The superior's behavior often conveys the leadership preference of the organization. If the superior is highly supportive with the leader, then the leader will likely be supportive with followers. If the superior is not supportive with the leader, then the leader will likely behave in a similar fashion with followers or will not remain in the organization. Because the superior often evaluates the leader's performance, the leader will most likely be sensitive to the superior's style preferences, and often reflect them in leadership behaviors. The organizational mission or culture may also encourage or discourage a leader's supportiveness.[18] Organizations that provide human services to clients (such as universities or hospitals), or that work with volunteers, seem to encourage a supportive leadership style.[19] Organizations that encourage high involvement and commitment by their staff also encourage supportiveness.[20] Other organizations may not encourage supportive leadership to the same extent, and the leaders may respond with less supportiveness. A recent study showed that female followers prefer their

▪ ▪ ▪ ▪ ▪ ▪ ▪ ▪ ▪ ▪ ──────── ▪ ▪ ▪ ▪ ▪ ▪ ▪ ▪ ▪ ▪ ────────

LEADERSHIP IN PERSPECTIVE
Supportiveness and Leader Gender

Many popular writers refer to a stereotypical female leadership style that features a high amount of supportiveness of their followers. Female leaders are said to demonstrate more caring for their followers, to be more concerned for their welfare and careers, to provide more helpful advice, and to be more considerate than most male leaders. A comprehensive summary of high-quality research on leadership style and gender was conducted by two female researchers. Although these researchers did find differences between male and female leaders, their findings for supportive leadership provides only limited support for the stereotypical leadership styles described by popular writers.

The researchers divided the studies comparing male and female leaders into three groups: (1) experimental studies conducted primarily with college students, (2) assessment center studies conducted on individuals who aspired to leadership positions (this group also contained many students), and (3) practicing leaders. In the first two groups, females playing the role of leaders were significantly more supportive than males. In the third group of studies that focused on actual leaders, there were no differences in supportiveness between male and female leaders.

Several possible explanations have been offered for these findings for actual female leaders. Female leaders may be compelled to adopt more stereotypical male styles as they advance in organizations, or they may find that other leadership behaviors that partially replace supportiveness are strongly needed. Further research on these issues indicates that female leaders may be more supportive than male leaders in female-dominated industries (such as nursing and early childhood education), but not in male-dominated industries (such as automotive, manufacturing, timber, or information technology). Female leaders may adapt their leadership style to fit the culture in male-dominated industries.

SOURCES: A. H. Eagly, and B. T. Johnson. Gender and leadership style: A meta analysis. In R. M. Steers, L. W. Porter, and G. A. Bigley, *Motivation and Leadership at Work.* New York: McGraw-Hill, New York, 1996, 315–345; and M. Gardiner and M. Tiggeman. Gender differences in leadership style, job stress and mental health in male and female dominated industries. *Journal of Occupational and Organizational Psychology,* 72 (1999), 301–315.

▪ ▪ ▪ ▪ ▪ ▪ ▪ ▪ ▪ ────────

leaders to be supportive more so than male followers.[21] Thus, organization and follower characteristics can clearly facilitate or limit the use of supportive leadership behaviors. The Leadership in Perspective box: Supportiveness and Leader Gender dispels a common myth about female leaders.

As one might expect, leaders from different countries and cultures may express their supportiveness differently. Supportive leaders in Great Britain are seen as people who share information and welcome followers' suggestions; those seen as supportive leaders in Japan and Hong Kong appear to focus on interactions with the group during and outside of work hours. Japanese leaders are known for spending much time with followers after work hours, eating and drinking while listening to follower concerns and building group solidarity. In the United States, leaders often provide most support for followers during work hours, with open-door policies and management by walking around. The focus of all these behaviors, though, is on caring and kindness, which is the hallmark of supportive leadership.

▮▮▮ Supportiveness and Followers' Behavior

One important issue for leaders is whether they should provide more interpersonal support to some subordinates than others. Most leaders would answer yes to this question. It is the rare leader who behaves the same toward each subordinate. To be effective, a leader needs to adapt to different subordinates. How can the leader decide who should receive more support and who should get less? This question addresses the leader's basic influence strategy.

One approach advocates that a leader should use interpersonal support as a reward.[22] This approach is closely aligned with behavioral psychology, and is based on the operant conditioning model of learning associated with B. F. Skinner. The rationale is that the leader should show most concern, be most considerate, and provide the greatest amount of encouragement for the best performers. The intended effect is to positively reinforce good performance. In turn, the thinking goes, the positive reinforcement increases the frequency of the good performance. Research supports the favorable impact of positive reinforcement on performance. It also indicates that leaders tend to show more support for high-performing followers.[23]

However, using supportiveness as positive reinforcement does not address the needs of followers whose performance is less than desired. These employees may need a concerned and encouraging leader to provide them with the confidence necessary to improve their performance. New or young employees who are striving to improve are often not the best performers. Given a nurturing and encouraging supportive leader, who also provides them with the needed task guidance, they may become very good or outstanding performers in the future. Tommy Lasorda, former manager of the Los Angeles Dodgers, attributes his success as a minor and major league manager to providing this type of supportive behavior to young baseball players.

Lasorda represents the approach that says that leaders should provide supportiveness as needed by individual followers rather than as a reward for high performance. Thus, his supportiveness can be a *facilitating condition* stimulating improved follower performance. In addition, of course, subordinates' needs vary over time, so that a normally secure, autonomous, and competent individual may experience personal problems that cause performance to decline, necessitating a temporary increase in supportiveness from the leader. When the problems are solved, the leader can reduce the interpersonal support. The subordinate will return to a normal level of performance, and will likely remember that the leader cared enough to respond with kindness when it was needed. Other workers see and hear about leaders who respond positively to followers in this manner. This helps explain why followers who have supportive leaders generally show a high level of job satisfaction.

In summary, leader supportiveness should be provided for followers who need it. Leaders stimulate and reward followers' performances in whatever ways they can. The use of interpersonal support may be the most immediately available stimulus or reward in a given situation, and most effective when leaders use it both ways. The Leadership in Action box on Stan Smith describes how he provided supportive leadership for followers with very positive results.

IIIIIIIIIIIIIIIIIIIIIIIIIIIIII

LEADERSHIP IN ACTION

Stan Smith

Until his recent retirement, Stan Smith managed a pantyhose manufacturing facility in the southwestern United States for Sara Lee Corporation. Under Stan's management, the plant was the most efficient of the five pantyhose manufacturers in the Sara Lee organization, and it employed about 800 employees working in three shifts. Stan displayed his supportive leadership by almost never being in his office. He was on the factory floor with his people. He knew the names of every employee on all three shifts.

Stan arrived at the plant early in the morning before the night shift left. He showed his concern for employees by immediately visiting every department, greeting workers, asking how things were going, answering questions, and inquiring about personal or work-related issues. He was present in the plant during the day shift, making the same rounds to each department, and did the same thing

one more time after the evening shift came in, before he went home for the night. He saw and either talked with or was available to every employee on all three shifts every single workday. He also expected this type of friendly and open behavior from his managerial staff.

Stan also conducted informational meetings during working hours with a different cross-section of employees each week. He fostered employee development by instituting a tuition reimbursement program for all employees who wished to take classes at the local colleges. They conducted classes in the plant (free of charge) on English as a second language, as well as other classes to help employees pass their high school equivalency examination. Stan was understandably popular with his employees, and they responded by throwing parties on his birthday, by being productive, and by exhibiting a very low turnover rate.

IIIIIIIII

III Effects of Supportive Leadership

When leaders are supportive, they help satisfy followers' needs for security, acceptance, esteem, and achievement, which makes the workplace more attractive for all concerned.[24] Followers typically respond to a leader's concern and kindness by themselves being considerate of others and of the organization. Since the Roman legions, military leaders who have seen to the needs of their followers before they saw to their own needs have typically derived intense loyalty from the followers in times of battle.[25] When leaders provide supportive leadership effectively, their followers often become committed to the organization,[26] are helpful and cooperative, and tend to imitate the leader.[27] These results of leader supportiveness are examples of followers' psychological reactions, shown previously in Figure 2-2. A leader who is supportive has other favorable effects—followers are usually more satisfied with their work and their supervision,[28–30] they report less job stress and burnout, their work groups show higher degrees of harmony and cohesiveness,[31] and they are less likely to be absent from work, tardy, file a grievance, or quit.[32] Supportive leadership also increases followers' self-confidence, lowers anxiety, and minimizes unpleasant and distracting aspects of the work situation.[33] Several recent summaries of research have also shown that when leaders are supportive, their followers often perform well on their jobs.[34–36]

Although not yet well researched, another follower reaction that may be influenced by supportive leadership is follower empowerment. In a leadership context, the term empowerment is related to motivation. Thus, empowerment is the process by which a leader enhances a follower's feelings of competence or ability to perform self-determination, and of the meaningfulness and significance of one's actions.[37] By trusting, respecting, and encouraging two-way communications with followers, a supportive leader can create a climate in which followers feel significant and meaningful, and believe they will receive the leader's time, help, and assistance when needed. This can increase followers' beliefs in their own capabilities. It can also increase the individuals' confidence that they can govern their own behavior to achieve what is expected of them. Such beliefs affect peoples' willingness to initiate new activities and persevere with tasks. Thus, leader supportiveness may be a key factor affecting employee empowerment.

Research in real and simulated organizations shows that supportive leadership has the strongest favorable effects on followers' job satisfaction, including increased satisfaction with supervision, intrinsic task satisfaction, and overall job satisfaction. Next to job satisfaction, leader supportiveness has its strongest effects on increased organizational commitment of followers on improved job performance.[38] However, the effects of a leader's supportiveness on followers are influenced by situational factors. In other words, the positive impacts of supportiveness are generally strongest in certain organizational situations or with certain types of followers. Most studies indicate that a wide range of situational factors should be considered to assess the degree of potential positive impact of a leader's support. Table 4-1 summarizes the impacts of supportive leadership.

Ongoing research outside the United States shows the same positive effects of leader supportiveness in almost every country studied. In Japan, Mexico, Taiwan, Turkey, and India, supportiveness has positive effects on followers' satisfaction and commitment.[39–42] Follower performance was also improved by leader supportiveness in Japan.[43] Positive effects of support were especially strong in Japan, Israel, and Germany when the leader was also directive.[44] Directive leadership is described in Chapter 5. The combination of leaders' supportive and directive behaviors may be particularly effective in highly industrialized countries. Although some writers have indicated that supportive leadership is less popular in a few countries, such as the Philippines and the People's Republic of China, supportiveness seems to be an important aspect of leadership in formal organizations in most countries. It appears that most followers around the world value a leader who shows concern for them, is considerate, listens, and tries to help them with their aspirations and problems.

TABLE 4-1 Effects of supportive leadership

Follower Benefits	*Organizational Benefits*
Satisfaction with work, job, and supervisor	Increased cohesiveness and harmony
Increased commitment to the organization	Lower turnover, absenteeism, lateness, and grievance rates
Reduced stress	
Increased self-confidence	Increased cooperation and helpfulness
Increased performance	Increased productivity

▬ ▬ ▬ Situations in Which Supportiveness May or May Not Be Effective

Even though supportiveness is an important element in most leaders' behavioral repertoire, certain situational factors (including follower characteristics) can make it more or less effective.[45,46] The remainder of this chapter addresses the situational dynamics of supportive leadership—what leaders should look for in a situation to know when supportiveness is most appropriate; how leaders can influence situations to make them more supportive; and how followers, situations, and supportive leaders influence one another.

The following Leadership Self-Assessment: Diagnosing Situations for Supportive Leadership provides descriptions of situations where supportive leadership may or may not be effective with followers.

The situations described in items 1, 2, 3, and 6 of the self-assessment would probably result in favorable consequences when a leader uses supportive leadership. These situations reflect a need for supportiveness that can enhance or increase the effectiveness of this leader behavior. Situational characteristics described in items 4 and 5 would likely decrease or neutralize the impact of a leader's supportiveness. These situations indicate followers who may resist or are immune to the positive effects of supportiveness. When these characteristics are present, a leader's supportive behaviors will likely produce little or no improvement in follower reactions. Followers in these situations may be subject to other types of influence, and their leaders must often adjust how they influence followers. Item 7 is an example of a situational characteristic that substitutes for followers' needs for supportiveness from their leader. When followers find their

---

LEADERSHIP SELF-ASSESSMENT

Diagnosing Situations for Supportive Leadership

Place an "✕" next to those situations in which you believe supportiveness will be most effective:

_____

1. _____ Followers are under high stress while trying to complete a dangerous task.

2. _____ Followers are new on the job, and are unsure of their abilities and insecure about keeping their positions.

3. _____ Followers are a small group of counselors in a student services department of a state university.

4. _____ Followers are very opinionated and stubborn in their point of view.

5. _____ Followers are a large group of people (more than 30) who work at widely varying tasks at different locations.

6. _____ Followers' work tasks require creativity and new learning, with much competition and possible conflict with other groups.

7. _____ Followers' work involves designing and testing computer programs. They are highly trained and competent, and obtain great personal satisfaction from their work.

LEADERSHIP IN ACTION
Herbert Kelleher

Herbert Kelleher founded Southwest Airlines and served as its chairman until 2001. He occasionally liked to poke fun at himself for the sake of his employees. Under his leadership, Southwest had record earnings as well as the top operating margin among the airline industry's large carriers.

Each year Kelleher threw a party for employees to introduce the airline's newest television advertising campaign. One ad showed Kelleher bumbling a ticket purchase with an expired credit card and missing his plane. Aside from appearing in ads, he showed concern for employees by boarding Southwest planes and joking with the flight crew. He also remembered employee names and sent them birthday cards. He regularly sent letters to all employees describing events in the airline industry and how they affected Southwest. He listened to employee concerns and took action—as when he interceded in labor negotiations over a petition by flight attendants

against certain types of uniforms. Kelleher's office was tiny, in a barracks-style building located at Dallas' Love Field. He shared this headquarters with other employees, and he made a clear effort to spread cost cutting equally throughout the company.

In addition to his bottom-line results, his concern for employees resulted in very high marks from employees and union officials. The profit-sharing plan offers both cash and stock ownership to employees. Southwest has not paid less than the maximum allowable cash bonus in 10 years, and has placed a substantial portion of the company's ownership in employee hands. The supportiveness and caring attitude he showed for employees, backed up by his actions for their benefit, resulted in a surprising sense of family at Southwest. One union boss admitted that "Southwest employees are more interested in the health of the company than most groups."

---

work tasks especially satisfying, and the basis for high follower commitment and performance, little interpersonal supportiveness by their leader is needed. Leaders can sometimes foster the development of these situational characteristics and thereby improve follower attitudes and performance in an indirect manner. These three types of situational characteristics are described in detail in the following sections as they relate to supportive leadership.

The Leadership in Action box on Herbert Kelleher describes his supportiveness of employees, who must maintain a friendly service orientation while working under stressful conditions. This type of situation calls for supportive behavior by the leader, and Kelleher seems to be effective in this role.

▪▪▪ Situational Factors That Enhance Effectiveness of Supportive Leadership

Several characteristics of work tasks and followers have been found to enhance (increase) the impact of supportive leadership. These characteristics make leader supportiveness especially useful to followers.

Task, Organizational, and Follower Characteristics

Individuals working at *job tasks that are dissatisfying or stressful* are particularly responsive to the kind, considerate, and understanding overtures of a supportive leader. Job conditions may be considered dissatisfying or stressful if (1) the task is dangerous or frustrating, (2) the task does not match the subordinate's needs, (3) subordinates are required to deal with hostile customers, or (4) subordinates face difficult job deadlines.[47] Admiral Richard E. Byrd, an American naval officer and polar explorer in the early 1900s, demonstrated supportiveness in a stressful and dangerous situation when he jumped into the icy Antarctic Ocean to rescue one of his crew members who had fallen overboard. Under conditions such as these, subordinates appreciate a leader who shows compassion and concern, and they respond with markedly improved psychological reactions.

Work tasks that are highly structured also tend to enhance the effects of supportive leadership. Highly structured tasks involve execution of rules and procedures that are simple, repetitive, and unambiguous. Once tasks of this nature have been learned, workers may view them as tedious and boring. Thus, workers appreciate a supportive leader who shows a kind and understanding attitude toward them, and who humanizes the working conditions. They respond to the supportive leader with significantly improved attitudes, and sometimes with improved task performance.[48] Structured work tasks are an important situational factor for several leadership behaviors described in this book.

Work tasks that require creativity or new learning may also enhance the impact of supportive leadership. Groups charged with a complex decision-making task often perform best under a supportive leader. And workers faced with new and unfamiliar work tasks perform higher-quality work with a supportive leader. It appears that by encouraging and showing confidence in subordinates, a supportive leader helps them overcome the anxiety often caused by a new complex task and allows them to more efficiently apply their collective energies toward effective performance.[49]

Several characteristics of the subordinate's work environment have also been found to enhance the impact of supportive leadership. Certain properties of the subordinate's work group can be particularly helpful, probably because an employee typically interacts with coworkers frequently during the workday. Discussions about the work itself, the leader, and the organization are common, and the evidence is clear that employees are influenced by their peers at work. A group that faces a lot of *conflict* with other groups inside or outside the organization is typically very responsive to a supportive leader.[50] The group apparently appreciates the leader's reassurance and concern for their difficult situation. A *group that is newly formed* is also highly influenced by a supportive leader. In new groups, problems of goal and role definitions are just being worked through, and group members need more support and attention from their leader than in other groups. When this supportiveness is present, they respond favorably with group cooperation and increased energy.[51] A dynamic feedback process also occurs with newly formed groups. This means that when group members respond to a supportive leader with increased cohesion and energy, this can cause the leader to respond with further increases in supportiveness. It thus appears that a newly formed work group offers unusually fertile ground for a supportive leader.

Studies have found that a *group that is highly cohesive* can enhance the effects of supportive leadership. A cohesive group has a high degree of solidarity, unity, and "felt closeness" among the members, and supportive leadership often pays off well in increased productivity as well as improved worker attitudes.[52] As with certain other leadership behaviors, however, this effect is likely dependent on the norms of the cohesive group. *Group norms* are shared beliefs among members about how they should or should not behave. A cohesive group is able to enforce its norms for member behavior very effectively because members are attracted to the group and wish to remain in it. If the group norms favor the leader, then the enhancing effect of group cohesion on supportive leadership will result. If group norms oppose the leader, however, the group may combine its efforts to resist the leader's influence, and cohesion can actually decrease the positive effects of a leader's supportive behaviors.

Overall organizational characteristics can also affect the impact of a leader's supportiveness. For example, a high degree of *organizational formalization* (i.e., explicit plans and goals, as well as standardized procedures and routines often associated with bureaucratic organizations) seems to make employees more responsive to a leader's supportive behaviors. The supportive leader is apparently seen as a rare source of concern and caring in an otherwise cold, machine-like organization, and is thus capable of instilling appreciation and especially improved attitudes in subordinates.[53]

The organizational or departmental *mission* can also enhance the impacts of a supportive leader. A recent analysis showed that the impact of supportive leadership on follower performance was greatest in educational organizations.[54] Although there were significant positive performance and attitudinal results in business, government, and military organizations as well, the impacts were stronger in schools between teachers and administrators. Similarly, several researchers have found that supportive leadership improves group effectiveness in service organizations and departments. These findings occurred in health and human service organizations, as well as service departments in manufacturing organizations.[55] Thus, the concerned and caring behavior of a supportive leader may be a particularly effective role model for subordinates whose jobs are to interact with and serve others.

A final environmental factor that can enhance the effect of a leader's supportiveness occurs when the *leader's superior is authoritarian* (i.e., the superior believes strongly in the need for rules and formal authority, and tends to dominate subordinates). In this situation, the leader's supportiveness may have an increased impact on group performance.[56] Here, subordinates apparently appreciate the buffering influence their immediate leader provides because it alleviates the tension created by the higher-level authoritarian manager.

Follower characteristics that enhance the impacts of supportive leadership include *low self-confidence, insecurity, and low self-esteem.*[57] Followers with these characteristics see the considerate and understanding leader as a source of comfort and encouragement, and therefore show positive reactions to this behavior. Followers who *expect their leader to be supportive* (perhaps because the predecessor was) or who have *high needs for achievement, autonomy, and esteem* also tend to be positively influenced by supportive leaders. First, a leader who meets their expectations will naturally improve followers' responses.[58] And second, because subordinates with these needs likely view the supportive leader as potentially helpful in achieving their goals, they also show higher satisfaction under this type of leadership.[59]

Influencing Situations to Increase the Impact of Supportiveness

Most leaders are interested in doing whatever they can to make followers more responsive to their leadership. As you probably noticed, many of the factors that enhance the impacts of supportive leadership reflect difficult or stressful situations for followers—stressful or dangerous job tasks, many formalized procedures to follow, external group conflict, authoritarian upper-level management, complex tasks, and low follower self-confidence, self-esteem, or security. We certainly do not advocate making jobs more stressful or difficult for followers just to increase the impacts of a leader's supportiveness, but leaders must be aware that stressful and difficult situations are common in organizations, and they may be difficult to change in the short run. In these situations, supportive leadership is the behavior of choice for the leader, and it should pay off with significant improvements in followers' reactions and behavioral outcomes. Creating smaller work groups or defining the group mission in terms of human service may also increase the impact of a leader's supportiveness. Organizational training and socialization programs that build followers' expectations of supportiveness and encourage strong needs for achievement, autonomy, and esteem in followers may also increase the impact of supportiveness. Figure 4-3 summarizes major situational

▪ ▪ ▪ ▪ **FIGURE 4-3** Situational factors that enhance the effectiveness of supportive leadership

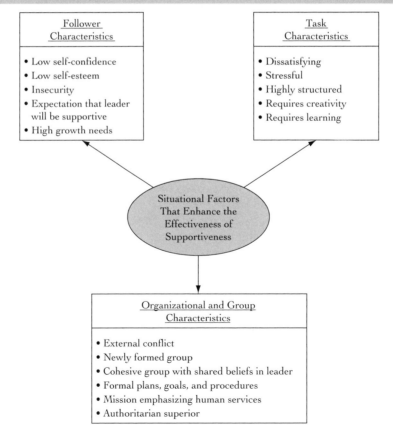

Follower Characteristics

- Low self-confidence
- Low self-esteem
- Insecurity
- Expectation that leader will be supportive
- High growth needs

Task Characteristics

- Dissatisfying
- Stressful
- Highly structured
- Requires creativity
- Requires learning

Situational Factors That Enhance the Effectiveness of Supportiveness

Organizational and Group Characteristics

- External conflict
- Newly formed group
- Cohesive group with shared beliefs in leader
- Formal plans, goals, and procedures
- Mission emphasizing human services
- Authoritarian superior

factors that increase the impacts of leader supportiveness. These situational factors help supportive leaders to have strong effects on followers' motivation, attitudes, and performance.

▬▬▬ Situational Factors That Neutralize Effectiveness of Supportive Leadership

Some characteristics of situations or followers make supportive leadership behavior less important because it has less of an impact on followers. This usually means that supportiveness is not an effective behavior pattern for leaders to use in that situation, and a different leadership approach is needed.

Task, Organizational, and Follower Characteristics

A *large organization or work group* can neutralize the impact of supportive leadership on subordinates.[60,61] Leaders are apparently more visible to members of smaller organizations or groups, and the supportive relationships with members of small groups are more intimate and decrease its impact. In large groups, the leader has less opportunity to interact personally with members because the leader is often spread too thin, reducing the overall impact of supportiveness on group performance and attitudes. Some leaders overcome this factor, such as Stan Smith described earlier, but it takes tremendous time and effort to interact with all the members of a very large group.

Followers who are *very dogmatic* (highly opinionated and unable to incorporate new information effectively) do not respond well to supportive leadership, effectively negating the favorable effects of this type of leadership.[62] These individuals are usually quite respectful of formal authority and prefer a strong directive type of leader. A supportive, concerned, and caring leader may be seen as weak or touchy-feelie, and will have little effect on their performance.

Three other situational factors have been proposed to possibly neutralize the effects of supportive leadership, although research has yet to validate these suggestions. These include a large spatial or geographic distance between leaders and subordinates, and the existence of little control by the leader over organizational rewards.[63] It is argued that a large spatial distance prevents adequate interaction with subordinates, and leaders who do not control organizational rewards will be largely ignored. Researchers also have proposed that followers who are highly trained professionals may resist supportive leadership, though the evidence is unclear at this time. As described with the mental health workers previously in this chapter, professional employees tend to value autonomy and self-control, and may resist certain supportive influence attempts by their hierarchical leader.

Overcoming Factors That Neutralize Supportive Leadership

Leaders should be aware of situational factors that neutralize the impact of supportive leadership so they can work around them. Large groups of followers or dogmatic individuals can be especially problematic. Leaders can break up such groups, or perhaps isolate or transfer dogmatic followers.

Overall, few situational characteristics appear to decrease the effectiveness of supportive leadership. This is not the case for other leadership behaviors described in later

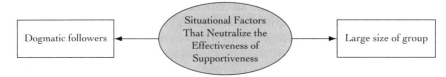

▪ ▪ ▪ ▪ **FIGURE 4-4** Situational factors that neutralize effectiveness of supportive leadership

chapters, but it does show that supportive leadership is clearly a very important part of a leader's behavioral repertoire. Figure 4-4 summarizes the major situational factors that can neutralize the positive effects of supportive leadership. These factors cause followers to resist or ignore a leader's support, but do not improve followers' motivation, attitudes, or performance.

LEADERSHIP SELF-ASSESSMENT
Supportive Leadership Communication

For each of the following leadership communications, indicate whether you feel it is supportive by placing an "×" in front of each supportive leadership communication.

1. _____ "I will explain the right way to solve the problem."
2. _____ "I would like to hear your feelings about that incident."
3. _____ "You did a great job on this project."
4. _____ "See me about the methods you will use to complete the project."
5. _____ "Your coworkers and I will cover for you during your absence."
6. _____ "I trust your judgment in this situation."
7. _____ "You must achieve the following goals by the end of the month."
8. _____ "How can I help you with your heavy workload?"
9. _____ "To prevent errors you will need to carefully follow my instructions."
10. _____ "You had a good idea for improving quality."
11. _____ "You can take Friday afternoon off to attend the professional development seminar."

KEY: Supportive communication items are 2, 5, 6, 8, and 11. Items 1, 4, 7, and 9 address directive communication. Items 3 and 10 address reward communication.

Questions

What differentiates the supportive statements from the nonsupportive ones?
Would the supportive leadership communications have a different impact on your behavior than the nonsupportive communications? Why?

SOURCE: Items adapted from research reported by D. A. Whetten and K. S. Cameron. *Developing Management Skills,* 4th ed. Reading, MA: Addison-Wesley, 1998.

▮▮▮ Situational Factors That Substitute for Supportive Leadership

Some situational or follower characteristics can directly improve follower and group attitudes and performance. At times these characteristics can make supportive leadership unnecessary.[64,65]

Task, Organizational, and Follower Characteristics

The strongest situational characteristic that substitutes for supportive leadership is the existence of a *work task that is intrinsically satisfying* to a worker.[66] When people find their work interesting and gratifying, they often derive all the encouragement and psychological support they need from their work, and require little, if any, interpersonal support from their supervisor to maintain positive job attitudes. When an occasional setback occurs, a small amount of leader supportiveness may help. But individuals who love their work are often challenged by temporary job setbacks, and need little encouragement by the leader to attack and overcome problems on their own.

Another situational characteristic that substitutes for supportive leadership is a *work task that provides its own feedback* concerning accomplishment. An example is repairing the brakes on a car and immediately testing them to be sure they work correctly. Research shows that most employees respond with very positive attitudes and motivation when they receive clear and direct feedback on their performance. When this feedback comes directly from their work, it is usually rapid, accurate, satisfying, and motivating.[67] Consequently, the need for a supportive, encouraging leader is reduced. This is especially true if the employee seeks autonomy and achievement on the job and also finds the work to be inherently satisfying.

When followers place an unusually *high degree of importance on tangible organizational rewards,* this can substitute for the need for supportive leadership.[68] Specifically, when people are motivated primarily by substantive rewards offered by the organization, such as pay raises, promotions, and benefits, they often place little value on a supervisor who concentrates on interpersonal support, encouragement, development, and a caring attitude. To these individuals, the proof is in the pudding, and a good leader is one who comes through with the tangible rewards they value. If these tangible rewards are made available, they will respond with favorable attitudes and performance. A leader who emphasizes a concerned, supportive approach without tangible rewards will have little influence on these followers.

Creating Factors That Substitute for Supportive Leadership

Creating jobs that are inherently satisfying may make supportive leadership less important, while increasing followers' satisfaction and freeing up the leader for other activities. However, intrinsically satisfying jobs must fit the job incumbent. For example, followers who want a challenging job will welcome a task that stretches their capabilities. But if a follower prefers a job that is highly repetitive and predictable, then a challenging job may not be appropriate. Building performance feedback into the challenging job will likely result in a more effective performer. If job redesign is not an option, the leader might increase the followers' interest and task satisfaction by switching the employee to a different job. Most employees come to an organization

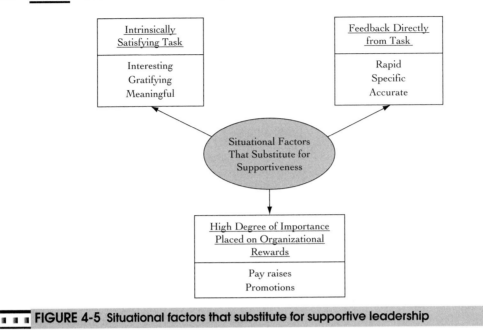

▪ ▪ ▪ ▪ **FIGURE 4-5** Situational factors that substitute for supportive leadership

with preexisting values and beliefs about the importance of tangible organizational rewards. If most of a leader's followers are primarily concerned with pay and promotion, then a reward system based on followers' performance may create favorable follower attitudes and performance with little or no supportiveness by the leader. Figure 4-5 summarizes the situational characteristics that have been found to substitute for supportive leadership. These factors directly improve followers' motivation, attitudes, and performance, and make supportive leadership at least partially unnecessary.

The Leadership in Action box: Substituting for Supportive Leadership with Young Athletes provides an example of how a leader's group can develop inherent satisfaction, motivation, and skills at tasks that provide their own feedback, and eventually require less interpersonal supportiveness from the leader.

▪ ▪ ▪ Assessing the Dynamics of Supportive Leadership

Hopefully the reader now realizes that there is a dynamic interaction among leaders, followers, and situational factors. The three key leadership tasks described in Chapter 1 (diagnosing situations, behaving appropriately, and modifying situations) reflect this dynamic interaction. Leaders diagnose situations and follower characteristics to determine if they will increase or decrease the effectiveness of supportive leadership (or other leadership behaviors). If situational conditions warrant supportiveness, they provide this leadership behavior. If factors exist that will neutralize the impacts of supportiveness, then the leader considers another leadership approach (described in the following chapters). Situational and follower characteristics thereby influence the type of behavior a leader uses to influence followers. Leaders also determine if followers and situations should be modified to eliminate factors that neutralize the effectiveness

LEADERSHIP IN ACTION
Substituting for Supportive Leadership with Young Athletes

One of the authors has spent several years coaching youth sports teams. In this situation, supportive leadership is especially effective. Many young participants on these teams have low self-confidence and are insecure about their abilities. They greatly want to improve their skills, their frequently vocal parents expect the coach to be highly supportive, and newly formed sports teams frequently have external conflicts with their opponents. The successful coach usually takes a developmental approach with players at this stage by carefully teaching them fundamental elements of the sport, showing concern for their safety and welfare, answering questions, and being sympathetic and encouraging when their performance is less than they hoped for. Under

this type of leadership, the young athletes generally improve, develop a cohesive team spirit, enjoy their experience, and have a successful season.

As these young athletes mature and develop their skills and confidence, the coach can often decrease the degree of interpersonal supportiveness. Competent players develop more interest in the sport and derive satisfaction from their own and the teams' performance. As the players and the team develop, their attitude and motivation are thus maintained at a high level with less interpersonal supportive behavior from the coach. Other leadership behaviors become important at this stage, such as providing guidance, direction, and recognition for good team performance.

---

of supportive leadership or to create factors that substitute for followers' needs for supportiveness. As described in this chapter, leaders can decrease stressful job situations, provide for followers' training, develop teams, or implement other actions to improve the work situation.

Thus, the leader can take a direct approach and provide a supportive, concerned, and encouraging climate for followers using supportive leadership behaviors described in this chapter. Or the leader can take an indirect approach by modifying and developing followers, groups, and other factors in the job situation to promote and maintain a supportive climate. The indirect approach increases followers' independence and self-confidence, and alleviates the need for the leader to provide interpersonal encouragement and consideration on a regular basis.[69] Some leaders may choose a combination of the direct and indirect approaches, depending on their time constraints, other duties, and the followers involved.

When a leader's direct or indirect actions improve followers' satisfaction, commitment, or performance, this reinforces the leader's approach and he or she will likely continue with the same influence strategy. If the results are not favorable, then the leader must rediagnose the situation to determine if a different strategy is needed to provide for followers' supportiveness needs. Followers' behaviors are therefore an important factor in a leader's decisions about providing direct or indirect forms of supportiveness. Providing support through direct interaction with followers probably produces results more quickly than the indirect approach. Thus, if followers are in an extremely stressful situation, direct supportiveness by the leader is best. But the

LEADERSHIP IN ACTION
Cleaster Mims

Cleaster Mims believed that her students were being placed on a "conveyer belt from the school house to the jail house." The same was true of the "boat people" and other immigrants to whom she taught English as a second language. Not enough was expected of the students because they were pigeonholed as low achievers. The teachers were failing the kids, and she knew this was wrong for the kids and wrong for society.

Cleaster heard Marva Collins speak about her West Side Preparatory School in Chicago, which emphasized academic excellence. She envisioned a similar program in Cincinnati and started to work. She enlisted community volunteers, found space in a church basement, and utilized cast-off furniture and supplies. She started the school without any books, but eventually obtained literature books from a Goodwill store. After five years the school had expanded from 41 students to more than 200. They purchased their own facility, and were considering boarding students.

Cleaster is president, CEO, principal, and founder of the school. She cares about doing the right things for her students. She developed a program to provide them with a supportive atmosphere that demonstrates a belief in their capabilities and their future. She believes that high expectations can create "a metamorphosis of the mind," if only someone will show they care. She also reflects a spiritual aspect of her leadership when she says: "I feel that I am chosen. When God chooses you, you cannot not do it and find any happiness in life." Her firm moral beliefs have helped her empower the school's teachers to carry out the school's mission.

SOURCE: Adapted from A. Shriberg, C. Lloyd, D. L. Shriberg, and M. L. Williamson. *Practicing Leadership: Principles and Applications.* New York: John Wiley & Sons, 1997.

indirect approach of follower development and situational modification can produce very favorable, long-lasting effects for followers and allow the leader more time to pursue other leadership activities.

SUMMARY

Supportive leadership is a pattern of behaviors involving concern, acceptance, consideration, respect, and a developmental approach toward followers. These behaviors can help preserve the integrity of work groups by building harmony and cohesiveness among members. Supportive leaders rely most heavily on their excellent communication skills, solid interpersonal relations, and technical competence at followers' tasks. These important skills are complemented when leaders make an effort to be sociable and agreeable, because by doing so, they show respect and acceptance of followers. The three sources of power that are most important to supportive leadership are expert power, referent power, and reward power.

Supportive leadership tends to strongly increase followers' satisfaction with their supervisor, work, and overall job situation. It also helps increase followers' commitment to their organization, lowers followers' stress, and increases group harmony, cohesiveness, and helpfulness. These follower and group psychological reactions usually result in increases in followers' performance, as well as reduced turnover, grievance rates, tardiness, and absenteeism.

Effective leaders diagnose situations and followers, and attempt to match their behavior to the needs of the situation. Supportiveness is likely to have the greatest direct impact on followers when situational and follower characteristics are present to enhance its effectiveness. But regardless of conditions, supportive leadership usually has some positive effect on followers.

In other situations, supportive leadership may have smaller direct impact on followers and therefore be less effective than other leadership behaviors. There may be conditions in which specific job factors promote high follower satisfaction, commitment, and possibly performance, without the need for supportive leadership behaviors.

Leaders can sometimes manipulate situational characteristics to make them more favorable. By modifying followers' jobs, work groups, or the organizational mission, leaders can increase the favorable direct effects of supportive behaviors on followers. Leaders can also influence followers indirectly by modifying their work tasks or selection procedures to decrease followers' needs for supportiveness by their leader. This strategy leaves time for the leader to address other follower needs.

Figure 4-6 presents a model of supportive leadership that summarizes the material presented in this chapter. Starting at the top of Figure 4-6, supportive behaviors by a leader are shown to influence follower or group psychological reactions, which in turn affect followers' behavioral outcomes. Situational factors that enhance or neutralize the effectiveness of leader supportiveness are shown on each side of the figure, with arrows intersecting the relationship between supportiveness and follower or group psychological reactions. These intersecting arrows indicate that situational and follower characteristics can increase or decrease a leader's effects on followers and groups. The arrows from the "Leader Supportiveness" box to the "Situational Factors" boxes indicate that leaders can sometimes manipulate situations to improve followers' reactions indirectly, and thereby enhance or substitute for supportive behaviors. Other dynamic effects occur among the boxes in Figure 4-6, but these are not shown, in order to prevent the figure from becoming overly complex.

Figure 4-7 is designed to show a leader how to use the model of supportive leadership presented in Figure 4-6. It describes the three key tasks for effective leadership (introduced in Chapter 1) as they apply to supportive leadership. Leaders first diagnose the situation by answering a series of questions regarding followers and their task situation ("1. Diagnosing the Situation"). These questions identify factors that can increase the impacts of supportive leadership. If the answer is "yes" to one or more of these questions, then supportiveness is probably needed and the leader should provide this type of leadership. If the answer is "no" to these questions, then a different leadership behavior pattern may be needed. Once the leader carries out the appropriate supportive behaviors ("2. Providing Supportive Leadership"), follower and situational characteristics should be examined to see if any exist that may be neutralizing the effectiveness of leader supportiveness. Eliminating these situational factors, if possible, should improve the leader's influence on followers ("3. Modifying Followers or Situations"). The leader should also consider the creation of factors that substitute for

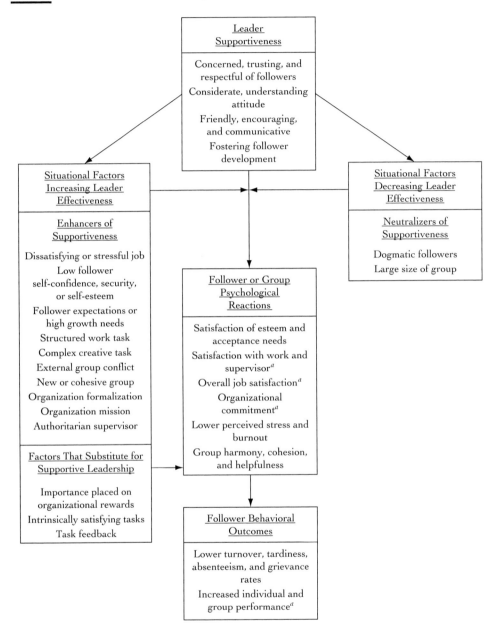

[a]These psychological reactions and outcomes have shown the most improvement from supportive leadership.

▮▮▮▮ **FIGURE 4-6 Leadership process model for supportive leadership**

supportiveness to provide for followers' needs without being present ("3. Modifying Followers or Situations"). The process outlined in Figure 4-7 emphasizes the leader's use of supportive behavior to directly satisfy followers' needs, as well as situational and follower development strategies that can indirectly satisfy followers' needs and make them less dependent on the leader.

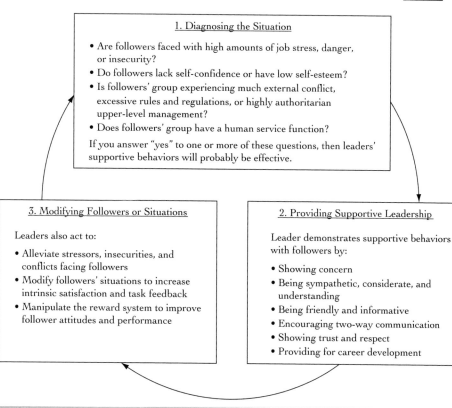

1. Diagnosing the Situation

- Are followers faced with high amounts of job stress, danger, or insecurity?
- Do followers lack self-confidence or have low self-esteem?
- Is followers' group experiencing much external conflict, excessive rules and regulations, or highly authoritarian upper-level management?
- Does followers' group have a human service function?

If you answer "yes" to one or more of these questions, then leaders' supportive behaviors will probably be effective.

3. Modifying Followers or Situations

Leaders also act to:

- Alleviate stressors, insecurities, and conflicts facing followers
- Modify followers' situations to increase intrinsic satisfaction and task feedback
- Manipulate the reward system to improve follower attitudes and performance

2. Providing Supportive Leadership

Leader demonstrates supportive behaviors with followers by:

- Showing concern
- Being sympathetic, considerate, and understanding
- Being friendly and informative
- Encouraging two-way communication
- Showing trust and respect
- Providing for career development

▪▪▪▪ **FIGURE 4-7 Applying the model of supportive leadership**

KEY TERMS AND CONCEPTS IN THIS CHAPTER ▪▪▪▪▪▪▪

- Achievement needs
- Authoritarian superior
- Cohesive groups
- Communication skills
- Creative task
- Dissatisfying tasks
- Dogmatic followers
- Empowerment
- Esteem needs
- Expert power
- External group conflict

- Feedback from task
- Followers' satisfaction
- Group norms
- Insecure followers
- Interpersonal skills
- Intrinsically satisfying task
- Organizational formalization
- Organizational mission
- Organizational rewards
- Referent power

- Relationship-oriented behaviors
- Reward power
- Self-confidence
- Self-esteem
- Supportive communication
- Supportive leadership behaviors
- Stressful task
- Task structure

REVIEW AND DISCUSSION QUESTIONS ▪▪▪▪▪▪▪

1. Describe specific supportive leadership behaviors that have influenced your behavior in an organization. Identify why each had an impact on your behavior.
2. What situations have you been in where you benefited from or wanted supportivness from a leader?
3. How might a leader develop the skills and abilities necessary to provide effective supportive behaviors?

4. Do you believe that leaders should be more supportive of the best performers, the average performers, or the poor performers? What are the reasons for your position?
5. What advice would you give a leader on how to use supportive leadership behaviors effectively?
6. Describe a situation you have experienced, observed, or heard about in which supportive leadership was not effective. Why was supportiveness not effective in this situation?
7. As a leader, how might you create situational factors to build your influence as a supportive leader?
8. Do you think supportive leadership would be effective by a supervisor in a coal mine? Why or why not?
9. Do you think supportive leadership would be effective by a supervisor of truck drivers for a package delivery company who are paid according to how many packages they deliver?

LEADERSHIP SELF-ASSESSMENT

When Are Supportive Behaviors Needed?

Objective: To help the reader apply chapter material by diagnosing situations for supportive leadership.

Instructions: Rate the following situations on whether they require supportive behaviors from the leader. Use the following scale for rating each situation: 5 = highly needed; 4 = needed; 3 = may or may not be needed; 2 = probably not needed; 1 = not needed.

1. Followers are soldering electrical parts onto circuit boards that will be installed in television sets by other workers.	1 2 3 4 5
2. Followers are assigned to handle customer complaints in a large department store.	1 2 3 4 5
3. Followers are sports writers who view and write about professional baseball and football games and players.	1 2 3 4 5
4. Followers work as tellers in a bank.	1 2 3 4 5
5. Followers are police officers who patrol urban areas with high crime rates.	1 2 3 4 5
6. Followers are trained volunteers who provide free family counseling and health advice to low-income families.	1 2 3 4 5
7. Followers are members of a closely knit and successful athletic team.	1 2 3 4 5
8. Followers are traveling sales persons who are paid exclusively based on commissions for their sales.	1 2 3 4 5
9. Followers are members of a newly formed team to develop a mission statement for the organization.	1 2 3 4 5
10. Followers are members of a competent team of computer engineers who are engrossed in designing a new computer and are very well paid.	1 2 3 4 5

Interpretation: If you rated items 1, 2, 4, 5, 6, 7, and 9 highly (a rating of 4 or 5), you correctly diagnosed that these situations normally require supportive leadership. The situations described in items 3, 8, and 10 normally do not require a high degree of supportiveness because other situational or follower characteristics often replace the need for supportiveness. Other leadership behaviors are probably needed in these situations.

■ ■■■■ C A S E   I N C I D E N T S ■■■■ ■

Don't Baby Them

Ann was relieved. The report was completed and it looked good. She thought it was the best market analysis the research section she supervised had ever done. She was especially proud because several members of her section were new and the group had not worked together extensively prior to this job. They had been pressured by upper management to rush its completion. The market analysis involved analyzing complex and detailed data. Because the report was completed ahead of schedule, she thanked each person in the section. Not only did she express her appreciation to the employees for knocking themselves out, she invited them to her house for pizza and drinks after work.

She could not wait to give the report to Tom Benson, the marketing director. When she put the report on Tom's desk, his first comment was, "So you finally got it done." Ann responded with, "Look, Tom, my section really went all out on this one. They

worked overtime to beat the schedule and did an outstanding job. Maybe some appreciation from you is in order."

"Now, Ann," Tom replied, "why baby them? They are paid to do their jobs and they did it. I do not see anything special about employees doing what they are assigned." ■

DISCUSSION QUESTIONS

1. How would you describe the leadership approaches of Ann and Tom?
2. What situational characteristics were important for a leader to consider in this case?
3. Do you think Ann's or Tom's leadership behaviors were the most appropriate for the employees and the situation? Why?
4. If you were Tom, would you have handled the situation differently? If so, how?

A Lack of Self-Confidence?

Ms. Jane Hunt manages the design department of a construction company. Ed Green is her most competent design engineer, and he can always be counted on to give a maximum effort on any assignment. Ed has an excellent educational background, having received a bachelors degree in mechanical engineering and a masters degree in civil engineering from a highly respected university.

Ed is very shy and Ms. Hunt feels that he is overly concerned about other people's

feelings. Ed cannot complete his projects without the contributions of technical writers, drafters, and typists. However, if he feels someone has a heavy workload, he does not delegate work to them. In fact, he sometimes fails to meet deadlines because he did not give the work to others for completion. If Ed's failure to meet deadlines continues, Ms. Hunt will not be able to assign him important projects. This could mean that Ms. Hunt would not be using Ed's ability effectively.

Everyone in the design department recognizes Ed's competence, but they also realize they can avoid doing his work because he is never demanding. They know that Ed will not insist that department standards be met, and he never complains about the quality of work done for him. When technical writing or drafting are not up to standards, he usually tells those doing the work, "Don't bother doing it over; it will be all right." Ms. Hunt knows that it is not all right when standards are not met, so she must have the work redone. Other employees have told Ms. Hunt they think Ed lacks self-confidence and does not realize his own high level of competence. ■

DISCUSSION QUESTIONS

1. Could Ms. Hunt use supportive leadership to positively influence Ed's job performance?
2. What specific supportive leadership behaviors would you recommend to Ms. Hunt to improve Ed's performance?

ENDNOTES ▪ ▪ ▪ ▪ ▪ ▪ ▪

1. Amabile, T. M., Schatzel, E. A., Monets, G. B., and Kramer, S. J. (2004). Leader behaviors and the work environment for creativity: Perceived leader support. *Leadership Quarterly, 15*, 5–32.
2. Bartol, K. M., and Butterfield, D. A. (1976). Sex effects in evaluating leaders. *Journal of Applied Psychology, 61*(4), 446–454.
3. Hendrick, H. W. (1979). Leaders' behavior, subordinate reactions, and perceptions of organizational climate and effectiveness. *Perception and Motor Skills, 49*(3), 803–816.
4. Bass, B. M. (1990). *Bass and Stogdill's Handbook of Leadership,* 3rd ed. Englewood Cliffs, NJ: Prentice Hall; Likert, R. (1967). *The Human Organization.* New York: McGraw-Hill; Fleishman, E. A. (1953). The description of supervisory behavior. *Journal of Applied Psychology,* 37, 1–6; Bowers, D. G., and Seashore, S. E. (1966). Predicting organizational effectiveness with a four-factor theory of leadership. *Administrative Science Quarterly,* 11, 238–263; and House, R. J., and Dessler, G. (1974). The Path-Goal theory of leadership: Some post hoc and a priori tests. In J. G. Hunt and L. L. Larson (Eds.), *Contingency Approaches to Leadership.* Carbondale, IL: Southern Illinois University Press.
5. DuBrin, A. J. (1998). *Leadership: Research Findings, Practices and Skills.* Boston: Houghton Mifflin.
6. Maslow, A. H. (1954). *Motivation and Personality.* New York: Harper & Row.
7. Mitroff, I. I., Mason, R. O., and Pearson, C. (1994). Radical surgery: What will tomorrow's organizations look like? *Academy of Management Executive,* 8(2), 11–21.
8. Van Maurik, J. (1994). Facilitating excellence: Styles and processes of facilitation. *Leadership and Organizational Development Journal,* 15(8), 30–35.
9. Hersey, P., and Blanchard, K. H. (1986). *Management of Organizational Behavior: Utilizing Human Resources,* 6th ed. Englewood Cliffs, NJ: Prentice Hall.
10. Blake, R. E., and Mouton, J. S. (1984). *The Managerial Grid III,* Houston, TX: Gulf Publishing.
11. Mann, F. C. (1965). Toward understanding the leadership role in formal organizations. In R. Dubin (Ed.), *Leadership and Productivity.* San Francisco: Chandler.
12. Bass, B. M., and Dunteman, G. (1963). Behavior in groups as a function of self, interaction, and task orientation. *Journal of Abnormal and Social Psychology,* 66, 419–428; Fleishman, E. A., and Salter, J. A. (1963). Relation between the leader's behavior and his empathy toward subordinates. *Journal of Industrial Psychology,* 1, 79–84; and Fleishman, E. A. (1957). A leader behavior description for industry. In R. M. Stogdill and A. E. Coons (Eds.),

Leader Behavior: Its Description and Measurement. Columbus, OH: Ohio State University, Bureau of Business Research.

13. Humphrey, R. H. (2002). The many faces of emotional leadership. *Leadership Quarterly,* 13, 493–504.

14. Avolio, B. J., and Bass, B. M. (1995). Individual Consideration viewed at multiple levels of analysis: A multi-level framework for examining the diffusion of transformational leadership. *Leadership Quarterly,* 6(2), 199–218.

15. Konovsky, M. A. (1986). Antecedents and consequences of informal leader helping behavior: A structured equation modeling approach. Doctoral diss., Indiana University; and Lindemuth, M. H. (1969). An analysis of the leader behavior of academic deans as related to the campus climate in selected colleges. Doctoral diss., University of Michigan.

16. Hunt, J. G., and Osborn, R. N. (1980). A multiple influence approach to leadership for managers. In P. Hersey and J. Stinson (Eds.), *Perspectives in Leader Effectiveness.* Ohio University, 47–62.

17. Wagner, L. W. (1965). Leadership style, hierarchical influence, & supervisory role obligations. *Administrative Science Quarterly,* 9, 391–420.

18. Halpin, A. W. (1955). The leader behavior and leadership ideology of educational administrators and aircraft commanders. *Harvard Educational Review,* 25, 18–32.

19. Rawls, J., Ulrich, R., and Nelson, O. (1973). A comparison of managers entering or reentering the profit and non-profit sectors. *Academy of Management Journal,* 3, 616–623; and Dragon, A. C. (1979). Leader behavior in changing libraries. *Library Research,* 1(1), 53–66.

20. Ansari, M. D. (1988). Leadership styles and influence strategies: Moderating effect of organizational climate. Paper presented at the International Congress of Psychology, Sydney, Australia; and Lombordo, M. M. (1983). I felt it as soon as I walked in. *Issues & Observations,* 3 (4), 7–8.

21. Vecchio, R. P., and Boatwright, K. J. (2002). Preferences for idealized styles of supervisors. *Leadership Quarterly,* 13, 327–342.

22. Podsakoff, P. M., Todor, W. D., and Schuler, R. S. (1983). Leader expertise as a moderator of the effects of instrumental and supportive leader behaviors. *Journal of Management,* 9(2), 173–185.

23. Barrow, J. C. (1976). Worker performance and task complexity as causal determinants of leader behavior, style and flexibility. *Journal of Applied Psychology,* 61, 433–440.

24. Henisath, D. (1998). Finding the word in leadership. *The Journal for Quality and Participation,* 21(1), 50–51.

25. Sayles, L. (1979). *Leadership: What Effective Managers Really Do . . . and How They Do It.* New York: McGraw Hill.

26. Dorfman, P. W., and Howell, J. P. (1988). Dimensions of national culture and effective leadership patterns: Hofstede revisited. In E. G. McGoun (Ed.), *Advances in International Comparative Management,* 3, 127–149; and Howell, J. P., and Dorfman, P. W. (1986). Leadership and substitutes for leadership among professional and nonprofessional workers. *Journal of Applied Behavioral Science,* 22, 29–46.

27. Kerr, S., and Slocum, J. W., Jr. (1981). Controlling the performances of people in organizations. In P. C. Nystrom, and W. H. Starbuck (Eds.), *Handbook of Organizational Design,* Vol. 2. New York: Oxford University Press.

28. Fisher, B. S., and Edwards, J. E. (1988). Consideration and initiating structure and their relationships with leader effectiveness: A meta-analysis. In *Best Papers Proceedings.* Anaheim, CA: Academy of Management, 201–215.

29. Fernandez, C. F., and Vecchio, R. P. (1997). Situational leadership theory revisited: A test of an across-jobs perspective. *Leadership Quarterly,* 8(1), 67–84.

30. Bartolo, K., and Furlonger, B. (2000). Leadership and job satisfaction among aviation fire fighters in Australia. *Journal of Managerial Psychology,* 15(1), 87.

31. Kerr, S., and Slocum, J. W., Jr., Controlling the performances of people in organizations; Fisher, B. M., and Edwards, J. E. (1988). Consideration and imitating

structure and their relationships with leader effectiveness: A meta-analysis. In *Best Papers Proceedings.* Anaheim, CA: Academy of Management Meeting, 201–215; and Seltzer, J., and Numeroff, R. (1988). Supervisory leadership and subordinate burnout. *Academy of Management Journal,* 31(2), 449–446.

32. Yukl, G. (1998). *Leadership in Organizations,* 4th ed. Upper Saddle River, NJ: Prentice Hall.

33. Ibid.

34. Wofford, J. C., and Liska, L. Z. (1993). Path-Goal theories of leadership: A meta-analysis. *Journal of Management,* 19(4), 857–876.

35. Dorfman, P. W., Howell, J. P., Hibino, S., Lee, J. K., Tate, U., and Bautista, J. (1997). Leadership in western and Asian countries: Commonalities and differences in effective leadership processes across cultures. *Leadership Quarterly,* 8(3), 233–274; and Dorfman, P. W., Howell, J. P., Cotton, B. C. G., and Tate, U. (1992). Leadership within the discontinuous hierarchy structure of the military: Are effective leadership behaviors similar within and across command structures? In K. E. Clark, M. B. Clark, and D. P. Campbell (Eds.). *Impact of Leadership.* Greensboro, NC: Center for Creative Leadership, 399–416.

36. Shea, C. M. (1999). The effect of leadership style on performance improvement on a manufacturing task. *The Journal of Business,* 72(3), 407–422.

37. Spreitzer, G. M. (1992). When organizations dare: The dynamics of individual empowerment in the workplace. Ph.D. diss., University of Michigan.

38. Podsakoff, P. M., MacKenzie, S. B., and Bommer, W. H. (1996). Meta-analysis of the relationships between Kerr and Jermier's substitutes for leadership and employee job attitudes, role perceptions, and performance. *Journal of Applied Psychology,* 81(4), 380–399.

39. Peterson, M. F., Smith, P. B., and Peng, T. K. (1993). Japanese and American supervisors of a U.S. workforce: An intercultural analysis of behavior meanings and leadership

style correlates. Working paper, Texas Tech University.

40. Misumi, J. (1985). *The Behavioral Science of Leadership: An Interdisciplinary Japanese Research Program.* Ann Arbor, MI: University of Michigan Press.

41. Howell, J. P., and Dorfman, P. W. A comparative study of leadership and its substitutes in a mixed cultural work setting. Paper presented at the Western Academy of Management Meeting, Big Sky, MT, March; and Ayman, R., and Chemers, M. M. (1982). The relationships of managerial behavior to effectiveness and satisfaction in Mexico. Paper presented at the International Conference of Applied Psychology, Edinburgh, Scotland.

42. Yeh, Q. J. (1995). Leadership, personal traits and job characteristics in R & D organizations: A Taiwanese case. *Leadership and Organizational Development Journal,* 16(6), 16–27.

43. Kenis, I. (1977). A cross-cultural study of personality and leadership. *Group and Organizational Studies,* 2, 49–60.

44. Ibid.

45. Hughes, R. L., Ginnett, R. C., and Curphy, G. J. (1996). *Leadership: Enhancing the Lessons of Experience,* 2nd ed. Boston: Irwin.

46. Hellriegel, D., Slocum, J. W., Jr., and Woodman, R. W. (1998). *Organizational Behavior,* 8th ed. Cincinnati, OH: Southwestern College Publishing.

47. Yukl, G. (1998). *Leadership in Organizations,* 4th ed. Upper Saddle River, NJ: Prentice Hall; Griffin, R. W. (1980). Relationships among individual, task design, and leader behavior variables. *Academy of Management Journal,* 23(4), 665–683; Fiedler, F. E., and House, R. J. (1988). Leadership: a report in progress. In C. Cooper (Ed.), *International Review of Industrial and Organizational Psychology,* Greenwich, CT: JAI Press.

48. Greene, C. (1979). Questions of causation in the Path-Goal theory of leadership. *Academy of Management Journal,* 22(1), 22–41; Indvik, J. (1986). Path-Goal theory of leadership: A meta-analysis. In *Proceedings of the Academy of Management Meeting,*

Chicago, 1986; House, R. J., and Dessler, G. (1974). The Path-Goal theory of leadership: Some post hoc and a priori tests. In J. G. Hunt, and L. L. Larson (Eds.), *Contingency Approaches to Leadership.* Carbondale, IL: Southern Illinois University Press; and Downey, A. K., Sheridan, J. E., and Slocum, J. W., Jr., (1976). The Path-Goal theory of leadership: A longitudinal analysis. *Organizational Behavior and Human Performance,* 16, 156–176.

49. Burke, W. W. (1965). Leadership behavior as a function of the leader, the follower, and the situation. *Journal of Personality,* 33, 60–81; and Schachter, S., Willerman, B., Festinger, L., and Hyman, R. (1961). Emotional disruption and industrial productivity. *Journal of Applied Psychology,* 45, 201–213.

50. Katz, R. (1977). The influence of group conflict on leadership effectiveness. *Organizational Behavior and Human Performance,* 20, 265–286.

51. Greene, C. N., and Schriesheim, C. A. (1980). Leader-group interactions: A longitudinal field investigation. *Journal of Applied Psychology,* 65(1), 50–59.

52. Schriesheim, J. F. (1980). The social context of leader–subordinate relations: An investigation of the effects of group cohesiveness. *Journal of Applied Psychology,* 65, 183–193; and Seashore, S. E. (1954). *Group Cohesiveness in the Industrial Work Group.* Ann Arbor, MI: University of Michigan, Institute for Social Research.

53. Indvik, J. (1986). Path-Goal theory of leadership: A meta-analysis. In *Proceedings of the Academy of Management Meeting,* Chicago; and Miles, R. H., and Petty, M. M. (1977). Leader effectiveness in small bureaucracies. *Academy of Management Journal,* 20, 238–250.

54. Fisher, B. M., and Edwards, J. E. (1988). Consideration and initiating structure and their relationships with leader effectiveness: A meta-analysis. In *Proceedings of the Academy of Management Meeting,* Anaheim, CA, 201–215.

55. Woodward, J. (1965). *Industrial Organization: Theory and Practice.* Oxford, England: Oxford University Press; Schneider, B. (1973). The perception of organizational climate: The customer's view. *Journal of Applied Psychology,* 57, 248–256; and Fleishman, E. A., Harris, E. F., and Burtt, H. E. (1955). *Leadership and Supervision in Industry.* Columbus, OH: Ohio State University, Bureau of Educational Research.

56. Hunt, J. G., Osborn, R. N., and Larson, L. L. (1975). Upper level technical orientation and first level leadership within a noncontingency and contingency framework. *Academy of Management Journal,* 18, 476–488.

57. Yukl, G. *Leadership in Organizations,* 4th ed.

58. Manheim, B. F., Rim, Y., and Grinberg, B. (1967). Instrumental status of supervisors as related to workers' perceptions and expectations. *Human Relations,* 20, 387–396.

59. Griffin, R. W. (1980). Relations among individual, task design, and leader behavior variables. *Academy of Management Journal,* 23(4), 665–683.

60. Greene and Schriesheim. Leader-group interactions: A longitudinal field investigation.

61. Koene, B. A. S., Vogelaar, A. L. W., and Soeters, J. L. (2002). Leadership effects on organizational climate and financial performance: Local leadership effect in chain organizations. *Leadership Quarterly,* 13, 193–215.

62. Weed, S. E., Mitchell, T. R., and Moffitt, W. (1976). Leadership style, subordinate personality, and task type as predictors of performance and satisfaction with supervision. *Journal of Applied Psychology,* 61, 58–66.

63. Kerr, S., and Jermier, J. M. (1978). Substitutes for leadership: Their meaning and measurement. *Organizational Behavior and Human Performance,* 22, 375–403.

64. DeVries, R. E. (1997). *Need for Leadership: A Solution to Empirical Problems in Situational Leadership Theory.* Ph.D. diss., Tilburg University, Netherlands.

65. Dorfman, P. W., Howell, J. P., Tate, U., and Cotton, B. C. G. (1992). Leadership within the "discontinuous hierarchy" structure of the military: Are effective leadership behaviors similar within and across command structures? In R. E. Clark, M. B. Clark, and D. P. Campbell (Eds.), *Impact of Leadership.* Greensboro, NC: Center for Creative Leadership.

66. Howell, J. P., and Dorfman, P. W. (1986). Leadership and substitutes for leadership among professional and nonprofessional workers. *Journal of Applied Behavioral Science,* 22(1), 29–46.

67. Kerr and Jennier. Substitutes for leadership: Their meaning and measurement.

68. Howell and Dorfman. Leadership and substitutes for leadership among professional and nonprofessional workers.

69. Ingens, O. M. (1995). Situational leadership: A modification of Hersey and Blanchard. *Leadership and Organizational Development Journal,* 16(2), 36–40.

Directive Leadership Behavior

Learning Objectives

After reading this chapter, you should be able to do the following:

1. Describe directive leadership and give examples of directive leadership behaviors.
2. Explain why directive leadership is important for individual followers and groups.
3. Explain why directive leaders do not need to be authoritarian, autocratic, or punitive to be effective.
4. Describe some of the personal traits, skills, and sources of power that leaders need to develop in order to be effective directive leaders.
5. Identify organizational factors that can encourage or discourage leaders from being directive.
6. Describe the major impacts directive leadership has on followers' psychological reactions and behaviors.
7. Identify organizational situations in which directive leadership is especially effective.
8. Identify situations in which directive leadership is probably not effective.
9. Explain how leaders can modify situations to make their directive leadership more effective.

Examples of Effective Directive Leadership

- A team member received a call from his team leader who was out of the country. The leader reviewed an updated production schedule with the member and said he was just checking in to stay aware of how things were going.
- An employee described her supervisor as someone who let her know what work needed to be done, informed her about the quality of her work and how she could improve, and discussed how to handle work-related problems with other employees.

- The supervisor walked along the production line checking the indicators on the machines and asking the operators if they had any problems.
- The production manager told a follower about a rush project that needed top priority and gave the follower suggestions about how to do the project.
- A manager met with an employee for two hours to establish performance goals for the coming year and to discuss the employee's action plans for attaining the goals.
- When Robert C. Hazard, Jr., left his position as CEO of Best Western to become CEO of Quality Inns, he left an organization of confident and capable personnel able to operate with little day-to-day direction. He moved to an organization that had declined and barely avoided bankruptcy. Its personnel needed a directive hands-on leader such as Hazard, who became involved in operations, telling individuals and groups what needed to be done and how to do it, and following up on results. This directive type of leadership behavior was needed to accomplish a turnaround for Quality Inns.[1–5]

▮▮▮ Definition, Background, and Importance of Directive Leadership Behaviors

These examples of leadership in organizations demonstrate effective directive leadership. Directive leadership involves leader activities that guide and structure the actions of group members. In these examples, the leader identified the followers' needs for guidance and information in performing their tasks, and provided the necessary inputs to meet those needs.

Leader directiveness has been studied for almost 50 years, and numerous behaviors have been attributed to this leadership pattern. Directive leadership involves defining roles in the group and clarifying for followers what they are expected to do to achieve specific performance goals.[6] Directive leaders also plan and schedule work to be done, assign responsibilities, and prioritize tasks for group followers.[7] They establish and maintain patterns of communication for explaining assignments, rules, and regulations, and use their expertise to improve followers' work methods and overcome obstacles. They also monitor and follow up on assignments and work methods to assure the intended results are obtained.[8] Other activities have recently been included as aspects of directive leadership. These include motivating followers to change or improve performance, and tracking followers' task skills, as well as training and coaching on new techniques and procedures.[9] An effective leader would probably not utilize all these behaviors in a situation in which directiveness is needed, but would likely select those directive behaviors that seem appropriate in the situation. Directive leadership behaviors are summarized in Figure 5-1.

Nondirective leaders are hesitant about specifying who, what, and how followers are to accomplish specific task assignments. Nondirective leaders make suggestions only when asked by followers, and they often let followers do the work any way they think best. Although this approach can be effective with highly trained and motivated followers, many situations require some type of direction from the leader.

Charles de Gaulle, French general and president, believed that men could not survive without direction any better than they could survive without eating, drinking, or sleeping. Most followers need some direction on the path toward successful effort.

FIGURE 5-1 Types of directive leadership behavior

Directive leadership alters followers' information, understanding, and ability to accomplish tasks. Directiveness can improve followers' performance capabilities by eliminating wasted effort and focusing attention on effective work methods and key aspects of task performance. Goal setting is a proven technique used by directive leaders for motivating follower performance. Goals provide concrete targets that focus attention and provide gauges for performance. Through directive leadership, a leader's intelligence and expertise can be effectively applied to resolving work-related problems.[10] Followers may recognize the need for directive leadership, especially when a crisis occurs, when ambiguity regarding management expectations exists, or when the methods for task performance are unclear. However, too much directiveness by a leader can create follower resentment and eventually cause grievances, absenteeism, and turnover.[11]

Some leaders believe their directiveness is more effective if they maintain a distinct psychological distance from followers.[12] If these leaders have little trust in followers, they may become closely controlling, as well as autocratic and authoritarian in their interpersonal relations. Authoritarian and autocratic leaders emphasize their formal authority, are cold and hostile, have little concern for followers' needs, and do not allow followers to participate in (provide input to) decision making that affects them on the job. Leadership experts have noted, however, that a leader can be directive without being a threatening autocrat.[13]

Effective leaders sometimes use one behavior pattern for making decisions and another pattern for executing decisions after they are made. Leadership in high-technology industries often requires highly trained technical professionals to participate in decision making by providing necessary technical input. High leader directiveness may be needed, however, in carrying out decisions with the same followers if they have little organizational experience in planning or allocating task assignments. Similar situations occur in small business organizations, in which a lack of established procedures, controls, or information systems fail to provide needed guidance to support independent follower action. Here, directive leadership is often needed. It seems clear that leaders can be directive without lording it over followers with their formal authority,

---

LEADERSHIP IN PERSPECTIVE
Frederick Winslow Taylor

Frederick Winslow Taylor was one of the best known management writers in the United States in the 20th century. He was one of the first individuals to study the activities of people at work. Taylor studied the supervision of men working in the steel industry around 1900, when steel making was very labor intensive. Large work gangs of foreign-born individuals with little education did strenuous physical labor. A firm hand, tempered with kindness, was needed in supervising these workers to assure they knew exactly what was expected of them and how to work according to Taylor's "scientifically" correct methods.[15] In Taylor's famous book, *Principles of Scientific Management*, published in 1911, he described how supervisors needed to be very directive with these workers.

The writings of Frederick Taylor were probably responsible for a strong emphasis by U.S. researchers on studying leadership at low levels in organizations. This emphasis on supervisory leadership lasted until the 1970s, and the study of what is now called directive leadership was a major part of this research. This directive leadership pattern is especially important for effective shop-level supervision of workers. It can also be important for leaders at other organizational levels, depending on the presence of other situational and follower characteristics.

---

being hostile and uncaring, or making important job-related decisions without follower input. In a study of managers' communication styles, researchers found effective directive leaders to be dynamic, informative, careful transmitters of information, as well as frank and open, and encouraging of two-way communication.[14]

Many of the leadership behaviors described here as directive leadership have a long history. Several were described in the early 1900s as aspects of Taylor's scientific management,[16] and later as initiating structure in the Ohio State leadership research program. The terms production oriented and concern for production were used in the 1950s, and work facilitation, goal emphasis, and task-oriented leadership were popular during the 1960s.[17–20] The term directive leadership became popular in the 1970s with the development of the Path-Goal theory of leadership.[21]

Some of the early measures of this leadership pattern included behaviors that are currently viewed as separate and distinct from a leader's directiveness. Two of these are continually pressuring followers to produce more, and threatening or taking punitive actions against followers for low performance. Some leaders use these behaviors, but they may not be productive. Threats and pressure often produce negative reactions, and are generally viewed as unnecessary to the clarification, guidance, and facilitative functions of directive leadership. Punitive leadership behavior will be discussed in Chapter 7. Constantly pressuring followers to produce more is not recommended with today's workforce, especially in developed countries, where the level of worker education has increased to the point that few workers will tolerate this type of leadership approach. Although there are exceptions in some countries with unique cultural beliefs, punitive and pressuring behaviors by leaders are typically omitted from current discussions and research on directive leadership.

▪▪▪ Ineffective Directive Leadership

Even though a leader may provide needed directive guidance in a clear manner, if not done in the appropriate context and with other needed information, the results can be inefficiency and ineffectiveness. Researchers provided the following example of ineffective directive leadership:

> A new manager clearly defined roles for followers on a project, specified goals to be met and methods to be used, and assured that members knew what was expected by the organization. The followers were experienced, well-meaning employees, however, who had not been receiving adequate performance feedback from their previous manager. These individuals consequently interpreted the leader's highly directive approach as a cue that their previous performance had been inadequate, and they began to change their behavior, which in reality was very effective, in an effort to please the leader. This had the effect of undercutting the reward system and eliminated previously effective behavior patterns.[22]

Later in this chapter we will describe the various situational contexts that make directive leadership most effective. In the above example, the timing and lack of prior feedback resulted in misinterpretation of the leader's directiveness. The timing and appropriateness of directive leadership behaviors for a particular task are critically important. Some tasks require structure and guidance during the goal-setting stage; others require clarification and performance feedback during execution. Some followers need guidance to relate their work to that of other employees; others need technical direction from the leader.[23] Effective leaders must carefully diagnose the type of direction needed by a follower and provide it in a timely fashion.

▪▪▪ Skills, Traits, and Sources of Power for Directive Leaders

Leaders can develop several skills, personal characteristics, and sources of power to help them effectively direct followers. Two skills are especially important for directive leaders. *Communication skills* are essential in specifying how followers are to accomplish tasks. Giving followers feedback on their performance also requires effective communication. Communication skills are essential in defining roles of followers and in defining communication patterns. The communication skill of obtaining understanding is necessary in clarifying performance expectations and describing work methods. To motivate followers, the leader must effectively communicate both desired behaviors and incentives for performance. The directive leader must also establish and maintain communication to explain assignments, rules, and procedures.

Leaders' competence at followers' tasks may determine their effectiveness in monitoring work methods to assure that results are obtained. Knowledge about processes, methods, and products is necessary in planning, scheduling, and assigning responsibilities. The directive leader may also need competence in the operation of equipment used by followers to help them accomplish tasks. In order to solve task problems, the leader may also need technical competence related to processes, materials, procedures, or equipment.

Although a number of personal traits are compatible with directive leadership, three traits seem most helpful. *Self-confidence* includes having high self-esteem, being decisive, and believing in one's ability. The leader with high self-confidence is more likely to attempt to influence followers, attempt difficult tasks, and set high goals. The leader with high self-confidence is not likely to express doubts or act indecisively, both of which can undermine directive leadership. The directive leader's self-confidence can help instill confidence in followers to carry out directions. To be effective, the directive leader needs to be self-confident without being overbearing. Too much self-confidence by a leader may be seen as arrogance, which can produce resentment. For most organizational situations, a moderately high level of self-confidence is probably best.

The term *assertiveness* refers to being direct in communication and expressing one's position on issues. Assertiveness helps the leader be directive in solving task problems and responding to difficult situations. Guiding followers and structuring the activities of followers often requires the directive leader to show assertiveness. The directive leader's assertiveness can help in informing followers of mistakes, setting high performance expectations, and making legitimate demands for quality performance.

To effectively direct the activities of followers, leaders can benefit from *relevant experience.* As with competence, experience can provide the leader with the knowledge necessary for guiding and structuring followers' activities. Experience can also be valuable to the leader in training followers in processes and procedures necessary to accomplish tasks. The leader's experience can be of great value in solving task problems, removing barriers to productivity, and achieving quality results. Finally, the more aware followers are of the leader's extensive experience, the easier it is for the leader to convey expertise. Relevant experience includes previous jobs, education, workshops, and coaching from higher-ups that increase a leader's task competence, communication skills, self-confidence, and assertiveness. These traits and skills are evident in effective coaches of college athletic teams. Successful coaches use their experience and expertise, as well as assertiveness and self-confidence, to communicate their knowledge and understanding to the players in a directive manner. With effort, leaders can build these skills and personal characteristics to increase the effectiveness of their directive leadership. The Leadership Self-Assessment box: Providing Effective Performance Feedback describes an important leadership skill.

Effective directive leaders often develop three sources of power to make their directions especially impactful. These are *legitimate power, expert power,* and *resource/connection power.* Two other sources of power that can make a leader's directions impactful are reward and coercive power, which will be discussed in Chapter 7.

Legitimate power supports directive leadership because followers' compliance is based on the belief that the leader has the right to provide the direction, and followers are obligated to comply. Followers normally perceive their leaders as having the right to influence because of the position they occupy. Managers usually have the legitimate right to assign specific tasks, schedule work, define work methods, and monitor performance.

Expert power helps directive leadership because followers believe that the leader has a high level of knowledge, skill, and ability for performing tasks. Expert power is especially useful in directive leadership because it enables the leader to make effective plans and strategies, solve problems, and achieve task objectives. When followers depend on the leader for advice and problem solving, the leader's ability to direct followers' behavior is enhanced. If expert power is to help the leader be more effective in providing direction, the follower must recognize the leader's expertise and believe the leader is trustworthy as a source of knowledge. When expert leaders use rational persuasion and apprise followers of the benefits of following their direction, followers usually cooperate and carry out the leader's requests.

LEADERSHIP SELF-ASSESSMENT

Providing Effective Performance Feedback

Instructions: Indicate the extent to which you would engage in the following behaviors when providing feedback to others on their performance, using the following scale: (5) almost always; (4) usually; (3) occasionally; (2) seldom; (1) almost never.

1. Provide specific examples of effective and ineffective behaviors.	5	4	3	2	1
2. Focus my feedback on the person's intent and motives.	5	4	3	2	1
3. Provide feedback that focuses on obtaining understanding and solving problems.	5	4	3	2	1
4. Provide feedback on situations, regardless of whether the person receiving the feedback has control over them.	5	4	3	2	1
5. Fix blame on individuals who are responsible for problems.	5	4	3	2	1
6. Avoid overloading individuals with too much feedback at one time.	5	4	3	2	1
7. Focus on the other person's needs and what will be helpful to him or her.	5	4	3	2	1
8. Criticize individuals when they deserve it.	5	4	3	2	1
9. Focus on the future in providing feedback and how future performance can be more effective.	5	4	3	2	1
10. Take into account the other person's attitudes, beliefs, and values to assure understanding of my feedback.	5	4	3	2	1

Interpretation: If you rated items numbered 1, 3, 6, 7, 9, and 10 as 4 or 5, then you are probably effective at giving feedback. These items focus on the receiver's behavior, understanding, needs, and values, and are oriented toward improving future performance. If you rated items numbered 2, 4, 5, and 8 as 4 or 5, you may be ineffective at providing feedback. These items do not focus on the receiver's behavior or are not oriented toward improving future performance.

SOURCES: Items based on K. Karp. The lost art of feedback. In J. W. Pfeiffer (Ed.), *The 1987 Annual: Developing Human Resources.* San Diego, CA: University Associates, 1987, 237–245; and J. Waldroop and T. Butler. The executive as coach. *Harvard Business Review,* November–December 1996, 111–130.

Resource/connection power in the form of access to important information also helps directive leaders because it enables them to provide followers with data and supporting information to justify their directions. When followers see that a leader's directions are justified by clear evidence of past performance, they are more likely to view the directions as helpful. Leaders may provide information on past performance, market demand, company operations, new technology, or other areas that can influence employees' task efforts and achievement. Followers and others willingly collaborate with leaders who provide them with information that they need. Figure 5-2 summarizes the skills, traits, and sources of power for effective directive leadership.

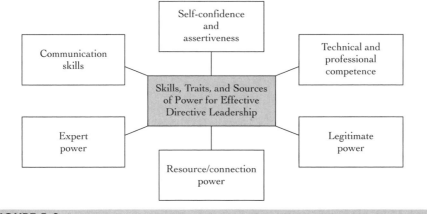

▪▪▪ **FIGURE 5-2** Skills, traits, and sources of power for effective directive leadership

▪▪▪ Facilitating and Limiting Conditions for Directive Leadership

Several writers have pointed out that leaders are often not completely free to choose their behavioral strategies because organizational requirements influence the amount of directive behavior required of the leader.[24–26] For example, leaders may be required to specify and enforce company standards, objectives, and work deadlines, or to coordinate followers' activities with other departments, all requiring directive leadership.[27] Leaders usually respond to a high degree of threat or stress by being directive.[28] The stress may come from pressure of the leader's superior for immediate results, from managers higher up in the organization, from low follower performance, or from a decline in organizational profits.[29–34] A highly bureaucratic climate with authoritarian policies and centralized decision making can also cause supervisors to be directive in their behavior.[35] These organizational conditions create expectations by superiors, and sometimes followers, that leaders should be directive. On the other hand, followers with high levels of education and job tenure may not appreciate directive leadership.

The Leadership in Action box: Women and Leadership in the America's Cup Race shows the importance of directive leadership in this highly stressful situation.

▪▪▪ Effects of Directive Leadership

As described earlier, the purpose of directive leadership is to help individuals and groups of followers perform work tasks efficiently and effectively. Because leaders usually possess greater authority, experience, and expertise than followers, they often provide information on management expectations for followers, and on performance plans, rules, and regulations. They also provide guidance on correct and updated work methods, and they schedule or assign tasks. They monitor and follow up on assignments, thereby motivating followers to avoid loafing. This section summarizes the overall impacts of directive leadership. In reading and thinking about these impacts, two factors should be kept in mind.

LEADERSHIP IN ACTION

Women and Leadership in the America's Cup Race

In 1995, a group of dedicated individuals set out to be the first women's team ever to enter the America's Cup sailing race. They had many difficulties, but eventually managed to race neck and neck with seven other teams composed exclusively of men. The lessons they learned about leadership made a vivid impression on all the crew members.

The team planners decided at an early stage to sail without a skipper. "We wanted teamwork to be the driving force behind the team. We thought that if we set things up so the leadership duties were shared, instead of having one person in charge, it would encourage working together as a team." They believed that the women would be more consensus oriented than men and would avoid the power struggles that had occurred on previous men's teams.

This decision to have no skipper prevented the team from developing and performing to its potential. The members did not resolve conflicts and differences. They strove to keep the appearance of harmony and a smooth façade rather than confronting difficult problems. The unresolved conflicts festered and continued to interfere with the team effort. For example, during the early races the helms person and tactician could not agree on a course of action. Because neither was the leader, neither could pull rank, so the team made and repeated mistakes in several races. A lack of clear directive leadership from a single skipper was clearly hurting the team's performance.

Anne Jardim is cofounder of the Simmons Graduate School of Management in Boston, the only all-female business school in the United States. Jardim was not surprised that the team had problems with a lack of leadership. She stated, "Women tend to generate teams of equals. We're not hierarchical—we operate by consensus. As a result, we don't generate leaders. Men are born followers; women aren't. Men need to establish hierarchies, find leaders; women don't. . . . The very idea that groups need leadership has to be taught to women, and it should have been hammered into your group."

The team planners decided to replace the tactician with a highly experienced skipper (team leader). This new skipper had the proven expertise to direct the team. By insisting that disagreements be faced and worked out, the skipper gained the respect and cooperation of all the crew members when quick decisions were needed. Eventually a "calm confidence settled over the boat."

The group came together, addressed the problems confronting them, and performed admirably. Although they did not win, they learned the importance of having a strong directive leader to address safety issues, tactics, and countless other quick decisions that arise during a race. These decisions require "one voice that can rise above the din of the water, the sails, the ropes, and the other crew members." Once the leadership and other conflicts were resolved, the group coalesced into the type of team that can compete in the America's Cup race.

SOURCE: Anna Seaton Huntington. A ship with no captain. *HR Magazine,* November 1997, 94–99. Reprinted with the permission of 'HR Magazine' published by the Society for Human Resource Management, Alexandria, VA.

First, much of the research on directive leadership has addressed its combined effects with supportive leadership. Consequently, in many studies it is difficult to distinguish separate effects for these two patterns of behavior. Where it is possible to separate the effects, we have done so. When the combined effects could not be clearly separated, we have reported them as combined impacts.

Second, the research on directive leadership indicates that its effects on followers are often strongly influenced by situational and follower characteristics. Usually, however, situational factors do not change the direction of directive leadership's effect. Instead, they change the amount of positive (or negative) effect. For example, if a follower is working on a highly structured task, the follower will likely see little need for directive leadership. Therefore, directiveness usually has a smaller impact (although it is usually still positive) on this follower's satisfaction than on one with a less-structured task. Lack of task structure usually means a follower welcomes a leader's directive guidance and tends to respond with considerably higher satisfaction. In both cases (high and low task structure) skillful directive leadership will often increase follower satisfaction, if only because it shows the leader is interested in the follower's performance. But the impact is usually largest in low task structure situations.

Effects on Follower and Group Psychological Reactions

Directive leadership has one of its most important psychological effects on followers' *role clarity*.[36–38] A follower's clear understanding of his or her correct role in accomplishing work tasks, as well as the follower's relationships with his or her leader and peers, is usually essential to effective task performance. When a leader provides information about expectations, guides a follower in the use of work methods, or assigns a task that utilizes the follower's ability, the leader is providing a clear picture for the follower of what needs to be done. This clear picture often relieves followers' uncertainty and tension; they know exactly how they are supposed to behave. The leader is providing structure for the follower. Most people welcome some structure and predictability in their lives. An example is when a college professor hands out a course syllabus early in the semester to clarify requirements and due dates for class assignments. This structure helps people concentrate on important issues, and the directive leader provides this by clarifying followers' roles. Thus, role clarity also often leads to positive employee attitudes and improved performance.[39]

Another follower psychological reaction to directive leadership, sometimes as the result of improved role clarity, is *follower satisfaction.* Satisfaction with the work one does, satisfaction with supervision, and overall satisfaction with one's job and organization have all shown improvements from a leader's directiveness.[39–44] Increases in follower satisfaction have been found with volunteers, nursing supervisors, fire fighters, school principals, departments in state governments, and numerous business settings. Some early measures of directive leadership, which included punitive, autocratic, and authoritarian dimensions, found decreases in follower satisfaction to result from leader directiveness. However, current measures of directive leadership that delete these other dimensions generally find positive impacts on follower satisfaction.

Another psychological reaction affected by directive leadership, often when combined with supportive leadership, is followers' level of *stress,* and a related outcome of stress—*job burnout.* Researchers have noticed that a leader's behavior can be a source of job stress or it can help followers avoid and cope with job stress. In early research that used punitive and autocratic definitions of directive leadership, a high degree of directiveness seemed to increase followers' stress. This is certainly understandable to anyone who has worked for a punitive autocratic leader. However, when assessed with current measures, which focus instead on information, expertise, and guidance, leader directiveness appears to lower followers' stress levels and increase their ability to deal with job stress.[45] This is supported by findings that directive leadership (as well as supportive leadership) results in lower job burnout among followers.[46]

The psychological reactions of the leader's group are also often affected by directive leadership. *Group cohesion* has been the most frequently studied group-level psychological reaction. Group cohesion refers to the *felt closeness,* or perceived solidarity, among group members. A cohesive group has a strong "we" feeling, and members have a sense of unity and togetherness with other group members. Cohesive groups are usually effective in controlling members' behavior, and thus the members usually act together in important task-related situations. Directive leaders who are not also arbitrarily punitive, autocratic, or authoritarian tend to have highly cohesive groups of followers.[47,48] Similar increases in group cohesion result when directive leadership is combined with supportive leadership.[49,50] Two other group psychological reactions that may be improved by directive leadership are the quality of relations among group members,[51,52] and the level of group motivation that is "focused on achieving organizational goals."[53] These results have been found consistently in business organizations, schools, and health care settings.

Effects on Followers' Performance and Behavior

Many researchers have studied the effects of directive leadership on followers' performance and behavior in different organizations. One finding was that in large organizations with several levels of management, directive leaders tend to receive higher *merit ratings* than nondirective leaders.[54–57] This is especially true in business organizations in which followers are working under time constraints—such as manufacturing departments. It is less true in service departments, where time constraints are often not critical. In schools, a high degree of directiveness combined with high supportiveness tends to result in high merit ratings for administrators.[58,59] This may indicate that in organizations that emphasize quality of human service, directive leadership is most effective when combined with supportiveness.

Studies of *followers' performance and productivity* as outcomes of directive leadership are generally also quite positive. Directive leaders usually have higher-performing or more-productive followers than nondirective leaders.[60–64] In addition, several researchers in education and health care settings have reported that increased leader directiveness resulted in improved department or organizational effectiveness and/or efficiency.[65,66] In educational and training settings, several studies show trainee or student scores on achievement tests to be higher when administrators and/or teachers are highly directive, sometimes when combined with supportive leadership.[67,68] Overall, it appears that the guidance, expertise, and attention to followers' task performance by directive leaders usually pays off.

Other outcomes of directive leadership have been studied to a lesser extent than those reported above, and the results are less consistent. Early measures of directiveness indicated that increased absenteeism, grievances, and turnover sometimes

LEADERSHIP IN ACTION
Directive Leadership in Mexico

Mexico has a culture that combines the histories of the Spanish Conquistadors who invaded Mexico in the 16th century and the Indians who occupied that country for thousands of years. The predominant leadership model of the Spaniards was militaristic and authoritarian. After arriving in the new world, their leaders burned their ships before proceeding overland. The Indian culture emphasized religious leaders who were considered omnipotent and their directions were never questioned. This dual history has resulted in a predominant leadership pattern in Mexico of the autocratic patron who makes decisions and gives clear directions to compliant followers.

Status differences are still predominant in Mexico, where high-status paternalistic leaders are expected to take care of and direct followers' activities. These cultural expectations reinforce the importance of strong directive leadership in Mexico. This is supported by recent research showing directive leadership improves followers' commitment, job clarity, and performance in business organizations in Mexico.

SOURCE: P. W. Dorfman, J. P. Howell, S. Hibino, J. K. Lee, U. Tate, and A. Bautista. Leadership in western and Asian countries: Commonalities and differences in effective leadership processes across cultures. *Leadership Quarterly,* 8(3), 1997, 133–274.

resulted, especially when the leader failed to also be supportive. One interesting early study showed that high levels of directiveness (which at that time still included authoritarian and autocratic behaviors) were tolerated by followers with no increases in grievances or turnover only when the leader was also highly supportive.[69] More recent studies with updated measures of leader directiveness show reductions in intentions to quit and no increases in actual turnover from directive leadership,[70] regardless of the level of a leader's supportiveness.[71]

Numerous researchers have found the directive leadership pattern to produce an impact in many countries.[72–74] In Japan, for example, directive leadership is highly acceptable to followers, because they view it as directly connected to accepting their organizations' mission and goals. Numerous studies in Japan have shown directive behaviors to result in high performance in many organizational settings.[75] Other researchers have reported positive impacts of directiveness (often along with supportive leadership) among Israeli foremen and nurses.[76] Recent studies of managers and supervisors in Mexico, Taiwan, and Korea also found positive impacts of leader directiveness on follower psychological reactions and perceptions.[77] One researcher also found directiveness to have important impacts on follower satisfaction and performance in Saudi Arabia.[78] Directive leadership is clearly an important part of a leader's behavioral repertoire in many countries.

Recently, researchers using updated statistical techniques have summarized the most extensive and consistent effects of directive leadership.[79,80] Modern directive leadership had strong positive effects on improved role clarity, satisfaction with

TABLE 5-1 Major effects of directive leadership

Follower Benefits	Organizational Benefits
Role clarity	Increased cohesiveness and harmony
Clear expectations	High-quality relations among group members
Satisfaction with work and supervisor	Reductions of intentions to quit
Satisfaction with organization	Group arousal focused on achieving organizational
Lower stress	goals
Increased performance	Improved efficiency and effectiveness

supervision, and overall job satisfaction. It also appeared to elicit a moderate to strong improvement in followers' satisfaction with work and their performance. Clearly, leader directiveness has important positive impacts on followers' role clarity, satisfaction, and performance. In addition, increased group cohesiveness and reduced stress may result from nonpunitive directive leadership. Though other psychological reactions of followers have been studied, the small number of studies or less-consistent results makes generalizations difficult at this time. Table 5-1 summarizes the major effects of directive leadership.

■■■ Situations in Which Directive Leadership May or May Not Be Effective

Certain situational factors make directive leadership more or less effective. We refer to these factors as the situational dynamics of directive leadership.[81] They include what leaders should look for in a situation to know when directive leadership is needed, and how leaders can help followers obtain directive guidance from other sources. Situational dynamics also address how directive leaders, followers, and situational factors affect one another.

The Leadership Self-Assessment: Diagnosing Situations for Directive Leadership provides descriptions of situations in which directive leadership may or may not be effective with followers.

Some of the situations described in the Leadership Self-Assessment reflect a need for directive leadership. The situations numbered 2, 3, 6, and 7 are examples in which followers typically need and respond favorably to directive behaviors by their leader. These situations therefore enhance the positive effects of directive leadership. Two of the situations have the opposite effect on leader effectiveness. The situations numbered 1 and 5 describe situations in which followers simply do not desire any direction by their leader. When the leader directs these followers regarding how their work should be done, they may become uncooperative. These situational characteristics can therefore decrease or neutralize the effects of directiveness on the followers described, and another leadership approach is needed. Two other situations described above actually replace or substitute for followers' needs for directiveness from their leader. The situations numbered 4 and 8 are examples of these situations, in which followers obtain guidance and direction from members of their

---

LEADERSHIP SELF-ASSESSMENT

Diagnosing Situations for Directive Leadership

Place an "×" next to those situations in which you believe leader directiveness will be most effective.

---

1. _____ Followers view themselves as capable and experienced individuals who desire to work independently without supervision by their leader.

2. _____ Followers are members of a large work group and they must coordinate their activities with one another to successfully complete their work tasks.

3. _____ The leader has a high degree of expertise at followers' work tasks and is very supportive of followers.

4. _____ Followers work in an organization in which clear written plans, procedures, and goals exist for their work, and feedback on their performance comes directly from a computer display of individual productivity.

5. _____ Followers work in a cohesive group of which the members usually meet their leaders' performance goals.

6. _____ Followers work on tasks that require them to follow specific procedures.

7. _____ Followers are new at their jobs, and need guidance from their leader about effective work methods and what the leader expects of them.

8. _____ Followers work in autonomous groups of which the members are highly trained and experienced, and help one another with task- and work-related problems.

---

work group or other sources, and require little or no direction by their leader. These situations often yield very favorable results for followers and leaders. The remainder of this chapter describes these three types of situations, and offers leadership strategies for influencing the situations to improve follower, group, and organizational results.

The Leadership in Action box: John F. Welch, Former Chairman and CEO of General Electric, shows how directive leadership can be used at the top of a very large corporation to drive company strategies. Welch was a highly effective directive leader.

■ ■ ■ Situational Factors That Enhance Effectiveness of Directive Leadership

Several task and environmental characteristics have been found to enhance the effects of directive leadership. These factors increase the effectiveness of directive leadership in influencing followers.

LEADERSHIP IN ACTION

John F. Welch, Former Chairman and CEO of General Electric

While chairman and CEO of General Electric (GE), John F. Welch directed a new quality program for the company's worldwide operations. He poured his energy into clarifying expectations and structuring activities for his people regarding the program. "You have to tell your people that quality is critical to survival, you have to demand that everyone gets trained . . . you have to say 'We must do this!'" An aspect of the quality control program Welch directed involved training "black belts" in statistical and other quality measures. He made his expectations clear to younger managers by informing them that they had no future at GE unless they became black belts. After their training, he assigned them to roam GE plants and held them responsible for setting up quality improvement projects on their own.

Shifting GE's emphasis from manufacturing products to supplying services was another strategy Welch directed. He provided planning and guidance for managers to help them emphasize services such as medical diagnostics, expanded spare parts and engine overhauls, and de-emphasized equipment sales with declining profit margins. He constantly clarified his expectations that managers must obtain and keep a dominant position in whatever business GE entered. He also assigned "stretch goals" to his managers, expecting them to attain huge gains in market power.

SOURCE: William M. Carley. Charging ahead: To keep GE's profits rising, Welch pushes quality control plan. *The Wall Street Journal*, January 13, 1997. Copyright 1997 by DOW JONES & CO INC. Reproduced with permission of DOW JONES & CO INC in the format Textbook via Copyright Clearance Center.

Task, Organizational, and Follower Characteristics

When followers' work tasks are *highly structured,* requiring a specific set of procedures for successful completion, leader directiveness usually results in high levels of follower and group performance.[82–87] A work task with high structure has predefined steps that enable a competent worker to perform effectively. Though followers may dislike directive leadership with structured, unambiguous tasks, their performance improves consistently when leaders are directive. This is probably because the existence of task structure gives the leader a clearly correct set of steps to use in guiding followers. By monitoring followers' performances, directive leaders also keep followers focused on their work. Two other task characteristics that increase the effects of leader directiveness are a high degree of *task interdependence* among followers and *direct communications between customers and followers.*[88,89] Task interdependence occurs when a follower must closely coordinate his or her work with others in order to achieve a high level of performance. An example is a group of medical workers in a hospital emergency room. An emergency room also often involves direct communications between various staff members and patients. Both of these situational conditions (combined, of course, with the life-and-death nature of the business) likely increase the importance of performing tasks correctly, which can increase followers' responsiveness to the leader's directive guidance.

The existence of a high degree of *stress* also often allows directive leadership to have a strong favorable impact on followers. This finding first occurred in early studies of military combat,[90] and has since been supported by studies in health care and numerous other organizations.[91,92] The emergency room example described in the previous paragraph is also a high-stress environment, necessitating directive leadership. Workers under high stress appreciate the guidance provided by a directive leader, and typically respond with high job satisfaction, low levels of job burnout, and high performance. The sources of stress studied have included stress with one's leader, the existence of internal group conflict, role conflict, and combat conditions. Two researchers recently reported findings supporting job stress as an enhancer of directive leadership, and they suggested that directive leaders who were highly experienced were particularly effective under stress, more so than directive leaders who were highly intelligent.[93] They cited earlier studies to justify this prediction, but research is beginning to appear that seems to justify their prediction in organizations.

When followers work in a relatively *large group* (more than four or five people), directive leadership usually has a favorable effect on followers' psychological reactions, including improved job satisfaction, group arousal, and group cohesion.[94,95] Some writers have suggested that this result occurs because larger groups are less cohesive. It seems likely, however, that a directive approach is necessary and effective in large groups primarily to guide and coordinate the large number of people so they do not act at cross purposes with one another.

Coordination is difficult with large groups, and leaders must give more attention to directing members to assure it is achieved. A *positive group performance norm* may also enhance the impact of directiveness on follower performance.[96] A performance norm is a shared expectation among group members about the amount or quality of performance they should achieve. When a group of followers has a positive performance norm, it shares a desire to help the leader reach performance goals and responds positively to his or her guidance. This positive attitude is often found on successful athletic teams.

When working in a *mechanistic organization structure* (a bureaucracy with many hierarchical levels and decisions communicated downward from higher levels), or when the leader's position is at a fairly low level within the structure, the impact of the leader's directiveness on followers' satisfaction is enhanced.[97,98] In an organization in which many decisions are made at higher levels and communicated downward, followers generally expect supervisory leaders to be directive to assure the decisions are carried out. Their positive reaction in the form of higher satisfaction may occur because the leader meets their expectations.

Certain leader characteristics or behaviors also increase the impact of directiveness on followers' performance or perceptions. A directive leader who possesses a high *need for achievement* (the desire to excel),[99] a high degree of *expertise* at the follower's task,[100] or a high degree of *supportiveness,*[101,102] typically has favorable impacts on individual follower performance, group performance, and subordinate role clarity.[103–105] The enhancing effect of supportiveness should not be interpreted to mean that all leaders should be highly directive and highly supportive of their followers. In fact, one researcher pointed out that a moderately high amount of directiveness and supportiveness (rather than extremely high on both) may be the optimal combination of these two leadership behaviors for many situations.[106] It is easy to imagine how leaders who are highly competent at followers' tasks, show concern for followers, and

LEADERSHIP IN PERSPECTIVE

Followers' Gender and Race

Two follower characteristics have often been assumed to influence the impact of directive leadership—gender and race. Reviews of empirical findings from laboratory studies[112] and field studies in real organizations[113] conclusively show that follower gender does not consistently increase or decrease the impact of directive leadership on followers' psychological reactions or behaviors.[114,115] Though studies have found significant differences related to follower gender, the findings are not consistent, and other situational factors have most likely affected the results and confused the interpretations. The same conclusion is appropriate for followers' race, although less good research is available on directive leadership and follower race than on gender. At this time, no clear, consistent evidence indicates that followers' race increases or decreases the impact of a leader's directiveness. Leaders may behave somewhat differently when followers are a different race, but the evidence does not show the impact of directive leadership to be consistently different. More research is needed in the area of race and leader effectiveness, especially with the increasing global integration of the U.S. economy.

display a strong desire for excellent performance, can be effective in directing their followers.

A small number of studies show follower characteristics can increase the effectiveness of leader directiveness. When ROTC cadets possessed a high need for achievement, their leader's directiveness resulted in high levels of follower satisfaction.[107] A similar result occurred for professional research and development workers who preferred their job requirements to be specific and clear.[108,109] *Followers who have high need for achievement* may welcome the leader's helpful direction in successfully completing their tasks. *High desire for clarity* by followers means they want and appreciate a leader's explanations and guidance for completing their job tasks.

Recent international studies have focused on how situational and follower characteristics enhance the impacts of directive leadership in various countries. One study of Mexican managers and professionals showed that followers who believed in the need for masculine (strongly assertive) leaders were more satisfied with directive supervision. This study also found that beliefs in paternalism (leaders should take care of followers) enhanced the impact of directiveness on followers' performance.[110] Another study found that a leader's task expertise was a consistent enhancer of directiveness in Japan, Taiwan, Korea, and Mexico.[111] More research is underway to better understand how situational and follower characteristics affect directive leadership in different cultures. The Leadership in Perspective box: Followers' Gender and Race describes research on these two follower characteristics and directive leadership.

Influencing Situations to Increase the Impact of Directiveness

Because high task structure increases the impact of leader directiveness on follower performance, leaders may be interested in building this task characteristic into followers' jobs. This can be done through job design programs that create clear stepwise methods and procedures for followers' job tasks. Certain types of jobs are obviously more suited to this approach than others, and more will be said about task structure later in this chapter. As noted, however, high task structure may also decrease the positive effect of directiveness on follower satisfaction, so leaders are best advised to also be supportive of followers. Training leaders to become experts in methods and procedures and to communicate this expertise via directive leadership should also significantly increase leaders' directive impacts on follower performance. Leader training that focuses on developing task expertise and providing supportive leadership behavior can enhance the favorable effects of directive leadership.

Stress on followers and a bureaucratic organization structure can also increase the effects of leader directiveness. Most leaders will not want to increase follower stress levels or to increase bureaucracy, but they should remember that directive leadership behavior is an effective strategy when followers face these job conditions. Increasing the size of followers' work groups, influencing the groups' production norm (through a group reward system), and recruiting followers who have a high need for clarity will increase the need for a leader's directiveness, and probably its impact. However, creating small groups and recruiting followers with low need for clarity can sometimes substitute for directive leadership, which can also improve followers' psychological reactions and performance, and give the leader added time for other tasks. Figure 5-3 summarizes the major situational factors that make directive leadership especially effective.

■ ■ ■ **FIGURE 5-3** **Situational factors that enhance the effectiveness of directive leadership**

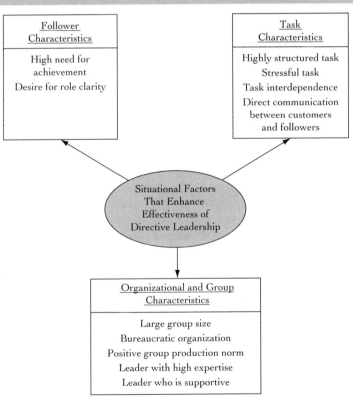

LEADERSHIP IN PERSPECTIVE
Combining Leadership Behaviors

Combining distinct leadership behavior patterns in different ways can affect how followers react. A recent study showed that one combination of supportive and directive leadership was better than others. Leaders who provided supportive behaviors (using statements such as "These are tough working conditions and I appreciate the extra efforts you are making"), *before* directive behaviors (such as "There are a number of tasks that you need to complete today") produced the most positive reactions from followers. Providing support immediately after directive leadership or after a long delay following directive leadership resulted in fewer positive and more negative reactions by followers. Because directive leadership implies an authority difference between leaders and followers, it appears that followers like to know the leader cares about them (through supportive behaviors) before he or she gives them instructions or performance expectations regarding their own behavior.

SOURCE: Gian Casimir. "Combinative aspects of leadership style: The ordering and temporal spacing of leadership behaviors." *Leadership Quarterly,* 12 (2001), 245–278.

▬▬ Situational Factors That Neutralize Effectiveness of Directive Leadership

Some situational characteristics can reduce or eliminate (neutralize) the impact of directiveness on followers. Most leaders would like to eliminate these situational factors if they can identify them. There are occasions, however, when these factors may be advantageous to an organizational unit or followers. This can occur in government or universities in which incompetent administrators become entrenched in their position and cannot be removed. In these situations, creating neutralizers is sometimes the only means to minimize damage to a group or organization.

Task, Organizational, and Follower Characteristics

Although a high degree of *task structure* was described earlier as increasing the impact of directive leadership on follower performance, the influence of task structure on the directive leadership–follower satisfaction relationship is quite different. When followers' work tasks are highly structured, the impact of leader directiveness on followers' intrinsic job satisfaction and general job satisfaction is actually reduced.[116–120] A recent summary of research on directive leadership confirmed this neutralizing effect for follower satisfaction.[121] It appears that when followers face job tasks with predefined procedures and steps, they dislike a leader reiterating these procedures to them through directive leadership, even though this reiteration can help their performance.

Characteristics of the follower's work group may also decrease the impact of directive leadership, although this is a complex situational factor. Studies of *group cohesion* (the solidarity or felt closeness among group members) indicate both neutralizing and enhancing effects. Cohesion among group members causes them to act together, cooperating with or resisting the leader. The key factor appears to be the type of *performance norm* that develops within the cohesive group. If a low performance norm exists, indicating little desire or effort by members to meet the leader's performance goals, then the impact of directive leadership on follower performance is decreased—a neutralizing effect.[122,123] This neutralizing effect is especially strong when the group is highly cohesive.[124] This neutralizing effect was observed in a county hospital in which an outside management team had been brought in by the board of directors to implement several new administrative systems. The existing middle management group disliked the outsiders and provided little cooperation in meeting the goals they were given. After a long and difficult implementation period, the systems were installed and the outside team left. Local managers replaced the outsiders and cooperation of the middle managers was restored.

High performance norms may increase (enhance) the impact of directive leadership. Clearly, a follower's work group affects how the follower reacts to a leader's directiveness. People respond to pressures by their fellow workers, and these pressures may enhance or overwhelm a leader's influence. It seems evident that task and group characteristics can be important situational factors that affect the impacts of directive leadership.

Two studies reported follower characteristics that decreased the impacts of a leader's directiveness. Leader directiveness had little impact when *followers were highly experienced.*[125] Also, the impact of directive leadership on followers' role ambiguity was reduced when *followers were highly competent* at their task and *desired independence* in their work.[126] These findings are consistent with other research indicating that experienced, capable followers who desire autonomy may resist directive leadership.[127]

Overcoming Factors That Neutralize Directive Leadership

Leaders should become aware of situational factors that neutralize the impacts of their directive behavior so they can either modify the situation or choose alternate behavioral strategies. Rather than creating a high degree of task structure for followers (which could improve performance but lower satisfaction), the leader might be better served by working to create high performance norms among followers. Leaders can influence group performance norms through group-based reward systems, and good-natured competition with other groups. Increasing one's own legitimacy through expertise, and effectively representing the group's interests are also effective strategies. Training programs that focus on creating these conditions will help the leader overcome possible neutralizers such as task structure and low group performance norms. It may also be advisable to hire capable followers who like to work independently without close supervision, even though directive leadership is probably not the most effective leadership behavior to emphasize with these followers. Other leadership behaviors such as providing rewards, to be discussed in Chapter 7, are effective in this situation. Figure 5-4 summarizes the situational characteristics that neutralize the effectiveness of directive leadership. When these characteristics exist, followers often ignore or resist a leader's directiveness, and leaders must use another type of influence to guide and motivate followers.

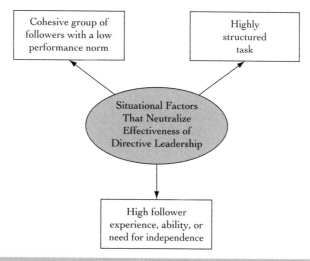

▪▪▪ FIGURE 5-4 Situational factors that neutralize effectiveness of directive leadership

▪▪▪ Situational Factors That Substitute for Directive Leadership

Effective leaders can often identify or create situational and follower characteristics that provide needed guidance and structure for followers. These factors can increase followers' ability to perform without continuous direction from the leader. Leaders can then perform other important functions, such as designing participation and reward systems or obtaining key resources. These activities can require considerable time and effort, and identifying factors that substitute for directive leadership is an important step toward making time available for these activities.

Task, Organizational, and Follower Characteristics

The strongest situational characteristic that substitutes for directive leadership is *autonomous work groups or team operations* in which followers interact frequently with one another and obtain guidance and input for their work tasks from coworkers.[128–130] When competent coworkers are available and followers are members of a work team with collective responsibilities for task accomplishment, direction from leaders can become unnecessary. Team structures of this type became increasingly common in large organizations during the late 1990s. Another important situational characteristic that replaces the need for directive leadership is a high degree of organizational formalization, for example, explicit plans, procedures, goals, and responsibilities assigned by the organization to specific followers. When tasks, work strategies, or methods are clearly specified in writing, there may be little need for directive leadership.[131,132] The substitution effects of clearly specified plans, procedures, and work methods are often found in organizational units with repetitive tasks and low levels of stress, such as a maintenance battalion in the peacetime military.

A third situational factor that can substitute for leader directiveness is built-in *feedback* from the follower's task.[133] This type of performance feedback is often

LEADERSHIP SELF-ASSESSMENT
Directive Attitudes and Behaviors

Indicate whether you mostly agree or mostly disagree with the following statements. Relate the statements to any work situation, including sports, community activities, or school activities, in which you have been responsible for the work of others. If a work situation does not come to mind, imagine how you would act or think.

	Mostly Agree	*Mostly Disagree*
1. I keep close tabs on productivity figures, and interpret them to the group.	___	___
2. I send frequent e-mail messages to group members, giving them information and guidance about work procedures.	___	___
3. I clearly specify the quality goals our group needs to achieve.	___	___
4. I maintain clear-cut standards of performance.	___	___
5. When I conduct a meeting, the participants can count on a clear agenda.	___	___
6. Specifying productivity goals at the beginning of each week is essential for good performance.	___	___
7. I schedule the work for our group members to assure tasks are completed on time.	___	___
8. I monitor and follow up on work that does not meet standards.	___	___
9. I spend at least 20 percent of my work week either doing my own planning or helping team members with their planning.	___	___
10. I spend a good deal of time instructing group members in how to solve technical or business problems.	___	___

If you responded "mostly agree" to eight or more of the above statements, you have a strong orientation toward directive leadership. If you responded "mostly disagree" to five or more of the statements, you may have a preference to use other leadership behaviors to influence followers.

SOURCE: Adapted from A. J. Dubrin, *Leadership: Research Findings, Practice, and Skills.* Boston: Houghton Mifflin, 1998, 92–93.

provided by computer displays of individual or group productivity,[134] which give followers frequent, up-to-date information on the effectiveness of their work methods and progress toward assigned goals. This feedback can alleviate the need for monitoring and direction by the leader. Competent followers can take timely action based on feedback received directly from the task. Fourth, a predictable flow of work that is often routine and repetitive has also been shown to substitute for directive leadership.[135,136] Once the *routine and predictable tasks* are mastered, workers have little need for direction by a leader. This occurs in food preparation work for fast food restaurant chains. Finally, one recent research study found a *large number of years* working for a given leader resulted in high performance by the follower and completely negated (neutralized) the influence of the leader's directive behaviors.[137] Years with a supervisor may be a useful way of measuring a follower's experience, confidence, job ability, or job savvy. Followers with these characteristics can provide their own job guidance with little or no direction needed from their leader.[138]

Creating Factors That Substitute for Directive Leadership

Creating situational factors that substitute for directive leadership may be best achieved by establishing autonomous work teams of followers. If the teams are provided with direct task feedback and authority to make and implement work-related decisions, this strategy can improve followers' psychological reactions and performance and give leaders more time. Of course, followers must be experienced, competent, and committed to performing well in order for autonomous work teams to have a desirable effect.

This strategy of granting independence to teams can be effectively complemented by designing production systems that provide a predictable flow of work and developing specific procedures to be used in performing tasks. Retaining highly experienced and capable followers who have worked with the leader for many years can provide another source of guidance and structure for group members who are less experienced, and can alleviate the need for the leader's directiveness. Figure 5-5 summarizes the situational characteristics that can substitute for directive leadership. These factors provide guidance and motivation for followers and make directive leadership at least partially unnecessary.

In the Leadership in Action box: A Need for Directive Leadership, Gerry Gladstone failed to recognize that the situational and follower characteristics he faced in Allied Machinery were very different from in his previous position. The new situational factors required more directive leadership behavior, which Gerry failed to provide. This led to his unsuccessful performance as president of Allied.

▪ ▪ ▪ **FIGURE 5-5** Situational factors that substitute for directive leadership

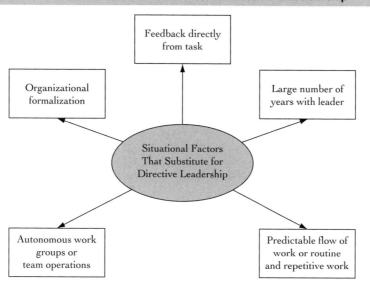

LEADERSHIP IN ACTION
A Need for Directive Leadership

Gerry Gladstone has had a lesson in leadership. He worked his way up to general manager of the machinery division of a large conglomerate. His division was one of the most profitable in the company when he accepted the presidency of Allied Machinery, a smaller competitor that was in need of new leadership to reverse its declining performance. A year later, Allied's performance is still declining, even though the industry is rapidly expanding. Gerry is beginning to realize he was spoiled in his earlier position. In his job as general manager in the conglomerate, Gerry learned to rely on high-quality subordinates and organizational support systems. Well-developed procedures for processing orders and inventory control, as well as sophisticated computer information systems, allowed him to use extensive participative leadership and delegation with followers. His democratic style included little directiveness, and he came to believe his style was the only way to lead.

The organization at Allied was quite different. The managers reporting to him had considerably lower capabilities and initiative than his former subordinates. They were accustomed to clear direction and close monitoring from their president. Allied did not have the well-developed procedures or the information system Gerry was accustomed to using. Without clear direction and follow-up from Gerry, his managers often made errors or failed to meet deadlines. Without adequate standardized procedures or reliable control systems, Gerry did not learn of the failures until too late. Allied's performance went from bad to worse in several key areas, and the board asked Gerry to resign as president a year after he took the job.

SOURCE: Adapted from J. P. Muczyk and B. C. Reimann. The case for directive leadership. *Academy of Management Executive,* 1(3), 301–311.

∎∎∎ Assessing the Dynamics of Directive Leadership

Leaders carry out the three key leadership tasks of diagnosing situations, behaving appropriately, and modifying situations when providing effective directive leadership. When leaders diagnose situations and find one or more characteristics that enhance the effectiveness of directive leadership (see Figure 5-3), they should be directive with followers. Followers in these situations respond positively to a directive leader. If the leader's situational diagnosis identifies factors that neutralize the effects of directiveness (see Figure 5-4), then other leadership behaviors will most likely be preferable.

A leader should also attempt to determine if situational characteristics can be modified to eliminate factors that neutralize directive leadership or create factors that substitute for directive leadership (see Figure 5-5). Leaders can improve the work situation and substitute for directive guidance from the leader by creating autonomous work teams; designing tasks that provide followers with direct performance feedback or are routine and predictable; designing and communicating goals, plans, and procedures for the work; or developing a cohesive group of followers with many years of experience.

When leaders act to modify situations in this manner, they force followers to take increased responsibility for managing their own work. They also empower followers by providing nonleader sources of guidance on the job, such as capable coworkers, standardized plans, goals, and procedures, and relevant work experience. Followers can turn to these sources to control and guide their own work efforts without requiring regular direction from the leader. This allows the leader to focus on other responsibilities.

When a leader provides direction resulting in favorable psychological reactions and behaviors from followers, this encourages the leader to continue the strategy. If the results are disappointing, the leader can shift his or her attention to the follower's work situation. When the leader identifies follower or situational characteristics he or she can modify to increase his or her influence on followers or to substitute for his or her directiveness with other sources of guidance, then the leader can benefit followers by working to change the situation. Followers' reactions and behaviors, as well as situational characteristics, thus affect the directive strategy of the leader. Directive leadership behaviors are often needed with some follower tasks, but they may not be necessary for all tasks. As followers gain experience and skill and identify coworkers who are knowledgeable and helpful, the leader can often decrease directive behaviors. This allows followers to develop into capable, self-managing performers who take pride in their work and are willing to help others on the job.

SUMMARY ▪▪▪▪▪▪▪

Directive leadership is a pattern of behaviors that involves providing guidance and structure for followers to help them carry out their tasks and effectively contribute to successful group performance. It involves defining roles of group members, clarifying expectations, planning and scheduling, explaining work methods, monitoring and following up on assignments, and motivating or coaching. Leaders can be directive without overemphasizing their formal authority and still allow followers to have input to decision making. Effective directive leadership improves followers' information, understanding, and ability to deal with work tasks.

Self-confidence and assertiveness are the two personal traits of directive leaders that seem to be most helpful. Effective directive leaders also develop good communication skills, competence, and experience, and they work to develop their own legitimate power, expert power, and resource/connection power (especially access to key information needed by followers). When carried out in a timely and effective manner, directive leadership increases followers' role clarity, satisfaction, and performance. It also probably increases group cohesion and reduces stress for followers.

Research shows that effective leaders adapt their directive behavior to the organizational situations they face. When important situational factors are present that enhance the impacts of directive leadership behavior, this behavior will be highly effective in influencing followers' psychological reactions and behavioral outcomes. When situational and follower characteristics are present that neutralize the impact of directive leadership behavior on followers, the leader had best try to modify the situation or use another behavioral strategy to influence followers. When situational factors exist that substitute for directiveness by a leader, this leadership behavior will be partially or completely unnecessary because the situation provides needed guidance and structure for followers on their work tasks. In these situations, the leader can decrease the

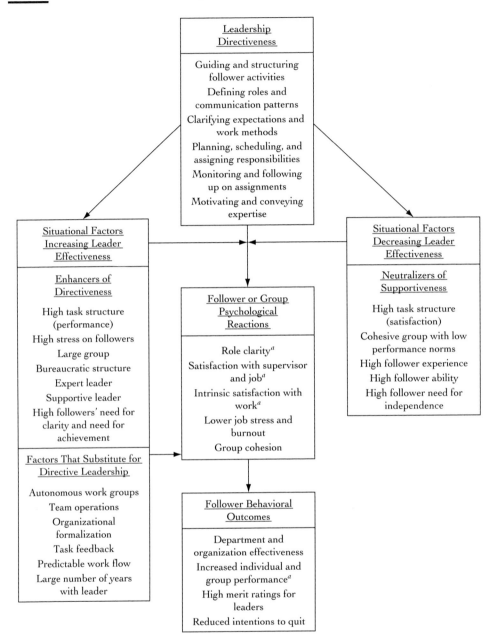

[a]These psychological reactions and outcomes showed the most improvement from directive leadership.

▪▪▪ FIGURE 5-6 Process model of the directive leadership process

amount of active guidance provided for followers and concentrate on other needed leadership behaviors that are often underattended.

Figure 5-6 describes a process model of directive leadership that summarizes many of the major findings regarding directive leadership behavior described in this chapter.

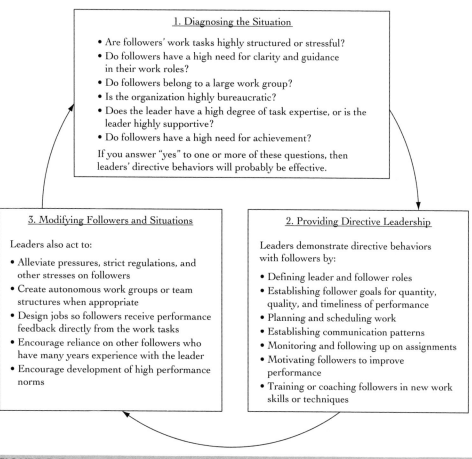

1. Diagnosing the Situation

- Are followers' work tasks highly structured or stressful?
- Do followers have a high need for clarity and guidance in their work roles?
- Do followers belong to a large work group?
- Is the organization highly bureaucratic?
- Does the leader have a high degree of task expertise, or is the leader highly supportive?
- Do followers have a high need for achievement?

If you answer "yes" to one or more of these questions, then leaders' directive behaviors will probably be effective.

3. Modifying Followers and Situations

Leaders also act to:

- Alleviate pressures, strict regulations, and other stresses on followers
- Create autonomous work groups or team structures when appropriate
- Design jobs so followers receive performance feedback directly from the work tasks
- Encourage reliance on other followers who have many years experience with the leader
- Encourage development of high performance norms

2. Providing Directive Leadership

Leaders demonstrate directive behaviors with followers by:

- Defining leader and follower roles
- Establishing follower goals for quantity, quality, and timeliness of performance
- Planning and scheduling work
- Establishing communication patterns
- Monitoring and following up on assignments
- Motivating followers to improve performance
- Training or coaching followers in new work skills or techniques

▪▪▪▪ **FIGURE 5-7 Applying the model of directive leadership**

Directive behaviors are shown at the top of Figure 5-6 influencing follower and group psychological reactions, which in turn affect followers' behavioral outcomes. Situational factors (including follower characteristics) that enhance, neutralize, or substitute for leadership directiveness are shown on each side of Figure 5-6, with arrows intersecting the relationship between directiveness and follower or group psychological reactions. These arrows indicate that the situational factors can increase or decrease the leader's effects on followers and groups. Arrows from the leadership directiveness box to the situational factor boxes show that leaders can sometimes modify situations to create more favorable leader–follower interactions. The arrow from the situational factor box on the left shows certain factors can affect follower or group reactions to substitute for the effects of directive leadership. To prevent Figure 5-6 from becoming too complicated, other possible dynamic effects among the boxes are not shown.

Figure 5-7 is designed to show a leader how to use the model of directive leadership presented in Figure 5-6. It describes the three key tasks for effective leadership (introduced in Chapter 1) as they apply to leadership directiveness. Leaders first diagnose the situation by answering a series of questions regarding followers and their task situation

("1. Diagnosing the Situation"). These questions identify the existence of situational factors that enhance the impacts of directive leadership. If the answer is "yes" to one or more of these questions, then directiveness is probably needed and the leader should provide this type of leadership ("2. Providing Directive Leadership"). At the same time, the leader should examine the follower and situational characteristics to see if important factors exist that can neutralize the effects of directiveness. The existence of one or more strong enhancers will likely overwhelm most neutralizers, but the leader would do well to eliminate neutralizers whenever possible. The creation of situational factors that substitute for directiveness should also be considered to help provide for followers' needs without active direction from the leader ("3. Modifying Followers and Situations").

KEY TERMS AND CONCEPTS IN THIS CHAPTER ▪▪▪▪▪▪▪

- Assertiveness
- Autonomous work groups
- Bureaucratic climate
- Cohesive groups
- Communication skills
- Directive leadership
- Expert power
- Group performance norms
- Initiating structure
- Intrinsic satisfaction
- Job burnout
- Legitimate power
- Mechanistic organizational structure
- Merit ratings
- Need for achievement
- Need for independence
- Organizational formalization
- Performance feedback
- Production oriented
- Resource/connection power
- Role clarity
- Satisfaction with supervisor and job
- Self-confidence
- Stress
- Supportiveness
- Task interdependence
- Task oriented
- Task structure

REVIEW AND DISCUSSION QUESTIONS ▪▪▪▪▪▪▪

1. Describe specific directive leadership behaviors that have influenced your behavior. For these leadership behaviors, identify why they had an impact on your behavior. If you have little or no work experience, think of one of your past teachers for this question.
2. Describe how a leader's values or beliefs could constrain the leader's effective use of directive leadership.
3. Should leaders be more directive of the best performers, the average performers, or the poor performers? What are the reasons for your position?
4. Why might employees who have directive managers show low levels of job satisfaction? Could the reasons be different for different individuals?
5. Describe how directive leadership might influence followers' feelings of empowerment.
6. What are the common situational characteristics that cause directive leadership to be highly effective?
7. Describe a situation you have experienced in which directive leadership was not effective. Explain why directiveness did not have a favorable impact on followers.
8. As a leader, how might you create situational factors to build your influence as a directive leader?
9. Do you think directive leadership would be an effective strategy for a supervisor of firefighters? Why or why not?
10. Do you think directive leadership would be an effective strategy for a supervisor of highly trained, experienced, and capable assemblers of desktop computers? Why or why not?

EXERCISE: ASSESSMENT OF DIRECTIVE LEADERSHIP BEHAVIORS ▪▪▪▪▪▪

Directions: Rate the following directive leadership behaviors by circling the number on the scale that best indicates your evaluation of their importance in supervising employees in a fast food restaurant.

	Low Importance				*High Importance*
1. Communicates authority as a leader	1	2	3	4	5
2. Clearly spells out performance expectations	1	2	3	4	5
3. Plans and schedules work for employees	1	2	3	4	5
4. Assigns responsibilities and tasks to individuals	1	2	3	4	5
5. Conveys to employees the methods to solve problems	1	2	3	4	5
6. Explains rules and procedures to employees	1	2	3	4	5
7. Monitors work methods to assure good results	1	2	3	4	5
8. Defines work roles for individuals	1	2	3	4	5
9. Identifies problems and acts decisively to solve them	1	2	3	4	5
10. Sets goals and priorities for employees	1	2	3	4	5

Compare your evaluations with a colleague's evaluations and discuss the results.

SOURCE: The items for this self assessment are derived from research by J. P. Howell and P. W. Dorfman. Leadership and substitutes for leadership among professional and nonprofessional workers. *Journal of Applied Behavioral Science,* 22(1), 1986, 29–46.

▪▪▪▪▪▪ **C A S E   I N C I D E N T S** ▪▪▪▪▪▪

Frances Hesselbein

Until she retired in 1990 at the age of 73, Frances Hesselbein was head of the Girl Scouts of America, one of the largest nonprofit organizations in the world. As national executive director, she oversaw a volunteer workforce of 750,000 people in 333 autonomous subsidiaries across the country, and managed an annual budget of $343 million. Praised by management guru Peter Drucker and studied by Fortune 500 managers, Hesselbein turned around a declining institution that had lost touch with social changes that began in 1970—including a reduction in volunteers as more women entered the work force, changing interests of teenage girls, and societal recognition of diversity.

Hesselbein obtained management experience as a partner in Hesselbein Studios with her late husband; he filmed TV commercials and promotions, and she wrote the scripts. She first became involved with the Girl Scouts as a troop leader in the 1950s. She moved up through the organization as a volunteer, advancing to a full-time paid director of an area council before becoming national executive director in 1976. To turn around eight consecutive years of eroding membership, Hesselbein first focused on redefining the Girl Scout's mission to be helping girls reach their potential. She then implemented a common planning system for the more than 300 autonomous regional councils. She initiated management training for both paid staff and volunteers. She encouraged the development of proficiency badges to support the increasing interest in areas such as business, the environment, and science. She insisted that uniforms be updated, and engineered a push to make the Girl Scouts more inclusive with expanded minority representation in both members and adult volunteers.

Hesselbein was sometimes subtle, but effective, in her guidance of the Girl Scouts organization. In handling controversial contemporary issues such as teen pregnancy and drug use, she avoided a top-down confrontation with conservative colleagues by developing a series of monographs on these subjects. These were distributed to autonomous regional councils to provide them with guidance and information in addressing these issues. She believed that follower development was a primary leadership role. A good example of this concern was described by a colleague. Before giving a telephone interview to a newspaper reporter, Hesselbein invited two young women from the media department into her office. She asked them to observe how she dealt with the key issues addressed by the interviewer, demonstrating her recognition that watching and listening are important aspects of the apprentice role. Frances Hesselbein is widely recognized as an effective leader and inspiring role model. ■

DISCUSSION QUESTIONS

1. In what ways did Frances Hesselbein provide directive leadership for the Girl Scouts of America?
2. What other leadership behaviors did she use in her position?

A Type of Direction

Scott Davis is the manager of a plant that manufactures camping equipment. The employees are highly trained and experienced in their jobs, and their performance has been excellent. Mr. Davis recently promoted Will Taylor to be supervisor of the department that manufactures sleeping bags. Will has worked in the plant for the past twelve years and has the best production record in the department.

After a month of Will's supervision, his employees in the sleeping bag department requested a meeting with Mr. Davis. They stated that Will was making it impossible for them to achieve their production goals. They characterized Will as a dictator and perfectionist.

Comments by the employees included: "Will is rejecting finished sleeping bags that meet quality specifications because they do not meet his criteria for perfection." "The only way to do the job is his way." "The job of supervisor has made him a dictator." "He demands that every work station be cleaned up twenty times a day." "He stands over us like we didn't know how to do our jobs." "He tells you that the job must be done exactly the way he would have done it." "If he keeps up his loud orders, we will need to get earplugs." ■

DISCUSSION QUESTIONS

1. What are possible problems in Will Taylor's directive style?
2. Would Will be more effective if he modified his methods of directiveness? If so, how?

3. What should Mr. Davis do to help Will improve his supervision?

ENDNOTES ▓ ▓ ▓ ▓ ▓ ▓ ▓

1. Klauss, R., and Bass, B. M. (1982). *Interpersonal Communication in Organizations.* New York: Academic Press.
2. Penley, L. E., and Hawkins, B. (1985). Studying interpersonal communication in organizations: A leadership application. *Academy of Management Journal,* 28(2), 309–326.
3. Yukl, G. (1998). *Leadership in Organizations,* 4th ed. Upper Saddle River, NJ: Prentice Hall.
4. Graen, G., Dansereau, F., Jr., and Minami, T. (1972). Dysfunctional leadership styles. *Organizational Behavior and Human Performance,* 7, 216–236.
5. Muczyk, J. P., and Reimann, B. C. (1987). The case for directive leadership. *Academy of Management Executive,* 1(3), 301–311.
6. Hellriegel, D., Slocum, J. W., Jr., and Woodman, R. W. (1998). *Organizational Behavior,* 8th ed. Cincinnati, OH: Southwestern.
7. Peterson, R. S. (1997). A directive leadership style in group decision making can be both virtue and vice: Evidence from elite and experimental groups. *Journal of Personality and Social Psychology,* 72(5), 1107–1121.
8. Muczyk and Reimann. The case for directive leadership.
9. Fiedler, F. (September 1987). When to lead, when to stand back. *Psychology Today,* 26–27.
10. Fiedler, F. E., and Garcia, J. E. (1987). *New Approaches to Effective Leadership: Cognitive Resources and Organizational Performance.* New York: Wiley.
11. Fleishman, E. A., and Harris, E. F. (1962). Patterns of leadership behavior related to employee grievances and turnover. *Personnel Psychology,* 15, 43–56.
12. Korman, A. K. (1966). "Consideration," "initiating structure" and organizational criteria—A review. *Personnel Psychology,* 18, 349–360.
13. Bass, B. M. (1990). *Bass and Stogdill's Handbook of Leadership,* 3rd ed. New York: Free Press.
14. Penley, L. E., and Hawkins, B. (1985). Studying interpersonal communication in organizations: A leadership application. *Academy of Management Journal,* 28(2), 309–326.
15. Taylor, Frederick W. (1911). *Principles of Scientific Management.* New York: Harper & Brothers.
16. Ibid.
17. Katz, D., Maccoby, N., and Morse, N. C. (1950). Productivity, supervision and morale in an office situation. Ann Arbor, MI: University of Michigan, Institute for Social Research.
18. Blake, R. R., and Mouton, J. S. (1964). *The Managerial Grid.* Houston, TX: Gulf.
19. Bowers, D. G., and Seashore, S. E. (1966). Predicting organizational effectiveness with a four-factor theory of leadership. *Administrative Science Quarterly,* 11, 238–263.
20. Fulk, J., and Wendler, E. R. (1982). Dimensionality of leader-subordinate interactions: A path-goal investigation. *Organizational Behavior and Human Performance,* 30, 241–264.
21. Indvik, J. (1986). Path-Goal theory of leadership: A meta-analysis. In *Proceedings of the Academy of Management,* 189–192.
22. Graen, G., Dansereau, F., Jr., and Minami, T. (1972). Dysfunctional leadership styles.

Organizational Behavior and Human Performance, 7, 216–236.

23. Bass, B. M. (1965). *Organizational Psychology.* Boston: Allyn & Bacon.

24. Stewart, R. (1967). *Managers and their Jobs: A Study of Similarities and Differences in the Way Managers Spent their Time.* London: Macmillan.

25. Stewart, R. (1976). *Contrasts in Management.* Maidenhead, England: McGraw Hill.

26. Stewart, R. (1982). *Choices for the Manager: A Guide to Understanding Managerial Work.* Englewood Cliffs, NJ: Prentice Hall.

27. Katzell, R. A., Miller, C. E., Rotler, N. G., and Venet, T. G. (1970). Effects of leadership and other inputs on group processes and outputs. *Journal of Social Psychology,* 80, 157–169.

28. Bass. *Bass and Stogdill's Handbook of Leadership.*

29. Greene, C. N. (1975). The reciprocal nature of influence between leader and subordinate. *Journal of Applied Psychology,* 60, 187–193.

30. Greene, C. N. (1979). Questions of causation in the Path-Goal theory of leadership. *Academy of Management Journal,* 22, 22–41.

31. Lowin, A., and Craig, J. R. (1968). Participative decision making: A model, literature, critique, and prescription for research. *Organizational Behavior and Human Performance,* 3, 68–106.

32. Fleishman, E. A., Harris, E. F., and Burtt, H. E. (1955). *Leadership and Supervision in Industry.* Columbus, OH: Ohio State University, Bureau of Educational Research.

33. Hall, D. T., and Mansfield, R. (1971). Organizational and individual response to external stress. *Administrative Science Quarterly,* 16, 533–547.

34. Bass, B. M., Brader, M. S., and Breed, W. (1967). Profitability and good relations: Which is cause and which is effect? (Brief No. 4). Pittsburgh, PA: University of Pittsburgh, Management Research Center.

35. Roberts, N. C. (1986). Organizational power styles: Collective and competitive power under various organizational conditions.

Journal of Applied Behavioral Science, 22, 443–458.

36. Fulk and Wendler. Dimensionality of leader-subordinate interactions: A path-goal investigation.

37. Indvik. Path-Goal theory of leadership: A meta-analysis.

38. Podsakoff, P. M., Toder, W. D., and Schuler, R. S. (1983). Leader expertise as a moderator of the effects of instrumental and supportive leader behaviors. *Journal of Management,* 9, 173–185.

39. Smith, E. E. (1957). The effects of clear and unclear role expectations on group productivity and defensiveness. *Journal of Abnormal and Social Psychology,* 55, 213–217.

40. Fulk, J., and Wendler, E. R. (1982). Dimensionality of leader-subordinate interactions: A path-goal investigation. *Organizational Behavior and Human Performance,* 30, 241–264.

41. Indvik. Path-Goal theory of leadership: A meta-analysis.

42. Kellogg, C. E., and White, D. D. (1987). Leader behaviors and volunteer satisfaction with work: The effect of volunteer maturation level. Paper presented at the Academy of Management meeting, New Orleans, LA.

43. Schriesheim, C. A., and Murphy, C. J. (1976). Relationship between leader behavior and subordinate satisfaction and performance: A test of some situational moderators. *Journal of Applied Psychology,* 61, 634–641.

44. House, R. J., Filley, A. C., and Kerr, S. (1971). Relation of leader consideration and initiating structure to R and D subordinates' satisfaction. *Administrative Science Quarterly,* 16, 19–30.

45. Graham, F. C. (1982). Job stress in Mississippi Cooperative Extension Service county personnel as related to age, gender, district, tenure, position and perceived leadership behavior of immediate supervisors. *Dissertation Abstracts International,* 43(7A), 2180.

46. Seltzer, J., and Numeroff, R. E. (1988). Supervisory leadership and subordinate burnout. *Academy of Management Journal,* 31, 439–446.

47. Berkowitz, L. (1953). An exploratory study of the roles of aircraft commanders. *USAF*

Human Resources Research Center and Research Bulletin, 53-65, 1–27.

48. Katzell, R. A., Miller, C. E., Rotler, N. G., and Venet, T. G. (1970). Effects of leadership and other inputs on group processes and outputs. *Journal of Social Psychology,* 80, 157–169.

49. Christner, C. A., and Hemphill, J. K. (1955). Leader behavior of B-29 commanders and changes in crew members' attitudes toward the crew. *Sociometry,* 18, 82–87.

50. Greene, C. N., and Schriesheim, C. A. (1980). Leader–group interactions: A longitudinal field investigation. *Journal of Applied Psychology,* 65, 50–39.

51. Nealy, S. M., and Blood, M. R. (1968). Leadership performance of nursing supervisors at two organizational levels. *Journal of Applied Psychology,* 52, 414–422.

52. Sheridan, J. E., and Vredenburgh, D. J. (1979). Structural model of leadership influence in a hospital organization. *Academy of Management Journal,* 22, 6–21.

53. Greene, C. N., and Schriesheim, C. A. (1980). Leader–group interactions: A longitudinal field investigation. *Journal of Applied Psychology,* 65, 50–39.

54. Rubenowitz, S. (1962). Job oriented and person oriented leadership. *Personnel Psychology,* 15, 387–396.

55. Dunteman, G. H., and Bass, B. M. (1963). Supervisory and engineering success associated with self, interaction, and task orientation scores. *Personnel Psychology,* 16, 13–22.

56. Fleishman, E. A., and Harris, E. F. (1962). Patterns of leadership behavior related to employee grievances and turnover. *Personnel Psychology,* 15, 43–56.

57. Fleishman, E. A., and Simmons, J. (1970). Relationship between leadership patterns and effectiveness ratings among Israeli foremen. *Personnel Psychology,* 23, 169–172.

58. Halpin, A. W. (1956). *The Leader Behavior of School Superintendents.* Columbus, OH: Ohio State University, College of Education.

59. Seeman, M. (1957). A comparison of general and specific leader behavior descriptions. In R. M. Stogdill and E. A. Coons (Eds.), *Leader Behavior: Its Description and Measurement.* Columbus,

OH: Ohio State University, Bureau of Business Research.

60. Indvik. Path-Goal theory of leadership: A meta-analysis.

61. Mann, F. C., Indik, B. P., and Vroom, V. H. (1963). *The Productivity of Work Groups.* Ann Arbor, MI: University of Michigan, Survey Research Center.

62. Gekoski, N. (1952). Predicting group productivity. *Personnel Psychology,* 5, 281–291.

63. Likert, R. (1955). *Developing Patterns of Management, General Management Series,* No. 178. New York: American Management Association.

64. Dagirmanjian, S. (1981). The work experience of service staff in mental health service organizations and its relationship to leadership style and organizational structure. *Dissertation Abstracts International,* 43(58), 1609.

65. Blaihed, S. A. (1982). The relationship between leadership behavior of the chief executive officer in the hospital and overall hospital performance. *Dissertation Abstracts International,* 43(7A), 2169.

66. Hemphill, J. K. (1955). Leadership behavior associated with the administrative regulations of college departments. *Journal of Educational Psychology,* 46, 385–401.

67. Hood, P. D. (1963). Leadership climate for trainee leaders: The army AIT platoon. Washington, DC: George Washington University, Human Resources Research Office.

68. Keeler, B. T., and Andrews, J. H. M. (1963). Leader behavior of principals, staff morale, and productivity. *Alberta Journal of Educational Research,* 9, 179–191.

69. Fleishman and Harris. (1962). Patterns of leadership behavior related to employee grievances and turnover.

70. Hunt, J. G., Osborne, R. N., and Martin, H. J. (1979). A multiple influence model of leadership. Unpublished manuscript. Carbondale, IL: Southern Illinois University Press.

71. Dorfman, P. W., Howell, J. P., Hibino, S., Lee, J. K., Tate, U., and Bautista, A. (1997). Leadership in western and Asian countries: Commonalities and differences in effective

leadership practices. *Leadership Quarterly,* 8(3), 233–274.

72. Ibid.

73. Matsai, T., Ohtsuke, Y., Kikuchi, A. (1978). Consideration and structure behavior as reflections of supervisory interpersonal values. *Journal of Applied Psychology,* 63, 259–262.

74. Misumi, J. (1985). *The Behavioral Science of Leadership: An Interdisciplinary Japanese Research Program.* Ann Arbor, MI: University of Michigan Press.

75. Misumi, J., and Peterson, M. F. (1985). The Performance–Maintenance (PM) theory of leadership: Review of a Japanese research program. *Administrative Science Quarterly,* 30, 198–223.

76. Fleishman, E. A., and Simmons, J. (1970). Relationship between leadership patterns and effectiveness ratings among Israeli foremen. *Personnel Psychology,* 23, 169–172.

77. Dorfman, Howell, Hibino, Lee, Tate, and Bautista. Leadership in western and Asian countries: Commonalities and differences in effective leadership practices.

78. Al Gattan, A. R. A. (1985). Test of the Path-Goal theory of leadership in the multinational domain. Paper presented at the Academy of Management meeting, San Diego, CA.

79. Indvik. Path-Goal theory of leadership: A meta-analysis.

80. Fisher, B. M., and Edwards, J. E. (1988). Consideration and initiating structure and their relationships with leader effectiveness: A meta-analysis. In *Best Papers Proceedings, Academy of Management,* 201–205.

81. Trevelyan, R. (1998). The boundary of leadership: Getting it right and having it all. *Business Strategy Review,* 9(1), 37–44.

82. Griffin, R. W. (1980). Relationships among individual, task design, and leader behavior variables. *Academy of Management Journal,* 23, 665–683.

83. Wofford, C., Jr. (1971). Managerial behavior, situational factors, productivity and morale. *Administrative Science Quarterly,* 16, 10–12.

84. Downey, A. K., Sheridan, J. E., and Slocum, J. W., Jr. (1976). The Path-Goal theory of leadership: A longitudinal analysis.

Organizational Behavior and Human Performance, 16, 156–176.

85. Indvik, J. (1986). Path-Goal theory of leadership: A meta-analysis.

86. Wolcott, C. (1984). The relationship between the leadership behavior of library supervisors and the performance of their professional subordinates. *Dissertation Abstracts International,* 45(5A), 1507.

87. Kahai, S. S., Sosik, J. J., and Avolio, B. J. (1997). Effects of leadership style and problem structure on work group process and outcomes in an electronic meeting system environment. *Personnel Psychology,* 50(1), 121–146.

88. Fry, L. W., Kerr, S., and Lee, C. (1986). Effects of different leader behaviors under different levels of task interdependence. *Human Relations,* 39, 1067–1082.

89. Childers, T. L., Dubinsky, A. J., and Skinner, S. J. (1990). Leadership substitutes as moderators of sales supervisory behavior. *Journal of Business Research,* 21, 363–382.

90. Halpin, A. W. (1954). The leadership behavior and combat performance of airplane commanders. *Journal of Abnormal and Social Psychology,* 49, 19–22.

91. Numeroff, R. E., and Seltzer, J. (1986). The relationship between leadership factors, burnout, and stress symptoms among middle managers. Paper presented at the Academy of Management meeting, Chicago.

92. Misumi, J., and Sako, H. (1982). An experimental study of the effect of leadership behavior on followers' behavior of following after the leader in a simulated emergency situation. *Japanese Journal of Experimental Psychology,* 21(1), 49–59. Cited in J. Misumi, *The Behavioral Science of Leadership: An Interdisciplinary Japanese Research Program.* Ann Arbor, MI: University of Michigan Press.

93. Fiedler, F. E., and Garcia, J. E. (1987). *New Approaches to Effective Leadership: Cognitive Resources and Organizational Performance.* New York: Wiley.

94. Greene, C. N., and Schriesheim, C. A. (1980). Leader–group interactions: A longitudinal field investigation. *Journal of Applied Psychology,* 65(1), 50–59.

95. Schriesheim, C. A., and Murphy, C. J. (1976). Relationship between leader behavior and subordinate satisfaction and performance: A test of some situational moderators. *Journal of Applied Psychology,* 61, 634–641.

96. Howell, J., and Frost, P. (1988). A laboratory study of charismatic leadership. *Organizational Behavior and Human Decision Processes,* 43, 243–269.

97. Nealy, S. M., and Blood, M. R. (1968). Leadership performance of nursing supervisors at two organizational levels. *Journal of Applied Psychology,* 52, 414–422.

98. Cooper, R., and Payne, R. (1967). *Personality Orientations and Performance in Football Teams: Leaders' and Subordinates' Orientations Related to Team Success.* Birmingham, England: University of Aston, Organizational Group Psychology.

99. Mayes, B. T. (1979). Leader needs as moderators of the subordinate job performance—Leader behavior relationship. Paper presented at the Academy of Management meeting, Atlanta, GA.

100. Podsakoff, P. M., Todor, W. D., and Schuler, R. S. (1983). Leadership expertise as a moderator of the effects of instrumental and supportive leader behaviors. *Journal of Management,* 9, 173–185.

101. Calloway, D. W. (1985). The promise and paradoxes of leadership. *Directors and Boards,* 9(2), 12–16.

102. Cleveland, H. (1980). Learning the art of leadership: The worldwide crisis in governance demands new approaches. Unpublished manuscript. Cited in B. M. Bass (1990). *Bass & Stogdill's Handbook of Leadership,* 3rd ed. New York: Free Press.

103. Podsakoff, Toder, and Schuler. Leader expertise as a moderator of the effects of instrumental and supportive leader behaviors.

104. Smith, E. E. (1957). The effects of clear and unclear role expectations on group productivity and defensiveness. *Journal of Abnormal and Social Psychology,* 55, 213–217.

105. Kellogg, C. E., and White, D. D. (1987). Leader behaviors and volunteer satisfaction with work: The effect of volunteer maturation level. Paper presented at the Academy of Management meeting, New Orleans, LA.

106. House, R. (1987). The "All things in Moderation" leader. *Academy of Management Review,* 12, 164–169.

107. Mathieu, J. E. (1990). A test of subordinates' achievement and affiliation needs as moderators of leader path-goal relationships. *Basic and Applied Social Psychology,* 11(12), 179–189.

108. Keller, R. T. (1989). A test of the Path-Goal theory of leadership with need for clarity as a moderator in research and development organizations. *Journal of Applied Psychology,* 74, 208–212.

109. Kroll, M. J., and Pringle, C. D. (1985). Individual differences and Path-Goal theory: The role of leader directiveness. *Southwest Journal of Business and Economics,* 2(3), 11–20.

110. Dorfman, P. W., and Howell, J. P. (1988). Dimensions of national culture and effective leadership patterns: Hofstede revisited. *Advances in International Comparative Management,* 3, 127–150.

111. Dorfman, P. W., Howell, J. P., Hibino, S., Lee, J. K., Tate, U., and Bautista, A. (1997). Leadership in western and Asian countries: Commonalties and differences in effective leadership practices. *Leadership Quarterly,* 8(3), 233–274.

112. Bartol, K. (1978). The sex structuring of organizations: A search for possible causes. *Academy of Management Review,* 3, 805–815.

113. Larwood, L., Wood, M. M., and Inderlied, S. D. (1978). Training women for management: New problems, new solutions. *Academy of Management Review,* 3, 584–593.

114. Marsh, M. K., and Atherton, R. M., Jr. (1981). Leadership, organizational type, and subordinate satisfaction in the U. S. Army: The hi-hi paradigm sustained. *Journal of Social Relations,* 9, 121–143.

115. Graham, F. C. (1982). Job stress in Mississippi Cooperative Extension Service county personnel as related to age, gender, district, tenure, position and perceived leadership behavior of immediate supervisors.

116. Jurma, W. E. (1978). Leadership structuring style, task ambiguity, and group member satisfaction. *Small Group Behavior,* 9, 124–134.

117. Badin, I. J. (1974). Some moderator influences on relationships between consideration, initiating structure, and organizational criteria. *Journal of Applied Psychology, 59,* 380–382.

118. Johns, G. (1978). Task moderators of the relationship between leadership style and subordinate responses. *Academy of Management Journal, 21,* 319–325.

119. Dessler, G. (1973). An investigation of the Path-Goal theory of leadership. Doctoral diss., Baruch College, City University of New York.

120. Kinicki, A. J., and Schriesheim, C. A. (1978). Teachers as leaders: A moderator variable approach. *Journal of Educational Research, 70,* 928–935.

121. Indvik. Path-Goal theory of leadership: A meta-analysis.

122. Howell, J., and Frost, P. (1988). A laboratory study of charismatic leadership. *Organizational Behavior and Human Decision Processes, 43,* 243–269.

123. Hernandez, S. R., and Kaluzny, A. D. (1982). Selected determinants of performance within a set of health service organizations. In *Proceedings, Academy of Management,* New York, 52–56.

124. Howell, J. P., and Dorfman, P. W. (1981). Substitutes for leadership: Test of a construct. *Academy of Management Review, 24,* 714–728.

125. Vecchio, R. P. (1987). Situational Leadership theory: An examination of a prescriptive theory. *Journal of Applied Psychology, 72,* 444–451.

126. Howell, J. P., and Dorfman, P. W. (1986). Leadership and substitutes for leadership among professional and nonprofessional workers. *The Journal of Applied Behavioral Science, 22*(1), 29–46.

127. Kerr, S., and Jermier, J. (1978). Substitutes for leadership: Their meaning and measurement. *Organizational Behavior and Human Performance, 22,* 374–403.

128. Manz, C. C., and Sims, H. P., Jr. (1987). Leading workers to lead themselves: The external leadership of self-managing work teams. *Administrative Science Quarterly, 32,* 106–129.

129. Wall, T. D., Kemp, N. J., Jackson, P. R., and Clegg, C. W. (1986). Outcomes of autonomous workgroups: A long-term field experiment. *Academy of Management Journal, 29,* 280–304.

130. Cherns, A. (1976). The principles of sociotechnical design. *Human Relations, 29,* 783–792.

131. Howell and Dorfman. Substitutes for leadership: Test of a construct.

132. Kerr and Jermier. Substitutes for leadership: Their meaning and measurement.

133. Schriesheim, C. A., and Denisi, A. S. (1981). Task dimensions as moderators of the effects of instrumental leadership: A two sample replicated test of Path-Goal leadership theory. *Journal of Applied Psychology, 66,* 589–597.

134. Cherns, A. (1976). The principles of sociotechnical design. *Human Relations, 29,* 783–792.

135. Wall, J. (1986). *Bosses.* Lexington, MA: D. C. Health.

136. Comstock, D. S., and Scott, W. R. (1977). Technology and structure of subunits: Distinguishing individual work efforts. *Administrative Science Quarterly, 22,* 177–202.

137. Mossholder, K. W., Niebuhr, R. E., and Norris, D. R. (1930). Effects of dyadic duration on the relationship between leader behavior perceptions and follower outcomes. *Journal of Organizational Behavior, 11,* 379–388.

138. Cox, C., and Makin, P. J. (1994). Overcoming dependency with contingency contracting. *Leadership and Organizational Development Journal, 15*(1), 21–27.

CHAPTER 6

Participative Leadership Behavior

Learning Objectives

After reading this chapter, you should be able to do the following:

1. Describe participative leadership behaviors and provide examples of specific leadership behaviors.
2. Explain why participative leadership can have positive influences on follower behaviors.
3. Describe skills and abilities that are needed to be an effective participative leader.
4. Describe the individual and organizational benefits that can result from effective participative leadership.
5. Identify characteristics of followers that make participative leadership highly effective and characteristics that make it ineffective.
6. Identify organizational and task characteristics that make participative leadership highly effective and characteristics that make it ineffective.
7. Describe how leaders can modify situations to increase the effectiveness of their participative leadership.
8. Explain how leaders can modify followers' work situations to make followers less dependent on the leader's participative leadership.

Examples of Effective Participative Leadership

1. When a leader asked for followers' input on a decision, he treated himself on par with them and did not emphasize any status differences between himself and followers. He did not coerce them to accept a solution he favored nor did he impose his opinions. In this manner, followers sensed a situation of trust, inspiration, and responsibility for making a good decision.
2. A team leader asked a team member for her opinion on a problem the leader was facing. The member described this as an encouraging sign of the leader's trust in her technical knowledge.

131

3. A department manager asked his immediate and highly experienced subordinates for help in designing a new office layout. He reviewed with them the needs of the department and then asked them to come up with a plan they all could agree on that would meet those needs. The new layout was approved with very few modifications and everyone was pleased with the results.

4. A team leader was asked if her team wanted to attend a special seminar that would last four to five hours, and she threw the question out to the team. In light of their work load, the team decided against attending. They indicated they appreciated the leader allowing them to say no to this opportunity.

5. Project managers often lack the technical knowledge needed to make important decisions on high-tech jobs. They supervise highly trained professional employees who are closer to the technical problems and have better information, but the manager may have broader knowledge than the technical professional on matters involving other parts of the system or on external pressures. By sharing their ideas through participative one-on-one or group discussions, the manager and the specialist can often arrive at better decisions than either deciding alone.[1–4]

These are examples of effective participative leadership behaviors by leaders.

▪▪▪ Definition, Background, and Importance of Participative Leadership Behaviors

Leaders make decisions on many issues—assigning people to jobs, obtaining supplies and equipment, modifying strategies or procedures, or nurturing new group members. For each decision, leaders weigh alternatives and select strategies they believe to be optimal. Many employees, volunteers, and other participants in today's organizations believe they have a right to be involved in or influence the decisions that affect them. Their reaction to a decision can be affected by the extent to which the leader consults them and allows them to provide input to the decision process. Employees often have extensive experience, information, training, and knowledge that can improve the quality of decisions. For these reasons, leaders often provide opportunities for followers to give input, especially when the decisions will affect followers in some way. When leaders involve followers in the decision processes, they are practicing participative leadership.

Managers and researchers have used two meanings for participative leadership. Historically, the most common meaning has been to involve followers in some way in decisions that leaders would otherwise make on their own—through consulting with individuals or holding meetings with groups of followers to discuss decision issues.[5] The leader often retains the final authority to make the decision, but followers provide information and ideas that the leader carefully considers in arriving at the final decision. The other meaning of participative leadership goes a bit further. Leaders involve followers in the decision process (such as discussing decision situations or evaluating alternatives), but also share decision-making power with followers by allowing them to directly affect the decision outcomes. Some writers believe that participation exists only when followers share decision-making power equally with the leader.[6,7]

In this book, participative leadership refers to numerous behaviors by leaders that involve and include followers in various aspects of the decision process. These behaviors include group discussion sessions or individualized one-on-one meetings in which leaders share decision-making power with followers. This definition thus includes the aspect of sharing the leader's power. It also includes leader actions such as obtaining information from followers, asking their opinions about decision alternatives, or obtaining their ideas about how particular strategies might be implemented. The latter activities may allow the leader to make the final decision, but followers have been involved in and indirectly influence the decision process by providing inputs and assessments that the leader then incorporates into deliberations and the final decision. Our definition of participative leadership includes elements of both of the earlier meanings used by managers and researchers.

Participative leadership includes describing a decision problem to a group of followers and asking for their input on the implications of various alternative solutions already developed by the leader. It also involves holding informal conversations with individual followers to draw their ideas out, and listening carefully to understand and incorporate their information into a decision solution. Participative leaders hold group meetings with followers to describe the decision situation and ask for followers' suggested solutions. They make sure that all group members who wish to express an opinion about a decision issue are given plenty of opportunity to do so, and assure the group members that all follower ideas and contributions are given serious consideration. When recommendations of followers are not implemented as part of the decision solution, participative leaders explain to followers why their suggestions were not included. When a leader and follower disagree, the participative leader may hold a discussion session to air both sides of the disagreement and help resolve the issue. Participative leaders sometimes even assign a decision problem to followers for their resolution.[8–11]

Many variations on these behaviors exist. The increasing level of education and increased feelings of equality in the workforce of the United States and other western countries have produced a widespread desire for upward mobility and interesting work. These factors have resulted in increased pressures from many workers for more participation opportunities. When followers in these countries describe their concept of an ideal leader, they usually include participative leadership behavior as one of the top three qualities.[12] Many individuals believe that participative leadership is a major part of effective leadership. Figure 6-1 summarizes major types of participative leadership behaviors.

Participation may also include individuals outside the leader's immediate group of followers, such as peers, upper-level leaders, or individuals outside the organization.[13] Even though decisions can sometimes benefit from this type of consultation, especially in highly technical environments, the traditional meaning of participative leadership focuses on inclusion of the leader's followers in decisions. This is the meaning used by most experts on participation, and their work will be summarized in this chapter.

In thinking about participative leadership in relation to the other leadership behaviors, the reader should keep in mind that participation deals with making decisions, whereas directive leadership (described in Chapter 5) often deals with executing a decision once it has been made. Leadership writers have noted that "a leader can be participative . . . by consulting employees during the decision-making phase, yet still be directive by following up closely on progress toward the ends that have been mutually decided on."[14] This approach might be appropriate for new followers who have up-to-date technical knowledge useful in making decisions, but little experience in how to implement that knowledge in a specific organization. Participative and directive leadership can often be used together in a complementary fashion to achieve effective results.

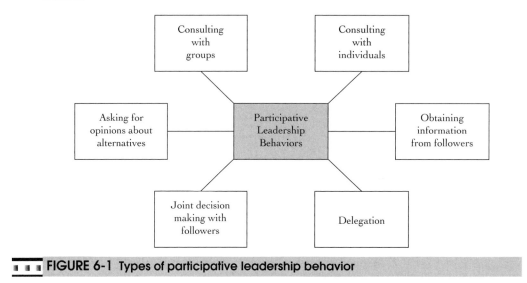

▪ ▪ ▪ **FIGURE 6-1 Types of participative leadership behavior**

In the United States and many other developed countries, individuals are taught and encouraged to participate in school, at home, at work, and in their communities. They therefore develop an expectation to participate, and the chance to participate leads to positive attitudes.[15] As noted, the rising education of the workforce in these same countries reflects a widespread desire for increased independence, achievement, influence, and personal growth. Participative leadership appeals directly to these needs of organizational members by providing opportunities for satisfaction, and this further increases follower morale and satisfaction. Thus rewarded, followers are often motivated to participate actively with their leader to assure continued satisfaction. In many developing countries (such as Mexico and the Peoples Republic of China), values other than participation are often emphasized, such as obedience, submission, and respect for authority. In these countries, participative leadership may not be effective.[16]

From a group or organizational standpoint, participative leadership improves the availability and flow of information for decision making. For example, followers often have more current information regarding work tasks than do leaders, and their involvement produces better decisions, made with more timely information. Participation also allows followers to learn more about implementing new programs or procedures after decisions are made.[17] Some writers have suggested that leaders use participative leadership because they believe it is politically correct and therefore necessary to increase the acceptance of the leader's ideas.[18] Clearly, participative leadership has many possible benefits. Bear in mind, however, that no single leadership behavior pattern is perfect for every situation. Research shows that most followers prefer a leader who adapts his or her leadership behavior pattern to fit the situation.[19] The situational factors that affect participative leadership are discussed later in the chapter.

One form of participative leadership has been common in Europe for several decades. Legislation in Sweden, Norway, the former Yugoslavia, and West Germany established workers' counsels to advise high-level decision makers or require union representation on boards of directors. These programs have been used extensively.

LEADERSHIP IN ACTION
Wilma Mankiller

Wilma Mankiller, former principal chief of the Cherokee Nation, is the only woman to have ever held this prestigious office. She was leader of the second largest tribe in the United States, with over 140,000 followers and a budget that exceeded $75 million.

As a participative leader, she found that developing teams is an ideal way to solve problems. According to Mankiller, consulting and collaborating with followers are the key ingredients of a good leader. These skills have also helped to revitalize the tribe. As an example of the faith that she placed in her followers, Mankiller says "after every major upheaval, we have been able to gather together as a people and rebuild a community and a government."

Because she is a woman, Mankiller met with opposition in the beginning of her term of office. But Mankiller feels that being a woman was eventually the key to her success. Studies in the 1980s and 1990s found that women often choose a participative approach to leadership. Wilma agrees. As a woman, she was "more of a team builder, my unscientific observations are that men make unilateral decisions and charge ahead. . . . There are exceptions to that, but women tend to . . . do things in a more consultative and collaborative way."

SOURCE: "Wilma Mankiller former Principal Chief of the Cherokee Nation," accessed at www.powersource.com/gallery/people/wilma.html

In the United States and Japan, the approach is more informal and flexible than in Europe. In these countries, the participative behaviors by a leader are based on a personal relationship between the leader and followers, not on national legislation. Leaders may have casual conversations with a single follower or a prescheduled meeting with an entire work group. This approach to participation allows the leader to adapt behavior to the needs of the situation. It may also permit followers to focus input on decisions that affect them most.[20] Experts on participative leadership believe that the informal approach provides more of an impact on individual and group productivity than the legislative approach.[21] Although many organizations have implemented quality circles, quality improvement groups, semiautonomous or self-managed work teams, and other programs, it is the informal approach that is described in this chapter.

One expert points out that in formal organizations, some participative leadership may be politically necessary to get a leader's decisions approved and implemented.[22] For example, upper management may want assurance that followers are committed to carrying out a decision. Follower involvement in making the decision may be important in obtaining this assurance. The Leadership in Action box: Wilma Mankiller describes participative behaviors by a Native American leader.

Some writers have described a continuum that shows how a leader can use degrees of participation to include followers in various types of decision situations.[23,24] Figure 6-2 shows these different degrees of participation. First, little or no participation is used under the autocratic decision approach—the leader makes the decision with or without

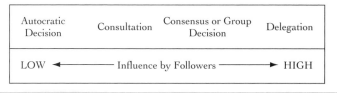

▪▪▪ **FIGURE 6-2 Degrees of participation**

SOURCE: Adapted from Gary Yukl. *Leadership in Organizations.* Upper Saddle River, NJ: Prentice Hall, 1998.

input from followers. Next, some participation takes place with the consultative approach—the leader obtains ideas and evaluations from followers, individually or as a group, and uses them to make the decision. With the consultation approach, the leader often obtains follower reactions to the decision option chosen. Increased levels of participation occur with consensus or group decision making, in which the leader and followers discuss the decision problem and make the decision together. With this approach, followers often have as much influence on the outcome as the leader. Finally, delegation represents the maximum amount of participation, in which the leader assigns a decision problem to one or more followers to decide. The leader may provide overall guidance or maintain veto power over the follower's decision.

Real leaders vary their use of these different forms of participation. Some leaders, for example, use consensus decision making only with one or two trusted followers; others prefer large group meetings in which all points of view are heard. Some leaders use delegation only after carefully specifying guidelines and limits to the decision option chosen, and may require that the final decision be subjected to the leader's approval before implementation.[25] Other leaders give followers complete freedom in arriving at and implementing a solution. Most leaders use different combinations of participation at different times, adapting them to each situation and group of followers.

Some writers have argued that delegation is a different form of decision making than participation and is more oriented to follower development.[26,27] However, research shows that followers see delegation as only one type of participation used along with other approaches to obtain their involvement.[28,29] Consultation and consensus decision making are also excellent learning opportunities for followers. Delegation is an end point in the continuum of participation, in which followers evaluate and make decisions on their own with a minimum of guidance and oversight by their leader, but it is certainly not the only participative procedure conducive to follower development.

Table 6-1 indicates some leadership actions that tend to improve the effectiveness of delegation.

▪▪▪ Ineffective Participative Leadership

As with other leadership behaviors, participative leadership can be used ineffectively. The following incidents describe leaders' use of participative leadership behaviors in an inappropriate manner:

1. A leader called a meeting, supposedly to obtain follower input on a decision problem. During the discussion it became apparent to followers that the leader

TABLE 6-1 Effective delegation

To Delegate Effectively	
Do	*Avoid*
Understand your authority and responsibility	Lack of agreement on authority and responsibility
Clearly communicate performance expectations	Lack of understanding of group's objectives
Make followers responsible for results	Involvement of followers not trained to effectively perform
Delegate challenging responsibilities	Showing a lack of confidence in followers
Show confidence in followers' ability to perform	Requiring "nothing less than perfection"
Reward accomplishment	Making followers feel insecure

had already made the decision, and the meeting's purpose was merely to give followers the perception of participation. When followers realized the leader's real objective, some tuned out the discussion entirely and said nothing, whereas others told the leader they favored the option he had already selected.

2. The department's morale was very low due to low wages and a poor benefits package. The manager decided to implement a participation program in which groups of workers in a given job category would discuss how their work could be done more efficiently. Workers saw the participation program as a gimmick to manipulate them and to divert their attention from real issues.

While participative leadership behavior can be used very effectively at times, these two incidents make it clear that in certain situations, and with certain leader motives, participative behaviors and techniques can be rendered not only ineffective but potentially disastrous. The Leadership in Perspective box describes the history of participative leadership and how it may not be effective in all cultures.

▅▅▅ Skills, Traits, and Sources of Power for Participative Leaders

Effective leaders typically develop specific traits, skills, and sources of power to help them carry out participative leadership with their followers. One very important leader trait with regard to participation is *integrity*. When the leader is honest with followers, they learn to trust the information and other input the leader provides. When the leader is known to be ethical in dealings both inside and outside the followers' group, they trust the leader to behave consistently with the group's values and to be fair to all group members. When the leader keeps his or her word, accurately represents the group's position in important issues, and gives credit to members for valuable contributions, follower loyalty and commitment to the group are generated.[40] When they feel trust, loyalty, and commitment, followers actively participate with the leader and other members in problem solving and decision making for the group's benefit.

LEADERSHIP IN PERSPECTIVE
History of Participative Leadership

In the year 529, St. Benedict described consultation with followers as an important part of leaders' decision making in the administration of monasteries.[30] In 1513, Machiavelli described a similar, though somewhat limited, approach in the administration of governmental affairs. In the 1850s, John Stuart Mill advocated participation in the administration of public affairs.

In U.S. industry in the late 1800s, independent craftsmen were prevalent, and so were strengthening labor unions. Both of these institutions tried to keep control of actual work methods in the hands of employees.[31] In the early 1900s, Frederick Taylor's scientific management sought to give control of work methods to management.[32] Taylor's success assured that management-centered control of workers' activities was prevalent, until research in the 1930s and 1940s addressed the shortcomings of management-centered decision making. During the 1950s and 1960s, writers developed management approaches that increased worker involvement in decision making. These approaches did not return control of work activities to workers; instead they simply included workers in discussions of important issues to improve collective effort and motivation, and to overcome resistance to the tremendous changes that were beginning to affect U.S. industry.[33]

Participative leadership has been written about and researched under several names, including consultative decision making, joint decision making, power sharing, decentralization, democratic management, and delegation. Famous early studies on democratic management included discussions of participative leadership as well as other leadership behaviors.[34,35] A classic study addressed participation as a method for overcoming resistance to change in an industrial organization.[36] Research programs at the University of Michigan clearly identified participative leadership as a key aspect of a leader's effectiveness.[37] The leadership research program at The Ohio State University included participation in early measures of consideration—a type of supportive leadership.[38]

Nearly all the new management programs developed in the past 30 years in the United States have included some attention to participative leadership. Many distinguished writers advocate participative approaches as the key to increasing the quality and competitiveness of U.S. industry.[39] However, not all countries and cultures value the individualism and independence that characterize the American culture and make participation so appealing there. Although participation is undoubtedly an important element in a leader's behavioral repertoire in the United States and other western countries, this is not necessarily the case elsewhere.

A leader's *socialized need for power* is another trait that helps them use participative behaviors effectively. Leaders whose personalities include a strong need for power like to influence and control their environment. The socialized form of need for power causes leaders to enjoy coaching and developing followers to build their influence over their environment. They are typically not aggressive or dominant with followers, and they are seldom defensive. They willingly take advice from others who have relevant knowledge, and are careful about abusing their position of power. These factors enable a leader to garner followers' ideas and cooperation in a participative manner and effectively address group problems and decisions.[41]

Leaders who are effective at *self-monitoring* can diagnose situations well and adapt their behavior based on social cues from their environment. These individuals learn from the feedback they receive from others, and develop an understanding of how their behavior affects others. They also are effective at resolving conflicts with others.[42] All these behavioral traits can help a leader obtain and keep group support that is needed for participative decision making.

Participative leaders also develop effective *listening skills*. These were described in Chapter 4 while discussing supportive leadership. In order to promote the trust and cooperation needed for effective follower participation, leaders must demonstrate active listening behaviors such as concentration, careful attention, and providing verbal and nonverbal feedback to followers. This shows that the leader values followers' ideas and input, and encourages their further participation.

Effective participative leaders often have a high level of *assertiveness skills*, but they are not aggressive. They stand up for their own and their group's rights, and make it easy for others to do the same. They are not hostile, domineering, or pushy. They do not polarize issues, but rather phrase their statements in order to open an honest dialogue with followers. They make honest statements about their own ideas and feelings, and show their willingness to address followers' ideas through mutual discussion and problem solving. These assertiveness skills model and encourage similar behaviors from followers, and they create a constructive environment for participative problem solving and decision making.[43]

Participative leaders also demonstrate *empathy* and *social insight*. They learn to understand their followers' attitudes, motives, and needs regarding key issues. They recognize the interests, goals, and values that followers have in common, and how they are aligned with their own. This empathy and insight usually comes from a leader's experience in participative problem-solving situations. They use this understanding to facilitate cooperation and discussion, to build harmony among followers, and to influence followers to pursue collective goals through participative discussions.

A final skill of participative leaders is *managing conflict* among followers. When two or more group members have interests or goals that seem incompatible, conflict and disagreement can disrupt the productive discussion needed for effective participation. It is important for leaders to determine the source of conflicts when they do occur and to address them proactively. Though conflict resolution strategies will vary with the situation, leaders must recognize that the followers' environment can be a critical factor in the amount of conflict followers perceive and experience. A leader's careful assessment of the organization's expectations of followers, the adequacy of resources, the degree of interdependence with others, and communication problems, may be important to resolving conflicts among followers. Conflicts between followers regarding values, beliefs, and goals are often addressed effectively by strategies that encourage collaboration and sharing of desired outcomes. Once conflicts are addressed, followers can get back to the business of joint problem solving and decision making.

Effective leaders usually attempt to develop and utilize at least three types of power to assist them in carrying out participative leadership. When leaders emphasize these sources of power, followers tend to respond well to participation opportunities.

A leader's *legitimate power* is important for gaining followers' confidence in the participative process. Followers need to know the leader has the authority to invite their involvement in making decisions. The leader must also be in a position to implement decisions that result from follower participation. If followers are uncertain about the leader's authority to use their input to implement group decisions, they will likely have little motivation to respond to participative behaviors by their leader. A leader's legitimate power thus gives followers confidence that their participation can have a meaningful and useful result.

A leader who has substantial *connection/resource power* can often minimize conflict and facilitate interactions among followers. Competition among members for scarce resources is a very common source of conflict in groups. Leaders who can provide ample resources eliminate this problem and allow members to concentrate their efforts on collaboration for problem solving and decision making. When members' work-related needs are met, they are unlikely to be anxious about their jobs and are more accommodating with coworkers, making collaboration and coalitions more likely. The leader who has connections and networks that include influential others outside the group will likely be highly respected by followers. This respect typically results in willing cooperation and active participation when leaders solicit followers' input for decisions.

A leader's *expert power* is also an asset to participative leadership, just as it is to supportive and directive leadership. The leader who has expert power can facilitate followers' participation by providing knowledge, skill, and ability that support their involvement in the decision-making process. The more important the decision, the greater the likelihood that the leader's expert power will be a factor in supporting follower participation. The leader can provide followers with needed knowledge, be available as a source of technical advice, provide rational explanations of processes, and refer followers to needed sources of assistance or information. Figure 6-3 summarizes the skills, traits, and sources of power for effective participative leadership.

▪ ▪ ▪ **FIGURE 6-3 Skills, traits, and sources of power for effective participative leadership**

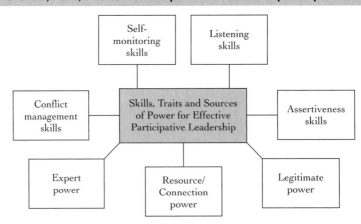

LEADERSHIP SELF-ASSESSMENT
Obtaining Effective Participation

Instructions: Indicate the extent to which you engage in the following behaviors when obtaining the participation of others in decision making, using the following scale: (5) almost always; (4) usually; (3) occasionally; (2) seldom; (1) almost never.

1. I take time to understand followers' preferences before trying to obtain their participation in decisions. 1 2 3 4 5
2. I involve everyone in making decisions, regardless of their needs and wants. 1 2 3 4 5
3. I provide others with clear information on the objectives and desired results of their participation. 1 2 3 4 5
4. I have people participate in decisions regardless of their knowledge or ability to make effective contributions. 1 2 3 4 5
5. I get input from others to clarify their reasons for suggesting alternative decisions or actions. 1 2 3 4 5
6. I make evaluative comments on the decision input from others before I fully understand their position. 1 2 3 4 5
7. After making comments about an individual's suggestions, I allow the individual to further explain his or her ideas. 1 2 3 4 5
8. I immediately let people know when they make suggestions that I disagree with. 1 2 3 4 5
9. I reward individuals who contribute ideas and suggestions with comments showing appreciation. 1 2 3 4 5
10. I take into account the other person's attitudes, beliefs, and values in order to obtain effective participation. 1 2 3 4 5

Interpretation: If you rated items 1, 3, 5, 7, 9, and 10 as 4 or 5, you are probably using participative leadership effectively. If you rated items 2, 4, 6, and 8 as 4 or 5, you may not use participative leadership effectively.

SOURCE: Items adapted from research by P. W. Dorfman, J. P. Howell, B. C. G. Cotton, and U. Tate. Leadership within the "discontinuous hierarchy" structure of the military: Are effective leadership behaviors similar within and across command structures? In K. E. Clark, M. B. Clark, and D. P. Campbell (Eds.), *Impacts of Leadership.* Greensboro, NC: Center for Creative Leadership.

▪▪▪ Facilitating and Limiting Conditions for Participative Leadership

Leaders do not all use the same amount of participation, and a given leader will usually vary the type or amount of participation used with followers in different situations.[44] Personal characteristics of leaders can influence their use of participative leadership. For example, although the leader's gender is not conclusively related to leader directiveness or supportiveness, current research shows that female leaders tend to use participative approaches to decision making more frequently than male leaders.[45] It may be that the social skills of women who have achieved leadership positions allow them to incorporate others more easily into the decision process, or perhaps female leaders are more frequently censured than male leaders when they are autocratic.[46] The Leadership in Action box on Wilma Mankiller is a good example of a female leader's participative approach.

Some studies have shown that leaders who have a lot of work experience or are highly educated are more participative.[47–50] These factors may allow the leader to be comfortable and secure with the leadership position and less threatened by potentially conflicting ideas. Followers often desire to be involved in decisions that affect them, and experienced or educated leaders may recognize and respond to their desires.

Leaders' perceptions of their followers also influence their use of participative leadership. For example, participative leadership is likely to be used in the following circumstances: when the leader perceives followers as having competence, expertise, or essential information to make a quality decision; when follower acceptance of the decision outcome is essential; when followers need to develop their decision skills; or when followers share organizational goals with the leader.[51–54] Several of these factors were described in Chapter 3 in connection with the Normative Decision-Making model. It is understandable that leaders carefully consider their followers when making a commitment to use participative leadership.

Some organizational factors constrain or prevent a leader from using participative leadership. For example, participation is difficult to use effectively when the leader works in a highly bureaucratic organization or has very little time to make a decision.[55,56] If the leader is highly authoritarian or there is a large social or occupational status difference between leader and followers, the leader may have less confidence in followers and therefore be less likely to involve them in decisions.[57,58] There is recent evidence that when the leader's followers are widely dissimilar regarding their age, education, or gender, the leader may be less participative.[59] These constraints make sense, although they are based on a limited number of research studies.

The appropriateness of participative leadership in different cultures and countries is difficult to determine because leadership practices must be consistent with the cultural norms in each society. These norms determine the amount and type of worker participation that is expected in that culture.[60] If there is a tradition or cultural imperative of participation (as in the United States), then participation is often expected; if there is a tradition of authoritarian decision making, then participation is not expected, and followers may dislike it.

In a classic study of international management, three well-known researchers surveyed leaders in fourteen countries. They found that leaders in all countries professed a belief in the importance of participation, but most of the leaders outside the U.S. did not trust the average follower's capability to show initiative and share leadership responsibilities.[61] Later studies showed this tendency was less pronounced but still present when leaders outside the U.S. described only followers of their own nationality. These findings probably result from cultural mandates that make leaders feel they should approve of participation even though they may not believe it is the most effective approach.

It is likely that the meaning of participative leadership is also different in different cultures. One writer noted that in Japan participation means that followers are given the honor of presenting their views to organizational superiors.[62] In the United States, participation often means that followers can present their ideas, *and* that those ideas

▪▪▪▪▪▪▪▪▪▪   ▪▪▪▪▪▪▪▪▪▪

LEADERSHIP IN PERSPECTIVE

What Are Groups Good at Doing?

Many years ago a famous learning psychologist named Robert Ladd Thorndike[63] conducted an experiment that showed how the type of problem was a critical factor in determining if an individual or a group was more effective at finding a solution. His results showed that groups were much better at solving crossword puzzles, but individuals were better at constructing them. Both of these tasks are complex, but there are important differences.

Vroom and Jago[64] pointed out that solving crossword puzzles involves solving a large number of small, loosely connected problems, each having one correct answer. One can begin anywhere, jump around randomly, and still solve the puzzle efficiently. Members of a group can work independently and effectively to solve the puzzle. In constructing crossword puzzles, however, there is no single correct solution, and any word added must be coordinated with previous words and those added later. Instead of being loosely coupled, the words must be tightly coupled in order and sequence, making coordination very important. Groups are less effective at completing this type of project, as they also are at writing a novel or composing a symphony. Groups can address themselves to large projects with numerous independent subtasks, but they are much less effective at combining complex patterns of highly interconnected tasks into a single integrated whole.

▪▪▪▪▪▪▪▪▪▪

are reflected in the decisions made. If there is no evidence that the followers' input is included in the decisions, then American workers are more likely to feel that genuine participation has not taken place. This distinction is another example of how cultural norms affect the meanings, expectations, and effectiveness of participation, as well as other types of leadership behavior. Leaders must consider the cultural norms and expectations of followers and peers when they use participative leadership.

The Leadership in Perspective box shows that group problem solving is highly effective at certain types of tasks, but not all tasks.

▪▪▪ Effects of Participative Leadership

Numerous books, chapters, and research articles published in the United States during the past 35 years have focused on the effects of participative leadership. A large portion of these publications are qualitative descriptions of specific management programs or other examples of participation in real organizations.[65–67] Another large group of studies is quantitative in nature, meaning that researchers actually measured the extent of participative leadership and its effect on followers' satisfaction, performance, commitment to decisions, and other important outcomes. These studies allow a good assessment of the real effects of participation, because the researchers are careful to rule out other possible causes of positive or negative results. Although researchers do not uniformly agree about what to conclude from this research, several recent summaries have helped to discern some general patterns.[68–71]

Effects on Follower and Group Psychological Reactions

Participative leadership has a very consistent favorable effect on the satisfaction of followers, including satisfaction with their leader, with their work, and general satisfaction with their organization and job situation.[72–75] Laboratory studies and studies of real organizations generally find that followers like participative leadership better than autocratic leadership, especially in the United States.[76] Several reasons are usually given for this finding. First, when asked to participate, followers can reflect their own interests and concerns in the outcomes of decisions that affect them. Second, participation gives followers an opportunity to utilize their own untapped talents, and this helps satisfy their needs for competence, self-fulfillment, and personal growth. Third, it allows followers to make a significant contribution to a valued group, thereby satisfying needs for esteem and accomplishment.

Participative leadership also improves followers' motivation and commitment to decisions. This commitment is often shown by less resistance to change produced by the decision, by smoother implementation of the decision option chosen, or by increased acceptance and motivation to make the decision work.[77,78] One writer described the reason for this result of participation by emphasizing that people support what they build.[79] By participating in the decision, followers often have their self-esteem tied to its outcome. They may also see it as beneficial to them, and they likely understand the reasoning behind the decision better than if they had not participated.

Effects on Followers' Performance and Behavior

A large number of studies have reported that participative leadership results in high levels of performance or productivity with followers or groups of followers.[80] These studies were conducted with many different types of followers and organizations, such as U.S. Army officers and NCOs,[81] library directors,[82] U.S. Army clerks,[83] aerospace firms,[84] light manufacturing firms,[85] and other types of formal organizations.[86,87] Although some researchers still disagree about whether improved performance results from participation, there are sound reasons for expecting improved performance. First, increased amounts of information are likely available from followers to help identify and evaluate alternative courses of action. Second, there is increased motivation to participate and to successfully implement decisions, because participation helps satisfy followers' esteem and social needs.

Numerous studies have indicated that the quality of decisions is improved with participative leadership.[88–91] A quality decision is highly likely to help attain organizational goals because it is well reasoned and consistent with available information and organizational goals and objectives.[92] High-quality decisions result from participation because more complete information is available to participants, and a more comprehensive discussion of the decision situation and possible alternatives often occurs.

Much of the research on decision quality deals with the model of participative leadership originally developed by Vroom and Yetton,[93] and further developed by Vroom and Jago.[94] Their model (described in Chapter 3) emphasizes follower and situational characteristics of each decision problem, and provides advice on how to use participative techniques to involve followers in decision making. These researchers report that the impact of participation on decision quality is highly affected by factors such as the existence of shared goals among followers, the amount of knowledge and information possessed by followers, group size, disagreement among participants, and the nature of the problem. These situational factors will be discussed in detail in the section on situational factors and participative leadership. Participative leadership affects decision quality, but the type and degree of impact depends on the decision situation.

Researchers also point to the development of followers as an outcome of participation. Including followers in discussions to generate and evaluate decision options develops their decision-making skills and may improve relations among followers. Participative discussions may also help integrate individuals and organizational goals and improve followers' self-management skills.

Participative leadership can also have several possible undesirable results. First, participative decision making usually takes more time than autocratic decisions, and this may be a critical factor in decision success (such as in a medical team facing an emergency). Participative discussions also take followers away from other tasks. Although they can benefit from the participative discussions, the urgency of their other tasks and decreased productivity during discussion sessions must be evaluated to determine which is more important. One writer also described the training costs for both leaders and followers to prepare them for effective consultation, group decision making, or delegation. Other support costs include meeting rooms and staff support to assure that necessary information is available to those who are participating in decisions.[95] Finally, some managers are not comfortable with participation and will resist if encouraged to use it. This resistance can cause resentment and lost productivity for those working with this manager, so the final decision to use participation should probably be left to the individual manager.

The impact of participative leadership in other countries depends on the norms and expectations that exist there. Studies in Western Europe generally find that participative leadership has positive effects, particularly on follower satisfaction.[96] One study compared the participative practices of German and British managers, and found they were quite similar in the degree of participation used for different types of decisions. As in the United States, the more formal education the managers had, the more they used participative leadership. These findings likely reflect the cultural similarities between the United States and Western Europe.

In the Middle East, the predominant cultures differ dramatically from that of the United States and Western Europe, and the impacts of participative leadership are more varied. One researcher found that Turkish supervisors were significantly less participative than Americans, and that the followers of Turkish supervisors were significantly less satisfied with participative leadership than were followers of American supervisors. The same researcher also found that Turkish supervisors were more authoritarian than Americans, which explained their low level of participativeness.[97] However, researchers in India found that Indian college students responded to participative leadership in a laboratory study by showing increased productivity.[98] In Nigeria, participative leadership was not effective in improving follower performance or satisfaction for construction workers and teachers.[99] Similar results occurred in Latin America and Asia. In a recent study of five countries, researchers showed that participative leadership had positive impacts in the United States only, and not in Mexico, Korea, Taiwan, or Japan.[100] It appears that participative leadership behaviors, as

TABLE 6-2 Major effects of participative leadership

Follower Benefits	*Group or Organizational Benefits*
Satisfaction with work and leader	Improved quality of decisions
General job satisfaction	Increased performance
Motivation	Smoother implementation of decisions
Commitment to decisions	Less resistance to change
Increased performance	
Improved development	

described here, may not be effective in certain countries in which the culture does not include egalitarianism and popular participation by all persons. Table 6-2 summarizes the major effects of participative leadership.

▪▪▪ Situational Dynamics of Participative Leadership

The effects or impacts of participative leadership often depend on the type of followers involved or the situation in which the leaders' participative behavior takes place. With certain types of followers or in specific situations, participation can be very effective. With other followers or other situations, participation may not be effective. The following sections of this chapter describe the situational and follower characteristics that may determine how much influence a participative leader has on followers. They also address how leaders can influence situations to allow for effective participation.

The Leadership Self-Assessment: Diagnosing Situations for Participative Leadership describes situations in which participative leadership may or may not be effective.

Several of the situations described in the self-assessment reflect a need for participative leadership. Items 1, 2, 5, 6, and 8 include follower and situational factors that can make participative leadership especially useful and effective with followers. Other situations can do the opposite—that is, they can make participation ineffective as an influence strategy. Items 3 and 4 are examples of such situations—that is, participative leadership will have little value to followers, or there is inadequate time to use participation effectively. Followers may reject a leader who attempts to use participative behaviors in these situations. Item 7 describes a situation in which an organizational factor substitutes for participative leadership by the leader. In this situation, written rules, procedures, and regulations provide clear guidance for leaders and followers in how decisions are to be made, making participation unnecessary. In this situation, the leader had best choose another strategy to influence followers. The situational and follower characteristics that make participative leadership highly effective, ineffective, or unnecessary are described in detail in the following sections.

The Leadership in Action box on Bob Gore describes his extremely participative leadership style, which helps produce responsibility and creativity throughout W. L. Gore & Associates.

LEADERSHIP SELF-ASSESSMENT
Diagnosing Situations for Participative Leadership

Place an "✕" next to those situations for which you believe participation will be most effective.

1. _____ Followers are working on tasks that are very important for the organization's success.

2. _____ Followers' acceptance and commitment are needed to successfully implement a decision.

3. _____ Followers' work tasks are highly predictable and repetitive, with no variation in the methods for completion.

4. _____ The leader must make several emergency decisions immediately, with very little time to gather input and information.

5. _____ The leader and followers work in an environment that is extremely uncertain and rapidly changing.

6. _____ Followers are highly competent, and possess knowledge and information needed to make an effective decision.

7. _____ An extensive set of written rules, regulations, and procedures exists to direct followers in their work and decision making.

8. _____ Followers have high needs for independence, and seek opportunities for achievement and self-fulfillment on the job.

▪▪▪ Situational Factors That Enhance the Effectiveness of Participative Leadership

When certain situational or follower characteristics are present, a leader's participative behaviors have very positive effects on followers' psychological reactions or behaviors. These situational and follower characteristics are enhancers of participative leadership.

Task, Organizational, and Follower Characteristics

When followers' *tasks are especially important* for the leader's group or organization, the impact of participative leadership on follower performance is usually strong and positive.[101–104] Followers carrying out important tasks are probably competent and take seriously their leader's invitations to influence decisions, with favorable results. Another important enhancer of participative leadership occurs when *follower acceptance or commitment to a decision are essential* to carry out the decision.[105,106] Inviting followers to participate in the decision process helps them understand and shape the decision process, thus increasing their ownership of the decision outcome and their acceptance and commitment to carry it out.

LEADERSHIP IN ACTION
Bob Gore, W. L. Gore & Associates

When Bob Gore was president and CEO of W. L. Gore & Associates, he was such a strong advocate of participative management that he referred to employees at every level as associates. W. L. Gore & Associates, makers of GORE-TEX® products, employs approximately 10,000 people worldwide with a very flat hierarchy. The lattice structure in their organization is intentionally decentralized to allow individuals to work across disciplines. Gore associates participate in business issues ranging from forecasting and planning to developing strategies for distribution and market positioning. Associates at Gore are also asked to participate in developing new product concepts, building teams, reorganizing, and troubleshooting—all issues that are important to the organization's success.

Bob Gore's style of participative leadership borrows heavily from the Socratic method of interactive questioning. Gore associates marvel at his ability to listen to them and interact with them by asking questions. One associate noted that "Gore made almost no statements during the whole 90-minute meeting, but instead asked hundreds of questions—from market forecasts to technical requirements to the associate's 'dream' for the business." Through this style of participation, associates at Gore are made to feel that not only are their ideas for the functional operations considered, but their vision for the organization as a whole matters.

Bob Gore is now chairman of the board of directors at W. L. Gore & Associates. His philosophy of leadership includes a healthy respect for the contributions of individuals. For Bob Gore, the contributions reside not only in the finished product or idea, but in the process by which the product or idea was conceived. For example, one associate was surprised to learn after her project was accepted that Bob Gore wanted to "access her thinking process" because he was so impressed with its value. At W. L. Gore & Associates, participative leadership allows employees to feel as though both their ideas and the processes by which ideas are conceived are valuable to the overall success of the organization.

SOURCES: S. W. Angrist. Classless capitalists. In P. L. Wright and S. P. Robbins (Eds.), *Organizational Theory,* Englewood Cliffs, NJ: Prentice Hall, 1978, 126–128; M. Pacanowsky. Team tools for wicked problems. *Organizational Dynamics,* 23(3), 1995, 36–51; and Heidi Cofran, W. L. Gore & Associates, Inc., personal communication, July 14, 2004.

Environmental uncertainty is another situational characteristic that enhances the impact of participation on followers or organizational performance.[107–110] Here, the input of followers is important in responding to a high degree of uncertainty faced by the group or organization. Participative leadership is an effective way of obtaining as much relevant information and as many ideas as possible in order to effectively address the uncertainty.

The conditions within the leader's group are also important to participative leadership. If the *group is harmonious* and *trusts the leader,* these conditions tend to enhance a participative leader's impact on group performance.[111] On the other hand, if *conflict* exists among followers, good conflict management skills enhance the leader's impact on group effectiveness.[112] Here, the leader is restoring the trust and camaraderie needed to encourage followers to participate wholeheartedly with the leader in decision making.

Certain characteristics of followers make them especially responsive to participative leadership behaviors. The characteristics that most frequently enhance participative leadership are *followers' job competence, expertise, knowledge, and information* relevant to the decision task. These follower characteristics increase the impact of leader participation behaviors on follower and group performance.[113–122] Furthermore, highly competent and knowledgeable followers often expect to have an impact on leadership decisions that affect them. As we will see, this expectation is not always present in other countries, but the enhancing effect of follower competence and knowledge has been found in many types of organizations in the United States.

Two other characteristics that can enhance the effects of leader participation on follower satisfaction and performance are *followers' needs for independence*[123–125] and *growth*.[126] In other words, followers who prefer to work independently or who seek self-fulfillment and achievement opportunities at work respond very positively to leader's efforts to involve them in decision making. They probably see the leader's invitation as a compliment to their capabilities, they value the chance to further develop and demonstrate their competence, their self-esteem is increased, and their positive attitudes and efforts are consequently heightened. A related follower characteristic that also enhances leader participativeness is *internal locus of control,* which is the tendency of certain people to see themselves as having personal control of their lives and environment.[127,128] These individuals do not believe in fate. They believe they control their own destiny through their own decisions and actions. When leaders solicit their input on decisions, they naturally respond positively with heightened satisfaction.

The amount of *participation followers expect* also enhances the impact of participation on their satisfaction, and sometimes on group performance. Followers expect participation when it is used by other leaders in the organization,[129] when it has been used for other decisions,[130] or when their prior leader used it in decision making. When a leader meets their expectations and involves them in decisions, they respond with improved satisfaction, and perhaps with improved performance. Figure 6-4 summarizes the situational factors that enhance the effectiveness of participative leadership.

Influencing Situations to Make Participative Leadership More Effective

The most potent enhancers of participative leadership are follower competence, knowledge, and information. Organizations can cultivate these factors with training and development programs, as well as selection and coaching for followers. Assigning competent followers to perform important tasks further enhances the impact of the leader's participation. Programs that increase the responsibility, autonomy, and importance of followers' work tasks can also enhance the impact of a leader's participativeness.

An uncertain environment also enhances participation's impact, although we do not advocate withholding information from followers simply to enhance a participative leader's impact. If a leader takes on a new project (such as developing a new product), having followers participate in decision making will likely be very effective because the activity is uncertain.

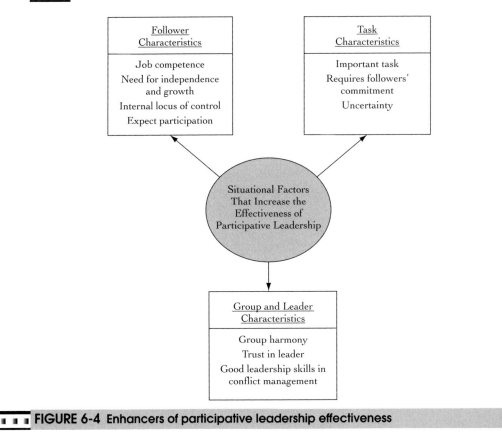

▪▪▪ **FIGURE 6-4** Enhancers of participative leadership effectiveness

Several other follower characteristics also enhance participation by a leader. For one, followers who expect to participate in decision making respond well to the opportunity. Here, precedence is important. When leaders use participation successfully in specific situations, they create the expectation among followers that they will use it in the future. Every manager knows the importance of precedent in the eyes of followers. Because followers who have a great need for independence, achievement, and self-fulfillment, or who believe they control their own destiny, respond well to participation, careful recruitment programs that bring these individuals into the organization should enhance the value of participative behaviors.

Organizational development and team-building programs can be used to build harmony and trust in the leader's group of followers. These conditions encourage collective team effort and enhance participative leadership. Such programs can be conducted by staff personnel, outside consultants, or managers who are experienced in team building.

The Leadership in Perspective box on participative leadership describes how economic and work force trends in the United States have created a situation in many organizations where participative leadership is especially popular.

LEADERSHIP IN PERSPECTIVE
Research on Participative Leadership

Victor Vroom and Arthur Jago have been studying participative leadership among managers in the United States for many years. They have noticed that the level of participation used by many managers has steadily increased since the 1970s. They note that the society and work force, as well as the products produced and the business environment, have all changed significantly since the days of Frederick Taylor and World War II. Vroom and Jago view the major reasons for the increase as an adaptation to current conditions. They also identified two critical aspects of these conditions that characterize today's organizations and encourage participation.

First, managers today face greater complexity in the decisions they make than managers faced decades ago. Technological innovations, foreign competition, and the changing role of government toward business mean that managers often do not have all the knowledge they need to make good decisions on their own. They must integrate the knowledge and capabilities of different specialists more than they used to in order to arrive at informed and effective decisions. This requires participative leadership.

A second major reason for increased participation by leaders is the nature of the labor force in organizations today. Followers are more educated than workers were earlier in this century. They often possess more ability to contribute toward effective decisions, and expect to be involved. Leaders who use an autocratic decision style will likely face greater resistance today than previously. Both of these situational factors—environmental complexity and an increasingly educated work force—probably have contributed to the increase in participative approaches taken by many of today's leaders.

SOURCE: Adapted from Victor H. Vroom and Arthur G. Jago. *The New Leadership.* Englewood Cliffs, NJ: Prentice Hall, 1988.

⊓⊓⊓ Situational Factors That Neutralize the Effectiveness of Participative Leadership

Situational factors exist that make participative leadership less important and therefore less effective with followers. When these factors exist, leaders should consider using other behavior patterns to influence followers.

Task, Organizational, and Follower Characteristics

A high degree of *task structure* in followers' work neutralizes the amount of satisfaction and performance that results from participative leadership.[131–135] Task structure refers to the existence of predictable and reliable methods for successful task performance. Repetitive tasks are often high in task structure, and research indicates that repetitive tasks decrease the impact of participative leadership.[136] Experienced leaders know that some workers appreciate predictable work methods and expect to have little influence on the leader's decisions. These workers often respond to nonparticipative leaders with satisfaction and good performance. For this type of worker, then, a high degree of task structure can decrease the effects of participative leadership.

A recent summary of research on participative leadership identified *task complexity* as a factor that neutralizes the impact of leader participativeness on follower satisfaction and acceptance of decisions.[137] This was the single most significant finding from this summary, and it may appear to contradict the neutralizing effects described previously regarding task structure. In fact, there has been a controversy among leadership researchers about how task characteristics affect the impact of participative leadership. However, task complexity in this summary seemed to involve problem-solving situations that required processing unusual information and dealing with considerable uncertainty. Individuals who perform such tasks are likely to be highly trained and experienced professionals, and they may require little input and discussion with their leader. Consequently, these individuals are not highly influenced by participative leadership behaviors. Professional workers are also usually satisfied and committed to their organizations, which is consistent with our expectations that the effect of task complexity is to neutralize the need for participative leadership.

The existence of *a large group* can also neutralize the effects of a leader's participative behaviors on followers' satisfaction. This is probably due to the difficulty of all members effectively sharing information and feeling they can influence a decision. Other researchers have reported that *short time deadlines,* emergencies, or a desire for quick results decrease the impact of participation on decision effectiveness.[138–140] The time requirements of many participative processes make them prohibitive or ineffective in these situations.

One set of follower characteristics has shown consistent, neutralizing effects on leaders' participation behaviors. When *followers are passive, apathetic, or willing to accept autocratic decisions,* participative leader behaviors do not improve follower satisfaction or commitment to decisions.[141–143] These followers apparently do not want to involve themselves with the leader in decision making, and when the leader tries to involve them, they react with low satisfaction and little commitment to decisions. Another follower characteristic that has neutralized the effects of leader participation in some situations is *follower authoritarianism.* Authoritarian followers prefer to have their behavior controlled by others. We would therefore expect them to prefer not to be consulted or involved in leadership decisions. This neutralizing effect was found in initial studies of parcel delivery workers and first-line supervisors,[144,145] but was not found in a later follow-up study.[146] Another researcher explored the possibility that the type of task may affect how authoritarian followers reacted to participation, and found the neutralizing effect occurred only when followers worked on highly repetitive tasks.[147] Recall that repetitive or structured tasks were also neutralizers of participation. When such tasks are performed by authoritarian followers, the neutralizing effect may be particularly strong. Figure 6-5 summarizes the situational and follower characteristics that neutralize the effectiveness of participative leadership.

Overcoming Factors That Neutralize Participative Leadership

Recall that leaders must know which situations are not compatible with participative leadership behaviors. If they can recognize these situations, leaders can modify or work around them when necessary.

▬▬▬ **FIGURE 6-5** Situational factors that neutralize the effectiveness of participative leadership

The followers' task structure and complexity are both possible neutralizers, especially when combined with certain types of followers. Task redesign can be used to manipulate the structure and complexity of followers' tasks, and selection procedures can help determine if specific personality types are well matched with certain jobs. A participative leader may wish to avoid placing authoritarian followers on jobs with high task structure, due to the neutralizing effect. Because highly trained professionals may be the only persons qualified to do complex problem-solving tasks, the leader may simply need to use behaviors other than participative ones to influence these individuals.

When leaders face emergency decisions or decisions with short time deadlines, participation is not effective. In some cases, the leader may be able to extend deadlines or learn of needed decisions sooner and thus provide more time for participative leadership. Emergencies and decisions with short time horizons do occur occasionally, and leaders are wise to avoid participative approaches when faced with these situations.

A large-sized group of followers can also neutralize the impact of participative leadership. In these situations, the leader may be able to create subgroups. These subgroups can operate with some autonomy but will allow the leader to involve members in useful discussions of decision issues. This approach may help prevent the isolation some individuals experience in large groups.

Followers who are passive and apathetic or are authoritarian and willing to accept a leader's autocratic decisions also neutralize the effectiveness of participative leadership behaviors. In the short run a leader can probably not do much to change these factors, and she should use other leader behaviors to influence followers. Charismatic leadership behaviors may be effective in overcoming apathetic and passive behavior. Over time, attrition and selection processes can bring in more involved and committed followers who appreciate and respond to participative leadership. The Leadership in Action box shows how General Motors has implemented participative leadership approaches to help solve productivity problems. Although GM met with difficulties, the participative approach seems to yield favorable results.

LEADERSHIP IN ACTION

Participative Leadership at General Motors

General Motors has been described as the world's largest corporate bureaucracy, with a long history of autocratic decision making by powerful top-level executives. In the late 1980s, GM had been through difficult times with tremendous foreign competition and inefficient production facilities. It had tried numerous programs to overcome the inefficiencies with limited success. Its chief executive officer, Roger Smith, agreed to try a more participative approach to involve employees in the decision process.

This change was difficult for the GM management. It required persuading managers to encourage and accept ideas and challenges from their subordinates, something they were unaccustomed to doing. It also involved convincing subordinates that the management really meant it when they asked for input. Given the long history of top-down decision making, this was probably the biggest hurdle.

After struggling with these difficulties, GM began to see some results. At the Lake Orion factory, managers began to involve plant workers in discussions with engineers on the full-sized models. Historically, workers found out about new models only when production began. But after introducing the participative approach, they were able to reduce product planning time by 6 months.

In the Buick City complex, managers got together with union leaders. They indicated that they needed to increase productivity, and showed figures that demonstrated how the plant was using more man-hours per car than any other GM plant. This participative approach resulted in faster production-line speed, a productivity level above the corporate average, and zero grievances. Participative leadership is having real bottom-line benefits at General Motors.

SOURCE: Adapted from *The Wall Street Journal,* January 12, 1988.

▪▪▪ Situational Factors That Substitute for Participative Leadership

One situational characteristic that substituted for participative leadership behavior among commissioned and noncommissioned U.S. Army officers was organizational formalization—the degree of formal rules, regulations, and procedures specified for followers to direct their activities.[148] When extensive rules and regulations were present, as is often the case in the military, the impact of leader participativeness on followers' satisfaction with their work was significantly reduced. However, the presence of organizational formalization also had a positive impact of its own on followers' satisfaction with work—replacing a normal impact of participative leadership. We should not assume from this single study that organizational formalization is always a substitute for a leader's participation. However, this study does show that formalization may substitute for this leadership behavior.

Creating Factors That Substitute for Participative Leadership

As noted earlier, the creation of factors that substitute for leadership helps free up a leader for other needed activities, adds to the stability of the leader's unit when the leader is absent, and helps followers take on added responsibility and become more independent. Because few researchers have attempted to identify factors that substitute for participative leadership, the only situational characteristic that has been confirmed to have substitution effects occurred in the sample of U.S. Army officers described earlier. The U.S. military probably operates with more formal rules and procedures than many nonmilitary leaders find comfortable. Although this potential leadership substitute is often under the control of the organization's management (more rules and procedures can always be created), it may require a very high degree of organizational formalization to completely substitute for participative leadership.

Although not yet tested by researchers, we believe that two other task characteristics may combine with individual follower traits to create substitutes for participation. Highly structured tasks, when performed by followers who are authoritarian or have a low need for independence, may substitute for participative leadership. The U.S. military may create this type of situation with their selection and socialization strategy. Highly complex tasks, when performed by highly trained or professional workers, may also substitute for participative leadership. Here again, recruiting and selecting well-trained and professional individuals for jobs of this type may create substitutes for participation. These possible substitutes are mostly speculative at this time and are therefore excluded from the summary figures later in this chapter.

▪▪▪ Assessing the Dynamics of Participative Leadership

A dynamic interaction occurs between a participative leader, followers' needs and expectations, and important situational factors. Research shows that situational and follower characteristics are generally three times more important than leadership characteristics in determining the amount of participation shown by a leader.[149] When leaders determine that situational and follower characteristics are present that will enhance the effects of participative leadership (see Figure 6-5), they should use participation to involve followers in decision making and problem solving. If the leader's diagnosis identifies factors that neutralize the effects of participation (see Figure 6-6), the leader should probably use other leadership behaviors to influence followers. If situational factors exist that substitute for participative leadership, then this leadership pattern is probably unnecessary, and the leader should look to other possible needs of their followers.

Effective participative leaders also assess situations and followers to determine if they can be modified. If leaders can eliminate factors that neutralize the positive effects of participation or create factors that enhance the effectiveness of participation, they can make the situation more favorable to participative leadership. As indicated earlier, leaders can provide training and development to increase followers' competence and job knowledge; redesign followers' jobs to increase their responsibility, complexity, and importance; use selection and job placement to create a group of followers who are independent, achievement oriented, nonauthoritarian, and expect participation; and use team building to create group harmony with small groups of followers. Moreover, leaders can sometimes get deadlines extended to allow time for effective participation. All these actions can create a situation in which participative leadership is highly effective. Leaders may also create formal written guidelines to inform decision makers how to make decisions without using participation, although this approach may be most useful in organizations that have historically relied heavily on written guidelines, rules, and procedures. Because only one situational factor has been found to clearly substitute for participative leadership, leaders had best concentrate their efforts on modifying situations to create enhancers and eliminate neutralizers of participative leadership.

Followers' reactions to the leader's efforts to modify their situation will affect the leader's future participative behaviors, as well as future efforts at situational modification. Followers thus influence the participative behaviors of their leader. Overall, however, with increasing levels of formal education and training of the working population in western countries, participative leadership seems to be a frequently effective leadership response to followers' needs. The Leadership in Action box on John W. Gardner describes ethical issues of participative leadership in the United States.

LEADERSHIP IN ACTION
John W. Gardner on Moral Leadership

John W. Gardner, who served six presidents of the United States in various leadership capacities, noted that the characteristics followers expect of an ethical leader are at least partly determined by the culture. But in the United States today, he believes that morally acceptable leaders are often identified by their objectives for their followers.

A continuing commitment to the development of human possibilities is a basic social objective and major goal of ethical leaders. He quoted Thomas Jefferson, who said, "We hope to avail the nation of those talents which nature has sown as liberally among the poor as the rich, but which perish without use, if not sought for and cultivated." In pursuing this objective, Gardner believes leaders have an obligation to encourage the active involvement of followers in decision making and the pursuit of group goals.

Gardner also quoted Al Sloan, who ran General Motors for 35 years, on this issue. Sloan said he worried about how to keep managers around the country awake and thinking about what they could contribute to the future of General Motors. "And the only way to do that is to push some decisions in their direction."

Gardner indicated that ethical leaders constantly strive to enliven individuals at every level of an organization to share in the leadership task of making decisions and carrying them out. This requires leaders who delegate, consult, and listen to followers, respect human possibilities, and remove obstacles to followers' participation. He ends by quoting Lyman Bryson, who stated, "A democratic way of doing anything is a way that best keeps and develops the intrinsic power of men and women."

SOURCE: John W. Gardner. *On Leadership.* New York: The Free Press, 1990. Adapted with the permission of The Free Press, a Division of Simon & Schuster Adult Publishing Group. Copyright © 1990 by John W. Gardner. All rights reserved.

SUMMARY ▄▄▄▄▄▄▄

Participative leadership consists of involving followers in making decisions that the leader would otherwise make alone. Participative behaviors include consulting with followers to obtain their input, meeting with groups of followers to jointly generate and explore alternatives, and delegating decisions to individuals or groups to make on their own with or without the final approval of the leader.

Participative leadership gives followers opportunities to satisfy needs for competence, self-control, independence, esteem, and personal growth. Participation has a long history as a leadership technique, and has been particularly popular in the United States and parts of western Europe for several decades. Female leaders or leaders who are highly experienced and educated tend to be participative with followers. Leaders also tend to use participative behaviors when followers are competent, when they share the organization's goals with the leader, when followers must implement the decision, or when they need to develop their decision skills.

Overall, the evidence shows that participative leadership improves followers' satisfaction and performance, although the effects are not strong and are most likely heavily influenced by characteristics of followers and the decision situation. Some evidence indicates that participation increases follower commitment to decisions and decision quality, but this also is likely affected by the situation. Participative leadership also has drawbacks: it takes time, removes followers from other tasks, requires training and other support, and may be resisted by some managers.

Leaders will be most effective with participative behaviors if they display them when enhancers of participation are present. In these situations, leaders will likely have strong positive effects on followers' psychological states and behavioral outcomes. Participative leadership will have less impact on followers when important substitutes or neutralizers are present. When these situational and follower conditions exist, leaders will likely be most effective if they avoid using participative leadership behavior and choose a different behavior pattern (such as directive or supportive leadership) to influence followers' psychological reactions and behaviors.

Figure 6-6 shows the Process Model of Participative Leadership, which summarizes material in this chapter on how situational factors influence the effects of participative leadership on follower psychological reactions and behavioral outcomes. Participative leadership behaviors are shown at the top of Figure 6-6, affecting follower and group psychological reactions, which in turn affect followers' behaviors and outcomes. Situational factors are shown on each side of Figure 6-6. The arrows from the situational factor boxes intersect the arrow connecting participative leadership behaviors with follower and group psychological reactions. This intersection shows that situational factors can increase or decrease the effects of participative leadership on followers' reactions. Participative leadership behaviors are also connected with arrows to situational factors, showing that leaders can modify the situations to make them more favorable for the leader's influence attempts. The factors that may substitute for participative leadership are shown at the left of Figure 6-6, with an arrow directly affecting follower reactions.

Figure 6-7 is designed to help the leader use the information summarized in Figure 6-6. It shows the three key leadership tasks of diagnosing situations, providing leadership, and modifying followers and situations. Leaders first diagnose the situation by answering the questions regarding followers and their work situation (1. Diagnosing

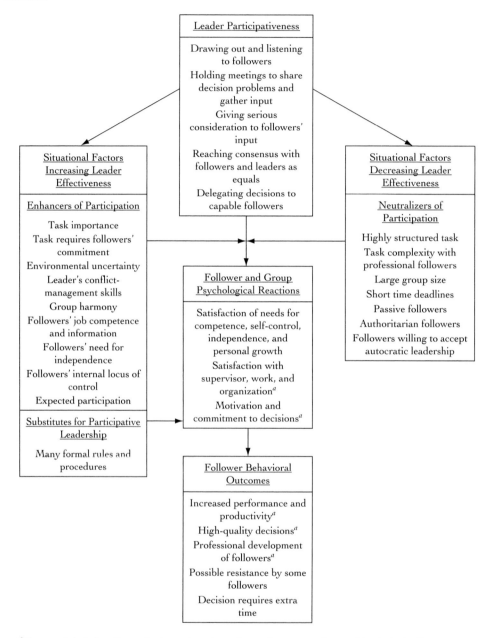

[a]These psychological reactions and outcomes have shown the most improvement from participative leadership.

▪▪▪▪ **FIGURE 6-6 Process Model of Participative Leadership**

the Situation). These questions assess the existence of factors that can increase or decrease the effects of participative leadership on followers' reactions. If the answer is "yes" to one or more of these questions, then followers will probably expect and value a participative approach by their leader. The leader then provides the appropriate

1. Diagnosing the Situation

- Are followers highly competent and knowledgeable? Do they work on important tasks? Is their commitment essential to carry out the leader's decisions?
- Do followers value achievement, independence, and self-fulfillment? Do they view themselves as controlling their own lives, feel harmony and trust with the leader, and expect to participate in decisions?
- Is the leader effective in obtaining follower input and skilled at conflict management?
- Is there much environmental uncertainty?

If you answer "yes" to one or more of these questions, followers will expect and value participative leadership.

3. Modifying Followers or Situations

Leaders also act to:

- Increase formal rules and procedures that prescribe how to deal with emergencies and short time deadlines
- Redesign tasks to increase their importance and followers' independence
- Build group harmony
- Develop followers' job competence and knowledge
- Eliminate highly structured tasks and large-sized groups
- Reassign followers who are passive, authoritarian, or desire autocratic leadership

2. Providing Participative Leadership

Leaders demonstrate participative behaviors with followers by:

- Holding informal conversations with individual followers to obtain information related to decisions
- Sharing decision problems with groups of followers to solicit their ideas or suggested solutions
- Assigning a decision problem to followers who are competent and desire to handle it
- Allowing air time for all followers who desire it when discussing decision problems
- Inviting input and discussion on points of disagreement regarding decision problems
- Explaining to followers why ideas or solutions are not implemented

FIGURE 6-7 Applying the Process Model of Participative Leadership

participative behaviors (2. Providing Participative Leadership). The leader also examines the followers' situation to determine if it can be modified to eliminate possible neutralizers or create enhancers of participative leadership. The leader might also determine if factors can be created that substitute for participation. If situations can be modified to improve the effectiveness of leaders and followers, then the leader does so (3. Modifying Followers or Situations). The leader then rediagnoses the situation and reconsiders the amount of participative leadership behaviors that are needed. Figure 6-7 is thus a dynamic model of continually diagnosing situations, providing participative leadership, modifying situations, rediagnosing situations, and so on. It represents the dynamic nature of the leadership process model described in this book.

KEY TERMS AND CONCEPTS IN THIS CHAPTER

- Acceptance of decisions
- Assertiveness skill
- Commitment to decisions
- Consensus group decisions
- Consultation
- Delegation
- Development of followers
- Empathy
- Environmental uncertainty
- Expert power

- Group harmony
- Growth needs
- Independence needs
- Joint decision making
- Legitimate power
- Listening skills
- Locus of control
- Managing conflict
- Organizational formalization

- Participative leadership
- Passive followers
- Quality of decisions
- Resource/connection power
- Self-monitoring
- Socialized need for power
- Task complexity
- Task structure

REVIEW AND DISCUSSION QUESTIONS

1. Describe participative leadership behaviors that had a positive effect on your behavior. Why did these leadership behaviors have a positive effect on you?
2. Describe participative leadership behaviors that were ineffective and had a negative effect on you. Why did these leadership behaviors have a negative effect on you?
3. Should most leaders be more participative with their followers? What are the reasons for your position?
4. Describe a situation in which someone delegated responsibility to you. Did the delegation result in effective or ineffective performance? Explain why.
5. Give several specific examples of situational factors that could cause participative leadership to be highly effective. For each, explain why they would increase the leader's impact on followers.
6. Give several specific examples of situational factors that could cause participative leadership to be less effective. For each, explain why they decrease the leader's impact on followers.
7. As a leader, how might you create situational factors to build your influence as a participative leader?
8. Discuss the values or benefits to leaders of creating factors that substitute for participative leadership.

CASE INCIDENTS

A Supervisor's Problem

You supervise one of several small final-assembly departments for a medium-sized producer of top-of-the-line camping equipment. You are not sure why, but the quality of camping lanterns produced in your depart-

ment has been declining. There have been some small changes recently in the lanterns' design, but employees in your department are experienced and knowledgeable about the lanterns, and their quality has been very good in the past. Morale in the department is good and employees usually take pride in the company's products. The lanterns are an important part of the company's product line, and customer complaints are increasing about the decreased quality. ■

use to help solve this production problem? Why?

2. Are there any other leadership behaviors or actions you recommend? If so, what are they?

DISCUSSION QUESTIONS

1. Considering the three patterns of leadership behavior described thus far in this book, which approach would you

EXERCISE: ACTIONS TO OBTAIN PARTICIPATION ▮▮▮▮▮▮▮

You supervise a group of copy editors in a medium-sized publishing firm. While talking with employees at the company recognition dinner, your manager became convinced that the employees in your department were not participating in departmental decisions. Employees told your manager that they had suggestions and ideas to improve the productivity in your department. They mentioned methods for cutting costs and increasing quality that impressed your manager. They also told him of grievances that he felt had the potential for producing major problems in employee relations. As a supervisor, you have been told to take courses of action to obtain employee participation on possible improvements in your department.

Evaluate the following list of actions to obtain participation from your employees. Which actions would you take? Why? Which actions would you avoid taking? Why?

1. Take a confidential survey of employees to obtain suggestions for improving the department.
2. Offer a monthly award for the best suggestion to cut costs or improve quality.
3. Provide employees with additional information on customers, quality control standards, costs, and how individual jobs contribute to department productivity.
4. Have the human resources department meet with employees to determine problems and complaints.
5. Become better friends with employees by participating with them in activities outside of work.
6. Have employees elect a representative group to evaluate ideas for improving productivity and make recommendations to you.
7. Establish a suggestion program so employees can make suggestions by using a suggestion box.
8. Listen in on employees' conversations whenever possible.
9. Have an open-door policy and encourage employees to provide input on pending decisions.
10. Hold weekly meetings with employees to share important issues with them and obtain their input.

Let's All Be Participative Managers

John Peterson is president of JP Chemical Corporation. He is committed to continually improving the company's management through the use of modern management practices. To get new ideas, he attended a management development seminar at a local university. The seminar focused on using participation to improve productivity and increase employees' commitment to their jobs. Mr. Peterson became convinced that all his managers needed to immediately implement participative management practices.

To insure implementation of participative management, Mr. Peterson sent an e-mail to all the company managers that stated: "I am convinced that we must immediately begin to practice participative management. The attachments to this e-mail are the handouts from the university management development seminar that explain how to practice participative management. I expect each of you to implement the practices in the attachments starting next week. As a company we are now committed to practicing participation. Any managers who do not implement participative practices will find it impossible to remain with this company." ▪

DISCUSSION QUESTIONS

1. Do you think Mr. Peterson's e-mail will result in effective participative practices by the managers? Why?
2. Do you think Mr. Peterson should have approached implementing participative practices in a different way? If so, how?

ENDNOTES ▪▪▪▪▪▪▪

1. Sinha, T. N., and Sinha, B. P. (1977). Styles of leadership and their effects on group productivity. *Indian Journal of Industrial Relations,* 13(2), 209–223.
2. Amabile, T. M., Schatzel, E. A., Moneta, G. B., and Kramer, S. J. (2004). Leader behaviors and the work environment for creativity: Perceived leader support. *Leadership Quarterly,* 15, 5–32.
3. Vroom, V. H., and Jago, A. G. (1988). *The New Leadership: Managing Participation in Organizations.* Englewood Cliffs, NJ: Prentice Hall.
4. Sayles, L. R. (1989). *Leadership: Managing in Real Organizations,* 2nd ed. New York: McGraw-Hill.
5. Bass, B. M. (1990). *Bass & Stogdill's Handbook of Leadership,* 3rd ed. New York: The Free Press.
6. Ibid.
7. Vroom and Jago (1988). *The New Leadership: Managing Participation in Organizations.*
8. Ibid.
9. Bass, *Bass & Stogdill's Handbook of Leadership.*
10. Muczyk, J. P., and Reimann, B. C. (1987). The case for directive leadership. *Academy of Management Executive,* 1(3), 301–311.
11. Wexley, K. N., and Snell, S. A. (1987). Managerial power: A neglected aspect of the performance appraisal interview. *Journal of Business Research,* 15, 45–54.
12. Graves, L. M. (1983). Implicit leadership theory: A comparison to two-dimensional leadership theory. In *Proceedings: Eastern Academy of Management,* Pittsburgh, PA, 93–95.
13. Yukl, G. (1998). *Leadership in Organizations,* 4th ed. Upper Saddle River, NJ: Prentice-Hall.
14. Muczyk and Reimann. The case for directive leadership.
15. Kenis, I. (1977). A cross-cultural study of personality and leadership. *Group and Organizational Studies,* 2(1), 49–60.

16. Lawler, E. E., III. (1986). *High Involvement Management.* San Francisco: Jossey-Bass.

17. Miller, K. I., and Monge, P. R. (1986). Participation, satisfaction and productivity: A meta-analytic review. *Academy of Management Review, 29, 727–753.*

18. Clark, A. W., and Witherspoon, J. A. (1973). Manager's conflict: Democratic management versus distrust of people's capacity. *Psychological Reports, 32(3), 815–819.*

19. Vroom, V. H., and Jago, A. G. (1995). Situation effects and levels of analysis in the study of leader participation. *Leadership Quarterly, 6(2), 169–181.*

20. Lawler, E. E., Renwick, P. A., and Bullock, R. J. (1981). Employee influence on decisions: An analysis. *Journal of Occupational Behavior, 2, 115–123.*

21. Vroom and Jago. *The New Leadership: Managing Participation in Organizations.*

22. Yukl. *Leadership in Organizations.*

23. Vroom and Jago. *The New Leadership: Managing Participation in Organizations.*

24. Tannenbaum, R., and Schmidt, W. H. (1958). How to choose a leadership pattern. *Harvard Business Review, 36, 95–101.*

25. Yukl. *Leadership in Organizations.*

26. Leana, C. R. (1987). Power relinquishment versus power sharing: Theoretical clarification and empirical comparison of delegation and participation. *Journal of Applied Psychology, 72(2), 228–233.*

27. Locke, E. A., and Schweiger, D. M. (1979). Participation in decision making: One more look. In B. M. Staw (Ed.), *Research in Organizational Behavior,* Vol. 1. Greenwich, CT: JAI Press, 265–339.

28. Bass. *Bass & Stogdill's Handbook of Leadership.*

29. Bass, B. M., Valenzi, E. R., Farrow, D. L., and Soloman, R. J. (1975). Management styles associated with organizational, task, personal and interpersonal contingencies. *Journal of Applied Psychology, 60, 720–729.*

30. Vroom and Jago. *The New Leadership: Managing Participation in Organizations.*

31. Ibid.

32. Taylor, F. W. (1911). *Principles of Scientific Management.* New York: Harpers.

33. Vroom and Jago. *The New Leadership: Managing Participation in Organizations.*

34. Lewin, K., and Lippitt, R. (1938). An experimental approach to the study of autocracy and democracy: A preliminary note. *Sociometry, 1, 292–300.*

35. Lippitt, R. (1940). An experimental study of the effect of democratic and authoritarian group atmospheres. *University of Iowa Studies in Child Welfare, 16, 43–95.*

36. Coch, L., and French, J. R. P. (1948). Overcoming resistance to change. *Human Relations, 1, 512–532.*

37. Likert, R. (1967). *The Human Organization: It's Management and Value.* New York: McGraw-Hill.

38. Bass. *Bass & Stogdill's Handbook of Leadership.*

39. Lawler. *High Involvement Management.*

40. Yukl. *Leadership in Organizations,* 4th ed.

41. Bass. *Bass & Stogdill's Handbook of Leadership.*

42. Dobbins, G. H., Long, W. S., Dedrick, E. J., and Clemons, T. C. (1990). The role of self-monitoring and gender on leadership emergence: A laboratory and field study. *Journal of Management, 16, 609–618.*

43. Hughes, R. L., Ginnett, R. C., and Curphy, G. J. (1996). *Leadership: Enhancing the Lessions of Experience.* Chicago: Irwin.

44. Hill, W. A. (1973). Leadership style: Rigid or flexible? *Organizational Behavior and Human Performance, 9, 35–47.*

45. Eagly, A. H., and Johnson, B. T. (1990). Gender and leadership style: A meta-analysis. *Psychological Bulletin, 108(2), 233–256.*

46. Jago, A. G., and Vroom, V. H. (1982). Sex differences in the incidence and evaluation of participative leader behavior. *Journal of Applied Psychology, 67, 776–783.*

47. Seversky, P. M. (1982). Trust, need to control, and the tendency to delegate: A study of the delegation behavior of superintendents. *Dissertation Abstracts International, 43(9A), 2851.*

48. Heller, F. A., and Yukl, G. (1969). Participation, managerial decision-making, and situational variables. *Organizational Behavior and Human Performance, 4, 227–241.*

49. Bass. *Bass & Stogdill's Handbook of Leadership.*

50. Jago and Vroom. Sex differences in the incidence and evaluation of participative leader behavior.

51. Field R. H. G., Read, P. C., and Louviere, J. J. (1990). The effects of situation attributes on decision making choice in the Vroom-Jago model of participation in decision making. *Leadership Quarterly,* 1, 165–176.

52. Vroom and Jago. *The New Leadership: Managing Participation in Organizations.*

53. Leana. Power relinquishment versus power sharing: Theoretical clarification and empirical comparison of delegation and participation.

54. Jago, A. G. (1978). A test of spuriousness in descriptive models of participative leader behavior. *Journal of Applied Psychology,* 63, 383–387.

55. Leana. Power relinquishment versus power sharing: Theoretical clarification and empirical comparison of delegation and participation.

56. Mohr, L. B. (1977). Authority and democracy in organizations. *Human Relations,* 30, 919–947.

57. Vroom, V. H. (1960). *Some Personality Determinants of the Effects of Participation.* Englewood Cliffs, NJ: Prentice Hall.

58. Mohr, L. B. (1977). Authority and democracy in organizations. *Human Relations,* 30, 919–947.

59. Somech, A. (2003). Relationships of participative leadership with relational demography variables: A multi-level perspective. *Journal of Organizational Behavior,* 24, 1003–1018.

60. Grunwald, W., and Bernthal, W. F. (1983). Controversy in German management: The Harzburg model experience. *Academy of Management Review,* 8(2), 233–241.

61. Haire, M., Ghiselli, E. E., and Porter, L. W. (1966). *Managerial Thinking: An International Study.* New York: Wiley.

62. Kerr, S. (1984). *Leadership and participation.* Working paper. Los Angeles: University of Southern California.

63. Thorndike, R. L. (1938). On what type of task will a group do well? *Journal of Abnormal and Social Psychology,* 33, 409–413.

64. Vroom and Jago. *The New Leadership: Managing Participation in Organizations.*

65. Peters, T. J., and Waterman, R. H., Jr. (1982). *In Search of Excellence: Lessons from America's Best-Run Companies.* New York: Harper and Row.

66. Lawler. *High Involvement Management.*

67. Kouzes, J. M., and Posner, B. Z. (1987). *Credibility: How Leaders Gain and Lose it, Why People Demand it.* San Francisco: Jossey-Bass.

68. Cotton, J. L., Vollrath, D. A., Froggett, K. L., Lengnick-Hall, M. L., and Jennings, K. R. (1988). Employee participation: Diverse forms and different outcomes. *Academy of Management Review,* 13, 8–22.

69. Leana, C. R., Locke, E. A., and Schweiger, D. M. (1990). Fact and fiction in analyzing research on participative decision making: A critique of Cotton, Vollrath, Froggett, Lengnick-Hall and Jennings, *Academy of Management Review,* 15: 137–146.

70. Wagner, J. A., III, and Gooding, R. Z. (1987). Shared influence and organizational behavior: A meta-analysis of situational variables expected to moderate participation-outcome relationships. *Academy of Management Journal,* 30, 524–541.

71. Wagner, J. A., III, (1994). Participation effects on performance and satisfaction: A reconsideration of research evidence. *Academy of Management Review,* 19(2), 312–330.

72. Dorfman, P. W., Howell, J. P., Cotton, B. C. G., and Tate, U. (1992). Leadership within the "discontinuous hierarchy" structure of the military: Are effective leadership behaviors similar within and across command structures? In K. E. Clark, M. B. Clark, and D. P. Campbell (Eds.), *Impacts of Leadership.* Greensboro, NC: Center for Creative Leadership.

73. Pace, L. A., Hartley, D. E., and Davenport, L. A. (1992). Beyond situationalism: Subordinate preferences and perceived leader impact. In K. E. Clark, M. B. Clark,

and D. P. Campbell (Eds.), *Impacts of Leadership.* Greensboro, NC: Center for Creative Leadership.

74. York, R. O., and Denton, R. T. (1990). Leadership behavior and supervisor performance: The view from the bottom. *The Clinical Supervisor,* 8(1), 93–108.

75. Indvik, J. (1986). Path-Goal theory of leadership: A meta-analysis. *Proceedings of the Academy of Management,* Chicago, 189–192.

76. Bass. *Bass & Stogdill's Handbook of Leadership.*

77. Delva, W. L., Wacker, J., and Teas, K. (1985). Motivational antecedents: A test of predictor models. *Psychological Reports,* 56, 447–461.

78. Tichy, N., and Devanna, M. (1986). *Transformational Leadership.* New York: Wiley.

79. Bass. *Bass & Stogdill's Handbook of Leadership.*

80. Kahai, S. S., Sosik, J. J., and Avolio, B. J. (2004). Effects of participative and directive leadership in electronic groups. *Group and Organization Management,* 29(1), 67–105.

81. Dorfman, Howell, Cotton, and Tate. Leadership within the "discontinuous hierarchy" structure of the military: Are effective leadership behaviors similar within and across command structures?

82. Solomon, R. J. (1976). An examination of the relationship between a survey feedback O. D. technique and the work environment. *Personnel Psychology,* 29, 583–594.

83. Reeder, R. R. (1981). The importance of the superior's technical competence in the subordinates' work. *Dissertation Abstracts International,* 42(6A), 2830.

84. Hinrichs, J. R. (1978). An eight-year follow-up of a management assessment center. *Journal of Applied Psychology,* 63, 596–601.

85. Bowers, D. G., and Seashore, S. E. (1966). Predicting organizational effectiveness with a four-factor theory of leadership. *Administrative Science Quarterly,* 11, 238–263.

86. Miller and Monge. Participation, satisfaction and productivity: A meta-analytic review.

87. Lawler. *High Involvement Management.*

88. Leana, C. R. (1985). A partial test of Janis' groupthink model: Effects of group cohesiveness and leader behavior on defective decision-making. *Journal of Management,* 11, 5–17.

89. Mitroff, I. I., and Mason, R. O. (1981). The metaphysics of policy and planning: A reply to Cosier. *Academy of Management Review,* 6, 649–651.

90. Mitroff, I. I. (1982). Dialectic squared: A fundamental difference in perception of the meanings of some key concepts in social science. *Decision Science,* 13, 222–224.

91. Lorge, I., Fox, D., Davitz, J., and Brenner, M. (1958). A survey of studies contrasting the quality of group performance and individual performance, 1920–1957. *Psychological Bulletin,* 55, 337–370.

92. Vroom and Jago. *The New Leadership: Managing Participation in Organizations.*

93. Vroom, V. H., and Yetton, P. W. (1973). *Leadership and Decision Making.* Pittsburgh, PA: University of Pittsburgh Press.

94. Vroom and Jago. *The New Leadership: Managing Participation in Organizations.*

95. Hammer, M., and Champy, J. (1993). *Reengineering the Corporation.* New York: Harper Business.

96. Drenth P. J. D., and Koopman, P. L. (1984). A contingency approach to participative leadership: How good? In J. G. Hunt, D. Hosking, C. A. Schriesheim, and R. Stewart (Eds.), *Leadership and Managers: International Perspectives on Managerial Behavior and leadership.* New York: Pergamon.

97. Kenis. A cross-cultural study of personality and leadership.

98. Sinha and Sinha. Styles of leadership and their effects on group productivity.

99. Ejiogu, A. M. (1983). Participative management in a developing economy: Poison or placebo. *Journal of Applied Behavioral Science,* 19(3), 239–247.

100. Howell, J. P., Dorfman, P. W., Hibino, S., Lee, J., Tate, U., and Bautista, A. (1994). Leadership in western and Asian countries: Commonalties and differences in effective leadership processes and substitutes across cultures. *Leadership Quarterly,* 8(3), 233–274.

101. Drenth and Koopman. A contingency approach to participative leadership: How good?

102. Bass, B. M., and Shackleton, V. J. (1979). Industrial democracy and participative management: A case for synthesis. *Academy of Management Review, 4*, 393–404.

103. Murnighan, J. K., and Leung, T. K. (1976). The effects of leadership involvement and the importance of the task on subordinates performance. *Organizational Behavior and Human Performance, 17*, 299–310.

104. Lawrence, L. C., and Smith, P. C. (1955). Group decision and employee participation. *Journal of Applied Psychology, 39*, 334–337.

105. Bass. *Bass & Stogdill's Handbook of Leadership.*

106. Vroom and Jago. *The New Leadership: Managing Participation in Organizations.*

107. Heller, F. A., and Wilpert, B. (1981). *Competence and Power in Managerial Decision-Making: A Study of Senior Levels of Management in Eight Countries.* London: Wiley.

108. Lawrence, L. C., and Lorsch, J. W. (1967). *Organization and Environment.* Boston, MA: Harvard University Press.

109. Burns, T., and Stalker, G. M. (1969). *The Management of Innovation.* Chicago: Quadrangle Books.

110. Roby, T. B., Nicol, E. H., and Farrell, F. M. (1963). Group problem solving under two types of executive structure. *Journal of Abnormal and Social Psychology, 67*, 550–556.

111. Bass, B. M., Valenzi, E. R., and Farrow, D. L. (1977). External environment related to managerial style. In *Proceedings, International Conference on Social Change and Organizational Development,* Dubrovnik, Yugoslavia.

112. Crouch, A. G., and Yetton, P. (1987). Manager behavior, leadership style, and subordinate performance: An empirical extension of the Vroom-Yetton conflict rule. *Organizational Behavior and Human Decision Processes, 39*, 65–82.

113. Dorfman, P. W., Howell, J. P., Hibino, S., Lee, J., Tate, U., and Bautista, A. (1997). Leadership in western and Asian countries: Commonalties and differences in effective leadership processes and substitutes across cultures. *Leadership Quarterly, 8*(3), 233–274.

114. Leana, C. R. (1986). Predictors and consequences of delegation. *Academy of Management Journal, 29*, 754–774.

115. Bass. *Bass & Stogdill's Handbook of Leadership.*

116. Bass, B. M., and Ryterband, E. C. (1979). *Organizational Psychology,* 2nd ed. Boston: Allyn & Bacon.

117. Filley, A. C., House, R. J., and Kerr, S. (1976). *Managerial Process and Organizational Behavior,* 2nd ed. Glenview, IL: Scott, Foresman.

118. Locke, E. A., and Schweiger, D. M. (1979). Participation in decision making: One more look. In B. M. Stow (Ed.), *Research in Organizational Behavior,* Vol. 1: 265–339. Greenwich, CT: JAI Press.

119. Fiedler, F., and Garcia, J. E. (1987). *New approaches to effective leadership: Cognitive resources and organizational performance.* New York: Wiley.

120. Heller and Wilpert. *Competence and Power in Managerial Decision-Making: A Study of Senior Levels of Management in Eight Countries.*

121. Hersey, P., and Blanchard, K. H. (1982). *Management of Organizational Behavior: Utilizing Human Resources,* 4th ed., Englewood Cliffs, NJ: Prentice Hall.

122. Vroom and Jago. *The New Leadership: Managing Participation in Organizations.*

123. Kenis, I. (1977). A cross-cultural study of personality and leadership. *Group and Organizational Studies, 2*(1), 49–60.

124. House, R. J., and Dessler, G. (1974). The Path-Goal theory of leadership: Some posthoc and a priori tests. In J. G. Hunt and L. L. Larson (Eds.), *Contingency Approaches to Leadership.* Carbondale, IL: Southwestern Illinois University Press.

125. Vroom, V. H. (1959). Some personality determinants of the effects of participation. *Journal of Abnormal and Social Psychology, 59*, 322–327.

126. Griffin, R. W. (1980). Relationships among individual, task design, and leader behavior variables. *Academy of Management Journal, 23*(4), 665–683.

127. Mitchell, T. R., Smyser, C. M., and Weed, S. E. (1975). Locus of control, supervision and work satisfaction. *Academy of Management Journal, 18,* 623–630.

128. House and Dessler. The Path-Goal theory of leadership: Some posthoc and a priori tests.

129. Lowin, A. (1968). Participative decision making: A model, literature, critique, and prescription for research. *Organizational Behavior and Human Performance, 3,* 68–106.

130. Miller, K. I., and Monge, P. R. (1986). Participation, satisfaction and productivity: A meta-analytic review. *Academy of Management Review, 29,* 727–753

131. Indvik. Path-goal theory of leadership: A meta-analysis.

132. Vroom, V., Grant, L. D., and Cotton, T. S. (1969). The consequences of social interaction in group problem solving. *Organizational Behavior and Human Performance, 44,* 77–95.

133. Shaw, M. E., and Blum, J. M. (1964). Effects of leadership style upon group performance as a function of task structure. *Journal of Personality and Social Psychology, 3,* 238–242.

134. Dunnette, M. D., Campbell, J. P., and Justaad, K. (1963). The effect of group participation on brainstorming effectiveness for two industrial samples. *Journal of Applied Psychology, 47,* 30–37.

135. Field, R. H. G. (1982). A test of the Vroom-Yetton Normative model of leadership. *Journal of Applied Psychology, 67,* 523–532.

136. Schuler, R. (1976). Participation with supervisor and subordinate authoritarianism: A Path-Goal theory reconciliation. *Administrative Science Quarterly, 21*(2), 320–325.

137. Wagner, J. A., III, and Gooding, R. Z. (1987). Shared influence and organizational behavior: A meta-analysis of situational variables expected to moderate participation-outcome relationships. *Academy of Management Journal, 30,* 524–541.

138. Bass, B. M., and Barrett, G. V. (1981). *People, Work and Organizations: An Introduction to Industrial and Organizational Psychology.* Boston: Allyn & Bacon.

139. Vroom and Jago. *The New Leadership: Managing Participation in Organizations.*

140. Hahn, C. P., and Trittipoe, T. G. (1961). *Situational Problems for Leadership Training: III. Review for Petty Officers of Leadership Research.* Washington, DC: Naval Contract Report, Institute for Research.

141. Vroom and Jago. *The New Leadership: Managing Participation in Organizations.*

142. Bass and Barrett. *People, Work and Organizations: An Introduction to Industrial and Organizational Psychology.*

143. Hahn and Trittipoe. *Situational Problems for Leadership Training: III. Review for Petty Officers of Leadership Research.*

144. Vroom. Some personality determinants of the effects of participation.

145. Kenis, I. (1978). Leadership behavior, subordinate personality, and satisfaction with supervision. *Journal of Psychology, 48*(1), 99–107.

146. Tosi, H. (1970). A reexamination of personality as a determinant of the effects of participation. *Personnel Psychology, 23,* 91–99.

147. Schuler. Participation with supervisor and subordinate authoritarianism: A Path-Goal theory reconciliation.

148. Dorfman, Howell, Cotton, and Tate. (1992). Leadership within the 'discontinuous hierarchy' structure of the military: Are effective leadership behaviors similar within and across command structures?

149. Vroom and Jago. Situation effects and levels of analysis in the study of leader participation.

7

Leader Reward and Punishment Behaviors

Learning Objectives

After reading this chapter, you should be able to do the following:

1. Explain how leaders can use rewards and punishments to have positive influences on followers.
2. Explain why leaders' use of rewards and punishments can sometimes have negative effects on followers.
3. Describe the skills and abilities that a leader needs to effectively use rewards and punishments.
4. Describe follower characteristics that can make leader reward and punishment behaviors highly effective, and characteristics that make them ineffective.
5. Describe organizational and task situations in which leader reward and punishment behaviors will likely be highly effective, and in which they may be ineffective.
6. Discuss how leaders can modify situations to increase the effectiveness of their reward and punishment behaviors.
7. Describe how leaders can modify followers' work situations to make them less dependent on the leader's reward and punishment behaviors.

▪▪▪ Examples of Effective Leader Reward and Punishment Behaviors

1. A supervisor established a policy that any member of the department who brought in a new client would earn 10 percent of the contracted fees.
2. In the McDonald's organization, the cook who makes the fastest high-quality hamburgers in the United States is awarded the title "All-American Hamburger Maker." This title implies great status in the company.
3. At the end of a very busy day, our supervisor told us we had done an excellent job and she appreciated our extra effort.
4. Because a head coach praised and rewarded players when they performed well, they were willing to accept his extreme reprimands and extra-grueling practice time when they performed poorly.

5. A supervisor expressed genuine disappointment to group members when their performance was well below standard.

6. A leader reduced a follower's rate of pay for repeated periods of low performance. This not only caused the punished follower to increase his efforts, but other followers also increased their performance to avoid similar punishment.[1–3]

The incidents described here are examples of effective leader reward and punishment behaviors.

⊓⊓⊓ Definition, Background, and Importance of Leader Reward and Punishment Behaviors

The use of rewards and punishments to influence followers' behavior is probably as old as the concept of leadership itself. Homer told of King Agamemnon promising rewards to Achilles, the great military leader, if he defeated the Trojans.[4] Military history is also filled with examples of followers being punished by their leaders for not being successful. Twentieth-century psychologists studied the impacts of rewards and punishments on experimental subjects and clarified how these influence strategies affected them.[5]

Early psychological research resulted in a principle of behavior known as the Law of Effect, which essentially states that a specific behavior will increase in frequency if it is followed by a reward. A corollary is that a behavior that is not followed by a reward (or is followed by a punishment) will decrease in frequency. The rationale for these principles is that people have innate tendencies to seek pleasure and avoid pain. Rewards bring pleasure and people consequently seek to attain them; punishments are painful and will therefore be avoided. Subsequent research findings from many areas of social behavior support these principles by showing that rewards and punishments can have strong effects on the behavior of animals and humans.[6–11]

In recent years, organizational researchers have focused on how leaders can effectively administer rewards and punishments in order to influence followers' behavior in specific ways. Leader reward behaviors provide desirable outcomes (positive reinforcers) for followers when they help achieve organizational goals.[12] Managers in high-performing organizations make a conscious effort to reward any action of organizational members that is valuable to the organization.[13] These managers recognize that tangible and intangible rewards that they control can help satisfy followers' needs for recognition, self-esteem, achievement, security, and physical necessities.

Because people enjoy being recognized and rewarded for a job well done, rewards improve followers' psychological reactions. A simple compliment or pat on the back are powerful rewards because they can be used frequently and on the spot with no time delay. In turn, followers' improved psychological reactions keep them committed to the organization. Providing meaningful rewards to followers when they perform well also gives them the information and incentives (motivation) they need to effectively direct their own behavior. The rewards tell followers what behaviors the leader sees as important, and they increase the chances followers will repeat those behaviors to obtain future rewards. When leaders reward good performance by followers they are putting their money where their mouth is, and this increases followers' confidence in the integrity of their leader and the organization.

Leader punishment behaviors provide *aversive* outcomes (punishment) or remove desirable outcomes when followers hinder achievement of organizational goals.[14] Many followers realize the importance of these behaviors when they are used carefully. A recent nationwide survey showed that almost 50 percent of workers believe that managers are too lenient with poor performers.[15] When leaders punish followers for rule violations, lack of effort, or poor performance, they provide followers with useful information on what behaviors the leader does not want. Followers generally recognize that it is useful to have information on what leaders want and what they do not want.

Formal leaders in organizations usually command numerous resources that can be used to reward or punish followers. Effective reward behaviors include giving special recognition to a follower whose work is outstanding, recommending a significant pay increase for someone whose performance is high, giving positive feedback when a follower performs well, acknowledging improvement in a follower's work, commending a follower who does better than average work, and informing the leader's boss when a follower does outstanding work.[16] Effective punishment behaviors are showing displeasure if a follower's work is below departmental standards, imposing fines for repeated rule violations, reprimanding a follower if his work is consistently below his capabilities, recommending that a follower receive no pay increase if his work is below standard, and giving undesirable job assignments to followers who are late to work.[17] Different leaders control different types of rewards and punishments, but all leaders use some type of rewards and punishments to influence their followers' behavior. Figures 7-1 and 7-2 summarize several types of leaders' reward and punishment behaviors.

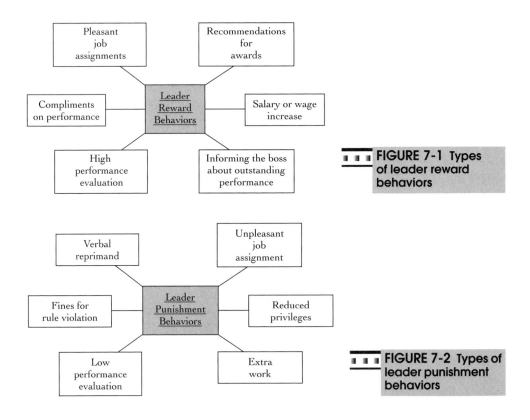

▪▪▪ **FIGURE 7-1 Types of leader reward behaviors**

▪▪▪ **FIGURE 7-2 Types of leader punishment behaviors**

▬▬ The Process of Social Exchange

The use of rewards and punishments by a leader has been described as a process of social exchange between the leader and followers.[18] The leader wants certain behavior from a follower such as attendance, a clean work area, responsiveness, or good performance. The leader also controls certain items that followers either want (rewards) or would like to avoid (punishments). An unwritten contract is established between the leader and followers that each will provide what the other wants. This contract is usually informal and is not specified in detail. As long as both perceive the contract as fair and the benefits to each party outweigh their costs, they will tend to have a mutually satisfying and productive relationship. This social exchange has been found in virtually all leader–follower relationships—soldiers and military leaders, voters and political bosses, street gang leaders and members, as well as managers and employees.[19]

Leader rewards and punishments may be tangible (a raise in pay or a demotion) or intangible (a compliment or a sarcastic remark). Both types can have significant impacts on followers. Research shows that organizational leaders use more intangible rewards to influence followers than tangible.[20] This is probably due to the ability of leaders to use intangible rewards such as praise, recognition, and appreciation on short notice. When a follower does something that the leader desires, an immediate compliment by the leader is very useful to assure the follower knows the leader is pleased with the behavior. When several of these informal rewards are followed by a tangible reward (such as a pay increase), the follower is effectively encouraged to repeat the desired behavior in the future. The Leadership in Action box describes an informal reward system used by military officers that was very effective.

■■■■■■■■■■■■■■■■■■■■■■■■■■■■■

LEADERSHIP IN ACTION
Informal Rewards in the Military

A management consultant was conducting a training session with a group of military officers. One colonel resisted the use of rewards to influence followers' behavior. Shortly thereafter, the colonel's superior officer, a general, decided to praise him for his handling of an important presentation. The general folded a piece of paper in half, wrote "Bravo" on the front, and wrote more specific complimentary remarks on the inside.

The general called the colonel in, praised him, and gave him the card. The colonel read the card, stood up abruptly, and walked out. The general was dumbfounded and thought he had offended the colonel. After a few minutes the general went to check on the colonel and found he had stopped at every office on the way out to show off his "Bravo" card. He was smiling and being congratulated by everyone who saw it. The colonel later printed his own recognition cards with "Wonderful" on the front.

SOURCE: Adapted from B. Nelson, *1001 Ways to Reward Employees.* New York: Workman Publishing, 1994.

■■■■■■■■■

▪▪▪ Contingent Rewards and Punishments

Effective use of rewards and punishments must be a consequence of specific follower behaviors. Another way of stating this is that the rewards and punishments must be contingent on the follower's behavior; that is, a follower must know that a compliment or pay raise is a direct result of specific behaviors or a high level of performance. Making the follower aware of this contingency allows the follower to focus efforts on repeating the behavior or performance to obtain the reward again. A similar process occurs with leader punishment. When the leader expresses dissatisfaction with a follower's poor attendance and states that repeated poor attendance will result in the follower's dismissal, the follower now has the knowledge needed to avoid further punishment. In both cases, making the reward or punishment contingent on specific follower behaviors and informing followers of this contingency provide the incentive and knowledge for followers to direct their behavior to attain rewards and avoid punishment.

In addition to clarifying the type of behavior or performance a leader prefers, tangible and intangible rewards also improve interpersonal relations and increase followers' satisfaction. Popular management writers have pointed out that everyone likes to be complimented and that tangible rewards are valued by followers.[21] It is probably best to give intangible rewards such as praise or compliments on an occasional basis. Complimenting a follower every day for coming to work on time will probably embarrass the follower or make the leader seem less than genuine. Some evidence from laboratory research indicates that tangible rewards provided by a leader may reduce the inherent satisfaction and motivation of followers when they complete certain challenging tasks. That is, in some research studies, tangible rewards appeared to cause followers to perform only for the tangible reward, not for the inherent interest in the task. However, this research is not well supported in real organizations in which people

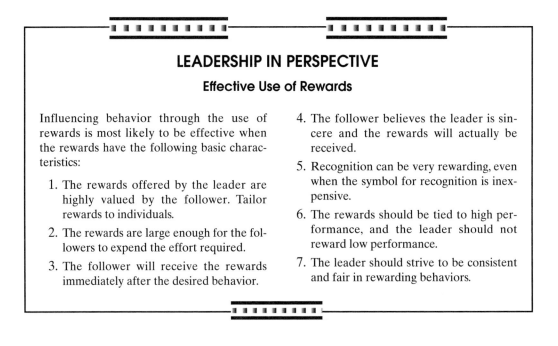

LEADERSHIP IN PERSPECTIVE
Effective Use of Rewards

Influencing behavior through the use of rewards is most likely to be effective when the rewards have the following basic characteristics:

1. The rewards offered by the leader are highly valued by the follower. Tailor rewards to individuals.

2. The rewards are large enough for the followers to expend the effort required.

3. The follower will receive the rewards immediately after the desired behavior.

4. The follower believes the leader is sincere and the rewards will actually be received.

5. Recognition can be very rewarding, even when the symbol for recognition is inexpensive.

6. The rewards should be tied to high performance, and the leader should not reward low performance.

7. The leader should strive to be consistent and fair in rewarding behaviors.

work for a living.[22,23] When people perform well at job tasks that they find interesting and challenging, they are usually happy and motivated to continue their good performance when a leader rewards them. The Leadership in Perspective box on guidelines for effective use of rewards provides leadership advice from research on leader reward behaviors.

Rewarding Desired Behavior

It is important for a leader to let followers know what tangible rewards are available and how they can obtain them. Leaders must be very careful about what is rewarded and how followers see the rewards as being distributed. One expert described numerous examples in which leaders say they want one thing and reward something else.[24] For example, organizational leaders may say they want followers who are original and think independently, but they reward those who conform. Orphanage directors say they want to place orphans with foster homes, but their salaries and budgets are based on the number of children living in the orphanage. In both of these situations, the rewards are not consistent with the stated goals. However, what is rewarded will be encouraged and probably repeated by those receiving the rewards. Leaders must carefully analyze which behaviors are rewarded and how the reward contingencies are viewed by followers. Table 7-1 provides examples of what leaders hope for and what often gets rewarded.

The Use of Punishment

Leaders' punishment behavior involves telling followers about possible punishments and administering them. The act of punishing involves imposing penalties and removing positive stimuli when followers demonstrate inappropriate or undesired behavior. B. F. Skinner was an influential psychologist and writer who argued that punishment was not effective, had undesirable side effects, and should be avoided. Some researchers and practicing leaders believe that punishment causes anxiety, passivity, withdrawal, or aggression toward the leader. Research reviews show, however, that these side effects are not common, and improvement in behavior is much more the rule.[25,26] Some have suggested that punishment is unethical or nonhumanitarian and reflects an eye-for-an-eye approach to leadership. This argument confuses punishment as a payback for past performance, with the current view of contingent punishment as future oriented, to help suppress or eliminate harmful behavior. Contingent punishment has been used effectively to suppress alcoholism and destructive workplace

TABLE 7-1 Examples of what is hoped for and what often gets rewarded

What Is Hoped For	*What Gets Rewarded*
Quality work	Fast work
Lasting solutions	Quick fixes
Creativity	Conformity
Cooperation	Aggressiveness
Simplification	Complication
Risk taking	Risk avoidance

behavior.[27-29] Leaders must evaluate the future consequences of undesirable or destructive behaviors if they do nothing to stop them. Many experts believe it is more humane to punish disruptive behavior and stop its recurrence than to ignore it and hope it will go away, thus allowing continued conflicts, hostility, and open insubordination to interrupt the activities of an entire group.

Some writers have suggested that punishment only eliminates undesirable behavior temporarily, until the threat of punishment is gone. This ignores the responsibility of leaders to regularly monitor follower activities and to reward the positive behaviors that replace those punished. Some managers believe that cohesion and esprit de corps are heightened if a group is subjected to harsh punishment. Fraternity initiations and basic military training seem to reflect this belief. Careful research shows, however, that harsh, noncontingent punishment *lowers* group cohesion, whereas less severe forms of punishment do not have this effect.[30]

When followers create conflict, repeatedly break rules, are hostile or insubordinate, or abuse drugs or alcohol on the job, some type of severe punishment is probably the most effective leadership strategy. In contrast, to eliminate lack of effort on the job, mild forms of punishment such as expressing disappointment or giving negative feedback are often adequate, especially when combined with promised rewards for good performance.

Refusing to comply with a leader's request is a common reason for imposing punishments such as a strong verbal reprimand, an unpleasant job assignment, or (if repeated) suspension or termination. A low level of effort resulting in low job performance will often be dealt with by withdrawal of privileges, not being considered for promotion, or a reduction in pay. For many followers, simply having one's poor performance or inappropriate behavior pointed out by the leader (known as negative

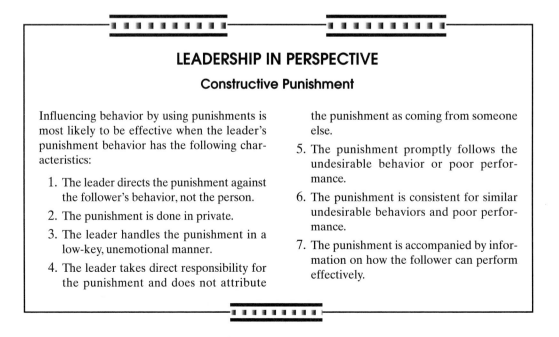

LEADERSHIP IN PERSPECTIVE
Constructive Punishment

Influencing behavior by using punishments is most likely to be effective when the leader's punishment behavior has the following characteristics:

1. The leader directs the punishment against the follower's behavior, not the person.

2. The punishment is done in private.

3. The leader handles the punishment in a low-key, unemotional manner.

4. The leader takes direct responsibility for the punishment and does not attribute the punishment as coming from someone else.

5. The punishment promptly follows the undesirable behavior or poor performance.

6. The punishment is consistent for similar undesirable behaviors and poor performance.

7. The punishment is accompanied by information on how the follower can perform effectively.

feedback) is sufficiently unpleasant to change the follower's behavior. Being told why their behavior was not appropriate and how to perform correctly in the future can be especially helpful to inexperienced followers. But followers must also be told what they have done correctly and that the leader recognizes and appreciates this behavior. Contingent reward behavior should be used with punishments whenever possible.

Management by exception is one type of contingent punishment behavior in which the leader monitors performance and does not acknowledge or reward desirable behaviors, but only intervenes with directiveness and punishment when followers do not perform well. This approach has *not* proven effective in industrial organizations, although there is some evidence it can be useful in military organizations.[31,32] The Leadership in Perspective box on guidelines for constructive punishment summarizes effective leadership approaches for using contingent punishment.

▪▪▪ Ineffective Leader Rewards and Punishments

Not all reward and punishment behaviors by leaders are effective. Ineffective use of leader reward behaviors are demonstrated by the following actions:

1. A leader was just as likely to praise a follower when he performed poorly as when he performed well. At first, followers liked getting the leader's praise, but it had no effect on their behavior. Because they had not earned the praise, after a while they began to view the leader as incompetent.
2. The owner-manager of a small retail business awarded bonuses equally to all employees whenever he felt he could afford it. The manager hoped the bonuses would encourage followers to increase their efforts and raise performance. But because the bonuses were not contingent on individual or group performance, employees had no way of knowing when or why they were awarded. The bonuses therefore had no effect on performance.

Ineffective use of leader punishment behaviors are demonstrated by the following actions:

1. A supervisor expressed extreme displeasure and criticized a follower's work, even though the follower had performed well compared to other group members.
2. A leader repeatedly punished his followers with severe verbal reprimands, unpleasant task assignments, and extra work. Because no followers were spared from the penalties and they were administered for trivial actions, the followers came to view them as part of the job, and they lost any impact they may have had if administered more selectively.
3. A leader always punished followers in public. The leader believed that embarrassing followers in front of their peers was an effective way to change their behavior. Followers reacted by resenting the leader and resisting her directions whenever they could.[33]

As the above examples show, rewards and punishments can be misused so that they have no effect or severely damaging effects. In most of these examples, rewards and punishments were not provided contingent on followers' performance, the punishment was excessive, or was not done in private. When leader rewards and punishments are not administered contingent on follower behaviors or performance, they have little

LEADERSHIP SELF-ASSESSMENT
Using Reward and Punishment Behaviors

Instructions: Indicate the extent you would engage in the following reward and punishment behaviors to influence followers. Use the following scale: (5) very frequently; (4) frequently; (3) occasionally; (2) seldom; (1) almost never.

1. I would give positive feedback to my followers when they perform well.	1 2 3 4 5
2. I would show my displeasure with followers when their work is below acceptable standards.	1 2 3 4 5
3. I would praise followers frequently, regardless of their performance.	1 2 3 4 5
4. I would be quick to acknowledge an improvement in the quality of a follower's work.	1 2 3 4 5
5. I would sometimes criticize a follower's work even if it is above acceptable standards.	1 2 3 4 5
6. When followers' work is not up to par, I would point it out to them.	1 2 3 4 5
7. Even when followers perform poorly on the job, I would still commend them.	1 2 3 4 5
8. I would reprimand followers now and then, even if they performed well, just to keep them in line.	1 2 3 4 5
9. I would offer a bonus to all followers who exceed performance standards for quantity and quality.	1 2 3 4 5

Interpretation: If you rated items 1, 4, and 9 as 4 or 5, you would probably use leader contingent reward behaviors effectively. If you rated items 2 and 6 as 4 or 5, you would probably use leader contingent punishment behaviors effectively. If you rated items 3 and 7 as 4 or 5, you would probably use noncontingent reward behavior. If you rated items 5 and 8 as 4 or 5, you would probably use noncontingent punishment behavior. Contingent reward and punishment behaviors are much more effective at influencing followers' behavior than noncontingent reward and punishment.

SOURCE: Adapted from research questionnaires originally developed by P. M. Podsakoff, P. W. Dorfman, J. P. Howell, and W. D. Todor. Leader reward and punishment behaviors: A preliminary test of a culture-free style of leadership effectiveness. *Advances in International Comparative Management*, 2, 95–138.

effect or a detrimental effect. The detrimental effect is especially pronounced when a leader administers noncontingent punishment behaviors.

▪▪▪ Skills, Traits, and Sources of Power for Rewarding and Punishing Followers

Leaders can develop behavioral traits, skills, and sources of power to help them use reward and punishment behaviors effectively. Leaders who *prefer to make their own decisions* and *take responsibility* for those decisions are often inclined to use rewards to influence followers. These leader traits are often accompanied by a high amount of *self-confidence* from the leader.[34,35] Leaders usually develop these personal factors through leadership experience, and these qualities allow leaders to act based on their own assessments of situations. They actively monitor followers' behavior and performance and use the information they obtain to effectively reward or punish followers.

Of course, leaders must be skilled at *accurately monitoring and measuring followers' performance* in order to provide rewards contingently. Performance evaluation is a notoriously difficult process to carry out accurately. Followers doing repetitive tasks are usually more easily evaluated than managerial or professional workers doing complex technical or service-oriented tasks. Thus, the leader must develop performance measures for followers that inspire their confidence. Skills at evaluating followers' performance are developed through experience as well as formal training.

Effective leaders often develop several sources of power to help them use reward and punishment behaviors. When leaders have *reward power* (control over important tangible rewards such as bonuses or promotions), they can use those rewards in exchange for certain follower behaviors and performances. High-level managers typically control more tangible rewards than low-level managers, although middle- and low-level supervisors usually control some tangible rewards. Leaders at all levels control intangible or social rewards, such as compliments and personal recognition. A leader's *coercive power* (control over important punishments such as demotion or termination) can be used to influence followers through punishment behaviors. Leaders in some organizations have more control over tangible punishments than in other organizations. Nearly all leaders control intangible and social punishments, such as negative performance feedback. Persistent reminders by a leader to carry out a task may remind the follower of the leader's coercive power without any actual mention of punishment. Today, leaders' abilities to use physical and many tangible punishments are highly restricted. But even the captain of an intramural softball team has the power to cheer for a player who gets an important base hit, or to suggest to another player the need for work on base-running skills.

A leader who holds a high-level position in an organization has a high amount of *legitimate power* that can be used to influence followers. Most followers are very respectful of leaders who work at high levels and respond quickly to their legitimate requests. These leaders also usually control major rewards and punishments that are important to followers. One recent study showed that a small amount of leadership behavior by a high-level leader had a much stronger effect on followers than a large amount of the same leadership behavior by a low-level leader.[36] The leader's legitimate power is one important factor that helps a leader use rewards and punishments effectively.

Leaders' *resource/connection power* can also be developed to help them use rewards and punishments to influence followers. When leaders cultivate contacts with high-level managers, they can sometimes obtain resources they can use to reward followers. Leaders often develop extensive networks in the organization to provide the political influence they may need to obtain approval for a follower's promotion. When followers are aware that their leader has extensive contacts at higher levels in the organization, they often view potential punishments as more significant because leaders at higher levels may become involved. This increases the potential impact of their leader's punishment behaviors. Figure 7-3 summarizes the traits, skills, and power sources that can be developed to help a leader effectively use rewards and punishments.

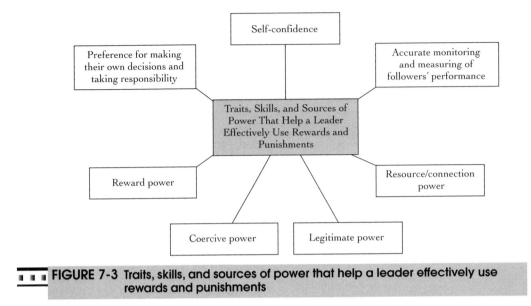

▪▪▪ **FIGURE 7-3** Traits, skills, and sources of power that help a leader effectively use rewards and punishments

▪▪▪ Facilitating and Limiting Conditions for Leader Rewards and Punishments

Two organizational factors can reduce or constrain a leader's ability to control important rewards: (1) labor contracts and civil service agreements that specify pay levels for employees; and (2) organizational reward systems, policies, or procedures that define in advance when employees will receive rewards, or that require time-consuming formal approvals of tangible rewards by upper management.[37] Leaders should probably emphasize intangible rewards and other leadership behaviors to influence followers in these situations.

As with leaders' reward behaviors, legal restrictions may significantly limit the use of certain types of punishment that were common in the past. For example, employment laws, previous court decisions, labor contracts, and civil service agreements severely limit managers' ability to dismiss employees. Legal limitations also exist for other types of disciplinary actions, such as demotions or suspension without pay.

Certain leadership characteristics may also limit a leader's use of contingent punishment behaviors. For example, one military study of multiracial groups showed that when both leaders and followers were the same race (black or white), the leader was less likely to use punishment than when leader and followers were of a different race.[38] Some researchers have found that male leaders are more inclined to use contingent reward and punishment behaviors than female leaders, but other studies show no differences between male and female leaders in using these behaviors.[39–42] More studies are needed on the effects of leaders' race and gender before definite conclusions are possible. The Leadership in Action box describes how one organizational leader used rewards to obtain high performance at Motorola.

LEADERSHIP IN ACTION

Robert Galvin, Past Chairman of Motorola

Robert Galvin's use of rewards at Motorola was partially responsible for the company's rise to the top of the semiconductor industry. Employees in Motorola's self-managed work teams can earn up to 41 percent of their base salaries in bonuses for meeting certain goals. According to Galvin, the only way the reward structure can work is if there is a clear and complementary relationship between employee performance and rewards. Workers receive financial rewards for innovation and for productive manufacturing of state-of-the-art technology that generates high profitability.

Galvin understood that employees would not take participation in decision making seriously unless they could share the rewards. Galvin believed that rewards should go to those who independently find imaginative ways to support the goals and philosophy of the corporation. For example, a production worker discovered that 10 percent of the screws being used broke during production. This worker took the initiative to call the vendor and work through the problem. At the end of the year, the company had realized considerable savings, which the workers shared. Another employee discovered that 40 percent of the gold used in their semiconductors was wasted during production. After eliminating over 50 places in which gold had been lost, the company reduced the waste to zero and shared the savings with the employees. Motorola established a reward program for production workers and administrative staff. For example, a group of secretarial workers pooled together all their loose office supplies and harvested a year's worth of supplies. Motorola shared the savings with employees for not having to buy office supplies.

Galvin also believed in rewarding entrepreneurial behavior, long-term thinking, and customer satisfaction. To encourage long-term thinking, Motorola measures and rewards managerial performance over as long as a six-year time frame. Galvin rewarded entrepreneurial behavior by promoting employees who successfully challenged inappropriate assumptions made by top management.

Galvin also used contingent punishments. When an internal audit revealed bookkeeping discrepancies in a Motorola sales department, Galvin directed 20 managers to make retribution by contributing $8,500 to charity. The results of Galvin's reward and punishment structure at Motorola included an increase in product quality and productivity, improvements in safety and cleanliness, need for less staff due to employees' willingness to carry an extra workload and share in the rewards, cooperation between shifts to keep production running smoothly, and decreased turnover as fewer people quit in search of greener pastures.

SOURCES: R. Galvin, What a message. *Across the Board,* 34(8), 1997, 12–14; J. O'Toole. *Vanguard Management.* New York: Berkley Books, 1985; and J. O'Toole. *Leading Change.* San Francisco: Jossey-Bass, 1995.

▪▪▪ Effects of Leader Rewards and Punishments

Followers enjoy leaders' reward behaviors because they help satisfy followers' needs for recognition, self-esteem, achievement, security, and physical necessities. When rewards and punishments are provided contingent on followers' performance, followers are aware of what the leader wants and does not want. In order to administer rewards and punishments contingently, leaders must monitor and evaluate followers' behaviors and performances. Monitoring and evaluation can have positive impacts on followers' psychological reactions and behavioral outcomes. The effects of leader reward and punishment behaviors are further described in this section.

Effects of Leader Reward Behaviors

Numerous studies of leaders' contingent reward behavior show that this behavior results in improvements in follower performance.[43-46] This favorable impact is also supported by research on behavior modification in organizations[47,48] and studies of leaders over time.[49-52] Other studies show the positive effects of contingent reward behavior on group productivity, enthusiasm, and cohesiveness,[53,54] and other follower behaviors including compliance with the leader's requests.[55-57] The popular management literature also indicates that tangible and intangible rewards are used extensively in effective organizations.[58,59]

Some writers have suggested that if leaders use reward power extensively, followers will view their relationship with the leader as strictly economic, and they will seldom do more than is required for the reward. They further suggest that extensive use of rewards will erode loyalty and commitment to the leader and the organization. However, many studies show that a leader's contingent reward behavior improves followers' psychological reactions, such as satisfaction with supervision, organizational commitment, and job clarity.[60-62] These findings and the fact that leader reward behavior also increases followers' ratings of their leader, imply that rewards do not erode followers' attitudes toward the leader or the organization.[63-65] Followers are generally happier with their leader and with those around them when they are well rewarded.

These positive effects assume rewards are provided contingent on follower behavior or performance. Studies of leader reward behaviors that are not contingent on follower performance generally show no effects or decreases in followers' psychological reactions and performance.[66]

There is a popular belief among experts on international leadership and management that a leader's contingent reward behavior is effective only in certain types of cultures. These cultures are usually described as individualist. Individualist cultures are composed of loosely knit social frameworks in which people are expected to look out for themselves, and emphasis is placed on individual initiative and independence (the United States is one example). In these cultures, leaders are assumed to spend a lot of time monitoring individual followers' behavior and performance, and guiding and controlling followers by appealing to their individual self-interests through contingent rewards and punishments. Cultures that are not individualist are often described as collectivist. These cultures have tight-knit social frameworks in which various groups (families, clans, or work groups) look after their members (the People's Republic of China is an example). Individuals in collectivist cultures are expected to look out for the group first (not themselves), and individual initiative and independence are not valued as highly as they are in individualist cultures. Here, individual guidance and control are maintained by group loyalty, not individual self-interest.

The belief that a leader's contingent rewards are effective only in individualist cultures has been contradicted by recent research findings from organizations in collectivist countries such as Taiwan, Japan, South Korea, and Mexico. These findings concern *intangible* (social) rewards, such as a leader's compliments, praise, and recognition for followers' good performance. Even in collectivist cultures, when leaders provide intangible rewards of this type contingent on followers' performance, they result in improvements in followers' psychological reactions, and sometimes performance.[67,68] These same results have been found in highly individualist business organizations in the United States. This evidence needs further corroboration, but it appears that performance-contingent social rewards by the leader have universally positive impacts on followers in both collectivist and individualist cultures. It may be that a leader's contingent *tangible* rewards have less impact in collectivist countries than in individualist countries. This possibility must be carefully tested in studies in both types of cultures before final conclusions are reached.

Effects of Leader Punishment Behaviors

Some early studies showed that a leader's use of punishment decreased followers' satisfaction with their leader,[69,70] or produced hostility, absenteeism, withdrawal, tension, and passivity in followers.[71–75] However, more recent studies show that contingent punishment behavior does *not* decrease follower satisfaction or performance,[76–78] probably because followers view contingent punishment as fair. In fact, several researchers have found that leaders' contingent punishment behavior can actually improve follower or group performance (primarily by eliminating undesirable behaviors) when used in combination with contingent reward behavior.[79–83] It appears that a leader's contingent punishment should only be used along with a liberal amount of contingent reward behavior by the leader.

A totally different pattern of results has occurred when leader punishment is not contingent on follower performance. This type of punishment often results in *decreases* in followers' satisfaction with work, supervision, and coworkers, and sometimes decreases in performance, commitment to the organization, role clarity, and group cohesion.[84–87] Followers react very negatively when they are punished for reasons unrelated to their behavior or performance.

Research evidence also suggests leader contingent punishment behaviors have an impact only in certain cultures. Contingent social punishment (such as reprimands or negative feedback) have had almost no effects on followers' psychological reactions or performance in studies of organizations in collectivist cultures.[88] In contrast, comparison studies from the United States found that contingent social punishment behaviors improved followers' organizational commitment and job clarity. It thus appears from this limited evidence that leaders' contingent punishment is primarily useful in individualist cultures. When leaders administer punishments that are not contingent on followers' behavior or performance, followers' reactions are universally negative. Table 7-2 summarizes the major effects of leaders' contingent rewards and punishments. The Leadership in Perspective box on punishment and moral leadership shows how this leadership behavior can result in followers' respect and trust.

▪▪▪ Situational Dynamics of Leader Rewards and Punishments

Although contingent reward and punishment behaviors often result in increased levels of performance and better attitudes, specific situational and follower characteristics may cause these leadership behaviors to have greater or lesser impact. The Leadership

TABLE 7-2 Major effects of leaders' contingent rewards and punishments

Follower Benefits	*Group or Organizational Benefits*
Improved performance	Improved productivity
Compliance with requests	Increased enthusiasm
Satisfaction with supervision	Cohesiveness
Commitment to the organization	
Role clarity	

Self-Assessment: Diagnosing Situations for Leader Rewards and Punishments describes when leaders' reward or punishment behaviors may or may not be appropriate.

A leader's contingent reward behaviors would probably be very effective in three of the situations described in the self-assessment. Items 1, 4, and 7 all include situational factors that make reward behaviors a useful influence strategy for leaders. The situations described in items 3 and 8 reflect a need for some type of punishment behavior by the leader. Here, the followers' behavior requires correction, and followers are likely to respond to reasonable punishments in a mature manner. Items 2, 5, and 6 describe situations in which neither reward nor punishment behaviors by the leader are likely to be effective with followers. Either the leader is unable to do a good job at evaluating

LEADERSHIP IN PERSPECTIVE
Punishment and Moral Leadership

Some managers do not believe in punishment. They believe that punishment hurts followers' feelings, and makes them resent and resist future leader requests. These managers maintain that rewards and other leadership behaviors are all that is necessary to obtain needed behavior from followers. But destructive follower behaviors sometimes require strong and immediate action by the leader. These follower behaviors can be damaging to other followers or the organization, and punishment is usually the quickest way to stop the damage and correct the behavior.

One example is sexual harassment, which causes personal physical or psychological harm to employees, damages careers, and creates legal liabilities for managers and organizations. Individuals who commit sexual harassment do not usually stop this behavior on their own. They often derive personal satisfaction from their power over others and do not want to relinquish this power. Leaders must make it clear to followers that sexual harassment will not be tolerated through training programs that define and give examples of inappropriate behavior, clear policies and procedures on reporting it, and the consequences (punishment) to those who sexually harass others. When incidents occur that are substantiated, leaders must follow through with the specified punishment to assure that everyone knows the leader is serious. Leaders who take firm punitive action in these situations develop a reputation for high moral conduct and promote trust and respect from followers.

LEADERSHIP SELF-ASSESSMENT

Diagnosing Situations for Leader Rewards and Punishments

Instructions: Place an "R" next to those situations in which you believe leader *reward* behavior can be effective in influencing followers; place a "P" next to those in which you think leader *punishment* behavior can be effective; and place an "N" next to those in which you believe *neither* of these leadership behaviors will be effective.

1. _____ The leader controls rewards that are important to followers, and has a reputation for administering those rewards in a fair and impartial manner.

2. _____ Followers are highly skilled design engineers doing complex work, and good performance measures for their work have not been developed at this time.

3. _____ The leader is held in high esteem by followers, and in the past has rewarded them for good performance. Recently, however, they have refused to follow the leader's directions on two consecutive assignments, resulting in poor performance.

4. _____ Followers' job performance is a direct result of their effort on the job.

5. _____ Followers work at locations that are physically distant from their leader, making it difficult for the leader to accurately gauge their performance on a regular basis.

6. _____ Followers are highly trained professionals who derive intense satisfaction from their work and place little value on the rewards controlled by the leader.

7. _____ The leader possesses a high degree of expertise at followers' work tasks, and has clearly explained to followers the criteria for good performance.

8. _____ A follower has been warned about demonstrating impolite and abusive behavior with other workers and customers, but this behavior has continued. The follower indicated she understands the necessity of treating coworkers and customers in a considerate manner, and she seems to be an emotionally stable individual.

---

followers' performance (making it very difficult to use rewards and punishments effectively), or followers are motivated by other factors that can substitute for leaders' rewards and punishments. Situational and follower characteristics that make leaders' rewards and punishments effective, ineffective, or unnecessary are described in the following sections.

▪▪▪ Situational Factors That Enhance the Effectiveness of Leader Reward and Punishment Behaviors

Certain situational and follower characteristics can increase or enhance the impact of leader's reward and punishment behaviors on followers' psychological reactions and behaviors. Practicing leaders are often very interested in these factors because they can make followers more responsive.

Task, Organizational, and Follower Characteristics

When leaders have *control over substantial tangible rewards,* they are a highly effective influence strategy because followers believe in the leader's ability to provide valued rewards that have been promised.[89,90] The *leader's rank* in the organization is closely related to control over rewards because higher-ranking leaders often have larger and more varied rewards at their disposal. A compliment or appreciative comment from a high-level leader can be very satisfying and encouraging to an employee who seldom interacts with anyone other than an immediate supervisor or coworkers. In general, control over valued rewards and high rank can enhance the effects of the leader's reward behavior on followers.[91]

Several factors related to the performance-appraisal process increase the effects of leaders' contingent reward behavior on followers' job performance. These factors especially increase the impacts of tangible rewards. Leader-provided tangible rewards have an especially strong impact on followers' performance when (1) *good measures of follower performance* are used by leaders to administer contingent rewards; (2) the *rewards and performance criteria are clearly explained* before the evaluation; and (3) *rewards are distributed fairly and in a timely fashion,* rather than arbitrarily or a long time after followers' performance.[92,93]

When leaders are recognized as experts in followers' tasks, this tends to increase the impact of the leader's contingent reward behavior on followers' psychological reactions, including their commitment to the organization, satisfaction with work, and job clarity.[94] *Leaders' expertise* increases followers' respect for the leader and their responsiveness to the leader's influence. When followers belong to a *cohesive work group,* the impact of a leader's contingent rewards on followers' performance can be enhanced.[95,96] As described in earlier chapters, the effect of a cohesive work group on the leader's influence depends on the groups' performance norms, but when the norms are positive and encourage high performance, the results are usually favorable.

When *rewards are valued and expected* by followers, the leader's reward behavior makes an especially large impact.[97–99] Moreover, *when followers' performance is determined by their skill and effort,* a leader's *contingent reward* behavior will have strong effects on followers' performance.[100] These situational factors are present at the Lincoln Electric Company in Cleveland, Ohio, where highly skilled employees are paid based strictly on the amount of good products they produce. They also receive quarterly bonuses from company profits. The size of bonus for each employee is determined by several indicators of their individual performance. Employees at Lincoln work very hard and are quite productive because they know they will be well compensated for their effort.

Regarding situational factors that increase the effectiveness of leaders' contingent punishment behavior, research showed that when individuals viewed a leader as having high status and esteem, they reacted more favorably to punitive behavior than when the leader had low status and esteem.[101] Thus, in this situation, the *leader's status and esteem* enhanced the effectiveness of punishment behavior, although another writer suggested that overuse of punishment by the leader may eventually undermine status and esteem.[102]

A *large variety of tasks* performed by followers also may enhance the impact of a leader's contingent punishment behavior.[103] In one line of research, which involved government workers, followers probably found contingent punishment to be helpful in clarifying appropriate and inappropriate behavior on the wide variety of tasks they perform. Task variety has not been studied extensively as a leadership enhancer, but this finding indicates it is worthy of more research. As indicated earlier, when leader *contingent punishment behavior was used concurrently with contingent reward behavior,* the effects of both were increased.[104]

Researchers have proposed several other leadership activities as potential enhancers of leader punishment behavior.[105] The leadership activities include assuring the punishment is consistent with organizational rules and policies, administering it in private and making it appropriately severe, allowing followers to express their opinions and appeal tangible punishments, and assuring that the leader's demeanor is not unpleasant. These behavioral factors are consistent with psychological research on learning, and leaders who keep them in mind are likely to yield positive results from their punishment behaviors.

Follower characteristics that may enhance the impacts of a leader's punishment behavior include the follower's belief in a just world (a belief that people get what they deserve), their positive affectivity (a general positive outlook and self-concept), and their effective emotional coping behaviors (lack of worry or negative thinking, not interpreting negative feedback personally, maintaining an optimistic and effective approach to life). Followers with these characteristics are probably mature individuals who will interpret reasonable punishments as useful feedback they can use to guide their future behavior. Each of these factors is worthy of future research to confirm its enhancing effects. Figure 7-4 summarizes the enhancers of leader reward and punishment behaviors from actual research. The Leadership in Perspective box: Rewards and Punishments in Team Sports shows how specific follower and situational characteristics enhance a coach's influence.

LEADERSHIP IN PERSPECTIVE
Rewards and Punishments in Team Sports

Basketball, football, and baseball players love to play their game. The best performing players on a team are normally part of the starting lineup. Therefore, being chosen as a starter is one of the most valued rewards a coach can give a player. The next most important reward a coach controls is playing time. The players who contribute the most to a team usually play the most minutes or innings in a game. The high value players place on starting and playing time, and the control of these factors by the coach, both enhance the coach's effects on the players' behavior and performance. However, because coaches can also withhold these two factors, they can be used to punish players for inappropriate behavior. Players are often pulled from the starting lineup or their playing time is reduced for missing practice, breaking team rules, lack of hustle, or poor performance. Effective coaches use the starting lineup and playing time as rewards for maximum effort and high performance and as punishments for inappropriate behavior by team members.

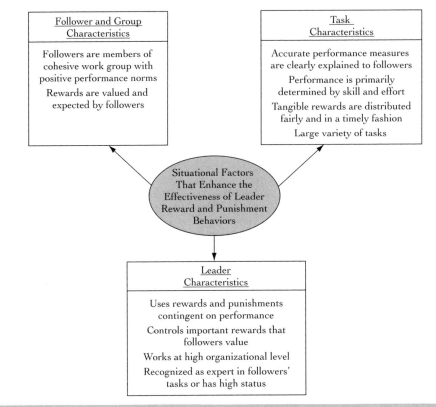

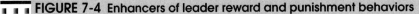

▐▐▐▐ **FIGURE 7-4** Enhancers of leader reward and punishment behaviors

Influencing Situations to Make Leader Rewards and Punishments More Effective

One set of factors that enhances the impacts of leader reward behavior deals with followers' performance and how it is evaluated by the leader. To assure that rewards are contingent on followers' performance, the leader must obtain and use accurate performance measures. These performance measures may be included in the organization's performance-evaluation system, or the leader may create them. Performance measures should be clearly explained, and the rewards identified for specific behaviors or performance levels. When followers achieve desired performance levels, rewards should be provided in an equitable and timely fashion.

Leaders who are at low levels in an organization and control few tangible rewards may attempt to negotiate with their superiors to obtain more reward power. They can also assure followers that they control some valued rewards (such as task assignments or work schedules). If leaders talk frankly with followers and think about their desires, values, and the work situation, they can often identify innovative and valued rewards. If these rewards are used along with intangible social rewards such as praise, they can overcome constraints on leaders' power to control other tangible rewards and enhance the leaders' impacts.[106]

Leaders can increase their task expertise by continually updating their skills and knowledge, and making themselves available to assist followers with task problems. They can encourage development of cohesive work groups by helping groups succeed at work tasks, providing resources for groups, and increasing opportunities and rewards for follower interaction. These strategies will increase the leaders' perceived expertise and cohesion among followers, and also will likely encourage group norms that are supportive of the leader. These factors should enhance the impacts of the leader's contingent reward behavior. The Leadership in Action box describes how different organizational leaders reward followers.

Increasing perceived expertise can also increase the leader's status and esteem in the eyes of followers. Superiors can increase a leader's status by making public statements about a leader's competence and accomplishments, as well as championing the leader to those outside the leader's group. These strategies can enhance both reward *and* punishment behaviors. If leaders use liberal doses of contingent reward behavior (tangible and intangible) along with carefully selected punishment behaviors, they can increase the impacts of both these behavioral strategies.

In implementing enhancers of contingent punishment behavior, leaders should assure that followers view punishments as contingent on their actions or performance. Making punishment consistent in all situations and for all followers also helps assure a maximum effect from the punishment. Consistency tells followers when to expect punishment, and they can use this knowledge to control their own behavior and avoid punishment.

LEADERSHIP IN ACTION
How Leaders Can Reward Followers

The following are examples of rewards used by leaders in several organizations:

A Pat-on-the-Back Award is given by managers to employees at Busch Gardens who do an outstanding job. Receiving the award is recorded in the employee's personnel file.

At Amway Corporation, employees who are commended in customers' letters are sent flowers.

When an employee at Pacific Gas & Electric has a noteworthy achievement, the manager rings a ship's bell.

As a reward for outstanding performance at South Carolina Federal Financial Services, the top managers serve lunch to the high-performance employees.

All employees who worked on the first Apple Macintosh computer had their signatures placed on the inside of all the Macintoshes manufactured.

The founder of IBM, Thomas J. Watson Sr., wrote checks on the spot to employees who were doing an outstanding job.

Managers at Bell Atlantic named cellular telephone sites after highly productive employees.

Mary Kay Cosmetics rewards the top independent sellers with pink Cadillacs and diamond rings.

▮▮▮ Situational Factors That Neutralize Leader Reward and Punishment Behaviors

Several situational characteristics can neutralize the effectiveness of a leader's contingent reward and punishment behaviors.

Task, Organizational, and Follower Characteristics

A *large spatial distance* between the leader and followers has neutralized the impact of leader contingent rewards on followers' psychological reactions and job performance. This distance is common in many service organizations, and its neutralizing effect has been found in studies of government workers in the United States and Taiwan, and in hospitals, universities, insurance companies, and public utilities in the United States.[107–109] Individuals who work at locations distant from their leader often have a high degree of job autonomy (independence from their leader). Examples of these types of workers are salespeople, technicians, construction workers, military personnel, other service and professional workers, and increasing numbers of individuals telecommuting from their homes. It is often difficult for a leader to regularly gauge performance and to reward followers in these situations. Contingent reward behavior may therefore not be especially effective. Although this limitation may apply especially to nontangible social rewards, leaders in these situations should probably emphasize other leadership behaviors to influence followers.

The existence of a closely knit *cohesive work group with antileader norms* can neutralize the impact of a leader's reward behavior on followers' satisfaction with work, satisfaction with coworkers, and job clarity.[110,111] When individuals work in a group with mutual support and camaraderie, they can derive many of their social rewards from coworkers rather than the leader. If followers do not value their leader's input, they may actually develop a norm of noncooperation with the leader. As noted earlier, however, a cohesive group can also enhance the effect of leader reward behavior when group members share a positive productivity norm.

Studies have also shown that a high degree of *organizational formalization* can neutralize the impact of a leader's contingent reward behavior on followers' performance and satisfaction.[112,113] Organizational formalization can also substitute for certain leadership behaviors. Written plans, goals, and guidelines can clarify task requirements for followers and facilitate effective performance, which can sometimes produce follower satisfaction without rewards from leaders. This situational characteristic is an important possible neutralizer or substitute for reward behavior, and must be carefully considered by leaders when attempting to use rewards to influence followers.

One other situational neutralizer of leader reward behavior has been suggested, although no studies have confirmed its effect. When followers' performance is largely determined by factors outside their control (such as bad luck, poor weather, machine breakdowns, or errors by other people), then the impact of leaders' contingent reward behavior is likely decreased.[114] This suggested neutralizer makes sense because a leader's rewards can affect only factors that are under followers' control. However, the effects of these situational factors are likely temporary. We suspect that once performance is under the control of the follower, a leader's contingent reward behavior will again become effective for influencing followers.

Two follower characteristics have also been noted as neutralizers of leaders' contingent reward behavior. First, *followers' indifference toward organizational rewards* can decrease the effect of leader rewards on follower performance.[115–117] Logically, if followers do not value the tangible or intangible rewards offered by a leader, those rewards will have little effect on their attitudes and behavior. Second, followers' *intrinsic task satisfaction* decreased the impact of a leader's contingent rewards on follower satisfaction in one study.[118] This finding should be further investigated.

Several writers have proposed other follower characteristics that may neutralize the impacts of a leader's contingent reward behavior. First, when followers do not believe they can perform well enough to receive rewards, they may not respond to a leader's promised rewards.[119] Second, if followers believe rewards are provided in a capricious and arbitrary manner and are not based on an accurate assessment of their performance, they will probably not respond to them.[120,121] These suggested neutralizers are consistent with research on motivation in organizations.[122] Future research is needed to verify their neutralizing effect on leaders' contingent reward behavior.

Two situational factors act as neutralizers of leaders' contingent punishment behavior. A *large spatial distance* between a leader and followers can decrease the impact of contingent punishment on followers' satisfaction.[123] Also, when workers have an opportunity to interact with one another in the leader's absence or *observe others disobeying the leader,* they are less likely to be influenced by a leader's punishment behavior.[124] It appears that spatial distance and a highly interactive (cohesive) group of followers with antileader norms may have the same neutralizing effects on a leader's contingent punishment behavior as on contingent reward behavior. Figure 7-5 summarizes situational factors that neutralize leader reward and punishment behaviors.

FIGURE 7-5 Situational factors that neutralize leader reward and punishment behaviors

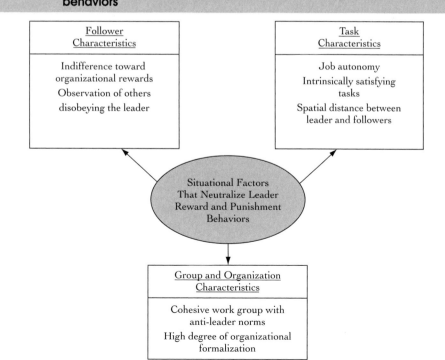

LEADERSHIP IN ACTION
Leading Social Workers

Social workers often work in poor urban or rural areas with high crime rates. They provide advice, counseling, and representation for individuals and families who need help in seeking employment, collecting welfare, or obtaining other social services. They usually meet with clients on their own with no manager present to administer organizational rewards or punishments. The type of individual who becomes a social worker is not motivated primarily by leaders' rewards and punishments. These individuals often feel a calling to help the less fortunate in our society. They undergo consider-

able formal education and practical training to prepare them to work independently. This education and training socializes them to take professional pride in the service they provide. They get considerable intrinsic satisfaction from helping their clients. These factors usually overcome any need for leaders' rewards and punishments to influence social workers to do their best for clients. Leaders in this situation should probably provide continuous training and development opportunities and resources to help the social workers serve their clients most effectively.

Overcoming Factors That Neutralize Leaders' Rewards and Punishments

When followers work autonomously or at a distance from the leader, it is difficult for the leader to adequately monitor their performance and behavior in order to administer contingent rewards and punishments. It is often best in these situations to foster development of followers' professionalism, work experience, intrinsic task satisfaction, additional training, and education. These substitutes for leaders' rewards and punishments are described in the next section of this chapter. The leader will also likely rely on other leadership behaviors that do not require continuous monitoring, such as supportive and charismatic ones.

When cohesive work groups with antileader norms, intrinsically satisfying tasks, or indifference toward organizational rewards neutralize leader reward behaviors, leaders can try to foster a professional pride in followers so that they will perform at high levels without regular monitoring and contingent rewards. Additional training or group development approaches may transform these follower and group characteristics into useful substitutes for leaders' rewards and punishments, providing motivation and guidance independent of the leader. The Leadership in Action box: Leading Social Workers describes how situational factors that neutralize leaders' rewards and punishments can be overcome.

Situational Factors That Substitute for Leader Reward and Punishment Behaviors

Some studies have shown that situational characteristics can act as substitutes for leaders' contingent reward and punishment behaviors. Several characteristics of the task, the organization, and followers can substitute for these leadership behaviors.

Task, Organizational, and Follower Characteristics

A high degree of organizational formalization (numerous plans, goals, or procedures to guide organizational members) or an *organization-wide reward system* can substitute for the impact of a leader's contingent reward behavior on followers' satisfaction or performance.[125,126] A formal organizational reward system that operates independently of the leader can be one aspect of overall plans, goals, and procedures designed to guide followers' activities. Examples occur with individuals who sell life insurance or real estate and earn a fixed commission on their sales regardless of their leader's behavior. Under these conditions, the guidance aspects of a leader's informal rewards and punishments can become less important to followers.

A closely knit, *cohesive work group with strong performance norms* can also substitute for a leader's contingent rewards.[127–129] Cohesive work groups are a good source of guidance and good feelings for followers. Also, the existence of a *leader with high expertise* at followers' tasks or *high rank,* can substitute for a leader's reward behavior.[130] Here, followers react favorably to requests by leaders with status, prestige, or know-how without requiring rewards for their behavior.

Much of the research reported in this section is quite recent and has been conducted outside the United States. In contrast, several studies in the United States have found *no* situational characteristics to substitute for leaders' contingent reward and punishment behaviors.[131–134] However, this may be partially due to inconsistent research methods. Also, many researchers have overlooked the distinctions between leadership enhancers, neutralizers, and substitutes, making it difficult for the reader to assess the results. The scarcity of findings in the United States may also be due to the individualistic nature of the culture. Individualism may make followers highly responsive to rewards or punishments from their leader. In fact, more follower characteristics than situational factors have been found to substitute for leaders' contingent reward and punishment behaviors in the United States. At this point, the limited evidence suggests that situational characteristics seldom act as substitutes for leaders' contingent reward and punishment behaviors in the United States, although situational substitutes may be more common in other countries.

Several characteristics of followers may substitute for leaders' contingent reward behavior. The most frequently occurring substitutes are with *followers who are highly professional,* have *extensive schooling,* or have *many years of work experience.* These factors all provide followers with relevant knowledge and ability that they can apply to their work tasks, independent of the leader's guidance. In turn, they can at least partially substitute for the impact of leaders' contingent reward behavior on followers' satisfaction, job clarity, and job performance in the United States and other countries.[135–137] Substitution effects of this type may also occur because a long period of training or experience has created in followers a high degree of pride in doing a good job and the desire to control their own behavior.[138,139] These individuals do not rely on leader-provided reinforcement for their motivation and job satisfaction.

Another follower substitute that may be related to the professionalism and experience of followers is *indifference toward organizational rewards.* This characteristic is found in followers who derive their motivation and satisfaction from sources other than the leader or their employing organization. They are usually committed to their work and derive pleasure from doing it well. These substitution effects have occurred most often in studies of managers.[140,141] *Intrinsic task satisfaction* is a

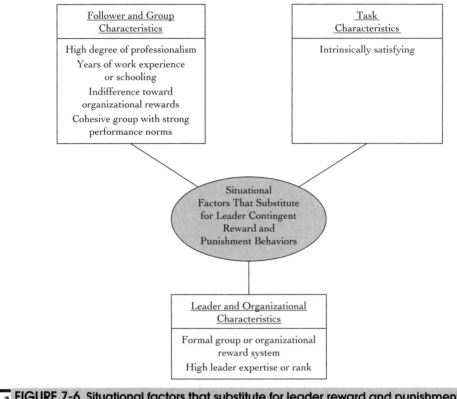

▪▪▪▪ **FIGURE 7-6 Situational factors that substitute for leader reward and punishment behaviors**

related characteristic that can also substitute for the effects of reward behavior on followers' satisfaction.[142,143] Thus, for followers who enjoy their work and derive their motivation and satisfaction from work activities rather than from their leader's reinforcement, the effects of the leader's contingent reward behavior can be minimal and unnecessary.

The pattern of findings for follower characteristics indicates strong substitution effects for followers who have considerable schooling, professional training, or experience, and who derive more satisfaction from doing their jobs well than from the rewards offered by their leader. The same may be true with regard to contingent punishment, but no research was available on that subject. We suspect, however, that many of the follower characteristics that substitute for leader reward behavior will do the same for intangible leader punishments. Figure 7-6 summarizes factors that may substitute for leaders' contingent reward and punishment behaviors.

Creating Factors That Substitute for Leader Reward and Punishment Behaviors

Follower characteristics are the most common substitutes for a leader's contingent reward behavior. Leaders who select or develop highly trained professional followers or those with considerable work experience can rely on those followers to carry out many required tasks on their own. The leader who develops followers and delegates important tasks will also increase followers' motivation and capabilities to work autonomously and without continuous reward behavior by the leader. Designing jobs and task assignments that match individuals with their interests will create high levels of intrinsic task satisfaction in followers, further increasing their desire to perform independently and at high levels. As the leader's group of followers becomes increasingly professional, experienced, and intrinsically satisfied with their work tasks, they will derive most of their motivation from these tasks and will be less reliant on leader-provided organizational rewards. This will free up the leader for other leadership activities.

Two situational characteristics that show the most promise to act as substitutes for leader reward behavior are cohesive work groups with strong performance norms, and group or organizational reward systems. Cohesive groups with strong performance norms can be developed by helping the group attain a high level of performance, providing adequate resources for the group, increasing the group's status, and increasing the opportunities for favorable interaction among group members. The weight of evidence indicates that cohesive groups with strong performance norms generally improve follower and group psychological reactions and performance. They may do this as enhancers or substitutes for leaders' reward and punishment behaviors. Group or organizational reward systems (such as gainsharing plans) also improve followers' psychological reactions and behaviors, possibly as substitutes for leader reward behaviors. Leaders should therefore encourage and work toward designing reward systems of this type to alleviate some of the needs for the leader to regularly provide tangible rewards contingent on followers' behaviors. Because empirical findings on substitutes for leader punishment behaviors are almost nonexistent, little can be said at this time regarding the creation of substitutes for this leader behavior.

▪▪▪ Assessing the Dynamics of Leader Reward and Punishment Behaviors

Leaders' reward and punishment behaviors, followers' background and personal characteristics, and the organizational situation all interact to affect how leaders influence their followers. If the leader's diagnosis of the situation identifies follower or situational characteristics that enhance the effectiveness of reward and punishment behaviors (Figure 7-4), then the leader can probably use this behavior pattern as an effective influence strategy with followers. If the leader's diagnosis identifies factors that neutralize the effects of a leader's rewards and punishments (Figure 7-5), the leader should consider other leadership behaviors to influence followers. If the leader diagnoses followers' characteristics that substitute for the leader's rewards and/or punishments (Figure 7-6), then these leadership behaviors may be unnecessary with these followers. The leader can then concentrate on other behavior patterns to satisfy follower needs. Leaders must consider situational and follower characteristics before using rewards and punishments to influence followers.

Effective leaders also diagnose situations to determine if they can make them more favorable. Leaders can sometimes create enhancers or eliminate neutralizers to make their reward and punishment behaviors more effective. Leaders can do this by developing accurate measures of followers' performance, negotiating with superiors for more control over valued rewards, administering them in a fair and timely manner, or increasing their own status and expertise through advanced technical training. They can also create cohesive follower groups with high-performance norms by providing adequate resources, helping followers succeed at tasks, advertising followers' achievements, and creating opportunities for favorable follower interactions. These and other possible strategies can create a situation in which a leader's rewards and punishments are particularly effective at influencing followers.

Leaders can also create substitutes for their rewards and punishments to enable followers to work independently. They can do this by hiring or developing highly professional and experienced followers who can perform well without the leader's regular guidance. Through individual follower development, careful delegation of challenging job tasks, thoughtful job design, and training experiences, individuals can become autonomous performers who are less reliant on their leaders for regular guidance and rewards. Leaders can also develop formalized group or organizational reward systems (such as gainsharing) that encourage or discourage specific follower behaviors and operate independently of the leader.

If important enhancers exist or can be created for a leader's reward and punishment behaviors, then followers will likely respond favorably to this behavior by their leader. However, if followers do not respond to the leader's rewards and punishments and the leader does not succeed at creating enhancers or eliminating critical neutralizers, then substitutes for this leadership behavior are needed. The leader should then attempt to create those follower or organizational characteristics that enable followers to perform effectively with little direct help from their leader. The leader thus uses rewards and punishments or modifies the followers' situation based on followers' reactions to the leader, as well as diagnosis of situational conditions and followers' characteristics.

SUMMARY ▪▪▪▪▪▪▪

Leader reward and punishment behaviors involve providing desirable outcomes (positive reinforcers) for followers when their behavior helps achieve organizational goals, and providing aversive outcomes (punishment) or removing desirable outcomes when their behavior hinders achievement of these goals. Rewards and punishments may be tangible (a raise or a demotion) or intangible (a compliment or expressing disappointment for low performance). Their use represents part of a social exchange between leaders and followers—leaders provide certain services, including rewards and punishments, and followers provide specific activities and task performance in return.

Rewards and punishments address our natural desire to seek pleasure and avoid pain. They also appeal to followers' needs for recognition, self-esteem, achievement, security, and physical necessities. When administered contingent on follower performance, rewards and punishments provide followers with information and motivational incentives that they need to effectively direct their own behavior. To effectively influence follower behavior, the leader must carefully monitor and measure follower behavior or performance, and administer rewards and punishments contingently.

Leaders' contingent reward behavior results in improved follower performance, compliance with leader requests, satisfaction, organizational commitment, role clarity, and follower ratings of the leader's effectiveness. Leaders' noncontingent reward behavior has little, if any, consistent impact on followers' psychological states or performance.

Leaders' contingent punishment behavior may have positive effects on follower performance when used in combination with leader contingent reward behavior. When used in this manner, contingent punishment does not decrease follower satisfaction, probably because followers view it as a fair complement to contingent reward behavior. When leader punishment behavior is not contingent on follower performance, decreases are likely in follower satisfaction, performance, commitment, role clarity, and group cohesion. Followers clearly react negatively when they do not know the reason for punishment.

Although a leader's contingent reward and punishment behaviors generally improve followers' psychological reactions and behaviors, certain situational and follower characteristics make these leadership behaviors more or less effective. Leaders need to be aware of these factors and select influence strategies that will maximize their effectiveness. Providing rewards and punishments and modifying followers' work situations are both useful strategies to influence followers' behavior.

Figure 7-7 presents a Leadership Process model of leader contingent reward and punishment behaviors. This model integrates the discussion of impacts of contingent reward and punishment with material on situational factors that can enhance, neutralize, or substitute for these leadership behaviors. Reward and punishment behaviors are shown at the top of Figure 7-7. Downward arrows show these leadership behaviors influencing follower and group psychological reactions, which in turn affect follower behavioral outcomes. Important situational factors are shown on each side of the figure, with arrows indicating how they affect the leadership process.

Figure 7-8 is shown to help the leader use the information from Figure 7-7 in a real leadership situation. Similar to comparable figures in earlier chapters, it shows the three key leadership tasks of diagnosing situations, providing leadership, and modifying followers or situations. Leaders first diagnose the situation by answering the questions in the first box ("1. Diagnosing the Situations"). They then provide the appropriate rewards or punishments ("2. Providing Reward and Punishment Behaviors"), and modify the situation to make it more effective by creating substitutes ("3. Modifying Followers or Situations"). The leader might also modify the situation by creating more enhancers or eliminating neutralizers, although these are not shown, in order to keep Figure 7-8 from becoming too complex. The leader then rediagnoses the situation and reconsiders the amount and type of reward and punishment behavior that is needed. If the answer is "no" to all the questions in the first box, then the leader should probably consider other leadership behaviors or assess the situation and followers for possible modification.

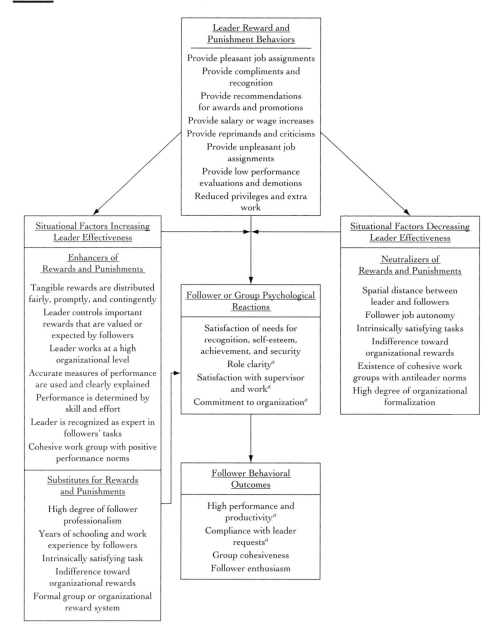

^{a}These psychological reactions and outcomes have shown the most improvement from leaders' rewards and punishments.

▄ ▄ ▄ ▄ **FIGURE 7-7 Leadership Process model of leader reward and punishment behaviors**

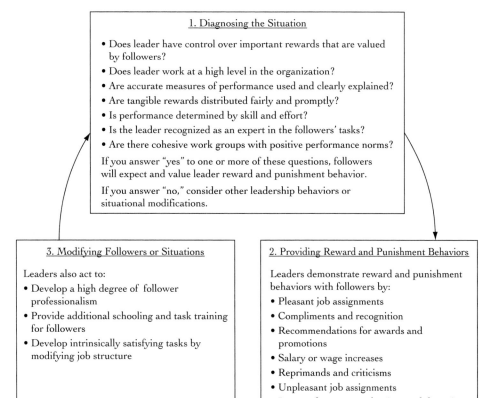

1. Diagnosing the Situation

- Does leader have control over important rewards that are valued by followers?
- Does leader work at a high level in the organization?
- Are accurate measures of performance used and clearly explained?
- Are tangible rewards distributed fairly and promptly?
- Is performance determined by skill and effort?
- Is the leader recognized as an expert in the followers' tasks?
- Are there cohesive work groups with positive performance norms?

If you answer "yes" to one or more of these questions, followers will expect and value leader reward and punishment behavior.

If you answer "no," consider other leadership behaviors or situational modifications.

3. Modifying Followers or Situations

Leaders also act to:
- Develop a high degree of follower professionalism
- Provide additional schooling and task training for followers
- Develop intrinsically satisfying tasks by modifying job structure

2. Providing Reward and Punishment Behaviors

Leaders demonstrate reward and punishment behaviors with followers by:
- Pleasant job assignments
- Compliments and recognition
- Recommendations for awards and promotions
- Salary or wage increases
- Reprimands and criticisms
- Unpleasant job assignments
- Low performance evaluations and demotions
- Reduced privileges and extra work

FIGURE 7-8 Applying the Leadership Process model of leader reward and punishment behaviors

KEY TERMS AND CONCEPTS IN THIS CHAPTER

- Coercive power
- Cohesive work groups
- Contingent punishment behaviors
- Contingent reward behaviors
- Coping behaviors
- Group cohesiveness
- Individualism
- Intrinsic task satisfaction
- Job autonomy

- Job clarity
- Law of Effect
- Leader punishment behavior
- Leader reward behavior
- Legitimate power
- Management by exception
- Organizational commitment
- Organizational formalization

- Organization-wide reward systems
- Performance norms
- Positive affectivity
- Professionalism
- Resource/connection power
- Reward power
- Satisfaction with supervision
- Social exchange

REVIEW AND DISCUSSION QUESTIONS

1. Describe a situation you have experienced or observed in which a leader effectively used rewards or punishments. Why was the leader's use of rewards or punishments effective in this situation?
2. Describe a situation you have experienced or observed in which a leader's use of rewards or punishments was not effective. Why was the leader's use of rewards or punishments not effective in this situation?
3. What situations have you experienced in which a leader's reward behavior was needed?
4. What situations have you experienced in which a leader's punishment behavior was needed?
5. Have you ever experienced a situation in which a leader was constrained from using a reward or punishment when it was really needed? If so, describe this situation.
6. As a leader, how could you create situational factors that would increase your influence when using rewards and punishments?
7. Do you think leader reward and punishment behaviors would be effective for a military commander? Why or why not? What about the leader of a volunteer group who wants to improve wildlife habitat?

▪▪▪▪▪ C A S E   I N C I D E N T S ▪▪▪▪▪

Choosing the Appropriate Leadership Behaviors

You manage an automotive accessories and repair department in a large department store. Profit margins of department stores are being squeezed by large discount chains, resulting in numerous department store closings nationwide. Auto accessories such as batteries, shock absorbers, and other items have always been a major profit center in your store, generating a large percentage of the stores' total revenue and earnings. Total sales of the automotive department have been at a moderate-to-low level during the winter and early spring, and the rest of the store has been doing even worse. The store manager is pressuring you to significantly increase sales in your department over the coming summer months to help make up for the low storewide sales.

The salespeople in your department are all fairly young (in their 20s and 30s), about

half graduated from high school (none attended college), and all have families with small children. They are paid on an hourly basis, and several of them have other jobs in their off-hours to supplement their income. They get along fairly well, but each is so busy and involved with their own family that there is little social interaction among them outside of work. They are generally experienced, capable, and highly independent.

From your experience, you know that store traffic always increases in the summer, and customers are interested in making sure their cars are comfortable, safe, and reliable for summer vacations. A successful salesperson in this department is one who is up to date on all product specifications, is outgoing and polite to customers, helps customers troubleshoot problems with their cars, and follows up on customer inquiries with an attempt to close each sale. All of these activities are directly related to the effort and skill of the salesperson. Your store has a reputation for quality products and service that the store management believes must be maintained. The store manager has emphasized that you must significantly increase the sales of your department or the entire store will be threatened with possible closing. The manager has confidence in you, and believes that department managers should have the freedom to lead and motivate their people as they see fit. ■

DISCUSSION QUESTIONS

1. What leadership behaviors are most needed in this case? Why?

Move the Supervisors?

Pam Hill is the site manager for a government contractor doing highly technical and complex design and testing of military systems. The work is being done on a military installation under the control of the military. Ms. Hill is responsible for two development teams that are working on the project. One team works the day shift and the other works the night shift.

The day shift (7:00 A.M. to 4:00 P.M.) is ahead of schedule and under budget. It has an excellent safety record, with no lost-time accidents. The day shift has been commended by the military commander for excellent security and has had no security violations. The team is highly cohesive and members cooperate with each other. The supervisor of the day shift has received very high performance evaluations from both management and team members.

The night shift (4:30 P.M. to 12:30 A.M.) is behind schedule and over budget. It has a poor safety record, with three lost-time accidents in the last month. The night shift has been written up twice for security violations, and a third violation could result in the government suspending the contract. Team members on the night shift have filed numerous grievances related to interpersonal conflict on the team, and they do not seem to cooperate with each other. The supervisor of the night shift has received very low performance evaluations from both management and team members.

Ms. Hill feels she must do something immediately to correct the problems on the night shift. To achieve a quick improvement in the situation she has decided to move the supervisor on the day shift to the night shift and to move the supervisor on the night shift to the day shift. ■

DISCUSSION QUESTIONS

1. If you were the supervisors involved, how would you interpret Ms. Hill's action?
2. Do you think this action by Ms. Hill will improve performance on the night shift? Why?
3. What effect do you think Ms. Hill's action will have on the day shift? Why?
4. If you were advising Ms. Hill, what actions would you advise her to take?

Leadership in a Women's Prison

The beep of a metal detector went off as Louise Miranda entered the doors of a women's prison in the southwest United States. She heard a voice from the radio on a guard's belt using a code system to identify who was entering the main doors. The doors were actually a series of steel bar sliding doors that opened and closed one at a time. As one door opened, the person entering would take a few steps in and walk toward another steel sliding door. As soon as the door behind closed securely, then one in front would open. Taking her first steps on the inside, where the general prison population lived, was an instant reality check for Louise; she realized that her thoughts and behavior were soon to change. As she walked through the halls toward the education department, the whistles and crude remarks from inmates began. She was on her way to meet the education director to discuss the expectations and duties for her new position as the law librarian.

Louise received no formal training, and was told that every inmate had a job they were required to go to at their scheduled times. Some had kitchen or janitorial duties, and some were allowed to attend school as their job. Louise was given responsibility for supervising four to seven inmate employees who worked in the prison library. Her duties included making up the work schedule, keeping track of the performance and behavior of her employees, and making sure that nothing unethical occurred in either the law library or the general library. She was told to gain the trust of the inmates, but not to become friends with them.

Assigning duties to specific workers was a delicate decision, as shown by the following example. The general population was permitted in the law library and general library Monday through Saturday. During this time, Louise rotated her employees between both libraries as needed. The law library workers were expected to help other inmates with their personal cases. Many of the inmates didn't have an attorney, due to lack of personal funds. The role of the library workers was not to aid the legal research, but to help and assist the inmates. Most of the workers were interested in the judicial process, and understood the research and paperwork needed to further the inmates' cases. The workers usually assisted the inmates as required, although many times they also found ways to gain personal items for themselves. These items varied from small things, such as cigarettes or extra food, to major items such as drugs or contraband. Extra attention was required on Sundays when "segregation" inmates were allowed an hour in the law library—one to five inmates at a time. These inmates were in lockdown, which meant spending only one hour a day outside their cell alone in a courtyard, and one hour a week in the law library. They had usually caused trouble, and were being punished by secluding them. They may have been involved in fights, been caught with drugs, or broken rules of the facility. Sometimes they were segregated for their own safety, due to threats from other inmates. Louise learned to keep in mind which of her employees could be trusted while assisting the segregation inmates.

Early on, Louise felt it was important to make it clear that she was not a fool and would not be intimated. She also tried to establish a positive working relationship with her workers so that other inmates would view her with trust and respect. Her regular workers are described below.

Lisa was soft spoken and educated. She had been convicted of first-degree murder. Her crime was not drug related, but rather the result of years of mental torture by her spouse. Background information on each worker was helpful in determining how to approach them. Lisa did not like to be in the spotlight. She served her time while trying to keep her record clean. This would enable her to get out of prison early due to good behavior.

Tanya was different—she was difficult to trust. She had been convicted on drug charges and homicide, and had no possibility of parole. When Tanya was working, Louise had to be very careful what she left on her desk. She locked up all the supplies, as well as other inmate's case files, or else they would disappear. Tanya had been in trouble, and in and out of segregation, many times. With no possibility of parole, Tanya developed the attitude that she had nothing to lose, so she caused problems whenever she pleased.

Ann was very gullible and had a strong desire to please others. Ann was difficult to trust because she had little backbone. Louise felt comfortable with Ann being the worker during segregation times only on an occasional basis. When asked to pass contraband or do something that was against the rules, Ann could usually say "no" once. But if asked several times, Ann would often agree even knowing the risks. Louise believed she needed to monitor Ann carefully, in order to keep her out of trouble.

Stacy was a reliable worker who had accepted her misbehavior and had a sincere attitude about turning her life around, once on the outside again. However, Stacy was not a self-starter. If there were new legal books to be checked in and shelved, the pile would sit there until another worker began the job or Louise started to do the job herself. Once Louise asked for help from Stacy, it was given right away with no questions asked. Stacy needed to see that what Louise asked of the workers was not something that she would not do herself.

Being inside the prison was uncomfortable for Louise. Knowing that the inmates lived there day and night for years at a time was unnerving. Knowing that she was able to leave after her shift was the only thing that kept her in good spirits. This was also a reminder that she needed to help her workers with issues in their personal lives in order to get the best out of them while working in the prison library. When she first began, she was told to keep in mind that these women are human beings, and not to treat them or think of them as their crime. She made every effort to maintain this perspective, although the crimes that were committed by these women were the second thing in her mind while in this position. ■

DISCUSSION QUESTIONS

1. Which leadership behaviors do you believe would be most effective for each of the four library workers and why?

SOURCE: This case was adapted from a case prepared by Marianne Carter.

ENDNOTES ▪▪▪▪▪▪▪

1. Yukl, G. A. (2002). *Leadership in Organizations,* 5th ed. Englewood Cliffs, NJ: Prentice Hall.
2. Hughes, R. L., Ginnett, R. C., and Curphy, G. J. (1996). *Leadership: Enhancing the Lessons of Experience,* 2nd ed. Chicago: Irwin.
3. Yukl, G. A., and Van Fleet, D. D. (1982). Cross situational, multimethod research on military leader effectiveness. *Organizational Behavior and Human Performance,* 30, 87–108.
4. Bass, B. (1990). *Bass and Stogdill's Handbook of Leadership,* 3rd ed. New York: Free Press.

5. Skinner, B. F. (1974). *About Behaviorism.* New York: Knopf.

6. Feldman, M. D., and MacCulloch, M. J. (1965). The application of anticipatory avoidance learning to the treatment of homosexuality: Theory, technique and preliminary results. *Behavior Research and Therapy, 2,* 165–183.

7. Bucher, B., and Lovaas, O. I. (1968). Use of aversive stimulations in behavior modification. In M. R. Jones (Ed.), *Miami Symposium on the Prediction of Behavior, 1967: Aversive Stimulation.* Coral Gables, FL: University of Miami Press.

8. Balke, B. G. (1965). The application of behavior therapy to the treatment of alcoholism. *Behavior Research and Therapy, 3,* 75–85.

9. Johnston, J. M. (1972). Punishment of human behavior. *American Psychologist, 27,* 1033–1054.

10. Rimm, D. C., and Masters, J. C. (1974). *Behavior Therapy: Technique and Empirical Findings.* New York: Academic Press.

11. Parke, R. D. (1972). Some effects of punishment on children's behavior. In W. W. Hartup (Ed.), *The Young Child: Reviews of Research,* Vol. 2, Washington DC: National Association for the Education of Young Children.

12. Szilagyi, A. D. (1980). Causal inferences between leader reward behavior and subordinate performance, absenteeism, and work satisfaction. *Journal of Occupational Psychology, 53,* 195–204.

13. Peters, T. J., and Waterman, R. H. (1982). *In Search of Excellence.* New York: Harper & Row.

14. Schriesheim, C. A., Hinkin, T. R., and Tetrault, L. A. (1991). The discriminant validity of the leader reward and punishment questionnaire (LRPQ) and satisfaction with supervision: A two sample, factor analytic investigation. *Journal of Occupational Psychology, 64,* 159–166.

15. Viega, J. F. (1988). Face your problem subordinates now! *Academy of Management Executive, 2,* 145–152.

16. Podsakoff, P. M., Todor, W. D., Grover, R. A., and Huber, V. L. (1984). Situational moderators of leader reward and punishment behaviors: Fact or fiction. *Organizational Behavior and Human Performance, 34,* 21–63.

17. Ibid.

18. Hollander, E. P. (1987). College and university leadership from a psychological perspective: A transactional view. Paper presented at the Invitational Interdisciplinary Colloquium on Leadership in Higher Education, National Center for Postsecondary Governance and Finance, Columbia University, New York.

19. Bass. *Bass and Stogdill's Handbook of Leadership.*

20. Ibid.

21. Peters and Waterman. *In Search of Excellence.*

22. Steers, R. M., Porter, L. W., and Bigley, G. A. (1996). *Motivation and Leadership at Work,* 6th ed. New York: McGraw-Hill.

23. Eisenberger, R., and Cameron, J. (1996). Detrimental Effects of Reward: Reality or Myth? *American Psychologist, 3*(11), 1153–1166.

24. Steers, Porter, and Bigley. *Motivation and Leadership at Work.*

25. Powell, J., and Azrin, N. (1968). The effects of shock as a punisher for cigarette smoking. *Journal of Applied Behavior Analysis, 1,* 63–71.

26. Kazdin, A. E. (1975). *Behavior Modification in Applied Settings.* Homewood, IL: Dorsey.

27. Harris, S., and Ersner-Hershfield, R. (1978). Behavioral suppression of seriously disruptive behavior in psychotic and retarded patients: A review of punishment and altercations. *Psychological Bulletin, 85,* 1352–1375.

28. Balke. The application of behavior therapy to the treatment of alcoholism.

29. Rimm and Masters. *Behavior Therapy: Technique and Empirical Findings.*

30. Blake, R. J., and Potter, E. H., III (1992). Novice leaders, novice behaviors, and strong culture: Promoting leadership change beyond the classroom. In K. E. Clark, M. B. Clark, and D. P. Campbell (Eds.), *Impact of Leadership.* Greensboro, NC: The Center for Creative Leadership.

31. Bass. *Bass and Stogdill's Handbook of Leadership.*

32. Colby, A. H., and Zak, R. E. (1988). Transformational leadership: A comparison of Army and Air Force perceptions. Report 88-0565. Maxwell AFB, AL: Air Command and Staff College, Air University.

33. Hughes, Ginnett, and Curphy. *Leadership: Enhancing the Lessons of Experience.*

34. Hinton, B. L., and Barrow, J. C. (1976). Personality correlates of the reinforcement propensities of leaders. *Personnel Psychology, 29,* 61–66.

35. Bass. *Bass and Stogdill's Handbook of Leadership.*

36. Dorfman, P. W., Howell, J. P., Cotton, B. C. G., and Tate, U. (1992). Leadership within the discontinuous hierarchy structure of the military: Are effective leadership behaviors similar within and across command structures. In K. E. Clark, M. B. Clark, and D. P. Campbell (Eds.), *Impact of Leadership.* Greensboro, NC: Center for Creative Leadership.

37. Yukl. *Leadership in Organizations.*

38. Scontrino, M. P., Larson, J. R., Jr., and Fiedler, F. (1977). Racial similarity as a moderator variable in the perception of leader behavior and control. *International Journal of Intercultural Relations,* 1(2), 111–117.

39. Kappelman, S. K. (1981). Teachers' perceptions of principals' bases of power in relation to principals' style of leadership. Doctoral diss., University of New Orleans.

40. Ansari, M. A. (1989). Effects of leader sex, subordinate sex, and subordinate performance on the use of influence strategies, *Sex Roles,* 20(5/6), 283–293.

41. Baker, L. D., Di Marco, N., and Scott, W. E., Jr. (1975). Effects of supervisor's sex and level of authoritarianism on evaluation and reinforcement of blind and sighted workers. *Journal of Applied Psychology,* 60, 28–32.

42. Szilagyi, A. D. (1980). Reward behavior of male and female leaders: A causal inference analysis, *Journal of Vocational Behavior,* 16, 59–72.

43. Williams, M. L., Podsakoff, P. M., and Huber, V. (1992). Effects of group-level and individual-level variation in leader behaviors on subordinate attitudes and performance. *Journal of Occupational and Organizational Psychology,* 65, 115–129.

44. Yammarino, F. J., and Bass, B. M. (1990). Long-term forecasting of transformational leadership and its effects among naval officers. In K. E. Clark and M. B. Clark (Eds.), *Measures of Leadership,* 151–170. West Orange, NJ: Leadership Library of America.

45. Podsakoff, P. M., Todor, W. D., and Skov, R. (1982). Effect of leader contingent and non-contingent reward and punishment behaviors in subordinate performance and satisfaction. *Academy of Management Journal,* 25, 810–821.

46. Szilagyi, A. D. (1980). Causal inferences between leader reward behavior and subordinate performance, absenteeism, and work satisfaction. *Journal of Occupational Psychology,* 53(3), 195–204.

47. Luthans, F., and Kreitner, R. (1975). *Organizational Behavior Modification.* Glenview, IL: Scott, Foresman.

48. Schneier, C. E. (1974). Behavior modification in management: A review and critique. *Academy of Management Journal,* 17, 528–548.

49. Greene, C. N. (1976). A longitudinal investigation of performance-reinforcing behaviors and subordinate satisfaction and performance. In *Proceedings, Midwest Academy of Management,* 157–185.

50. Greene, C. N. (1976). Causal connections among cohesion, drive, goal acceptance, and productivity in work groups. Paper presented at the Academy of Management meeting, Kansas City, MO.

51. Sims, H. P., and Szilagyi, A. D. (1978). A causal analysis of leader behavior over three different time lags. Paper presented at the Eastern Academy of Management meeting, New York.

52. Sims, H. P. (1977). The leader as manager of reinforcement contingencies: An empirical example and a model. In J. G. Hunt and L. L. Larson (Eds.), *Leadership: The Cutting Edge.* Carbondale, IL: Southern Illinois University Press.

53. Podsakoff, P. M., and Todor, W. D. (1985). Relationships between leader reward and punishment behavior and group process

and productivity. *Journal of Management,* 11, 55–73.

54. George, J. M. (1995). Asymmetrical effects of rewards and punishments: The case of social loafing. *Journal of Occupational and Organizational Psychology,* 68(4), 327–338.

55. Herold, D. M. (1977). Two-way influence processes in leader-follower dyads. *Academy of Management Journal,* 20, 224–237.

56. Thamhain, H. J., and Gemmill, G. R. (1974). Influence style of project managers: Some project performance correlates. *Academy of Management Journal,* 17, 216–224.

57. Warren, D. I. (1968). Power, visibility, and conformity in formal organizations. *American Sociological Review,* 6, 951–970.

58. Kouzes, J. M., and Posner, B. Z. (1987). *The Leadership Challenge: How to Get Extraordinary Things Done in Organizations.* San Francisco: Jossey-Bass.

59. Peters and Waterman. *In Search of Excellence.*

60. Williams, Podsakoff, and Huber. Effects of group level and individual-level variation in leader behaviors on subordinate attitudes and performance.

61. Dorfman, P. W., Howell, J. P., Hibino, S., Lee, J. K., Tate, U., and Bautista, A. (1997). Leadership in western and Asian countries: Commonalities and differences in effective leadership processes across cultures. *Leadership Quarterly,* 8(3), 233–274.

62. Yammerino, F. J., Spangler, W. D., and Dubinsky, A. J. (1988). Transformational and contingent reward leadership: Individual, dyad, and group levels of analysis. *Leadership Quarterly,* 9(1), 27–54.

63. Hollander, E. P. (1992). The essential interdependence of leadership and followership. *Current Directions in Psychological Science,* 1(2), 71–75.

64. Korukonda, A. R., and Hunt, J. G. (1989). Pat on the back versus kick in the pants: An application of cognitive inference to the study of leader reward and punishment behaviors. *Group and Organization Studies,* 14(3), 299–324.

65. Fox, L. D., Rejeski, W. J., and Gauvin, L. (2002). Effects of leadership style and group dynamics on enjoyment of physical activity.

American Journal of Health Promotion, 14(5), 277–283.

66. Podsakoff and Todor. Relationships between leader reward and punishment behavior and group process and productivity.

67. Fahr, J. L., Podsakoff, P. M., and Cheng, B. S. (1987). Culture-free leadership effectiveness versus moderators of leadership behavior: An extension and test of Kerr and Jermier's "Substitutes for Leadership" model in Taiwan. *Journal of International Business Studies,* 18, 43–60.

68. Dorfman, Howell, Hibino, Lee, Tate, and Bautista. Leadership in western and Asian countries: Commonalities and differences in effective leadership processes across cultures.

69. Bachman, J. G., Smith, C., and Slesinger, J. A. (1966). Control, performance and satisfaction: An analysis of structural and individual effects. *Journal of Personality and Social Psychology,* 4, 127–136.

70. Weschler, I. R., Kahane, M., and Tannenbaum, R. (1952). Job satisfaction, productivity and morale: A case study. *Occupational Psychology,* 26, 1–4.

71. Bachman, J. G., Bowers, D. G., and Marcus, P. M. (1968). Bases of supervisory power: A comparative study in five organizational settings. In A. S. Tannenbaum (Ed.), *Control in Organizations,* New York: McGraw-Hill.

72. Ivancevich, J. M., and Donnelly, J. H. (1970). An analysis of control, bases of control, and satisfaction in an organizational setting. *Academy of Management Journal,* 13, 427–436.

73. Riecken, H. W. (1952). Some problems of consensus development. *Rural Sociology,* 17, 245–252.

74. Sheridan, J. E., and Vredenburgh, D. J. (1978). Usefulness of leadership behavior and social power variables in predicting job tension, performance, and turnover of nursing employees. *Journal of Applied Psychology,* 63, 89–95.

75. Martinko, M. J., and Gardner, W. L. (1982). Learned helplessness: An alternative explanation for performance deficits. *Academy of Management Review,* 7, 195–204.

76. Arvey, R. D., Davis, G. A., and Nelson, S. M. (1984). Use of discipline in an organization: A field study. *Journal of Applied Psychology,* 69, 448–460.

77. Podsakoff, Todor, Grover, and Huber. Situational moderators of leader reward and punishment behaviors: Fact or fiction?

78. Podsakoff, Todor, and Skov. Effect of leader contingent and noncontingent reward and punishment behaviors on subordinate performance and satisfaction.

79. Arvey, R. D., and Ivancevich, J. (1980). Punishment in organizations: A review, propositions, and research suggestion. *Academy of Management Review,* 51, 123–132.

80. Podsakoff, Todor, and Skov. Effect of leader contingent and non-contingent reward and punishment behaviors on subordinate performance and satisfaction.

81. Korukonda and Hunt. Pat on the back versus kick in the pants: An application of cognitive inference to the study of leader reward and punishment behaviors.

82. Williams, M. L., Podsakoff, P. M., and Huber, V. (1992). Effects of group-level and individual-level variation in leader behaviors on subordinate attitudes and performance. *Journal of Occupational and Organizational Psychology,* 65(2), 115–129.

83. Podsakoff, P. M., and Todor, W. D. (1985). Relationships between leader reward and punishment behavior and group processes and productivity. *Journal of Management,* 11(1), 55–73.

84. Podsakoff, Todor, Grover, and Huber. Situational moderators of leader reward and punishment behaviors: Fact or fiction?

85. Podsakoff, P. M., Dorfman, P. W., Howell, J. P., and Todor, W. D. (1986). Leader reward and punishment behaviors: A preliminary test of a culture-free style of leadership effectiveness. *Advances in International Comparative Management,* 2, 95–138.

86. Williams, Podsakoff, and Huber. Effects of group-level and individual-level variation in leader behaviors on subordinate attitudes and performance.

87. Podsakoff and Todor. Relationship between leader reward and punishment behavior and group process and productivity.

88. Dorfman, Howell, Hibino, Lee, Tate, and Bautista. Leadership in western and Asian countries: Commonalities and differences in effective leadership processes across cultures.

89. Hughes, R. L., Ginnett, R. C., and Curphy, G. J. (1993). *Leadership: Enhancing the Lessons of Experience.* Homewood, IL: Irwin.

90. Arvey, R. D., and Ivancevich, J. M. (1980). Punishment in organizations: A review, propositions and research suggestions. *Academy of Management Review,* 5, 123–132.

91. Howell, Dorfman, Hibino, Lee, and Tate. Leadership in western and Asian countries: Commonalities and differences in effective leadership processes and substitutes across cultures.

92. Lawler, E. E., III. (1971). *Pay and Organizational Effectiveness.* New York: McGraw-Hill.

93. Luthans, F., Paul, R., and Baker, D. (1981). An experimental analysis of the impact of contingent reinforcement on salespersons' performance behavior. *Journal of Applied Psychology,* 64, 314–323.

94. Howell, Dorfman, Hibino, Lee, and Tate. Leadership in western and Asian countries: Commonalities and differences in effective leadership processes and substitutes across cultures.

95. Podsakoff, Todor, Grover, and Huber. Situational moderators of leader reward and punishment behavior: Fact or fiction?

96. Howell, Dorfman, Hibino, Lee, and Tate. Leadership in western and Asian countries: Commonalities and differences in effective leadership processes and substitutes across cultures.

97. Ilgen, D. R., Fisher, C. D., and Taylor, M. S. (1979). Consequences of individual feedback on behavior in organizations. *Journal of Applied Psychology,* 64, 349–371.

98. Bennis, W. G, Berkowitz, N., Affinito, M., and Malone, M. (1958). Authority, power, and the ability to influence. *Human Relations,* 11, 143–155.

99. Bass. *Bass and Stogdill's Handbook of Leadership.*

100. Yukl. *Leadership in Organizations.*

101. Iverson, M. A. (1964). Personality impressions of punitive stimulus persons of differential status. *Journal of Abnormal and Social Psychology,* 68, 617–626.

102. Bass. *Bass and Stogdill's Handbook of Leadership.*

103. Podsakoff, Todor, Grover, and Huber. Situational moderators of leader reward and punishment behavior: Fact or fiction?

104. Brass, D. J., and Oldham, G. R. (1976). Validating an in-basket test using an alternative set of leadership scoring dimensions. *Journal of Applied Psychology,* 61, 652–657.

105. Ball, G. A., Trevino, L. K., and Sims, H. P., Jr. (1992). Understanding subordinate reactions to punishment incidents: Perspectives from justice and social effect. *Leadership Quarterly,* 3(4), 307–333.

106. Hughes, Ginnett, and Curphy. *Leadership: Enhancing the Lessons of Experience.*

107. Podsakoff, Todor, Grover, and Huber. Situational moderators of leader reward and punishment behavior: Fact or fiction?

108. Fahr, Podsakoff, and Cheng. Culture-free leadership effectiveness versus moderators of leadership behavior: An extension and test of Kerr and Jermier's "Substitutes for Leadership" model in Taiwan.

109. Podsakoff, P. M. Niehoff, B. P., MacKenzie, S. B., and Williams, M. L. (1993). Do substitutes for leadership really substitute for leadership? An empirical investigation of Kerr and Jermier's Situational Leadership model. *Organizational Behavior and Human Decision Processes,* 54, 1–44.

110. Podsakoff, Dorfman, Howell, and Todor. Leader reward and punishment behaviors: A preliminary test of a culture-free style of leadership effectiveness.

111. Podsakoff, Niehoff, MacKenzie, and Williams. Do substitutes for leadership really substitute for leadership? An empirical investigation of Kerr and Jermier's Situational Leadership model.

112. Podsakoff, Dorfman, Howell, and Todor. Leader reward and punishment behaviors: A preliminary test of a culture-free style of leadership effectiveness.

113. Podsakoff, Todor, Grover, and Huber. Situational moderators of leader reward and punishment behavior: Fact or fiction?

114. Yukl. *Leadership in Organizations.*

115. Podsakoff, Todor, Grover, and Huber. Situational moderators of leader reward and punishment behavior: Fact or fiction?

116. Ilgen, Fisher, and Taylor. Consequences of individual feedback on behavior in organizations.

117. Podsakoff, Dorfman, Howell, and Todor. Leader reward and punishment behaviors: A preliminary test of a culture-free style of leadership effectiveness.

118. Ibid.

119. Larson, J. R. (1984). The performance feedback process: A preliminary model. *Organizational Behavior and Human Performance,* 33, 42–76.

120. Ibid.

121. Bass. *Bass and Stogdill's Handbook of Leadership.*

122. Pinder, C. (1998). *Work Motivation in Organizational Behavior,* Upper Saddle River, NJ: Prentice Hall.

123. Fahr, Podsakoff, and Cheng. Culture-free leadership effectiveness versus moderators of leadership behavior: An extension and test of Kerr and Jermier's "Substitutes for Leadership" model in Taiwan.

124. Stotland, E. (1959). Peer groups and reactions to power figures. In D. Cartwright (Ed.), *Studies in Social Power.* Ann Arbor, MI: University of Michigan, Institute for Social Research.

125. Howell, Dorfman, Hibino, Lee, and Tate. Leadership in western and Asian countries: Commonalities and differences in effective leadership processes and substitutes across cultures.

126. Markham, S. E. (1988). The pay-for-performance dilemma revisited: An empirical example of the importance of group effects. *Journal of Applied Psychology,* 73, 172–180.

127. Howell, Dorfman, Hibino, Lee, and Tate. Leadership in western and Asian countries: Commonalities and differences in effective leadership processes and substitutes across cultures.

128. Bass. *Bass and Stogdill's Handbook of Leadership.*

129. Tsur, E. (1983). The kibbutz way of life—Structure and management of the kibbutz. *Kibbutz Studies,* November 1983, 23–31.

130. Howell, Dorfman, Hibino, Lee, and Tate. Leadership in western and Asian countries: Commonalities and differences in effective leadership processes and substitutes acrosss cultures.

131. Podsakoff, Niehoff, MacKenzie, and Williams. Do substitutes for leadership really substitute for leadership? An empirical investigation of Kerr and Jermier's Situational Leadership model.

132. Dorfman, Howell, Cotton, and Tate. Leadership within the discontinuous hierarchy structure of the military: Are effective leadership behaviors similar within and across command structures?

133. Podsakoff, Dorfman, Howell, and Todor. Leader reward and punishment behaviors: A preliminary test of a culture-free style of leadership effectiveness.

134. Howell, Dorfman, Hibino, Lee, and Tate. Leadership in western and Asian countries: Commonalities and differences in effective leadership processes and substitutes across cultures.

135. Podsakoff, Dorfman, Howell, and Todor. Leader reward and punishment behaviors: A preliminary test of a culture-free style of leadership effectiveness.

136. Howell, Dorfman, Hibino, Lee, and Tate. Leadership in western and Asian countries: Commonalities and differences in effective leadership processes and substitutes across cultures.

137. Jacoby, J., Mazursky, D., Troutman, T., and Kuss, A. (1984). When feedback is ignored: Disutility of outcome feedback. *Journal of Applied Psychology,* 69, 531–545.

138. Parsons, C. K., Herold, D. M., and Turlington, B. (1981). Individual differences in performance feedback preferences. Paper presented at the Academy of Management meeting, San Diego, CA.

139. Bass, B. M. (1967). Social behavior and the orientation inventory: A review. *Psychological Bulletin,* 68, 260–292.

140. Podsakoff, Dorfman, Howell, and Todor. Leader reward and punishment behaviors: A preliminary test of a culture-free style of leadership effectiveness.

141. Howell, Dorfman, Hibino, Lee, and Tate. Commonalities and differences in effective leadership processes and substitutes across cultures.

142. Podsakoff, Dorfman, Howell, and Todor. Leader reward and punishment behaviors: A preliminary test of a culture-free style of leadership effectiveness.

143. Howell, Dorfman, Hibino, Lee, and Tate. Leadership in western and Asian countries: Commonalities and differences in effective leadership processes and substitutes across cultures.

Charismatic Leadership Behavior

Learning Objectives

After reading this chapter, you should be able to do the following:

1. Describe the behaviors that charismatic leaders use to influence followers.
2. Explain why charismatic leaders can have such strong effects on followers.
3. Describe examples of effective and ineffective charismatic leadership.
4. Describe several personal traits, skills, and power sources of effective charismatic leaders.
5. Describe the major favorable effects of charismatic leadership.
6. Explain the risks that some charismatic leaders can create for followers.
7. Identify situations in which charismatic leadership is especially effective.
8. Identify situations in which charismatic leadership may not be needed.
9. Explain how leaders can modify situations to make charismatic leadership more effective.

Examples of Effective Charismatic Leadership

- A leader viewed her job as transferring a dream to others in the organization so they would value the dream as she did. She used emotional terms in describing the dream to excite her followers and to get them to buy into it with all their creative energies.
- A new company president talked personally with every company employee in every branch during his first year as president. He told them of his vision for the company, but avoided trying to get them to adopt his vision. Instead, he encouraged them to develop a vision for their group or department. He was amazed to see how his vision stimulated harmony among the resulting department and branch visions.
- Mahatma Gandhi showed how symbols and role modeling by a leader provide a simplified message that can inspire charismatic effects in followers. The spinning

wheel that Gandhi often used, for example, symbolized self-reliance, the value of cottage industries, and the demand for Indian independence. Cleaning his own toilet modeled self-reliance and humility as important values in the passive resistance action plan he advocated against the British.

- Franklin Delano Roosevelt demonstrated how charismatic leaders often project an image of unusual mental abilities. He developed an excellent memory and seized information from many sources, thus conveying the impression that he had a powerful mind and a wide range of knowledge. Roosevelt kept material ready to impress listeners whether they were business people or coal miners. This practice increased his perceived competence and insight in followers' eyes, and thereby raised their faith and confidence in him.

- The company credo at Johnson & Johnson demonstrates how charismatic leadership can become a permanent part of an organization. Created by General Robert Wood Johnson more than 60 years ago, the credo emphasizes honesty, integrity, and respect for people. Senior managers still emphasize these values when they gather to discuss the credo every few years, to keep its ideas current. They also spend considerable time ensuring that employees live by the credo. The current CEO stated, "If we keep trying to do what is right, at the end of the day we believe the marketplace will reward us."

These examples demonstrate effective behaviors used by charismatic leaders to influence their followers.

▪ ▪ ▪ Definition, Background, and Importance of Charismatic Leadership Behaviors

Charisma is a Greek word meaning divine gift of grace. It is found in Biblical references to the Holy Spirit, and was also used to describe the roles of specific members of the early Christian church. Max Weber, a famous German sociologist, expanded the meaning of charisma to apply to a type of authority or influence based on exceptional characteristics of an individual person.[1] Weber believed these exceptional characteristics were often shown by heroic acts and/or by advocating a revolutionary mission or program of action to resolve some crisis. These exceptional characteristics were further demonstrated by repeated successes in carrying out the mission.

Weber's interpretation of charisma as an important type of social influence is consistent with the way most people use this term today. Leaders are described as charismatic if they are perceived as having exceptional (almost magical) qualities that inspire extreme devotion, commitment, and trust; when followers identify themselves with the leader and become emotionally involved in the leader's mission; and when followers feel increased self-esteem due to their association with the leader.[2] The meaning of charisma has thus changed from being an endowment of divine grace from God to an endowment of exceptional qualities, high esteem, and referent power from followers.[3]

Some experts believe it is primarily a leader's personal characteristics and behaviors (such as self-confidence, rhetorical skills, or expressed vision of the future) that cause the leader to be perceived as charismatic. Others believe the situational context surrounding the leader (such as the existence of a crisis), or characteristics of followers (such as low self-esteem or low self-confidence), cause people to perceive charismatic qualities in a leader. Most recent scholars believe that the leader's characteristics and behaviors, the followers' characteristics, and situational factors combine to cause a leader to be viewed as charismatic. When followers view a leader as charismatic, they ascribe or attribute charismatic qualities to the leader.[4] We therefore define *charismatic leadership* as an attribution made by followers about leaders who exhibit certain personal traits, abilities, and behaviors, and who have unusually strong influence on followers' emotions, values, beliefs, attitudes, and behaviors. In all walks of life and throughout organizations we find gifted charismatic leaders who advocate radical solutions to critical problems and followers who are unquestioningly and magnetically attracted to these leaders.[5]

Most of the leadership behaviors described thus far in this book are considered transactional because they involve an informal exchange or transaction of some sort between leaders and followers. An example of this transaction occurs when followers provide competence and effort in exchange for useful direction and rewards provided by the leader. These leadership activities usually appeal to followers' existing needs and values. In contrast, some experts believe that charismatic leaders raise followers' needs and values, and therefore promote dramatic changes (often called transformations) in individual followers, groups, and organizations. Followers are apparently motivated by their emotional involvement with a charismatic leader and their commitment to the leader's mission, which is satisfying in itself. This distinction between transactional and charismatic leaders is especially important in descriptions of transformational and visionary leadership, which include charisma, and are described later in this chapter.

Some scholars have emphasized the impacts of charismatic leaders on group motivation, cohesion, and collective inspiration,[6] and de-emphasized the effects on individuals. Others have noted that charisma is in the eye of the beholder, and different persons perceive it differently. One follower may perceive a leader's speech as inspirational and moving, whereas another may see it as trite, flowery, and the work of a charlatan. Recent research shows that charismatic leaders have stronger impacts on individuals rather than on groups.[7,8] It seems that individuals are more likely than an entire group to attribute special charismatic qualities and high esteem to a leader. We will see, however, that very successful charismatics can sometimes have significant influence over large groups of people.

Charismatic leadership involves describing a desirable mission or vision of the future with goals, opportunities, and roles for followers that have a moral dimension and appeal to followers' needs and values. Charismatic leaders also make inspirational speeches that are emotionally expressive, intolerant of the status quo, and motivational with regard to the mission. They use impression-management techniques (displaying extreme confidence in themselves, focusing on progress and success, not mentioning failures) in order to appear competent and trustworthy. They role model their own behavior for followers to emulate by setting high performance standards for themselves, having high expectations for followers, showing confidence in followers' abilities to meet these standards, and showing determination, optimism, and self-confidence. They demonstrate creative, innovative behavior, risk taking, and self-sacrifice to show their courage and convictions about achieving the mission. They also engage in frame alignment, which involves describing followers' tasks, events, and the environment in ways that make them organized, interpretable, meaningful, and understandable for followers to help guide their actions.

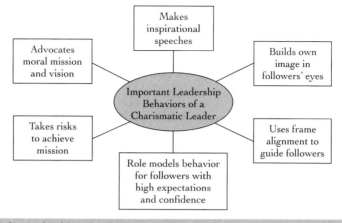

FIGURE 8-1 Important leadership behaviors of a charismatic leader

These behaviors tend to produce loyalty, dedication, trust, and commitment to the leader, emotional involvement in the leader's mission, increased self-esteem, and belief in the leader's values and moral correctness. These impacts are most likely when the leader also exhibits certain personal characteristics often associated with charismatic leadership—such as self-confidence, belief in the moral rightness of his or her position, and outstanding speaking ability. Specific follower and situational characteristics may also contribute to these effects, with the result that followers view their leader as charismatic. Figure 8-1 summarizes the major charismatic leadership behaviors.

Many people believe that only a small number of individuals can successfully carry out these leadership behaviors and be viewed as charismatic by their followers. However, two research studies showed that people can learn to carry out charismatic behaviors and have predictable charismatic effects on followers.[9,10] Although these studies were conducted in research laboratories, they involved highly realistic organizational work tasks, and imply that many individuals in real organizations may learn to demonstrate charismatic behaviors and have charismatic effects on followers. The Leadership in Action box on Anita Roddick describes an effective charismatic leader.

Charismatic Leadership has Strong Effects

Over 70 years ago, Sigmund Freud[11] described a major reason why charismatic leaders have such strong effects on followers. Freud believed that followers resolve inner conflicts between their self-image and what they think they should be by making the charismatic leader a representative of their ideal self. To followers, the leader becomes an ideal person whose behavior is a model they can emulate. By totally accepting a leader and his or her revolutionary ideas, followers fulfill the human desire to go beyond their self-interests and become more noble and worthy. By emulating this leader or ideal person, followers can become their ideal self.

Some writers believe this process is most common for followers who lack a strong sense of personal identity[12]—that is, people who are unsure of who they are, where they are going in life, and what basic values and beliefs they wish to live by. When these

LEADERSHIP IN ACTION

Anita Roddick, Founder of the Body Shop

In 1976, in Brighton, England, a school teacher named Anita Roddick took an idea from her kitchen table and built it into an empire with over 1,400 shops in 46 countries and an estimated worth of $650 million by 1995. How did she do it? Roddick did it with her charismatic style encompassing a vision of global leadership, indomitable courage and passion, and a developmental approach to followers.

Roddick's vision of global leadership began with a desire to supply women around the world with cosmetics, soaps, and lotions made from all natural products that have not been tested on animals. Her commitment to running a socially and environmentally responsible company is symbolized in her ideology and message to other corporations to charge their leaders to be "true planetary citizens." To this end, Roddick has advocated reductions in world poverty, violence against women, and nuclear testing. Roddick models her socially active role by sacrificing profits; she will not do business in countries she believes are not attempting to address her social and environmental causes.

Anita, as she insists on being called by her employees at every level, is considered an inspirational leader who generates passion among The Body Shop employees. She emphasizes strong personal relationships with her employees and tries to spend as much time with them as possible. Roddick insists that every Body Shop store is equipped with a VCR so she can send employees messages regarding her latest advances in social causes and remind employees that their work efforts are making an important contribution to larger social and environmental issues. Roddick also engages in frame alignment, as she promotes an image of female beauty that runs contrary to that fostered by the media. As employees learn The Body Shop philosophy, they are encouraged to view women of every shape, size, and ethnicity as completely beautiful.

Another aspect of Roddick's charismatic style of leadership is signified by heavy doses of futuristic thinking and dissatisfaction with the status quo. In her office is a sign that reads "Welcome to the Department of the Future." Roddick refers to her style of leadership as "benevolent anarchism." She inspires creativity by encouraging employees to question what they are doing and how they are doing it, in the hope of finding better working methods. Above all, Roddick tells her employees "to have fun, put love where labor is, and go in the opposite direction to everyone else." Anita Roddick's passion for social and environmental causes, her personal acceptance and belief that all women are beautiful, and her style of forward-thinking inspirational leadership, have contributed to The Body Shop's overwhelming success.

SOURCES: N. J. Adler, Global leadership: Women leaders. *Management International Review,* 37(1), 1997, 171–196; N. Kochran. Anita Roddick: Soap and social action. *World Business,* 3(1), 1997, 46–47; and C. P. Wallace, Can The Body Shop shape up? *Fortune,* 133(7), 1996, 188.

individuals are on their own, they often feel uneasy and have a sense of drifting through life. Charismatic leaders provide these followers with a strong identity, including important goals, beliefs, and values, and thus improve followers' self-esteem and sense of purpose.[13] This process by which followers connect with charismatic leaders is called *personal identification,* and it helps explain why they will actively defend the leader against critics or other attackers. They are really defending their own ideal self, which they are striving to become.

Several scholars have noticed that charismatic leaders often surface during crises.[14] During a time of crisis, the leader is viewed as a savior who will fulfill unmet needs. A similar situation occurs when followers are undergoing a major transition. In these situations, traditional methods are not working, and the charismatic leader's radical ideas represent a break from the old ways that created the need for change. The crisis or major transition creates a sense of drifting, uncertainty, and anxiety, which the leader resolves through vast knowledge, moral authority, and embodiment of follower ideals and values. When followers personally identify with a charismatic leader in this manner, they often experience euphoria. This is because the leader's perceived omnipotence and moral authority overshadow the internal guilt and hostility that often accompany an individual's conflicts between the real self and the ideal self. The charismatic leader overcomes their internal conflicts, and they are free at last to be the person they have dreamed they could be.

Another process that helps explain the extreme effects of charismatic leadership is known as *internalization.* In this case, followers adopt the leader's ideals and goals and become inspired to attain them because the goals are inherently satisfying; it is the leader's goals that inspire followers, not the leader as an individual. Through careful rhetoric, the leader causes followers to believe their own values will be achieved by carrying out the leader's objectives. This is often done by articulating a vision with ideals that include followers' values and self-concepts. Attaining this vision is a way to realize followers' values as well as their ideal self-concept. The leader describes followers' tasks as meaningful, noble, morally correct, and even heroic. This gives a moral quality to followers' task performance, and makes their actions inherently satisfying. It feels right to actively pursue the leader's goals because they are worthwhile and necessary to attain important values shared by the leader and followers.

The two psychological processes of identification and internalization often occur together as the charismatic leader weaves a spell over followers. Followers of Mahatma Gandhi and Martin Luther King Jr. undoubtedly believed strongly in their leader's goals and values (internalization), and also saw their leader as a model of their ideal person at the time and in the situation they faced (identification). Followers of Adolf Hitler and Jim Jones undoubtedly identified with their leaders and internalized many goals and values contained in their mission. Although some charismatic leaders exploit their followers and others benefit them, the psychological processes involved in influencing followers are quite similar.

Another process, called *social identification,* helps to further explain the strong impacts of charismatic leaders, and is closely related to followers' personal identification with the leader. It means that followers define themselves in terms of membership in a group or organization. In these situations, charismatic leaders create a connection in followers' minds between their self-concepts and the shared values and identities of their group.[15] The leaders provide the group with a unique identity through their rhetorical skills and the vision they describe of the group's past and future accomplishments. They emphasize the group identity via group slogans, symbols (flags, emblems, uniforms), rituals (singing the organizational song, saluting the flag, reciting the company creed), and ceremonies (initiation of new members, giving awards to outstanding members).[16]

Both identification and internalization are involved in social identification, but the focus of social identification is the group rather than the leader. The leader describes the group's past, present, and future in the form of a collective mission that provides followers with a sense of continuity and order, and helps them interpret their experiences. Followers develop the feeling that they are a part of something very meaningful, and their motives are aroused to help carry out the collective mission.

Another social process has been described recently that may strengthen the impacts of identification and internalization. This process, called *social contagion,* is based on findings from social psychology. The concept assumes that most people share a heroic image as part of their self-concept. When a crisis or period of extreme change occurs, causing followers to feel anxious or frustrated, a skilled charismatic leader can activate this heroic aspect of followers' identities and cause them to behave with unusual

---

LEADERSHIP IN PERSPECTIVE
Ethical and Unethical Charismatic Leadership

Charismatic leaders often produce results, but they also create risks for followers. Well-known charismatics like Adolf Hitler, Jim Jones, and Charles Manson have carried out evil or immoral missions, and brought death and destruction on their followers. Jane Howell and Bruce Avolio describe what they believe to be the qualities of ethical and unethical charismatic leaders and their effects on followers, which are summarized in the following table:

Key Characteristics and Behaviors

Ethical Charismatic Leaders	Unethical Charismatic Leaders
Uses power to serve others	Uses power for personal gain or impact
Aligns vision with followers' needs and aspirations	Promotes own personal vision
Considers and learns from criticism	Censures critical or opposing views
Stimulates followers to think independently and question the leader's views	Demands that own decisions be accepted without question
Uses open, two-way communication	Uses one-way communication
Coaches and develops followers, and shares recognition with followers	Is insensitive to followers' needs
Relies on internal moral standards to satisfy organizational and societal interests	Relies on convenient external moral standards to satisfy self-interests
Develops followers' ability to lead themselves	Selects and produces obedient, dependent, and compliant followers
Uses crises as learning experiences, to develop a sense of purpose in the mission and vision, and to emphasize the leader's intention to do right	Uses crises to solidify own power base, minimize dissent, and increase dependence of followers
Avoids the trappings of success; rather, shares credit with followers and stays humble	Success brings delusions of invincibility, greatness, and extreme emphasis on image management

Based on their research, Howell and Avolio suggest that the following organizational practices can create and sustain ethical charismatic leaders:

• Top management commitment and enforcement of a clear code of ethical conduct

• Recruiting, selecting, and promoting managers with high moral standards

• Developing performance standards and rewards that emphasize respect for people

• Providing leaders with education and training that teaches them how to integrate new and old perspectives and diverse points of view

• Training individuals who have the necessary personality characteristics, social skills, and motivations to acquire ethical charismatic leadership behaviors

• Identifying and celebrating heroes and heroines who exemplify high moral conduct

These practices should lead to a culture of ethical responsibility that promotes moral development, acceptable standards for leaders' conduct, and long-term success for the organization.

SOURCE: Based on J. M. Howell and B. J. Avolio. The ethics of charismatic leadership: Submission or liberation? *Academy of Management Executive,* 6(2), 1992, 43–54.

▮▮▮▮▮▮▮▮▮

devotion to a great cause. When other followers observe this devotion, their heroic self-images may also be activated, causing them to lose their inhibitions and replicate the observed behavior. In other words, extreme devotion to leaders and their cause becomes contagious and spreads throughout a group via social influence of one member on another.

Charismatic leaders probably cause all these processes to occur with their followers. They encourage personal and social identification through their value-laden speeches and their emphasis on a righteous mission and vision of the future. They cause followers to internalize their goals, values, and beliefs about the future, and to obtain intrinsic satisfaction from the pursuit of those goals. Their influence is heightened by social influence processes that cause followers to give themselves over to the collective spirit and enthusiasm of their fellow group members. Charismatic leadership is a complex process, and charismatic leaders make use of numerous social and psychological processes to exert strong effects on followers. The Leadership in Perspective box: Ethical and Unethical Charismatic Leadership shows how these influence processes can be used for moral or immoral purposes.

▮▮▮ Examples of Ineffective Charismatic Leadership

Charismatic leadership is not always an effective influence strategy. The following examples demonstrate how charismatic leadership can sometimes result in unpleasant consequences.

1. One charismatic leader took advantage of a crisis situation to solidify his power base. Followers hungered for a resolution to the crisis and looked to the leader for a magical solution. The leader used his power base to minimize follower dissent and to help attain his personal vision. Followers became dependent on the leader for guidance and lost their self-confidence to think on their own. When the crisis ended and the leader was unable to adapt his vision to the changed environment, followers were unable to be self-guiding. The leader blamed the followers for his and their inadequacies.

2. A leader described a vision of the future and energized followers to strive for that vision, but in doing this she created expectations in followers that were unrealistic and unattainable. When the results were far short of what was envisioned, followers felt the leader had misled them. They became frustrated and angry with the leader who created their unrealistic expectations.

3. A previously successful charismatic leader became trapped by followers' expectations that the leader's magic would continue indefinitely. This caused the leader to take high risks when the situation no longer warranted it. When the leader's risky actions were not successful, he suffered a loss of magic in followers' eyes, and a crisis in leadership resulted.

4. Leadership in an organization was focused on a single charismatic individual. Thus, the time, energy, expertise, and interests of that leader limited the organization's ability to deal with various issues. During a time of extreme change, when different issues required different types of competencies, these limits became problematic because the single leader did not possess expertise in all the needed areas.

In all these situations, followers developed an overreliance on a single charismatic leader. Either the leader was unable to meet their expectations, or he or she did not prepare them to meet the demands of the mission and the environment. A slower leadership approach that focused on solidifying gains and developing expertise throughout the organization may have been more effective in these situations. The Leadership Self-Assessment box describes some personal tendencies of charismatic leaders.

▬▬▬ Skills, Traits, and Sources of Power for Charismatic Leaders

Charismatic leaders work hard at developing critical skills so they can have extraordinary effects on followers. For one thing, charismatic leaders develop outstanding *communication and rhetorical skills*.[17] They can provide emotionally stimulating descriptions of an ideal future, and they can outline a mission to achieve their vision that generates excitement and commitment by followers. They relate follower values, aspirations, and beliefs to their vision, and incorporate moral dimensions to bind followers together with them in carrying out the mission. They often relate followers' historical roots to their mission, and provide a broad picture of the importance of followers' collective roles in a historical context. They may relate their mission to wider social movements, such as environmentalism, religious purity, or political equality and freedom. These activities clearly require considerable verbal skills, and successful charismatic leaders develop these skills.

Charismatic leaders often develop personal characteristics that support and enhance their verbal skills. They are usually *assertive, dynamic, outgoing,* and often *forceful.* They are not shy or timid in dealing with others. They are verbally and nonverbally expressive of their ideas and feelings. When holding public office, they seem to enjoy interacting with the press and other members of the public. As they gain experience and achieve short-term goals, their *self-confidence* and *self-assurance* usually

LEADERSHIP SELF-ASSESSMENT
Do You Have Charismatic Tendencies?

To investigate your charismatic tendencies, answer the questions below. *Fortune* devised this quiz with the help of Jay Conger, an expert on charismatic leadership. If your present situation does not apply to the questions, imagine how you would react if placed in the situation.

1. I worry most about
   a. my current competitors
   b. my future competitors

2. I'm most at ease thinking in
   a. generalities
   b. specifics

3. I tend to focus on
   a. our missed opportunities
   b. opportunities we've seized

4. I prefer to
   a. promote traditions that made us great
   b. create new traditions

5. I like to communicate an idea via
   a. a written report
   b. a one-page chart

6. I tend to ask
   a. "How can we do this better?"
   b. "Why are we doing this?"

7. I believe
   a. there's always a way to minimize risk
   b. some risks are too great

8. When I disagree with my boss, I typically
   a. coax him or her nicely to alter his or her view
   b. bluntly tell him or her, "You're wrong."

9. I tend to sway people by using
   a. emotion
   b. logic

10. I think this quiz is
    a. ridiculous
    b. fascinating

▪ ▪ ▪ ▪ ▪ ▪ ————————————————————————————————————— ▪ ▪ ▪ ▪ ▪ ▪

ANSWERS TO SELF-ASSESSMENT

Charismatic types tend to give the following answers: 1.b; 2.a; 3.a; 4.b; 5.b; 6.b; 7.a; 8.b; 9.a; 10.b. If you respond to seven or more of these questions in this way, you have strong charismatic tendencies.

▪ ▪ ▪ ▪ ▪ ▪ ▪ ▪ ▪ ▪

increases. This, in turn, increases the strength of their conviction in their ideas, mission, and goals. This strong conviction is needed to convince followers the mission and goals are achievable.[18,19]

Furthermore, charismatic leaders usually have or develop a *high need for power.* This refers to leaders' desire to influence and sometimes control their environment, often including other people. This characteristic is sometimes complemented by a *low degree of authoritarianism.* Individuals who are low in authoritarianism do not require absolute obedience to authority, show restraint in using their power, and do not dominate or manipulate others exclusively for their own ends.[20] The pattern of high power need and low authoritarianism is particularly effective for high-level leadership positions in large formal organizations.[21] It may be that low authoritarianism tempers a leader's power needs, making these leaders more concerned with their followers' welfare and causing them to demonstrate more caring behaviors.

When a charismatic leader is *highly authoritarian,* a high need for power may result in a domineering and manipulative leader, such as Jim Jones or Adolf Hitler. These charismatic leaders become dominant, manipulative, and narcissistic—having a grand sense of self-importance and a need for constant attention and admiration by followers.[22] They can be highly influential, but their goals are usually self-oriented and the consequences for followers can be detrimental or disastrous.

Effective charismatic leaders often develop two types of power to help them exert extraordinary influence on followers. They develop *referent power* from their achievements and personality, their strongly held beliefs and values that support the vision, and their willingness to take personal risks to carry out the mission. Referent power causes followers to feel affection for the leader, to identify with the leader and his or her vision, to emulate the leader's behavior, and to adapt their beliefs and values to fit the leader's.[23] Followers respond to the charismatic leader's personal appeals because they want to be like the leader, whom they admire and look up to for guidance and inspiration.

Charismatic leaders also develop *expert power* by accumulating extensive knowledge and understanding of problems facing followers and the means to overcome those problems. They work diligently to simplify and interpret a complex environment to help followers understand key issues that concern them. They become skilled at designing and communicating a strategic mission to achieve the shared vision. They also use their knowledge and expertise to provide rational explanations of the benefits of pursuing the mission, and serve as role models for important behaviors to carry it out. Because of these factors, followers view the leader as having a high degree of expertise, so they trust her, willingly obey her requests, and accept her directives without question.[24]

FIGURE 8-2 Key skills, characteristics, and sources of power for charismatic leadership

Some charismatic leaders make use of the *legitimate power* of their high-level position in an organization. By controlling many resources and having extensive staff help, they give the impression of having vast amounts of personal knowledge and understanding of situations. They build on this perceived expert power by emphasizing their own past successes and de-emphasizing failures, and by being forceful in proposing and implementing strategies for followers to carry out. Historians have noted that Franklin Delano Roosevelt, our 32nd president, was particularly adept at building his expert and referent power with the public. Figure 8-2 summarizes key power sources, skills, and characteristics for charismatic leadership.

▪▪▪ Facilitating and Limiting Conditions for Charismatic Leadership

Several organizational characteristics may predispose leaders to use charismatic leadership behaviors and followers to view their leaders as charismatic. The number of studies of these factors is quite small, however, so much of the literature on organizational factors that precipitate charismatic leadership is still at the theoretical stage.

Max Weber believed that a *crisis* was essential for charismatic leadership to emerge. Followers experience anxiety and distress during crises, and they yearn for a way out of their predicament. A leader who confidently explains the reasons for the crisis and advocates a radical mission that involves followers in resolving the crisis is often seen as a savior with exceptional powers of understanding, foresight, and vision (charisma). Recent studies show that a crisis is not essential for charismatic leadership to occur, but *followers' anxiety or distress* can create an opportunity for charismatic leaders to emerge. Many organizational factors can create anxiety and stress in followers. Periods of radical social change, such as political revolution or disrupted family patterns, the impending financial failure of an organization, the stress of starting a new business, or severe competition that threatens followers' livelihood, can all cause followers who feel inadequate, fearful, or alienated, to hunger for an all-encompassing solution to their problems.[25–28] In some cases, leaders have precipitated crises through enflamed rhetoric or other actions, resulting in anxiety, distress, and fear, which cause followers to seek a charismatic savior.

Some evidence indicates that groups with a *history of charismatic leaders* are more likely to attribute charismatic qualities to their leaders. In these situations, the followers have mental images of an effective leader who possesses many charismatic qualities, and as a result, followers tend to look to leaders who have these qualities. It may also be helpful for a leader to hold a *high-level office* (such as president), or to have a *history of success* as a leader, in order to be viewed as a charismatic leader.[29,30] These factors likely combine with a leader's characteristics, skills, and behavior to produce the image followers identify as a charismatic leader.

Little has been written and almost no research has been conducted on factors that prevent or limit charismatic leadership from occurring. Several writers have noted that charisma is transitory in nature, occurring as long as the factors causing followers' anxiety, fear, and distress are present.[31] When these factors are removed, followers may prefer to maintain the status quo, and thus seek other leaders with a less revolutionary vision. The political fate of Winston Churchill after the end of World War II is a case in point. Churchill was ousted as prime minister of Britain when his arrogant and combative leadership style no longer fit with the new peacetime attitudes of British voters. Some have suggested that charisma can be prolonged through institutionalization of the leader's mission in an organization's processes, but this appears to be difficult. Others have noticed that followers who work closely with a charismatic leader often perceive fewer or different charismatic qualities than those who are physically distant.[32,33] Followers who are highly educated or professional may also attribute fewer charismatic qualities to a leader.[34] These possible constraints on the emergence of charismatic leadership will likely receive attention by researchers in the future. The Leadership in Perspective box: Spirituality and Charismatic Leadership describes the extreme power and danger of some charismatic leaders.

▬▬▬ Effects of Charismatic Leadership Behaviors

Charismatic leadership has the most immediate effects on followers' *emotional attachment* to the leader, their *emotional arousal* (excitement), and their *motivation* regarding the leader's mission.[35,36] These emotional effects are often strong. When followers have a leader who skillfully demonstrates charismatic behaviors, they often feel inspired and exhilarated, and they attribute charismatic traits to that leader.

Effects on Follower and Group Psychological Reactions

When followers view a leader as charismatic, they place a high degree of *respect, trust, loyalty,* and *acceptance* in the leader and his or her judgment, and are loyal to the leader's mission.[37–40] Followers may also experience increased *self-esteem, self-assurance,* and belief that their work for the leader is highly *meaningful* and *important*.[41,42] Because these psychological reactions all contain a large emotional component, followers often experience the effects of charismatic leaders as unusually strong and memorable.

These positive emotional reactions explain the most frequently repeated finding from research on charismatic leadership behavior. Followers of charismatic leaders are

LEADERSHIP IN PERSPECTIVE
Spirituality and Charismatic Leadership

Several writers have emphasized that charismatic leadership emerges from a leader's spirituality, personal philosophy, and inner vision. James Kouzes and Barry Posner described Major General John Stanford as an example. Stanford was a charismatic leader who commanded the U.S. Army's Military Traffic Management Command, and later became an inspirational superintendent of public schools in Seattle, Washington. Stanford firmly believed he knew the secret of success in life: "The secret of success is to stay in love." He explained this to mean that leadership is an affair of the heart. Loyal followers must be convinced that the leader passionately believes in his or her vision of the future and believes in each of them. Anita Roddick, Nelson Mandela, Mahatma Gandhi, and Martin Luther King Jr. are examples of passionate charismatic leaders who also demonstrated this process.

However, other writers point out that leaders who are viewed in spiritual terms often evoke strong personal identification in followers who suffer from fear, guilt, or alienation. Gary Yukl gave an example of a young man experiencing an identity crisis because he had no clear concept of an ideal self, due to weak or abusive parents. This individual could develop a strong emotional attachment to a charismatic gang leader who symbolizes an ideal self. Another individual who has caused great harm to others may experience extreme guilt. He could identify with a charismatic religious leader who represents strong moral values, vicariously experience this leader's moral superiority, and overcome his guilt. When followers attribute intense spirituality and inner vision to charismatic leaders, this may reflect a weakness in followers' psychological or social condition or character. This can be a dangerous situation for followers, as shown by charismatics like David Koresh, Adolph Hitler, and Charles Manson. Followers must be sure that their spiritual charismatic leaders also have the qualities of an ethical charismatic described earlier in this chapter.

SOURCES: Based on J. Kouzes and B. Posner, *The Leadership Challenge: How to Keep Getting Extraordinary Things Done in Organizations.* San Francisco: Jossey-Bass, 1995; and G. Yukl, *Leadership in Organizations,* 4th ed. Upper Saddle River, NJ: Prentice Hall, 1998.

---

usually more *satisfied* with the leader, their work, and their overall job and organization. These effects of charismatic leaders on followers' satisfaction are often quite strong.[43–48] Followers' positive emotional states and high satisfaction levels help explain the high levels of *organizational commitment* and *low levels of stress* and *low job burnout* reported by followers in studies of charismatic leaders.[49,50]

When followers become emotionally attached to a leader, when they are excited and internally motivated by a vision and rhetoric, and when their own self-esteem and self-assurance are heightened, they respond positively to a leader's requests for extreme effort, self-sacrifice, perseverance, and commitment. These responses explain how charismatic leadership can sometimes inspire high performance in followers.

Effects on Followers' Performance and Behavior

A large volume of research explores the effects of charismatic leadership on follower and group performance, using performance ratings of the charismatic leader as their outcome variable, rather than more direct quantitative measures of follower performance or productivity. In these studies, followers and superiors have rated their charismatic leaders as highly effective in diverse groups and organizations.[51–56]

These findings support the strong emotional effects of charismatic leaders. However, because the performance measures are based on perceptions of those who work with the charismatic leader, the overall positive impression of the leader could result in both the charismatic attributions and the positive performance perceptions. In other words, if followers are impressed with a leader's behavior, skills, and past achievements, they may assume the leader is charismatic and evaluate the leader as highly effective regardless of her actual performance in her current position. If this occurs, then the charismatic leader's behavior has not caused the positive performance perceptions. Instead, the general positive impression of the leader has only made him or her appear effective.

When people believe that charismatic leaders are effective, these positive impressions can impose an important bias on their ratings of the leader's actual effectiveness. Researchers recently adjusted for this bias by having one follower rate a leader's charisma and a second follower rate the leader's effectiveness. With this more careful approach, charismatic leadership behavior was not related to perceived effectiveness. Only when the same followers rated the leader's behavior and effectiveness was there a relationship between charisma and effectiveness. A comprehensive review of studies of this type shows that this perceptual bias can make charismatic leadership appear more effective than it really is.[57] Clearly, few solid conclusions can be drawn from research on *perceived effectiveness* of charismatic leaders.

Recently, some researchers have carefully measured one or more aspects of follower or group performance under a charismatic leader. One experimental study of business students doing a business simulation with trained leaders showed that charismatic leaders produced high-quality performance among followers (higher than supportive leaders, and about the same level as directive leaders). Followers of charismatic leaders also generated more possible courses of action in the simulation than did followers of directive or supportive leaders.[58] Also, a study of church ministers found that when church members saw their minister as charismatic, they attended church more often and church membership increased.[59] Another study of managers and supervisors in a distributing company showed that charismatic leaders had higher-performing followers than noncharismatic leaders.[60]

Charismatic leadership also improved follower performance among petrochemical workers and U.S. Army commissioned and noncommissioned officers. In these situations, charismatic leaders created positive psychological reactions in their followers (especially trust in the leader and commitment to the organization), and these improved psychological reactions resulted in better performance on the job.[61,62] Some researchers have measured aspects of group, department, or division performance in relation to charismatic leadership. Business-unit performance in a financial institution, and in one audit committee, have improved under charismatic leaders, and so has technological innovation.[63–65] Two recent studies in large business organizations in the United States showed positive effects of CEO charismatic leadership on their companies' performance only when the organizational environment was highly uncertain.[66,67]

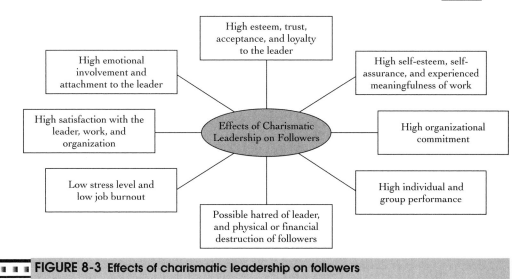

▪ ▪ ▪ ▪ **FIGURE 8-3** Effects of charismatic leadership on followers

It seems safe to conclude that charismatic leadership can improve follower and group performance, although the effects are probably not any stronger than other important leadership behaviors.[68,69] It appears from the research thus far that the effects of charismatic leadership on followers' attitudes and emotional reactions are considerably stronger than the effects on their performance.[70] The situations in which these impacts are most likely to occur will be addressed in the following sections of this chapter. Because charismatic leadership has the most immediate effects on followers' psychological reactions, such as emotional attachment to the leader, motivation, and arousal, these are likely the factors that transmit the leader's effects onto follower or group performance.

Charismatic leaders, however, do not always create positive follower reactions. For example, charismatics sometimes inspire strong opposition and hatred in individuals who favor the old order of things.[71] This finding is consistent with the conclusion of one writer that charismatic leaders who transform followers, organizations, and governments are either loved or hated by members of their constituency. It is also supported by a historical study that found that charismatic U.S. presidents experienced either an assassination attempt during their first term, were reelected, or both.[72] John F. Kennedy, Martin Luther King Jr., Malcolm X, and Mahatma Gandhi are examples of charismatic leaders who faced attacks by individuals who violently opposed their missions. Both charismatic leaders and their followers can face large risks. Figure 8-3 summarizes the effects of charismatic leadership. The Leadership in Perspective box describes the current status of research on charismatic leadership outside the United States.

▪ ▪ ▪ Transformational Leadership

Transformational leadership is closely related to charismatic leadership. Transformational leaders are said to influence followers to adopt new values and visions, and transcend personal goals and interests for achievement of collective goals.[73–75] The term "transformational" comes from the changes these leaders create in

LEADERSHIP IN PERSPECTIVE
Charismatic Leadership in Other Countries

Several examples of charismatic leaders from outside the United States have been given in this chapter. These examples demonstrate that followers respond favorably to these leaders in other countries. This conclusion is supported by research showing that charismatic leadership behaviors improve followers' attitudes and perceptions in Mexico and several Asian countries. However, there is little research evidence at this time that charisma improves follower or group performance outside the United States. One ongoing international study has shown that individuals believe charismatic leadership is effective in their culture, but this research has yet to relate charismatic behaviors to actual measures of follower performance in these countries.

Some have suggested that charismatic leaders need to adapt their behavior to the culture. They might be more participative in India and Japan than in Pakistan or Taiwan because workers expect participation in India and Japan. We suspect future international research will show that charismatic leadership improves followers' performance outside the United States. However, the actual behavior of charismatic leaders may vary to fit the followers' cultural expectations.

SOURCES: Based on P. W. Dorfman and J. P. Howell, Managerial leadership in the United States and Mexico: Distant neighbors or close cousins? In C. K. Granrose and S. Oskamp (Eds.), *Cross-Cultural Work Groups,* 234–264. Thousand Oaks, CA: Sage, 1997; P. W. Dorfman, International and cross-cultural leadership research. In P. J. Punnett and O. Shenker (Eds.), *Handbook for International Management Research,* 267–348. Cambridge, MA: Blackwell, 1996.

followers' values, goals, visions, and sense of purpose. In its most recent form, transformational leadership consists of four components: *idealized influence (attributed and behavioral), inspirational motivation, individualized consideration,* and *intellectual stimulation.* Idealized influence (attributed) involves a socialized charisma of the leader, focusing on whether the leader is perceived as competent, self-confident, and committed to higher-order ideals and ethics. Idealized influence (behavioral) involves charismatic actions of the leader related to values, beliefs, and missions. Inspirational motivation includes such behaviors as articulating appealing visions, focusing followers' efforts, and modeling appropriate behaviors to energize followers. Intellectual stimulation includes frame alignment behaviors by the leader that help followers view problems and issues they face from a new perspective, and think creatively to solve those problems.[76] Individualized consideration refers to supportive behaviors for followers such as showing concern for their needs and well being, giving encouragement and compliments to them to improve their self-confidence, and facilitating their development.

Transformational leadership is clearly related to several follower and group outcomes. It has a direct impact on followers' emotions, optimism, and frustration, which may influence followers' performance.[77] Followers led by transformational leaders are more likely to identify with values and beliefs of the leader and the group, have increased self-efficacy and collective efficacy, and develop higher levels of dependence on the leader.[78] They may also develop critical thinking skills, be more safety conscious, exert extra effort for task performance, and have more cohesive groups.[79–81]

Charismatic leadership and transformational leadership are frequently viewed as interchangeable. Both include many similar behaviors, such as developing and articulating an inspirational vision, advocating a moral mission that reflects followers' values and needs, arousing followers' emotions to identify with the leader and the mission, role modeling, frame alignment, and inducing extra effort from followers to achieve high levels of performance.[82–86] Both charismatic leadership and the most recent version of transformational leadership also include attributions by followers about the leader's characteristics, behaviors, and capabilities. In fact, three of the four overall components of transformational leadership reflect aspects of charismatic leadership—idealized influence, inspirational motivation, and intellectual stimulation. The fourth component, individualized consideration, reflects supportive behaviors described in Chapter 4, and is not typically included in descriptions of charismatic leadership. It represents an important difference between transformational and charismatic leadership.

Because transformational leaders are both charismatic and supportive of their followers, they are more concerned with their followers' welfare, their visions and missions directly reflect followers' values and needs, and they create conditions that facilitate followers' development and performance. Leaders who are truly transformational often avoid certain charismatic tactics such as impression management, precipitating apparent crises, or withholding information. Charismatic leaders sometimes use these tactics to build their own image in followers' eyes as omniscient saviors who are bigger than life, and they can generate emotional bonds with the leader that may be exploited for the leaders' own benefit. Real transformational leaders reflect their supportiveness (individualized consideration) for followers by being nonauthoritarian and showing restraint in their use of power. They may thus be more willing to delegate important tasks to followers (to facilitate their development) than other charismatic leaders. A recent study clearly demonstrated that supportive behaviors are an important complement to charismatic leadership. It showed that supportiveness by military officers was more important than charismatic behaviors in creating followers' trust, motivation, and willingness to sacrifice for their group.[87]

In theory, transformational leadership is different from transactional leadership. With transformational leadership, followers are more aware of the importance of task outcomes, and they may transcend their self-interest for achievement of group interests, have higher self-confidence, and exert more effort for task performance. Transactional leadership, on the other hand, appeals to followers' self-interest. It involves an exchange relationship, in which followers exert effort for the purpose of getting contractual benefits in return from the leader or group.

However, transformational and transactional leadership are not mutually exclusive.[88] Leadership scholars developed and tested a Full Range Leadership theory (FRLT), which includes both transformational and transactional leadership.[89–93] FRLT focuses on nine leadership factors. Five of them are transformational leadership factors: *idealized influence (attributed), idealized influence (behavior), inspirational motivation, intellectual stimulation,* and *individualized consideration.* These transformational leadership factors exactly match the components of transformational leadership. The three transactional leadership factors are *contingent reward leadership, management by exception (active),* and *management by exception (passive).* Contingent reward leadership refers to clarifying task roles and requirements and providing rewards to followers based on their task performance (similar to the directive and reward behaviors described in Chapters 5 and 7). Management by exception (active) refers to leadership behaviors aimed at keeping track of operations to prevent problems from occurring and to ensure that standards are met (this process was also described in Chapter 5 as directive leadership). Management by exception (passive) describes the leader's intervention after work-related problems occur. The final leadership factor is nontransactional *laissez-faire leadership,* which involves a total abandonment of the leader's responsibility and authority. The Multifactor Leadership Questionnaire (MLQ) is the instrument used to measure the Full Range Leadership theory behaviors, and has been used in many leadership-related studies.[94] These studies show that elements of both transformational leadership and transactional leadership are important to group performance.[95] The FRLT elements that reflect charismatic leadership (idealized influence, inspirational motivation, intellectual stimulation), supportive leadership (individualized consideration), directive leadership (active management by exception), and contingent reward leadership have the most consistent favorable effects on group performance.

▬▬▬ Situational Dynamics of Charismatic Leadership

The remainder of this chapter describes the situational and follower characteristics that make charismatic leadership more or less effective. We also describe strategies for influencing situational and follower characteristics to improve the effectiveness of charismatic leadership. The continual interaction between charismatic leaders, their followers, and environmental factors are emphasized. Because only a small portion of the research on charismatic leadership has dealt with situational and follower characteristics, some of the findings described in these sections are still tentative. The Leadership Self-Assessment: Diagnosing Situations for Charismatic Leadership describes when charismatic leadership behaviors may or may not be effective.

The following sections explain how these and other situational and follower characteristics influence effective charismatic leadership.

▬▬▬ Situational Factors that Enhance Charismatic Leadership

For many years, almost no studies were conducted on situational factors that enhance the effectiveness of charismatic leadership. This is probably because researchers focused on understanding the behaviors and characteristics of these leaders. Recently, researchers have become more interested in situational enhancers. These findings are described here, followed by several conclusions made by leadership experts based on historical descriptions of charismatic leaders. Each of these sources provides evidence about when charismatic leaders should be most effective.

LEADERSHIP SELF-ASSESSMENT

Diagnosing Situations for Charismatic Leadership

Place an "×" next to those situations in which you believe charismatic leadership is appropriate.

1. _____ Followers work in an industry that is extremely competitive, with rapid technological change and constant threats of mergers and takeovers by other companies.

2. _____ Followers work in an organization that emphasizes peer reviews of their performance, collegial decision making, and a culture of self-management.

3. _____ There is a long history of charismatic leaders in the organization.

4. _____ Followers' work involves providing social services to low-income recipients.

5. _____ Followers are highly experienced, educated, older employees who hold high-level positions in the organization, and work at tasks that they find interesting and enjoyable.

6. _____ Followers are voluntary members of a self-help organization designed to assist its members in overcoming alcohol and drug addiction.

Charismatic leadership has been found to be highly effective in four of these situations. Items 1, 3, 4, and 6 describe situations in which followers usually respond positively to a charismatic leader. In these situations, followers may be highly stressed and anxious about the future, expect their leader to be charismatic due to a history of charismatic leaders in their organization, or work at tasks that are morally gratifying but probably under rewarded. These situations often enhance the effectiveness of charismatic leadership. The situations described in items 2 and 5 may have the opposite effect. Here, followers may be highly trained and experienced, enjoy their work, and have considerable status in their organization, or their organization may emphasize independence, self-control, and equality of power and influence. In any of these situations, followers may not feel the need for an inspirational and dynamic charismatic leader. They are probably accustomed to charting their own course in carrying out job duties, and their organization has rewarded their independence and self-management in the past.

Organizational and Environmental Characteristics

Recent studies of chief executive officers (CEOs) in large business organizations and historical analyses of charismatic leaders show that environmental conditions or events can enhance the impacts of charismatic leadership.[96,97] Charismatic CEOs generated high levels of company financial performance *only* when the economic, technical, or cultural *environment was highly uncertain*.[98,99] Culture shocks, a general decline in cultural values, absence of behavioral norms, or extreme crises that threaten the life or well-being of followers may turn a charismatic leader into a savior in the followers' eyes. In these situations, there is a lack of clarity regarding appropriate goals, or few environmental cues are available to guide behavior. Followers have no structure or guidance other than the leader, and may be grateful for a mission and role model to guide them in a constructive manner.[100] Conditions such as these were faced by Gandhi in India before its independence, Hitler in post–World War I Germany, Martin

Luther King Jr. in the United States during the 1950s and 1960s, and Lee Iacocca with Chrysler Corporation in the 1980s. In each of these situations, followers faced extremely difficult existing conditions or possible disaster, causing them to look to a charismatic leader to save them from their intolerable situation.

Researchers also found that charismatic leaders had stronger positive effects on project quality in research groups that worked on new concepts and ideas than in groups that developed existing products and technology.[101] This finding is consistent with the tendency of charismatic leaders to describe a vision and mission that includes a major change from the status quo. The research group projects involved more uncertainty and had more potential for groundbreaking advancements than did the development of existing products. In research groups, high-technology industries, and new business start-ups, major changes can happen quickly as breakthroughs occur in new materials, processes, technology, or markets. Researchers recently noted that charismatic leadership had more impact in entrepreneurial firms, in which change often occurs quickly, than in large well-established companies. Charismatic leaders who envision these changes can inspire followers to persist with excitement and vigor, and to change the current ways of thinking and doing things in their field. In situations in which *rapid change* is likely, charismatic leadership may be highly effective.

In a study of managers and professional workers in Asia, researchers found that a leader's *expertise* and *rank*, as well as the existence of extensive *formal plans, goals, and procedures,* all enhanced the effects of charismatic leadership on followers' satisfaction and commitment to the organization.[102] When followers viewed their leaders as high in rank or as experts in followers' tasks, or when there was considerable documentation to guide followers in their activities and to support the leader's mission, charismatic leadership tended to be more effective at improving followers' attitudes. Leaders who are experts and hold a high status or rank can intensify the super-human image of a charismatic leader, and therefore enhance their effects on followers.[103] Extensive plans, goals, and procedures that support the leader's vision may help clarify how followers can carry out the leader's mission to achieve the vision. Each of these situational factors has been found in previous studies to enhance other leadership behaviors, but this is the first time they have been studied in conjunction with charismatic leadership.

The *culture* of the leader's organization or group may enhance the impacts of charismatic leadership in at least two ways. First, an organization, group, or society may have a *history of charismatic leadership* that causes followers to attribute charisma to their leaders and respond favorably to charismatic behaviors. In Jewish and Muslim cultures, there is a strong history of having charismatic prophets as leaders of the people; in Japan, leaders have traditionally been viewed as men of exemplary courage and self-sacrifice; and in the United States, leaders are historically seen as strong, outspoken individuals with a vision of the future.[104] This is especially true in the U.S. military, in which charismatic leadership often has strong effects.[105] Alcoholics Anonymous (AA) was started by a charismatic individual and has maintained the culture of divine inspiration to help lead individuals out of their difficulties with alcohol.

A second way in which culture may enhance charismatic leadership is through its relationship with *followers' tasks*.[106] For example, if a task reflects the dominant social values of a culture, followers can become morally involved in pursuing these values through their task. Such conditions occur for military leaders during wartime and when members of AA try to save alcoholics from their addiction. They were also in place when Lee Iacocca saved tens of thousands of Chrysler employees from losing their jobs. In these situations, a charismatic leader's vision, inspirational speeches, and inno-vative behavior may instill followers with a feeling of correctness and moral striving that can result in persistent, high-energy devotion.

Followers who have feelings of *self-doubt, helplessness, anxiety, cynicism, insecurity, isolation, distress,* or *low self-esteem* are particularly susceptible to the influence of charismatic leaders.[107–110] These conditions may accompany a loss of control over one's environment, perhaps due to culture shocks or other social crises. Individuals in these situations respond to a confident, persuasive charismatic leader who resolves their feelings of anxiety, isolation, and distress by directing their efforts toward a morally worthwhile goal. Charismatic leaders also involve these followers in meaning-ful, self-fulfilling activities that increase their self-esteem.

International researchers identified several other follower characteristics that enhanced the effects of charismatic leadership on follower satisfaction and commit-ment. Followers' number of *years of schooling* was an enhancer in Korea and Mexico; *followers' high rank* was an enhancer in Taiwan and Mexico; and *followers' profession-alism* was an enhancer in Korea.[111] These factors are related—followers with more years of schooling will typically have higher rank and a more professional attitude toward their work, organization, and leaders. It appears that workers in these countries who progress in organizations and have professional attitudes see a lot of value in charismatic leadership. Each of these countries has a predominantly collectivist orien-tation toward life and work. Collectivism implies sacrifice for the good of the group or organization, and responsiveness to leaders, who are often viewed as highly charis-matic. It may be that followers who are trained, competent, and successful adhere very closely to the collectivist cultural patterns that are approved in their country. This may be less true in individualistic countries, such as the United States. These cultural pat-terns may be key factors affecting enhancers of charismatic leadership.

Several writers have suggested that when *followers' needs, values, and identities* are congruent with a charismatic leader's vision, they will likely respond with very positive attitudes and commitment to carry out that vision.[112,113] Others believe that followers who have an *expressive orientation* to their work life and a *principled orientation* to social relations may be more susceptible to the influence of charismatic leaders.[114] Expressively oriented individuals view work as more than just an exchange of their time for money and other extrinsic rewards; they see it as a means of expressing who they are. Principle-oriented people try to maintain a clear code of conduct in dealings with others, as opposed to letting the situation entirely dictate their behavior. Because charismatic leaders usually have a moral element to their mission, followers with these characteristics are likely to identify with these leaders. Figure 8-4 summarizes the findings from research on enhancers of charismatic leadership.

Influencing Situations to Make Charismatic Leadership More Effective

Many of the enhancers described refer to some type of follower distress, anxiety, isola-tion, or extreme uncertainty. We do *not* advocate that leaders or organizations create these difficulties for organizational members simply to give charismatic leadership behaviors more impact (although some leaders have actually resorted to this strategy). It seems clear, however, that organizations should be alert to the presence of these follower conditions and equip their leaders with charismatic behavioral skills. When coached, leaders can learn to identify and define a mission with a moral dimension, make emotionally expressive speeches to arouse followers to support the mission,

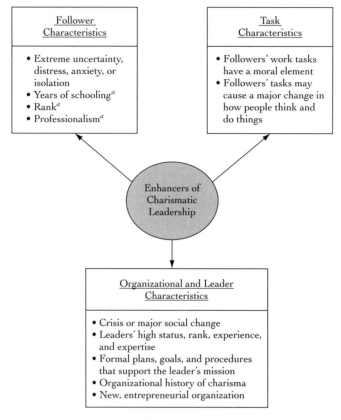

a These enhancers may vary depending on the followers' culture.

▪ ▪ ▪ ▪ **FIGURE 8-4** Enhancers of charismatic leadership

manage followers' impressions, and model desired behaviors for followers. These charismatic behaviors should allow leaders to respond to enhancing conditions when they exist among followers.

   Because building a leader's status, rank, and expertise may enhance the impacts of charismatic leadership, organizations can provide champions, mentoring, and training programs. These will help leaders build their reputation, status, technical skills, and eventually, increase their rank in the organization. Providing staff assistance to help leaders develop plans, goals, and procedures (organizational formalization) consistent with the mission should also enhance a charismatic leader's impact. Internal communications can emphasize charismatic characteristics and accomplishments of past leaders in the organization, which can create a history of charisma in the organization. It may also cause current and future leaders to emulate charismatic behaviors, and followers to respond positively to the leader's behavior.

   In one international study described earlier, each follower characteristic identified as an enhancer of charismatic leadership reflects some aspect of follower empowerment—years of schooling, rank, or degree of professionalism.[115] Although certain cultural characteristics of these countries may have caused employees to become highly responsive to charismatic leadership, programs in these organizations that provide education and

▮▮▮▮▮▮▮▮▮▮▮▮▮▮▮▮▮▮▮▮▮▮▮▮▮▮

LEADERSHIP IN ACTION

Orit Gadiesh, A Charismatic Leader

"True North!" This refers to the set of principles that Orit Gadiesh has used to lead consulting firm Bain & Co. to expand operations and increase revenues by 25 percent a year. True North, defined by Gadiesh as that which is virtuous and right, has made Gadiesh one of the most powerful women in business.

Her looks and nervy style get her noticed. Her skirts start eight inches above the knee and her hair is magenta. It is not unusual to see Orit Gadiesh sit down at a serious meeting and throw her high-heeled feet on the table. However, it is her "intense passion" about being true to herself and her clients that makes Orit so charismatic, according to Tom Tierney, former worldwide managing director at Bain. "She is complex, intense, driven, painfully direct, sometimes ribald, and a lot of fun."

Her father was a commander in the Israeli army. She served two years in army intelligence before enrolling in the Harvard Business School, where she graduated in the top 5 percent of her class. She was hired by Bain & Co. right out of Harvard as one of their first female consultants. She impresses people with her high energy level and her ability to pull the emotional levers of others.

She leads an organization of consultants who are frequently instrumental in making major changes in their clients' organizations. The individuals in these organizations are often experiencing anxiety and distress from problems when the consultants arrive. Gadiesh's expertise and position inspire respect and admiration in her firm's consultants and clients. Her success as a charismatic leader stems from these factors, as well as being a brilliant consultant who can inspire and empathize with clients and her staff.

Though head of one of the most secretive firms in the industry, Gadiesh still manages to spend 70 percent of her time with clients. This is the type of role modeling she provides for Bain & Co. members, where she is seen as a generous mentor for junior consultants. She constantly reminds herself, "If I were the client, how would I feel about this?" It is this empathy, intense passion, and energetic style that creates the "Orit mystique," making her an impressive charismatic leader.

SOURCE: P. Sellers. What exactly is charisma? *Fortune,* January 15, 1996, 68–75. From "What Exactly Is Charisma?," P. Sellers, FORTUNE. © 1996 Time Inc. All rights reserved.

▮▮▮▮▮▮▮▮▮

training, promote professional affiliations, and encourage company loyalty and promotion from within may also increase the impacts of charismatic leadership. The Leadership in Action box on Orit Gadiesh describes how her charismatic style is especially effective for dealing with clients of the consulting firm she leads.

▮▮▮ Situational Characteristics that Neutralize Charismatic Leadership

Little research exists on factors that neutralize the effects of charismatic leadership. Leadership experts have suggested, however, that in organizational situations that call for *routine reliable performance* in pursuit of *pragmatic goals* (such as a post office),[116] charismatic leadership would not likely be effective. These situations normally lack the crises or unusual opportunities that make extraordinary inspiration and effort particularly helpful. Although this prediction has not been tested directly, two recent empirical studies may contradict it. In a laboratory study involving a business simulation, researchers found that a low productivity norm did not neutralize the effect of charismatic leadership on follower performance or satisfaction.[117] A study of real business managers later confirmed this lack of neutralizing effect.[118] Even though workers doing routine tasks with pragmatic objectives may often have a low productivity norm, it is uncertain at this time whether these situational factors neutralize charismatic leadership.

When followers and leaders are *equal in power,* another expert predicted charismatic leadership would have little effect on followers. Although equality of power between leaders and followers might seem highly unusual in most organizations, it can happen. One situation in which this could occur is in a high-technology organization in which technical personnel have information, knowledge, and expertise equal to or greater than their hierarchical leader. This also may occur in universities or health service organizations, in which highly trained professionals report to administrators whose knowledge base in certain areas is less extensive than that of their followers. To date, no studies have tested this prediction, so we do not know if this factor can actually neutralize the effects of charismatic leadership.

In summary, although several writers have made interesting predictions, the research is very sparse on possible neutralizers of charismatic leadership. At this time, no research supports the suggestion that situational or follower characteristics can reliably neutralize the impacts of charismatic leadership.

▪▪▪ Situational Factors that Substitute for Charismatic Leadership

Several types of formal organizational procedures have been described as substituting for charismatic leadership. These factors may make charismatic leadership unnecessary.

Task, Organizational, and Follower Characteristics

Group bonus-pay plans may induce group motivation and commitment to goal achievement in lieu of charismatic leadership. As another example, organizational requirements for *peer review committees, tenure regulations, and consensus decision making* may substitute for the possible influence of charismatic leaders in universities and colleges.[119] Similar requirements and procedures also apply in many health service organizations. Federal and state regulators, as well as funding and accrediting agencies, often specify policies and procedures for these organizations in great detail. This structured atmosphere can inhibit the flexibility and creativity needed for charismatic leaders to influence organizational members.

Charismatic leadership may not be needed in organizations that value independence and *self-management* among employees, commonly found in universities or Theory Z–type business organizations. Theory Z organizations emphasize clear, detailed goal statements and supportive policies that encourage individuals to transcend self-interests and focus on the good of the organization. Hewlett-Packard, a highly successful manufacturer of computers and information systems equipment, is one example. This type of organization may inspire high motivation without a charismatic leader.

One recent empirical study identified two other situational substitutes for charismatic leadership.[120] First, formal organizational *plans, goals, and procedures* substituted for charismatic leadership in Mexico. In this case, the mere existence of formal plans and procedures seemed adequate to obtain follower satisfaction and commitment, and actually alleviated the need for charismatic leadership. Second, a high level of *task expertise by the leader* also alleviated the need for charismatic leadership behaviors in both the United States and Mexico. Although these factors can also be enhancers, they sometimes substitute for specific leadership behaviors by encouraging task expertise and autonomy among followers or by providing formal goals and guidance. It appears that situational factors may sometimes substitute for the impacts of charismatic leadership, at least in the United States and Mexico. However, since several of the Mexican organizations in this research were affiliated with United States corporations, this connection may explain why the substitution effects were similar in both countries. More research is needed to verify these substitution effects.

Some researchers have suggested that certain follower characteristics may substitute for charismatic leadership. They proposed that followers will resist charismatic leadership if they are *self-confident, highly educated,* and *have a strong belief in human equality.*[121] Such individuals are expected to be more careful, discerning, and independent in making decisions about their own behavior and in their judgments of others (including leaders), and to be less likely to surrender their judgment to a charismatic leader. They also often perform well on job tasks. These follower characteristics may be most effective as substitutes for charisma in individualistic cultures, such as the United States. One study found that *followers who were older, had many years of work experience,* and worked at *tasks that they found enjoyable and satisfying* also demonstrated positive attitudes without the need for charismatic leadership.[122] These individuals are usually highly confident, knowledgeable, and high in status, causing them to be independent thinkers. Although a single study cannot confirm a certain substitution effect, these findings support the idea that specific follower characteristics may make charismatic leadership unnecessary. Figure 8-5 summarizes findings on substitutes for charismatic leadership.

Creating Factors That Substitute for Charismatic Leadership

Several organizational actions may create substitutes for charismatic leadership. Selection programs that induct older employees with considerable work experience into the organization and on-the-job training programs that build more work experience may result in a more independent workforce that has less need for a charismatic leader. In addition, job design programs that make jobs inherently satisfying will cause employees to derive positive attitudes and feelings from their work rather than from a charismatic leader. Also, creation of formal plans, goals, and procedures can provide guidance and direction for employees in place of the mission and role modeling provided by a charismatic leader. Finally, programs that develop leaders' competence and expertise and eventually result in their promotion to higher levels may encourage followers to emulate these leaders and themselves become more independent. All of these programs may make followers less dependent on a charismatic leader for motivation, inspiration, and guidance. The Leadership in Action box on Nelson Mandela describes how his charismatic leadership effectively addressed the difficult political and social situation of South Africa.

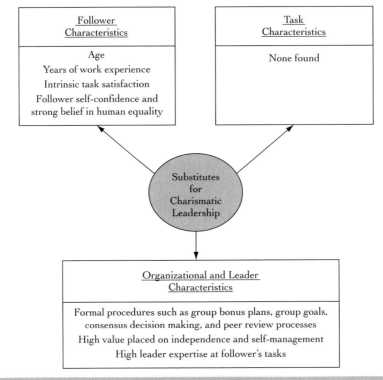

▪▪▪ **FIGURE 8-5 Substitutes for charismatic leadership**

▪▪▪ Assessing the Dynamics of Charismatic Leadership

Effective charismatic leaders are especially sensitive to followers and situations. As they carry out the three key leadership tasks of diagnosing situations, behaving appropriately, and modifying situations, charismatic leaders shape their vision, mission, and communications to fit followers' perceptions of themselves and the environment. In this way, they inspire followers to persist with unusually high effort to reach their goals.

In diagnosing situations, charismatic leaders look for current and future culture shocks or crises that create anxiety and distress in followers. They also engage followers by identifying tasks that have a moral component and a high potential for major change. They build their own status and expertise, develop organizational procedures, and describe historical charismatic leaders to give followers a sense of continuity and respect for their own charismatic efforts. They also may include followers in their mission who are highly educated, professional, and hold a high rank, to add to the legitimacy of the mission. When these follower and environmental factors are present, a leader should use the charismatic behaviors described in Figure 8-1 to influence followers.

▪ ▪

LEADERSHIP IN ACTION
Nelson Mandela

Nelson Mandela, the past president of South Africa and a 1993 Nobel Peace Prize winner, was born in the rural village of Qunu, in what was then the black homeland of Transkei. After a brutal and harsh 27 years of imprisonment on charges of treason and sabotage, Mandela then led his country with his unique style of charismatic leadership.

South Africa has a long history of poverty and apartheid. Apartheid is the oppressive system of all the laws and regulation that had kept black South Africans in an inferior position to whites for centuries. It is easy to imagine that isolated, anxious, and helpless South Africans longed for a leader with the courage and principle to free them from apartheid, just as Moses freed the children of Israel from Egypt.

Twenty-seven years of harsh prison life certainly steeled Mandela. During the period in prison, he talked about politics, developed his vision of a nonracist society in which white and black would live together in harmony, and even strengthened his courage and principle. Soon, the prison became known as Mandela University. His strong beliefs and courage allowed him to speak clearly to white audiences and convince them that they must take responsibility for the past and act according to democratic principles. He also spoke realistically to black audiences, telling them that material needs would not be satisfied immediately.

His charismatic behaviors included providing a clear vision of a nonracist society, making the personal sacrifice of 27 years in prison for his beliefs, and speaking his beliefs to anyone who would listen. Two critical situational factors made Mandela's charismatic behaviors especially effective: (1) the feelings of anxiety and helplessness of black South Africans due to apartheid and extreme poverty, and (2) a tremendous expectation among South Africans and the world community that South Africa must change from a white-dominated society to a democratic one. A Harvard professor once described Mandela as "a small man who has taken on the giant forces of evil, and it looks like he is going to win. All of us, black and white, need to know that David can still beat Goliath."

SOURCE: Nelson Mandela. *Long Walk to Freedom.* Boston: Little, Brown and Company, 1994.

▪ ▪ ▪ ▪ ▪ ▪ ▪ ▪ ▪ ▪

If none of these factors are present, effective charismatic leaders consider modifying environmental or follower characteristics to improve the situation. They may create enhancers by redefining followers' tasks to contain a new moral component or more potential for major change, increase their own status by having their supporters tell stories of the leader's past successes, build their expertise through continuous training, or promote and develop competent followers who support the leader's mission. Each of these actions can enhance the effects of charismatic leadership behaviors.

Charismatic leaders who are concerned with their followers' development may also consider modifying environmental and follower characteristics to create factors that substitute for charismatic leadership. Leaders can do this by providing followers with valuable work experiences that are inherently interesting and satisfying, and helping followers succeed at their tasks to build their self-confidence. Leaders can also develop standard procedures for group bonuses or tenure that do not depend on the leader, or peer review committees that develop and evaluate followers. They can encourage consensus decision making or self-management to make followers less dependent on the leader. This type of situational modification can cause followers to look more to themselves and peers in decision making and problem solving, and to be less reliant on a charismatic leader for guidance and inspiration. This may free up the leader to perform other needed activities that have received little attention in the past.

When a leader correctly diagnoses important enhancers and provides charismatic leadership behaviors, the effects on followers are usually favorable. The leader will continue this successful strategy, at least until follower or situational factors change significantly. If the leader misdiagnoses the situation, and the effects of charismatic leadership behaviors are disappointing, then the leader considers other behaviors, or perhaps modifies other situational and follower characteristics. Leaders may create enhancers to increase their effect on followers, or substitutes to make followers more capable, confident, and independent of the leader. Either strategy can result in improved attitudes and performance by followers. Effective charismatic leaders thus adapt their behaviors and strategies to fit both the situation and followers' reactions and performance. Charismatic leadership behaviors may be needed when followers face threatening and highly uncertain situations. As the environment changes and followers experience success at overcoming their problems, they probably have less need for a charismatic inspirational leader and can operate on their own as independent and competent groups of individuals.

SUMMARY ▪▪▪▪▪▪▪

Charismatic leadership is an attribution (causal explanation) made by followers about a leader who exhibits certain personal characteristics, abilities, and behaviors, and has unusually strong influence on followers' emotions, values, beliefs, attitudes, and behaviors. Charismatic leaders are found in many different organizational contexts, in which they often advocate radical solutions to critical problems and reflect a personal magnetism that inspires unquestioning loyalty, esteem, and emotional attachment in their followers. Their effects on followers appear to result from a combination of leader characteristics and behaviors, follower characteristics, and situational factors.

The key leadership behaviors of charismatic leaders include describing a mission or vision of the future that appeals to followers' moral values and growth needs, making inspirational speeches, using impression management to enhance their image in followers' eyes, role modeling behaviors for followers that reflect high expectations and confidence in followers, demonstrating creative risky behavior for the sake of the mission, and using frame alignment to help followers develop shared perspectives of events and environmental factors that help guide follower behavior.

The strong effects of charismatic leaders on followers often occur because followers identify with the leader and his or her lofty goals, beliefs, and values. This identification, in turn, enhances followers' self-esteem and sense of purpose. Followers may also view the leader's mission and ideals as inherently satisfying because the leader convincingly describes their achievement as a way to realize followers' values and self-concepts. Here, followers internalize the leader's goals because they feel right and are necessary to attain shared values. Charismatic leaders may convince followers to invest their identities in a group.

Charismatic leadership inspires follower's emotional involvement and attachment to the leader. Followers hold charismatic leaders in high esteem and show trust, acceptance, and loyalty to the leader. They often experience increased self-esteem and self-assurance, and view their work with the leader as meaningful and important. Followers of charismatics are very highly satisfied with their leader, their work, and their overall job and organization. Their organizational commitment can be high, and stress levels and rate of job burnout are often low. For followers who do not buy in to the leader's mission, charisma may inspire strong opposition.

Although followers of charismatic leaders consistently rate their leaders as highly effective, fewer studies have measured actual follower or group performance under charismatics. The evidence is accumulating, however, that the favorable effects of charismatic leadership on followers' emotional and psychological reactions often create improvements in follower and group performance. Charismatic leadership is also risky—attacks on the leader and follower destruction are both possible outcomes.

Charismatic behaviors are most likely to have positive effects on followers' psychological reactions and behaviors when important enhancers are present. These organizational and follower conditions (described in Figure 8-4) tend to make charismatic leadership behaviors highly effective with followers. When a leader finds these conditions, the use of charismatic behaviors described in this chapter and summarized in Figure 8-1 is recommended.

When substitutes for charismatic leadership behaviors are present (described in Figure 8-5), these situational and follower characteristics provide followers with motivation or positive attitudes without charismatic leadership. This leadership pattern is therefore less necessary, and the leader should choose a different set of behaviors to influence followers.

Figure 8-6 summarizes material from this chapter on the behaviors, effects, and important situational factors affecting charismatic leadership. Figure 8-6 shows charismatic leadership behaviors at the top, with arrows pointing downward to show that these behaviors affect follower and group psychological reactions. These psychological reactions result in specific follower behaviors and performance. Situational factors that may enhance or substitute for the effects of charismatic leadership are shown on the left side of the figure. No factors have yet been found that neutralize the effects of charismatic leadership.

Figure 8-7 shows how a leader can apply the information in Figure 8-6 to a real leadership situation. The leader diagnoses the situation by answering the questions at the top of Figure 8-7. These questions help identify enhancers that will probably cause followers to respond favorably to charismatic leadership. If the answer is "yes" to one or more of these questions, the leader should provide this type of leadership behavior and monitor the results. These behaviors are shown by the items listed on the right of Figure 8-7. The leader can then try to modify situational factors to make the charismatic behaviors more effective. Leaders may also consider creating factors that can substitute for the effects of charismatic leadership, to make followers less dependent on the leader. These actions are shown on the left of Figure 8-7. The leader then rediagnoses the situation to determine if charismatic behaviors are still needed, and the dynamic cycle of situational diagnosis, providing charismatic leadership, and situational modification begins again.

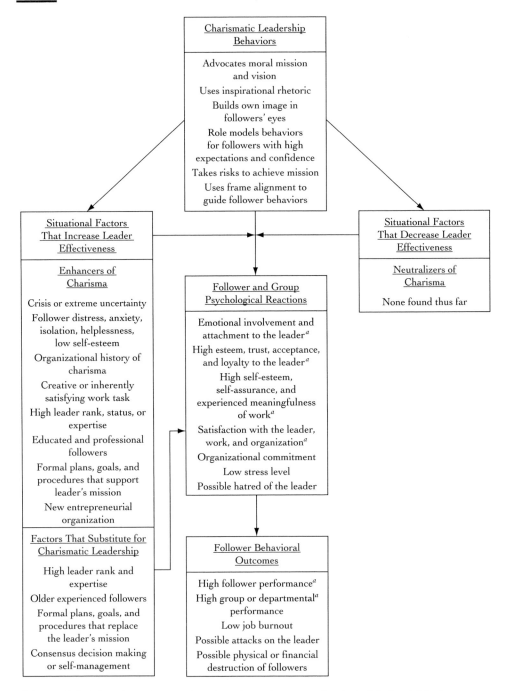

[a]These psychological reactions and outcomes have shown the most improvement from leaders' charismatic behaviors.

▪▪▪▪ **FIGURE 8-6 Process model of charismatic leadership**

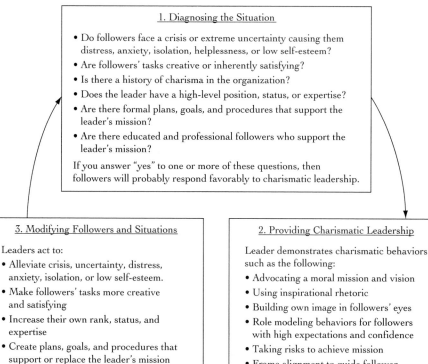

FIGURE 8-7 Applying the model of charismatic leadership

KEY TERMS AND CONCEPTS IN THIS CHAPTER ▪▪▪▪▪▪▪▪

- Charismatic leadership
- Consensus decision making
- Culture shocks
- Expressive orientation
- Extreme crisis

- Internalization
- Personal identification
- Principled orientation
- Professionalism
- Self-management

- Social contagion
- Social identification
- Theory Z organization

REVIEW AND DISCUSSION QUESTIONS ▪▪▪▪▪▪▪

1. Which of the charismatic leadership behaviors described in this chapter do you believe are most important in influencing followers? Why?

2. Think of a charismatic leader you have known, read about, or have seen in a film. Describe how that leader used one or two of the leadership behaviors described in this chapter. What situational or follower characteristics were present that enhanced this leader's effectiveness?

3. Do you think the followers of the charismatic leader described in Question 2 were influenced through personal identification, social identification, internalization, or social contagion? If these leaders used some other influence strategy with followers, describe this strategy and how it differs from those described here.

4. If you have ever worked with or observed a charismatic leader, describe the effects the leader had on you. Are these effects consistent with those described in this chapter?

5. Why do you think charismatic leaders have stronger effects on followers' attitudes and emotions than on follower and group performance?

6. Can you think of a situation you have experienced, observed, or heard about in which charismatic leadership was not needed? If so, describe this situation.

7. Think of your current job situation or a job you would like to have. Do you believe charismatic leadership would be effective in this situation? Why or why not?

8. Do you believe charismatic leadership would be effective for a group of maintenance personnel in an office building? Why or why not?

9. Do you believe charismatic leadership would be effective for the captain of a football team? Why or why not?

EXERCISE: ANALYZING CHARISMATIC LEADER COMMUNICATION ▪▪▪▪▪▪

After reading Dr. King's speech that follows, analyze the charismatic communication characteristics by answering the questions that follow the speech.

I Have a Dream

Martin Luther King Jr. delivered the following address on the steps of the Lincoln Memorial in Washington, D.C., on August 29, 1963.

I say to you, my friends, that in spite of the difficulties and frustrations of the moment I still have a dream. It is a dream deeply rooted in the American Dream.

I have a dream that one day this nation will rise up and live out the true meaning of its creed: "We hold these truths to be self-evident; that all men are created equal."

I have a dream that one day on the red hills of Georgia the sons of former slaves and the sons of former slave owners will be able to sit down together at the table of brotherhood.

I have a dream that one day even the state of Mississippi, a desert state sweating in the heat of injustice and oppression, will be transformed into an oasis of freedom and justice.

I have a dream that my four little children will one day live in a nation where they will not be judged by the color of their skin but the content of their character.

I have a dream today.

I have a dream that one day the state of Alabama, whose governor's lips are presently dripping with the words of interposition and nullification, will be transformed into a situation where little black boys and girls will be able to join hands with little white boys and white girls and walk together as sisters and brothers.

I have a dream today.

I have a dream that one day every valley shall be exalted, every hill and mountain shall be made low, the rough places will be made plain, and the crooked places will be made straight, and the glory of the Lord shall be revealed, and all flesh shall see it together.

This is our hope. This is the faith with which I return to the South. With this faith we will be able to transform the jangling discords of our nation into a beautiful symphony of brotherhood. With this faith we will be able to work together, to pray together, to struggle together, to go to jail together, to stand up for freedom together, knowing that we will be free one day.

This will be the day when all of God's children will be able to sing with a new meaning, "My country 'tis of thee, sweet land of liberty, of thee I sing. Land where my fathers died, land of the pilgrim's pride, from every mountainside, let freedom ring."

And if America is to be a great nation this must become true. So let freedom ring from the prodigious hilltops of New Hampshire. Let freedom ring from the mighty mountains of New York. Let freedom ring from the heightening Alleghenies of Pennsylvania!

Let freedom ring from the snowcapped Rockies of Colorado!

Let freedom ring from the curvaceous peaks of California!

But not only that; let freedom ring from the Stone Mountains of Georgia.

Let freedom ring from every hill and molehill of Mississippi. From every mountainside, let freedom ring.

When we let freedom ring, when we let it ring from every village and every hamlet, from every state and every city, we will be able to speed up that day when all of God's children, black men and white men, Jews and Gentiles, Protestants and Catholics, will be able to join hands and sing in the words of that old Negro spiritual, "Free at last! Thank God almighty, we are free at last!"

1. How would you rate the charismatic appeal of King's speech? (If feasible, listen to the speech on tape or watch it on video to better comprehend the nonverbal aspects of the speech.)

2. What specific charismatic elements can you identify in this famous speech?

3. What situational or follower characteristics were present that enhanced the effects of this speech?

4. Would a speech of this emotional intensity be appropriate in a work setting? Explain your reasoning.

SOURCES: Andrew J. Dubrin. *Leadership: Research Findings, Practices, and Skills.* Boston: Houghton Mifflin Company, 1998, 78–79. The reprint of Dr. King's speech is used by arrangement with The Heirs to the Estate of Martin Luther King Jr., c/o Writers House, Inc., as agents of the proprietor. Copyright 1963 by Martin Luther King Jr. copyright renewed 1991 by Coretta Scott King.

▪▪▪▪▪▪ C A S E   I N C I D E N T ▪▪▪▪▪▪

Charismatic Leadership: A Follower's Perspective

Deborah Layton grew up in a house of secrets. She was 16 before her parents told her she was Jewish. Later they informed her that the grandmother who supposedly died of a heart attack actually committed suicide, and her mother had fled Nazi Germany. She was sent to a British boarding school to curb her adolescent rebellion. These early experiences resulted in lack of trust and extreme feelings of insecurity in Deborah.

When she was 17 and on summer vacation, her brother Larry introduced her to Jim Jones at the first People's Temple in northern California. Larry was already a member of the Temple, and he believed it would help him survive the atomic war he expected. Jones wore dark glasses indoors and out, his hair was glossy black, he wore sweeping robes, and liked to be called Father of his flock.

Deborah describes herself at this time as "young and unanchored." She was charmed when Jones fixed his penetrating brown eyes on her and warmly invited her to "join me and my family of all races." He claimed to have "hundreds of followers working to feed the hungry, house the homeless and help addicts get clean." She further states, "The people that joined the People's

Temple were really good people. They were innocent. They were naïve. . . . They were looking for something larger than themselves to be involved in."

Deborah joined the People's Temple and became a trusted financial officer for Jones. He later told her "You are the only one I can really trust." But she began to learn about another side of Jim Jones and the People's Temple. Beatings of members who disagreed with Jones and fake healings were increasingly common. When the Temple was moved to Jonestown, a jungle encampment 250 miles from the capital of Guyana, she knew she had entered a prison. In Jonestown, the residents who were able worked the fields, and the population subsisted on rice. "Dissent was unthinkable. Offenders sweltered in 'The Box,' a 6-by-4-foot underground enclosure. Misbehaving children were dangled head-first into the well late at night. . . . Loudspeakers broadcast Jones' voice at all hours." Once he barked out the warning, "White night!" This meant they were about to be attacked and everyone was to take poison punch.

Deborah escaped in May 1978 when she was chaperoning a youth group in the capital city. She spread the alarm that Jones was planning a mass suicide, but few listened.

Finally on November 17, a group of reporters and concerned family members arrived, led by U.S. Representative Leo Ryan. They toured Jonestown and spent the night. The next day, as they were about to board their plane to leave with about 20 defectors, they were ambushed. Ryan and four others were killed. Deborah's brother, Larry, was posing as a defector and was one of the shooters. He is now serving a life sentence in federal prison.

In Jonestown, Jim Jones was orchestrating the mass suicide of all its residents. Poison punch was squirted into babies' mouths. Then adults were instructed to drink the poison. Some were shot by security guards. Jones was shot through the head. In all, over 900 of Jones' followers died. ■

DISCUSSION QUESTIONS

Discuss this incident in groups and answer the following questions:

1. What situational or personal characteristics caused Deborah Layton to become a follower of Jim Jones' charismatic leadership?
2. Why did so many residents of Jonestown choose to stay when their life there was so harsh and punishing?

SOURCE: Las Cruces Sun News, November 15, 1998.

EXERCISE: WHAT DOES AND DOES NOT INSPIRE? ▪▪▪▪▪▪▪

1. Divide the class into groups of five or six people per group.
2. **a.** Have members of half the groups think of a situation or incident they experienced in which a leader inspired them to do their best and created a high degree of commitment to their task. Have them write down what the leader did in this situation to inspire them.
   b. At the same time, members of the other groups think of a situation or incident they experienced in which a leader failed to inspire them to do their best and resulted in low commitment to their task. Have them write down what the leader did or did not do in this situation that caused them to be uninspired and uncommitted. (10 minutes)
3. Now have members of each group describe their incidents to their own group, and explain what they identified as key leadership actions in that situation. Have one member in each group create a list of leader actions that resulted in high inspiration and high commitment or low inspiration and low commitment for their members. (20–30 minutes)

4. The instructor will now call on each group, and create a list of unique leader actions for the class that resulted in high inspiration and commitment and another list that created low inspiration and lack of commitment. (10–15 minutes)

5. This can be followed by a short lecture on inspirational skills for creating a group vision (see Jay Conger. Inspiring others: The language of leadership. *Academy of Management Executive,* 5(1), 1991, 31–45).

ENDNOTES ▪▪▪▪▪▪▪

1. Weber, M. (1947). *The theory of social and economic organization,* T. Parsons (Trans). New York: Free Press.

2. House, R. J. (1977). A 1976 theory of charismatic leadership. In J. G. Hunt and L. L. Larson (Eds.), *Leadership: The Cutting Edge,* 189–207. Carbondale, IL: Southern Illinois University Press.

3. Bass, B. M. (1990). *Bass and Stogdill's Handbook of Leadership,* 3rd ed. New York: Free Press.

4. Yagil, D. (1998). Charismatic leadership and organizational hierarchy: Attribution of charisma to close and distant leaders. *Leadership Quarterly,* 9(2), 161–176.

5. Ibid.

6. House, R. J., and Shamir, B. (1993). Toward the integration of transformational, charismatic and visionary theories. In M. M. Chemers and R. Aymon (Eds.), *Leadership theory and research: Perspectives and directions.* New York: Academic Press.

7. Yammarino, F. J., and Bass, B. M. (1990). Transformational leadership and multiple levels of analysis. *Human Relations,* 43, 975–995.

8. Avolio, B. J., and Yammarino, F. J. (1990). Operationalizing charismatic leadership using a levels-of-analysis framework. *Leadership Quarterly,* 1(3), 193–208.

9. Howell, J. M., and Frost, P. J. (1989). A laboratory study of charismatic leadership. *Organizational Behavior and Human Decision Processes,* 43, 243–269.

10. Kirkpatrick, S. A., and Locke, E. A. (1996). Direct and indirect effects of three core charismatic leadership components on performance and attitudes. *Journal of Applied Psychology,* 81(1), 36–61.

11. Freud, S. (1922). *Group Psychology and the Analysis of Ego.* London: International Psychoanalytic Press.

12. Downton, J. V. (1973). *Rebel Leadership: Commitment and Charisma in the Revolutionary Process.* New York: Free Press.

13. Freemesser, G. F., and Kaplan, H. B. (1976). Self-attitudes and deviant behavior: The case of the charismatic religious movement. *Journal of Youth and Adolescence,* 5(1), 1–9.

14. Bass. *Bass and Stogdill's Handbook of Leadership.*

15. Shamir, B., Zakay, E., Breinin, E., and Popper, M. (1998). Correlates of charismatic leader behavior in military units: Subordinates' attitudes, unit characteristics, and superiors' appraisals of leader performance. *Academy of Management Journal,* 41(4), 387–409.

16. Yukl, G. (1998). *Leadership in Organizations,* 5th ed. Upper Saddle River, NJ: Prentice Hall.

17. Shamir, B., Arthur, B. B., and House, R. (1994). The rhetoric of charismatic leadership: A theoretical extension, a case study, and implications for research. *Leadership Quarterly,* 5(1), 25–42.

18. Simonton, D. K. (1988). Presidential style: Personality, biography, and performance. *Journal of Personality and Social Psychology,* 55(6), 928–936.

19. House. A 1976 theory of charismatic leadership.

20. House, R. J., Spangler, W. D., and Woycke, J. (1991). Personality and charisma in the U.S. presidency: A psychological theory of leader effectiveness. *Administrative Science Quarterly,* 36, 364–396.

21. Dubrin, A. J. (1998). *Leadership: Research Findings, Practice, and Skills.* Boston: Houghton Mifflin.

22. Post, J. M. (1993). Current concepts of the narcissistic personality: Implications for political psychology. *Political Psychology,* 14(1), 99–121.

23. Halpert, J. A. (1990). The dimensionality of charisma. *Journal of Business Psychology,* Summer 1990, 5, 401.

24. Ibid.

25. Cell, C. P. (1974). Charismatic heads of state: The social context. *Behavioral Science Research,* 4, 255–304.

26. Trice, H. M., and Beyer, J. M. (1986). Charisma and its routinization in two social movement organizations. *Research in Organizational Behavior,* 8, 113–164.

27. Roberts, N. C. (1984). Transforming leadership: Sources, processes, consequences. Paper presented at the Academy of Management meeting, Boston.

28. Kets de Vries, M. F. R. (1988). Origins of charisma: Ties that bind the leader and the led. In J. A. Conger and R. N. Kanungo (Eds.), *Charismatic Leadership: The Elusive Factor in Organizational Effectiveness.* San Francisco: Jossey-Bass.

29. Bass. *Bass and Stogdill's Handbook of Leadership.*

30. Puffer, S. M. (1990). Attributions of charismatic leadership: The impact of decision style, outcome and observer characteristics. *Leadership Quarterly,* 13, 177–192.

31. Bass. *Bass & Stogdill's Handbook of Leadership.*

32. Conger, J. A., and Kanungo, R. N. (1987). Toward a behavioral theory of charismatic leadership in organizational settings. *Academy of Management Review,* 12(4), 637–647.

33. Yagil. Charismatic leadership and organizational hierarchy: Attribution of charisma to close or distant leaders.

34. Bass, B. M. (1985). Leadership: Good, better, best. *Organizational Dynamics,* 13(3), 26–40.

35. House and Shamir. Toward the integration of transformational, charismatic and visionary theories.

36. Bass. Leadership: Good, better, best.

37. Maranell, G. M. (1970). The evaluation of presidents: An extension of the Schlesinger polls. *Journal of American History,* 57, 104–113.

38. Smith, B. J. (1983). An initial test of a theory of charismatic leadership based on responses of subordinates. Doctoral diss., University of Toronto.

39. Podsakoff, P. M., MacKenzie, S. B., Moorman, R. H., and Fetter, R. (1990). Transformational leader behaviors and their effects on followers' trust in leader, satisfaction, and organizational citizenship behaviors. *Leadership Quarterly,* 1(2), 107–142.

40. Willner, A. R. (1984). *The Spellbinders: Charismatic Political Leadership.* New Haven, CT: Yale University Press.

41. Carlton-Ford, S. L. (1992). Charisma, ritual, effervescence, and self-esteem. *Sociological Quarterly,* 33(3), 365–387.

42. House and Shamir. Toward the integration of transformational, charismatic and visionary theories.

43. Deluga, R. J. (1991). The relationship of leader and subordinate influencing activity in naval environments. *Military Psychology,* 3(1), 25–39.

44. Yammarino, F. J., and Bass, B. M. (1990). Transformational leadership and multiple levels of analysis. *Human Relations,* 43(10), 975–995.

45. Kirby, P. C., Paradise, L. V., and King, M. I. (1992). Extraordinary leaders in education: Understanding transformational leadership. *Journal of Educational Research,* 85(5), 303–311.

46. Podsakoff, MacKenzie, Moorman, and Fetter. Transformational leader behaviors and their effects on followers' trust in leader, satisfaction, and organizational citizenship behaviors.

47. House, R. J., Woycke, J., and Fodor, E. M. (1988). Charismatic and noncharismatic leaders: Differences in behavior and effectiveness. In J. A. Conger and R. N. Kanungo (Eds.), *Charismatic Leadership: The Elusive Factor in Organizational Effectiveness.* San Francisco: Jossey-Bass.

48. Howell and Frost. A laboratory study of charismatic leadership.

49. Peterson, M. F., Phillips, R. L., and Duran, C. A. (1989). A comparison of Japanese performance-maintenance measures with U. S. leadership scales. *Psychologia—An International Journal of Psychology in the Orient, 32,* 58–70.

50. Seltzer, J., Numeroff, R. E., and Bass, B. M. (1987). Transformational leadership: Is it a source of more or less burnout or stress? Paper presented at the Academy of Management meeting, New Orleans, LA.

51. Hater, J. J., and Bass, B. M. (1988). Superiors' evaluations and subordinates' perceptions of transformational and transactional leadership. *Journal of Applied Psychology, 73,* 695–702.

52. House, Woycke, and Foder. Charismatic and noncharismatic leaders: Differences in behavior and effectiveness.

53. Yammarino, F. J., Spangler, W. D., and Bass, B. M. (1993). Transformational leadership and performance: A longitudinal investigation. *Leadership Quarterly, 4*(1), 81–102.

54. Deluga, R. J. (1992). The relationship of leader and subordinate influencing activity in naval environments. *Military Psychology, 3*(1), 25–39.

55. Waldman, D. A., Bass, B. M., and Yammarino, F. J. (1990). Adding to contingent reward behavior: The augmenting effect of charismatic leadership. *Group and Organizational Studies, 15*(4), 381–394.

56. Kirby, Paradise, and King. Extraordinary leaders in education: Understanding transformational leadership.

57. Fuller, J. B., Patterson, C. E. P., Hester, K., and Stringer, D. Y. (1996). A quantitative review of research on charismatic leadership. *Psychological Reports, 78,* 271–287.

58. Howell and Frost. A laboratory study of charismatic leadership.

59. Onnen, M. K. (1987). The relationship of clergy leadership characteristics to growing or declining churches. Doctoral diss., University of Louisville.

60. Waldman, D. A., Bass, B. M., and Einstein, W. O. (1987). Leadership and outcomes of performance appraisal processes. *Journal of Occupational Psychology, 60,* 177–186.

61. Podsakoff, MacKenzie, Moorman, and Fetter. Transformational leader behaviors and their effects on followers' trust in leader, satisfaction, and organizational citizenship behaviors.

62. Dorfman, P. W., Howell, J. P., Cotton, B. C. G., and Tate, U. (1992). Leadership within the discontinuous hierarchy structure of the military: Are effective leadership behaviors similar within and across command structures? In K. E. Clark, M. B. Clark, and D. P. Campbell (Eds.), *Impact of Leadership.* Greensboro, NC: Center for Creative Leadership.

63. Howell, J. M., and Avolio, B. J. (1993). Transformational leadership, transactional leadership, locus of control, and support for innovation: Key predictors of consolidated-business-unit performance. *Journal of Applied Psychology, 78*(6), 891–902.

64. Howell, J. M., and Higgins, C. A. (1990). Champions of technological innovation. *Administrative Science Quarterly, 35*(2), 317–341.

65. Spangler, W. D., and Braiotta, L. (1990). Leadership and corporate audit committee effectiveness. *Group and Organization Studies, 15*(2), 134–157.

66. Waldman, D. A., Ramirez, G. G., House, R. J., and Puranam, P. (2001). Does leadership matter? CEO leadership attributes and profitability under conditions of perceived environmental uncertainty. *Academy of Management Journal, 44*(1), 134–143.

67. Tosi, H., Misangyi, V. F., Fanelli, A., Waldman, D. A., and Yammarino, F. (2004). CEO charisma, compensation, and firm performance. *Leadership Quarterly, 15,* 405–420.

68. Fuller, Patterson, Hester, and Stringer. A quantitative review of research on charismatic leadership.

69. Shamir, B., Fakay, E., Breinin, E., and Popper, M. (1998). Correlation of charismatic leader behavior in military units: Subordinates' attitudes, unit characteristics, and superiors appraisals of leader performance. *Academy of Management Journal, 41*(4), 387–409.

70. Lowe, K. B., Kroeck, K. G., and Sivasubramaniam, N. (1996). Effectiveness of correlates of transformational and

transactional leadership: A meta-analytic review of the MLQ literature. *Leadership Quarterly,* 7, 489–508.

71. Tucker, R. G. (1970). The theory of charismatic leadership. In D. A. Rustow (Ed.), *Philosophers and Kings: Studies in Leadership.* New York: Braziller.

72. House, Woycke, and Fodor. Charismatic and noncharismatic leaders: Differences in behavior and effectiveness.

73. Bass, B. M. (1985). *Leadership and Performance Beyond Expectations.* New York: Free Press.

74. Bass, B. M., and Avolio, B. J. (1990). The implications of transactional and transformational leadership for individual, team, and organizational development. In W. Pasmore and R. W. Woodman (Eds.), *Research in Organizational Change and Development,* Vol. 4, 231–272. Greenwich, CT: JAI Press.

75. Burns, J. M. (1978). *Leadership.* New York: Harper & Row.

76. Hughes, R. L., Ginnett, R. C., and Curphy, G. J. (2002). *Leadership: Enhancing the Lessons of Experience,* 4th ed. Boston, MA: McGraw-Hill.

77. McColl-Kennedy, J. R., and Anderson, R. D. (2002). Impact of leadership style and emotions on subordinate performance. *Leadership Quarterly,* 13, 545–559.

78. Kark, R., Shamir, B., and Chen, G. (2003). The two faces of transformational leadership: Empowerment and dependency. *Journal of Applied Psychology,* 88, 246–255.

79. Dvir, T., Eden, D., Avolio, B. J., and Shirir, B. (2002). Impact of transformational leadership on follower development and performance: A field experiment. *Academy of Management Journal,* 45, 735–744.

80. Pillai, R., and Williams, E. A. (2004). Transformational leadership, self-efficacy, group cohesiveness, commitment, and performance. *Journal of Organizational Change Management,* 17, 144–159.

81. Barling, J., Loughlin, C., and Kelloway, E. K. (2002). Development and test of a model linking safety-specific transformational leadership and occupational safety. *Journal of Applied Psychology,* 87, 488–496.

82. Conger, J. A., and Kanungo, R. (1998). *Charismatic Leadership in Organizations.* Thousand Oaks, CA: Sage Publications.

83. Bass. *Leadership and Performance Beyond Expectations.*

84. Bass and Avolio. The implications of transactional and transformational leadership for individual, team, and organizational development.

85. House. A 1976 theory of charismatic leadership.

86. Hughes, Ginnett, and Curphy. *Leadership: Enhancing the Lessons of Experience.*

87. Shamir, Zakay, Breinin, and Popper. Correlates of charismatic leader behavior in military units: Subordinates attitudes, unit characteristics, and superior appraisals of leader performance.

88. Yukl, G. (2002). *Leadership in Organizations,* 5th ed. Upper Saddle River, NJ: Prentice Hall.

89. Avolio, G. J., and Bass, B. M. (1991). *The Full Range Leadership Development Programs: Basic and Advanced Manuals.* Binghamton, NY: Bass, Avolio & Associates.

90. Avolio, B. J., Waldman, D. A., and Yammarino, F. L. (1991). Leading in the 1990s: Towards understanding the four I's of transformational leadership. *Journal of European Industrial Training,* 15, 9–16.

91. Bass, B. M. (1998). *Transformational Leadership: Industrial, Military, and Educational Impact.* Mahwah, NJ: Lawrence Erlbaum Associates.

92. Avolio, B. J., Bass, B. M., and Jung, D. I. (1995). MLQ multifactor leadership questionnaire: Technical report. Redwood City, CA: Mindgarden.

93. Bass, B. M., and Avolio, B. J. (Eds.) (1994). *Improving Organizational Effectiveness Through Transformational Leadership.* Thousand Oaks, CA: Sage Publications.

94. Avolio, Bass, and Jung. MLQ multifactor leadership questionnaire: Technical report.

95. Bass, B. M., Avolio, B. J., Jung, D. I., and Berson, Y. (2003). Predicting unit performance by assessing transformational and transactional leadership. *Journal of Applied Psychology,* 88, 207–218.

96. Conger, J. A., and Kanungo, R. N. *Charismatic Leadership: The Elusive Factor in Organizational Effectiveness.* San Francisco: Jossey-Bass, 1988.

97. Bass. Leadership: Good, better, best.

98. Tosi, Misangyi, Fanelli, Waldman, and Yonemarino. CEO charisma, compensation, and firm performance.

99. Waldman, Ramirez, House, and Puranam. Does leadership matter? CEO leadership attributes and profitability under conditions of perceived environmental uncertainty.

100. Shamir, B., House, R. J., and Arthur, M. B. (1993). The motivational effects of charismatic leadership: A self-concept based theory. *Organizational Science,* 4, 1–17.

101. Keller, R. T. (1992). Transformational leadership and the performance of research and development project groups. *Journal of Management,* 18(3), 489–501.

102. Howell, J. P., Dorfman, P. W., Hibino, S., Lee, J. K., and Tate, U. (1994). Leadership in western and Asian countries: Commonalities and differences in effective leadership processes and substitutes across cultures. New Mexico State University, Bureau of Business Research.

103. Hollander, E. P. (1978). *Leadership Dynamics: A Practical Guide to Effective Relationships.* New York: Free Press.

104. Bass. *Bass and Stogdill's Handbook of Leadership.*

105. Fuller, J. B., Patterson, C. E. P., Hester, K., and Stringer, D. Y. (1996). A quantitative review of research on charismatic leadership. *Psychological Reports,* 78, 271–287.

106. House, R. J., Woycke, J., and Fodor, E. M. (1988). Charismatic and noncharismatic leaders: Differences in behavior and effectiveness. In J. A. Conger and R. N. Kanungo (Eds.), *Charismatic Leadership: The Elusive Factor in Organizational Effectiveness.* San Francisco: Jossey-Bass.

107. Madsen, D., and Snow, P. G. (1983). The dispersion of charisma. *Comparative Political Studies,* 16, 337–362.

108. Newman, R. G. (1983). Thoughts on superstars of charisma: Pipers in our midst.

American Journal of Orthopsychiatry, 53(2), 201–208.

109. Freemesser, G. F., and Kaplan, H. B. (1976). Self-attitudes and deviant behavior: The case of the charismatic religious movement. *Journal of Youth and Adolescence,* 5(1), 1–9.

110. Bass. *Bass and Stogdill's Handbook of Leadership.*

111. Howell, Dorfman, Hibino, Lee, and Tate. Leadership in western and Asian countries: Commonalities and differences in effective leadership processes and substitutes across cultures.

112. Shamir, House, and Arthur. The motivational effects of charismatic leadership: A self-concept based theory.

113. Yukl. *Leadership in Organizations.*

114. Shamir, House, and Arthur. The motivational effects of charismatic leadership: A self-concept based theory.

115. Howell, Dorfman, Hibino, Lee, and Tate. Leadership in western and Asian countries: Commonalities and differences in effective leadership processes and substitutes across cultures.

116. House, Woycke, and Fodor. Charismatic and noncharismatic leaders: Differences in behavior and effectiveness.

117. Howell, J. M., and Frost, P. J. (1989). A laboratory study of charismatic leadership. *Organizational Behavior and Human Decision Processes,* 43, 243–269.

118. Howell and Avolio. Transformational leadership, transactional leadership, locus of control, and support for innovation: Key predictors of consolidated-business-unit performance.

119. Bass. Leadership: Good, better, best.

120. Howell, Dorfman, Hibino, Lee, and Tate. Leadership in western and Asian countries: Commonalities and differences in effective leadership processes and substitutes across cultures.

121. Bass. Leadership: Good, better, best.

122. Howell, Dorfman, Hibino, Lee, and Tate. Leadership in western and Asian countries: Commonalities and differences in effective leadership processes and substitutes across cultures.

CHAPTER

9

Boundary Spanning and Team Leadership

Learning Objectives

After reading this chapter, you should be able to do the following:

1. Describe boundary spanning leadership behaviors and provide specific examples of these behaviors.

2. Explain why boundary spanning behaviors can have positive effects on followers.

3. Describe skills, abilities, and sources of power that leaders need to be effective at boundary spanning.

4. Describe the individual and organizational benefits that can result from effective boundary spanning behaviors.

5. Describe an approach to negotiation that will maximize benefits for all parties

6. Describe team leadership as an important role that requires effective boundary spanning and other leadership behaviors.

7. Identify follower, organizational, and task characteristics for which boundary spanning leadership behaviors would be highly effective and for which they would not be effective.

▬▬ Examples of Effective Boundary Spanning

- The new superintendent of a manufacturing plant successfully convinced his autocratic boss to purchase a new piece of material-processing equipment that was badly needed, but had been vetoed by the boss when proposed by the previous superintendent. The new superintendent carefully prepared his boss by making an appointment with him to tour the plant, where the conditions spoke for themselves. The superintendent added to the visual clues with a description of how the old equipment hampered the plant. The boss had no option but to agree about the problem, and asked "What do you propose?" The superintendent responded with a carefully worked out proposal that the boss approved almost immediately.[1]

- A manager at Data General protected and facilitated a group of young, creative, and motivated computer design engineers to help them design a faster computer than the competition. Data General at this time was internally competitive, highly political, and resource poor. The leader obtained workspace that was isolated— encouraging considerable interaction among the team members and discouraging interaction outside the team. He articulated overall project requirements, negotiated deadlines, stayed out of internal disputes, obtained required resources wherever he could, and buffered the team from organization politics. The team developed a high degree of camaraderie during the project, and completed the project successfully in record time.[2]

- The manager of a staff department demonstrated effective negotiation skills when asked by a production manager about getting assistance from one of his key staff members. "There is no way I can get Harry to work on that, even though he is the one you want and could do it best. But I could get Harry to look over Bill and Jane's work, to be sure it's consistent with the way you like things done." The production manager agreed, the work was successfully completed, and the working relationship between production and the staff department was strengthened.[3]

All organizations and groups have boundaries of some type that determine who is and who is not a member. Leaders have much of the responsibility for establishing and maintaining these boundaries. The incidents described above demonstrate effective boundary spanning leadership. *Boundary spanning leadership* is defined as leader actions that establish and maintain a group's integrity through negotiating with nongroup members, resolving disputes among followers and subgroups, obtaining resources, establishing influence networks, and helping followers deal with the external environment.

Boundary spanning activities may include interacting with superiors on behalf of the group to obtain resources or approval for changes, or buffering the group from unreasonable demands. They can also include lateral interactions with other individuals and groups to obtain and provide information, coordinate activities, and resolve disputes. Internal boundary spanning is similar to lateral interactions, except the focus is on providing information, coordinating, and resolving disputes among subgroups and members within the leader's immediate group. One study found that 70 to 80 percent of the boundary spanning activities in a large formal organization were carried out by leaders.[4]

As organizations and their environments have increased in complexity, these boundary spanning activities have become more important and time consuming. Several developments inside modern organizations contribute to this trend, including more worker participation in decision making, autonomous or self-managed teams, advances in information technology, and specialized staff units.[5] All of these increase the need for resources, information, and coordination. Boundary spanning interactions can be complicated because several groups are often involved, each with its own norms, values, goals, and loyalties. These interactions also occur sporadically and are difficult for leaders to predict. They therefore interrupt other important leadership activities, and may interfere with departmental procedures. Boundary spanning can also be time consuming for the leader, especially when negotiating with another group or persuading a superior to approve a major change in departmental plans, procedures, or objectives.

The following are examples of boundary spanning leadership behaviors:

1. Defining and modifying organizational or unit boundaries so members know who is and who is not a member.
2. Protecting and representing the group while resisting unreasonable demands and responding to outside influence.
3. Managing interactions between leaders and followers, among followers themselves, and among subgroups within the leader's unit, including helping to resolve stalemates and conflicts.
4. Negotiating with upper management and other outsiders to obtain resources for the unit and to arrange for distribution of the unit's output.
5. Identifying and describing for group members what they should attend to in the environment and what they should ignore to help them make sense of developments that may affect them (otherwise known as frame alignment).
6. Developing and maintaining networks inside and outside the leader's own organization, and using these networks to describe the unit's activities, accomplishments, and capabilities in order to increase its legitimacy, image, and power.
7. Obtaining, filtering, and storing valuable information from the unit's environment, putting the information into a useful form, and disseminating it to unit members.

By defining and protecting the group boundaries and mission, the leader establishes and maintains a shared identity that builds cohesion and cooperation among members. Managing interactions among various follower and subgroup roles within the unit helps maintain this shared identity and prevents the unit from fracturing into combative subgroups. Obtaining resources and building influence networks increases the potential performance and reputation of the group, which increases future support and further builds cohesion. Identifying key dimensions of the environment, regularly scanning these environmental dimensions, and conveying information to members in a useful form helps make members sensitive to the unit's welfare. These activities also allow the group to adapt to new technical developments, innovations in organizational design, legal issues, trends in related fields, interest groups, and other external issues to keep the unit in sync with its environment. Figure 9-1 summarizes major boundary spanning behaviors by leaders.

▪▪▪ Examples of Ineffective Boundary Spanning

Some leaders recognize the importance of boundary spanning activities, but they are unsuccessful at carrying them out. The following incidents describe examples of ineffective boundary spanning activities by leaders:

- A new department manager was faced with an urgent request from his boss that required critical input from another department. When contacted by the new manager, the other department head said he could not provide the needed input in the near future, if at all. The new manager became indignant and saw the other manager as inefficient and an obstacle. Because he was new in the organization, he decided against trying to bully or threaten the other manager. He opted instead for a strategy of trying to fool the manager into believing he would share credit for meeting the boss' request. The other department manager saw through

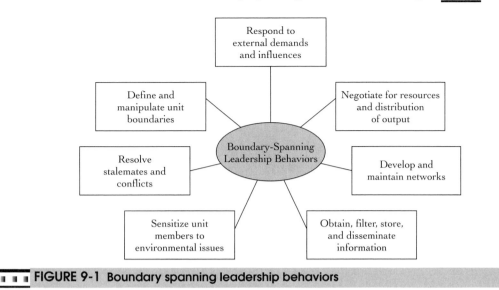

▮▮▮▮ **FIGURE 9-1 Boundary spanning leadership behaviors**

this and the new manager lost credibility in the organization. He did not realize that effective managers must build long-term relationships and count on friendship and respect to obtain the cooperation they need.

- A young supervisor with a recent college degree described her inability to obtain needed resources from another department as "just a misunderstanding, a communication problem. When the situation is clarified, they will cooperate and come through for us." However, the supervisor did not get the resources to the extent that she wanted, regardless of her repeated efforts to "get them to listen." Her mistaken assumption was that the organization was one big happy family in which everyone had the same interests and goals. Other departments had different interests and were often rewarded for things that were not consistent with the new supervisor's needs.

- A new manager of a highly professional group of research-and-development workers was anxious to please her superior. She saw her job as representing upper-level management to the R&D workers. She became a mouthpiece for upper management, conveying all their concerns and requests directly to the employees. The R&D personnel began to see her as not standing up for them in maintaining the independence they needed to pursue new ideas for products, and as passing down unreasonable management requests with deadlines that were not realistic. They wanted a manager to buffer them from unreasonable requests and to serve as an advocate in obtaining flexibility and resources to pursue projects they believed were potentially valuable to the company. The new manager lost their respect because she did not realize that she was responsible to her people as well as to upper management.

Each leader in these incidents failed to realistically assess some aspect of their group or its environment. Accurate perceptions of the group's needs as well as important environmental factors are essential for effective boundary spanning leadership.

▬▬▬ Importance of Boundary Spanning

Organizations have traditionally been viewed as having relatively fixed boundaries, and the leader's job included focusing on exchanges of resources and information between the organization and its environment. Early experts described a key leadership function as the defense of organizational integrity. They pointed out that a leader's influence with higher-ups affected the leader's influence on followers and unit performance.[6]

One organizational expert, writing in 1961, distinguished between *representative* functions and *linking-pin* functions of leaders. He described representatives as spokespersons for their own group, and their loyalties were entirely to that group. Linking pins were viewed as members of two or more interacting groups, with loyalties to both; they fulfill a liaison role, helping to coordinate and resolve conflicts among groups.[7] Today, boundary spanners play both representative and linking-pin roles, depending on the situation. Organizational boundaries are no longer fixed, but are constantly changing. The leader's job frequently includes engaging in boundary modification and redefinition, as work teams, departments, and organizations are divided, merge, or acquire one another.

Another writer described ten key leadership roles that managers play; seven involve some sort of boundary spanning:

1. Figurehead—Performing symbolic acts, such as representing the organization at social gatherings
2. Liaison—Forming and maintaining networks outside the unit, including making new contacts, keeping in touch with important outsiders, and doing favors
3. Monitoring—Obtaining information from outside the leader's unit that may help the overall unit's performance
4. Disseminator—Passing information on to insiders or to subunits about other subunits
5. Spokesperson—Transmitting information and expressing value statements to outsiders
6. Disturbance handler—Dealing with conflicts among subordinates or subunits, loss of subordinates, strikes, and other crisis situations
7. Negotiator—bargaining for the unit in dealing with others over resources and constraints; buffering the unit and its members from higher-ups and outsiders.[8]

In this era of rapid change, increasing interdependence, and networking between and within organizations, boundary spanning activities require increasing amounts of a leader's time and effort. The flexible nature of boundaries, complex environments, and increasing importance of networks also mean that boundaries offer less protection than before. Advocacy groups, government regulators, courts, and professional standards committees all penetrate today's organizations, and their view of appropriate procedures may differ markedly from the leader's. One researcher noted that 93 outsiders entered an inner-city school during one week to perform some type of service.[9] These outsiders are not socialized into the organization's norms and practices in the way of employees. Consequently, leaders have little control over them. They create both learning opportunities and risks of subversion. Leaders are usually responsible for dealing with these outsiders and the impacts of their activities on the organization.

Organizations today are composed of increasingly diverse groups of people. Employees identify with ethnic groups, age groups, gender groups, religious groups, and many others. For many people, their personal lives are no longer distinct from their work lives. They often work at home and on weekends, they rely on their employers for child care, elder care, and health care, and their friendships are work related. These factors continually change employees' expectations of organizations, requiring leaders to actively manage evolving boundaries among followers and between followers and the organization. One result of these changes is that followers often view leaders as more powerful than leaders view themselves. So leaders must continually clarify their role, including powers and limitations in dealing with followers' roles.

In organizations of the 21st century, information will increasingly be viewed as the major resource. The information-processing function of leaders, in which leaders convert raw data to summaries, conclusions, and inferences, is especially important. Information that is thus converted is difficult for other organization or group members to verify, but it slowly becomes part of an organization's collective intelligence, which, once created, tends to be well accepted. Thus, the information processing aspects of a leader's boundary spanning activities have long-term implications for the organization's strategies and actions.

The leadership self-assessment on the next page provides specific examples of boundary spanning behaviors.

▪▪▪ Skills, Traits, and Sources of Power for Effective Boundary Spanning

Leadership researchers have not carefully studied the personal characteristics of boundary spanners. It appears, however, that effective boundary spanners should have a high *internal locus of control*. That is, they should believe in their own abilities to influence environmental factors. Having confidence in one's abilities is essential for success in dealing with environmental demands and constraints.

Descriptions of boundary spanning also imply several important skills that leaders should develop to effectively carry out these behaviors. For example, many boundary spanning activities require effective *communication skills*. Such skills are critical to advocating for the group, persuading outsiders to support the group, and influencing individuals and subgroups to look beyond turf battles and cooperate for the sake of the unit. Communication skills also include *telling stories* about past successes (such as when a coach describes how a team rallied to win an important game) or *creating slogans* (such as an automobile-leasing firm proclaiming "We try harder!"). These activities help establish a "we" feeling among unit members, and consequently shape the unit or organization's boundaries. *Political* and *negotiation skills* are also critical for boundary spanning in order to place the unit in a favorable position to influence its environment. *Conflict-management skills* are key to overcoming internal and external disputes that can threaten the unit's supply of resources and freedom of action. Leaders can develop these boundary spanning skills through formal education and training experiences (such as membership in a Toastmasters club), relevant work experiences, and coaching or mentoring programs. These skills should enable leaders to effectively represent their people, buffer them from environmental jolts, and obtain

LEADERSHIP SELF-ASSESSMENT
Boundary Spanning Leadership

Think of a team, committee, or other group you have participated in that had an identifiable leader. If you have trouble thinking of a group of your own, then think of a leader you have observed, read, or heard about. Describe the leader's boundary spanning behaviors using the rating scale for the items below.

	Hardly Ever					*Almost Always*	
	1	2	3	4	5	6	7
1. Establishes procedures that shield employees from unnecessary interference so that they can perform their jobs effectively and productively	1	2	3	4	5	6	7
2. Resists unrealistic demands on the work group from outsiders (customers, vendors, other departments)	1	2	3	4	5	6	7
3. Filters out irrelevant material while keeping the team supplied with information important to the work group	1	2	3	4	5	6	7
4. Persuades upper management and outsiders to appreciate and support the work group by telling them about its abilities, activities, and accomplishments	1	2	3	4	5	6	7
5. Coordinates activities with other groups	1	2	3	4	5	6	7
6. Actively seeks out any additional resources (extra supplies, materials, tools, or equipment) needed to complete our work	1	2	3	4	5	6	7
7. Forms contacts with people outside of the work group who can provide useful information	1	2	3	4	5	6	7
8. Attends social events to develop contacts and find out what is happening in other parts of the organization	1	2	3	4	5	6	7
9. Collects relevant information and verifies its accuracy before confronting employees about interpersonal conflicts	1	2	3	4	5	6	7
10. Encourages members to resolve conflicts in a constructive manner	1	2	3	4	5	6	7
11. Promptly addresses employee concerns about poor treatment by coworkers (for example, sexual harassment, racial slurs, etc.)	1	2	3	4	5	6	7
12. Introduces new employees to everyone in the department	1	2	3	4	5	6	7
13. Provides accurate information directly to employees about past or future events in order to prevent or dispel rumors	1	2	3	4	5	6	7

Those items that you rated as 6 or 7 indicate a high level of boundary spanning behavior by this leader. Why do you think this leader was so active in using these behaviors? Describe any environmental or group characteristics that made these boundary spanning behaviors especially important.

the resources and cooperation needed to facilitate their group and organization's performance.

In nearly any organizational situation, leaders who are recognized as experts in their group or organizational tasks are highly respected. They convey an image of competence to group members and outsiders alike. This competence or *expert power* causes others to listen carefully and often to react favorably to what the expert leader says.[10] This tendency to elicit positive reactions from others is extremely helpful to leaders' boundary spanning efforts. When leaders possess expert power, outsiders and group members hesitate to question or challenge their arguments, and they are more likely to go along with the leader's requests. This ability to influence others through rational persuasion can result in adequate resources, cooperative agreements, and favorable relationships with outsiders who can help the group achieve its goals. Leaders often develop expert power through continuous learning and training programs, formal education, and meaningful work experiences.

In addition to task expertise, when leaders are highly respected or admired for other reasons, their boundary spanning behaviors are probably more effective. This *referent power* may result from the leader's past accomplishments, high status, or a magnetic personality. It often complements expert power in helping the leader represent the group effectively. Others in the organization can help build a leader's referent power by emphasizing the leader's achievements and potential for future accomplishments.

Effective boundary spanners usually develop networks of relationships with important individuals and groups outside the leader's group or organization.[11] These networks help build the leader's *resource/connection power,* which is critical to keeping the leader's group well supplied with the resources needed to accomplish its goals. The leader's connections also help obtain cooperation with other groups through the leader's efforts at consultation and collaboration. In organizations working with sophisticated technology, such as those conducting complex medical procedures or complicated manufacturing operations, willing cooperation from other departments can be essential to effective performance.

Two other sources of power can especially help leaders with boundary spanning inside their own group. Leaders who hold a high-level position in the organization are likely to be respected due to their position. In other words, the leader's efforts to resolve disputes among subgroups or members of the leader's group will likely be influential due to the leader's *legitimate power* of position. Followers will probably assume that high-level leaders also possess *reward and coercive power* due to their position, and may be anxious to keep on these leaders' good side. Although many leaders do not emphasize their formal position or control over rewards and punishments, these power sources are implied when a high-level leader makes a suggestion or offers to help two followers work out a disagreement that is interfering with the group's performance.[12] Although legitimate power is usually bestowed on a leader by the organization, all leaders control some types of rewards and punishments—either tangible (such as a bonus or a demotion) or intangible (a compliment or a reprimand). Effective leaders typically make use of several of these power sources when carrying out boundary spanning activities. Figure 9-2 summarizes important skills and power sources for boundary spanning leadership.

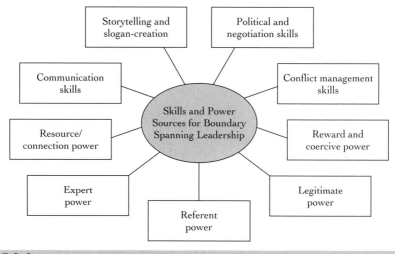

▮▮▮▮ **FIGURE 9-2 Skills and power sources for boundary spanning leadership**

▮▮▮ Negotiation in Boundary Spanning

Everyone is a negotiator. Buying a car or home, searching for a job, hiring an employee, or trying to get your boss to increase your department's budget all involve negotiations. Because leaders are the primary boundary spanners in organizations, they are required to negotiate formal or informal agreements on a regular basis. *Negotiation* is a series of communications between two parties who are trying to reach an agreement that satisfies their interests. Some of these interests are shared by the two parties and some are not shared. In organizations, as well as family life, when decisions are made that affect numerous people, these decisions usually involve some negotiation.[13]

Many people believe there are two types of negotiators: hard and soft. Hard negotiators see their situation as a contest of wills, in which the party who takes an extreme position and holds out the longest usually wins. Unfortunately, taking a hard position often causes the other party to do the same, and creates hard feelings that can damage their future relationship. Soft negotiators want an agreeable settlement without conflict, so they often make several concessions and end up feeling exploited, unhappy, and resentful.

There is another approach, often called *principled negotiation,* that can avoid some of the drawbacks of the hard or soft approaches. This approach involves looking for mutual gains between the two parties as much as possible. When interests are in conflict, the resolution should be based on some fair, independent standard rather than the will of either party. This approach involves no trickery; instead, it is designed to help people settle negotiations in a reasonable and decent manner.

Whatever approach is used for negotiations should result in meeting the legitimate interests of both parties as much as possible. It should also resolve conflicting interests in a fair manner, consider the impacts on the surrounding community, be doable, and not damage the relationship between the parties involved. It is also desirable if the approach does not take too much time and does not leave the parties exhausted.

One tactic often used in negotiation is called *positional bargaining.* Here, each party takes a position, argues for it, and then hopefully makes concessions to reach a compromise. This tactic can result in people getting stuck in their position because their ego is involved. The more they defend their position, the more stuck they become. Less attention is given to satisfying both parties' needs and more is given to winning or not giving in. Arguing over positions is also time consuming and exhausting. An agreement may be a split-the-difference deal that is unsatisfying to both parties, endangering their future relationship.

Principled negotiation attempts to avoid these problems and satisfy the criteria described above. This approach involves six basic principles, as described next.[14]

Separate the People from the Problem

People perceive things differently, they miscommunicate, and they are influenced by emotions. These factors get entangled with objective facts during negotiations. In organizations, most negotiations are not a one-shot deal, so it is important to maintain the relationship after the negotiation. This means dealing with people problems directly, not through concessions in the negotiation. Improving perceptions is a first step, and can be accomplished by viewing the negotiation from the other party's perspective, not expecting your worst fears, avoiding placing blame on the other party if you are unhappy with their offer or response, emphasizing areas you agree on, and making your proposals consistent with your values. Handling emotions requires acknowledging their importance and understanding their source, allowing others to let off steam, not responding to outbursts, and making symbolic gestures of friendship. These behaviors should provide a better understanding of both perspectives, keep emotions from interfering with substantive discussions, and facilitate real understanding by both parties. They will also help build a working relationship and facilitate the current negotiation.

Focus on Interests, Not Positions

Each party to a negotiation has specific interests they hope to achieve. These interests reflect their needs, desires, concerns, and fears. These interests are the basis for bargaining positions that people adopt, and they must be addressed to satisfactorily conclude the negotiation. Some of the parties' interests are compatible and some conflict, but they must be identified to facilitate useful discussion. Asking why the other party takes a specific position helps identify their interests. Asking what the other side sees you wanting from them can also be helpful. Then ask yourself why they have not given you what they think you want. What are their interests that prevent them from agreeing? These interests must be met to some degree to conclude the negotiation. Talking about your own and the other party's interests helps move the discussion away from positions. Focusing on the future (not past actions) and having concrete options you could agree with, while being flexible, also helps avoid the "digging in" problem with positional bargaining. These behaviors keep the discussion fixed on satisfying both parties' interests.

Invent Options for Mutual Gain

People rarely develop options when entering a negotiation. This causes them to dig in to specific positions and show little creativity. Developing options requires brainstorming with colleagues or friends to produce ideas that may later become options for negotiation. The number of options can be increased by viewing the problem from the perspectives of different experts or thinking of limited agreements that might be satisfactory for the time being. Exploring options with the other party to the negotiation involves you both in trying to satisfy each other's interests. This also helps in identifying shared interests and creating new possibilities. To be seriously considered, every option must appear to be legitimate (fair, legal, and honorable). Basing an option on precedent (prior negotiations) usually increases its legitimacy. Avoid threats ("Take it or I'm outta here"), because they do not contribute to legitimacy. Consider how the other party might be criticized if they accept an option. Compose every option you propose so that a simple "yes" would be realistic and doable.

Insist on Using Objective Criteria

Focus your negotiation strategy on some standard or objective criteria that is independent of the personal will of either party. Standards of fairness, efficiency, or expert judgment are usually more helpful in evaluating and discussing proposals than trying to force each other to back down from their position. Other independent standards that might be used in a negotiation are market value, precedent, equal treatment, reciprocity, or tradition. Describe the standards you are using to the other party. Try to use reason in your negotiation and be open to reason by the other party. One way to do this is to ask "What is your reasoning?" or "How did you arrive at that proposal?" Never yield to pressure tactics such as threats, bribes, or manipulative appeals to trust ("You trust me, don't you?"). Evaluate proposals using objective standards, and make concessions only when your objective evaluation indicates they are appropriate.

Know Your BATNA

BATNA stands for *best alternative to a negotiated agreement.*[15] People negotiate to produce a better result than if they did not negotiate. The best alternative use of your assets (without any negotiation) is your BATNA, and should be considered a measuring point that is used to evaluate any proposed agreement. If you accept any proposal that is less than your BATNA, then your negotiation has failed because it resulted in a worse situation than without any negotiation. Knowing your BATNA before you begin negotiating will help you identify any proposal that you should reject, and will help you make the most of your assets.

Preparation Is the Key

Before you begin negotiating, you should inform yourself about the standards that apply to your negotiation, as well as your major interests, your BATNA, and the options that are acceptable to you. You should also have some idea about the other party's interests and his or her BATNA. Doing your research and being prepared will often suggest a strategy to your negotiation, and will help you prepare your first offer. Table 9-1 describes 10 guidelines to be used in negotiation that can help you reach a favorable agreement.

▬▬▬ Effects of Boundary Spanning

Leaders' boundary spanning activities have produced favorable results in many organizational situations. For example, *coordination* problems were almost completely eliminated among legal, judicial, and mental health departments in a city government

TABLE 9-1 Guidelines for negotiation

1. Know your BATNA, but do not reveal it during negotiations.

2. Research the other party's BATNA by putting yourself in their position and considering their alternatives.

3. Set high aspirations, because they will usually result in a better agreement.

3. If possible, make the first offer, because it is highly predictive of the final settlement.

4. Counteroffer soon after receiving an offer in order to show your willingness to negotiate.

5. Do not state a range of values that are acceptable to you for a final settlement. This forfeits important bargaining space.

7. Make bilateral (not unilateral) concessions and expect a concession in return. Fewer small concessions are better than many larger ones, Do not offer more than one concession at a time.

8. Use objective rationale to support your offers.

9. Appeal to norms of fairness.

10. Do not fall for the even split ploy. If you have made a generous offer and theirs is extreme, splitting the difference may result in an unfair settlement.

▪▪▪▪▪▪▪▪▪

SOURCE: Leigh L. Thompson. *The Mind and Heart of the Negotiator,* 2nd ed. Upper Saddle River, NJ: Prentice Hall, 2001. © 2001. Adapted by permission of Pearson Education, Inc., Upper Saddle River, NJ.

when managers of these units engaged in extensive external boundary spanning activities.[16] In business organizations, when leaders went to bat to defend followers and kept their superiors informed regarding group activities, these leaders received *higher performance evaluations.*[17] High performance evaluations were also given to school principals by superintendents and teachers when principals were active in boundary spanning by obtaining resources for their schools and disseminating information to outsiders.[18]

Boundary spanning is also important for project managers in research and development departments.[19] These managers often obtain important technical and career information from external sources and then convey it to personnel in their departments. This activity can result in improved staff development and socialization, especially among younger personnel. These improvements produce *lower turnover* and *higher promotion* rates for these personnel than those who have managers who are less active in boundary spanning.[20] Other studies show that followers' *satisfaction, morale,* and *confidence in the leader* are increased by effective boundary spanning.[21]

Leaders can also experience negative consequences from their boundary spanning activities. For example, managers in research and development organizations reported a high level of *role conflict* when they were heavily involved in boundary spanning. The boundary requirements of their different roles created varying demands and multiple loyalties that were difficult for these managers to juggle. Leaders in human service organizations also reported high levels of *stress* and *job burnout* associated with their boundary spanning duties.[22] Although leaders' boundary spanning activities have favorable effects on their organizations and followers, the negotiations and haggling that may accompany these activities can clearly take their toll on leaders.

▪▪▪ Situational Enhancers, Neutralizers, and Substitutes for Boundary Spanning

The amount of boundary spanning activities required of a leader is often related to factors in the organization's environment.[23] A highly uncertain environment often requires more boundary spanning. In these situations, the leaders need to monitor the environment in order to gather information and adapt to unforeseen changes that might affect the organization. But researchers have also found that predictable and controllable environments encouraged boundary spanning by company managers to influence that environment.[24] Here, the boundary spanners were able to create and exploit opportunities for their organization as they interacted with outside individuals and organizations. In both situations, the *organizational environment* enhanced the need for external boundary spanning, but the objectives of the boundary spanners differed depending on the nature of the environment and the organization's position.

Internal organizational factors can also enhance a need for boundary spanning activities by leaders. When followers' *tasks are uncertain and difficult* (such as designing new computer software or hardware), leaders spend much time in boundary spanning activities.[25] Here, the group members often need information and guidance from other sources in order to complete their tasks, and boundary spanners are active in obtaining this information. If the leader's *group is central* to the organization's activities and engages in highly interdependent operations with other organizational groups, then boundary spanning activities are enhanced.[26] A lot of coordination with other groups is needed in these situations, and boundary spanners provide this coordination by anticipating and solving problems before they get out of hand.

A leader is likely to be highly effective when he or she responds to these environmental, task, and organizational situations with boundary spanning behaviors. Leaders are also most likely to be successful in boundary spanning efforts when they are *familiar with the organization's operations,* have *extensive leadership experience,* and have *many internal and external connections* (connection power).[27] These factors increase respect for the leader by followers and others who interact with him or her, thereby enhancing the effectiveness of the leader's boundary spanning behaviors. When the leader is responsible for one or more *self-managed work teams,* boundary spanning activities are also especially important. These teams are increasingly common in organizations, and are described in the following section.

On the other hand, research indicates that boundary spanning activities are less important in certain settings. For example, numerous *formal policies, procedures,* and *written guidelines* substituted for many boundary spanning activities among noncommissioned U.S. Army officers.[28] Formalized procedures are very prevalent in military organizations. These procedures may assure that certain needs of followers are met, and they need not rely on the leader's boundary spanning activities to provide for them.

Some studies have also reported that older followers, or those with higher rank and years of service, are less affected by boundary spanning activities of their leaders.[29] These individuals may be in a position to satisfy their own needs without the leader's help, whereas younger, less-experienced followers may depend on the leader's boundary spanning. *Followers' age, rank, and years of experience* may thus neutralize the effects of the leader's boundary spanning. Although the information is sparse, it does appear that the leader must consider situational and follower characteristics in order

TABLE 9-2 Enhancers, neutralizers, and substitutes for boundary spanning leadership

Enhancers of Boundary Spanning	Substitutes for Boundary Spanning	Neutralizers of Boundary Spanning
Environmental uncertainty versus predictability	Numerous formal organizational procedures	Older followers with many years of service
Task uncertainty and difficulty		Followers with high rank
Centrality of leader's unit		
Leader's experience and familiarity with organizational operations		
Leader's extensive internal and external networks		
Team-based organization structure		

to assess the need for the boundary spanning function. The three types of situational and follower characteristics that affect boundary spanning leadership are summarized in Table 9-2. The Leadership in Action box on Bill Gates describes a current example of boundary spanning.

▪▪▪ Team Leadership—A Key Situational Factor

Organizations today face tremendous competitive pressures from international firms for marketing their products and services. They also face competition for raw materials, as increasingly free and open societies worldwide make more demands on our planet's limited natural resources. They face demands from investors, consumer groups, and government regulators to be more efficient and profitable, more socially responsible, and more proactive on environmental and employee issues. In response to these complex pressures, leaders in many organizations are changing the way work processes are organized and new technology is implemented. These organizations often implement team-based approaches in which groups of people work together on collective tasks, when previously a manager tried to coordinate numerous individuals doing different portions of the collective task.

A *work team* is a group of individuals, usually about 5 to 15, who work interdependently to achieve a common goal. The essence of the team is that members work together in a coordinated and cooperative effort to achieve their common purpose. These members bring different perspectives and wider expertise to solve organizational problems, and they often make better decisions than individuals. Different types of teams are popular in organizations today, including cross-functional teams, process improvement teams, quality circles, and top management teams. Each type of team has similar properties, issues, and problems that must be addressed by the leader and team members.

The leadership of work teams, often called team leadership, is a popular topic in organizations because of the widespread use of team structures. Although some organizations have shown significant improvements with a team structure, other team

LEADERSHIP IN ACTION

Bill Gates, Boundary Spanner

Bill Gates is chairman and cofounder of Microsoft, and one of the world's richest people. He has created the dominant computer software company by staying abreast of rapid technological developments in the computer industry and negotiating agreements with other companies that have potentially valuable products. Microsoft then modifies, repackages, and markets these products to the expanding market for computer software. Gates' boundary spanning activities of obtaining information and negotiating agreements have allowed Microsoft to achieve its position in the software market.

Gates dropped out of Harvard in 1975 to found Microsoft. Its first product was an adapted version of the programming language BASIC for the first personal computer—the Altair 8800 (both were invented by other people). In 1980, Gates made a deal with IBM to build operating systems for their personal computers. Microsoft bought Q-DOS from another company and revised it for IBM's PCs. Microsoft created its famous Windows operating system based on a window–mouse system pioneered years earlier by Xerox Corporation. Most of Microsoft's products were made possible through agreements that Gates negotiated with other companies.

In the early 1990s, e-mail and the Internet were becoming popular, and the World Wide Web emerged in 1994. Gates negotiated a licensing agreement with another company to provide a Web browser called Internet Explorer. In the late 1990s, the U.S. Justice Department brought suit against Microsoft for exerting monopoly power in the computer software industry. Gates became active in representing and defending his company against these charges. Most observers agree that he was highly effective in this role.

Gates has used boundary spanning behaviors in gathering and disseminating information to Microsoft employees (he is an avid e-mail user), negotiating with other companies for new products and markets, and buffering Microsoft from charges of monopoly power. In the fast-changing and uncertain computer software industry, Gates' boundary spanning skills have produced incredible success for Microsoft.

SOURCE: D. Galernter. Bill Gates—Software strongman. *Time,* December 7, 1998, 201–205.

---

approaches have failed. One major reason for this failure is the team leadership by the person who is formally responsible for the team's performance.[30] Team-based organizations usually require leaders to provide operational employees with increased knowledge about organizational and technical processes, increased quality of information for decision making, and increased authority and responsibility to implement their ideas. Team structures often result in employees relying more on their coworkers for guidance and support than on their formal superior. These changes require a shift in leadership strategy from that used in traditional organizations. This often causes team leaders to be uncomfortable with their new responsibilities. This section focuses on teams and the behaviors needed to lead them effectively. We first describe several types of teams that are growing in popularity—cross-functional teams, self-managed teams, virtual teams, and top management teams.

Cross-Functional Teams

Cross-functional teams are groups of individuals with a shared goal who represent different functions or areas of expertise in an organization, and whose combined efforts are required to achieve the team's goal. These teams are usually used for planning and carrying out complex activities that require much cooperation, coordination, and joint problem solving by all members of the team.[31] Examples include product development teams, multidisciplinary quality improvement teams, consulting teams that address specific market segments, program development teams in a medical center or university, or cross-functional management teams that manage an entire product family within the 3M Corporation.[32] These teams often include personnel from all levels of the organization, and sometimes key customers or suppliers who are important to the organization. Cross-functional teams are used frequently in organizations with fast-changing markets in which adapting to varying customers needs is especially important.

Cross-functional teams are composed of individuals from diverse backgrounds, interests, organizational roles, and cultural backgrounds. The team's purpose often involves highly technical or scientific work that requires specialized knowledge from numerous sources. Members of the team are usually also members of a functional department or other unit in the organization. Because of this, they often have little or no experience in working with other cross-functional team members, and the team leader has little or no formal authority over the members' performance in the team. Being a team leader in a cross-functional team is a difficult assignment.

Self-Managed Teams

Self-managed teams are usually composed of workers from the same functional unit who are responsible for a block of work necessary to produce a product or deliver a service to an internal or external customer. A large portion of the authority and responsibility usually given to a manager is assigned to the team. The team often has the authority to plan, schedule, and assign work to members, and to make and implement decisions related to production and personnel.[33] Variations of self-managed teams are sometimes called self-directed, self-governing, or self-led teams. These teams are closely related, and differ primarily in the degree to which they carry out tasks previously done by their manager. Because self-managed teams are so popular, much of the recent research on work teams has focused on them.

The activities and responsibilities of self-managed teams vary considerably, partly due to the experience and developmental level of the teams themselves. Early in its life, a team will begin to regulate its own member's task assignments, vacation and training schedules, attendance, monitor team performance, and do some problem solving regarding quality or interpersonal issues. As a team matures and gains confidence, its members often contact suppliers and customers directly regarding the team's product or service. Team members become involved in their own planning, goal setting, hiring, equipment acquisition, and budgeting decisions. Very mature teams may make many of these decisions on their own, and also manage their own overtime needs, conduct performance appraisals, or discipline members regarding performance problems.[34]

Self-managed teams are usually given considerable independence, and they often help develop their own work processes, resulting in processes that work better. Having direct customer contact causes them to take more ownership for meeting their commitments to customers. They are often involved with acquiring and implementing new technology, frequently resulting in more efficient and effective operations.[35] Members of these teams are usually multiskilled; in fact, the pay system normally encourages employees to master all the job tasks carried out by their team. Members are also often assigned team roles in addition to their job tasks. These team roles are usually rotated, and may include recognizer, innovator, monitor, communicator, task master, and internal leader. The team usually reports to a formally designated leader, often called a team coach or facilitator. The team coach or facilitator is in the formal position of a first-line supervisor, but the coach's functions under the self-managed team structure are very different from the traditional foreman.[36]

Virtual Teams

Virtual teams are groups of individuals who are geographically or organizationally dispersed and who collaborate via various types of information technology to achieve a common goal. They may include customers or suppliers and they may be permanent or temporary. Some companies, such as British Petroleum, report favorable results with virtual teams because they can bring a wide degree of expertise to help solve problems without requiring the physical presence of all team members. Research is just beginning on virtual teams, but it appears that establishing clear goals and schedules for accomplishment, coordinating members' efforts, and facilitating the team's discussions and decision making are key issues for making virtual teams effective.[37]

Top Management Teams

Most organizations have a CEO or president, a chief operating officer, and several other top-level managers who head separate divisions within the organization. The CEO is usually in charge and consults with the other top-level managers on operational decisions and frequently on strategic issues. Some organizations have adopted a team approach to top-level leadership. Here, a group of top-level executives collectively take responsibility for organizational operations, and sometimes work with the CEO to develop a consensus on organizational strategies.[38] Some writers claim that this team approach promotes creativity in problem solving, brings diverse perspectives to bear on major organizational issues, and increases commitment to decisions.[39]

Top management teams can also overcome weaknesses of the CEO and create excellent developmental experiences for participating managers. They may be especially appropriate in dealing with complex, rapidly changing environments. Their effectiveness appears to depend on the development of a clear team identity and shared vision for the organization, doing real work together (such as collectively analyzing and solving organizational problems), giving team members responsibility for organization-wide programs, staggering member turnover to assure some continuity of membership, providing significant compensation based on overall organizational performance, and skilled CEO leadership.[40–42] These factors can help avoid the process losses that result from poor communication, hidden agendas, lack of trust, and flawed decision making that prevent some top management teams from realizing their potential.

Effective Leadership Behaviors for Team Leaders

Research on the teams described above shows they are less likely to be successful without a competent leader. The most important leadership behaviors for a team leader will vary with the experience and level of development of a team. From the beginning, however, cross-functional and self-managed teams need leaders who can effectively perform the boundary spanning activities described earlier in this chapter.[43,44] These teams are especially in need of the buffering, linking, communicating, resource acquisition, and mediating efforts of leaders if they are to maintain their autonomy and self-control, and still deal effectively with their environment. One recent study of creative teams found boundary spanning to be the most important role of the team leader that influenced team effectiveness.[45] The boundary spanning role for these teams requires emphasis on reducing uncertainty for the team by finding and sharing information on organizational and other departments' goals, team performance, new technology, performance of competitors, pay levels, and sources of raw materials. One team leader described his most important role as getting the team whatever information or other resources they needed. Negotiating implicit or explicit contracts and agreements with outsiders is also important. Team boundary spanning involves advocacy for the team, such as making the team's case to managers who are skeptical, indifferent, or actually oppose the team concept. Publicizing team successes, rebutting arguments or proposals that could harm the team, being vigilant for other forces that could unintentionally damage team independence or performance, and working to prevent mistakes from destroying the team are all part of the team leader's advocacy activities. Taking over functions from upper management, negotiating increased autonomy for the team, and opening doors for the team and its members are also important. The leader often encourages joint training and decision making with other teams when issues concern both teams. Helping team members develop an accurate shared understanding of their operating environment and how the team should respond to that environment is also an aspect of leaders' boundary spanning.

Another aspect of the boundary spanning role that often gives team leaders problems is *mediating conflicts* within the team and with other teams. Experienced team leaders try to avoid giving advice on a solution to the conflict; rather, they concentrate on asking questions to help guide the team to its own solution. As team members become comfortable with their roles and participation, they begin to assert themselves, and conflict usually occurs within the team. The effective team leader usually acknowledges the frustration of members and asks questions such as "Have you talked with this individual about that?" or "Have you looked at it from his viewpoint?" The leader may help the team develop objective feedback for a problem member, and rehearse with them what they will say when they discuss the issue with him or her. When conflict occurs with other teams, the leader urges the team to acknowledge unproductive behavior by both teams and define the issues as shared needs rather than opposing views. The team is urged to stay focused on problem solving and look for points of agreement. It is often wise not to stifle occasional outbursts of anger, but to follow up on them with a restatement of the issues.

Early in a team's life, a leader's *directive* behaviors are important for the team's development and eventual performance.[46,47] Two researchers reported that the most advanced self-managing teams started with supervisors who were highly directive in the early stages.[48] The same appears to be true for virtual teams. The leader is active in providing or helping the team understand its mission and goals, as well as strategies and action steps to achieve them. The leader may describe role requirements of team members and provide benchmarks for the team to gauge its own progress. Newcomers to the team often seek information and feedback from the team leader, who shapes their perceptions of the team.[49]

Much of the research on team leadership emphasizes the importance of the leader's *supportive behaviors* to provide encouragement for team members and to help them treat mistakes as learning opportunities as the team takes on new tasks. Active listening that is empathetic and respectful without passing judgment, validates and alleviates member concerns, and mirrors back to the team what the leader hears, is an important behavioral skill for the supportive team leader. The leader also arranges for or conducts training in communication and interaction skills to help team members communicate more openly and honestly, to keep communication focused on work issues and behaviors rather than individuals, and to gauge team expectations and reactions when they consider word choice.[50] The leader provides mentoring by using experience and an understanding of organizations to give informal guidance and career counseling. The supportive team leader facilitates team development by identifying needed skills and providing training in these skills, and helping the team address problems as they work through the stages of team development.

Team coaching is a major aspect of a team leader's supportiveness. It involves interacting with the team to help members use their collective expertise and skills to successfully accomplish the team's goals.[51] Examples might be encouraging a second-chance meeting, or suggesting that a devil's advocate be assigned when a major decision is faced by the team. This can help the team learn to avoid the groupthink syndrome, which is especially important in top management teams. Another example could be asking the team thoughtful questions about their planned procedures for developing a new product. Asking questions, paraphrasing, encouraging and modeling flexibility and openness to new ideas, soliciting contributions from quiet team members, insisting that all members respect ideas and input from others, celebrating achievements, and dealing with dysfunctional members are all team coaching activities that can help develop the group process skills of the team. These process skills are essential for the team to function effectively as a viable and ongoing organizational entity. The team coaching aspect of supportiveness was recently shown to significantly improve a team's process skills.[52]

Encouraging *participative decision making* is a team leader's behavior that reflects a particularly important aspect of the team's process skills. All leaders, whether appointed or elected, face decisions regarding how participative they want to be. In many of the teams described here, a consensus style of decision making is expected. In Chapter 3, we described the Vroom-Yetta-Jago model of participative decision making that helps a leader choose a decision style. Effective team leaders usually try to develop team members' process skills and commitment to the team goals to make consensus decision making more effective.

Effective leaders of self-managed teams sometimes allow teams to make mistakes, as long as they are not devastating to the team. If the leader sees the team about to make a serious error, he or she will often ask key questions such as, "Why do you think that is right?" or "Have you viewed it from this perspective?" *Modeling* self-regulation is also important to encourage members' self-development and self-control. The leader helps the self-managed team handle production problems that are beyond its experience or expertise, such as managing raw materials with unusual properties. The leader also provides *rewards and recognition* to the team through positive feedback when the team performs well, and by enacting a policy of skill-based pay to encourage members to master all the tasks facing the work team.

Creating Team-Based Substitutes for Leadership

Throughout the process of developing many of these teams, the team leader works steadily to create team-based leadership substitutes for many behaviors previously performed by the first-line supervisor. The leader's negotiations with upper management, delegation of administrative tasks, and team development efforts are all designed to encourage the team to control its own behavior for high performance. *Continuous training* is conducted to increase the relevant knowledge among team members that can alleviate much of the need for direction by the team leader. *Delegation with coaching* is designed to increase members' abilities, experience, and confidence, so that leader direction and support are less necessary. *Team development* that increases cohesion and encourages positive performance norms can help maintain the morale of the team and improve member attitudes and motivation with less need for leader supportiveness or charismatic behaviors. The philosophy of empowering the team to take collective responsibility for management activities encourages a strong *need for independence* within the team that increases members' desire to act without the leader's guidance.

Developing these leadership substitutes also involves teaching and coaching the team and its members in several skills of self-leadership.[53] *Self-observation* involves gathering information on team behavior and performance, as well as on the factors that affect performance, and comparing this information with team goals. *Self-goal setting* involves setting shared team goals. *Antecedent modification* involves actively influencing the task environment by removing environmental stimuli that encourage undesirable behavior, and increasing exposure to stimuli that encourage desirable behavior (such as changing the team's workspace). *Self-reward and self-punishment* means team members reinforce desirable performance by providing tangible or intangible rewards for members in return for important behaviors. It also involves punishing behaviors that do not help the team (such as agreeing to work overtime for too much socializing). *Rehearsal* is practicing a key performance or team maintenance activity. *Strategic planning* involves examining team standards of performance as well as goals and tactics, and interactively creating a shared team vision of goals and strategies to accomplish them. Avoiding *groupthink* tendencies means being careful of assuming the group is inherently more moral or less vulnerable than other groups, not pressuring deviants to keep quiet, and avoiding retreat from difficult problems faced by the group. Leader comments such as "We can do this!" are often helpful in difficult situations to avoid this retreat mentality. These behaviors by team leaders are designed to help the team operate more independently of the leader with flexibility and creativity.

Effects of Team Leadership

Increasing amounts of evidence indicate that when leaders carry out the behaviors described here, the results are favorable. Research and case studies credit well-led teams with increased productivity, improved quality of work, more positive attitudes, less member absenteeism, and a desire by members to stay in the team.[54] Company reports also point to major cost savings, improved work quality and attitudes, some productivity improvements, and reduced need for supervisors.[55]

The movement toward work teams appears to be a major trend in organizations. Increasingly, effective team leaders will be required to make these teams successful. Boundary spanning activities, as well as the other leadership behaviors described in this section, will be essential for team leaders.

SUMMARY ▮▮▮▮▮▮▮

Boundary spanning with the organization's environment appears to be particularly needed when a team or organization faces a rapidly changing, complex, resource-poor, or threatening environment, or when the environment presents unique information or opportunities for the organization to exploit. Boundary spanning inside the organization or team is especially needed when conflict exists between teams or team members, or the leader's unit and other units are highly specialized, interdependent, or use complex technology requiring extensive coordination and cooperation. Finally, when an organization is composed of work teams that operate with some independence from

▮▮▮ **FIGURE 9-3 Process model of boundary spanning leadership**

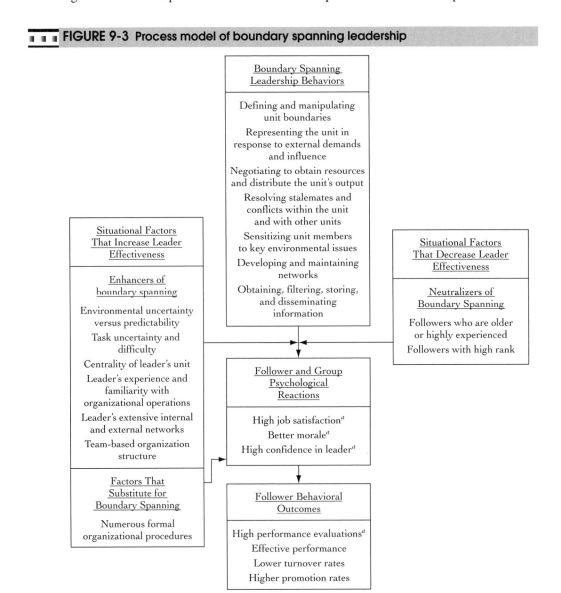

[a]These psychological reactions and outcomes have shown the strongest improvement from a leader's boundary spanning.

higher management, boundary spanning will be especially important. These situational factors are very common in today's organizations, making boundary spanning an important type of leadership behavior. Leaders may be especially effective at boundary spanning when they are good communicators, assertive, knowledgeable, and experienced in organizational operations, and have many connections outside their group or department. Negotiation and team leadership skills are especially important for boundary spanning in organizations of the 21st century.

Figure 9-3 describes a process model of boundary spanning leadership. It summarizes the major boundary spanning leadership behaviors and how they affect follower reactions, which in turn affect followers' behaviors and outcomes. Boxes at each side of Figure 9-3 show how situational factors influence the effectiveness of the leader's boundary spanning.

Figure 9-4 describes how leaders can use the process model of boundary spanning leadership. The box at the top of Figure 9-4 (1. Diagnosing the Situation) describes diagnostic questions leaders can ask to determine if boundary spanning leadership is needed. If the answer is "yes" to one or more of these questions, then the leader should

▪▪▪▪ **FIGURE 9-4** Applying the process model of boundary spanning leadership

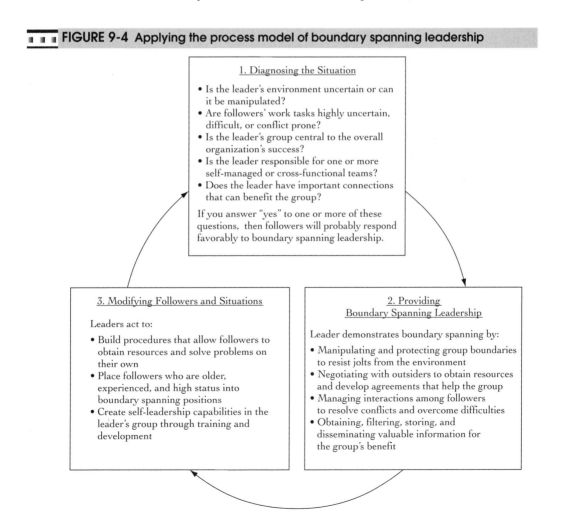

1. Diagnosing the Situation

• Is the leader's environment uncertain or can it be manipulated?
• Are followers' work tasks highly uncertain, difficult, or conflict prone?
• Is the leader's group central to the overall organization's success?
• Is the leader responsible for one or more self-managed or cross-functional teams?
• Does the leader have important connections that can benefit the group?

If you answer "yes" to one or more of these questions, then followers will probably respond favorably to boundary spanning leadership.

3. Modifying Followers and Situations

Leaders act to:
• Build procedures that allow followers to obtain resources and solve problems on their own
• Place followers who are older, experienced, and high status into boundary spanning positions
• Create self-leadership capabilities in the leader's group through training and development

2. Providing Boundary Spanning Leadership

Leader demonstrates boundary spanning by:
• Manipulating and protecting group boundaries to resist jolts from the environment
• Negotiating with outsiders to obtain resources and develop agreements that help the group
• Managing interactions among followers to resolve conflicts and overcome difficulties
• Obtaining, filtering, storing, and disseminating valuable information for the group's benefit

carry out boundary spanning behaviors (2. Providing Boundary Spanning Leadership). The leader should then assess the situation to determine if it can be modified to make followers more independent of the leader's boundary spanning activities (3. Modifying Followers and Situations). After taking feasible actions to modify the followers' situations, the leader then returns to the first box and rediagnoses the situation to determine if boundary spanning is still needed. The leader thus carries out the three key leadership tasks of diagnosing situations, providing boundary spanning leadership, modifying the situation, and so on, in a continuous and dynamic process.

KEY TERMS AND CONCEPTS IN THIS CHAPTER ▪▪▪▪▪▪▪

- Active listening
- Antecedent modification
- BATNA
- Boundary spanning behaviors
- Communication skills
- Conflict-management skills
- Cross-functional teams
- Delegation

- Environmental uncertainty
- Groupthink
- Leadership roles
- Linking-pin functions
- Locus of control
- Negotiation skills
- Political skills
- Positional bargaining
- Principled negotiation

- Rehearsal
- Representative functions
- Self-managed teams
- Team development
- Top management teams
- Virtual teams
- Work teams

REVIEW AND DISCUSSION QUESTIONS ▪▪▪▪▪▪▪

1. Describe boundary spanning behaviors you have engaged in or observed. Which of these boundary spanning behaviors were effective and which were ineffective? Why?
2. List the skills and abilities needed for effective boundary spanning. Now describe how you can improve your skills and abilities for this leadership behavior.
3. Describe situational factors you have observed or heard about that show a need for boundary spanning behaviors.
4. Describe a situation you observed or heard about where a leader negotiated on a group or organization's behalf. Was the leader effective in the negotiation? Could he or she have been more effective? How?
5. Describe an organization in which you think a leader's boundary spanning would be especially needed. Why is it needed?
6. Think of an effective team and an ineffective team you have belonged to. Why was one team more effective than the other? What could have been done to make the ineffective team effective?

EXERCISE: BOUNDARY SPANNING WITH THE BOSS ▪▪▪▪▪▪▪

Leonard Sayles described an effective boundary spanning strategy that middle managers can use to influence their boss. First, managers must accept the fact that their boss has a different perspective than they do. The boss may be viewing things with a longer-term perspective, maintaining a larger picture than the manager's own department. Second, managers must realize that the job involves built-in role conflict. They will always be in the middle between upper management's concerns and followers' concerns. However, managers must not be a sieve, passing down everything that comes from above. Nor can they simply immerse themselves in the workgroup and pretend to be just one of the gang. Third, managers must learn to be persuasive with their boss by developing presentation skills, assembling convincing information, designing tables and graphs, and articulating an appealing line of argument. Sayles adds that when attempting to persuade the boss to approve a big decision, the manager should present the problem in stages so that no solution will be immediately apparent. This will keep the boss from forming a conclusion before you have presented your entire case. The example of a new superintendent of a manufacturing plant on the first page of this chapter demonstrates this approach. Once a boss has made a decision, it is next to impossible to get that decision reversed. Bringing the boss through each phase of the problem with the solution still unclear increases the chances of getting your solution accepted.

After reading this description of boundary spanning with the boss, meet with two or three other students and develop responses to the following questions.

1. Why can't managers be "just one of the gang"?
2. Why does Sayles believe a supervisor should present a problem in stages to his or her boss, rather than proposing a final solution at the beginning? Do you agree with this approach? Why or why not?
3. What preparation should a supervisor do before trying to persuade his or her boss to approve an important decision?

SOURCE: L. R. Sayles. *Leadership: Managing in Real Organizations,* 2nd ed. New York: McGraw-Hill, 1989.

▪▪▪▪ C A S E   I N C I D E N T S ▪▪▪▪

Can the Conflict Be Resolved?

You supervise the shipping department for a tool manufacturing company. There are seven packers who put tools in individual boxes and place them in cartons for shipment. Each packer works alone to box his or her share of the tools each day. Rebecca Garcia finishes her work in about half the time required by the other packers. Because she finishes faster, Rebecca takes longer breaks and has more time for lunch than the other packers. On breaks and after she has completed her work for the day, Rebecca usually works on assignments for the college courses she is taking. Rebecca does not seem to have much in common with the other packers and spends little time talking with them.

All the packers receive the same pay and there is no extra pay for greater output. The company policy is that the pay for jobs that are primarily manual labor is to be on an hourly basis, with all employees doing the same job receiving the same hourly pay rate.

The other packers frequently complain about Rebecca's longer breaks and her study-ing. You have encouraged Rebecca to work toward a degree, and approved her studying during breaks as long as she did her share of the work. Even though the other packers agree that Rebecca gets her share of the work done, they have requested that you assign her more work. You know that if you don't take action there will be continuing conflict between Rebecca and the other packers. ▪

DISCUSSION QUESTIONS

1. What do you believe is the main cause of the conflict among the packers?
2. As supervisor, should you continue to allow Rebecca to take longer breaks and study on the job? If you do, how will you explain your action to the other packers?
3. How can you maintain productivity and resolve the conflict between Rebecca and the other packers? What boundary spanning behaviors would be involved in your proposed solution?

Henry Ford, An Historical Business Leader

Henry Ford (1863–1947) was the son of an Irish immigrant and farmer, born near Dearborn, Michigan. His involvement with automobiles began when he experimented with machinery on his parents' farm, and later built combustion vehicles. Ford founded his own automobile company, the Ford Motor Company, in 1903, when he felt ready to market the automobile that he built. The Ford Motor Company was almost put out of business five weeks after it began, because Ford was denied a license to manufacture automobiles when he refused to pay licensing fees to the holder of a patent on "road engines." Ford fought the patent case in court and finally won in 1911. The Ford Motor Company targeted average income customers and achieved great success, becoming one of the major automakers in the world.

Ford, as founder and leader of the company, deserved great credit for its success. Ford was called the "father of the modern assembly line." Ford's assembly line revolutionized production and greatly improved efficiency. At first, workers on the line earned a daily wage of $2.38 and worked 9 hours a day. However, they quickly tired of their repetitive tasks, resulting in a high turnover rate. In 1913, Ford had to hire 963 workers to maintain every 100 on the payroll. To keep a workforce of 13,600 employees, Ford implemented training programs and a program of bonuses and benefits, including a medical clinic, athletic fields, and playgrounds for workers' families. But the turnover problem was not solved, so Ford took a bold and radical step. He announced in 1914 that the company would pay eligible workers $5.00 a day and would cut daily working hours from 9 to 8 hours. The $5.00 wage was almost double the average daily wage in the industry, and it shocked the whole nation. Ford was acclaimed as the friend of the worker and a humanitarian by some, but attacked as a mad socialist by others. Many businessmen and shareholders considered his decision reckless, but Ford ignored this criticism. He believed that a happy workforce would lead to a high level of productivity, and that retaining workers would reduce costs. The high-pay policy worked. Between 1914 and 1916, the company's profits increased from $30 million to $60 million. Ford later said, "The payment of five dollars a day for an eight-hour day was one of the finest cost-cutting moves we ever made."

Ford was an autocratic and authoritarian leader. He refused to implement suggestions to modernize the Model T, which had been a highly profitable vehicle. Sales of the Model T dropped and production ended in May 1927, resulting in a company closure for several months until the Model A was launched in December. During the 1930s, Ford used labor spies and company police to prevent workers from unionizing. It was not until 1941 that he signed a union contract with the United Automobile Workers. His dictatorial style once resulted in a lawsuit by shareholders for not consulting them about his decision to use funds from profits for production expansion rather than dividends. He was eventually required by a court to pay $19 million in dividends.

Ford was notorious for his anti-Jewish attitudes. In 1919, he purchased a newspaper called *The Dearborn Independence,* in which he published a document purporting to describe a plan for global Jewish domination. This document is regarded by virtually all historians as a pretext for anti-Semitism in the early 20th century. Ford also published several other anti-Jewish articles, which were included in a volume titled *The International Jew, the World's Foremost Problem.* Some evidence indicated that Ford provided financial support for Adolf Hitler during Hitler's early political career. In 1938, the Ford Motor Company opened an assembly plant in Germany, aiming to supply trucks to the Wehrmacht. In the same year, Ford was awarded and accepted the Grand Cross of the Order of the German Eagle, the highest honorary award given to foreigners by the Nazi government.

Ford had a strong passion for automobiles. Despite financial setbacks, he never gave up his vision to build automobiles that ordinary people could afford. He did not hesitate to take risks when the company was in difficult situations, and used his power to remove obstacles in managing the company. He actively developed a social network with high-level government officials, who gave him information on legal and regulatory issues. Ford was a forceful business leader who was driven by the pursuit of profits, but he did not ignore society's needs. The Ford Foundation gave over $10 billion to charity.

Ford is remembered as a pioneer of the automobile industry, the father of the modern assembly line, a dictatorial leader, and a powerful anti-Semite. He displayed his unique leadership in starting Ford Motor Company and leading it through many successes and setbacks. ∎

DISCUSSION QUESTIONS

1. What kind of leadership behaviors does Henry Ford display?
2. Why was he effective?
3. Would he be effective today as CEO of a major auto maker? Why or why not?

ENDNOTES

1. Sayles, L. R. (1989). *Leadership: Managing in Real Organizations,* 2nd ed. New York: McGraw-Hill.
2. Kidder, T. (1981). *The Soul of a New Machine.* New York: Little Brown.
3. Sayles. *Leadership: Managing in Real Organizations.*
4. Katz, R., and Tushman, M. L. (1983). A longitudinal study of boundary spanning supervision on turnover and promotion in research and development. *Academy of Management Journal,* 26(3), 437–456.
5. Kerr, S., Hill, K., and Broedling, L. (1986). The first-line supervisor: Phasing out or here to stay. *Academy of Management Review,* 11(1), 103–117.
6. Selznick, P. (1957). *Leadership in Administration.* Evanston, IL: Row Peterson; Pelz, D. (1958). Influence: A key to effective leadership in the first line supervisor. *Personnel,* 29, 209–217; and Hills, R. J. (1963). The representative function: Neglected dimension of leadership behavior. *Administrative Science Quarterly,* 8, 83–101.
7. Likert, R. (1961). *New patterns of management.* New York: McGraw-Hill.
8. Mintzberg, H. (1973). *The Nature of Managerial Work.* New York: Harper & Row.
9. Gilmore, T. N. (1982). Leadership and boundary management. *Journal of Applied Behavioral Science,* 18, 343–356.
10. Dorfman, P. W., Howell, J. P., Cotton, B. C. G., and Tate, U. (1992). Leadership within the "discontinuous hierarchy" structure of the military: Are effective leadership behaviors similar within and across command structures? In K. E. Clark, M. B. Clark, and D. P. Campbell, *Impact of Leadership,* 399–416. Greensboro, NC: Center for Creative Leadership.
11. Au, K. Y., and Fukuda, J. (2002). Boundary spanning behaviors of expatriates. *Journal of World Business,* 37, 285–296.
12. Yukl, G. (1998). *Leadership in Organizations,* 4th ed. Upper Saddle River, NJ: Prentice Hall.
13. Thompson, L. (2001). *The Mind and Heart of the Negotiator.* Upper Saddle River, NJ: Prentice Hall.
14. Fisher, R., Ury, W., and Patton, B. (1993). *Getting to Yes: Negotiating Agreement Without Giving In.* New York: Penguin.

15. Thompson. *The Mind and Heart of the Negotiator.*

16. Steadman, H. J. (1992). Boundary spanners—A key component for the effective interactions of the justice and mental health systems. *Law and Human Behavior,* 16(1), 75–87.

17. Kerr, Hill, and Broedling. The first-line supervisor: Phasing out or here to stay.

18. Hills. The representative function: Neglected dimension of leadership behavior.

19. Elkins, T., and Keller, R. T. (2003). Leadership in research and development organizations: A literature review and conceptual framework. *Leadership Quarterly,* 14, 587–606.

20. Katz and Tushman. A longitudinal study of boundary spanning supervision on turnover and promotion in research and development.

21. Dorfman, Howell, Cotton, and Tate. Leadership within the "discontinuous hierarchy" structure of the military: Are effective leadership behaviors similar within and across command structures?; and Hills. The representative function: Neglected dimension of leadership behavior.

22. Steadman. Boundary spanners—A key component for the effective interactions of the justice and mental health systems.

23. Louis, M.R., and Yan, A. (1996). The migration of organizational functions to the work unit level: Buffering, spanning and bringing up boundaries. Working paper, Boston University.

24. Schwab, R. C., Ungson, G. R., and Brown, W. B. (1985). Redefining the boundary spanning-environment relationship. *Journal of Management,* 11(1), 75–86.

25. Ito, J. K., and Peterson, R. B. (1986). Effects of task difficulty and interunit interdependence on information processing systems. *Academy of Management Journal,* 29(1), 139–149.

26. Friedman, R. A., and Podolny, J. (1992). Differentiation of boundary spanning roles: Labor negotiations and implications for role conflict. *Administrative Science Quarterly,* 37(1), 28–47.

27. Steadman. Boundary spanners—A key component for the effective interactions of the justice and mental health systems.

28. Dorfman, Howell, Cotton, and Tate. Leadership within the "discontinuous hierarchy" structure of the military: Are effective leadership behaviors similar within and across command structures?

29. Dorfman, Howell, Cotton, and Tate. Leadership within the "discontinuous hierarchy" structure of the military: Are effective leadership behaviors similar within and across command structures?; and Katz and Tushman. A longitudinal study of boundary spanning supervision on turnover and promotion in research and development.

30. Stewart, G. L., and Manz, C. C. (1995). Leadership of self-managed work teams: A typology and integrative model. *Human Relations,* 48(7), 747–770.

31. Yukl. *Leadership in Organizations.*

32. Parker, G. M. (2003). *Cross Functional Teams: Working with Allies, Enemies, and Other Strangers.* San Francisco: Jossey-Bass.

33. Deeprose, D. (1995). *The Team Coach.* New York: AMACOM-American Management Association.

34. Thompson. *The Mind and Heart of the Negotiator.*

35. Deeprose. *The Team Coach.*

36. Manz, C. C., and Sims, H. P. (1987). Leading workers to lead themselves: The external leadership of self-managing teams. *Administrative Science Quarterly,* 32, 106–139.

37. Zigurs, I. (2002). Leadership in virtual teams: Oxymoron or opportunity. *Organizational Dynamics,* 31(4), 339–351.

38. Yukl. *Leadership in Organizations.*

39. Edmondson, A. C., Roberto, M. A., and Watkins, M. D. (2003). A dynamic model of top management team effectiveness: Managing unstructured task streams. *Leadership Quarterly,* 14, 297–325.

40. Thompson, L. (2004). *Making the Team: A Guide for Managers,* 2nd ed. Upper Saddle River, NJ: Prentice Hall.

41. Hambrick, D. C. (1995). Fragmentation and the other problems CEOs have with their TMTs. *California Management Review,* 37(3), 110–127.

42. Hambrick, D. C. (1997). Corporate coherence and the TMT. *Planning Review,* 25(5), 24–29.

43. Zaccaro, S. J., Rittman, A. L., and Marks, M. A. (2001). Team leadership. *Leadership Quarterly,* 12(4), 451–483.

44. Druskat, V. U., and Wheeler, J. V. (2003). Managing from the boundary: The effective leadership of self-managing work teams. *Academy of Management Journal,* 46(4), 435–457.

45. Kolb, J. A. (1992). Leadership of creative teams. *The Journal of Creative Behavior,* 26(1), 1–9.

46. Zaccaro, Rittman, and Marks. Team leadership.

47. Weinkauf, K., and Hoegl, M. (2002). Team leadership activities in different project phases. *Team Performance Management: An International Journal,* 8(7/8), 171–182.

48. Walton, R. E., and Schlesinger, L. A. (1979). Do supervisors thrive in participative work systems? *Organizational Dynamics,* Winter 1979, 25–38.

49. Major, D. A., Kozlowski, S. W. J., Chao, G. T., and Gardner, P. D. (1995). A longitudinal investigation of newcomer expectations, early socialization outcomes, and the moderating effects of role development factors. *Journal of Applied Psychology,* 80(3), 418–431.

50. Versteeg, A. (1990). Self directed work teams yield long term benefits. *Journal of Business Strategy,* November–December 1990, 11(6), 9–12.

51. Hackman, J. R. (2002). *Leading Teams: Setting the Stage for Great Performances.* Boston: Harvard Business School Press.

52. Edmondson, A. C. (2003). Speaking up in the operating room: How team leaders promote learning in interdisciplinary action teams. *Journal of Management Studies,* 40(6), 1419–1451.

53. Neck, C. P., Stewart, G., and Manz, C. C. (1996). Self-leaders within self-leading teams: Toward an optimal equilibrium. In M. M. Beyerlein, D. A. Johnson, and S. T. Beyerlein, *Advances in Interdisciplinary Studies of Work Teams: Team Leadership* 3, 43–65: Greenwich, Conn.: JAI Press.

54. Cohen, S. G., and Baily, D. E. (1997). What makes teams work: Group effectiveness research from the shop floor to the executive suite. *Journal of Management,* 23, 239–290; Huselid, M. A. (1995). The impact of human resource management practices on turnover, productivity, and corporate financial performance. *Academy of Management Journal,* 38, 635–672; MacDuffie, J. P. (1995). Human resource bundles and manufacturing performance: Organizational logic and flexible production systems in the world auto industry. *Industry and Labor Relations Review,* 48, 197–221; and Stewart and Manz. Leadership of self-managed work teams: A typology and integrative model.

55. Smith, P. B., Peterson, M. F., and Misumi, J. (1994). Event management and work team effectiveness in Japan, Britain and USA. *Journal of Occupational and Organizational Psychology,* 67, 33–43.

10

Building Social Exchanges and Fairness

Learning Objectives

After reading this chapter, you should be able to do the following:

1. Describe and provide examples of leadership behaviors that build social exchanges with followers.

2. Explain why effective leaders' social exchange behaviors can have a positive influence on individual and group performance.

3. Describe how to develop and maintain effective leader–member exchanges.

4. Describe the skills, traits, and sources of power that help leaders build effective social exchanges with followers.

5. Identify situational factors that enhance, neutralize, or substitute for leader exchange behaviors.

6. Describe and give examples of three types of organizational justice that are important to followers.

7. Identify behaviors used by leaders to maintain organizational justice.

8. Describe the effects of leaders' exchange behaviors.

Examples of Effective Social Exchange Behaviors

- The new manager asked about and discussed each group member's job expectations, as well as the member's concerns and expectations of the manager. He also used active listening skills to decipher important issues and how they were raised by group members. The manager also shared some of his own expectations about his new job, the members' jobs, and their working relationship.

- Noting which group members responded well to early task assignments, the leader carefully selected increasingly complex tasks for them with longer time horizons, and eventually began to delegate administrative duties to these group members.

- With group members who continued to perform well and expressed positive attitudes toward their task assignments and the leader, the leader began to allow more freedom in the choice of approaches to tasks with statements such as, "I'll support you in whatever you decide."
- The leader expressed understanding and some agreement with a follower's position on an important issue, before explaining her own position. Rather than stating outright her preferred strategy for dealing with the issue, she prefaced her strategy by saying "I was just wondering if we might consider another approach...."

The above incidents demonstrate effective leadership behaviors that build social exchanges with followers. *Leaders' social exchange behaviors* define followers' and leaders' roles and obligations in relation to one another as they work to achieve group and organizational goals.

Several types of exchange behaviors occur between leaders and followers. For example, Chapter 7 described leaders' contingent reward and punishment behaviors as effective influence strategies when provided in exchange for specific follower actions such as effective performance or poor attendance. Recent research on leader–follower exchanges, sometimes called leader–member exchanges (LMX), has produced interesting insights into how leaders solicit their followers' assistance in achieving goals and how various exchanges affect followers. Certain patterns are discernible in these exchanges, and effective leaders must be aware of these patterns, how they develop, and how they affect individual and group performance.

Early in a leader–follower relationship, an informal process occurs called *role making*.[1] Roles are standard or repeated patterns of behavior that often become expected or required of a person in a specific functional relationship. Roles in organizations are only partially specified by job descriptions, and are usually more completely defined by the interactions of leaders and followers. Leaders play certain roles vis-à-vis their followers or groups, and followers play specific roles vis-à-vis their leader.

Leaders usually have a vested interest in the role performance of followers, and they therefore exert pressure on followers in the form of role expectations. For example, they expect followers to be punctual, to come to work regularly, and to give careful attention to leader requests. A leader's expectations of a given follower may be based on the follower's test scores, recommendations, interviews, or initial interactions. Over time, these role expectations help the follower define an appropriate role in the leader's group. Followers also have expectations of their leaders. Examples may be fairness in distributing rewards and punishments, creativity in problem solving, and provision of task guidance when needed. The responses of a specific leader and follower to early role expectations often define the type of exchange that will develop between them.[2]

New leaders frequently find themselves short on time or energy to adequately attend to all aspects of their job. They therefore look for dependable individuals in the group for help. Leaders usually perceive some followers as more experienced and ready for added responsibility and duties than others. The leader then invests more time and energy to develop this subset of group members, and maintains this disproportionate attention to preserve their contributions. This subgroup is sometimes called the leader's *ingroup,* and their roles become much more than merely complying with leader requests and completing prescribed duties. They are expected to become committed to the unit's activities and goals, to be more dependable, to give more time and energy, to become more involved in administrative activities, and to be more responsive to the leader's wishes than other group members. In return, the leader offers ingroup members wider latitude in their roles; increased attention, information, and support; added influence on the unit's operation; and increased responsibility for the unit's performance.[3] These added inputs and latitude may help the leader obtain the extra commitment and assistance needed to run the unit effectively. These exchanges between a leader and ingroup members are sometimes called *high-quality* exchanges, because they are based on a high degree of trust, reciprocity, and implicit obligations between the leader and ingroup members.[4]

A leader's time limitations and unique personal characteristics lead to a range of exchanges—many that are less intense than ingroup exchanges. Some followers inevitably evolve a more distant relationship with their leader. These individuals are sometimes called *outgroup* members, and their exchange with the leader is referred to as *low-quality*—reflecting lower levels of trust, interaction, support, rewards, decision influence, and little or no involvement in administrative activities. With outgroup exchanges, the job description defines the leader–follower exchange, with little need for any other social exchange.

Leaders generally devote more time and attention to developing ingroup members, and as a result, they may receive extra effort, loyalty, and support from these followers. Outgroup members receive less of the leader's time and developmental efforts, and they may bring less effort and commitment to their roles as group members. Once these exchanges are established, they seldom change. Given the time that leaders invest in ingroup members, they usually do not wish to replace them. Ingroup and outgroup exchanges are both theoretically fair and equitable to leaders and followers. Both parties to an ingroup exchange may provide a high degree of input, and both parties to an outgroup exchange may provide lower inputs. In practice, however, outgroup members often report wanting more information, attention, support, and latitude from their leader. In some situations, a middle group may emerge that falls between the ingroup and outgroup in terms of effort and commitment provided and attention and support received from the leader.

Understanding social exchanges between leaders and followers is important because they affect follower attitudes and behaviors as well as the leader's ability to carry out his or her responsibilities. High-quality (ingroup) exchanges allow followers to feel competent and valued by their leader. This helps satisfy their esteem and growth needs, and they experience more career success (promotions). Low-quality (outgroup) exchanges often frustrate followers, resulting in poorer attitudes and less career success in the organization. Research shows that when leaders are trained in how to develop more high-quality exchanges, the improvement in attitudes and behaviors of outgroup members are most pronounced because leaders finally acknowledge and address their previously unsatisfied needs for esteem and growth.

▪▪▪ Developing the Leader–Follower Exchange

Leaders and followers bring numerous characteristics to their early interactions. Research has shown that surface characteristics, such as similarity of gender or race, do not usually affect the quality of leader–follower exchanges,[5] but other personal characteristics do affect who becomes an ingroup or outgroup member. Factors such as education level, experience, work ethic, or career aspirations influence how close a leader and follower feel toward one another. Leaders also view these factors as indicative of followers' skill level, motivation to assume increased responsibility, and trustworthiness.[6] Early task assignments given by the leader reflect these initial impressions.

The leader may delegate a challenging task to the follower, or perhaps ask the follower to carry out a task that is outside of the formal job description. In this way, the leader is assessing the follower's competence, motivation, and trustworthiness. If the follower hesitates to complete the task assignment, asks for an explanation regarding why he or she is assigned this task, or performs it poorly, then this has clear implications for the development of an ingroup or outgroup exchange.[7] High-quality (ingroup) exchanges are usually based on the successful completion of a series of assignments or tests given by the leader to the follower.[8]

Of course, some followers may not wish to invest the extra effort in their work to successfully complete the leader's tests/assignments. These followers prefer a lower-quality (outgroup) exchange, with fewer expectations, as well as fewer rewards and benefits. But high-quality exchange followers typically have more authority to carry out assignments, receive more preparation and special information that can help them complete their tasks, and are given more support from the leader in high-pressure situations. If a follower's effort, diligence, performance, and feelings expressed in these early assignments are consistent with the leader's positive impressions of the follower, then a basis for an ingroup exchange is established.[9]

The leader then begins to engage in *accommodating behaviors,* which are meant to further define the follower's role in relationship to the leader, by showing the leader's willingness to consider or adapt to the follower's ideas and concerns. The leader eventually uses *aligning behaviors,* which bring the leader and follower closer together by minimizing power differences between them. These accommodating and aligning behaviors are also used to maintain the leader–follower exchange as the leader and ingroup members face problems as a team of colleagues rather than as a hierarchically organized group. The following leadership behaviors are used in this process of building and maintaining the leader–follower exchange:

1. Delegating tasks to certain followers and monitoring their performance, effort, diligence, and feelings expressed toward the task and the leader.
2. Negotiating a follower's expanded role by first politely acknowledging the follower's other duties and responsibilities, responding to follower concerns, and sometimes using humor to soften an additional role expectation.
3. Being especially polite when expressing an objection or disagreement with something the follower has said or done. This often takes the form of offering understanding and some agreement with the follower's position to establish a common ground before objecting, in order to avoid polarizing differences and negatively impacting the exchange.
4. Framing choices for followers by describing a decision situation and often revealing the alternative the leader prefers, but letting the follower make the decision.
5. Demonstrating that the leader's values and goals converge with those of the followers. This is often done through spiraling agreement patterns. For example, the leader states an opinion or describes an idea and waits to see if the follower agrees or extends the idea by building on the leader's opinion. As this convergence evolves, either party may complete the statement the other was about to make.

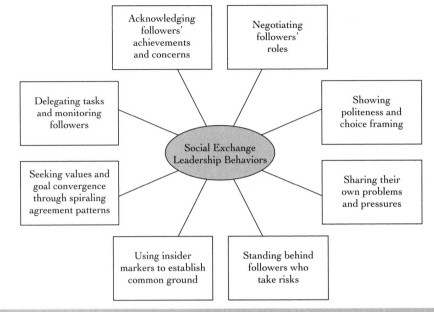

▪▪▪ FIGURE 10-1 Important social exchange behaviors used by leaders

6. Establishing a common ground with a follower through the use of *insider markers*, such as informal address forms, jargon or slang, insider joking, friendly teasing, laughter, and informal discussion that assures a shared common knowledge.

7. Showing high supportiveness of followers by standing behind them when they take risks or try innovative approaches to complex problems. The leader is also very careful to keep promises and commitments.

8. Sharing pressures, problems, and responsibilities with select followers who recognize their complexity and are able and willing to help the leader make sense of complex problems and find viable solutions.[10]

9. Enacting fair reward distributions and processes, and keeping promises to followers.

In general, leaders build and sustain high-quality exchange relationships through aligning and accommodating moves that emphasize similarities between leader and follower, mutual supportiveness, membership in the ingroup, and relations that are more collegial than hierarchical. Figure 10-1 summarizes important social exchange behaviors used by leaders. The Leadership in Action box: The New Department Head demonstrates the use of several social exchange behaviors.

▪▪▪ Examples of Ineffective Social Exchange Behaviors

Some leadership behavior patterns cut off possible high-quality exchanges between leaders and followers. These behaviors are not effective in developing followers' capabilities and willingness to take on added responsibilities. The following are examples of

LEADERSHIP IN ACTION
The New Department Head

The new department head of a university department had no management experience when he assumed the position. Thus he carefully selected two highly experienced individuals in the department to advise him and keep him informed. Both had been colleagues with the new leader for many years, and they all had high levels of trust and respect for each other. These two individuals formed the new leader's ingroup during his first two years in the position.

The new department head used accommodating behaviors, such as insider joking, laughter, and teasing, as well as acknowledging the significant responsibilities and contributions of his two ingroup members. He expressed agreement with their positions on key issues and supported them when they took risks. He also used aligning behaviors, such as politeness when disagreeing with these members, spiraling agreement patterns, and choice framing, to help achieve values and goals congruence. These social exchange behaviors resulted in a high degree of commitment by the ingroup members to help the new leader succeed. They devoted considerable extra time to discussing strategic issues with him and reacting to his ideas prior to their implementation. They also let him know when other department members were unhappy with key decisions or practices, but were unwilling to confront the leader. The department head's social exchange behaviors created an ingroup that provided him with valuable help as he learned the ropes of his new leadership position.

these ineffective social exchange behaviors:

- In dealing with followers, the leader constantly referred to formal role prescriptions as specified in the employment contract. The leader repeatedly emphasized his formal authority and the obligations of each group member to be bound by the contract.
- The leader's interaction with a follower was brief, with specific questions directed at the follower and little time or effort provided for exchanging ideas on issues. The questions were designed to gather information on the follower's performance on specific tasks.
- A leader showed little understanding of a follower's job problems and needs, and blamed all the problems on the follower's lack of effort. When the follower attempted to explain her perceptions of the problems, the leader constantly interrupted her and ignored her explanation.

Each of these examples shows a leader who has low expectations of a follower, and has no apparent interest in hearing the follower's ideas or allowing any latitude in the follower's behavior. These leaders probably stifle the follower's motivation and future development.

⚊⚊⚊ Skills, Traits, and Sources of Power for Building Social Exchanges

Effective leaders can develop specific skills, traits, and sources of power that will help them build social exchanges with followers. As they are for many leadership behaviors, *communication skills* are especially valuable in building social exchanges. Leaders who use verbal and nonverbal skills to acknowledge a follower's capabilities and job responsibilities, respond to followers' concerns, and use insider joking, good-natured teasing, and informal discussion, can minimize the social distance between themselves and followers. Learning to build on a follower's ideas can create spiraling agreement patterns that build convergence in thoughts, values, and goals. Leaders who share their own pressures and responsibilities with followers encourage followers to do likewise. Finally, active listening by the leader helps to build and maintain an open dialogue with followers as they gain the necessary knowledge and confidence to interact with the leader to solve group problems.

Other skills that can help leaders build social exchanges with followers include *empathy* and *social perceptiveness*. When leaders show a genuine appreciation for followers' problems, feelings, and anxieties, followers often feel they have more in common with the leader. When leaders demonstrate understanding of followers' difficulties and support their efforts to solve problems creatively, they convince followers that the leader is on their side. When a leader learns to sense followers' problems as they develop and helps followers act to address these problems, the leader is viewed as a confidant and helper who the follower can trust. *Flexibility* by a leader in responding to followers' concerns, and allowing followers to try new approaches to problem solving, can also build followers' trust in the leader. *Career mentoring skills* are also helpful in building social exchanges. These skills are usually based on the leader's own work experience, and involve efforts to discuss job and career goals with followers.[11] Leaders can develop each of these skills through training, practice, and capable coaching from other experienced leaders.

Four sources of power are also useful to leaders in building social exchanges with their followers. When leaders acquire *referent and expert power,* followers usually want to get to know them and emulate their traits and behaviors. Followers are then easily influenced to take on extra tasks and responsibilities to help the leader. These leaders are also effective at *choice framing* for followers, conveying their preferred approach to a decision situation, and being relatively sure that followers will implement a solution that is consistent with the leader's preferences. When followers emulate the leader's behavior and decision making, they feel in sync with the leader, creating the "we" feeling that characterizes high-quality (ingroup) exchanges.

Effective leaders also use *legitimate and reward power* to acknowledge extra effort, commitment, and loyalty by specific followers. When a leader praises a follower's continued efforts, shows fondness for a loyal follower, or spends extra time explaining a complex organizational issue to a follower, he or she makes that individual feel like a valued member of the leader's group. This is especially true if the leader holds a high-level position in the organization. These leader activities encourage further follower efforts to help the leader and to advance the group's goal achievement. These added efforts create more appreciative gestures by the leader, which gradually creates a higher-quality exchange with this follower.[12]

As described in earlier chapters, leaders can develop referent and expert power through knowledge gained from continuous training and work experience, and through publicizing past accomplishments and supporting statements made about the leader by higher-level leaders. Most leaders possess the power to administer intangible but significant rewards. Examples are appreciative comments and behaviors directed at followers, and extra time spent with a follower who shows an unusual capability and willingness to learn. When a leader selectively directs gestures of approval at individual followers, this can increase the value of this approval and build on the leader's reward power.

One recent study of electronics and telecommunications workers addressed a possible constraint on leaders' social exchange behaviors. Disabled followers generally had lower-quality social exchanges than nondisabled followers.[13] However, this constraint was overcome when followers engaged in specific ingratiation behaviors with their group leader, such as doing favors for the leader, expressing similar opinions as the leader, and expressing approval of the leader's decisions. A few writers have pointed to some other possible constraints. *Strong union contracts* may specify a violation if a leader treats some employees differently than others. *Limitations on the leader's time or emotional resources* may also prevent him or her from engaging in high-quality exchange behaviors with all followers. Future research may verify if these or other organizational factors constrain leaders from developing high-quality exchanges with followers.

▮▮▮ Fairness or Justice in Social Exchanges

An important requirement for the development of high-quality (ingroup) exchanges is that both the leader and follower view the exchange as fair or just. Each party gives something to the exchange and gets something back, and when both parties view these inputs and returns as fair, then a stable relationship is established.[14] Leaders' fairness or justice is therefore an important aspect of their leadership, and is critical to the social exchanges they develop with followers. Fairness is important to followers because they are concerned with resource allocation, reward distribution, job assignments, decision making, performance evaluation, and many other administrative matters. Fairness can become an ethical issue when one person is treated differently from another. One influential writer stated that leaders have a moral "duty of fair play."[15] This duty requires leaders to recognize the interests and aspirations of all parties as legitimate. This may limit leaders' ability to pursue their self-interests in a given social exchange.

Perceived fairness must be present in order to establish trust, which is needed for mutual cooperation. Fairness, trust, and cooperation are all necessary to promote high-quality exchanges. Studies show that perceptions about a leader's fairness also shape people's judgments of his or her ethics.[16] For one thing, unethical leaders often ignore situations involving unfair or questionable behavior in their organization as long as they benefit (Enron is one example of this tendency). However, this type of behavior by leaders can backfire on an organization and draw government legal action, increased regulation, public criticism, customer or stockholder dissatisfaction, and employee turnover or retaliation.[17] Followers respond favorably to leaders who fulfill their promises and agreements, show integrity by dealing with all individuals in a straightforward and fair manner, and pay attention to followers' concerns. These leadership behaviors often result in high-quality exchanges in which followers go beyond their job requirements for the sake of their leader and group.[18]

Organizations and their environments will continue to change rapidly during the 21st century. Organization members will face a lot of uncertainty about the future of their organizations and their roles in those organizations. Specifically, resources are shrinking in many organizations, organizations frequently acquire or merge with one another, and international competition as well as advancing technology threaten the future of many organizations and their members. Social exchanges between leaders and followers that people have relied on in the past are uncertain, and people are increasingly concerned about their own welfare. In uncertain times, people usually look to their leader for assurances of fair treatment. Regardless of their philosophy or preferred pattern of behavior, effective leaders recognize that fair treatment is essential for successful leadership.[19]

Several writers have noted that a leader's fairness is in the mind of the beholder, and followers often form their perceptions of a leader's fairness quickly. A leader's truthfulness, kindness, consideration, values, ethics, and integrity are often mentioned as elements of a leader's fairness.[20] Judgments of a leader's fairness are not arbitrary, but are based on moral principles that followers consider legitimate.[21] What they consider legitimate depends on their culture, economic environment, history, and many other factors. Most experts indicate that moral judgments should be based on sound principles and an impartial consideration of the interests of each individual.[22] Generally speaking, however, when a leader breaks some mutual understanding or agreement, whether explicitly stated or implied, most followers consider this as unfair.

Sometimes a group or organization establishes specific norms that govern a leader's decision making and behavior, and a leader must adhere to these norms to be considered fair. For example, in a large Japanese business organization, the reward system was based primarily on the needs of each employee. A person's salary was primarily determined by factors such as the size of their family, whether they owned their own home, and how far they drove to work. The performance of the employee was only a minor factor. The employees in that organization considered this a fair reward system. This example shows how existing norms can affect judgments of fairness. The Leadership in Perspective box describes how fairness perceptions can affect professional sports teams.

Types of Fairness or Justice

Researchers have described three types of fairness or justice as important to followers—distributive, procedural, and interactional. *Distributive fairness* refers to the outcomes (rewards) a follower receives in relation to his or her inputs (efforts or abilities). This is often called an *equity* comparison. Followers evaluate what they receive for their efforts and skills, and compare it to what others similar to them are receiving. If the two outcomes are comparable, the leader is considered fair. Some experts believe that these equity comparisons are fundamental to human nature, and this makes a leader's fair distribution of rewards an extremely important leadership behavior. However, the example of the Japanese business organization described earlier shows that cultural differences can affect employees' perceptions of fair treatment. In the United States and many other western countries, there is a widespread belief that

LEADERSHIP IN PERSPECTIVE
Pay, Fairness, and Professional Sports

Organizations adopt different types of pay policies to motivate employees. Some emphasize large pay differentials between numerous organizational levels, hoping this will motivate employees to invest high effort in job performance, develop their own competence, and take more responsibilities in order to move up in the organization. Other organizations deemphasize pay differentials and have fewer levels, with the hope that people will perceive greater fairness in the organization resulting in cooperation and teamwork. If an organization's performance depends primarily on individual effort and competence (such as a legal firm), then a policy with high pay differentials may work best. However, if an organization's performance depends on teamwork and cooperation (such as a film production crew), then deemphasizing pay differentials may be best.

Professional baseball is a highly competitive industry in which both individual performance and teamwork are important. Players often compare their salaries with others on their team and in their league. If they believe their compensation is not consistent with other players, they often conclude they are treated unfairly and ask for a new contract or to be traded. Salaries for outstanding players have become highly inflated in recent years, resulting in perceived unfairness by many ballplayers. Recent research also shows that teams with large pay differentials win fewer division championships and perform less well financially. The researcher concluded that the lower performance was due to players' perceptions of unfairness resulting in less cooperation and teamwork. Team managers have a difficult problem of motivating both individual performance as well as teamwork.

those who do more should receive more. This means that an employee who works harder than others and contributes significantly more to the group's performance deserves a larger reward than those who contribute less (this is often called *distributive justice*). When leaders distribute rewards contingent on followers' performance (as recommended in Chapter 7), their behavior reflects this cultural belief. In other cultures, however, equality or an individual's needs are considered more important than the relative contribution of an employee. In these situations, followers may expect rewards to be distributed equally to everyone, or differentially based on individual followers' needs (for example, those with larger families should receive more). Here, a leader who distributes rewards based on followers' performance is seen as unfair. In the United States, however, if a leader distributes rewards equally or based on followers' needs, those who contribute the most may believe the leader is unfair to them. These examples show that leaders must be aware of the existing cultural values and beliefs affecting how people are rewarded for their work. To be viewed as fair, leaders should consider these values and beliefs when they distribute rewards to their followers.

Procedural fairness describes followers' assessment of the procedures used to make decisions that affect them, such as resource allocations and reward distributions. Followers generally consider procedures fair if rules are clearly explained and consistently followed, rules reflect existing cultural values and beliefs, followers are given a chance to voice their opinions, and errors are corrected whenever they are found. If the procedures used are considered fair, then followers will likely accept a decision even if they are not happy with the amount of the distribution. For example, a low pay raise will often be accepted as long as the organization's procedures for performance evaluation and rewards are clear, reasonable, consistently followed, and allow for followers' input.

Interactional fairness refers to the quality of interpersonal communication and treatment the follower receives from a leader. Is she honest, consistent, unbiased, informative, and careful in carrying out the procedures? If so, then the leader is usually viewed as fair. All three types of fairness are important, but interactional fairness may have the most immediate effects on followers. Studies show that leaders who clearly communicate fair procedures are viewed favorably by followers even when resource allocations seem unfair.[23,24]

Interactional fairness flows from the leader's behavior with the follower, and is thus under the direct control of the leader. These interactions leave a vivid impression on followers, because the leader essentially represents the organization to them. Followers assess these interactions as indicators of their standing in the organization, and this influences their self-worth. We believe leader–follower interactions exert the primary influences on followers' perceptions of a leader's fairness.

How to Demonstrate Fairness or Justice

Leaders have the responsibility to lead their followers and their organizations toward fair and just decision making and action. In this regard, *supportive leadership* is one of the most important behaviors leaders use to assure followers and others of their concern for fairness and ethics. Supportive leaders respect followers' views and rights as mature adults; they are honest and open with information about rewards, plans, and procedures; and they are courteous, kind, and concerned for the development of followers. These supportive behaviors show leaders' respect for followers and their willingness to treat them fairly. Two types of information provided by the leader are particularly helpful in assuring a fair and ethical social exchange. Providing information to followers about procedures for resource allocation, reward policies, or decision criteria shows followers that the leader has nothing to hide. Providing explanations for why policies exist or certain decisions are made provides the follower with a clearer image of the rationale behind them. These explanations are particularly effective if they address the reasoning and assumptions behind the decisions or policies, rather than blaming upper management or making excuses.

Leaders' contingent reward behavior is generally viewed as a sign of fairness in western countries. Leaders who use this behavior effectively try to assure equity among followers by basing reward allocations on accurate information on follower performance. Such leaders are also consistent and unbiased in carrying out procedures and making judgments for all followers. Leaders in the United States may use equality as a guideline for distributing resources or rewards when group solidarity, harmony, and follower cooperation are needed, or when followers' performance is determined by factors outside of their control.[25] In these situations, the leader's behavior is usually seen as fair and just.

Leaders' boundary spanning behavior is particularly important with regard to fairness issues during times of major change in organizations and their environments. By

LEADERSHIP IN ACTION
The Four-Way Test

The following code of ethical conduct has been emphasized by several public service organizations in the United States for many years. It is short and simple, but has broad application to all types of organizational activities. Labor and contract negotiators have found the Four-Way Test especially useful as a set of overall guiding principles.

THE FOUR-WAY TEST

1. Is it the truth?
2. Is it fair to all concerned?
3. Is it profitable or beneficial to all concerned?
4. Will it build friendship among all concerned?

The four points can provide general guidelines to be followed and used as a test for any decision or action. In a given situation, all of these guidelines may not be entirely satisfied, but they do provide a set of useful criteria that are easily remembered. The more an individual strives to use these guidelines, the more salient they become to his or her choice of behavior.

---

actively and consistently representing followers' fairness concerns to higher-ups and influencing these individuals to ensure fair treatment of followers, leaders show their allegiance and concern for followers. *Participative leadership* is also important for fairness; it includes encouraging followers to voice their views on issues and decisions that affect them. This allows followers to raise their concerns, and shows the leaders' respect for them. In most western countries, when followers are allowed to affect the outcomes of decisions, they usually view their leader as very fair.

When implementing decisions, *directive* leaders who observe followers on the job can assure followers that they base their allocation and reward decisions on fair and accurate information. Directive leaders can also demonstrate competence at the followers' tasks, assuring followers that the leader can recognize good performance. Each of these leadership behaviors can be powerful tools for effective leaders to assure followers that fairness will be emphasized in their group and organization. Most leaders rely on several behavioral strategies to convey this message to followers. The Leadership in Action box describes a code of conduct used by many leaders.

▪▪▪ Effects of Leaders' Social Exchange Behaviors

Leaders' social exchange behaviors have a strong effect on the attitudes of followers. Group members who are the focus of leaders' high-quality exchange behaviors are highly *satisfied* with their leader, work, and organization. They also have favorable *perceptions of their organization's climate, high commitment* to the organization, *fewer feelings of inequity,* and perceive *few social differences* between themselves and the leader.[26] They may have *fewer thoughts about quitting* and more *influence on* decision making with the leader, and they are more *ingratiating* by doing personal favors and complimenting the leader.[27]

Leaders tend to reciprocate in high-quality exchanges by providing *high performance ratings* and *faster promotions* for ingroup members.[28,29] Interestingly, ingroup members receive high performance ratings regardless of their actual performance.[30] In other words, it is not clear if the actual performance of ingroup members exceeds that of other followers.[31] However, once a leader has selected an ingroup, the leader seems to have a favorable image of these followers, and maintains this image through positive evaluations and recommendations for promotion. This tendency or bias may also be reflected in a study of nurses that showed leaders reporting more altruistic behavior by ingroup members.[32] This positive image, or *halo,* is also shown in the tendency of leaders to attribute good performance by ingroup members to hard work and high ability, whereas good performance by outgroup members may be attributed to luck.

It is often stated that ingroup members who are the focus of high-quality leader exchange behaviors have less turnover than other followers.[33] However, summaries of studies show that the impacts of these leadership behaviors on turnover are uncertain. Whereas some researchers find reduced turnover among ingroup members, others report no difference between ingroup members and other followers.[34] There is also evidence that ingroup members do not necessarily spend more hours working than other followers, and they may not reduce the leader's administrative duties by taking on more of those duties themselves.[35] It appears uncertain, then, whether followers who are involved in high-quality exchanges actually do more for the leader.

One group of researchers trained leaders in high-quality exchange behaviors. They found that both ingroup and outgroup members improved their performance and satisfaction under the trained leaders, but the largest improvements occurred for outgroup members.[36] This may indicate that the high degree of leader trust, attention, and involvement contained in these behaviors is useful for all followers, and that outgroup members may be highly responsive to the opportunities provided by these leadership behaviors.

Overall, the leadership behaviors designed to produce high-quality exchanges definitely improve follower attitudes, and they have the potential to improve follower performance. Leaders should, however, be careful not to be too selective about which followers are the focus of these behaviors. Followers who the leader initially views as outgroup members may have much to contribute if given the opportunity, attention, and support by their leader. Figure 10-2 summarizes the effects of a leader's social exchange behaviors.

▪▪▪ Situational Enhancers, Neutralizers, and Substitutes for Leaders' Exchange Behaviors

Although only a few studies have addressed situational factors and leaders' exchange behaviors, their results point to some factors that may enhance, neutralize, or substitute for these leadership behaviors. For example, when followers had highly *routine* or highly *challenging work tasks,* these factors increased the impact of leaders' high-quality exchange behaviors on followers' performance. For routine tasks, the added attention and high expectations by the leader probably motivated the followers. With challenging tasks, the leader's strong support and high expectations may have given followers confidence to meet the challenges. Leaders' high-quality exchange behaviors were less effective when followers' tasks were neither routine nor particularly

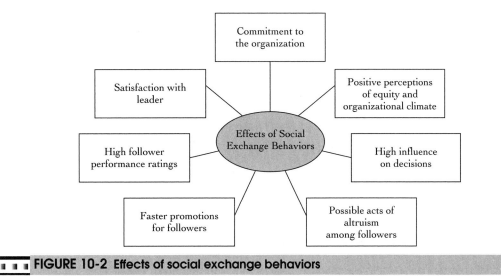

FIGURE 10-2 Effects of social exchange behaviors

challenging (tasks that possess variety, but require little creativity, such as construction or retail sales jobs).[37] Also, followers who were *achievement oriented* and liked to be challenged responded favorably to the developmental opportunities provided by greater job latitude, decision involvement, and delegation, which were part of the high-quality exchange behavior by their leader.[38] Thus, it seems possible that these situational factors may enhance the impacts of leaders' social exchange behaviors.

One situational factor, the redesign of followers' jobs, may substitute for leaders' exchange behaviors in work organizations. *Job redesign* approaches are intended to create satisfaction, commitment, and motivation among nonmanagement employees. When these programs have been combined with *goal setting,* they have promoted both positive attitudes and high performance. By emphasizing increased worker autonomy and self-determination, these programs may operate in place of the intensive leader–follower interactions that characterize high-quality exchanges. These possible substitution effects should be tested in future research.

Researchers have identified two situational characteristics that may neutralize the effects of leaders' exchange behaviors. These are (1) a *lack of trust* between a leader and followers, and (2) *peer-group pressure* to ostracize followers who do extra work. A lack of trust could interfere with the mutual confidence needed in a high-quality exchange, and peer pressure may inhibit an ingroup member from putting in the extra effort expected by the leader. As yet, no empirical research has tested the possible neutralizing effects of these situational factors.

SUMMARY ▪▪▪▪▪▪▪

One reason that leaders develop high-quality exchanges with specific followers is to help fulfill the leader's responsibilities. When leaders have too many responsibilities and certain followers are underutilized (that is, they welcome more opportunities to achieve and challenge themselves on the job), then leaders' social exchange behaviors may create high-quality exchanges that benefit the leader and these followers.

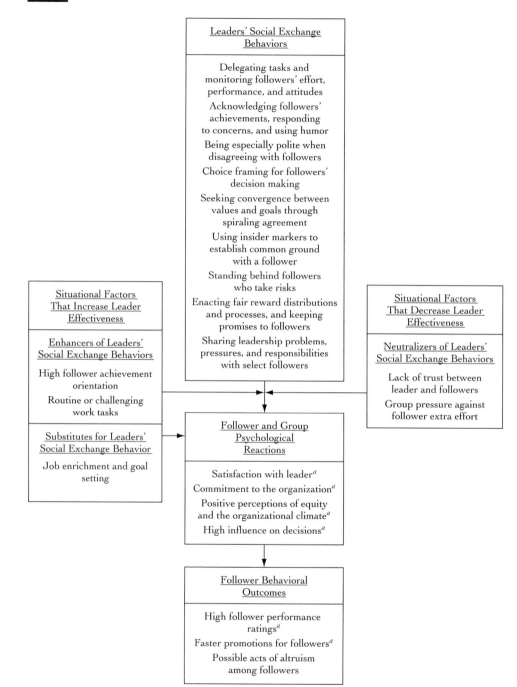

[a]These psychological reactions and outcomes have shown the most improvement from leaders' social exchange behaviors.

▪▪▪ FIGURE 10-3 Tentative process model of leaders' social exchange behaviors

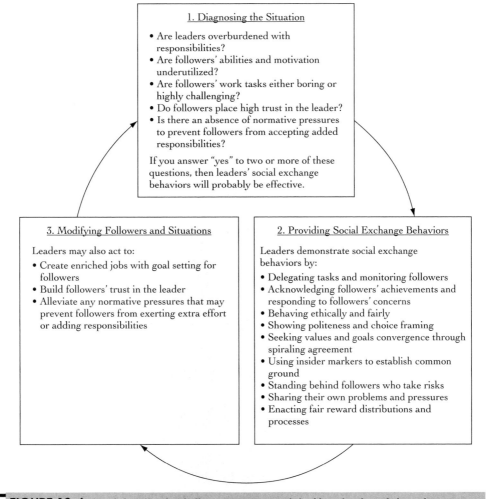

▪▪▪▪ FIGURE 10-4 Applying the tentative process model of leaders' social exchange behaviors

However, there must be mutual trust between leaders and followers and an absence of normative pressure (contractual or otherwise) that may prevent followers from accepting additional duties and responsibilities.

The reader should remember that social exchange behaviors by a leader may be most effective with followers who have previously had *low-quality exchanges*. The potential of these outgroup members is often underestimated, and leaders' social exchange behaviors may unleash this potential.

Figure 10-3 summarizes much of the information about leaders' social exchange behaviors. These behaviors are shown at the top of Figure 10-3 affecting follower reactions, which in turn influence follower outcomes and behaviors. Situational factors on the left of Figure 10-3 may enhance or substitute for social exchange behaviors. Situational factors on the right may neutralize the effectiveness of social exchange behaviors. The situational factors shown are tentative until further research is carried out on the effects of these organizational characteristics.

Figure 10-4 describes how leaders can use the tentative process model of leaders' social exchange behaviors. The first box (1. Diagnosing the Situation) describes several questions that determine the need and appropriateness of leaders' social exchange behaviors. If the leader answers "yes" to two or more of these questions, then the leader should probably provide social exchange behaviors. The second box (2. Providing Social Exchange Behaviors) shows several social exchange behaviors that can be used to create high-quality exchanges with followers. Recall that followers who the leader may have viewed as outgroup members may benefit from these behaviors as well or more than followers the leader viewed more favorably. Once the leader has enacted these social exchange behaviors, he or she assesses the followers' situation to determine if it can be modified to improve follower and group effectiveness (3. Modifying Followers and Situations). This situational modification can either make the exchanges more effective (create enhancers) or alleviate the need for social exchange behaviors by the leader (create substitutes). In either case, any modifications carried out should help followers work more effectively on their own or in close cooperation with their leader. Once any modifications are implemented, the leader rediagnoses the situation, provides needed exchange behaviors, and so on, in a dynamic process.

KEY TERMS AND CONCEPTS IN THIS CHAPTER ▪▪▪▪▪▪▪

- Accommodating behaviors
- Achievement oriented
- Aligning behaviors
- Boundary spanning
- Choice framing
- Distributive fairness

- Empathy equity comparison
- Ethics
- Fairness
- Goal setting
- Interactional fairness

- Normative pressures
- Procedural fairness
- Social exchange behaviors
- Social perceptiveness
- Spiraling agreements

REVIEW AND DISCUSSION QUESTIONS ▪▪▪▪▪▪▪

1. Describe a situation you have experienced or heard about in which leader–member exchange behaviors were effective. Why did these leader–member exchange behaviors have a positive effect?
2. Describe a situation you have experienced or heard about in which leader–member exchange behaviors were ineffective or produced undesirable effects. Why were these leader–member exchange behaviors ineffective?
3. What can a leader do to develop the skills and abilities necessary to build effective social exchanges with followers?
4. When you are in a leadership position, what are specific leadership behaviors you could use to support followers when they take risks or try innovative approaches to problem solving?
5. Describe how as a leader you would use reward power to create positive social exchanges that would result in extra effort and high commitment by followers.
6. What behaviors make you feel that you are being treated fairly or unfairly by the leader? Why do you feel some leadership behaviors are fair and others unfair?

EXPERIENTIAL EXERCISE: ASSESSING YOUR SOCIAL EXCHANGE ▪▪▪▪▪▪▪

Think of a leader you now have or have had in the past. You can use any type of leader, such as an employer, supervisor, coach, military officer, committee chairman, or manager. Use the scale below to describe your relationship with your leader.

1. Do you know where you stand with your leader? That is, do you usually know how satisfied your leader is with what you do?

1	2	3	4	5
Rarely	Occasionally	Sometimes	Fairly often	Very often

2. How well does your leader understand your job problems and needs?

1	2	3	4	5
Not at all	A little	A fair amount	Quite a bit	A great deal

3. How well does your leader recognize your potential?

1	2	3	4	5
Not at all	A little	Moderately	Mostly	Fully

4. Regardless of how much formal authority he or she has built into his or her position, what are the chances that your leader would use his or her power to help you solve problems in your work?

1	2	3	4	5
None	Small	Moderate	High	Very high

5. Again, regardless of the amount of formal authority your leader has, what are the chances that he or she would bail you out at his or her expense?

1	2	3	4	5
None	Small	Moderate	High	Very high

6. Do you have enough confidence in your leader that you would defend and justify his or her decision if he or she were not present to do so?

1	2	3	4	5
Strongly confident	Confident	Neutral	Not confident	Strongly not confident

7. How would you characterize your working relationship with your leader?

1	2	3	4	5
Extremely ineffective	Worse than average	Average	Better than average	Extremely effective

If you rated five of the items above with a 4 or 5, then you probably have a high-quality (ingroup) social exchange with this leader. Describe any behaviors the leader has demonstrated that led (or could have led) to a high-quality social exchange.

If you rated five of the items with a 1 or 2, then you probably have a low-quality (outgroup) social exchange with this leader. Describe any behaviors the leader has demonstrated that led (or could have led) to a low-quality social exchange.

Meet with three to five other members of your class. Share your responses with other members of your group. Compile a list of leadership behaviors that led to high-quality social exchanges, then compile a list of behaviors that led to low-quality social exchanges. Compare your lists with the leadership behaviors described in this chapter.

SOURCE: Adapted from G. B. Graen and M. Uhl-Bien. Relationship-based approach to leadership: Development of leader-member exchange (LMX) theory of leadership over 25 years: Applying a multi-level multi-domain perspective. *Leadership Quarterly,* 6(2), 1995, 219–247.

▪ ▪ ▪ ▪ ▪ ▪ C A S E   I N C I D E N T ▪ ▪ ▪ ▪ ▪ ▪

The Improvement Suggestion

Brian James is the team leader of a production team that manufactures furniture. Part of the manufacturing process includes gluing and nailing the components that make up the frames of furniture pieces.

Richard Marks, a member of the production team, learned from a friend of a new type of wood adhesive. Richard conducted tests with the new adhesive and determined it formed a stronger bond than the adhesive currently being used. Richard obtained cost data that indicated the new adhesive would be half the cost of the current adhesive. Richard's tests also indicated that the new adhesive alone would produce a stronger bond than the old process of both gluing and nailing.

Richard suggested the change in adhesives to Mr. James, who then sold the idea to top management. Mr. James never told management it was Richard's suggestion. Mr. James received all the credit for the process improvement and was awarded a cash bonus for the suggestion. ▪

DISCUSSION QUESTIONS

1. How do you think Mr. James' actions will affect his future social exchanges with the team?
2. What fairness and ethics issues are raised by the leader's behavior in this situation?
3. If team members think Mr. James' behavior was unfair and unethical, what should he do to create positive reactions from the team?

ENDNOTES ▪▪▪▪▪▪▪

1. Dienesch, R. M., and Liden, R. C. (1986). Leader-member exchange model of leadership: A critique and further development. *Academy of Management Review,* 11(3), 618–634; and Wayne, S. J., and Greene, S. A. (1993). The effects of leader-member exchange on employee citizenship and impression management behavior. *Human Relations,* 46(12), 1431–1440.
2. Dansereau, F., Graen, G., and Haga, W. J. (1975). A vertical dyad linkage approach to leadership within formal organizations. *Organizational Behavior and Human Performance,* 13(1), 46–78.
3. Liden, R. C., Wayne, S. J., and Stilwell, D. (1993). A longitudinal study on the early development of leader-member exchanges. *Journal of Applied Psychology,* 78(4), 662–674.
4. Graen, G. B., and Scandura, T. A. (1986). Toward a psychology of dyadic organizing. In B. M. Staw and L. L. Cummings (Eds.), *Research in Organizational Behavior,* Vol. 9. Greenwich, CT: JAI Press.
5. Augusta, C. Y., Hartman, S., and Galle, W. P. (2002). An investigation of relationships between communication style and leader-member exchange. *Journal of Communication Management,* 6(3), 257–268.
6. Gomez, C., and Rosen, B. (2001). The leader-member exchange as a link between managerial trust and employee empowerment. *Group and Organizational Management,* 26(1), 53–69.
7. Scandura, T. A. (1999). Rethinking leader-member exchange: An organizational justice perspective. *Leadership Quarterly,* 10(1), 25–40.

8. Schriesheim, C. A., Neider, L. L., and Scandura, T. A. (1998). Delegation and leader-member exchange: Main effects, moderators, and measurement issues. *Academy of Management Journal,* 41(3), 298–318.

9. Dienesch and Liden. Leader-member exchange model of leadership: A critique and further development.

10. Fairhurst, G. T. (1993). The leader-member exchange patterns of women leaders in industry: A discourse analysis. *Communication Monographs,* 60(4), 321–351.

11. Scandura, T. A., and Schriesheim, C. A. (1994). Leader-member exchange and supervisor career mentoring as complementary constructs in leadership research. *Academy of Management Research,* 37(6), 1588–1602.

12. Cogliser, C. C., and Schriesheim, C. A. (2000). Exploring work unit context and leader-member exchange: A multi-level perpective. *Journal of Organizational Behavior,* 21, 487–511.

13. Colella, A., and Varma, A. (2001). The impact of subordinate disability on leader-member exchange relationships. *Academy of Management Journal,* 44(2), 304–315.

14. Dansereau, F., Alluto, J. A., and Yammarino, F. J. (1984). *Theory Testing in Organizational Behavior: The Variant Approach.* Englewood Cliffs, NJ: Prentice Hall.

15. Rawls, J. (1958). Justice as fairness. *Philosophical Review,* 67, 164–194.

16. Singer, M. S. (1996). The role of moral intensity and fairness perception in judgments of ethicality: A comparison of managerial professionals and the general public. *Journal of Business Ethics,* 15, 469–474.

17. Groner, D. M. (1996). Ethical leadership: The missing ingredient. *National Underwriter,* 100(51), 41–43.

18. Deluga, R. J. (1995). The relation between trust in the supervisor and subordinate organizational citizenship behavior. *Military Psychology,* 7(1), 1–16.

19. Meindl, J. R. (1989). Managing to be fair: An exploration of values, motives, and leadership. *Administrative Science Quarterly,* 34, 252–276.

20. Bobocel, D. R., and Farrell, A. S. (1996). Sex based promotion decisions and interactional fairness: Investigating the influence of managerial accounts. *Journal of Applied Psychology,* 8(1), 22–35; and Sashkin, M., and Williams, R. L. (1990). Does fairness make a difference? *Organizatinal Dynamics,* 19(2), 56–71.

21. Zajac, E. E. (1995). *Political Economy of Fairness,* Cambridge MA:, MIT Press; and Rachels, J. (1993). *The Elements of Moral Philosophy,* 2nd ed. New York: McGraw-Hill.

22. Rachels. *The Elements of Moral Philosophy.*

23. Folger, R., and Konovsky, M. A. (1989). Effects of procedural and distributive justice on reactions to pay raise decisions. *Academy of Management Journal,* 32, 115–130.

24. Tyler, T. R., and Lind, E. A. (1992). A relational model of authority in groups. *Advances in Experimental Social Psychology,* 25, 115–191.

25. Meindl, J. R. (1989). Managing to be fair: An exploration of values, motives, and leadership; and Wagstaff, G. F. (1994). Equity, equality and need: Three principles of justice or one? An analysis of "equity as desert." *Current Psychology: Developmental, Learning Personality, Social,* 13(2), 138–152.

26. Wayne, S. J., Liden, R. C., and Sparrowc, R. T. (1994). Developing leader-member exchange: The influence of gender and ingratiation. *American Behavioral Scientist,* 37(5), 694–714; and Wilhelm, C. C., Herd, A. M., and Steiner, D. D. (1993). An investigation of leader-member exchange effects. *Journal of Organizational Behavior,* 14(6), 531–544.

27. Scandura, T. A., Graen, G. B., and Novak, M. A. (1986). When managers decide not to decide autocratically: An investigation of leader-member exchange and decision influence. *Journal of Applied Psychology,* 71(4), 579–584; Dockery, T. M., and Steiner, D. D. (1990). The role of initial interaction in leader-member exchange. *Group and Organization Studies,* 15(4), 395–413; and Wayne, S. J., and Ferris, G. R. (1990). Influence tactics, affect, and exchange quality in supervisor-subordinate interactions: A laboratory experiment and field study. *Journal of Applied Psychology,* 75, 487–499.

28. Graen and Scandura. Toward a psychology of dyadic organizing.

29. Vecchio, R. P. (1997). Are you in or out with your boss? In R. P. Vecchio (Ed.), *Leadership: Understanding the Dynamics of Power and Influence in Organizations.* Notre Dame, IN: University of Notre Dame Press.

30. Duarte, N. T., Goodson, J. R., and Klich, N. R. (1993). How do I like thee? Let me appraise the ways. *Journal of Organizational Behavior,* 14(3), 239–249; and Rosse, J. G., and Kraut, A. T. (1983). Reconsidering the vertical dyad linkage model of leadership. *Journal of Applied Psychology,* 56(1), 63–71.

31. Scandura. Rethinking leader-member exchange: An organizational justice perspective.

32. Wayne and Greene. The effects of leader-member exchange on employee citizenship and impression management behavior.

33. Rosse and Kraut. Reconsidering the vertical dyad linkage model of leadership.

34. Vecchio, R. P. (1985). Predicting employee turnover from leader-member exchange: A failure to replicate. *Academy of Management Journal,* 28(2), 478–485;

Graen, G. B., Liden, R. C., and Hoel, W. (1982). Role of leadership in the employee withdrawal process. *Journal of Applied Psychology,* 67: 868–872; and Ferris, G. (1985). Role of leadership in the employee withdrawal process: A constructive replication. *Journal of Applied Psychology,* 70(4), 777–781.

35. Rosse and Kraut. Reconsidering the vertical dyad linkage model of leadership.

36. Graen, G. B., Wakabayashi, M., Graen, M. R., and Graen, M. G. (1990). International generalizability of American hypotheses about Japanese management progress: A strong inference investigation. *Leadership Quarterly,* 1(1), 1–24.

37. Dunegan, K. J., Duchon, D., and Uhl-Bien, M. (1992). Examining the link between leader-member exchange and subordinate performance: The role of task analyzability and variety as moderators. *Journal of Management,* 18(1), 59–76.

38. Graen, G. B., Scandura, T. A. and Graen, M. R. (1986). A field experimental test of the moderating effects of growth need strength on productivity. *Journal of Applied Psychology,* 71(3), 484–491.

CHAPTER 11

Followership

Learning Objectives

After reading this chapter, you should be able to do the following:

1. Describe followership behaviors and provide specific examples of followership behaviors.
2. Explain why effective followership behaviors can have positive influences on group and organizational performance.
3. Describe ineffective followership behaviors and the negative influences they can have on group and organizational performance.
4. Identify how group members can become more effective in followership behaviors by increasing their technical competence and developing social skills.
5. Identify follower characteristics that are helpful in carrying out followership behaviors.
6. Identify organizational and task characteristics in which followership behaviors would be highly effective and in which they would not be effective.

Examples of Effective Followership

- A member of a new-product development team found out that no one was taking responsibility for coordinating engineering, marketing, and manufacturing. "She worked out an interdepartmental review schedule that identified the people who should be involved at each stage of development. Instead of burdening her boss with yet another problem, this woman took the initiative to present the issue along with a solution."[1]
- A welder in a large railroad-car assembly plant liked being a welder but avoided being a boss. "Although he stood on the lowest rung of the hierarchy in the plant, everyone knew Joe, and everyone agreed that he was the most important person in the entire factory. . . . The reason for his fame was simple: Joe had apparently mastered every phase of the plant's operation, and he was now able to take anyone's place if the necessity arose. Moreover, he could fix any broken-down piece of machinery, ranging from huge mechanical cranes to tiny electronic monitors. . . .

Joe not only could perform these tasks, but actually enjoyed it when he was called upon to do them."[2]

- A CEO described one of his best followers. "[He] is a great devil's advocate. . . . He will ask the questions nobody ever thought of, and he will take the opposite side of everything. But he is a deal maker, not a deal breaker and that's very unique."[3]
- A leader described an effective follower as someone who was continually mastering organizationally useful skills. Her personal standards for her own performance were generally higher than the organization required, and she continually updated her skills in any way she could.

These incidents are examples of effective *followership,* which is an essential role in all leadership situations. The *American Heritage Dictionary* defines a follower as "one who subscribes to the teachings of another; an attendant, servant or subordinate; one who emulates . . . or agrees with another; one who accepts guidance or leadership of another."[4] As the above examples demonstrate, the behavior of effective followers today is more proactive than implied by these definitions.

The heroic leader who embodies all the best traits and behaviors of classical and current theories of leadership probably does not exist. All leaders, successful or not, have weaknesses and gaps in their leadership styles. Effective followers fill in for these gaps and weaknesses. One researcher pointed out that followers contribute a lion's share of the effort that goes into achieving organizational goals.[5]

Leadership cannot exist without followers. Leadership takes place within the context of a specific group of followers,[6] and leadership and followership are interdependent, complementary roles.[7] Leaders regularly adjust their own behavior to fit follower's characteristics and behaviors. Followers forego rewards like money, status, and fame that go with leadership, and instead find meaning in working with their leader and coworkers. In Japan, the follower role is a highly valued tradition. Bushido is a traditional Japanese term for a faithful follower to one's lord. Although the lord has been replaced by the modern corporation, this traditional follower role is still associated with high social standing in Japan.

However, effective followers today are not yes men or sheep, who do whatever the leader desires. Numerous factors influence the roles of followers in organizations. Today, these factors include scarce resources, increased foreign competition, higher operating costs, increasing education of the work force, changing attitudes toward formal authority, increased technology in the workplace, and reductions in the number of middle-management positions in large organizations. All these developments are causing followers to take on more responsibilities than in the past. Proactive followers who take responsibility for organizational tasks and improvements, who demonstrate self-management individually and in groups, and who carry out activities previously performed by leaders are increasingly common in many organizations.[8]

In today's organizations, followership is defined as an interactive role individuals play that complements the leadership role and is equivalent to it in importance for achieving group and organizational performance. The followership role includes the degree of enthusiasm, cooperation, effort, active participation, task competence, and critical thinking an individual exhibits in support of group or organizational objectives, without the need for star billing.

In formal organizations, most individuals (including leaders) spend much of their time as followers. No matter how many subordinates one has, he or she usually also has one or more bosses. Many military experts believe the first step in developing leadership potential is teaching individuals how to be good followers. Research shows that the same individuals who are nominated as the most desired leaders are also nominated as the most desired followers.[9] The characteristics of good leaders are also characteristics of good followers, and one of the important skills of followers may be the ability to shift easily between leadership and followership roles.[10]

The following are effective followership behaviors:

1. Demonstrating job knowledge and competence while working without close supervision and completing work tasks on time.
2. Demonstrating independent critical thinking by developing one's own opinions and ideas that show inventiveness and creativity.
3. Showing initiative in taking on responsibilities, participating actively, seeing tasks through to completion, and taking responsibility for one's own career development.
4. Speaking up frequently to offer information, share viewpoints, or take issue with decisions or actions that may be unethical or ill-advised.
5. Building collaborative and supportive relationships with coworkers and the leader that result in partnerships for achieving organizational goals.
6. Exerting influence on the leader in a confident and unemotional manner to help the leader avoid costly mistakes. Effective influence tactics often include logical persuasion, mobilizing coalitions, and being persistent and assertive. Flattery and praise of the leader are used sparingly.
7. Showing up consistently when needed, and accurately representing the leader's interests and views.
8. Competently spanning group or organizational boundaries when needed to acquire resources, export products, manipulate or interpret the environment, and provide key information for the organization.
9. Setting work goals that are action oriented, challenging, measurable, and aligned with group and organizational goals.
10. Demonstrating proper comportment for the organization. This may include manner of speech, dress, grammar, and etiquette.
11. Demonstrating a concern for performance, as well as a supportive and friendly atmosphere, within the work group.[11]

The followership role fulfills important personal needs for individuals. It provides for comradeship with valued others, and thus helps satisfy one's social needs. It allows individuals to serve others, and thus confirms a favorable self-concept and personal identity for many people. In addition, effective followers often identify with the leader and his or her mission. This identification with a respected leader and a worthwhile mission can enhance followers' self-concepts. By helping to shape and reinforce one's self-concept, the followership role satisfies individual needs for self-esteem and self-actualization. Followership roles also provide for personal growth of individuals by helping them become more mature and effective performers, or even future leaders, thus helping to satisfy human needs for competence and self-determination. Figure 11-1 summarizes the major followership behaviors.

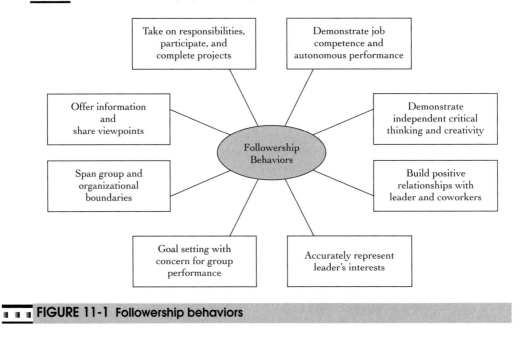

▮▮▮ **FIGURE 11-1 Followership behaviors**

▮▮▮ Examples of Ineffective Followership

Some follower behaviors are very common, but ineffective. Here are some examples:

- Hawkeye Pierce, in the TV series *MASH,* was a capable cynic who sarcastically criticized the leader's actions, often withheld his own efforts, and gradually sunk into disgruntled acquiescence.[12]
- Conformist followers are intellectually lazy because they "allow the leader to make the moral decisions for which they are responsible and . . . readily do what they are told."[13]
- Passive followers "act morally only under someone else's prodding."[14]
- Pragmatic followers "avert their eyes from wrongdoing rather than stop it or. . . are unwilling to disturb the status quo to do something worthwhile."[15]
- Apathetic, passive, or cynical followers exhibit a spectator-like noninvolvement that invites abuse by unethical leaders.[16]
- Ineffective followers expect training and development to be served to them. These individuals attend seminars and training experiences only if their organization sends them. They require a parental leader to care and feed their development or they become obsolete.

These followers are ineffective because they are not actively participating with the leader in individual and group development and performance. In contrast, the Followership in Action box shows an effective follower.

FOLLOWERSHIP IN ACTION
Taking Responsibility in a Difficult Situation

Pilots of passenger airlines are operational leader–managers, and their decisions have major impacts on cost and safety of the passengers. A major pilot error can cost tens of millions of dollars, as well as hundreds of lives. Pilots must have the ability to rapidly evaluate complex situations and arrive at effective decisions. A case occurred where the captain on an international flight arrived for the preflight check in a drunken condition. The ground staff carefully ignored his condition and said nothing. When the first officer arrived, however, things were different. Drawing the older captain aside, the first officer asked him in a firm tone, "Captain, will you turn yourself in, or will I have to turn you in?" The captain went immediately to the chief pilot's office and voluntarily grounded

himself. Getting control of his drinking problem took the captain six months, but he returned to flying without any further problems with alcohol. The effective followership behavior of the first officer demonstrated concern for the organization and the captain. The first officer demonstrated both job competence and a willingness to speak up when necessary. He took responsibility even though the captain was his superior in rank. After the captain got control of his alcohol problem, positive relations developed between the two pilots that lasted for years and contributed to organizational effectiveness. In this situation, the followership behavior of the first officer was clearly in the best interest of the airline, the customers, and the two individuals involved.

▪▪▪ Importance of Followership

Followers have historically been thought of as dependent individuals who need to be told what to do. Followership was viewed as a passive role, akin to clay, awaiting the leader's creative force. The heroic leader was expected to determine the direction, pace, and result of everyone's efforts, while assuring that the organization was profitable, produced excellent quality, had outstanding employment conditions, guaranteed employees' jobs, maximized performance, and transformed followers' lives.[17] Organizations have emphasized leadership initiatives with rewards for outstanding leadership performance. Organizational researchers, university faculties, and management trainers have produced leadership programs, books, articles, and seminars offering leadership prescriptions to help guide groups and organizations toward higher performance.

However, in the 1990s, many organizational members came to resent leaders with ridiculously high salaries and bonuses, extreme status symbols, and golden parachutes. The ability of leaders to meet the increasing number of expectations placed on them came into question. Followers now want a larger role in making organizational decisions, in carrying out those decisions, and in reaping the benefits. In the next decades we will see followership roles being emphasized in organizations. The popularity of work teams, productivity improvement groups, employee ownership, empowerment, and gainsharing all point to a larger role for followers in organizations of the future.

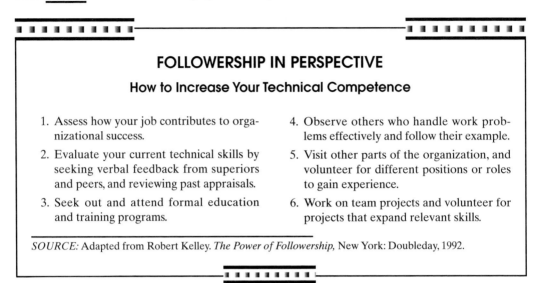

FOLLOWERSHIP IN PERSPECTIVE
How to Increase Your Technical Competence

1. Assess how your job contributes to organizational success.

2. Evaluate your current technical skills by seeking verbal feedback from superiors and peers, and reviewing past appraisals.

3. Seek out and attend formal education and training programs.

4. Observe others who handle work problems effectively and follow their example.

5. Visit other parts of the organization, and volunteer for different positions or roles to gain experience.

6. Work on team projects and volunteer for projects that expand relevant skills.

SOURCE: Adapted from Robert Kelley. *The Power of Followership,* New York: Doubleday, 1992.

Followership roles provide growth and development experiences for individuals to prepare them for greater responsibilities. As individuals develop, they typically contribute more to group or organizational performance. They also increase their self-confidence and become more willing to make moral judgments about possible unethical actions contemplated or taken by their leaders. By becoming proactive regarding ethical issues, they may prevent major mistakes that could cause serious damage to their organization. As noted earlier, followership roles can satisfy psychological needs for comradeship, service to others, identification with a valued cause, self-determination, and self-esteem. Followership roles help organizations address increased competition, high costs of operation, and organizational downsizing (by taking over some management functions) that characterize many major industries today.[18] They also help their organizations by increasing their technical competence, as detailed in the Followership in Perspective box: How to Increase Your Technical Competence.

▪▪▪ Skills, Traits, and Sources of Power for Effective Followership

Although the research on followership is sparse, a few writers have suggested traits and skills that should help fulfill the followership role in formal organizations. When a follower develops a high degree of *expertise or technical competence,* often resulting from extensive *education* or *relevant work experience,* the follower is usually more capable of self-management and less reliant on a leader for direct guidance on the job. When followers develop good *social skills,* they can build cooperative relationships with leaders and coworkers. Cooperation builds cohesion and avoids cliques that subvert the group's objectives. Followers who are *friendly* and *agreeable* may also help the unit by building effective relationships with important outsiders.[19] Followers who share *attitudes and values* with their leader and coworkers are also likely to build effective relationships.[20]

FOLLOWERSHIP IN PERSPECTIVE

Followers' Strategies for Building Effective Relations with Leaders

1. View your own and the leader's success as interdependent.

2. Try to understand the leader's personal and organizational objectives.

3. Recognize and complement the leader's weaknesses and limitations.

4. Keep the leader informed about activities, developments, and changes in the group.

5. Clarify your own role with the leader.

6. Adapt to the leader's style of leadership.

7. Show up prepared to perform.

SOURCE: Adapted from Robert Kelley. *The Power of Followership,* New York: Doubleday, 1992.

Flexible followers can adapt to changing demands and environments without being paralyzed by the stressful ambiguity that accompanies rapid change. Leaders usually appreciate a *sense of humor,* and they rate this quality highly in followers.

Followers provide an audience for leaders. As such, another requirement for effective followership is a *readiness to accept the leader's influence* without being yes men. This involves listening and learning without feeling threatened or sensing any loss of status. This readiness may result from follower maturity, including a sense of confidence and self-esteem. With charismatic leadership, however, the readiness may reflect followers' feelings of helplessness due to a perception that the situation is more than they can handle on their own. For whatever reason, effective followers must address the leader with a willingness to engage in the dynamic interaction of followership vis-à-vis leadership.

When followers are intelligent, competent, and possess critical thinking skills, others will probably view them as having *expert power.* If a follower's expertise is complemented with sociability, flexibility, and the ability to handle stress, the follower will likely possess *referent power.* Both these sources of power can make followers more effective and influential with the leader and coworkers.

A *leader's expectations and perceptions* of the follower may influence the followers' willingness to engage in certain followership behaviors. For example, if a leader has high expectations for a follower, this can result in constructive and proactive followership behaviors, such as speaking up and exerting influence on the leader. However, low expectations and perceptions can cause followers to be overly tentative, afraid to speak up, and unwilling to take unpopular (but needed) positions on important issues.[21] A similar result may occur when a leader's beliefs, philosophy, or style is *not compatible with followers.* In this case, followers may not be willing to carry out the active followership behaviors needed to help the leader meet objectives. Certain leaders simply rub followers the wrong way. When this occurs, the follower should consider the followers' strategies for building effective relations with leaders, described in the Followership in Perspective box. If the follower is unable or unwilling to attempt these strategies, then he or she had best seek another position with a leader who is more compatible.

∎∎∎ Effects of Followership

A limited number of research studies have been carried out on the effectiveness of the followership behaviors and skills described above. These studies show that followership behaviors resulted in *higher performance ratings* by superiors.[22] We believe that these followership behaviors will also result in increased *motivation, satisfaction,* feelings of *empowerment,* and group *cohesion.* Much more research is needed to verify whether objective performance and productivity measures, or other follower reactions, are related to these followership behaviors.

∎∎∎ Situational Enhancers, Neutralizers, and Substitutes for Followership

We believe that the active followership behaviors described in this chapter are valuable in virtually any leader–follower relationship. There are probably specific situations, however, in which the followership behaviors are especially needed and effective.

Enhancers of followership may be common in many organizations today. When the *leader is frequently absent or distant from followers,* the followership behaviors involving task competence, taking initiative, actively participating, and thinking independently may be especially critical for team performance. When followers' *work tasks are highly complex or interdependent,* then followers' task competence and activities that build cooperation with coworkers are probably especially important for group performance. When the followers' group faces *frequent emergencies, high-risk situations,* or *rapid change,* then the followership behaviors of speaking up, task competence, proactive initiative, and concern for performance are probably especially important.

Because it is an essential role in the leadership process, there can be no complete substitutes for followership. However, there may be substitutes for specific followership behaviors. This might occur when the leader is very active in external boundary spanning by gaining resources for the unit, building and maintaining networks with key outsiders, and facilitating important exchanges for the group. Here, the followers' external boundary-spanning behaviors may be unnecessary. When the leader is unusually adept at critical thinking, creativity, and inventiveness, this may at least partially alleviate the need for followers to demonstrate these characteristics. We have difficulty imagining, however, any substitutes for followers' task competence, active participation, taking responsibility, building positive relations with coworkers, and several other followership behaviors.

One situational factor might possibly decrease (neutralize) the favorable effects of followership behaviors. A domineering, autocratic, and self-centered leader may want nothing but yes men as followers, who flatter the leader and do not think for themselves. This type of leader may not value competent followers who show initiative and speak their mind. In these situations, the competent follower should work on building better relations with the leader or seek another position.

Although there is no research data, we suspect that neutralizers and substitutes for followership behaviors are quite rare. Future research is clearly needed to better understand how followership behaviors interact with situational characteristics. The Followership in Perspective box offers suggestions for building cooperative relationships with coworkers. These strategies may help create a cohesive group of followers, which can be an effective substitute for other leadership behaviors described in this book.

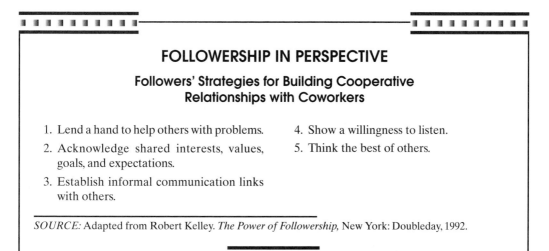

FOLLOWERSHIP IN PERSPECTIVE

Followers' Strategies for Building Cooperative Relationships with Coworkers

1. Lend a hand to help others with problems.

2. Acknowledge shared interests, values, goals, and expectations.

3. Establish informal communication links with others.

4. Show a willingness to listen.

5. Think the best of others.

SOURCE: Adapted from Robert Kelley. *The Power of Followership,* New York: Doubleday, 1992.

SUMMARY ▮▮▮▮▮▮▮

Followership is a necessary element in the leadership process. Most followership behaviors described in this chapter are needed to achieve group goals. However, certain followership behaviors may be especially important in specific situations. For example, when leaders are frequently distant from followers, when followers' tasks are complex or interdependent, or when followers face frequent high risks, emergency situations, or rapid change, the followership behaviors of speaking up, taking initiative, acting competently, building relationships with coworkers, and thinking independently can be especially important. Although research on these behaviors is sparse, we believe that nearly all leaders prefer this type of followership to having yes men or sheep who simply do as they are told and nothing more. The changes occurring in organizations in the 21st century will make these followership behaviors increasingly important. Because nearly all leaders in organizations report to higher-level leaders, these followership behaviors are useful for virtually all organizational members.

Figure 11-2 depicts a tentative process model of followership that summarizes much of the information in this chapter. Followership behaviors are shown at the top of Figure 11-2 affecting group and follower reactions, which in turn affect follower outcomes. Boxes at either side of the figure show how certain situational factors can enhance, neutralize, or substitute for the effectiveness of followership behaviors. Although the relationships shown in Figure 11-2 are based on sparse research, we believe they will be strongly confirmed in the future.

Figure 11-3 shows how followers can apply the information contained in Figure 11-2. The questions contained in the first box (1. Diagnosing the Situation) at the top of Figure 11-3 help identify situations where followership behaviors will be especially needed and effective. If the answer is "yes" to one or more of these questions, then active followership behaviors (2. Providing Followership) are needed, and the followers should carry them out. The follower can then assess the situation to determine if modifications

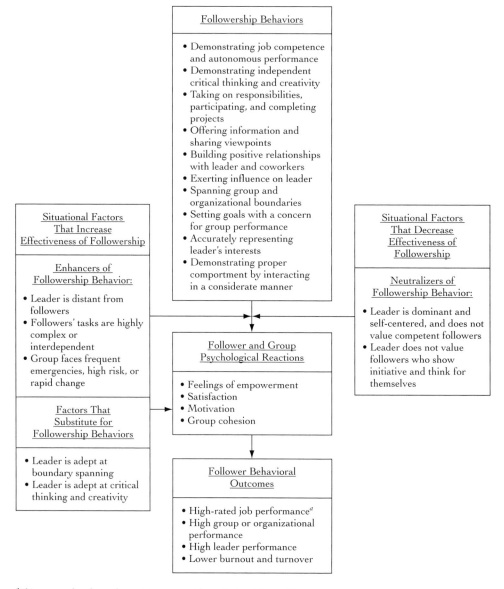

Followership Behaviors

- Demonstrating job competence and autonomous performance
- Demonstrating independent critical thinking and creativity
- Taking on responsibilities, participating, and completing projects
- Offering information and sharing viewpoints
- Building positive relationships with leader and coworkers
- Exerting influence on leader
- Spanning group and organizational boundaries
- Setting goals with a concern for group performance
- Accurately representing leader's interests
- Demonstrating proper comportment by interacting in a considerate manner

Situational Factors That Increase Effectiveness of Followership

Enhancers of Followership Behavior:

- Leader is distant from followers
- Followers' tasks are highly complex or interdependent
- Group faces frequent emergencies, high risk, or rapid change

Factors That Substitute for Followership Behaviors

- Leader is adept at boundary spanning
- Leader is adept at critical thinking and creativity

Situational Factors That Decrease Effectiveness of Followership

Neutralizers of Followership Behavior:

- Leader is dominant and self-centered, and does not value competent followers
- Leader does not value followers who show initiative and think for themselves

Follower and Group Psychological Reactions

- Feelings of empowerment
- Satisfaction
- Motivation
- Group cohesion

Follower Behavioral Outcomes

- High-rated job performance[a]
- High group or organizational performance
- High leader performance
- Lower burnout and turnover

[a]This outcome has shown the most improvement from effective followership.

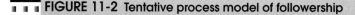

▪▪▪▪ **FIGURE 11-2 Tentative process model of followership**

can be made to make the followership behaviors more effective (3. Modifying Followers and Situations). Enterprising followers can sometimes increase the distance from their leader, or identify rapidly changing environmental factors that will increase the leader's appreciation for their active followership. Once these situational factors are addressed, the follower then reevaluates the questions in the first box, provides the needed followership behaviors, and so on, in a dynamic fashion.

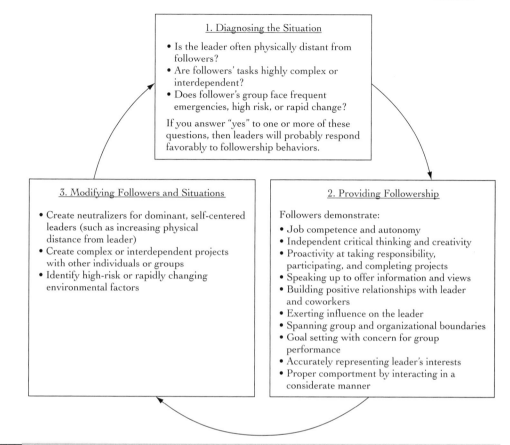

▪ ▪ ▪ **FIGURE 11-3 Applying the tentative model of followership**

KEY TERMS AND CONCEPTS IN THIS CHAPTER ▪▪▪▪▪▪▪

- Boundary spanning
- Comportment
- Empowerment
- Followership

- Goal setting
- Group cohesion
- Leader expectations
- Leader perceptions

- Social skills
- Technical competence

REVIEW AND DISCUSSION QUESTIONS ▪▪▪▪▪▪▪

1. Describe a situation you have experienced or heard about in which followership behaviors positively contributed to group productivity. Why was the followership effective in this situation?

2. Describe a situation you have experienced or heard about in which certain followership behaviors decreased the effectiveness of a group. Why was followership not effective in this situation?

3. As a follower, which of the situational characteristics described in this chapter have had the most impact on your desire to engage in followership behaviors? How could these characteristics that encouraged you to engage in followership behaviors be created by a leader?

4. Think of your current job or a job you would like to have. What skills or abilities could you develop to become a more effective follower in this situation?
5. What followership behaviors do you think would contribute the most to improving patient care in a hospital? Why?
6. How could followership behaviors improve customer service in a fast food restaurant?

FOLLOWERSHIP SELF-ASSESSMENT

Effective Followership Behaviors

Instructions: Indicate the extent to which you engage in the following followership behaviors when you are a member of a group or team, using the following scale: 5 = almost always; 4 = usually; 3 = occasionally; 2 = seldom; 1 = almost never.

1. I work at improving my knowledge, skills, and abilities in ways that will improve group performance.	1	2	3	4	5
2. I contribute to solving problems faced by the group with independent thinking and creativity.	1	2	3	4	5
3. I take responsibility and actively participate to help achieve group objectives.	1	2	3	4	5
4. I support group members and try to help them improve their contribution to the group.	1	2	3	4	5
5. I set personal goals that are action oriented, challenging, measurable, and supportive of group goals.	1	2	3	4	5
6. I behave in ways that are considered acceptable by the group, and interact in a considerate manner.	1	2	3	4	5
7. I show up when the group needs me, and accurately represent the leader's interests and views.	1	2	3	4	5
8. I try to obtain resources and information needed by the group from sources outside the group.	1	2	3	4	5
9. I try to influence the leader in a confident and unemotional manner to avoid costly mistakes.	1	2	3	4	5
10. I try to build positive working relationships with group members and the leader that are cooperative and supportive.	1	2	3	4	5

Interpretation: Total the numbers you circled for the 10 items. The following scores indicate the extent of your engagement in followership behaviors:

40–50: Highly engaged in followership behaviors

30–39: Moderately engaged in followership behaviors

20–29: Occasionally engaged in followership behaviors

0–19: Seldom engaged in followership behaviors

SOURCES: Items adapted from material presented by R. E. Kelley. *The Power of Followership.* New York: Doubleday, 1992; and E. P. Hollander. The essential interdependence of leadership and followership. *Current Directions in Psychological Science,* 1(2), 1992, 71–75.

▪▪▪▪ C A S E   I N C I D E N T ▪▪▪▪

Can Ralph's Followership be Improved?

You work as a programmer in the computer center of a service organization. As a member of a programming and systems design team, you work with six other professionals. With the exception of Ralph Hughes, the members of the team get along very well together. If Ralph was not on your team, you could be more productive, and jobs would be more enjoyable.

Ralph repeatedly resists the ideas of other team members, and thereby blocks progress at improving the system. He is very aggressive in finding fault with suggestions from others. In attacking one of your ideas, he said, "Why do you keep coming up with these bright ideas to make more work? Why don't you try selling them to IBM?" On another occasion, Ralph responded to your idea with, "That's what I would expect from someone who knew nothing about this system." He often prevents team members from making suggestions by interrupting them with comments like, "I have something important to say."

As a result of Ralph's uncooperative behavior, discussions often turn into arguments, with people shouting at him. You have never worked with anyone who is as hard to get along with as Ralph. You often leave work angry with Ralph, and wish he would get fired. ▪

DISCUSSION QUESTIONS

1. How can you respond to Ralph so that he would be encouraged to develop positive followership behaviors?
2. What could the team members do to change Ralph's followership behaviors?

ENDNOTES ▪▪▪▪▪▪▪

1. Kelley, R. E. (1988). In praise of followers. *Harvard Business Review,* November–December, 142–148.
2. Kelley, R. E. (1992) *The Power of Followership.* New York: Doubleday.
3. Ibid.
4. *The American Heritage Dictionary,* 2nd college ed. (1985). Boston: Houghton Mifflin.
5. Kelley. *The Power of Followership.*
6. Hughes, R. L., Ginnett, R. C., and Curphy, G. J. (1996). *Leadership: Enhancing the Lessons of Experience,* 2nd ed. Chicago: Irwin.
7. Heller, T., and Van Til, J. (1982). Leadership and followership: Some summary propositions. *Journal of Applied Behavioral Science,* 18(3), 405–414; and Hollander, E. P. (1992). Leadership, followership, self, and others. *Leadership Quarterly,* 3(1), 43–54.
8. Lee, C. (1991). Followership: The essence of leadership. *Training,* 28(1), 27–35; and Kelley, R. E. *The Power of Followership.*
9. Bass, B. (1990). *Bass and Stogdill's Handbook of Leadership,* 3rd ed. New York: Free Press.
10. Hollander, E. P. (1992). The essential interdependence of leadership and followership. *Current Directions in Psychological Science,* 1(2), 71–75; and Hollander, E. P. (1993). Legitimacy, power, and influence: A perspective on relational features of

leadership. In M. M. Chemers and R. Ayman (Eds.), *Leadership Theory and Research: Perspectives and Directions.* New York: Academic Press.

11. Gilbert, G. R., and Hyde, A. C. (1988). Followership and the federal worker. *Public Administration Review,* 48(5), 962–968; Kelley. *The Power of Followership;* Gilbert, G. R., and Whiteside, C. W. (1988). Performance appraisal and followership: An analysis of the officer in the boss/subordinate team. *Journal of Police Science and Administration,* 16(1), 39–43; and Hafsi, M., and Misumi, J. (1992). The leader-follower's mutual effect: Developing a performance–maintenance interactional model. *Psychologia: An International Journal of Psychology in the Orient,* 35(4), 201–212.

12. Kelley. *The Power of Followership.*

13. Ibid.

14. Ibid.

15. Ibid.

16. Gardner, J. (1990). *On Leadership.* New York: Free Press.

17. Nicoll, D. (1986). Leadership and followership: Fresh views on an old subject. In John D. Adams (Ed.), *Transforming Leadership: From Vision to Results,* Alexandria, VA: Miles River Press.

18. Flower, J. (1991). The art and craft of followership: A conversation with Robert Kelley. *Healthcare Forum,* January/February 1991, 56–60; and Buhler, P. (1993). Managing in the 90s: The flipside of leadership—cultivating followers. *Supervision,* March 1993, 17–19.

19. Kelley. *The Power of Followership;* and Hughes, Ginnett, and Curphy. *Leadership: Enhancing the Lessons of Experience.*

20. Shamir, B., House, R. J. and Arthur, M. B. (1993). The motivational effects of charismatic leadership: A self concept based theory. *Organizational Science,* 4, 1–17.

21. Lippitt, R. (1982). The changing leader-follower relationships of the 1980s. *Journal of Applied Behavioral Science,* 18(3), 395–403.

22. Gardner. *On Leadership;* and Gilbert and Hyde. Followership and the federal worker.

CHAPTER 12

Leadership Ethics and Diversity

Learning Objectives

After reading this chapter, you should be able to do the following:

1. Explain why ethical leadership is so important in organizations.
2. Describe major ethical issues that leaders face, and approaches for addressing those issues.
3. Explain how leaders can create an ethical climate in their organization.
4. Describe the role of spirituality in creating an ethical organizational climate.
5. Explain the competitive advantages of diversity for organizations.
6. Describe leadership strategies and behaviors for creating a multicultural organization.

An Example of Leadership Ethics

Numerous scandals have been reported in the popular press in recent years involving the questionable behavior of leaders in business and public organizations. These incidents have made leaders' ethics a major topic of discussion among practicing leaders and behavioral scientists who study leadership. The collapse and highly publicized investigation of Enron has probably attracted more recent attention to leadership ethics than any other single case.

Enron began in 1985 with the merger of two pipeline companies that were in the energy delivery business. In 1988, when the deregulation of electric power took place, Enron redefined its business as an energy broker. It specialized in bringing buyers and sellers of electric power together, and gained revenues from the differences between buying and selling prices. Viewing the company as a broker encouraged Enron personnel to adopt aggressive and clever strategies similar to Wall Street brokers (who have produced ethics scandals of their own). Jeffrey Skilling, former president, CEO, and COO at Enron, encouraged employees to be independent, innovative, and aggressive in developing new products, services, and related businesses while the Internet age was beginning. Producing income for the company was all that mattered, so that rule breaking was approved if it created value for Enron.[1]

Enron's early profits and growth earned positive evaluations from the press and financial community. This created pressure to sustain the early success to keep the stock price high. This was essential to keep a high credit rating, which affected the trust placed in Enron by its customers, and consequently, future revenues. High stock prices also protected the value of the large fortunes of Enron executives, obtained from huge bonuses in the form of stock options. Enron executives developed a deceiving web of pseudo-partnerships with newly created "investment companies" that were actually Enron subsidiaries. These pseudo-partnerships were used to hide debt from Enron shareholders and to report earnings on transactions before they actually took place. In one situation, Enron recorded a profit of over $110 million on a partnership that failed in its first venture and was abandoned. Enron executives referred to these deceptive accounting strategies as timing issues, not unethical behavior.

When these practices were made public, the investment community began to lose confidence in Enron. Loans became due, pseudo-partnerships began to fail, customers lost trust in Enron, and it could not meet its obligations. Jeffrey Skilling resigned suddenly, citing personal reasons, and sold his Enron stock totaling $66 million. Enron was forced to restate prior earnings to more accurately reflect its real profit picture, its stock price fell, and employees began to lose their investments in the company (investments that Enron executives had encouraged). Executives blamed each other, claimed ignorance of the questionable accounting tactics used to hide debt and create false profits, seized computers and destroyed files with important records, and claimed the fifth amendment when testifying before a congressional committee.

Enron eventually filed for bankruptcy, and many employees lost their entire investments and retirement pensions. Several executives face charges for illegal activities. The executives had encouraged and modeled an organizational culture of individualism, innovation, aggressive cleverness, and excess, at the expense of compassionate, honest, and responsible leadership. Personal ambition and greed overshadowed everything else, creating an atmosphere in which unethical and illegal activities occurred with regularity and were almost never questioned. One writer noted that "Just as the destiny of individuals is determined by personal character, the destiny of an organization is determined by the character of its leadership."[2]

The case of Enron is not unique. Leaders such as John Gutfreund at Salomon Brothers, "Chainsaw" Al Dunlap at Scott Paper and Sunbeam Corporation, and John Rigas at Adelphia Communications demonstrated similar behaviors that were eventually brought to light. These leaders lost their credibility and the trust that is necessary for effective leadership. They also did tremendous damage, financially and professionally, to many people. These unethical leaders demonstrate the importance of leadership in establishing an ethical climate in an organization. Leaders are the prime example that followers emulate when it comes to ethical or unethical behavior.

▬▬▬ Ethics and Leadership

The word *ethics* derives from the Greek word *ethos,* meaning character. Ethics is the study of morality (right and wrong) and the moral choices people make in their relationships with others. Discussions of ethics typically involve descriptions of good or bad behavior, and often include references to a society's values or standards of conduct for a profession. The press reports about Enron executives, John Gutfreund, Al Dunlap, and John Rigas demonstrate the importance the public places on ethical leadership today. As one expert on ethics recently stated, "The moral triumphs and failures of leaders carry a greater weight and volume than those of non-leaders."[3]

Ethics concerns how we should behave in the roles that society gives us. Leaders are often in roles that can determine the well-being of others, and they sometimes influence the broader good. When we study leadership we hope to understand how to become a *good* leader. But *good* has two meanings—technically good (effective) and morally good. Some leaders are effective, but not very ethical. Others may be highly ethical, but not particularly effective. A leader is usually known and described for his or her accomplishments (effectiveness). Unless there is a major setback or scandal, we hear little about ethical questions such as: What were the leader's intentions? How did the leader go about achieving the goal? Was the goal itself good?[4] Doing things right and doing the right things are both important aspects of good leadership.

⊤⊤⊤ Ethical Issues

Several ethical issues are common to most leadership positions. Perhaps the most important and most difficult ethical issue is the leader's *power*. Power is the basis for a leader's influence on followers. The more power a leader has, the more likely that followers will comply with the leader's wishes. In Chapter 2, we described several types of power used by leaders and noted that leaders use different types of power in different situations. But the old axiom that "power corrupts, and absolute power corrupts absolutely" rings true. The greater a leader's power, the greater the potential for abuse. This can be seen in the horrible treatment of millions of people by dictators such as Hitler, Idi Amin, Pol Pot, and Stalin. The greater the formal power differential between a leader and followers, the greater the probability that the leader will make demands on followers when friendly requests would work just as well. A friendly request usually creates a better emotional climate.[5]

Edwin Hollander described several corrupting influences of power: (1) Power may become desired as an end in itself and be sought at any cost; (2) Power differences may cause followers to give the leader false positive feedback and create an elevated sense of self-worth in the leader; (3) This may, in turn, cause the leader to devalue followers' worth and to avoid regular contact with followers or mistreat them (as often occurs with dictators).[6] One scholar described another common corrupting influence that she labeled the *Bathsheba Syndrome.* In the Old Testament, David first appeared as a young shepherd who defeated the enormous enemy Goliath. God selected David as the next leader because he had a "good heart," and he became a great leader whom God favored. While he was king, he saw the beautiful Bathsheba bathing and had her brought to him. He lay with her and she became pregnant, but she was married to Uriah, one of David's military leaders. David recalled Uriah from the war and tried to get him drunk so he would sleep with Bathsheba and thus hide David's transgression. But Uriah refused to enjoy himself while his men were still fighting, demonstrating the moral commitment of a good leader to his followers. So David ordered Uriah to the front lines of the fiercest battle and he was killed. The prophet Nathan then confronted David with his sin, and God punished David.[7]

Stories like this have been replayed over and over in scandals such as Watergate, President Clinton and Monica Lewinski, and Enron. Leaders' power gives them privileges that others do not have. The leaders indulge themselves and then use their power to cover up their indulgence. Their inflated sense of self-worth causes them to believe they are not subject to the same norms and laws that affect other people. They believe they can control outcomes, and often commit greater transgressions trying to cover themselves. The murder of Uriah is worse than David's seduction of Bathsheba, and many believe Clinton's lying to the American public was worse than his adultery. In each case, however, someone exposes the leader and they are held to the same moral standards as everyone else. A leader's failure to acknowledge the ethical limits of power causes a loss of credibility and trust, and does devastating damage to the leader and his or her constituency.[8]

The issue of *moral standards* for a leader's behavior also poses ethical issues for followers. Some people say leaders should be held to a higher moral standard than others. Does this mean it is acceptable for others to live by a lower moral standard? Most would hesitate to agree with this implication. The person is rare who has never lied or failed to keep a promise. So a higher moral standard means we would probably have a shortage of leaders and would most likely become disillusioned with them when they were unable to meet the higher standards. A more realistic expectation is that leaders will be held to the same standards as everyone else, but that they will fail less often than others in living up to those standards. Kings, presidents, and corporate executives are not above the existing laws and norms of society, but they should be meticulous in their respect and adherence to these laws and norms to maintain the respect of their followers.

Another ethical issue for leaders is *moral consistency*. If leaders' behavior does not match their stated values, they will lose the trust of their followers and colleagues. Lack of trust makes it difficult to obtain the cooperation needed to be effective. A leader's moral inconsistencies are more open to public scrutiny than other people's and they are often used as a tool to attack a leader's character. Tim Eyman was leader of a citizen's group that focused on holding politicians accountable for how they spent taxpayers' dollars. A Seattle newspaper revealed that Eyman paid himself $45,000 from the money raised to support one of the group's ballot initiatives. Politicians whom he had called corrupt used this report to discredit Eyman and his citizen group. At first he denied the charge, and then later admitted his inconsistent behavior. Leaders such as Eyman who do not behave consistently with their stated ethical values risk being labeled hypocrites.

The relationship between *ethics and effectiveness* can be a complicated ethical issue for some leaders. A suicide bomber may achieve his goal of instilling terror in a population and bringing public attention to his cause (he is effective). His fellow terrorists may view his suicide as altruistic, but most people would view killing innocent people as unethical. Robin Hood stole from the rich and gave to the poor. Even though his motives were altruistic, stealing is generally considered unethical. Similarly, politicians sometimes achieve worthwhile goals for their constituencies using questionable tactics.

The phrase "He may be a son of a bitch, but he is our son of a bitch" hints at a double standard when judging some leaders. As with Robin Hood, some followers will excuse unethical behavior if it is effective and they benefit. Martin Luther King Jr. was highly effective at making gains in social justice for the civil rights movement, and he empowered and disciplined his followers to use nonviolent techniques (he used and encouraged ethical means). But his extramarital affairs and plagiarism in writing his doctoral dissertation are generally considered unethical. The secretary-general of the United Nations has limited formal power. The moral authority derived from completely ethical behavior is absolutely essential if the person in this position is to be effective.[9] Judging a leader as good involves complex assessments of the leader's achievements and the means used to reach those achievements. It also often involves the perspective of the person who is judging the leader.

Leaders also make *moral mistakes* that cause unfortunate consequences, although their intentions were ethical. A Swiss Christian charity raised considerable money to buy the freedom of an estimated 200,000 enslaved children in Sudan. Their freedom program unwittingly created a large market for slaves, causing slavery to increase. The president of South Africa, Thabo Mbeki, attacked what he saw as exploitation of the public by big business by stating that it was not clear that HIV caused AIDS. He believed the pharmaceutical industry was scaring people to increase their revenues. This type of statement is highly unfortunate in an area heavily damaged by the AIDS epidemic. Cases such as these involve the complex relationship between ethics and effectiveness or competence. An ethics expert poses this question: Were these leaders unethical or just incompetent? These examples show that leaders must be competent enough to make good ethical judgments, while they strive to be effective. The process of moral reasoning is a means for making ethical judgments, and is described later in this chapter.

The ethicist Rushworth Kidder believes that most of us are out of shape when it comes to making ethical judgments. He encourages us to practice dealing with these issues by reading about ethical theories and discussing ethical cases with colleagues. This can sharpen our skills at recognizing and dealing with ethical issues. Figure 12-1 summarizes important ethical issues for leaders. The Leadership in Action box on John Gutfreund describes an analysis of one case of unethical behavior by a business leader.

▪▪▪▪ **FIGURE 12-1** Ethical issues for leaders

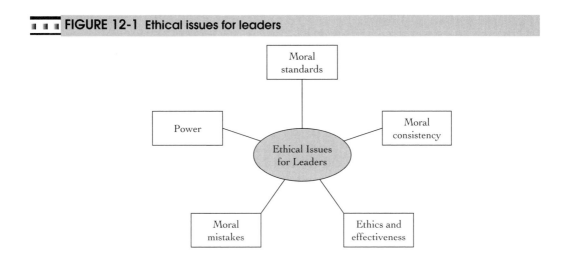

LEADERSHIP IN ACTION

John Gutfreund and the Salomon Brothers Scandal

Salomon Brothers, Inc., a large investment banking company, admitted in August 1991 that it had seriously violated several U.S. Treasury auction rules by submitting illegal bids for Treasury bills. The company eventually paid a fine of $290 million. This scandal was regarded as a product of a greedy and power-hungry organizational culture. The pure profit-driven culture of Salomon Brothers was closely linked to the leadership of John Gutfreund, the CEO of the company at that time. Organizational expert Ed Schein described the relationship between Gutfreund's leadership behavior and the culture at Salomon Brothers by focusing on five major issues.

First, *what leaders pay attention to.* Gutfreund focused on short-term business profits. No evidence showed that Gutfreund ever developed a long-term strategy for the company. As a trader, Gutfreund believed in instantaneous decision making. Employees were forced to pursue immediate profit, and the long-term outcomes and ethics of their behaviors were ignored.

Second, *how leaders react to crises.* In reaction to the knowledge of the Treasury bills scandal in 1991, Gutfreund tried to cover it up. When this attempt failed, he lied and tried to absolve himself from any responsibility. There is no evidence that he ever took action against those who submitted the illegal bids.

Third, *how leaders behave.* Gutfreund's career was marked with hard work, aggression,

and betrayal of people who trusted him. While Gutfreund was CEO at Salomon Brothers, he engineered the sale of the company to Philip Brothers. He did not even discuss this sale with Billy Salomon, who had been his mentor and still owned most of the company that bore his name. Billy Salomon was bitter and humiliated about this betrayal that earned Gutfreund $32 million. Gutfreund's behavior provided a model for his employees regarding how to succeed in the company—ethics and trust are sacrificed for financial gain.

Fourth, *how leaders allocate rewards.* Gutfreund promoted a profit-based compensation policy. At Salomon Brothers, greed, aggression, and complete loyalty to the company were rewarded. Evasion and bending of government regulations were encouraged and rewarded, and ethics were ignored.

Finally, *how leaders hire and fire individuals.* Gutfreund selected ambitious young people and provided them with a chance for large financial gains. However, the company never had specific performance guidelines, and performance was measured subjectively. Dismissal decisions were usually made by Gutfreund based on his own judgment. This led to vague and inconsistent management, which created space for employees to cross ethical and legal boundaries.

John Gutfreund's leadership produced great financial gains, but it was eventually very costly to the company.

SOURCES: R. R. Sims and J. Brinkman. Leaders as moral role models: The case of John Gutfreund at Salomon Brothers. *Journal of Business Ethics,* 35, 2002, 327–339; www.sbam.com/SBAM/html/history.html; elitewatch.911review.org/Salomon_Smith_Barney.html.

▪▪▪ Approaches to Ethical Behavior

For centuries, philosophers and writers have suggested different approaches or general guidelines for the ethical behavior of leaders. This section describes several major approaches that have been popular with different groups. When reading and thinking about these approaches, it is probably best at this point not to select a single approach for your own behavior. You may need to combine several approaches to resolve an ethical problem, or you might find that a specific approach is best to deal with certain types of ethical dilemmas. It can often be enlightening to apply more than one approach to a specific ethical problem to see what learning and insight you gain from each approach. Each approach focuses on a different aspect of ethical behavior. By considering multiple approaches in this manner, you will engage in *moral learning,* and you should be better equipped to deal with different ethical issues you will face as a leader.

The German philosopher Immanuel Kant described what he called the *categorical imperative,* which specified that individuals should always do what is right, regardless of the consequences. He believed we are duty bound to follow universal truths that are part of our conscience. This approach is sometimes called *obligation ethics* because it states that we are obligated to follow specific rules or moral laws. When we feel guilty it is because we have violated one or more of these moral laws. Using this approach, we should ask ourselves: "Would I want others to behave as I did?" If the answer is "yes," the behavior is ethical; if the answer is "no," the behavior is unethical. Using this type of moral reasoning, behavior such as telling the truth and helping the needy are always right (ethical). Other behaviors such as lying, cheating, and stealing are always wrong (unethical).[10]

Those who adhere to this approach usually show persistence and consistency in their behavior, and they are less likely than others to compromise their personal standards. Most people believe, however, that there are sometimes exceptional situations in which thoughtful people might violate one of these rules and still behave ethically. Telling a lie or stealing an expensive medication to save a child's life are examples. In these situations, people sometimes choose the lesser of two evils, and many believe their choice is ethical.

Another ethical guideline, called *utilitarianism,* states that ethical decisions must be based on their consequences. Although most people probably consider the likely outcomes and impacts of their decisions, this approach maintains that we should behave so as to create the greatest good for the greatest number of people. It is sometimes called *consequential ethics* or *ethics of responsibility.* Advocates of utilitarianism may endorse general guidelines for behavior, but allow situations to affect the application of those guidelines. A person might tell a lie to protect a group that has suffered great misfortune, and still believe that lying is usually wrong because it is misleading and often harmful. Utilitarians would view this behavior in this situation as ethical.

The utilitarian approach is often used by leaders in decision making. One expert described the case of President Harry Truman, who made the final decision to drop atomic bombs on Hiroshima and Nagasaki to hasten the end of World War II. Truman judged that the benefits of dropping the bombs (to save lives from a planned invasion of Japan) outweighed the costs of lives lost from the bombs. This decision also shows some of the difficulties of using utilitarianism as a sole ethical guideline. Identifying all the relevant consequences of a decision can be difficult, especially when leaders represent diverse groups or when their decisions have far-reaching effects. Calculating the costs and benefits of all the effects is often complex and usually uncertain. For this reason, two utilitarian leaders might make different decisions when faced with the same ethical problem. Historians have very different opinions about Truman's decision to drop the bombs, which destroyed highly populated cities and helped initiate the nuclear age. Another criticism of the idea that leaders should always do the greatest good for the greatest number arises in many developed countries, where we believe that minorities also have basic rights and deserve equal treatment. All important decisions should not favor only the majority of stakeholders.[11]

Altruism is often described as another approach to ethical behavior. Altruistic leaders are concerned for the welfare of others, and their actions are designed to help others even if they result in a cost to themselves. Some writers believe that leaders are only truly effective if their behavior is guided primarily by the criterion of benefiting others.[12] Others maintain that looking out for the interests of others is part of a leader's job.[13] Altruism is often contrasted with selfishness, which involves benefiting oneself at the cost of others. Complete altruism and complete selfishness are extreme motivations for behavior, and most leaders demonstrate aspects of both. Confucius equated altruism with the Golden Rule, "Do unto others as you would have them do unto you." This guideline occurs in numerous cultures, perhaps because it describes how to transform self-interest into a concern for others. It thus bridges altruism and self-interest.[14]

Altruism seems to be a universal value across the world. The Dalai Lama, Judaism, and Christianity all emphasize an ethic of compassion and loving others as we love ourselves. Mother Teresa's religious order practices this type of altruistic mission in India. Societies and organizations function more smoothly when people help one another in their daily activities. It may be that altruism is more important for leaders than it is for followers, because leaders exert influence on behalf of followers and are often responsible for followers' welfare.[15]

Altruism is a popular ethical perspective because it is an ancient and contemporary guide for behavior. It is healthy for societies and organizations, it helps leaders connect self-interest with others' interests and keep their leadership responsibilities in the forefront, and acts of pure altruism can inspire our own behavior. Though popular, altruism may be difficult in practice. Fierce wars have been fought by religious groups whose faith includes altruistic teaching. Leaders who behave altruistically may not be completely ethical: Recall Robin Hood, and the terrorist whose behavior was designed to benefit others, but can still be judged as unethical by many people.[16] Classifying a leader's behavior as ethical or unethical is a complex process.

Virtue ethics is a very old approach for explaining and encouraging ethical behavior. The central idea of virtue ethics is that leaders and other individuals who have high moral character are most likely to make wise ethical choices in their behavior and decision making. Virtues are "deep-rooted dispositions, habits, skills, or traits of character that incline persons to perceive, feel and act in ethically right and sensitive ways."[17] Early Greek and Chinese philosophers described the virtues of ideal leaders. Advocates of virtue ethics tend to describe the character traits and qualities of the ideal leader as an ethical role model.

LEADERSHIP SELF-ASSESSMENT
Describing Leaders

Take a blank sheet of paper and divide it into two columns. In one column, list the character traits and qualities of an ideal political leader. In the other column, list the traits and qualities of an ideal business leader. When you finish, compare the two lists.

Are there more similarities than differences between the lists? If so, why? If not, why not?

SOURCE: Adapted from Craig Johnson. *Meeting the Ethical Challenge of Leadership.* Thousand Oaks, CA: Sage, 2001.

Try completing the Leadership Self-Assessment: Describing Leaders. Research shows that there are usually more similarities than differences between character traits and qualities of ideal political and business leaders. Americans typically describe ideal political leaders as having integrity, showing restraint, being respectful, exercising good judgment, persisting during adversity, and being able to rally followers. Americans, Europeans, and Australians describe ideal business leaders as being honest, forward looking, inspiring, and competent.[18,19] Aristotle and Plato described good leaders as having prudence (caution and good judgment), justice, courage, and self-restraint. Early Chinese philosophers listed simplicity, patience, and compassion. A single list of virtues is probably not as important as combining a set of desirable characteristics to create a strong ethical character for a leader.[20]

Character formation is a long and often difficult process. Individuals typically make progress in some areas, but not in others. High-level leaders often have their moral weaknesses made public along with their accomplishments. Martin Luther King Jr. and President Bill Clinton's moral weaknesses were described earlier. Presidents Franklin Delano Roosevelt and John Kennedy also had moral indiscretions that became widely known. For some leaders, character building is a lifelong process. Persistent emotional and mental effort is required to build the type of character that inspires trust and respect from followers.

Immoral personal behavior by high-level political leaders has fueled a debate among ethicists and the general public about personal and public morality. Some argue that there is a clear distinction between a leader's personal life and professional behavior. This group maintains that Presidents Clinton, Roosevelt, and Kennedy's behavior is irrelevant to their performance in office. Others believe that personal and public morality cannot be separated because both reveal important information about the leader's character. A leader who lies or cheats on his spouse will likely lie to followers when it is convenient. Both situations erode the trust and respect needed for effective leadership.

A final approach to ethical behavior is closely related to character building and virtue ethics. This approach is called *moral learning,* and involves gradual changes in beliefs, attitudes, values, and habits obtained through prolonged effort by a leader to behave in a just, prudent, and truthful manner. Moral learning is a process of human development. It involves more than following fixed moral laws or general guidelines such as "the greatest good for the greatest number." It does more than point out limits beyond which a leader's behavior may be harmful (such as not cheating customers). Moral learning is an inherently positive process that causes leaders to want to create benefits for people, such as more jobs or a higher-quality work experience. It also causes leaders to make decisions and act in accordance with their conscience, while using all available information to formulate careful, prudent judgments.

Moral learning focuses on an ethic of excellence. It teaches leaders to strive for a higher good and to take the most ethical approach, even if it is costly in terms of the leader's personal preferences, income, career, or the welfare of other stakeholders. The higher good may be the moral example the leader sets for followers and future leaders. It may be a moral stand that tells competitors and other interested parties the type of leader and organization they are dealing with. Moral learning extends to followers, as the leader strives to instill the ethic of excellence in their behavior to increase their ability to make better decisions in the future.[21]

James Rest suggested several elements of moral learning that ethical leaders acquire through effort and experience.[22] Leaders must first become *sensitive to ethical problems*. They must be alert to violations of peoples' rights, issues of fairness and consistency, and the implications of actions and decisions for current and future stakeholders. Leaders must also become *competent in making moral judgments,* which include identifying, evaluating, and deciding on courses of action that address ethical problems. Leaders must be *motivated to behave ethically* and make ethical decisions. Moral values often conflict with other values and motivations, such as security, enjoyment, and personal achievement. Ethical leaders must learn to give precedence to moral values in order to develop a reputation for ethical behavior. And leaders must be *willing to take moral action,* often in the face of criticism, distractions, fatigue, and other obstacles. Overcoming these factors is often difficult and requires courage, a positive attitude, good interpersonal skills, determination, and persistent hard work.[23]

The elements of moral learning are related to one another. For example, what we judge to be immoral will likely affect our motivation and willingness to take ethical action. Individuals are typically stronger in some elements of moral learning than others. A new leader may be extremely sensitive to ethical issues, but lack the experience to make confident moral judgments about an ethical course of action. Becoming aware of the different elements of moral learning should help individuals focus their learning efforts. Several sources of learning are especially useful for leaders' ethical development.

Selecting good leadership *role models* that exhibit consistent ethical behavior is one major learning source. Leaders usually learn about virtuous behavior by observing and imitating ethical leaders. Leaders who demonstrate ethical behavior every day provide the most learning, rather than the leader who engages in a single heroic act. Consistently ethical (not necessarily heroic) leaders give the observer the chance to observe ethical behavior in different situations with different stakeholders. One writer noted that most of life is lived in the daily valleys, not on the heroic peaks. We need role models who live consistently ethical lives to help us develop the elements of moral learning over time through the moral choices and actions we take every day. Ethical leaders as role models can be found in schools, business, public organizations, history books, literature, or movies and plays.

Hardships are another source of moral learning. Highly admired leaders often suffered great hardships, such as Nelson Mandela and Abraham Lincoln. Hardships are particularly vivid learning experiences because they are unplanned, often intensely personal, and usually involve some loss to the individual. Major types of hardships described by researchers at the Center for Creative Leadership include business failures, major career setbacks, personal trauma, and dealing with problematic employees, mergers, acquisitions, or downsizing. Hardships can sensitize us to ethical issues, and overcoming hardships can improve our moral judgment, motivation, and willingness to act on ethical issues. Treating hardships as learning experiences helps us maximize our development as ethical leaders.

Developing a *value-driven mission* can help guide us in moral learning and in choosing moral behaviors and decisions. We will discuss personal values in more detail in Chapter 13. Our values affect our perceptions of people and situations, how we think about individual and organizational success, our relationships with other people, how we solve problems, the risks we take, and how we distinguish between ethical and unethical behavior. Values also have a major influence on the moral choices we make in work and life in general. If a person values honesty, they will likely choose not to lie. If they value humility, they will probably not promote themselves (that is, they will not toot their own horn when interacting with others). But having worthwhile values does not guarantee leaders will live by them. Other factors, such as social or family pressure, time deadlines, or personal ambition, can intrude on a leader's judgment and cause him or her to behave in ways that are inconsistent with some core values.

Developing a value-driven mission statement involves incorporating your core values into a clear statement of what you wish to accomplish in your career. Abraham Lincoln's mission was to preserve the union and eliminate slavery. Oscar Schindler's mission during World War II was to save Jews from death and destruction in Nazi concentration camps. Mother Teresa's mission was to reduce suffering. A clear value-driven mission can keep a leader focused on core values and help prevent other factors from diverting his or her behavior.

One expert has noted that the most useful mission statements can be stated in one sentence, are easily understood, and can be committed to memory.[24] Writing a value-driven mission statement begins with the leader assessing his or her family experience and other background that resulted in the values, interests, and strengths that describe who he or she is. This process also involves examining the leader's motivations—what excites him or her, or makes him or her feel worthwhile and fulfilled? What arouses her passion or enthusiasm? Issues that evoke these motivations typically reflect the leader's core values, and they make up the primary content of a value-driven mission statement. Experts suggest that these mission statements begin with "My mission is to . . . ," followed by one or more verbs such as "achieve," "create," or "improve." This should be followed by a value, principle, or purpose the leader wishes to commit themselves to, such as "financial security," "happiness," or "equal opportunity." The statement ends by identifying the person(s) or entity that is the focus of your mission, such as your family, profession, clients, customers, employees, or church members. Examples might be "My mission is to achieve financial security for my family members" or "My mission is to create equal opportunity for all my employees." This mission statement should reflect

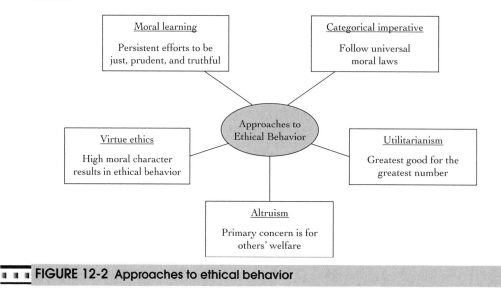

▪▪▪▪ FIGURE 12-2 Approaches to ethical behavior

enough of the leader's core values and self-concept to inspire ethical activities on and off the job. Committing themselves to a value-driven mission affects how leaders perceive their environment, and helps them learn to promote their ethical values in different areas of life. Figure 12-2 summarizes the various approaches to ethical behavior.

▪▪▪ Creating an Ethical Climate

Worthwhile values and a value-driven mission provide a basis for the ethical climate of an organization. This climate is the shared perceptions among organizational members of the organization's policies, practices, and procedures regarding ethical behavior. Specific actions by leaders also contribute to this ethical climate.

Followers often watch leaders to obtain cues about what is important in their organization. We noted earlier that selecting a good leadership role model was important for moral learning. *Role modeling* emphasizes visible behaviors and may include demonstrations of how to implement specific values. It is therefore helpful in establishing an ethical organizational climate. Sometimes visible actions by a leader require no explanation, as one business leader described in the following example. "Some years ago, I was running one of our plants. I had just taken over and they were having some financial troubles. . . . Most of our management was flying first class. . . . I did not want. . . my first act to be to tell everybody that they are not gonna fly first class anymore, so I just quit flying first class. And it wasn't long before people noticed it and pretty soon everybody was flying coach. . . . They got the message."[25]

The same type of modeling by a leader can convey negative cues. Suppose an organization's ethics policy prohibits employees from accepting gifts from clients, but employees notice a group of executives sitting in a client's box at a professional baseball game. Employees will likely conclude that the ethics policy can be ignored. It does not matter if the executives paid for their own seats at the game and were simply visiting with a client between innings. Employees see the leaders' actions and make inferences about what is really expected.

Leaders must expect followers to observe their behavior, and the leaders must think about how it will be interpreted before they act. If they consistently demonstrate integrity by exhibiting behaviors that reflect socially approved values, their behavior will help determine a healthy ethical climate for the organization.

A leader's *directive behavior* also conveys important information regarding the ethical climate. By clearly specifying ethical policies and practices through organizational codes of ethics, continuing education and training on ethical issues, implementing internal ethics committees to respond to employees' concerns and questions, and insuring regular coverage of ethical issues in the company newsletter, leaders help keep ethical considerations in the forefront of followers' behavioral decisions.

Ethical leaders also use *contingent reward and punishment* behaviors to establish a climate of ethical behavior. They do this by rewarding individuals and groups who accomplish goals by acting in ways that are consistent with organizational values. This often requires developing a set of measures for ethical behavior so leaders can accurately identify actions that deserve a reward. The literature on organizational citizenship behavior provides a set of concepts that have been suggested as indicators of ethical behavior. These behaviors include *altruistic behavior* (such as going out of your way to help other employees), *conscientiousness* (such as doing a better job than expected), *courtesy* (such as giving advance notice of upcoming projects), *civic virtue* (such as regular attendance and active participation in meetings), and *sportsmanship* (such as not complaining and not making mountains out of mole hills). Individuals who demonstrate these behaviors encourage a culture that values consideration and helping of all participants. Leaders who watch for and reward organizational citizenship behaviors help create a climate that emphasizes these values.

Ethical leaders also discipline employees who fail to adhere to company values. One executive described how two leaders handled sexual harassment cases in their respective organizations. Both cases involved a pattern of harassment that was well documented. The ethical leader was quick to dismiss the wrongdoer. The leader then sent an e-mail message to all employees explaining the ethics violation (harassment), the general circumstances of the incidents, and the consequences to the employee and the company. This type of e-mail became a pattern for the leader each time an ethics violation occurred. The other leader delayed taking action regarding the harassment, and this allowed the rumor mill to take over. People began to believe that the leader was condoning the unethical conduct. The harassing individual was then allowed to quietly resign, and was given glowing recommendation letters (with no mention of the harassment) that allowed him to obtain a position of greater responsibility in another organization. The individual's departure was attributed to "personal reasons" and nothing more was said about the incident. The first leader used the harassment incident (and others similar to it) to emphasize a climate of justice, personal responsibility, and fair treatment. The second leader's behavior demonstrated that unethical behavior may be ignored or used to benefit the perpetrator. Both actions by these leaders help set a precedent for their respective organizations. One encourages a climate in which ethical conduct is expected and valued, the other may actually encourage unethical behavior.

Participative leadership behavior is also essential for establishing an ethical climate. Ethical leaders provide forums for dialogue and discussion of ethical assumptions and practices in the organization. The focus of these dialogues is to increase understanding of ethical approaches and assumptions. Understanding different ethical approaches helps people assess their own and others' behavior, and knowingly select ethical courses of action. Freedom of dissent should be an element in these discussions. This involves supporting individual responsibility to speak out if a person believes the organization is acting unethically.[26] Levi Strauss and Motorola both encourage open, honest communication, including permission to dissent. Leaders who fail to support dissent leave their organization's ethical practices unquestioned, and may doom their organization to repeating ethical failures.

Ethical leaders also organize discussions of past actions of the organization that have ethical implications. These discussions require everyone to think about and learn from these past actions by exchanging ideas and asking leaders for an explanation or clarification of the reasons and objectives of these actions. Examining ethical blunders often results in important learning, especially for people who were not closely involved with the incident or decision under discussion. Discussing sound ethical actions or decisions can also provide useful reference points for organizational members. This practice of involving followers in discussions of real ethical incidents in the organization encourages everyone to examine organizational responses and processes, and makes ethical assumptions and approaches clearer to everyone involved. This allows for more discussion about whether these existing assumptions and approaches are appropriate for the future. With this practice, the leader continuously tests the validity of the existing ethical assumptions and approaches through dialogue with employees, and helps establish a climate of ongoing moral and ethical learning.

When these leadership actions are successful in creating a strong ethical climate for an organization, the organizational values often become adopted by individual members as personal values. They thus become moral imperatives, and actions consistent with these values are seen as the right thing to do. Leaders can reinforce this process by emphasizing specific behaviors as the only ethically acceptable alternative.

Managers at a construction site used this strategy by posting a sign that read: "Wear your hard hat—it's the right thing to do." The leadership of a military installation posted a sign that read: "Unfriendly eyes are watching: It's your DUTY to safeguard information." Even if all employees do not adopt the organization's values as their own, research shows that when people learn the ethical rules and expectations of their organization, they usually follow them whether they agree with them or not.[27]

⠿ Charismatic or Transformational Leadership and Ethics

In Chapter 8, we described transformational leadership as primarily composed of elements of charismatic leadership. James McGregor Burns initially described transforming leadership as motivating followers to strive for higher-level values and morality. His description involved raising the consciousness of followers to reflect real societal needs and values rather than personal self-interest. Transformational leadership was based on Burns' model, and currently specifies idealized influence (charisma), inspiration, intellectual stimulation, and consideration as key elements. Bass and Steidlmeier[28] recognized that these four elements are themselves morally neutral, and can be used to benefit or oppress followers. Howell and Avolio[29] proposed that real transformational leaders were motivated by social power motives rather than the desire for personal power. Their social motives were altruistic and primarily aimed at benefiting the group, organization, or society.

Charismatic or transformational leaders are considered unethical when their behavior reflects a self-serving or egotistical bias rather than altruistic values. They are either totally committed to benefiting their own self-interest, or their commitment to social values is so weak that they are overwhelmed by self-serving temptations. This explanation of unethical charismatic or transformational leaders is inadequate, however, because it excludes many whose behavior is unethical for another reason. Some charismatic or transformational leaders behave unethically because they are so committed to other-oriented values that they mistakenly believe generally applicable moral requirements do not apply to them. Their position can be described by the classic phrase "the ends justify the means," and they believe their excessive behavior is necessary and therefore acceptable because their motives are for the long-term benefit of the larger group or society. One example of this was Mao Zedong's repression, torture, and executions to "raise the standards of health and literacy" and "revive the revolutionary spirit of ordinary people."[30] Another was President Harry Truman's decision to drop the first atomic bombs on civilian populations at Hiroshima and Nagasaki, which was justified as necessary to end World War II in the Pacific. Many writers have judged these actions as ethical mistakes because they violated normal moral expectations in order to achieve their higher-order values.

The theory of transformational leadership assumes that the leader knows (and followers do not know) what values followers should be inspired to achieve,[31] or that followers are unable to resist the temptations of pursuing their own selfish interests in order to strive for the greater good. One writer recently described this assumption: ". . . followers sometimes act on what they want because they do not know what they [really] need."[32] This type of assumption about the ignorance of followers and the superior knowledge and insight of transformational leaders is probably unhealthy. It encourages leaders to believe they are so superior that normal ethical requirements do not apply to their behavior. One wonders if the popularity of charismatic or transformational leadership in corporate America, combined with this assumption of superior knowledge, has resulted in the abuses and violations of public trust that seem so common in large corporations recently. As we noted in Chapter 8, charismatic or transformational leadership can be dangerous, partly because of the ethical risks these leaders are inclined to take, and their implications for followers and other stakeholders.

⣿ Spirituality

In addition to their interest in ethical issues, many leaders have turned to spirituality for moral guidance at work. The following assumptions are implicit in the spirituality movement in work organizations: (1) Spirituality is part of our nature as humans; (2) The content of our work and the context (environment) help determine our total work experience; (3) The work context or content today are often injurious to the human spirit and may be getting worse; (4) Embracing spirituality at work may help counteract these injurious trends and benefit organizations, their members, and communities.[33]

Spirituality describes an awareness by individuals of the human need to grow or develop internally toward their vision of an ideal self. This growth process is very personal (that is, it may be different for each person), and the individual must not become alienated or estranged from their own self or their ideal self in order to remain spiritually healthy. This means a spiritually healthy person accepts themselves as they are but continually strives to become more similar to their vision of their ideal self. Spirituality in leadership involves this constant striving toward the ideal self, as leaders fulfill their roles, responsibilities, and relationships in organizations. For most leaders, this means incorporating higher-order (often religious) values into their leadership behavior.

Organizational leaders and researchers often describe two processes as necessary to enact their spirituality at work—self-reflection and connection. Leaders use different techniques to reflect on (or think about) their inner self and their ideal self— religious practices, meditation, and astrology were all used by leaders in one study.[34] These methods often allow individuals to clear their minds and focus more clearly and objectively on their spiritual condition. Nearly all leaders also describe some type of connection—a need to relate to something—as key to their spirituality. Some describe connecting with their inner self and emphasize self-growth or self-realization. Others describe connecting with something external—a higher entity, power, deity, or God.

Organizational leaders use numerous practices to encourage the self-reflection and connection needed for their own and their followers' spiritual growth. These practices include prayer, discussing and fostering followers' self-actualization, stating and modeling value systems or codes of ethics, group or individual meditation, chanting mantras, or organization-wide communications with religious content. In a study of Asian leaders in a multireligious and multiethnic context, one researcher found religious practices to be the dominant means used to enact spirituality at work.[35] These leaders relied on their faith to guide their self-reflection and connect them with an external source of guidance and protection.

Another writer on spirituality in leadership in the United States reached the same conclusion. James Bailey maintains that religion and spirituality are inseparable. A spiritual connection may be seen in nature, modern technology, new age perspectives, or traditional religious institutions. Religions usually view spirituality as a *focus* on reflection and connection with individuals or entities such as God, Mohammed, Jesus, Buddha, or Allah. This focus implies a faith that is practiced by leaders in all areas of their life, including work organizations. Bailey cites a papal encyclical by Pope John Paul II entitled *On Human Work,* in which he argues that work is a unique human activity that has value because it is intimately connected with human striving for connectedness with God.[36] The excerpt contained in the Leadership in Action box describes the experience of a consultant to several high-level business executives.

The current interest in spirituality in leadership and work organizations may reflect a resurgence of interest in religion in the general population. Several researchers have concluded that spirituality in leadership can result in improvements in creativity and innovation, teamwork, decision making, morale, integrity, values, and ethics in organizations.[37–40] They also point to a sense of personal satisfaction, inner peace, a sense of being guided or protected, and enhanced organizational reputation.[41] Improvements in the moral character of employees are often described by leaders who advocate spirituality at work.

Critics of spirituality at work often claim that organizations cannot accommodate diverse spiritual beliefs. But researchers report that committed leaders find ways to

LEADERSHIP IN ACTION

A Consultant's Description of Spirituality Among CEOs

Several years ago, I was consulting with a group of 12 CEOs whom I think most would agree were first-rate managerial leaders. They were members of an ongoing group that met monthly to discuss their organizational problems. In the midst of their discussions, one of them described a business decision with which he had recently been confronted. It involved an extraordinarily complex set of circumstances. If he made the wrong decision, his business went bankrupt. If he made the correct decision, his business survived. He made the correct decision.

"How did you make it?" one of his colleagues asked.

"God only knows," was his reply.

Taking a leap of faith worthy of Kierkegaard, I asked, "What does God know that we don't?"

And he told us. In fact, he told us that every night for a week, he had gotten on his knees and prayed that God would lead him to the correct decision. Finally, he was convinced that God had spoken to him and he responded to God's command.

After what seemed to be an interminable silence, another CEO said, "I'll be God damned, I thought I was the only one in this bunch who prayed when I got in trouble."

Then, one by one, they began to discuss their prayer lives.

On the basis of what I learned from that experience and a lot of similar ones, I have found that many major decisions at the highest level of all kinds of organizations are made on the basis of prayer. Furthermore, I find that leaders who wield extraordinary influence in a wide variety of venues are deeply concerned about the spiritual side of their leadership roles, and they are starved for opportunities to discuss it. But when they do discuss their spiritual concerns, they mostly do so using words such as "God," "Allah," "religion," "prayer," "church," "worship," "Jesus," and "Buddha." They do not talk about "work spirit," "spirit," "organizational transformation," "open space," "energy sources," and "organization as community."

SOURCE: J. B. Harvey. Reflections on books by authors who apparently are terrified about really exploring spirituality in leadership. *Leadership Quarterly,* 12(2), 2001, 377. Copyright © 2001 with permission from Elsevier.

include a diversity of spiritual beliefs and practices for the benefit of everyone involved. Seeking inclusive frameworks for diversity of spiritual beliefs may become a critical skill for leaders of the future. Figure 12-3 summarizes the approaches for creating an ethical organizational climate.

▪▪▪ Diversity

The United States population, the workforce, and the buying public are rapidly changing. The population is getting older, it is composed of increasing numbers of ethnic and racial groups with varying cultural backgrounds, and an increasing number of women are working full time and are attaining high-level positions in organizations. The age, race, gender, ethnic heritage, mental and physical capabilities, and sexual orientation of

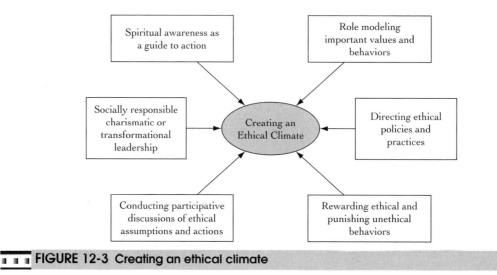

▪▪▪ **FIGURE 12-3 Creating an ethical climate**

organizational members and customers are becoming the basis for identifiable groups that demand respect and equal treatment. The U.S. population and the workforce are not a melting pot in which all groups blend together, but rather a "salad" of diverse groups of people who want to maintain their own beliefs and customs and still participate fully in organizations. Organizations are also increasingly global in their orientation, and they employ individuals and market products and services to people in different parts of the world with widely varying cultural beliefs and practices. Leaders in the new millennium face the difficult task of integrating these diverse groups of individuals into a unified effort to achieve organizational goals efficiently and effectively.

Diversity refers to the multiple social, cultural, physical, and environmental differences among people that affect the way they think, feel, and behave.[42] Diversity includes race, ethnicity, gender, age, mental and physical abilities, sexual orientation, religion, social class, and other dimensions that create important differences among people. How these differences are perceived and interpreted are influenced by culture. We can think of culture as the shared mental programming of a group of people. Culture tells us who we are, what groups we belong to and identify with, and how we should behave. Culture also provides us with certain perspectives and attitudes toward people who are different from us, and tells us how we should act toward these people. Our own culture surrounds us so completely that we are often unaware of it, and we may not realize there are very different views of the world and different ways of responding to people and situations.[43]

Because different groups often have different cultures, their values, norms, and behavior patterns frequently vary. Different groups may also address ethical issues in different ways. Behaviors that are totally acceptable in one group or culture may be unacceptable in others. One example of this occurs with the U.S. Foreign Corrupt Practices Act of 1977, which forbids bribery of foreign individuals to facilitate business transactions. However, in many African, Asian, and Middle Eastern countries, bribery is accepted as common practice. Another example is when U.S. companies do business in Mexico, the common response to a request is *"no problema,"* apparently meaning the request will be easily met. However, many U.S. business people have been frustrated when they learned that *"no problema"* is a way for Mexicans to smooth over relations with foreigners and to protect their own interests. U.S. managers sometimes view this response as lying. The treatment of women is another issue that varies widely among cultures. Scandinavian countries have done much to promote equality between men and women, but Saudi Arabia and Japan view women's roles as caring for the home, and they are excluded from leadership positions. Individuals from Scandinavia may view Saudis or Japanese as morally wrong in their treatment of women. *Ethnocentrism* is the tendency to perceive the world from our culture group's point of view.[44] Our values, norms, and practices become the standard for judging other cultural groups. If their norms and behavior are different from our own, they are viewed as wrong.

Cultures play an important role in maintaining a society and group of people. They structure behavior to help perpetuate the species, pass on hard-earned lessons to future generations, and provide knowledge about how to obtain food and shelter, care for the sick, cope with death, and deal with the living.[45] Cultures change over time, however, as new ideas and concepts arise that are more effective in dealing with problems. These changes often come from other cultures. Arabic numerals are better than Roman numerals, so they became the common means of counting and performing mathematical operations throughout the known world. Printing from China allowed the creation of books, which were much more efficient to pass on knowledge and history than handwritten scrolls. Music, art, language, and foods from other cultures all enrich our lives and open us up to other ways of living. Diverse cultures thus provide us with new information, ideas, techniques, and ways of dealing with life and people that enrich our experience as human beings.

Between the years 2000 and 2015, only 15 percent of the individuals entering the U.S. workforce will be white males. People of color represent the majority population in at least 16 of the top 25 urban markets in the United States. Globalization is one of the most significant trends in the 21st century. Increasing numbers of organizations are involved in operations in other countries. Organizations must draw their members and customers from this changing population, and leaders must acknowledge and value these differences to improve organizational operations and outcomes.

There are many competitive advantages that accrue to an organization when its leaders truly appreciate diversity and act to integrate diverse groups in their organization. One key benefit for organizations that promote diversity is being able to attract and hire the best personnel available. As labor pools shrink and their composition changes, it will be increasingly important to draw from all available workers to obtain the most competent people. Marketing also benefits from diversity in organizations. Including employees from different ethnic groups and different countries helps organizations design and deliver products for these diverse markets. Diverse perspectives in organizations help avoid overconformity to norms from the past and thereby improve creativity and problem solving because a wider range of alternatives are considered. With more ideas available, organizations are less likely to become rigid in their procedures and can respond in a more flexible manner to frequent environmental changes. Cost savings should also accrue to organizations that move quickly to promote diversity because they will become more experienced and efficient at integrating individuals from different groups into their operations. Figure 12-4 summarizes these competitive advantages of diversity in organizations.

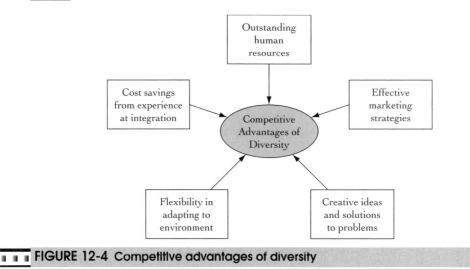

▮▮▮ **FIGURE 12-4 Competitive advantages of diversity**

Barriers to Diversity

Ethnocentrism is the tendency to view the world from our own cultural perspective, and to judge others' values, norms, and behaviors as wrong if they differ from our own. The effects of extreme ethnocentrism were demonstrated in the late 1800s when the U.S. Bureau of Indian Affairs forced Native Americans to send their children to reservation schools and punished these children if they spoke their tribal languages. In Australia, government representatives once kidnapped aboriginal children and placed them with white families.[46] An ethnocentric perspective will prevent organizational leaders from taking the actions that are needed to obtain and integrate a high-quality workforce needed to deal with the challenges of the 21st century. Two major tendencies emerge from an ethnocentric view that are major barriers to diversity.

Stereotypes are labels we use to typecast all members of a group (with whom we have little contact) as though they are all clones from the same mold.[47] Stereotypes make our interactions with members of unfamiliar groups easy, because they provide predetermined attitudes toward these individuals and ways of interacting with them. They cause us to perceive all members of one group as, for example, ignorant, musical, boring, uncaring, or power hungry. Stereotypes discourage us from recognizing and appreciating differences among people, and these differences may be important for effective organizational performance.

A related tendency is *prejudice* toward certain groups of people. Prejudice is the prejudgment of something without adequate knowledge of the facts. When we are prejudiced toward a group of people, we often develop negative opinions about them with little or no prior experience to support those opinions. This prejudice may be based on rumors or learned from others in our cultural group. Most of us have some prejudices in that we prefer to socialize with people from our own age group or ethnic group. Strong negative prejudice can be very damaging because it produces discrimination. For example, police in some urban areas believe that young, male African Americans are prone to commit crimes. Consequently, the police are more likely to stop and question young, black males, and to quickly use force if there is any sign of resistance.[48] Another example occurs in many business organizations in which there has been a prejudicial belief that women are not suited for high-level leadership positions. This resulted in women being excluded from executive positions—frequently referred to as the "glass ceiling."

Leaders need to recognize their own ethnocentric views, stereotypes, and prejudices, and encourage others to challenge their beliefs. Training and development programs (described later in this chapter) should begin with top-level leaders because their commitment is needed to make diversity programs work throughout the organization. Diversity among high-level leaders must also be a part of any successful diversity management program.

Diversity Among Leaders

In the United States, the most common image of an effective organizational leader is a white male who was born in the U.S.[49] This means that leadership positions are often dominated by white males who are U.S. born. This image is also reflected in personnel policies and practices that create barriers for women, minorities, and foreign nationals who aspire to leadership positions. Today, these barriers are probably most difficult to overcome for those seeking top-level leadership positions.

In spite of the difficulties and barriers, the representation of minorities in leadership positions has increased considerably. In 1972, women held only 18 percent of managerial and administrative positions in the U.S.; by 2002, this figure was 46 percent.[50] In Fortune 500 companies, the percentage of women serving as CEOs and corporate officers is at an all-time high. In 1990, 13.2 percent of black men and 19.2 percent of black women were employed as managers or professionals; in 2000 these numbers had increased to 17.7 percent and 25.2 percent, respectively.[51] Male and female black leaders are visible at all levels in U.S.-based corporations. These changes probably reflect federally mandated programs such as affirmative action, as well as diversity awareness and diversity management initiatives in organizations. They may also result from the evolution of many leadership roles in organizations away from a hierarchical power-based style toward a more supportive and participative style.

Early studies showed that girls are socialized to show consideration and caring for others, and boys are socialized to compete and perform. Leadership scholars often assumed that women would therefore place more importance on satisfying others' needs, and men would value equity and fairness in allocating rewards.[52] Researchers later found that women emphasized establishing rapport in their communications, whereas men focused on establishing reporting relationships.[53] The actual research findings on differences in leadership behavior between men and women are often unclear. A "feminine" leadership style is often described as highly supportive and caring of followers' needs, which seems consistent with findings on socialization processes for girls. Research shows that when college students or women who aspire to leadership are studied in experiments or assessment centers, they do show more supportiveness than men in these simulated leadership situations. However, studies of men and women who have *attained* leadership positions show no differences in the amount of supportiveness given to followers.[54] This may be due to women adapting their leadership style to match a male leadership prototype, or it may reflect another finding that women leaders have higher power needs than other professional women.[55]

Whatever the reason, the popular belief that female leaders show more caring and support for their followers than male leaders is not supported by scientific research.

There is one difference between men and women leaders that is supported by research. Women who have attained leadership positions show a more participative, democratic style with their followers than do male leaders.[56] Women leaders have also been found to be more effective in leadership positions that are viewed as less masculine (such as in education or social service organizations).[57] These organizational situations probably include a large portion of highly trained service-oriented followers who appreciate a participative leader who consults with them in decision making. Male leaders have been found to be more effective in leadership positions viewed as more masculine (such as manufacturing or military organizations). A more directive leadership style is probably prototypical of these organizational situations. The Leadership in Action box describes a female leader who has excelled in a traditionally masculine leadership role.

Masculinity is a personality characteristic reflecting assertive, aggressive, and confrontational tendencies. This characteristic is found in individuals who emerge as leaders in studies of leaderless groups (that is, where no formal leader has been appointed). Although both men and women may possess these masculine tendencies, there is evidence that female leaders receive more negative responses and fewer positive responses in groups than male leaders. Thus, even though females can be effective in leadership positions, they likely face negative social interpretations that decrease their opportunities for promotions and challenging assignments. These negative interpretations may also cause them to leave organizations. Many of these women become entrepreneurs and are quite successful running their own business organizations.

There is relatively little research comparing white leaders versus leaders of color. Studies of black managers show they perceive race to negatively impact their performance appraisals, pay, recognition, and promotion. They often feel less accepted in their organizations than whites, and have fewer opportunities for forming networks that can provide important psychosocial support.[58] Early research showed black leaders to be more supportive of followers, whereas white leaders were more directive and possibly more coercive, especially with black followers.[59,60] A comparative study of Asian American managers and Caucasian American managers showed only minor differences in influence tactics, although both groups used different tactics when influencing subordinates as compared to supervisors.[61] There is not enough research yet to make definitive conclusions about leadership style differences between white leaders and leaders of color.

The combination of sex and race can, however, be especially meaningful to certain individuals. Black women in the United States have historically worked at many arduous jobs at the bottom of the labor market that many white men and women avoided. And black male managers report that they need to be especially careful when meeting with white female subordinates to assure their behaviors are not misread. A stereotypical perception of black men as sexual predators who love every white woman can affect the promotion opportunities and responsibilities given to effective black managers.[62] Discrimination can be especially severe for men who are large and dark complexioned. Black male leaders indicate they must constantly exert special care in their body language and leadership behavior so as not to intimidate white females or other personnel.

LEADERSHIP IN ACTION
CEO Kathleen Ligocki

Kathleen Ligocki is a corporate leader who believes that being a woman has been an advantage in her career. Ms. Ligocki had no intention of having a career in business. She obtained a degree in liberal studies and needed money for graduate school, so she took a job as a factory foreman at General Motors. She learned to enjoy the pace and culture of the factory and moved into numerous other positions at GM and Ford, including sales, engineering, purchasing, finance, strategy, mergers, and general management. She moved 18 times in 23 years. She eventually became CEO of Ford Mexico and Ford vice president for Canada, Mexico, and North America strategy, before recently accepting the position of president and CEO for Tower Automotive, Inc.

Tower Automotive makes metal body structures and other component parts for the major automakers. Tower reported $2.8 billion in sales last year, but it also has a lot of long-term debt and is being pressured by automakers to reduce costs and prices. It employs over 12,000 people in 14 countries. Ms. Ligocki plans to diversify the customer mix at Tower Automotive by decreasing the percentage of its sales to Ford and GM and increasing sales to overseas producers like Toyota and Renault-Nisson.

Ms. Ligocki believes that women typically learn to listen before they seek to satisfy their own needs, and this gives them an advantage in organizations by helping to build bridges with others. She noted that listening without judging can create a bond between people that facilitates cooperation. She has also indicated that the situation is changing for women in business. "When I joined, it was all about adapting to the dominant norm." But the auto industry is starting to realize other styles of leading and working are also valuable for business.

Ligocki is a high-energy individual who is sociable and easy to like. She works 70 to 80 hours per week and is almost never in her office. Traveling and visiting with colleagues, coworkers, and customers keeps her in touch with current conditions. She has studied and speaks several languages, and believes they help her understand how people think in different cultures. With Towers' business projected to grow in Europe and Asia, this insight into other cultures will be valuable.

"The auto industry is a tough business," Ligocki noted. She believes that people must enjoy the challenge to be successful. She has a determination to succeed at each new position, and does not complain about stress because she loves her work.

SOURCES: Ligocki takes unusual path to CEO role in male-dominated industry. *Las Cruces Sun News,* July 18, 2004; From art history student to CEO. *Women Working,* July 18, 2004, www.creativeexpansions.com/feature/index/php?id=29; and Rachel Miller. Kathleen Ligocki: Supplying fresh ideas for Ford. *Road and Travel Magazine,* www.roadandtravel.com/celebrities/kathleenligocki.htm.

Cultural differences can also affect the values and behaviors of leaders in different countries. For example, in Thailand (which is high in power distance, a cultural characteristic reflecting a tendency to accept unequal distributions of power in society), close directive supervision is expected. However, in the United States (which is lower in power distance), a more democratic participative approach is valued.[63] Another example was reported by international researchers who found that participative leadership was not effective in traditional Mexican organizations, but an autocratic directive approach was often expected.[64] A similar finding was reported in Russia.[65] Much cross-cultural research is currently ongoing, but it is safe to say that cultural differences must be considered in managing people from different countries and cultural backgrounds. Leadership behaviors that are effective with workers who are born and raised in the United States may not be effective in other countries or with individuals who are not born and raised in the United States.

Creating a Multicultural Organization

Leaders of a diverse workforce face many obstacles, including prejudices and stereotypes, lack of understanding of other cultures, and fear by the majority of losing their advantaged status. But leaders can create and direct certain programs that help overcome these obstacles. These programs can help change the organization and its members from an *ethnocentric* cultural perspective ("our way is the right way") toward a *multicultural perspective,* in which there is a true appreciation of the value of diversity for solving organizational and societal problems.

One major goal of diversity programs deals with *acculturation,* which is how cultural differences between the dominant culture group and the minority culture group are resolved or addressed. This can be done through *assimilation,* in which the minority group is expected to adopt the norms and values of the majority group. It can also be addressed through *separatism,* in which little adaptation of either group occurs. These two strategies usually add very little to the organization's competitiveness, and often result in resentment and conflict. A more constructive alternative is for the organization to try to create *pluralism,* in which both the majority and minority group cultures partially adapt to each other. With pluralism, members of the minority culture are encouraged to enact behaviors from their own culture as well as the majority culture, and thereby retain a sense of their own cultural identity.[66]

Training and orientation programs are a key strategy for creating pluralism. Two types of training are common—*awareness building* and *skill building.* Awareness building generally provides an introduction to the importance of diversity, as well as information on types of diversity, workforce demographics, and exercises to get participants to think about diversity issues. Skill building usually provides information about cultural norms of specific groups and how they might affect employee behavior in the organization. McDonnell Douglas developed a program on gender differences in work behaviors that includes mixed gender role plays and some gender discussions. Hewlett-Packard does training on cultural differences in communication styles between American Anglos and Mexican, Indochinese, and Filipino employees. Data from a Canadian study showed that even the simplest form of diversity training increased participants' awareness and appreciation for diversity in organizations.[67]

Language training can also be important for organizations that employee Hispanics, Asian Americans, or foreign nationals. Offering second-language training to Anglos as well as minorities shows a commitment to valuing languages other than English. These classes are generally conducted on company time and at company expense. Directing that diverse groups be represented on key committees and including diversity in mission statements also shows the value placed on different perspectives. Establishing minority advisory groups to meet with top-level leaders on how the internal organizational environment might be improved demonstrates leadership concern and support for these initiatives.

Formal integration of minorities at all organizational levels is required to create an organization in which a person's culture-identity group is unrelated to their job status. This requires that education and skill levels must be the same for all groups. In the past, this has been a problem for Hispanics and Blacks. *In-house education* programs have addressed this issue in many companies, such as Aetna Life Insurance, Quaker Oats, Eastman Kodak, and Digital Equipment Corporation. Joint programs with colleges and universities are needed to promote equal educational achievement that is necessary to keep U.S. business organizations competitive.

Affirmative action programs are the starting point for many diversity programs by bringing minorities into organizations. *Career development plans* that provide advice, coaching, and promotional paths for minorities are also useful. Xerox has an excellent development program that provides a national network for minorities, career paths, and support to move minorities into professional and management positions.[68] *Management appraisal and reward systems* must include (and emphasize) recruitment and development of minority employees. Benefits and work schedules must also be flexible to help employees balance work and family roles. *Childcare, parental leave,* and *flexible work schedules* are common, and some companies allow professionals or managers to work part-time for several years and remain eligible for promotion.

Informal integration is also essential to maintain minority participation and full contribution to organizational activities. Company-initiated *mentoring programs* are helpful, although these programs work best if they operate as informally as possible. Surveys show that racial and ethnic minorities have less access to mentors than do nonminorities. *Company-sponsored social events* also help with forming informal networks. Some organizations encourage *minority support groups* to help members exchange information and provide social support.

Programs to eliminate prejudice, stereotypes, and discrimination in hiring, promotion and compensation decisions are needed to create a bias-free organization. *Seminars* in sexual harassment, racism, and civil rights are common. *Bias-reduction training* focuses on exposing individuals' prejudices and stereotypes, and participants in these sessions report more positive attitudes toward minorities. *Focus groups* of employees are also being used more frequently to expose and dispel stereotypes and to help participants build working relationships with people they view as different. *Task forces* are used to monitor organizational policies and practices to identify any evidence of unfairness.[69]

Although some conflict is often healthy for organizations to prevent rigidity in procedures and practices, conflict that results from resentment of minority-based initiatives can be destructive. Survey feedback (using anonymous questionnaires to obtain input from employees) regarding diversity programs and issues is especially helpful with this problem. If it exists, actual data from company records should be obtained and used to respond. Several organizations track the length of time taken for various groups to become fully integrated into the organization. One company found the time varied according to gender and race, with black females taking the longest. Another firm demonstrated that promotion rates for white men were seven times higher than for white women, and sixteen times higher than for women of color. These differences in promotion rates were not supported by differences in performance. This type of data is usually helpful in convincing all parties to support needed changes.

These programs can help move organizations toward multiculturalism. Multicultural organizations reflect pluralism, formal and informal integration of minority group members, lack of prejudice, stereotyping, and discrimination, and low levels of intergroup conflict. By doing this, they reduce alienation and build commitment among minority employees and create an environment in which all organizational members can maximize their potential.

Leadership for Diversity

Directive leadership is needed in organizations to establish diversity-related programs and to emphasize their importance for organizational competitiveness. This was effectively carried out by the president of a large engineering firm when he publicized the goal or vision for their diversity efforts: ". . . to significantly improve the company's ability to hire, retain, and use people from all social and cultural backgrounds and to improve the performance of the organization by tapping the full potential of the entire workforce."[70] Another example occurred when leaders in a large consumer electronics firm required that all employees enroll in 40 hours of diversity training per year. Courses were taught throughout the organization. Top-level leaders must be involved to symbolize to organizational members that diversity is a high-priority issue. This was demonstrated when the top-level managers in a manufacturing plant opened and closed every session of diversity awareness training in the plant. It was also shown when a general manager conducted feedback meetings on the results of a diversity assessment of the organization's climate, and when a vice president of human resources designed and conducted a series of seminars on the principles of managing diversity. These examples show top-level leaders providing direction for their organizations' diversity efforts as well as *role modeling* behaviors for other managers. Leaders who demonstrate zero tolerance for sexual harassment and derogatory comments about personnel from foreign affiliate organizations are also providing important role modeling of multicultural values.

Leaders must also use *supportive* behaviors, such as mentoring to help minority individuals adapt to organizational conditions that are new to them. Leaders must listen to followers' frustrations and concerns, and coach them as they work through needed adjustments on the job. Whenever possible, leaders also provide support through work and family policies dealing with flextime, childcare, eldercare, and part-time work to demonstrate that the organization values and respects employees who are trying to balance work and family responsibilities. Leaders also use *boundary-spanning* behaviors as they help followers build networks and connect with support groups composed of others who have had similar experiences. These informal networks and connections are crucial for fully integrating minority members into organizational operations. Leaders also use *participative leadership* when they support internal advocacy groups, and conduct feedback sessions and discussions on the results of diversity programs. This helps leaders obtain input from followers to keep these programs relevant and oriented to followers' problems and concerns.

Leaders' contingent reward behavior is also essential to assure that diversity efforts are taken seriously. Including a rated behavior in performance appraisals on the extent to which managers value and promote diversity is a good place to start. This will help leaders develop a list of diversity-competent behaviors to be included in future training sessions. Including diversity issues in goal-setting sessions and as criteria for promotion decisions will send a clear message to organization members on the importance

⊩⊩⊩ FIGURE 12-5 Leadership for diversity

of diversity. Informally, leaders should recognize and compliment followers for success in completing diversity training and development programs, and for applying the training to their work situation. They must also celebrate the promotion of nontraditional minorities into positions of increasing responsibility.

Leaders who recognize that people are similar in some ways and different in other ways are best prepared to realize the values and benefits of diversity.[71] Looking for similarities between themselves and others who initially appear quite different brings out the commonalities among people. This can reduce resentment and conflict that is sometimes associated with diversity because it creates common reference points to guide future interactions.[72] Leaders who look for these similarities and demonstrate patience, flexibility, and a willingness to listen are best able to implement the leadership behaviors and diversity programs described previously. Their organizations should be well prepared to effectively utilize the rich and diverse workforce of the 21st century. Figure 12-5 summarizes leadership behaviors that help promote diversity and multiculturalism in organizations.

SUMMARY   ⊩⊩⊩⊩⊩⊩⊩

Recent scandals involving executives in large U.S. business organizations have made most people skeptical about the ethical practices of organizational leaders. Ethics is the study of morality (right and wrong) and the choices people make in their relationships with others. Leaders deal with numerous ethical issues in organizations, including power, moral standards, moral consistency, moral mistakes, and ethics versus effectiveness. Different approaches have been suggested for dealing with these issues, such as following universal moral laws, the greatest good for the greatest number, having a primary concern for others' welfare, promoting high moral character in leaders, and persistently striving to be just, prudent, and truthful in one's behavior. Creating an ethical organizational climate requires leaders to role model ethical behaviors, direct and reward ethical policies and practices, punish unethical behavior, participatively discuss ethical assumptions and practices, and use charismatic or transformational leadership behaviors in a socially responsible manner. Many leaders are turning to spiritual or religious practices to help them deal with ethical issues.

Diversity refers to the multiple social, cultural, physical, and environmental differences among people that affect the way we think, feel, and behave. Our organizations, markets, and the general population are all composed of increasingly diverse groups of people. Leaders must act to include these diverse groups if organizations are to successfully recruit qualified personnel, market their products or services, and solve problems in creative and responsible ways. Overcoming barriers such as ethnocentrism (the belief that my ways are always right and others are wrong), stereotypes, and prejudice requires much effort by leaders. Important leadership activities include initiating and directing diversity seminars and training; supporting the creation of flexible personnel policies, mentoring programs, and career development; boundary spanning to help minorities build networks and support groups; participating in training and discussion sessions on diversity issues and programs; and rewarding and recognizing those who promote and participate in diversity programs. These behaviors can help create an ethical organizational culture in which all organizational members can maximize their potential.

KEY TERMS AND CONCEPTS IN THIS CHAPTER ▐▐▐▐▐▐▐

- Acculturation
- Affirmative action
- Altruism
- Assimilation
- Awareness building
- Categorical imperative
- Charismatic or transformational behavior
- Contingent reward and punishment
- Directive behavior

- Diversity
- Ethics
- Ethnocentrism
- Feminine leadership style
- Hardships
- Moral consistency
- Moral learning
- Moral mistakes
- Moral standards
- Multiculturalism
- Participative behavior

- Power
- Prejudice
- Role models
- Skill building
- Spirituality
- Stereotypes
- Supportive behavior
- Utilitarianism
- Value-driven mission
- Virtue ethics

REVIEW AND DISCUSSION QUESTIONS ▐▐▐▐▐▐▐

1. Why are leaders' ethics currently such a hot topic?
2. Describe the advantages and disadvantages of the different approaches for dealing with ethical issues by leaders.
3. Which leadership strategies or behaviors do you think would be most effective for creating an ethical organizational climate? Does your response depend on the type of organization? If so, why?
4. Why do you think that research on female leaders shows they are not more supportive of their followers than male leaders?
5. Why is a truly diverse workforce often difficult for an organization to achieve?
6. Do you believe a multicultural workforce is really possible in a large organization? Why or why not?

▪ ▪▪▪▪ C A S E   I N C I D E N T S ▪ ▪▪▪▪

Multiply-Abused Children

Save the Kids is a nonprofit group that pushes for tougher laws against those who sexually abuse children. Currently, Save the Kids is in its biggest lobbying effort ever in an attempt to get the state legislature to pass a law that requires convicted sex offenders to register their whereabouts with local police departments. The organization's founder, Steve Hanson, is convinced that such a law can significantly reduce the number of child abuse cases in the state. Unfortunately, contributions aren't keeping up with expenses, and Save the Kids may have to drastically reduce its lobbying efforts just as the sex offender registration bill comes before the legislature. Chances are, this law will pass only if Save the Kids keeps up its lobbying campaign. Mr. Hanson is now raising money for Save the Kids through a series of speeches. To encourage contributions, Hanson knowingly exaggerates both the number of convicted sex offenders in the state and the number of children who are abused every year. ▪

DISCUSSION QUESTIONS

1. Do you agree with Mr. Hanson's decision to exaggerate to raise money for Save the Kids? Why or why not?
2. Does the amount of exaggeration make a difference in your evaluation of Mr. Hanson's action? What if he decides to exaggerate only slightly? What if he greatly inflates the figures?
3. Do Mr. Hanson's intentional lies make a difference in how you evaluate his decision? What if he exaggerated because he didn't check his facts carefully?
4. How do you determine whether someone is justified in lying? What standards do you use to determine whether you should tell the truth?

SOURCE: Craig E. Johnson. *Meeting the Ethical Challenges of Leadership.* Thousand Oaks, CA: Sage, 2001, 36.

EXPERIENTIAL EXERCISE: BENEFITS OF MULTICULTURALISM ▪ ▪ ▪ ▪ ▪ ▪ ▪

Imagine yourself 5 years from now in a mid-level management position. Assume you are working for a company you chose after receiving several job offers upon graduating from college. You have done well with this company, having received two promotions thus far, and you are pleased with your progress.

The top-management team has reached the conclusion that the company must initiate programs to diversify the workforce, including the management personnel. They have directed all mid-level managers to explain to their department members the benefits of achieving a multicultural organization. You have called a meeting of your department members for this afternoon. You now need to outline the major points of your presentation. You begin by writing, "If we can be successful in creating a multicultural organization that truly values diversity of all types, our company will _____.

1. Complete this presentation by writing down the benefits of a multicultural organization that you will emphasize in your presentation.
2. Now describe the programs or policies that are needed to create this multicultural organization.

SOURCE: Adapted from T. Cox, Jr. *Creating the Multicultural Organization.* San Francisco: Jossey-Bass, 38.

Three Chinese Companies

Company A, Company B, and Hotel X are three state-owned enterprises in the southern part of the People's Republic of China. Company A is a shipbuilding company. Company B is a financial services conglomerate, and Hotel X is a subsidiary of Company B.

Company A suffered financial losses for two consecutive years in the mid-1990s. The newly appointed general manager (GM), Mr. F, identified three problems in the company: (1) incompetence of the top management team (TMT); (2) lack of motivation and initiative among employees and managers; and (3) ineffective enforcement of rules and regulations. To tackle the first problem, Mr. F replaced the old TMT with technically competent and performance-oriented managers that had integrity and were honest. To motivate employees, Mr. F and his new TMT announced at the first plenary meeting of the enterprise that employees' effort and performance would affect their rewards and employment status, and that idleness and poor performance would lead to dismissal from the company. To enforce rules and regulations, Mr. F and his TMT consulted with company employees to revise and reduce the number of rules in order to gain commitment. Task goals were specified, and reward and punishment were linked to achievement of business goals. In addition to reforming the managerial policies and practices in the company, Mr. F also

worked to establish a new culture of frugality, self-restraint, integrity, and service orientation by role modeling and communicating values and visions. Mr. F and his TMT's effort paid off. After one year, the company's sales improved, overhead was reduced, and the business became profitable. This favorable trend continued in the ensuing years.

Company B experienced heavy losses beginning in the mid-1990s. Although a new GM was appointed to turn the company around, it took an entire year to get approval from the provincial government to appoint a new TMT. The new GM and TMT eventually failed to prevent the company from being liquidated. Company B's bankruptcy was linked with three corrupt former company leaders: Mr. H, the former headquarters GM and Communist Party secretary; Mr. V, also a Communist Party secretary, and a former GM in an affiliated company; and Mr. O, the former GM in another affiliated company. All three leaders used their position power to create benefits for themselves, their families, and people with whom they had special *guanxi* (relationships). They pushed three-man rule inside the company, and took revenge against anyone who dared to speak up, either through dismissal or removal from their original positions. Outside the company, they actively developed a powerful social network for themselves through bribery and entertaining government officials at company expense. The model set by the top managers fostered a self-serving culture in the company. As a result, employees at all levels engaged in private business deals during office hours. Morale was extremely low, rules and regulations were not enforced, and junior staff avoided making suggestions to their managers, who were busy moonlighting in their personal businesses.

Hotel X was one of over 100 affiliated companies of Company B. Hotel X adopted Western-style hotel procedures in the early 1980s, but management was reluctant to update rules and regulations. Forty percent of the rules and regulations were not strictly enforced, and managers failed to abide by the rules themselves. There were no incentives for performance beyond the minimum requirements. Although a performance-based reward system was once proposed by the GM, it was rejected by the TMT at Company B headquarters. The GM attempted to make changes and build a strong organizational culture, but he eventually gave up because of a lack of cooperation from other managers who had strong connections with government officials and the TMT at Company B headquarters. Managers had a passive, uncaring attitude and morale was low. Employees at all levels were satisfied with minimal performance and were reluctant to make any upward suggestions. ▪

DISCUSSION QUESTIONS

1. Describe the organizational cultures in the three organizations.
2. What leadership behaviors of the leaders foster the organizational cultures in the three organizations?
3. What role did the leaders' ethics play in the performance of these three organizations?

SOURCE: L. J. Huang and R. S. Snell. Turnaround, corruption, and mediocrity: Leadership and governance in three state owned enterprises in mainland China. *Journal of Business Ethics,* 43, 2003, 111–124.

ENDNOTES ▪▪▪▪▪▪▪

1. Sims, P. R., and Brinkman, J. (2003). Enron ethics (Or: Culture matters more than codes). *Journal of Business Ethics,* 45, 243–256.
2. Josephson, M. (1999). Character: Linchpin of leadership. *Executive Excellence,* 16(8), 13–14.
3. Ciulla, J. B. (2003). Ethics and leadership effectiveness. In J. Antonakis, A. T. Cianciolo, and R. J. Sternberg (Eds.). *The Nature of Leadership.* Thousand Oaks, CA: Sage, 302–327.
4. Ibid.
5. Johnson, C. E. (2001). *Meeting the Ethical Challenges of Leadership.* Thousand Oaks, CA: Sage.
6. Hollander, E. (1995). Ethical challenges in the leader-follower relationship. *Business Ethics Quarterly,* 5, 55–65.
7. Ciulla. Ethics and leadership effectiveness.
8. Ibid.
9. Ibid.
10. Johnson. *Meeting the Ethical Challenges of Leadership.*
11. Ibid.
12. Kanungo, R. N., and Mendonca, M. (1996). *Ethical Dimensions of Leadership.* Thousand Oaks, CA: Sage.
13. Ciulla. Ethics and leadership effectiveness.
14. Ibid.
15. Kanungo and Mendonca. *Ethical Dimensions of Leadership.*
16. Ciulla. Ethics and leadership effectiveness.
17. Johnson, R. (1996). *Ethics in Human Communication,* 4th ed. Prospect Heights, IL: Waveland Press, 11.
18. Johannesen, R. L. (1991). Virtue ethics, character, and political communication. In

R. E. Denton (Ed.), *Ethical Dimensions of Political Communication.* New York: Praeger, 69–90.

19. Kouzes, J. M., and Posner, B. Z. (1993). Credibility: How leaders gain and lose it, why people demand it. San Francisco: Jossey-Bass.

20. Johnson. *Meeting the Ethical Challenges of Leadership.*

21. Argandona, A. (2001). Management and acting "beyond the call of duty." *Business Ethics: A European Review,* 10(4), 320–330.

22. Rest, J. (1986). *Moral Development: Advances in Research and Theory.* New York: Praeger.

23. Johnson. *Meeting the Ethical Challenges of Leadership.*

24. Jones, L. B. (1996). *The Path: Creating Your Own Mission Statement for Work and for Life.* New York: Hyperion.

25. Trevino, L. K., Hartman, L. P., and Brown, M. (2000). Moral person and moral manager: How executives develop a reputation for ethical leadership. *California Management Review,* 42(4), 128–142.

26. Gottlieb, J. Z., and Sanzgiri, J. (1996). Toward an ethical dimension of decision making in organizations. *Journal of Business Ethics,* 15, 1275–1285.

27. Dickson, M. W., Smith, D. B., Grojean, M. W., and Erhart, M. (2001). An organizational climate regarding ethics: The outcome of leader values and the practices that reflect them. *Leadership Quarterly,* 12(2), 197–217.

28. Bass, B., and Steidlmeier, P. (1999). Ethics, character, and authentic transformational leadership behavior. *Leadership Quarterly,* 10, 181–217.

29. Howell, J., and Avolio, B. (1992). The ethics of charismatic leadership: Submission or liberation? *Academy of Management Executive,* 6(2), 43–54.

30. Glover, J. (1999). *Humanity: A Moral History of the Twentieth Century.* New Haven, CT: Yale University Press.

31. Rost, J. C. (1991). *Leadership for the Twenty-First Century.* New York: Praeger.

32. Price, T. (2003). The ethics of authentic transformational leadership. *Leadership Quarterly,* 14(1), 67–81.

33. Fernando, M. (2003). Enacting spirituality at work: An empirical study. Paper presented at the National Academy of Management meeting, Seattle, WA.

34. Ibid.

35. Ibid.

36. Bailey, J. R. (2001). Review of *Spirit at Work: Discovering the Spirituality in Leadership. Leadership Quarterly,* 12(3), 367–368.

37. Neck, D., and Milliman J. (1994). Thought self leadership: Finding spiritual fulfillment in organizational life. *Journal of Managerial Psychology,* 9(6), 9–16.

38. Fort, T. (1996). Religious belief, corporate leadership, and business ethics. *American Business Law Journal,* 33(3), 451.

39. Greenleaf, R. K. (1970). *The Leader as Servant.* Indianapolis, IN: The Robert K. Greenleaf Center for Servant Leadership.

40. Senge, P. (1990). The leader's new work: Building learning organizations. *Sloan Management Review,* 31(3), 33–45.

41. Fernando, M. Enacting spirituality at work: An empirical study.

42. Harvey, C., and Allard, M. J. (1995). *Understanding and Managing Diversity: Readings, Cases, and Exercises,* 2nd ed. Upper Saddle River, NJ: Prentice Hall.

43. Ibid.

44. Johnson, C. E. (2001). *Meeting the Ethical Challenges of Leadership: Casting Light on Shadow.* Thousand Oaks, CA: Sage.

45. Sowell, T. (1991). A world view of cultural diversity. *Society,* 29(1), 37–44.

46. Ibid.

47. Harvey and Allard. *Understanding and Managing Diversity.*

48. Johnson, *Meeting the Ethical Challenges of Leadership.*

49. Hooijberg, R., and DiTomaso, N. (1996). Leaders in and of demographically diverse organizations. *Leadership Quarterly,* 7(1), 1–19.

50. Eagly, A. H., and Carli, L. L. (2003). The female leadership advantage: An evaluation of the evidence. *Leadership Quarterly,* 14(6), 807–834.

51. Livers, A. B., and Caver, K. A. (2003). *Leading in Black and White: Working Across the Racial Divide in Corporate*

America. Greensboro, NC: Center for Creative Leadership.

52. Brockner, J., and Adsit, L. (1986). The moderating impact of sex on the equity-satisfaction relationship: A field study. *Journal of Applied Psychology, 71,* 585–590.

53. Tannen, D. (1990). *You Just Don't Understand: Men and Women in Conversation.* New York: Ballantine.

54. Eagly, A. H., and Johnson, B. T. (1990). Gender and leadership style: A meta-analysis. *Psychological Bulletin,* 108, 233–256.

55. Hooijberg and DiTomaso. Leaders in and of democratically diverse organizations.

56. Eagly and Johnson. Gender and leadership style: A meta-analysis.

57. Eagly, A. H., Karou, S. J., and Makhijani, M. G. (1995). Gender and the effectiveness of leaders: A meta-analysis. *Psychological Bulletin,* 117, 125–145.

58. Hooijberg and DiTomaso. Leaders in and of democratically diverse organizations.

59. Adams, E. F. (1978). A multivariate study of subordinate perceptions of and attitudes toward minority and majority managers. *Journal of Applied Psychology,* 63(3), 277–288.

60. Kipnis, D., Silverman, A., and Copeland, C. (1973). Effects of emotional arousal on the use of supervised coercion with black and union members. *Journal of Applied Psychology,* 57, 38–43.

61. Xin, K. R., and Tsui, A. S. (1996). Different strokes for different folks? Influence tactics by Asian-American and Caucasion-American managers. *Leadership Quarterly,* 7(1), 109–132.

62. Livers and Caver. *Leading in Black and White.*

63. Howell, J. P., and Dorfman, P. W. (1988). A comparative study of leadership and its substitutes in a mixed cultural work setting. Unpublished manuscript.

64. Howell, J. P., DelaCerda, J., Martinez, S., Bautista, A., Ortiz, J., Prieto, L., and Dorfman, P. W. (2003). Societal culture and leadership in Mexico. Submitted for publication.

65. Welsh, D. H. B., Luthans, F., and Sommer, S. M. (1993). Managing Russian factory workers: The impact of U.S. based behavioral and participative techniques. *Academy of Management Journal,* 36(1), 58–80.

66. Cox, T., Jr. (1991). The multicultural organization. *Academy of Management Executive,* 5(2), 34–47.

67. Ibid.

68. Ibid.

69. Ibid.

70. Cox, T., Jr. (2001). *Creating the Multi-Cultural Organization.* San Francisco: Jossey-Bass.

71. Loden, M., and Rosener, J. B. (1991). *Workforce America: Managing Employee Diversity as a Vital Resource.* Homewood, IL: Business One Irwin.

72. Ofoic-Dankwa, J. C., and Julian, S. D. (1995). The diversimilarity approach to diversity management: A primer and strategies for future managers. In C. Harvey and M. J. Allard (Eds.), *Understanding and Managing Diversity: Readings, Cases, and Exercises,* 2nd ed. Upper Saddle River, NJ: Prentice Hall.

CHAPTER 13

Leadership Development and Organizational Change

Learning Objectives

After reading this chapter, you should be able to do the following:

1. Describe leadership development and the three major processes involved in the leadership development programs at the Center for Creative Leadership.

2. Describe the four types of leadership development programs that are popular in the United States.

3. Explain why clarifying one's personal values is an important part of a leader's development.

4. Describe the difference between an individual's personal vision and leadership vision.

5. Identify several guidelines a person can follow to become a more active listener.

6. Describe several tactics a leader can use to be a persuasive speaker.

7. Describe other skills that leaders need to effectively carry out leadership behaviors.

8. Describe the major types of change affecting organizations today, and how they affect leaders and those preparing for leadership.

9. Distinguish between the two major patterns of change occurring in organizations.

10. Describe the classic model for implementing change developed by Kurt Lewin.

11. Describe a learning organization and the three major leadership roles needed to create and maintain a learning organization.

12. Explain some actions that leaders can take to help their followers cope with change.

▀▀▀ Leadership Development

Leadership development can be defined as expanding an individual's capabilities to effectively carry out leadership behaviors and processes. These behaviors and processes should enable members of the leader's group or organization to work together in productive and meaningful ways. Leadership development usually focuses on developing the individual's beliefs, attitudes, capabilities, or skills for a variety of leadership roles or positions. These may include a management position with formal authority, an officer in a sorority or fraternity, head of a church committee, and an organizer of a neighborhood group to improve home security. Leadership development is probably affected by many factors, including genetics, childhood experiences, and adult learning. The focus of leadership development programs, as described in this chapter, is on what adults can learn and develop to become more effective leaders.[1]

The Leadership Self-Assessment: Assessing Your Emotional Intelligence at Work is designed to provide feedback to the reader on several capabilities that are important for effective leadership. These capabilities are a part of what has been called *emotional intelligence,* which includes self-awareness, impulse control, self-confidence, adaptability, optimism, and initiative.[2] When you complete the self-assessment, imagine yourself in your current job or a job you hope to have in the near future.

The Center for Creative Leadership (CCL) is an institution that conducts training activities and applied research in an effort to understand and improve the leadership capabilities of people in organizations. Its training and development programs are widely respected in the United States and abroad. The approach to leadership development used at CCL emphasizes three key processes that are central to its programs. These three processes are *assessment, challenge,* and *support,* and they are referred to by many leadership development experts.[3]

Assessment provides information to individuals about where they stand—their strengths and weaknesses. People develop most quickly when they build on their own strengths while working to improve on their weaknesses. Self-assessments and assessments by others encourage people to evaluate themselves, and provide benchmarks to measure future development. Assessments also help people understand what strengths they can rely on in exerting leadership and where they can work to become better leaders. The self-assessment was designed to help the reader with this type of understanding.

Challenge occurs for people when their accustomed ways of dealing with situations no longer work. They begin to question the adequacy of their current skills and approaches to problems, and to recognize the need for new capabilities in order to be successful in the future. Everyone develops habitual ways of thinking and behaving, but organizational situations change over time and this requires leaders to adapt and change accordingly. Situations that are new to the leader often occur when coworkers or followers leave, or the leader is transferred, promoted, or changes jobs. Ambiguous job tasks or conflicts with the boss, coworkers, or family often challenge leaders, as do disappointments, losses, and other hardships. These challenging situations motivate people to learn by stimulating their *need for competence*—the desire to deal effectively with one's environment. They therefore provide prime opportunities for leaders to learn and develop their capabilities.

Support prevents challenges from overwhelming people. The best sources of support are other people whose opinions and views are valued by the individual.

LEADERSHIP SELF-ASSESSMENT

Assessing Your Emotional Intelligence at Work

The following 25 statements represent aspects of emotional intelligence (EI). Using a scale from 1 to 4 (1 is low; 4 is high), estimate how you rate on each trait.

_____ I usually stay composed, positive, and unflappable, even in trying times.

_____ I can think clearly and stay focused on the task at hand under pressure.

_____ I am able to admit my own mistakes.

_____ I usually or always meet commitments and keep promises.

_____ I hold myself accountable for meeting my goals.

_____ I am organized and careful in my work.

_____ I regularly seek out fresh ideas from a wide variety of sources.

_____ I am good at generating new ideas.

_____ I can smoothly handle multiple demands and changing priorities.

_____ I am results oriented, with a strong drive to meet my objectives.

_____ I like to set challenging goals and take calculated risks to reach them.

_____ I am always trying to learn how to improve my performance, including asking advice from people younger than I am.

_____ I readily make sacrifices to meet an important organizational goal.

_____ The company's mission is something I understand and can identify with.

_____ The values of my team—or of our division, department, or the company—influence my decisions and clarify the choices I make.

_____ I actively seek out opportunities to further the overall goals of the organization, and enlist others to help me.

_____ I pursue goals beyond what is required or expected of me in my current job.

_____ Obstacles and setbacks may delay me a little, but they don't stop me.

_____ Cutting through red tape and bending outdated rules are sometimes necessary.

_____ I seek fresh perspectives, even if that means trying something totally new.

_____ My impulses or distressing emotions don't often get the best of me at work.

_____ I can change tactics quickly when circumstances change.

_____ Pursuing new information is my best bet for cutting down on uncertainty and finding ways to do things better.

_____ I usually don't attribute setbacks to a personal flaw (mine or someone else's).

_____ I operate from an expectation of success rather than a fear of failure.

Scoring and interpretation: Add your ratings for all 25 items. A score below 75 indicates a need for improvement. Remember, however, that EI is not a permanent state. As Goleman notes in *Emotional Intelligence* and *Working with Emotional Intelligence,* "Emotional intelligence can be learned, and we can each develop it, in varying degrees, throughout our lives. It is sometimes called maturity."

SOURCE: George Manning and Kent Curtis. *The Art of Leadership.* Boston: McGraw-Hill, 2003; and Daniel Goleman, *Working with Emotional Intelligence.* New York: Bantan Books, 1998. Copyright © 2003 The McGraw-Hill Companies. Reprinted with permission.

This includes coworkers, bosses, family members, and colleagues who actively listen to the leader's descriptions of difficulty, provide ideas on how to approach problems, encourage, reassure, and inspire the leader to continue trying, and act as cheerleaders for the leader's successful efforts. Support from valued others keeps a person motivated to learn and develop by building their self-efficacy beliefs. *Self-efficacy* reflects a person's confidence in their ability to deal effectively with the challenges they face. A high degree of self-efficacy is essential for people to persist in dealing with difficult situations and to maintain the effort to overcome challenges. A leader's supporters are essential to give leaders the self-confidence they need to continue on their path of development.

Jay Conger is a leadership scholar who has surveyed and experienced numerous popular leadership development programs in the United States. Conger has classified these programs into four major types corresponding to their primary emphases: personal growth, conceptual understanding, feedback, and skill building.[4]

Personal growth programs often include psychological testing designed to assess the individual's current leadership skills and attitudes. They also include experiential exercises, which may involve simulated organizational situations that require problem solving or action by a leader. They may also include outdoor adventure activities that encourage personal reflection on a person's own behavior, values, or desires. These programs are designed to promote self-awareness, personal responsibility, and communication skills of participants.

Leader development programs that focus on conceptual understanding are more application oriented than personal growth programs. They usually involve lectures to help participants understand the leadership process, and case discussions of actual leadership issues and problems. These programs probably increase participants' understanding of the leadership process. However, leadership behaviors and skills are complex and often require some type of experience or modeling before people can carry them out effectively.

Programs that emphasize feedback provide participants with knowledge of their strengths and weaknesses regarding key skills and attitudes needed to carry out important leadership behaviors. CCL emphasizes assessments and extensive testing that result in feedback from the Center's trainers and other program participants. This multisource feedback approximates a currently popular type of developmental program in work organizations called *360-degree feedback*. With 360-degree feedback, the leader receives input on his or her leadership skills and behaviors from peers, followers, managers, and sometimes clients or customers. CCL and other feedback-intensive programs also provide extensive experiential exercises and simulations to give participants the chance to practice the capabilities they need to improve to become more effective leaders.

Leadership development programs that emphasize skill building provide instruction in key leadership skills and behaviors in 3- to 4-hour modules. These are usually followed by experiential exercises and case studies that are designed to demonstrate these skills in action. These programs often have a large role-playing component to allow participants to practice and obtain feedback from trainers and participants on their skill development.

In addition to these programs conducted by professional trainers working with leaders from a variety of organizational settings, many work organizations conduct their own in-house leadership development activities. These programs often involve assigning a *mentor* to each leader. A mentor is usually a manager who is considerably more experienced than the leader being mentored, and often works at a higher level in the organization, though he or she is not the manager of the leader being mentored. Mentors can help a leader learn the ropes in a new position, and facilitate skill building and career advancement. Mentoring relationships can be formal (the mentor is assigned to a leader) or informal (a friendly agreement), and may last for many years. Informal relationships may be most effective. *Executive coaching* is also used for higher-level leaders. Coaches may be internal or external consultants who help identify competencies that leaders need to develop, provide perspective and feedback, and act as sounding boards for the executive. These programs are often shorter term than mentoring relationships, but they can be helpful in leadership skill development for high-level positions.

Action learning is also used by some large organizations, such as General Electric. This involves seminars and training modules in leadership, along with challenging task assignments in the organization. The leader often works with a team of other leaders from their own organization on a leadership or organizational problem in a part of the company separate from their own. The team may be assigned to study a problem in governmental relations for a South American division, or to design a start-up plan for a new plant in a rural area of the southern United States. These organizational programs emphasize developmental activities on the job, but they also provide the conceptual background, feedback, and skill building found in the programs conducted by professional training organizations.

These leadership development programs have considerable overlap in the techniques they utilize. Elements of all four types of programs are probably needed for individuals to significantly improve their effectiveness as leaders. A conceptual understanding of leadership behaviors and processes, followed by feedback and skill development with some personal growth experiences, can all contribute to an individual's maturity as a leader. Used together, these processes can provide self-awareness of one's motives, values, and skills that help leaders make difficult choices often required of them. They also provide the understanding and skill-based knowledge to help leaders carry out their visions with followers.

The remainder of this section on leadership development will describe in detail several key areas that are emphasized in the previously mentioned leadership development programs. These key areas include clarifying personal values, developing a personal and leadership vision, competencies and skills for effective leadership behavior, and learning from experience. The emphasis will be on helping the reader to develop their own self-awareness, vision, skills, and the ability to continue their learning through on-the-job experience. Figure 13-1 summarizes the four major types of leadership development programs.

Values and Self-Awareness

Values are the standards, guideposts, and principles we use to guide our behavior. They remind us what is right or wrong, good or bad, worthy or unworthy. Values provide the internal moral compass that leaders can refer to when faced with ethical challenges, rapid change, or ambiguous situations requiring an immediate response. A leader's behavior in these situations may reflect his or her clarity of values more than intelligence, training, or rational analysis. Possessing a clear understanding of one's values helps the

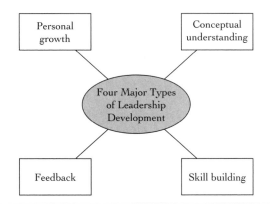

FIGURE 13-1 Four major types of leadership development

leader's followers know where they stand on issues, which is helpful when potential conflicts arise. Organizations are sometimes held together by a core set of values that are emphasized and acted on throughout the organization.

Ben & Jerry's Homemade Holdings is a good example of how values helped an organization stay together and become successful. Ben Cohen and Jerry Greenfield were friends from high school who shared the values of friendship, equality, creativity, social responsibility, having fun at work, and the love of ice cream. Adhering to these values helped them create a successful business that grew much larger than they envisioned.[5]

Core values are the most important standards people use to guide their behavior and decisions in life and as a leader. Developing a clear idea about one's core values is not easy. It is important, however, because it influences where you give your attention, the choices you make, and the positions you defend and fight for when conflict arises. Becoming clear about your core values takes time and mental effort to honestly reflect on how you really want to live your life.

Some values that are common to business people include power, ambition, financial success, helping others, success as an entrepreneur, honesty, integrity, and respect for others. The Leadership Self-Assessment: How Often Do You Value These Things? asks you to rate each general value according to how often you think of it in relation to your life or your behavior.

Did you include most of these values as "Always Valued" or "Often Valued"? This is true of many managers who have used this self-assessment for the first time. In reality, people cannot hold many core values at the same time and behave consistently. It is a good idea to reexamine your "Always Valued" list and ask yourself: Did you rate some values as "Always Valued" because they were socially correct? Were some values more important to you in the past? Did your thoughts about another person who is important to you affect your "Always Valued" list? Now try to reassign some values from your "Always Valued" list to a more accurate category. Do the same for your "Often Valued" list. This process should result in eight or ten items in your "Always Valued" list. You have now made significant progress in identifying your core values.

Go through your "Always Valued" list and write down how you demonstrate each value in your actions. If you listed "Challenge," how do you seek out and respond to

LEADERSHIP SELF-ASSESSMENT
How Often Do You Value These Things?

Read each value in the list below and think about its importance to you. Using the table with five columns labeled "Always Valued" to "Never Valued," write each value below the heading that best describes how often you think about it in connection with your life and your behavior. Add to the list any other values that are important to you.

Achievement—A sense of accomplishment; mastery; goal achievement

Activity—Fast-paced, highly active work

Advancement—Growth, seniority, and promotion resulting from work well done

Adventure—New and challenging opportunities; excitement; risk

Aesthetics—Appreciation of beauty in things, ideas, surroundings, personal space

Affiliation—Interaction with other people; recognition as a member of a particular group; involvement; belonging

Affluence—High income; financial success; prosperity

Authority—Position and power to control events and other people's activities

Autonomy—Ability to act independently with few constraints; self-sufficiency; self-reliance; ability to make most decisions and choices

Balance—Lifestyle that allows for a balance of time for self, family, work, and community

Challenge—Continually facing complex and demanding tasks and problems

Change and variation—Absence of routine; work responsibilities, daily activities, or settings that change frequently; unpredictability

Collaboration—Close, cooperative working relationships with groups

Community—Serving and supporting a purpose that supersedes personal desires; making a difference

Competency—Demonstrating high proficiency and knowledge; showing above-average effectiveness and efficiency at tasks

Competition—Rivalry with winning as the goal

Courage—Willingness to stand up for one's beliefs

Creativity—Discovering, developing, or designing new ideas, formats, programs, or things; demonstrating innovation and imagination

Diverse perspectives—Unusual ideas and opinions; points of view that may not seem right or be popular at first, but bear fruit in the long run

Duty—Respect for authority, rules, and regulations

Economic security—Steady and secure employment; adequate financial reward; low risk

Enjoyment—Fun, joy, and laughter

Fame—Prominence; being well known

Family—Spending time with partner, children, parents, or extended family

Friendship—Close personal relationships with others

Health—Physical and mental well-being; vitality

Hedonism—Pursuing pleasure as a way of life

Helping others—Helping people attain their goals; providing care and support

Humor—The ability to laugh at oneself and life

Influence—Having an impact or effect on the attitudes or opinions of other people; persuasiveness

Inner harmony—Happiness; contentment; being at peace with oneself

Integrity—Acting in accordance with moral and ethical standards; honesty; sincerity; truth; trustworthiness

Justice—Fairness; equality; doing the right thing

Knowledge—The pursuit of understanding, skill, and expertise; continuous learning

Location—Choice of a place to live that is conducive to one's lifestyle

Love—Involvement in close, affectionate relationships; intimacy

Loyalty—Faithfulness; dedication to individuals, traditions, or organizations

Order—Stability; routine; predictability; clear lines of authority; standardized procedures

Personal development—Dedication to maximizing one's potential

Physical fitness—Staying in shape through exercise and physical activity

Recognition—Positive feedback and public credit for work well done; respect and admiration

Responsibility—Dependability; reliability; accountability for results

Self-respect—Pride; self-esteem; sense of personal identity

Spirituality—Strong spiritual or religious beliefs; moral fulfillment

Status—Being respected for one's job or association with a prestigious group or organization

Wisdom—Sound judgment based on knowledge, experience, and understanding

Always Valued	*Often Valued*	*Sometimes Valued*	*Seldom Valued*	*Never Valued*
___	___	___	___	___
___	___	___	___	___
___	___	___	___	___
___	___	___	___	___
___	___	___	___	___
___	___	___	___	___
___	___	___	___	___
___	___	___	___	___
___	___	___	___	___
___	___	___	___	___
___	___	___	___	___
___	___	___	___	___
___	___	___	___	___

SOURCE: Adapted from R. J. Lee and S. N. King, *Discovering the Leader in You: A Guide to Realizing Your Personal Leadership Potential.* Center for Creative Leadership. Greensboro, NC: Jossey-Bass, (2003) 60–61.

challenges in your life? If you indicated "Family," how do you show this value in your daily behavior? Do this for each value in your "Always Valued" list, then evaluate which values you most clearly live out in your daily behavior.

The last phase of this exercise involves getting help from friends who know you well. Ask them about each of the values in your "Always Valued" list. Do they see or hear you showing these values in your behavior? Which values seem most consistent with your behavior? Do they see or hear inconsistencies (lack of congruence) between your "Always Valued" list and your behavior? Are there values not shown on your list that consistently show up in your behavior? Most of us have blind spots, and feedback from others can make us aware of these.

This exercise helps clarify your core values so you are aware of what drives your actions. Sometimes situations may force us to behave in certain ways that are not consistent with our values. Different values may also conflict with one another. Thinking of each core value in relation to other values and situational factors makes us realize that compromises are often essential in organizations. These conflicts can also cause you to evaluate which values in the "Always Valued" list are most important to you. This does not mean one is unimportant, only that another value may be more important at this time. Later in your life a different value may be more important.

Now that you have a good idea about your core values, it is often useful to evaluate the core values in the profession, industry, or organization in which you are working or plan to work. What values are rewarded in this profession, industry or organization? What values are consistent with a good leader in these situations? You might answer these questions using the values and categories shown in the self-assessment. This information is probably most available via discussion with several individuals working in these situations. Now compare these values with your own core values. Are they congruent or incongruent? If incongruencies occur (and they usually do), you should probably give careful thought to how you want to respond to these situations.

When leaders' actions are congruent with their values, this often reassures followers because they know they can trust a leader to be consistent. Values such as loyalty and integrity in a leader create followers' trust that the leader will be above board in his or her actions, and this builds the leader's influence on followers.

The emphasis on becoming aware of our personal values stems from the belief that society and organizational expectations have caused many of us to lose touch with our true values and passions. Exploring our own values may help us reconnect with our true selves and let these values emerge in our work and our roles as leaders. This self-awareness can give us a deeper understanding of who we are and help us to design work and lead others in tasks that are more fulfilling.

Vision

Robert Lee and Sara King described two types of vision that are important for a person's development as a leader.[6] An individual's *personal vision* is a picture of the person's ideal life as he or she views it. It is an ideal image of the person's future, and may include family, work, leisure, location, friends, or whatever the individual views as important. It will also reflect the personal values identified earlier in the Leadership Self-Assessment: How Often Do You Value These Things? A *leadership vision* is a part of the personal vision that involves an ideal image of the type of leader the person

LEADERSHIP SELF-ASSESSMENT
You, Fifteen Years from Now

Think about where you would be sitting and reading this book if it were fifteen years from now and you were living your *ideal* life. What kinds of people would be around you? What does your environment look and feel like? What might you be doing during a typical day or week? Don't worry about the feasibility of creating this kind of ideal life. Just let the image develop, and place yourself in the picture.

Try doing some "free writing" around this vision of yourself fifteen years from now, or else speak your vision into a tape recorder or talk about it with a trusted friend. When doing this exercise, many people report that they experience a release of energy, feeling more optimistic than they had even moments earlier. This kind of envisioning of an ideal future can be a powerful way to connect with the real possibilities for change in our lives.

SOURCE: From D. Goleman, R. Boyatzis, and R. McKee. *Primal Leadership.* Boston: Harvard Business School, 2002.

wants to be. Your leadership vision can include leadership roles or positions you hope to hold, achievements as a leader, and how your leadership will fit into your personal vision.

To begin and sustain real development as a leader, scholars believe you must tap into the motivational force of your ideal self.[7] This is because development involves changing one's habits, skills, and behaviors, which is hard work. Making changes that last requires a strong commitment to your future vision of yourself. This is especially true during times of increasing responsibilities, stress, and rapidly changing organizations. The personal vision must not focus on obstacles that might prevent you from achieving your ideal life, only the characteristics of that ideal state with you in it. Now try the Leadership Self-Assessment: You, Fifteen Years from Now, which asks you to begin thinking about your own personal vision.

Your *ideal self* described in this exercise can be influenced by your *ought self*—the person you think you should become. The ought self may be determined by expectations from our parents, spouse, boss, friends, colleagues, or any other person who has special significance to us. As we go through our lives, so many different people provide input (expectations) to our ought self that we can lose track of our ideal self. We lose sight of our dreams and begin behaving only to please others' expectations—following our ought self. Taking the time to uncover your ideal self is important if you are to have a happy, fulfilling career as a leader, or in any occupation. Obtaining a rich, holistic view of your ideal life is needed to provide the emotional involvement and motivation required to persist in your self-development toward what really matters to you.

LEADERSHIP SELF-ASSESSMENT
Personal Best Exercise

A "personal best" experience is an event (or series of events) that represent your personal standard of excellence. It is a time when you performed at your very best. It may be something you measure yourself by. When you select a personal best experience, you might use this criteria: "When I think about this experience, it makes me smile." Describe this experience in writing. Try to include in your description why this experience is a good example of your personal best. How does your description compare with your core values and your personal vision you described earlier?

Your leadership vision is your mental picture of yourself as the leader you would like to become. If you aspire to be a leader, it is based on your personal vision and values. It will include what you are trying to accomplish as a leader in your field of work, and possibly as a leader outside of work (for example, in your community or a public service organization).[8] It may include how leadership can help you carry out your personal vision and values. It will probably include a description of how you relate to followers and other people that you and your group deal with.

To begin thinking about your leadership vision, try the Leadership Self-Assessment: Personal Best Exercise. This exercise is designed to bring out your feelings and beliefs about excellence through a written description of something you experienced.

This self-assessment is designed to help you think about excellence in your own behavior. A leadership vision should be similar in that it should describe excellence in your future behavior as a leader. Asking yourself some of the following questions may help you clarify your leadership vision:

1. Do you seek or willingly accept leadership roles in groups?
2. Are there specific leadership roles that really capture your attention and energize you? If so, describe them (examples may be leader of a sports team or starting your own business).
3. Who are your leadership role models? Why did you choose them and do they have characteristics similar to your own?
4. Do you seek and enjoy using power? Do you admire others who have power? When do you feel powerful and how do you use power?
5. What ideals, goals, or issues have you or are you willing to fight for?
6. Do you believe that a leadership position will allow you to express your creativity? If so, how?[9]

These questions point out that having a clear leadership vision can help a person make intelligent decisions about the leadership role he or she seeks or accepts. It can also help you guide your own development as a leader. A leadership vision that is consistent with your core values and your personal vision can help you navigate your own career by providing a picture of your own true north. It will be a regular reminder of where you are heading. It thus becomes a standard by which you can evaluate your current actions by asking yourself, "Is what I am doing consistent with my leadership vision?" and "Am I making concessions and trade-offs in my leadership role that are seriously diverting me from my vision of myself?" It provides a steady benchmark to help you judge your own behavior as a leader.

Another input to your leadership vision is a realistic estimate of the costs and benefits of leadership. Table 13-1 provides a list of many of these costs and benefits. Leadership trainers indicate that leaders typically list financial rewards and pride of accomplishment as their major rewards. Look through these lists and think about how important these costs and benefits are to you.

Now try writing out your own leadership vision—your ideal image of yourself as a future leader. Who are you leading in this vision? What type of group or organization is it? What are its goals and values? What experiences have you had to prepare you for

TABLE 13-1 Possible costs and benefits of leadership

Costs	*Benefits*
Physical energy	Pride of accomplishment
Long hours	Financial rewards
Too many meetings	Self-validation
Constant obligations	Impact on people and events
Responsibility	Service to others
Caretaking	Meaning
Less time for nonleadership work and interests	Attention and recognition
	Personal prominence
Visibility ("being in a fishbowl")	New connections and acquaintances
Public duties	Helping others grow
Isolation from peers	Perquisites of office
Less freedom of expression	More resources for family
Pressure to produce	Personal status
Stress on family	Singular achievements
Less time for family	Heightened experience
Less time for other pursuits	More autonomy
Emotional strains	Travel linked to recreation
Very little feedback	Good relocations
Less useful feedback	Change
Too much travel	Control
Bad relocations	Respect
Job insecurity	Inclusion

this leadership role? How did you obtain this position? What are the major costs and benefits of this leadership role? How long do you want to stay in this leadership role?

If you give careful thought to your leadership vision, you will probably revise it several times. This will show that you are serious about this important process in your development as a leader. It is a good idea to review this vision often, along with your core values and personal vision. They will help you proceed with confidence in your own development and career as a leader, and they will keep you mindful of your own true north.

Skill Development

Regardless of how gifted individuals are, they are novices when they assume their first leadership position. Scholars have noted that leaders develop somewhat different skills through their careers.[10] Though some conceptual, technical, and interpersonal skills are needed by nearly all leaders, the relative importance of these often shift as leaders move up the hierarchy. A leader's technical competence and conceptual expertise generally develop with education, training, and work experience that provide a variety of challenges. Much of a leader's competence and expertise is organization-specific, and it aids leaders in problem solving and task facilitation because it reflects the organization's technology and industry characteristics. However, interpersonal skills are important for all levels of leadership, and this skill area is often the focus of many leadership development programs. The leader's ability to empathize with followers, communication skills such as inspiring, persuading, and active listening, rewarding others, team skills, conflict management, and the ability to learn from experience are needed by all leaders. The Leadership Self-Assessment: The Interpersonal Skills Checklist will provide you with information on interpersonal skills that are important for leadership.

As pointed out in the self-assessment, improving your skills takes persistence and self-discipline to put forth the long-term effort needed for lasting change. Several important interpersonal skills are described in this section, along with suggestions to help you improve your skills in each area.

Communication Skills

Communication is the means leaders use to influence their followers. Communication skills are needed to carry out all the leadership behaviors described in this book. Oral and written communication skills are essential to show followers the leader cares about their welfare, to provide the direction needed in ambiguous situations, to convey an inspiring vision of the future, or to establish a working relationship with another department or organization. Effective communication has already been addressed at different places in this book. At this point, we will emphasize two communication skills that are prerequisites for effective performance in many leadership positions: active listening and persuasion.

Most people assume listening is a passive process. They tend to relax and let the speaker expend the effort, while they take in the message and often daydream. Unfortunately, most listeners retain only about 25 percent of what they hear, and poor listening is one of the main reasons that leaders fail.[11] Good listening is really an active process that requires effort by listeners in order to be effective. *Active listening* involves using your energy and effort to concentrate fully on the speaker and the message you are receiving. Try completing the Leadership Self-Assessment that addresses your listening skills.

LEADERSHIP SELF-ASSESSMENT
The Interpersonal Skills Checklist

Below are a number of specific aspects of behavior that suggest a person needs to improve his or her interpersonal skills related to leadership and influence. Check each statement that is generally true for you. You can add to the reliability of this exercise by asking one or two other people who know you well to rate you, then compare your self-analysis with their analysis of you.

Developmental Needs and Areas for Improvement

1. I'm too shy and reserved. _____
2. I bully and intimidate others too frequently. _____
3. I tell others what they want to hear rather than emphasizing the truth. _____
4. I have trouble expressing my feelings. _____
5. I make negative comments about group members too readily. _____
6. Very few people pay attention to the ideas I contribute during a meeting. _____
7. My personality isn't colorful enough. _____
8. People find me boring. _____
9. I pay too little attention to the meaning behind what team members and coworkers are saying. _____
10. It is very difficult for me to criticize others. _____
11. I'm too serious most of the time. _____
12. I avoid controversy in dealing with others. _____
13. I don't get my point across well. _____
14. It's difficult for me to make small talk with others. _____
15. I boast too much about my accomplishments. _____
16. I strive too much for individual recognition instead of giving credit to the team. _____
17. Self-confidence is my weak point. _____
18. My spoken messages are too bland. _____
19. My written messages are too bland. _____
20. I relate poorly to people from cultures different from my own. _____
21. I read people poorly. _____
22. _____ _____
   (Fill in your own statement.)

(Continued)

Now that you (and perhaps one or two others) have identified specific behaviors that may require change, draw up an action plan. Briefly describe a plan of attack for bringing about the change you hope to achieve for each statement that is checked. Ideas might come from personal development books or from this course. After formulating an action plan, you will need self-discipline for its successful implementation. For example, if you checked, "People find me boring," you might want to expand your fund of knowledge by extensive reading and by talking to dynamic people. You will then need the self-discipline to continue your quest for ideas and to incorporate some of these ideas into your conversation.

SOURCE: A. J. Dubrin, *Leadership: Research Findings, Practice, and Skills,* 4th ed. New York: Houghton Mifflin, 2004, 466–467. Copyright © 2004 by Houghton Mifflin Company. Reprinted with permission.

LEADERSHIP SELF-ASSESSMENT

Listening Skills

Select the response that best describes the frequency of your actual behavior. Write the letter A, U, F, O, or S on the line before each of the 15 statements.
   (A: Almost always; U: Usually; F: Frequently; O: Occasionally; S: Seldom)

_____ 1. I like to listen to people talk. I encourage others to talk by showing interest, smiling, nodding, and so forth.

_____ 2. I pay closer attention to people who are more similar to me than I do to people who are different from me.

_____ 3. I evaluate people's words and nonverbal communication ability as they talk.

_____ 4. I avoid distractions; if it's noisy, I suggest moving to a quiet spot.

_____ 5. When people come to me and interrupt me when I'm doing something, I put what I was doing out of my mind and give them my complete attention.

_____ 6. When people are talking, I allow them time to finish. I do not interrupt, anticipate what they are going to say, or jump to conclusions.

_____ 7. I tune people out who do not agree with my views.

_____ 8. While the other person is talking, or professors are lecturing, my mind wanders to personal topics.

_____ 9. While the other person is talking, I pay close attention to the nonverbal communications to help me fully understand what they are trying to communicate.

_____ 10. I tune out and pretend I understand when the topic is difficult for me to understand.

_____ 11. When the other person is talking, I think about and prepare what I am going to say in reply.

_____ 12. When I think there is something missing or contradictory, I ask direct questions to get the person to explain the idea more fully.

_____ 13. When I don't understand something, I let the other person know I don't understand.

_____ 14. When listening to other people, I try to put myself in their position and see things from their perspective.

_____ 15. During conversations, I repeat back to the other person what has been said in my own words to be sure I correctly understand what has been said.

If people you talk to regularly were to answer these questions about you, would they have the same responses that you selected? To find out, have friends fill out the questions with you in mind rather than themselves, then compare answers.

To determine your own score, give yourself 5 points for each A, 4 for each U, 3 for each F, 2 for each O, and 1 for each S for statements 1, 4, 5, 6, 9, 12, 13, 14, and 15. Place the numbers on the line next to your response letter. For items 2, 3, 7, 8, 10, and 11, the scores are reversed: 5 points for each S, 4 for each O, 3 for each F, 2 for each U, and 1 for each A. Place these score numbers on the lines next to the response letters. Now add your total number of points. Your score should be between 15 and 75. Mark your score on the continuum below. Generally, the higher your score, the better your listening skills.

15 – 20 – 25 – 30 – 35 – 40 – 45 – 50 – 55 – 60 – 65 – 70 – 75
Poor listener   Good listener

SOURCE: R. N. Lussier and C. F. Achua, *Leadership: Theory, Application, Skill Development,* 2nd ed. Eagan, MN: Thomson South-Western. © 2004. Reprinted with permission of South-Western, a division of Thomson Learning.

Most people assume they are good listeners, however they fail to retain 75 percent of what they hear. Listening skills are critical for effective leadership because virtually everyone wants to be heard. Effective listening gives the speaker a sense of self-worth.

There are several guidelines to help you become a better listener. These should be kept in mind and practiced (with effort) if you are to improve your listening skills. Listening is the primary way we learn about the world and the basis of good communication skills. If you practice using these guidelines, you will become a better listener and a more effective leader.

1. *Use your extra mental time productively.* Most people speak at a rate of about 125 words per minute, but we can listen, think, and process information at about 350 to 450 words per minute. This means we have a considerable amount of extra mental time. Most people use this time to daydream, doodle, or think about something besides the speaker's message. Using this extra mental time productively means to review the speaker's message in your head as you receive it, paraphrase the message in your own words, and place the message in your own context by deciding how it affects you. Avoid mentally arguing with the speaker while you are listening.

2. *Avoid interruptions, distractions, and other activities.* If you start to daydream or doodle, take a deep breath and refocus on the message. Do not play with your pen, paper clips, or other distracting items while you are listening. Ask questions and maintain eye contact with the speaker. Try to avoid phone calls or interruptions by other people.

3. *Listen to the entire message.* Do not assume you know what a speaker is going to say before the entire message is completed. Watch for the speaker's gestures, pauses, and points of emphasis to help you identify the speaker's major objective or concern. Sometimes leaders need to act as sounding boards to hear followers talk about their worries or concerns about issues such as changing technology, plant closings, or personnel issues. Followers may want to talk about personal issues that could affect their work. The leader must remember that active listening is essential to satisfy followers' need to be heard.

4. *Try to place a structure on the message.* Tried and true structures such as who, what, where, when, and why are often helpful. Using literary techniques in paraphrasing messages can often make the message more memorable. Examples are rhyming, alliteration (red right returning), or word association (a merger is like a marriage). These techniques can increase the amount of a message that is retained by the listener.

5. *Take notes and give feedback.* Applying a structure to a message is often easier when taking notes. Develop your own form of shorthand with abbreviations of frequently used words (such as "w/" for the word "with," or "re" for the word "regarding"). Notes provide a record of an important message that can be reviewed later. They can also help in giving feedback to the speaker when the listener missed an important point. Feedback shows the speaker you are listening and not daydreaming, and motivates him or her to convey the message accurately and completely. Feedback also shows the speaker that you are taking responsibility for your own understanding. During the next week, try to use one of these five guidelines in your own life. Review them occasionally, and through practice and effort, you will steadily improve your listening skills.

Persuasive oral communication is a hallmark of famous leaders throughout history, including Napoleon Bonaparte, Winston Churchill, Abraham Lincoln, Franklin Roosevelt, and John F. Kennedy. Each of these leaders was able to formulate and present messages that persuaded and inspired followers to act in certain ways. Leaders at all levels find persuasive communication skills to be useful, and often essential, to effective performance. Several tactics are helpful to experiment with and remember in framing persuasive communication.

1. *Build your credibility.* Be well prepared with information, data, and other influential persons who support your position or message. Anticipate objections and know beforehand how you will respond. Explain why your background provides you with expertise on the subject. Build trust by emphasizing similarities between yourself and your audience, and explain how they will benefit by agreeing with your position.

2. *Choose your language carefully.* Certain words or terms have persuasive power, though this power may change with time. "Freedom" and "democracy" have been powerful terms for many years in the United States. Currently, words such as "empowerment," "outclassing," "surpassing," "bonding," and "virtual" are in vogue, and imply rapid advancement, early success, and being on the cutting edge. Avoid profanity in order to be seen as more attractive and persuasive. Avoid a lot of pauses or gaps in your message, and meaningless words and phrases such as "uhm," "kind of," "maybe," "like," "you know," "she goes"

(meaning she says), and "I guess." These phrases and terms convey a lack of self-confidence and powerlessness in a leader.

3. *Orient your message to the listeners.* Appeal to their needs and wants by putting yourself in their position. Include stories that show your familiarity with listeners' perspectives and how your message can help them.

4. *Think about nonverbal messages.* People are viewed as more persuasive when they make eye contact with listeners, use facial expressions and gestures that imply relaxation and sociability, and use hand or body movements that convey meaning and are easily recognizable (such as hello, good by, crazy, I don't know). Touching people increases persuasiveness if done appropriately (usually on the hand or arm). Being well dressed and neatly groomed increases respect and persuasiveness of a leader.

Some of these tactics may be easier for you to use than others. Remember to build on your strengths and rely on tactics that feel most comfortable and appropriate to your audience.

Empathy

The ability to empathize with other people involves understanding their thoughts and feelings. Empathy is a key element of emotional intelligence that was described earlier in this chapter. Seeing things from a follower's viewpoint is essential for effective supportive leadership behavior, as well as directive, participative, and charismatic leadership. When leaders understand followers' thoughts and feelings, they can provide the emotional support, direction, involvement, or inspiration that the follower is seeking from the leader. Empathy is thus a key skill for leaders to accurately diagnose followers' needs and adapt their behavior to meet those needs.

Athletic coaches often describe their job as getting inside their players' minds in order to motivate them. Empathy was part of a training program to improve a sales staff's ability to respond to customers' emotions that were expressed during sales calls. This training resulted in greater increases in sales for those attending the program than for those who did not attend.[12]

A manager of a system of retirement homes described how he empathizes with his employees. He walks in their shoes in each facility for a day. He dresses the way they dress and carries out tasks assigned to him by managers in each facility for an entire workday. With this program, he began to realize in person the stresses they faced every hour they were on the job. He also gained the respect of the residents, who enjoyed seeing the manager cleaning rooms, delivering laundry, and struggling with equipment.[13]

Developing empathy with followers and others involves doing whatever is necessary to experience followers' perspectives, frustrations, and concerns. It may involve walking in their shoes, having town meetings with employees every week in which concerns are aired and questions answered, or spending time with employees in other ways. One plant manager spent most of his time out of his office with his people. He told the middle managers to do the same, even if their paperwork was late because of it. He learned the names of all the employees in his plant and tried to speak with each of them every day. He told one of the authors that after a while he could feel problems in the plant when he was talking with his people, well before they mentioned the problems to any of the managers. He was tuned into his people so well that they saw him as one of them. They gave a celebration party for him each year on his birthday. The key method to achieve empathy with followers is to spend time with them while making a concerted effort to be an active listener.

Rewarding Others

The power of carefully administered rewards in influencing followers was discussed in Chapter 7. It was explained that when rewards are contingent on current performance, they are most powerful at motivating high future performance. That is, when a follower is rewarded for a job well done, he or she is most likely to repeat that high job performance in the future. We also mentioned that social rewards in the form of personal recognition were especially powerful motivators because they can be used by a leader on the spot and they cost nothing.

Some people have difficulty rewarding or complimenting others for good work. The best way to develop this skill is to practice. Some experts suggest that leaders should look for things that followers are doing well and tell them immediately. The leader should also tell the follower how their performance was an important contribution to the group or organization and that he or she appreciates the skill and effort they have shown on the job. The more often leaders recognize high performance of followers, the more often followers will respond with continued high performance.

To begin practicing this skill of recognizing others, try the following exercise with a group you are currently working with. This can be a class group, study group, work group, sorority or fraternity group, or any other group you meet with regularly to accomplish some goal(s) other than socializing. Write a short note to each person in the group telling them how they have contributed to the group's performance or to your experience in the group. The person may have contributed important ideas, resolved a conflict, spoken for the group, or provided some other important service for the group. That person may have made you more relaxed in the group, encouraged you, or made the group more enjoyable in some other way. At your next meeting with this group, tell the other members you are practicing the skill of rewarding and recognizing others, and give them each their note. Do this activity once or twice in each group you belong to and you will soon find it is very easy and enjoyable. It will also encourage positive group behaviors by other group members.

Goal Setting

Research clearly shows that goal setting is an effective program to increase individual and group motivation and performance. When individuals have specific performance goals, they consistently outperform their peers who have no goals. Goals provide a clear purpose for a person's work. They also provide a standard to help managers evaluate and reward their employees' performance.

Goal setting can be a large part of leaders' directive and charismatic behaviors. Several guidelines are helpful to remember for leaders when setting goals for their followers or their organization. When these guidelines are used consistently by leaders, they can increase their skill and effectiveness at goal setting and improve their followers' performance.

1. Goals must be specific, clearly measurable, and describe a single end result.
2. Goals should be difficult, but achievable and acceptable to followers.
3. Leaders should be available to coach and support followers' efforts to achieve goals.

4. Goals should specify a time limit for their accomplishment.

5. Followers should provide input to help set their goals in order to be committed and satisfied with the goal-setting process.

Learning from Experience

Leadership scholars recently pointed out that leadership development occurs as much at work as it does in specially designed training programs.[14] Although most companies include some type of classroom experience, many increasingly recognize that this is not enough to continue participants' development as leaders. Many top-level executives trace their development from a pivotal or transformational experience that often occurred early in their career.[15] Something occurred that taught the young leader to always respect and listen to those around him, or the importance of building supportive networks with those outside his or her own job situation. These findings point to the importance of learning from our own work experience if we are to continue our development as leaders.

Experts describe the ability to learn as ". . . recogniz[ing] when new behaviors, skills, or attitudes are called for, engag[ing] in activities that provide the opportunity to learn or test new skills and behaviors, and work[ing] to develop a variety of learning tactics in order to acquire the needed skills or behaviors."[16] A certain degree of cognitive development and a desire to face a challenge and succeed are needed to continue learning from our experience, but people can improve their ability to learn. They can make a concerted effort to develop new perspectives and they can expand on their learning tactics.

Many people learn from classroom-type lectures and discussions, and others learn by participating in experiential exercises or case discussions. Interacting with other people in a group situation to discuss leadership issues is a learning tactic favored by some. In order to continue our learning and development as leaders, we need to cultivate multiple methods or tactics for learning. If we usually learn through classroom lectures with question-and-answer formats, we need to seek out opportunities to try out our ideas in hands-on situations. This may mean joining a campus or community organization and taking on a leadership role, or forming a study or discussion group to further explore our understanding and get others' reactions to our ideas. Sometimes learning opportunities occur that may not fit our preferred learning tactic. In these cases, we need to be willing to switch tactics and expand our understanding in a new way. When a learner is blocked and cannot grasp a concept or issue, it often means he or she is using the wrong learning tactic for that situation. Researchers have found that effective learners are able to adapt their learning tactics appropriately to fit the situation.[17]

In order to absorb new learning, most people need time and an atmosphere conducive to reflection on the new information they are receiving. They need to integrate that information with their preexisting knowledge, assumptions, and behaviors to plan their future behavior. Whatever learning approach is favored or available to you, a useful tool to facilitate reflection and integration is a *learning journal*. After a class, group discussion, or exercise, try writing in your journal for a few minutes about the experience. You might simply summarize what happened, describe your reaction to it, what you believe you learned, and how the experience and your learning fits in with your prior experience, knowledge, and behavior. Eventually you will probably notice patterns in your learning and behavior, which usually causes more reflection and integration of current and prior learning. This is the time to begin to think and write about how this new learning will affect your future behavior as a leader.

A supportive relationship with your boss is extremely helpful as you expand your learning tactics and develop your skills as a leader. A supportive relationship can encourage a person who is low in self-confidence to try new approaches to problems and take some risks. Research shows that taking on a variety of assignments that challenge a person's abilities leads to development as a leader. Job assignments that stretch and challenge people push them out of their comfort zone and force them to question the adequacy of their existing skills and approaches. Challenging tasks require people to develop new skills to deal with the new assignments if they are to succeed. Challenge may be provided by novel job assignments, difficult goals such as starting something from scratch, ambiguity regarding a boss's expectations of how to approach a problem, or dealing with some type of conflict, loss, or failure. These situations stimulate people to confront their weaknesses and develop new skills.

A supportive leader who views task assignments as developmental experiences (not do or die situations) and provides feedback to the learner can be an incredible asset to your learning as a leader. Early in your career, it is wise to search out a supervisor who will be supportive of your development. Even if he or she is not exactly in the department or organization where you would most like to work, he or she may be that pivotal person who provides you with the challenge, feedback, and support needed to become an effective leader.

A mentor also can often provide support needed to enhance learning from experience. Mentors are usually senior managers outside the reporting line of the developing leader or manager. They may be formally assigned to a junior-level leader, or the mentoring relationship may develop informally. Informal relationships tend to be most effective. Mentors can provide support as role models, counselors, feedback sources, sounding boards, cheerleaders, or reinforcers. They may even help the junior leader negotiate with his or her boss for challenging job assignments. A personal closeness often develops between the mentor and junior leader that helps open the relationship to allow honest sharing of ideas, aspirations, fears, and frustrations that all leaders experience. Mentors can provide both career support (such as advocacy, feedback, or coaching) and psychosocial support (emotional and interpersonal bonding) that are needed by young leaders and managers. These relationships often evolve into friendships, and may last 20 or 30 years. They often have a strong positive influence on a leader's development and success. Seeking out a willing mentor is an excellent learning tactic for a young leader or manager. Although women and people of color have more difficulty finding good mentors, the positive influence on their development as leaders is well worth the persistent effort to locate the right person.

Several guidelines have been developed from research and organizational practices to enhance your ability to learn from experience. Using these guidelines with effort should help you continue your development as a leader throughout your career.

1. Always believe the research that shows people can learn and improve as leaders, regardless of their upbringing, personality, or intelligence. Leadership skills are developed through persistent effort.

▪ ▪ ▪ **FIGURE 13-2** Major leadership skills

2. Become aware of your favored learning tactics and try to expand the repertoire of tactics you use. Seek learning opportunities that require you to utilize new learning tactics.
3. Start and keep a learning journal to record your experiences and learning as a leader.
4. Find a boss or mentor who will support your career and psychosocial development.
5. Seek out variety and challenging job assignments that will stretch your skills and understanding of the complexity of leadership.
6. Seek feedback from peers, followers, superiors, and customers to better understand how you affect people. Discuss this feedback with these individuals to learn how you can utilize the results. Use active listening during these sessions, and avoid being defensive.

Figure 13-2 summarizes the major skills leaders can develop to increase their effectiveness.

▪ ▪ ▪ Leading Organizational Change

This section focuses on leading change efforts in organizations. Leadership development, addressed previously in this chapter, is a critical technique for implementing and supporting change in organizations. This was demonstrated in AstraZeneca, one of the five leading pharmaceutical companies in the world. It was created by the merger in 1999 of Astra (a Swedish-based company) and Zeneca (a British-based company)—both global companies with strong track records in producing and marketing prescription drugs.

The senior leaders at AstraZeneca recognized that many mergers do not achieve their goals due to cultural conflicts between personnel in the original companies. This is especially true for mergers of organizations based in different countries. The managers took proactive steps to address these potential conflicts by encouraging discussions at the lowest level of the stated vision and values of the new company. They also initiated a leadership development program to support the major changes involved in integrating the two organizations. They recognized that leadership could be a powerful vehicle for supporting the massive change effort.

The development program began with the top-level leaders from different parts of the company. These leaders were to focus on developing the culture and realizing the values for the new organization, as well as establishing trust, working with differences, being flexible, and leading remote teams. They utilized change experts from Sweden, the United Kingdom, and the United States, and formed Business Challenge Groups (a form of action learning), in which group members helped one another with real problems and challenges they were facing in the new organization. This experience, and subsequent reflection and discussion of organizational problems and possible solutions, increased their recognition that many of their problems were common in any organization experiencing major change. They also realized how a variety of differences could contribute to solving problems, how the parts of the organization were interconnected, and how their environment was different from the past and required a future-oriented perspective. Other leadership development programs emerged from this executive program. These included leaders at various levels throughout the organization, and gave participants the chance to mix together and exchange views, develop networks in the company, dialogue with the executive leaders, and form a common perspective. These programs focused on a deeper understanding of the health care industry, AstraZeneca's objectives and strategy, developing their ability to work with people from different disciplines and cultural backgrounds, and increasing their ability to learn from experience. They thus were able to help one another change to fit the new organization, and developed tools, contacts, and perspectives to help their followers adapt to and implement their new organizational culture.[18]

This example shows the importance of leadership in implementing major change in a very large organization. But many of the problems faced by AstraZeneca are faced by any organization that makes major changes in its technology, structure, strategy, or culture. Change is omnipresent in our world today, and many changes affecting organizations must be addressed by leaders if their organizations are to survive and prosper.

Major Types of Change Affecting Organizations

Change can be thought of as a process that makes something different, alters, or transforms it. Change seems to occur wherever we look today, although several areas of change are especially relevant for organizations. One type of change we hear about almost daily is technological change. Changes in physical technology involve new equipment, software, information processing, materials, and products that were not available a few years ago. New social technology involves recent changes in human processes that facilitate organizational performance, such as programs in quality improvement, environmental responsibility, and self-managed teams. Developments in physical and social technology seem to occur every week, and they affect the operations, recruiting, training, and interactions of people in organizations.

Globalization is another major area of change affecting organizations. New information technology has made us all aware of events throughout the world almost as they occur. Political and governmental changes, armed conflicts, and terrorist activities are reported and reacted to by public leaders with little or no lead time to prepare. Technological developments, marketing strategies, governmental decisions, and economic shifts that affect organizations doing business in different countries require timely responses by business leaders. Global competition for the production and sale of products and services, and for the extraction and use of natural resources, is intense, often predatory, and controversial.

Population changes are also having major affects on organizations. In the United States, the population is getting older. This places considerable strain on health and human service organizations at a time of rising health care costs. Permeable borders permit high levels of population movement through immigration into developed countries, which adds to the strains on social services and economies. Exploding populations of young people in parts of the world combine with global information technology to create demands for products and services that organizations cannot meet and people cannot afford.

Political, economic, and social changes in recent decades have made the world a freer place, but that freedom is costly and often limited. International corporations discover myriads of regulations and cultural restrictions when they begin operations in different countries. Scandals of worker exploitation, dumping of faulty products, and unfair allocation of resources make managers more careful and watchful. Political, cultural, and religious conflicts arise that were kept in check by previous authoritarian governments, but can now prevent organizations from operating in certain areas.

A growing worldwide concern for environmental issues causes many organizations to plan and proceed more carefully in their operations. These issues affect decision-making processes regarding extraction, export, and use of natural resources, plant location, and provision of goods and services. They also affect the demand for products that are environmentally safe and the flow of capital into and out of certain industries.

News reports about the need for higher ethical and quality standards make clear demands on many organizational leaders to change their traditional ways of thinking and acting. Demands for increased accountability in education and other public service organizations place major requirements on leaders and service providers. Revelations about fraudulent practices produce changes in regulations and enforcement, training, selection, and socialization of leaders.

These issues are examples of the types of change affecting organizations and their leadership today and in future decades. They are having major effects on leaders and those preparing for leadership positions. Some major effects are listed below:

1. *The leader's role as change agent.* Leaders are increasingly expected to anticipate important changes in their organization and environment, implement these changes, and help and support organizational members in adapting to the changes. Some current writers even define leadership as the process of managing change.

2. *Individual and organizational flexibility.* As environments change, organizations and their employees must willingly adapt their behaviors and skills to fit those changes. Many popular management programs that concentrate on issues such as quality assurance, productivity improvement, and diversity are designed to make the organization and its employees more flexible in the face of changing market expectations, shareholder demands, or workforce composition.

3. *Importance of teams.* Futurists claim that knowledge is doubling every 5 years or less. As knowledge develops it becomes more specialized, and people become experts in increasingly specialized fields. However, organizations and their environments are becoming more complex. These two trends mean that leaders alone do not have the answers to many of the organizational problems they face. They need to rely on groups or teams of diverse, specialized experts who can work together to solve problems.

4. *Learning as a lifelong process.* The rapid accumulation of knowledge also means that much of our learning must be updated, modified, or replaced if we are to remain current in our fields of work. Continuous education and learning must be emphasized, encouraged, and provided by leaders to enable employees to contribute to their changing organizations.

Leaders in specific organizations will undoubtedly have other major issues they must address and roles to carry out. We believe, however, that these four issues are generalizeable to leaders in nearly all organizations now and in the future. They reflect a continuously changing environment, accumulating knowledge with specialization, and essential adaptability needed to keep organizations viable in a rapidly evolving world.

Organizational Culture

Most large change efforts in organizations involve some aspects of organizational culture.[19] Organizational culture is difficult to define, but it is usually thought of as including one or more of the following elements shared among organizational members: group norms (for example, "a fair day's pay for a fair day's work"), common jargon (for example, a "big plate" is a large piece of glass in construction), traditions (such as graduation ceremonies), espoused values (such as "quality service is our motto"), climate (the feeling conveyed by how people interact), and shared meanings and mental models (for example, "learn by doing" is a mental model for some colleges). These elements reflect relatively stable ways of thinking, perceiving, or feeling by organizational members. Over time, they generally form a consistent pattern that characterizes each organization. This pattern is the essence of an organization's culture.[20]

We can define organizational culture as the accumulated shared learning represented by common basic assumptions about how an organization solves its problems of coordination, cooperation, and adaptation to its environment. These assumptions are considered valid and are taught to new members as the appropriate way to think, perceive, and feel regarding organizational issues. The shared assumptions represent a common history of a stable membership, and they satisfy the human need for consistency and parsimony in placing meanings on organized activity. Organizational culture is a relatively stable factor that interacts with other situational factors to affect people's behavior. Groups within organizations may also develop cultures of their own, though they are usually constrained somewhat by the organization's culture. Culture can change, but it often requires considerable effort by organizational leaders and other members to bring about these changes. The Leadership in Action box describes an organization for which the leader established an effective culture.

LEADERSHIP IN ACTION
Culture in W. B. Doner & Company

W. B. Doner & Company is an international advertising agency with offices in Michigan, Maryland, and throughout the world. Doner creates award-winning advertising for major companies worldwide. Doner employees pride themselves on their creative work. In order to succeed in the highly competitive advertising industry, top-level leaders designed a distinctive organizational culture that encourages creativity, requires teamwork, and rewards entrepreneurial behavior. According to Chairman and CEO Alan Kalter, for Doner to successfully compete with those companies listed on the stock exchange, Doner needs to be quicker, smarter, and understand who they are. The company's founder, Rod Doner, established the core value of "creative first, everything else second." He constantly emphasized improving the quality of their products. During the past 60 years, Doner developed and nurtured an organizational culture that enabled it to succeed, evolve, and grow in a very competitive industry.

SOURCE: Adapted from Robert N. Lussier and Christopher F. Achua, *Leadership: Theory, Application, Skill Development,* 2nd ed. Eagan, MN: Thomson South-Western.

Two Patterns of Organizational Change

Several writers have described two different patterns of change in organizations.[21,22] The two patterns include different processes that initiate and guide change. As will be shown in the following section, they also imply different leadership roles and behaviors depending on which pattern is considered appropriate.

One pattern is often called *episodic* change because it occurs infrequently, when there is a perceived misalignment between an organization's way of operating and environmental demands. Episodic change is often dramatic and is preceded by a condition called inertia. Inertia is the inability of an organization to change as rapidly as its environment. Inertia often results from well-established organizational routines, outdated structure, top management with long tenure, old technology, or complacency from previously successful performance. Something triggers episodic change by indicating the seriousness of the misalignment with environmental reality. The trigger may be consistently poor organizational performance, a major environmental shift, new top management, or failure of strategic initiatives. Inertia usually builds slowly and eventually triggers an episodic change to replace whatever is viewed as misaligned. This is the goal of episodic change: to replace the organizational framework within which people work. The new framework is intended to be better aligned with the organization's environment. The leader's role is as a prime mover who creates the change by telling people what must be done. This type of change is sometimes called *transformational,* and is often implemented by transformational leaders.

The other change pattern is called *continuous* or *incremental* change because it is steadily evolving and accumulates over time. Continuous change involves ongoing modifications in work processes or social interactions. It is initiated by alert reactions to organizational instabilities, and includes improvisation, experimentation, accommodation, and learning throughout the organization. This approach assumes that in interconnected systems such as organizations, even marginal changes can have far-reaching effects. Small, continuous adjustments can accumulate to create substantial organizational change. The changes with this pattern involve redirecting organizational activities within an established framework, rather than replacing it with a new framework. Continuous change involves altering a range of people's skills, including strengthening some existing skills, rather than a specific action of replacement. The leader's role with this change pattern is to role model how to identify and highlight problem areas and processes, improvise, discuss and reframe how they are viewed and carried out, and encourage these learning behaviors in organizational members.

Some experts have argued that in a world of global competition, rapid technological change, deregulation, and political turmoil, choosing a pattern of incremental change can spell failure for many organizations.[23] Others maintain that both change patterns have value in different situations. Researchers described successful firms in the computer industry using both approaches to change when appropriate.[24] A mixture of continuous modifications within the current overall strategic framework and "additional episodic initiatives that are outside the current strategy"[25] may be ideal for some environments. Diagnosing the organization and its environment, and assessing their degree of compatibility—now and in the future—will determine the pattern of change a leader chooses for his or her organization. The next section will describe different models for implementing change in organizations.

The Classic Model for Implementing Change

The classic model for implementing change in any human system was developed by Kurt Lewin.[26] Change experts often refer to this model, and its three major elements are part of countless change efforts. Although it has recently been associated primarily with episodic organizational change, many of the ideas in the model have relevance for continuous change. The three elements of Lewin's model are unfreezing, changing, and refreezing, and are described below along with important subprocesses within each element.

Unfreezing

This process involves creating a motivation to change. Organizational members must perceive that things are not right with their group or organization, perhaps due to some crisis or external threat. This establishes a sense of urgency. Edgar Schein described three subprocesses to unfreeze people from their established ways: (1) There must be enough disconfirming data to cause serious discomfort that established patterns of working are no longer appropriate; (2) The disconfirming data should be directly relevant to desired goals or values; and (3) Organization members must perceive the possibility of resolving the problem of disconfirming data while maintaining their organization's integrity. Otherwise, they will likely deny the validity of the data.[27]

Charismatic leadership can be especially relevant during this phase. As described in Chapter 8, charismatic leadership behaviors are effective during times of crises or a high degree of uncertainty. Leaders may use their charismatic rhetorical skills to highlight threats to the organization, as well as opportunities that are not evident to others. By describing a favorable ideological vision of the future, the leader may provide the sense of psychological safety that organization members need to believe so that they can act successfully to address the problem. Without a considerable amount of convincing disconfirming data that is related to goal achievement, an ideological vision may have little or no effect on organization members. When they are ready to listen (they have a sense of urgency), a well-developed and communicated vision can be effective.

Changing

Here, followers typically look to their leader for guidance in determining new ways of behaving, perceiving, or thinking. The leader may enlist experts from inside or outside the organization, but he or she must have a plan of action with specific goals for followers to point toward.

Several leadership issues are important during the changing phase. The leader needs to enlist the support of a strong guiding coalition of individuals from inside the organization. This is sometimes called a *support platform,* and ideally should be composed of individuals who have power, credibility, respect, and are well liked. They should understand the obstacles, fears, and political issues involved in the change effort, and provide continued vocal support for the leader's change efforts. The leader's boundary-spanning behaviors are important in assembling this coalition to obtain the cooperation and support of key individuals from outside his or her own group or area of operation.

If the leader has not already developed a vision for the change effort, it is valuable to do so at this stage. The vision should include the goals of the change. It should clearly describe the future as a significant improvement over the current situation, and it must have the active endorsement and commitment of the leader's guiding coalition. The vision must be effectively and repeatedly communicated by the leader in a consistent and persuasive manner with the constant support of coalition members. The charismatic leadership behavior of making inspirational speeches is especially valuable at this stage to keep followers focused on the changes being made.

Directive leadership behavior is also needed to set a clear direction for the change, articulate what is expected, and continually monitor the progress. Defining roles and responsibilities, clarifying required behaviors, and building measurement mechanisms to evaluate the change are also directive behaviors needed by the change leader.[28,29]

Supporting followers is also critical to any successful change effort. Gaining their active cooperation and commitment to carry out the needed change activities is essential. It is not enough to merely overcome their resistance to change. The leader must enable or empower employees by providing needed resources, training, and information, and have the discretion to make decisions and to carry out the change. Supportive behaviors by the leader include removing obstacles and adapting existing structures, rules, policies, or procedures to facilitate the change effort. Psychological support is also needed for followers because they may become discouraged or disheartened when their efforts do not produce results as quickly as they hoped. Active listening to followers' frustrations, encouraging, coaching, empathizing, and showing confidence in followers are all critical supportive behaviors needed by leaders.

Looking for and rewarding short-term gains is also important to maintain the momentum for a major change program. Leaders should make liberal use of contingent reward behavior, giving visible recognition and celebrating small wins as changes are implemented. The confidence and enthusiasm from celebrating small wins will create the drive to take on bigger challenges and speed up the completion of the overall change effort.[30]

Refreezing

This involves reinforcing the changed behaviors, processes, structures, technology, or whatever has been changed. It must include some type of data confirming that the changes are appropriate, and thus remove the anxiety or sense of urgency that motivated the change efforts. Leaders can obtain confirming data through boundary-spanning efforts with environmental sources (such as customers or other market sources), other stakeholders (such as shareholders or financial sources), or from internal sources (such as upper-level management or respected individuals outside the leader's group). Once this confirming data is obtained and distributed, the changes become institutionalized as part of the organization's operations and culture. Old ways are replaced with new ways, and the organization is stabilized to prevent a reversal to the old ways.

Schein maintains that Lewin's model describes any change process at the individual, group, or organizational level. It describes the conditions and processes that must take place for lasting change to occur. Although the three phases may overlap, each one is important for a change to be successful. Unfreezing is needed to overcome natural resistance to change, and without refreezing, the organization may revert to its prechange condition. Leaders of change should attend to these three phases and the leadership behaviors they require to be effective in implementing major change in their organization.

An Alternative Model for Implementing Change

Several writers have described another model for implementing change that corresponds with the continuous change pattern explained earlier. This approach assumes that we do not know what the future will be like except that it will be different than today.[31] The leader's major effort with this model is to shape the organization's culture to encourage and facilitate continuous learning. The leader's goal is to develop a *learning organization* that will be able to continuously diagnose environmental needs and implement whatever changes are appropriate. Peter Senge goes further in describing a learning organization. Senge believes that increasing an organization's adaptability to its environment is only the first stage of a learning organization. He notes that the desire to learn is with us from childhood, though it may have been discouraged by competition for grades in school or performance evaluations at work. Continuous learning is what makes companies survive, and encouraging this learning makes many top-level business leaders successful.[32] He refers to this continuous learning as *generative learning* because it encourages people to generate new ideas and to experiment, explore, create, and expand their capabilities. Generative learning concentrates on anticipating environmental changes before they occur and imagining ideal strategies to address these changes. It involves thinking about what clients might need and developing products to address these needs. Learning organizations that use generative learning continually collect data from their environment. They create knowledge from this data and from past experience, share this knowledge throughout the organization, and continuously transform themselves to reflect this knowledge and insight. This is the type of learning organization developed by Larry Bossidy of Allied Signal (one of the top performing companies on the Dow Jones Industrial Average), Roger Enrico of PepsiCo, Andy Grove of Intel, and Jack Welch, former head of General Electric.

Senge maintains that the motivation for generative learning and continuous change comes from a creative tension between a highly desirable vision of what might be and a realistic assessment of current reality. The gap between these two generates the tension. The vision as described by the leader must contain enough of followers' values and aspirations to be important to them. The assessment of current reality must be vivid and accurate so followers are convinced that it is valid and unacceptable in light of the possible vision.

Charismatic leaders are skilled at describing both the desirable vision of the future (for example, "I have a dream . . .") and the reality of the current situation (such as the "shameful conditions of prejudice and racism"). Senge notes that the undesirable picture of current reality is just as important as the favorable vision of the future. In fact, some charismatic leaders have been accused of exaggerating their unfavorable description of the present in order to enlarge the gap and create more tension to motivate followers. If followers discover this type of exaggeration, the leader loses credibility and his or her influence is eroded.

Several experts on organizational change have described the roles and behaviors of leaders in creating and maintaining a learning organization. Senge classified the major leadership roles as *designer, teacher,* and *steward* of a learning culture. Schein emphasized the unique and powerful role of leaders in creating and embedding an organization's culture. The leader's role is the key element that can make a learning organization effective.

Leader as Designer

We like to use the term *social architect* to describe the designer role of leaders. By designer, we do not mean that leaders create new or different boxes and draw lines on an organization chart. Leaders create visions, guidelines, and processes that affect how people interact, what they interact about, and how the results of those interactions affect the organization.

Vision creation and communication were described in Chapter 8. To inspire followers, the vision must include the core values, purposes, and aspirations that are critically important to them. It must be very different from the current situation, be clearly relevant to followers' actions, and be communicated in a persuasive and inspiring manner. Charismatic leaders are usually skilled at these tasks, and these skills are valuable at this stage.

As designer of a learning culture, the leader also establishes ideals or values of the organization in the form of policies, strategies, and processes that embody the vision. To engage people at all levels, these guidelines and processes must include input from as many segments and levels of the organization as possible. This is facilitated when the leader concentrates on posing questions and engages in active listening regarding guidelines that he or she has proposed. The leader must not be shy about outlining the ideals and processes of the learning organization, but must gather input and reflect this input in the social architecture that is actually implemented. This calls for some directive leadership followed by an element of participation.

One expert described several guidelines and processes that are the core of learning organizations. These items represent key elements of a social architecture that encourages continuous organizational learning.

1. Ideas and knowledge flow freely throughout the organization. The culture is characterized by solidarity and sociability, with no barriers to sharing, teamwork,

or innovation. The norms encourage flow of ideas, knowledge, and cooperation across groups, inspiring creativity and multiple perspectives. Interpretations, capabilities, and practices evolve through dialogue, improvisation, and storytelling.

2. Learning leadership is dispersed throughout the organization. Top-level leaders unearth assumptions and mental models that underlie current organizational activities, and gently encourage questioning their current and future usefulness. Middle- and lower-level leaders become coaches, teachers, learning models, and colearners. They also encourage a climate of sharing experiences and experimentation.

3. Open dialogues to obtain multiple perspectives are created at all levels. These dialogues are preferably informal, but may range from deeply questioning current basic assumptions to hallway discussions in which people share insights, observations, and experiences. Ideas are discussed based on their merit rather than who proposed them. Criticism of current policies is encouraged and debated, with the objective of creating as many shared assumptions and mental models as possible.

4. Individual improvement and development, as well as organizational renewal, are continually emphasized. Individuals and groups constantly gather data for feedback on their activities, and address this feedback in dialogues with others. These activities are done within a consciously maintained supportive climate to result in personal growth, competence enhancement, added flexibility, and increased performance to meet stakeholders' rising expectations.[33]

A large amount of supportive and participative leadership behaviors are needed in establishing and implementing these guidelines. Leaders must be available and actively engage their followers and peers to create an atmosphere of open dialogue. This should improve the organizational climate and make individuals feel free to express their ideas, criticisms, and proposals with the expectation that they will be truly heard.

Leader as Teacher

By assuming the role of teacher, leaders take responsibility for ensuring that what is learned is communicated throughout the organization. They constantly seek opportunities to dialogue with others about the organization, its environment, and the assumptions and mental models people have of both. They tend to obtain a more complete picture of the tacit assumptions in their organization through their teaching efforts.

Senge described research on General Motors, in which the unspoken assumption for many years was that cars were status symbols, so styling was more important than quality. This tacit assumption kept GM from reacting to foreign competition that emphasized quality first, until it was almost too late. Assumptions such as this affect how people perceive the environment, as well as problems, opportunities, and their own behavior. All these are important change issues. By surfacing and discussing tacit assumptions, leaders can teach themselves and other organizational members a more accurate view of reality. This view can help people see the patterns and causal mechanisms that produce events, and allow them to develop proactive organizational responses before events place them in a reactive (defensive) position.

Followers benefit from being taught by experienced individuals from their own organization. They experience continued development as individuals and as leaders while addressing the real challenges of change. Leaders as teachers recognize that people develop winning strategies and form the real strength of an organization, so they focus on developing people to prepare them to do just that.

Leaders as teachers also make extensive use of participative and supportive leadership behaviors, along with the charismatic behavior of role modeling. Recognizing and rewarding followers for breakthroughs in their thinking and actions is also an important leadership behavior used by leaders as teachers.

Leader as Steward

This role is briefly described by Senge, but is less frequently mentioned by other change experts. Senge indicates that leaders have two stewardship roles in learning organizations. The first role is directed toward the people they are leading in their own organization. It reflects an appreciation for the strong impacts a leader can have on followers. People can thrive under supportive and foresightful leaders who work to help them prepare for the future. People can also suffer tremendous emotional, professional, and economic losses under ineffective leaders. Leaders who take responsibility for the welfare and development of their followers, fulfill this stewardship role. They demonstrate their commitment through their actions on followers' behalf. They religiously avoid ever placing their own welfare ahead of their people.

The second stewardship role reflects the leader's commitment to the organization's mission. When leaders are engaged in a worthy purpose, this ignites their motivation to learn and help others learn in order to carry out the purpose. They become proactive in turning conversations into learning experiences. Amid busy schedules, they focus their attention on their own and others' learning. They attend and participate in as many dialogue sessions as possible to demonstrate the importance they place on learning. They allocate resources and reward learning initiatives, share breakthroughs and learning accomplishments with others, and recruit people who will bring new perspectives into the organization. In short, leaders as stewards do all they can to embed and encourage continuous learning in their organization's culture.

In their role as stewards, leaders exhibit role modeling, contingent reward behavior, and boundary spanning inside and outside their organizational unit. They demonstrate responsibility for followers' learning by supporting their efforts through providing resources to support learning initiatives. They also use participative behaviors to engage followers and colleagues in discussions about keeping the learning process moving forward. Table 13-2 summarizes the leadership behaviors needed in fulfilling the three leader roles in a learning organization.

TABLE 13-2 Important leadership behaviors in a learning organization

- Vision creation, including core values, purposes, and aspirations
- Directiveness regarding values, policies, and processes
- Participation regarding knowledge sharing, mental models, assumptions, and the learning process
- Supportiveness for individual development and creative learning
- Rewarding and recognizing improvements and breakthroughs
- Boundary spanning to keep the organization connected and informed
- Role modeling responsible behaviors, and dialoguing

Denial, Avoidance, and Resistance to Change

One reality of change that all leaders must keep in mind is that change causes stress. Change involves a risk because we do not know how it will affect us. New work methods, new habits, new software, new people, new boss, and new rules all involve moving out of our comfort zone and into the unknown. Most people try to avoid or minimize stress. They may do this by denying the need for change, avoiding it entirely, or blaming others for fixing things that are not broken.[34]

Denial and avoidance of change can turn into resistance that many writers believe must be overcome. Experts have recently noted, however, that resistance to change can be healthy and valuable for an organization. It can convey information to the change leader that certain things should be kept as is or simply modified instead of completely replaced. Resistance can tell leaders that there are values, mental models, or processes that reflect important organizational history and culture, and discarding them may mean a loss of identity for employees. Some continuity is needed in order for people to maintain their organizational identity. Leaders must listen carefully to the sources of denial, avoidance, and resistance to change, and consider if they are motivated by stress avoidance alone or if important change issues should be reexamined before they are implemented as planned.

Helping People Cope

There are numerous actions leaders can take to assist their followers when changes are ongoing. Some of these actions have been described in previous sections of this chapter, but are presented here as techniques for helping employees deal with major changes in their work.

1. Provide as much information to employees as possible. Communicating before, during, and after a major change process can help prevent misunderstandings, false rumors, and conflict. Communicating in person is the best method. It allows for immediate questions and answers.
2. Actively listen to what people say and how they say it. Acknowledge others' feelings and share your own feelings. Paraphrase what you hear to show understanding.
3. Provide training, coaching, and guidance to help followers develop the skills and capabilities they will need. This will aid people in dealing with adjustments, disruptions, or dislocations that often occur with major changes.
4. Help people set goals that focus on key tasks and priorities for the change process. Encourage and express high expectations, but be patient.
5. Develop an implementation team with ad hoc task forces to involve followers in planning, implementing, and evaluating change activities. Although time consuming, this will pay off in avoiding major mistakes and giving people some control over the change process. Avoid micromanaging the process, and empower the teams to implement change.
6. Support the change process in every way possible. Utilize different opportunities to repeat your own and the organization's commitment to the change. Provide staffing, facilities, and funds as needed. Back up decisions made by those implementing the change whenever possible.
7. Acknowledge, reward, and celebrate accomplishments and contributions of all those involved in the change process.[35,36]

When these actions are taken by leaders in an honest and sincere manner, followers are likely to commit their own energies to making the change process successful. Follower commitment is the key ingredient to a successful change effort.

Evaluating Change

Writers on organizational change seldom address the importance of evaluating the results of change efforts. They seem to assume that change is inherently valuable to people and organizations in general. Evaluation is essential if we are to know whether or not specific changes are beneficial to the organization and its people.

For evaluations to be credible to everyone involved, they should be carried out by an evaluation committee or task force composed of people from all levels of the change effort. The leader may or may not be a member of this committee, but he or she should provide input as needed and expect regular reporting on the committee's findings. The committee's discussions will likely be more honest and open if the leader is not a regular member. The evaluation committee should have benchmarks or guidelines to gauge all phases of the change process. These guidelines may come from industry associations, other organizations, or be worked out by the committee itself in advance. The evaluation should be based on actual data from the organization or group undergoing the change. Perceptions and opinions are subjective and often biased. Actual data from organizational operations must be monitored to show real results of change efforts. Improvements will take time while people adjust to the changes, but improvements must be demonstrated at some point to justify the change process.

Summary ▪▪▪▪▪▪▪

Leadership development involves expanding a leader's capabilities to effectively carry out needed leadership behaviors and processes. One of the key factors in this development is adult learning, which is the major focus of this chapter. Most leadership development experts emphasize three key processes: assessment, challenge, and support. Development programs usually emphasize one or more of these processes. The three processes encourage personal growth, conceptual understanding, self-knowledge, and skill building in leaders. A lot of development takes place within a leader's own organization via interactions with mentors and coaches, and through action learning, in which leaders work with other leaders to discuss and address real organizational problems.

A leader's personal values provide guideposts to help steer the leader's development in the right direction. Activities that help leaders obtain a clear picture of their values allow them to plan rewarding careers and be sure their behaviors are congruent with these values. This congruence is important in obtaining followers' trust.

A leader's vision is also important in guiding his or her development. A personal vision (a picture of the leader's ideal life) and a leadership vision (a picture of the ideal leader he or she wants to become) can provide confidence and guidance to the leader as he or she develops, and help maintain awareness of his or her true north.

Major skills needed for most leadership positions include communication skills (especially active listening and persuasion), empathy, rewarding others, and learning from experience. Exercises and guidelines provided in this chapter are useful in developing each of these skill areas.

Change is a process that makes something different, alters it, or transforms it. Change is occurring in almost every aspect of organizational operations. The leader's role is tremendously important in guiding change efforts in organizations. Leaders act as change agents (anticipating, implementing, and supporting needed change), encourage flexibility and team approaches to problems, and emphasize continuous learning as part of their organization's culture.

Organizational change is often described as episodic (in which infrequent adjustments help the organization better fit its environment) or continuous (involving ongoing modifications in work processes and social interactions). Both approaches have been found useful for understanding and addressing organizational change. The classic model for implementing a major organizational change involves unfreezing current views, behaviors, and approaches; changing the behaviors, process, structure, or technology as needed; and refreezing the views, behaviors, and approaches through positive reinforcement and positive feedback. This approach was developed by Kurt Lewin and was originally based on the episodic view of organizational change, although many current scholars still believe it applies to any change occurring in organizations. An alternative model for implementing change assumes that change is continuous and unpredictable. The leader's strategy with this approach is to shape the organization's culture to encourage and facilitate continuous learning. Organizations with this type of culture are called learning organizations, and they continuously diagnose environmental needs and implement the changes that are appropriate. Leaders in learning organizations actively encourage new ideas, as well as experimentation, exploration, and creativity to expand peoples' capabilities. These organizations anticipate environmental changes and future client needs, and take action to address them before they cause problems.

Peter Senge described three major roles for leaders in building a learning organization. The leader as designer creates visions, guidelines, and processes that affect how people interact, what they interact about, and how the results of their interactions affect the organization. The leader as teacher actively ensures that what is learned is communicated throughout the organization. The leader as steward has two functions: (1) he or she assumes responsibility for followers' welfare and development through showing support and foresight to help them prepare for the future; (2) he or she assures that the continuous learning that is encouraged will help the group or organization achieve its mission. Many of the leadership behaviors described in this book are useful for carrying out these three leadership roles.

Organizational changes always meet with resistance from some personnel. This is often due to stress and the fear of not knowing how the changes will affect them. Leaders should be sure that the resistance does not indicate the possible loss of important values, mental models, or processes that are important for followers' identity and commitment to the organization. Helping people cope with the stress of change is essential, and specific actions were offered in this chapter for leaders to use in providing this help and support for followers. Some evaluation of the results of organizational change efforts is essential in order to learn if the changes benefited the organization and its people. This evaluation must be based on actual data from the organization (not simply the opinions of those involved), and should be carried out by a group of credible individuals from different levels of the organization.

KEY TERMS AND CONCEPTS IN THIS CHAPTER

- 360-degree feedback
- Action learning
- Active listening
- Assessment
- Challenge
- Changing
- Continuous, incremental change
- Emotional intelligence
- Empathy

- Episodic change
- Executive coaching
- Ideal self
- Leader as designer
- Leader as steward
- Leader as teacher
- Leadership development
- Leadership vision
- Learning journal
- Learning organization

- Mentor
- Organizational culture
- Ought self
- Personal vision
- Persuasive communication
- Refreezing
- Self-awareness
- Support
- Unfreezing
- Values

REVIEW AND DISCUSSION QUESTIONS

1. Describe the type of leadership development program that you think would be most helpful for your own development as a leader.
2. Describe your core values and how you show these values in your behavior.
3. Describe your personal vision and your leadership vision. How are these two visions related to one another?
4. Describe a leadership position you would like to have in the future. What are the major costs and benefits to a person in this position?
5. Which key leadership skills do you already possess? Which skills do you need to develop? Describe how you can develop these needed skills.
6. Describe how you can become a more active listener.
7. Describe how you can become a more persuasive speaker.
8. What industry(or industries) do you plan to work in? Describe the types of change that strongly affect organizations in this industry.
9. Describe the organizational culture that existed in an organization in which you worked or are familiar with. How could this culture be improved to make the organization more effective and efficient?
10. As a future leader, how would you create a learning organization in which you plan to work? Be as specific as possible.

EXPERIENTIAL EXERCISE: LEADERSHIP ROLES

As a useful exercise to begin planning your own development as a leader, describe the kinds of leadership roles you would like to pursue. These roles may be a leader in a campus organization, a voluntary community or church group, a political party, a business or governmental organization, or some other situation. You might describe a series of roles you hope to fulfill, leading to a certain position as your ultimate leadership goal. Share your list of leadership roles with friends, classmates, or those you work with. Ask for their input on how you can prepare yourself for these leadership roles.

EXPERIENTIAL EXERCISE: YOUR LEARNING JOURNAL

After reading this chapter, take 20 minutes to think about what you learned from it. You might begin by reviewing the major issues and guidelines described in this chapter. Then write down your thoughts and feelings about these issues. Now select one or two issues that were more meaningful to you than the others. Describe how these issues or guidelines apply specifically to your development as a leader or to a needed change in an organization you participated in. Then describe how the issues or guidelines can be used to further your own development as a leader or to change and improve the organization.

ENDNOTES ▪▪▪▪▪▪▪

1. Van Velsor, E., McCauley, C. D., and Moxley, R. S. (1998). Our view of leadership development. In C. D. McCauley, R. S. Moxley, and E. Van Velsor (Eds.), *Handbook of Leadership Development.* San Francisco: Jossey-Bass.

2. Goleman, D. (1998). What makes a leader? *Harvard Business Review,* 76(6), 92–105.

3. Van Velsor, McCauley, and Moxley. Our view of leadership development.

4. Conger, J. (1992). *Learning to Lead.* San Francisco: Jossey-Bass.

5. Cohen, B., and Greenfield, J. (1997). *Ben and Jerry's Double Dip: Lead with Your Values and Make Money, Too.* New York: Simon & Schuster.

6. Lee, R. J., and King, S. N. (2001). *Discovering the Leader in You: A Guide to Realizing Your Personal Leadership Potential.* Center for Creative Leadership. Greensboro, NC: Jossey-Bass.

7. Goleman, D., Boyatzis, R., and McKee, R. (2002). *Primal Leadership.* Boston: Harvard Business School Press.

8. Lee and King. *Discovering the Leader in You: A Guide to Realizing Your Personal Leadership Potential.*

9. Ibid.

10. Mumford, M. D., Marks, M. S., Connelly, M. S., Azccaro, S. J., and Reiter-Palmon, R. (2000). Development of leadership skills: Experience and timing. *Leadership Quarterly,* 11(1), 87–114.

11. Berhnut, S. (2001). Managing the dream: Warren Bennis on leadership. *Ivey Business Journal,* 65, 36.

12. Hughes, R. L., Ginnett, R. C., and Curphy, G. J. (2002). *Leadership: Enhancing the Lessons of Experience,* 4th ed. Boston: McGraw-Hill/Irwin.

13. Dubrin, A. J. (2004). *Leadership: Research Finding, Practice, and Skills,* 4th ed. New York: Houghton Mifflin.

14. Day, D. V. (2001). Leadership development: A review in context. *Leadership Quarterly,* 11(4), 581–613.

15. Bennis, W. G., and Thomas, R. J. (2002). *Geeks and Geezers.* Boston: Harvard Business School Press.

16. McCauley, Moxley, and Van Velsor. Our view of leadership development.

17. Van Velsor, E., and Guthrie, V. A. (1998). Enhancing the ability to learn from experience. In C. D. McCauley, R. S. Moxley, and E. Van Velsor (Eds.), *Handbook of Leadership Development.* San Francisco: Jossey-Bass.

18. Hyde, A., and Paterson, J. (2002). Leadership development as a vehicle for change during a merger. *Journal of Change Management,* 2(3), 266–271.

19. Yukl, G. (2002). *Leadership in Organizations,* 5th ed. Upper Saddle River, NJ: Prentice Hall.

20. Schein, E. (1992). *Organizational Culture and Leadership.* San Francisco: Jossey-Bass.

21. Weick, K. E., and Quinn, R. E. (1999). Organizational change and development. *Annual Review of Psychology,* 50, 361–386.

22. Chapman, J. A. (2002). A framework for transformational change in organizations. *Leadership and Organizational Development Journal,* 23(1), 16–25.

23. Nadler, D. A., and Tushman, M. L. (1990). Beyond the charismatic leader: Leadership and organizational change. *California Management Review,* 32(2), 77–97.

24. Brown, S. L., and Eisenhardt, K. M. (1997). The art of continuous change: Linking complexity theory and time-paced evolution in relentlessly shifting organizations. *Administrative Science Quarterly,* 42, 1–34.

25. Weick and Quinn. Organizational change and development.

26. Lewin, K. (1951). *Field Theory in Social Science.* New York: Harper & Row.

27. Schein. *Organizational Culture and Leadership.*

28. Nadler and Tushman. Beyond the charismatic leader: Leadership and organizational change.

29. Waldersee, R., and Eagleson, G. (2002). Shared leadership in the implementation of re-orientations. *Leadership and Organizational Development Journal,* 23(7), 400–407.

30. Lussier, R. N., and Achua, C. F. (2004). *Leadership: Theory, Application, Skill Development,* 2nd ed. Eagan, MN: Thomson South-Western.

31. Schein. *Organizational Culture and Leadership.*

32. Senge, P. (1990). The leader's new work: Building learning organizations. *Sloan Management Review,* Fall 1990, 7–23.

33. Snell, R. S. (2002). The learning organization, sense giving and psychological contracts: A Hong Kong case. *Organization Studies,* 23(40), 549–573.

34. Lee and King. *Discovering the Leader in You: A Guide to Realizing Your Personal Leadership Potential.*

35. Manning, G., and Curtis, K. (2003). *The Art of Leadership.* Boston: McGraw-Hill.

36. Liesser and Achua. *Leadership: Theory, Application, Skill Development.*

14

Integration and Conclusions

Learning Objectives

After reading this chapter, you should be able to do the following:

1. Summarize the general effects of leadership behaviors on follower reactions and outcomes.

2. Identify leadership behaviors that most consistently increase the quantity or quality of performance by individuals and groups.

3. Describe the leadership styles that result from various combinations of leadership behaviors.

4. Identify the combinations of leader characteristics and skills that complement the different leadership styles.

5. Identify follower and situational characteristics that impact the effectiveness of different leadership styles.

6. Describe two general strategies leaders can use to influence the attitudes and performance of individuals and groups.

7. Describe several dimensions of culture that are important for leaders to consider when working in different regions of the world.

8. Explain the concept of equifinality in leadership, and how it can be applied to increase leadership effectiveness.

▫▫▫ General Effects of Leadership Behaviors

All the leadership behaviors described in this book have some effects on followers and their groups. Most of these effects are favorable, though as we have noted, many situational and follower characteristics influence the direction and strength of these effects. Table 14-1 summarizes the general effects of the leadership behaviors on follower reactions and outcomes. Although the effects described in Table 14-1 depend somewhat on situational and follower characteristics facing the leader, they are usually as specified in the table.

TABLE 14-1 General effects of leadership behaviors on followers[a]

Leadership Behaviors	Quantity or Quality of Individual or Group Performance	Supervisor Ratings of Individual or Group Performance	Individual Role Clarity or Development	Individual Satisfaction, Commitment, or Motivation	Group Cohesion	Individual Turnover, Burnout, or Intent to Quit
Directive[b]	Positive	Positive	Strongly positive	Strongly positive	Positive	Negative
Supportive	Positive	Positive	Positive	Strongly positive	Positive	Negative
Participative	Small positive	Probably positive	Probably positive	Positive	Probably positive	Probably negative
Contingent reward	Positive	Positive	Positive	Positive	Probably positive	?
Contingent punishment	Probably positive[c]	?	?	?	?	?
Charismatic	Positive	Strongly positive	?	Strongly positive[d]	?	Negative
Building social exchanges	?	Strongly positive	Probably positive	Strongly positive	?	?
Boundary spanning	Probably positive	Positive	?	Positive	?	Probably negative
Followership	Probably positive	Positive	?	Probably positive	Probably positive	?

▪▪▪▪▪▪▪▪▪▪

[a]A positive effect means a leader's behavior resulted in an increase in followers' performance, attitudes, role clarity, or group cohesion. A negative effect means a leader's behavior resulted in a decrease in followers' burnout, turnover, or intent to quit. A question mark (?) means research results are either contradictory or there are too few studies to draw a conclusion.

[b]Positive effects of directive and supportive leadership were often found when both leadership behaviors were provided together by the leader.

[c]When used in conjunction with contingent reward behavior.

[d]Most followers react very positively to charismatic leadership, although some individuals can react very negatively.

As shown in Table 14-1, directive, supportive, contingent reward, and charismatic leadership behaviors have been most consistent at increasing the *quantity or quality of performance* by followers and groups. The other leadership behaviors may improve the quantity or quality of followers' performance, but the effects are either small or require further research for complete verification. Charismatic and social exchange behaviors by leaders strongly increased the *performance ratings* they received from their supervisors. Directive, supportive, contingent reward, and boundary-spanning behaviors also produced favorable ratings of leaders by their supervisor. Directive leadership produced the strongest improvements in followers' *role clarity,* although supportive and contingent reward leadership behaviors also improved this follower reaction.

Supportive, directive, charismatic, and social exchange behaviors produced the strongest improvements in followers' attitudes, such as *satisfaction* and *commitment* to the organization as well as *motivation.* Recall, however, that charismatic leadership behavior can also produce strong negative reactions from followers. Participative and contingent reward leadership behaviors also improved followers' attitudes, but not as strongly as other leadership behaviors. Directive and supportive leadership behaviors improved *group cohesion,* whereas directive, supportive, and charismatic leadership behaviors all decreased followers' *turnover, burnout,* and *intentions to quit.* Notice that contingent punishment behavior resulted in a "Probably positive" effect on followers' performance only when used along with contingent reward behavior. There were no other reliable effects of contingent punishment behavior on the follower reactions and outcomes shown in Table 14-1.

▪▪▪ Typical Leadership Styles

The leadership behaviors described in this book are usually used in combination with one another. These combinations often result in several typical *leadership styles* found in many organizations. Some of these styles are described in this section. In the real world, many leaders do not fit precisely into any of these types. Some leaders may combine several of these styles. We believe, however, that readers with experience in real organizations will recognize some of these styles. The description of each is followed by a figure summarizing when the style could be effective and how the leader might enact the style and modify the situation as needed.

Coach

A leader with this style places maximum importance on developing followers' potential to perform well.[1] Coaches are usually highly *directive* with followers, spending considerable time explaining expectations about quantity, quality, and rules and procedures, outlining useful methods to complete tasks, and clarifying task assignments. They are also *supportive* by showing concern and consideration for followers as individuals and expressing confidence in them as they develop. Coaches may slowly increase the amount of *participation* they use with followers as they develop. That is, as followers' knowledge and ability increase, coaches increase the amount they involve them in decision making and the scope of tasks delegated to them.

Coaches probably use *contingent (intangible) reward* behavior to reinforce followers' development and good performance, showing appreciation for their efforts through compliments and recognition. They most likely use very little *contingent punishment* behavior; rather, they allow followers' performance to speak for itself. Coaches may not reprimand followers solely for low performance, but they would do so for extreme cases of disruptive follower behavior.

Coaches spend considerable time with their followers, and they generally have *good interpersonal and communication skills.* Most coaches have a fairly high *socialized need for power,* which is a strong desire to build influence through others. In the process, they help the followers to become independent performers to support their goals. Many coaches also may have a high *need for affiliation,* which means they enjoy spending time interacting with others and like to feel valuable and accepted by others.

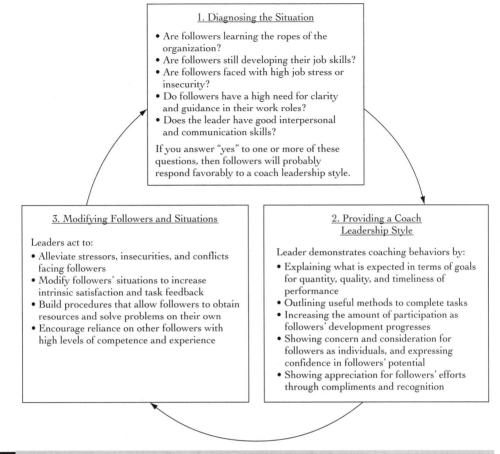

1. Diagnosing the Situation

- Are followers learning the ropes of the organization?
- Are followers still developing their job skills?
- Are followers faced with high job stress or insecurity?
- Do followers have a high need for clarity and guidance in their work roles?
- Does the leader have good interpersonal and communication skills?

If you answer "yes" to one or more of these questions, then followers will probably respond favorably to a coach leadership style.

3. Modifying Followers and Situations

Leaders act to:
- Alleviate stressors, insecurities, and conflicts facing followers
- Modify followers' situations to increase intrinsic satisfaction and task feedback
- Build procedures that allow followers to obtain resources and solve problems on their own
- Encourage reliance on other followers with high levels of competence and experience

2. Providing a Coach Leadership Style

Leader demonstrates coaching behaviors by:
- Explaining what is expected in terms of goals for quantity, quality, and timeliness of performance
- Outlining useful methods to complete tasks
- Increasing the amount of participation as followers' development progresses
- Showing concern and consideration for followers as individuals, and expressing confidence in followers' potential
- Showing appreciation for followers' efforts through compliments and recognition

▪▪▪▪ **FIGURE 14-1 Applying the coach leadership style**

Coaching is often an effective leadership style for followers who are learning the ropes of the organization and are still developing their job skills. The directive and supportive aspects of this style may be less effective for followers who are highly trained and experienced at their job tasks or who have other sources of guidance and encouragement readily available, such as helpful and proficient coworkers or specialized training personnel. In these situations, the coach's participation and reward behaviors should be emphasized.

Tommy Lasorda, former manager of the Los Angeles Dodgers, was described earlier. Lasorda's coaching style of leadership combined directive leadership with a lot of supportiveness for young players, followed by compliments and recognition as players became more proficient. He eventually used participation by consulting with veteran players on key decisions. He is well known for his success in developing young players. Figure 14-1 summarizes the coach leadership style.

Human Relations Specialist

Leaders with this style emphasize keeping followers happy and comfortable, assuming they will respond with effective performance.[2] These leaders are highly *supportive* by showing concern for followers' welfare, happiness, and comfort. They are often also highly *participative,* especially when followers have the desire to be involved in management decision making. They consult often with followers and delegate frequently. These leaders often use *boundary spanning* to represent their people to those outside, obtaining resources needed for their comfort. They are usually *not directive* with followers, spending little time defining management expectations. They seem to assume that followers know best what to do. If performance problems occur, they often appeal to followers to get together and help figure out what to do. They may *modify situations* to make the followers' work more comfortable and pleasing to them.

Human relations specialists have *good interpersonal skills* in order to interact in a pleasant manner with followers. They likely have high *need for affiliation* and *nurturance,* and they enjoy seeing followers happy and comfortable in the work situation. This type of leadership style is useful when followers are recovering from some traumatic event, such as a disaster or a merger or major downsizing that involved layoffs or a reorganization of work. It can be used effectively as a short-term strategy to restore equilibrium among followers so they can settle into their new routines. It is not usually an effective leadership style for achieving high levels of performance, unless the leader's followers are unusually competent, highly trained individuals who rely on one another for any needed job guidance.

The human relations specialist style was shown by an interim coach of a youth swimming team. This coach filled the position after the previous coach was asked to leave for mistreating the swimmers and driving kids away from the sport. The interim coach showed concern and supportiveness for the remaining swimmers and solicited input from their parents on how to rebuild team morale. She did not direct any major changes in team procedures or swimming techniques and did not differentiate rewards among team members. Instead, she treated all members equally with the same caring attitude. She was effective at providing stability, and kept the team together until the new coach was hired. Figure 14-2 summarizes the human relations specialist style of leadership.

Controlling Autocrat

Individuals using this leadership style are often obsessed with controlling the actions of those around them.[3] They are highly *directive* with followers, giving detailed instructions regarding work methods, output expected, quality standards, rules, and regulations. They use contingent and noncontingent *punishment* extensively. Followers often see these leaders as arbitrary and unfair. They usually do *not* use much participative, supportive, rewarding, or boundary-spanning leadership behaviors in dealing with followers.

Controlling autocrats have a high *personal need for power,* meaning they constantly desire to control their environment and other people around them. They often have *poor interpersonal skills* and dominate followers with *authoritarian* demands. They are frequently *dogmatic* in their beliefs, and do not value new input or criticism from others. This leadership style may achieve results under emergency conditions, when time is short and the stakes are high. In most organizational situations, however, this style produces so much resentment among followers that they do not willingly cooperate with the leader and usually seek other positions as soon as possible.

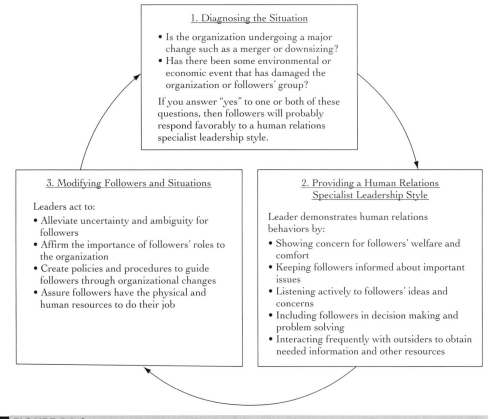

1. Diagnosing the Situation

- Is the organization undergoing a major change such as a merger or downsizing?
- Has there been some environmental or economic event that has damaged the organization or followers' group?

If you answer "yes" to one or both of these questions, then followers will probably respond favorably to a human relations specialist leadership style.

3. Modifying Followers and Situations

Leaders act to:
- Alleviate uncertainty and ambiguity for followers
- Affirm the importance of followers' roles to the organization
- Create policies and procedures to guide followers through organizational changes
- Assure followers have the physical and human resources to do their job

2. Providing a Human Relations Specialist Leadership Style

Leader demonstrates human relations behaviors by:
- Showing concern for followers' welfare and comfort
- Keeping followers informed about important issues
- Listening actively to followers' ideas and concerns
- Including followers in decision making and problem solving
- Interacting frequently with outsiders to obtain needed information and other resources

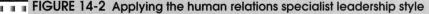

▮▮▮▮ **FIGURE 14-2 Applying the human relations specialist leadership style**

A supervisor who worked for a government contractor on a construction project used the controlling autocratic style to enforce government specifications and meet a short project deadline. When the project was later extended to include another phase with no specific deadline, the supervisor continued using the same controlling autocratic style. Followers who cooperated to meet the earlier deadline saw no reason for this close direction and control during the new phase. They began to resent the supervisor when he gave them no freedom to determine how they did their work and he threatened to lower their pay or fire them if they did not follow his detailed directions. Their dissatisfaction was shown by increased absenteeism and turnover among the workers. Figure 14-3 summarizes the controlling autocrat style of leadership.

Transformational Visionary

This style is currently very popular in the management literature, and is thought to create extreme devotion and extraordinary effort among followers.[4] This type of leader uses *charismatic* behaviors extensively, giving inspirational speeches using metaphorical language, often describing current conditions as immoral and intolerable, and outlining a future vision that is radically different from the status quo. These leaders are also highly *supportive* of followers, showing concern and consideration for

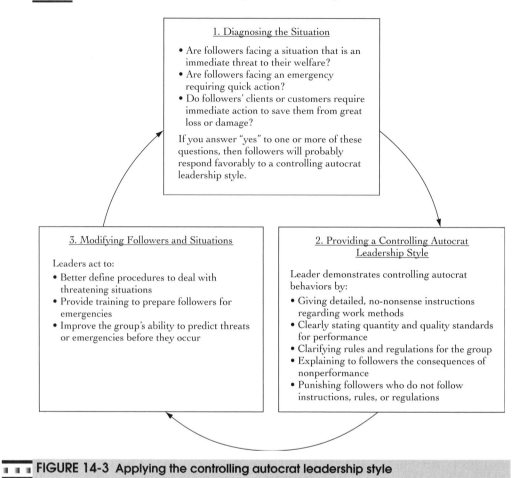

1. Diagnosing the Situation

- Are followers facing a situation that is an immediate threat to their welfare?
- Are followers facing an emergency requiring quick action?
- Do followers' clients or customers require immediate action to save them from great loss or damage?

If you answer "yes" to one or more of these questions, then followers will probably respond favorably to a controlling autocrat leadership style.

3. Modifying Followers and Situations

Leaders act to:

- Better define procedures to deal with threatening situations
- Provide training to prepare followers for emergencies
- Improve the group's ability to predict threats or emergencies before they occur

2. Providing a Controlling Autocrat Leadership Style

Leader demonstrates controlling autocrat behaviors by:

- Giving detailed, no-nonsense instructions regarding work methods
- Clearly stating quantity and quality standards for performance
- Clarifying rules and regulations for the group
- Explaining to followers the consequences of nonperformance
- Punishing followers who do not follow instructions, rules, or regulations

▪▪▪ **FIGURE 14-3** Applying the controlling autocrat leadership style

them as individuals. They may try to develop followers' leadership skills through *mentoring* relationships in which they dialogue, demonstrate, and encourage followers to try new and challenging tasks. They use *boundary-spanning behaviors* to represent followers and groups effectively to outsiders and to gain acceptance, resources, and cooperation needed to carry out the mission. Perhaps surprisingly, these leaders are often *not participative* with followers. That is, they do not necessarily consult with followers or solicit input for decision making. They are usually very self-confident, and although they may occasionally consult with a few key advisors, they consciously project an image of assuredness and certainty in the mission and strategy they outline for followers.

Transformational visionaries have excellent *communication skills* that they use to convey their mission and vision in a convincing manner. They also have a high *socialized need for power*, desiring to build their influence and move the group or organization toward their vision. They use *impression management skills* to create a positive image, which further enhances their confidence and the confidence of followers in their leadership. Transformational visionary leaders may also be highly *intelligent and creative* in defining a vision and mission for followers, in cleverly relating that mission to strong follower desires and needs, and in communicating that mission through emotional speech patterns and their own behavior.

This leadership style is highly effective when followers are frustrated, stressed, or unhappy with their current situation. This may occur because of an intolerable political or organizational administration, a dangerous emergency, rapid change, prolonged discrimination, economic hardship, or other personal factors that have weakened followers. It is not clear whether transformational visionary leaders are effective when followers are not experiencing extreme stress and frustration.

Larry Bossidy used the transformational visionary leadership style to stop the decline of Allied Signal in the early 1990s. When Bossidy took over as CEO, Allied Signal was overextended with too many operations and too much debt, and was rapidly losing cash. He first focused on selling certain divisions, cutting staff, and combining operations. He then developed a company vision and mission for the future, with goals that people found attractive. He visited workers at all levels to describe the mission, and encouraged and supported their efforts to contribute toward the goals. He focused on teamwork to pull employees together to save the company and help it prosper. Today, Allied Signal is a successful defense and auto parts conglomerate, its stock has soared, and employees take pride in the fact that they saved the company.[5] Figure 14-4 summarizes the transformational visionary leadership style.

The Transactional Exchange

This leadership style is based on exchanges of benefits and contributions between the leader and followers.[6] The leader provides guidance, attention, and benefits to particular followers based on their input to the group. Directive leadership behavior is a major element of this style. Leaders tell followers their expectations, and clarify the procedures and work methods needed to complete tasks. They also make extensive use of contingent reward behavior, providing compliments and recognition, as well as extra time, attention, and other rewards for followers, when they perform well. They also use contingent punishment behavior by letting followers know when they have not performed well. Transactional exchange leaders may reprimand followers for repeated rule violations and low effort leading to poor performance. These leaders also build close social exchanges (create ingroups) with selected followers whom they view as effective or potentially effective performers. They often exclude others from close social exchanges.

Transactional exchange leaders often have high achievement motivation, setting high goals for themselves and their groups, and focusing their intense effort on achieving those goals. They are sometimes described as single-minded in their pursuit of these goals. They also often have good interpersonal and communication skills, which they concentrate on their highest-performing followers. These leaders can be effective with followers who are very rational in their approach to tasks and who view their time with the leader as an opportunity to benefit themselves professionally. This style may be less effective in situations in which the leader has few rewards at his or her disposal, or the methods are unclear and extensive creativity is required.

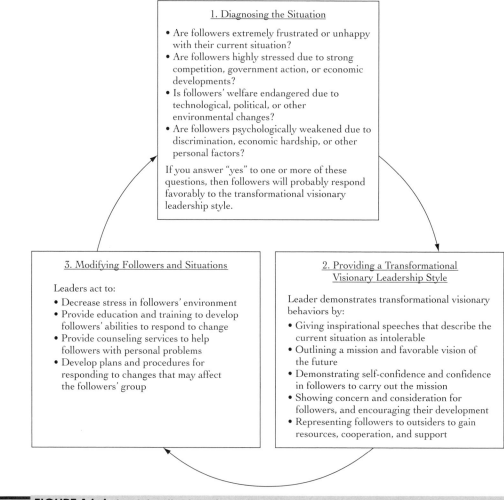

1. Diagnosing the Situation

- Are followers extremely frustrated or unhappy with their current situation?
- Are followers highly stressed due to strong competition, government action, or economic developments?
- Is followers' welfare endangered due to technological, political, or other environmental changes?
- Are followers psychologically weakened due to discrimination, economic hardship, or other personal factors?

If you answer "yes" to one or more of these questions, then followers will probably respond favorably to the transformational visionary leadership style.

3. Modifying Followers and Situations

Leaders act to:
- Decrease stress in followers' environment
- Provide education and training to develop followers' abilities to respond to change
- Provide counseling services to help followers with personal problems
- Develop plans and procedures for responding to changes that may affect the followers' group

2. Providing a Transformational Visionary Leadership Style

Leader demonstrates transformational visionary behaviors by:
- Giving inspirational speeches that describe the current situation as intolerable
- Outlining a mission and favorable vision of the future
- Demonstrating self-confidence and confidence in followers to carry out the mission
- Showing concern and consideration for followers, and encouraging their development
- Representing followers to outsiders to gain resources, cooperation, and support

▪▪▪ **FIGURE 14-4** Applying the transformational visionary leadership style

The transactional exchange style was used when the Trans-Alaska Pipeline System was under construction. The contractors hired skilled and unskilled labor to work in isolated areas and under severe weather conditions for very high wages. Supervisors expected workers to put in 10- to 12-hour days and work 6 or 7 days per week. All their living needs were provided for by the company when they were on the job, so many workers saved substantial amounts of money. The supervisors were highly directive and rewarded good performance by rehiring workers who went south every few weeks for rest and relaxation. They enforced strict rules of conduct when workers were on the job or in the enclosed living facilities the companies provided. They also expected employees to show up for work on time. Supervisors made these expectations clear to employees when they first arrived, and when employees complied with expectations, the monetary rewards were very significant. Figure 14-5 summarizes the transactional exchange leadership style.

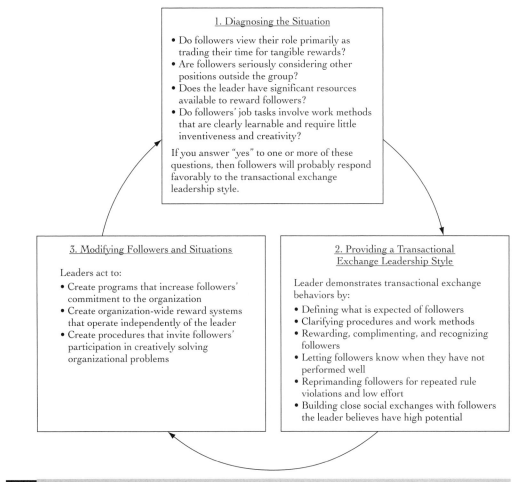

1. Diagnosing the Situation

- Do followers view their role primarily as trading their time for tangible rewards?
- Are followers seriously considering other positions outside the group?
- Does the leader have significant resources available to reward followers?
- Do followers' job tasks involve work methods that are clearly learnable and require little inventiveness and creativity?

If you answer "yes" to one or more of these questions, then followers will probably respond favorably to the transactional exchange leadership style.

3. Modifying Followers and Situations

Leaders act to:

- Create programs that increase followers' commitment to the organization
- Create organization-wide reward systems that operate independently of the leader
- Create procedures that invite followers' participation in creatively solving organizational problems

2. Providing a Transactional Exchange Leadership Style

Leader demonstrates transactional exchange behaviors by:

- Defining what is expected of followers
- Clarifying procedures and work methods
- Rewarding, complimenting, and recognizing followers
- Letting followers know when they have not performed well
- Reprimanding followers for repeated rule violations and low effort
- Building close social exchanges with followers the leader believes have high potential

▪▪▪ **FIGURE 14-5 Applying the transactional exchange leadership style**

Servant

The term *servant leader* has recently appeared in the popular management literature to describe a variation on the coach and transformational visionary styles. As with coaches, servant leaders' primary concern is for their followers. They view their leadership position as most useful when they are meeting followers' needs. They place service before self-interest, and are not concerned with acquiring power, prestige, financial reward, or status. This means assuring that followers are growing as persons, becoming healthier, freer, morally mature, and autonomous in their work and life. In this sense, the servant leader is a servant first and a leader second.

Some writers describe a spiritual element as part of servant leadership.[7] These leaders urge followers to seek the power of their human spirit and let their conscience guide them as they accept their responsibilities. This can mean that servant leaders are extremely open and willing to share their own pain and frustrations with followers.

LEADERSHIP IN ACTION
Abraham Lincoln as a Servant Leader

The people were divided and the nation was at war. Prejudice, cruelty, sickness, and death all waited at the door. In this hour, Abraham Lincoln called to Washington a soldier from the field. He wanted to talk with him about something important. The soldier was a good-hearted man, but he had neglected his mother. He had not written her for 2 years, and she believed him killed. She had asked the president if he could locate his grave.

Lincoln talked with the young man sternly, but not unkindly. He told him that he must write his mother every week beginning now, or be court martialed for a crime worse than treason: ingratitude. The record shows that one hour later, the young man left. About the time spent, Lincoln said, "It needed doing."

SOURCES: D. T. Phillips. *Lincoln: Executive Strategies for Tough Times.* New York: Warner, 1992; and D. T. Donald. *Lincoln.* New York: Touchstone, 1996.

Servant leaders are often supportive, participative, and charismatic with their followers. They are excellent listeners; they seek to fully understand their followers' problems and concerns and to affirm their confidence in the followers. They try to provide followers with whatever they need to do their jobs and grow as individuals. They engage with followers in problem solving. They think the best of others and strive for moral excellence. They inspire trust by being trustworthy (that is, they are totally honest, avoid controlling followers, and focus on others' well being). They effectively communicate a vision and mission that is exciting and challenging. Servant leaders are also competent at followers' tasks, often challenge the status quo, and look for opportunities to assist others. They emphasize and model ethical behavior for followers, oppose injustice in the organization, and encourage followers to tell them what they need to perform their jobs better.[8] The Leadership in Action box on Abraham Lincoln describes an example of servant leadership.

The servant leadership style is probably most effective when followers are discouraged or face a long, difficult task. Their discouragement may come from past leaders who have made unrealistic promises or exploited followers, or from a lack of confidence in their own ability. They need a leader who is trustworthy, supports their development, and provides encouragement and confidence in their abilities.

Mother Teresa is an example of a highly committed servant leader. She devoted her life to serving the sick and poor population of India, and inspired hundreds of followers and millions of dollars in donations. On a smaller scale, in one manufacturing plant, managers give assembly-line workers time off to read thought-provoking books to help develop their minds.[9] Figure 14-6 summarizes the servant leadership style.

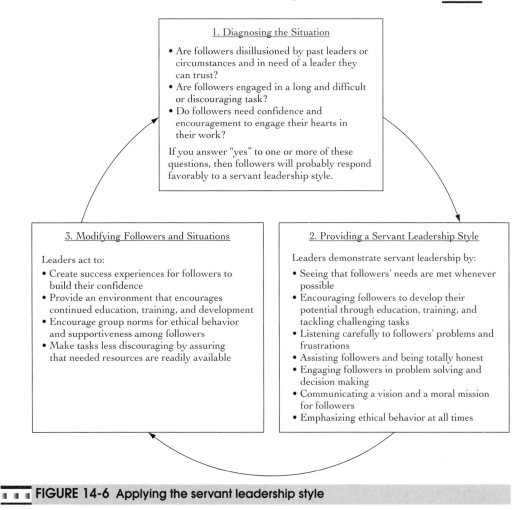

1. Diagnosing the Situation

- Are followers disillusioned by past leaders or circumstances and in need of a leader they can trust?
- Are followers engaged in a long and difficult or discouraging task?
- Do followers need confidence and encouragement to engage their hearts in their work?

If you answer "yes" to one or more of these questions, then followers will probably respond favorably to a servant leadership style.

3. Modifying Followers and Situations

Leaders act to:
- Create success experiences for followers to build their confidence
- Provide an environment that encourages continued education, training, and development
- Encourage group norms for ethical behavior and supportiveness among followers
- Make tasks less discouraging by assuring that needed resources are readily available

2. Providing a Servant Leadership Style

Leaders demonstrate servant leadership by:
- Seeing that followers' needs are met whenever possible
- Encouraging followers to develop their potential through education, training, and tackling challenging tasks
- Listening carefully to followers' problems and frustrations
- Assisting followers and being totally honest
- Engaging followers in problem solving and decision making
- Communicating a vision and a moral mission for followers
- Emphasizing ethical behavior at all times

▪▪▪▪ **FIGURE 14-6** Applying the servant leadership style

▪▪▪ Creating Leadership Enhancers and Substitutes

In addition to describing effective leadership behaviors in this book, we have also emphasized how follower characteristics and situational factors can enhance or substitute for specific leadership behaviors and affect the attitudes and performance of individuals and groups. Incompetent leaders have often been saved by followers who knew the ropes and ignored the leader's directives, while relying on their own job knowledge and experience to complete their tasks in a competent manner. Experienced leaders know that environmental factors can play a key role in many group performance situations. Plentiful supplies may allow a group to easily recover from early mistakes; technological breakthroughs or market shifts can give an organization a sudden competitive advantage; or an act of God may destroy an important competitor and give an organization a virtual monopoly. Internal organizational factors such as company programs for job redesign, gainsharing, goal setting, empowerment, autonomous work groups, and self-management can be leadership substitutes and significantly affect employee attitudes and performance. These programs are all created, controlled, and influenced by leaders in organizations.

Leaders have two general strategies to influence followers. First, they can use the behaviors described in this book, which have direct effects on followers' reactions and behaviors. Second, they can modify or develop organizational programs and environmental factors that help guide and shape followers' behavior and performance. This second strategy involves creating leadership enhancers or substitutes, and it may take longer to show favorable effects on followers. However, many organizational programs have the potential to foster increased ability, motivation, and performance among followers. For example, company-wide reward systems or goal-setting programs may *enhance* a leader's effectiveness by making followers increasingly responsive to leaders. Other programs that emphasize job redesign, empowerment, autonomous work groups, or self-management can allow followers to govern their own work behavior more effectively and actually substitute for certain behaviors leaders have often provided in the past.

We emphasize that leadership substitutes *do not* eliminate the need for leadership in organizations. They can, however, reduce or eliminate the need for leaders to do certain things that have occupied much of their time. The time a leader devotes to supervising of operations, providing interpersonal strokes to bolster follower confidence, or monitoring performance of individuals and groups, can all be drastically reduced by creatively modifying situations and followers to create substitutes. Substitutes can have enduring effects, as when a challenging job becomes a lasting source of motivation for an employee, or when a gainsharing program engages all employees in actively achieving organizational goals. The evidence from research shows that organizational programs that create these leadership substitutes can foster increased productivity and improve employee attitudes and behaviors.

One educational expert recently described how substitutes for leadership can be developed in schools as a strategy to foster morality and virtue, as well as high-quality performance among teachers, students, administrators, and involved community members.[10] At an early stage of a school's development, the leader provides the behaviors described in this book to guide and motivate staff members to work on tasks that are needed for goal accomplishment and to create satisfying experiences in the process. At this early stage, the leader's behavior directly affects followers' actions, attitudes, and performance.

At a more evolved stage of a school's development, the leader encourages a culture or a *sense of community,* with norms and goals for excellence and achievement. This culture includes shared values, commitments, and obligations to work professionally, and collegiality to carry out those norms and goals. These *norms, shared values, professionalism,* and *collegiality* represent substitutes for leadership that glue the school together by governing and guiding members' behavior and engaging them in intrinsically satisfying work as an organizational community. These substitutes thus provide much of what school leaders have traditionally provided through directive, reward and punishment, or even charismatic leadership behaviors. Guidance, motivation, and satisfaction come from increasingly self-managed members of the school community, who rely on each other to obtain help, advice, ideas, encouragement, and feedback to carry out their shared values, norms, and goals.

Such substitutes for leadership may be the only leadership strategy that adequately addresses the complex and changing demands that now face organizations. These substitutes empower individuals to develop their own problem-solving abilities, to communicate and cooperate with their colleagues, and to develop and enforce codes of ethics that define individual duties and moral responsibilities. By creating more self-management, organizational leaders are freed up for boundary-spanning activities needed to obtain the political, resource, moral, and administrative support to foster organizational performance and development.

This work on substitutes for leadership in schools represents one application of the situational modification strategy for leadership. In the long run, this approach is designed to help organizational leaders, members, and clients achieve human and organizational goals with efficiency and integrity.

▪▪▪ Globalization and Cross-Cultural Leadership

Globalization is probably the most significant trend affecting business today. Large business organizations cannot ignore the production and marketing of products and services in other countries. Microsoft operates in over 60 countries, Toyota produces in 39 countries, and one Chinese company conducts business in over 160 nations. Effective leadership is critical to the success of multinational companies. To be effective, leaders must adapt their leadership behavior to the national culture and societal institutions where they are situated.[11]

It may seem obvious that leadership approaches must reflect the tremendous differences among cultures. Early experts noted that it is probably useless to try to use participative leadership in authoritarian cultures in which more people believe in the divine right of kings than in Jeffersonian democracy.[12] Leadership and organizational practices can be quite dissimilar in different cultures, such as large Korean business organizations (chaebols), in which basing pay on seniority (not performance) is preferred in order to maintain group harmony,[13] and in Japan, where frank discussions of followers' performance are avoided at work, but often take place after work while socializing with workers (often over food and drink). These practices differ from those in most organizations in North America and Western Europe. In recent years, cross-cultural researchers have begun to address which cultural values, norms, and beliefs are most important for leadership, and how effective leaders adjust their styles to fit these cultural characteristics.

One of the authors is a co-investigator for the Global Leadership and Organizational Behavior Effectiveness (GLOBE) Project, which is probably the largest cross-cultural leadership research project ever conducted. It began in the early 1990s and is still ongoing, with 170 co-investigators throughout the world. Bob House, a world-class leadership researcher and writer, initiated and directs the GLOBE Project. Over 17,000 leaders and managers have been studied from 950 different organizations in 62 countries. The GLOBE Project has identified nine cultural dimensions that are most important for effective leadership. The dimensions are: power distance, uncertainty avoidance, humane orientation, institutional collectivism, ingroup collectivism, assertiveness, gender egalitarianism, future orientation, and performance orientation. These dimensions are described in Table 14-2, along with specific statements that represent each dimension.

Some researchers have suggested that institutional collectivism and ingroup collectivism are two of the most important dimensions of cultural variation. Others

TABLE 14-2 GLOBE Project dimensions of culture that are important for leadership

Culture Dimension	*Statement Describing Each Specific Dimension*
Power Distance: The degree to which members of a collective expect power to be distributed equally.	Followers are expected to obey their leaders without question.
Uncertainty Avoidance: The extent to which a society, organization, or group relies on social norms, rules, and procedures to alleviate unpredictability of future events.	Most people lead highly structured lives with few unexpected events.
Humane Orientation: The degree to which a collective encourages and rewards individuals for being fair, altruistic, generous, caring, and kind to others.	People are generally very tolerant of mistakes.
Institutional Collectivism: The degree to which organizational and societal institutional practices encourage and reward collective distribution of resources and collective action.	Leaders encourage group loyalty even if individual goals suffer.
Ingroup Collectivism: The degree to which individuals express pride, loyalty, and cohesiveness in their organizations or families.	Employees feel great loyalty toward this organization.
Assertiveness: The degree to which individuals are assertive, confrontational, and aggressive in their relationships with others.	People are generally dominant in their relationships with each other.
Gender Egalitarianism: The degree to which a collective minimizes gender inequality.	Boys are encouraged more than girls to attain a higher education. (Scored inversely.)
Future Orientation: The extent to which individuals engage in future-oriented behaviors such as delaying gratification, planning, and investing in the future.	More people live for the present than for the future. (Scored inversely.)
Performance Orientation: The degree to which a collective encourages and rewards group members for performance improvement and excellence.	Students are encouraged to strive for continuously improved performance.

▪ ▪ ▪ ▪ ▪ ▪ ▪ ▪ ▪

SOURCE: Adapted from R. J. House, P. J. Hanges, M. Javidan, P. W. Dorfman, and V. Gupta (Eds.). *Culture, Leadership, and Organizations: The GLOBE Study of 62 Societies*. Thousand Oaks, CA: Sage, 2004.

believe in the importance of power distance in determining which type of leadership is best. GLOBE Project researchers hope to identify which culture dimensions are most important in different regions of the world.

GLOBE Project researchers have also identified 21 leadership dimensions (including behaviors, traits, and skills) that can be important for leadership in different cultures. These leadership dimensions reflect many of the leadership behaviors, traits, and skills described in this book. Examples of GLOBE Project leadership dimensions include integrity, modesty, collaborative, performance oriented, humane, participative, diplomatic, and charismatic. Investigators are currently studying the effects of these leadership dimensions on follower and organizational performance in the different cultures included in the study. This should provide definitive information for leaders on which leadership styles work best in specific types of cultures.

Several preliminary findings by different researchers provide some indication of where specific leadership approaches are most effective and where the results are unclear. Leaders' supportiveness improves followers' attitudes in nearly every country studied.[14] This is not surprising because supportive leaders show concern for followers and are considerate and available to listen to their problems. Cross-cultural studies of directive leadership are often inconclusive, although there is some indication that this leadership behavior is especially effective in the Middle East.[15] Middle Eastern countries tend to be high in ingroup collectivism, power distance, and humane orientation culture dimensions, and low in gender egalitarianism, future orientation, and performance orientation. Some measures of directive leadership still include elements of autocratic and authoritarian behavior, so these findings may not be totally comparable to current studies that exclude these outdated elements of directiveness.

Leaders' contingent reward behavior has resulted in high levels of followers' satisfaction and commitment in many different cultures.[16,17] This leadership behavior can also encourage high followers' performance, but this may be most prevalent in individualistic cultures. The impacts of leaders' reward behavior may also vary in different cultures, depending on whether the leader uses tangible or intangible rewards. Leaders' contingent punishment behavior may be most impactful in highly individualistic cultures such as the United States.

The cross-cultural findings regarding participative leadership provide some evidence about where this pattern is most effective. Cultures that are moderate or low in power distance and uncertainty avoidance (such as the United States) probably encourage participative practices by leaders, and followers likely respond favorably. In cultures that are high in power distance and uncertainty avoidance (such as many countries in Eastern Europe), participation is less likely to be effective with followers. Participation is a major leadership dimension in the GLOBE Project study, so more results should soon be available regarding these tentative conclusions.

Proponents of charismatic or transformational leadership believe that this leadership behavior pattern is effective in virtually all cultures.[18,19] They admit, however, that a charismatic leader's behavioral strategy may need to be adapted to cultural and other situational factors. This was demonstrated by two very different charismatic leaders— Mahatma Gandhi and General George Patton. Gandhi's exhortations of love and acceptance for others aroused the need for affiliation among followers. This was consistent with the high level of humane orientation in Indian culture and the strategy of peaceful resistance used against the British occupation of India. General Patton's speeches to his troops in World War II evoked negative images of the enemy, which aroused power motives in the soldiers. Power motives are consistent with a wartime military culture, and are probably needed for success in combat. There is strong evidence that charismatic leadership improves followers' satisfaction and commitment, especially in western cultures. Its effects on follower and organizational performance appear to be highly situational, however, as noted in Chapter 8. The GLOBE Project study includes charismatic leadership as a major component, so it should provide clearer evidence on the cross-cultural effectiveness of this leadership behavior pattern.

Global business is often described as good business. Government, educational, health-related, philanthropic, and religious organizations are all becoming more global in their operations. Although our understanding of effective cross-cultural leadership is still quite limited, the GLOBE Project should provide a major step forward to increase our understanding of this important topic.

█ █ █ Equifinality in Leadership

The systems concept of equifinality refers to the fact that a final goal can be achieved from many starting points and via numerous means. Viewing organizations as systems, the final goal is usually a state of high productivity and positive follower attitudes. Many suggestions have been given in this book regarding how leaders can demonstrate specific behaviors or modify situational and follower characteristics in order to improve the performance of followers and organizations. Other recommendations addressed ways to improve follower attitudes, and decrease job burnout and turnover in organizations. The findings presented in Table 14-1 show that these outcomes and follower reactions can be attained by more than one type of leadership behavior.

For example, Table 14-1 indicates that followers' individual performance can often be significantly improved by directive, supportive, contingent reward, or charismatic leadership behaviors. Follower satisfaction and commitment are improved by most of the core leadership behaviors, and group cohesion, role clarity, and turnover can be improved by a smaller number of leadership behaviors. Of course, any leadership behavior is most effective when provided in the correct situations, but more than one type of leadership behavior can produce favorable results. This demonstrates the equifinality of the different behaviors available to leaders. Some leadership behaviors may have stronger effects on a given outcome than others, but leaders usually have behavioral choices regarding how to influence followers.

High-level organizational leaders can also use various approaches to overcome leadership problems experienced by lower-level leaders. For example, problem leaders can be trained to use a specific leadership behavior more effectively, or to use a different leadership behavior to achieve a desired outcome. When training is not a viable option due to a leader's stubbornness or some other factor, problem leaders can be replaced or transferred to different duties. If replacement is difficult due to seniority, tenure, or other constraints, a higher-level leader can modify situational or follower characteristics to *enhance* the problem leader's effects on followers. Alternatively, leadership substitutes can be created to fill in for weaknesses in the leader's behavioral skills. Because substitutes are often durable, this approach can allow the problem leader to concentrate on those aspects of leadership that match his or her skills.[20] These approaches demonstrate equifinality for high-level leaders in solving leadership problems in their organizations.

Both approaches to situational modification can improve leadership effectiveness. Creating enhancers often increases a leader's control of the situation and the direct effects of a leader's behavior on followers. Followers who lack competence, self-confidence, or self-esteem, are insecure, or have a high fear of failure may need regular interaction with the leader to maintain their sense of well-being and focus on the job.

Enhancers facilitate followers' interactions with and responsiveness to the leader, usually making their reactions and performance more favorable.

Creating leadership substitutes, the other approach to situational modification, often increases followers' control of the situation. For followers who are highly trained or educated, professionally oriented, and independent in their work, substitutes are useful. They can make such employees even more capable of performing well on their own, and even less reliant on their leader. A leader's interpersonal guidance, support, personal recognition, and inspirational speeches are then less necessary in achieving favorable follower reactions and performance.

Thus, both approaches to situational modification can result in improved follower reactions and performance.[21] The correct approach often depends on the type of followers. Substitutes for leadership are appropriate to many current workforce and organizational trends, such as increasing levels of formal education and professionalism, networked computer systems, computer integrated manufacturing, and telecommuting. These trends emphasize worker competence and autonomy without the leader's frequent input, and they are common in highly developed countries. If leadership substitutes are implemented carefully, they will allow more freedom and independence for organizational employees. They will also allow leaders to spend more time on increasingly important boundary issues, building productive exchanges with all employees, and developing followers' abilities to perform on their own.

SUMMARY

Although the leadership behaviors described in this book are most effective in specific situations, their most frequent impacts were described in Table 14-1. Directive, supportive, contingent reward, and charismatic leadership behaviors are the most consistent at improving followers' and groups' actual performance. Directive leadership also strongly improves followers' role clarity, and charismatic and social exchange behaviors result in higher performance ratings by the leader's superior. Supportive, directive, charismatic, and social exchange behaviors produce strong improvements in followers' satisfaction, commitment, and motivation—although charismatic leadership can also produce strong negative reactions by followers. Participative and contingent reward leadership also improve followers' attitudes, but not quite as strongly as the other leadership behaviors. Supportive, directive, and charismatic leadership all reduce followers' turnover, burnout, and intentions to quit, and directive and supportive leadership increase group cohesion.

A leader's style is usually some combination of the leadership behaviors described in this book. Leaders often have distinctive styles, and several such styles are described in this chapter—including the coach, human relations specialist, controlling autocrat, transformational visionary, transactional exchange, and servant. Each of these styles is appropriate for different situations.

Leaders can use two general strategies to influence followers and groups. First, they can influence followers and groups directly by exhibiting the leadership behaviors described in this book. Second, they can influence followers and groups indirectly by modifying the situation to create enhancers or substitutes for leadership. The second approach often takes longer to show its favorable effects, but these effects may last longer than the effects from the first approach. Both approaches are needed in organizations of the 21st century.

Globalization is probably the most significant organizational trend affecting today's organizations. This means that leaders must adapt their behaviors to reflect the culture in which they work. Researchers have identified several dimensions of culture that are important for leaders to consider. Research is currently underway to identify the specific leadership behaviors that best serve different cultural situations.

Equifinality describes the fact that a final goal can be reached from many starting points and via numerous means. Because improvements in followers' attitudes and performance can be obtained from different leadership behaviors, enhancers, and substitutes, leaders usually have choices in how to influence followers. These choices represent equifinality in leadership, and correctly matching their behavioral choices with the situation is the key to effective leadership.

KEY TERMS AND CONCEPTS IN THIS CHAPTER **!!!!!!!**

- Assertiveness
- Boundary spanning
- Coach leadership style
- Commitment
- Controlling autocrat leadership style
- Equifinality
- Followership
- Future orientation
- Gender egalitarianism
- Globalization

- Group cohesion
- Human relations specialist leadership style
- Humane orientation
- Impression management skills
- Ingroup collectivism
- Institutional collectivism
- Leadership styles
- Need for affiliation
- Performance orientation

- Personal need for power
- Power distance
- Role clarity
- Servant leadership style
- Social exchanges
- Socialized need for power
- Transactional exchange leadership style
- Transformational visionary leadership style
- Uncertainty avoidance

REVIEW AND DISCUSSION QUESTIONS **!!!!!!!**

1. What four leadership behaviors have been most consistent at increasing the quality or quantity of performance by followers and groups? Why do you think these leadership behaviors consistently increase performance?
2. Describe specific situations in which charismatic and social exchange behaviors improved your opinion of a leader's performance. Why did these behaviors work so well?
3. Describe a leader you have observed or heard about who used a coach leadership style. What situational characteristics contributed to the effectiveness of this leader's coaching?
4. Identify situations you have observed or heard about in which leaders who used a human relations specialist leadership style were effective or ineffective in achieving high levels of performance. What situational factors made the human relations specialist leadership style effective or ineffective?
5. Think of a controlling autocrat leader you have observed or heard about. What behaviors did the leader use to influence followers? Was the controlling autocrat leader effective? How did followers react to the controlling autocrat leader?
6. Why do you think that the transformational visionary leadership style is currently very popular? How effective would transformational visionary leaders be in influencing your behavior?
7. Of the leadership styles presented in this chapter, which is the closest to your preferred style as a leader? How would you modify the style to better fit your preferred leadership style?
8. Describe why globalization has important implications for leadership in the 21st century.
9. Explain the concept of equifinality in leadership. How could you use this concept to be a more effective leader?

▪▪▪▪ C A S E   I N C I D E N T S ▪▪▪▪

Gaining Compliance

Jim Stanley has accepted his first supervisory job after graduating in the top 5 percent of his college class with a degree in management. Jim's new position is supervisor of the purchasing department for a state government agency. By working hard in the agency's training program and spending considerable time studying on his own, Jim has gained an in-depth understanding of the agency's policies on how jobs are to be done. From Jim's first day on the job, he has carefully explained to employees how the agency's policies and procedures are to be followed in accomplishing all work. Even with repeated explanations, some employees insist that they be allowed to do their jobs their own way, which Jim feels is not according to agency policies.

Jim took David Murphy aside, one of the employees who continually refuses to cooperate, and said, "You are going to have to do the job according to agency procedures."

David replied, "No, sometimes you have to be practical and get around the agency's bureaucratic procedures. The way I do the job is the most effective way."

Jim responded, "I am not going to be a party to getting around agency policies and procedures. You either do it the way I told you, or I'll recommend that you be replaced."

David retaliated with, "If you knew anything about management, you'd realize that you should support employees. We can do the best job when we do it our own way."

Jim is beginning to wonder if there is any way to get through to David that things must be done according to agency policies and procedures. Jim knows that David thinks that because he is a civil service employee, he cannot be fired or the subject of severe disciplinary action. ▪

DISCUSSION QUESTIONS

1. How would you characterize Jim Stanley's leadership style? What leadership behaviors seem to dominate Jim's attempts to influence David's behavior?
2. What situational and follower factors should Jim take into account in deciding which leader behaviors would be effective?
3. What advice would you give Jim about how to effectively influence the behavior of his employees and achieve the objectives of the agency?

Leadership in a Sexual Assault Recovery Center

La Grange Sexual Assault Recovery Services is a nonprofit organization to aid the recovery of victims of sexual assault. Their goal is to help transition the clients from victim to survivor. La Grange was first organized in 1993 by a small group of feminists because there were no services available to victims of sexual abuse in the area. The cofounders of La Grange were Shannon White and Jean Martin. Shannon White was a professional trainer and consultant, and Jean Martin was an educator of the deaf. The idea behind the structure of the organization was to emphasize a feminist ideology, in which there was consensus decision making, a collaborative work environment, and a connected and supportive staff. Jean Martin was the executive director and Shannon White was the main advocate trainer. The board consisted of citizens from the helping professions, such as psychotherapy, social work, health, education, and one previous client.

La Grange currently serves about 40 new clients a month, and continues to aid in the recovery of former clients. The state has a high annual number of sexual assaults, especially incest. La Grange has grown steadily, and provides essential resources and services that a victim needs to transition to a survivor and maintain mental and emotional health. Crisis intervention is the main service provided by La Grange, although ongoing group and individual counseling are also available.

The care providers of La Grange consist of trained victim's advocates, sexual assault nurse examiners (SANEs), and psychotherapists who specialize in victimization and recovery. SANEs are specifically trained and certified to collect forensic evidence and address the specialized needs of victims of sexual assault. The clients of La Grange range from 3-year-old victims and their families to 87-year-old senior citizens. About 90 percent are female, and they include a wide range of ethnicities, races, orientations, education levels, social classes, and religions. The wide variety of clients and their needs suggests that a leader of La Grange should be very likeable and have referent power, in order to establish and maintain the relationships and loyalties in the community that help make the organization successful. Strong networking and consciousness-raising skills would also be essential to continue educating the public

about the effects of sexual abuse, as well as the need to aid in the recovery of the victims, their families, and their friends. A leader of La Grange would also need to be sensitive to the needs and emotional states of those around him or her, be caring, and be able to communicate that caring appropriately.

In 1994, one year after the founding of La Grange, Jean Martin resigned as executive director and Shannon White took over this duty. Shannon inspired those who worked with her to feel the importance of the work at hand. Although she wanted the organization to be based on feminist principles, there was a sense of hierarchy, with Shannon in charge. She discussed problems with individual board members prior to the meetings to achieve general consensus before the group gathered to discuss the issues. In the community, Shannon was either loved or hated, but the connections she made were strong and long lasting. Shannon White left La Grange in 1996 to further her education, and because of personal conflicts with the idea of crisis intervention and societal norms. She believed that sexual assault was a norm of society, not a crisis. She felt that the goal of La Grange should be to increase awareness of the problem as a defect in socially acceptable behaviors, rather than trying to "fix" the victim after the damage was done.

In 1996, Carla Melendrez took over as executive director. Carla has a background in social services with a specialization in working with individuals who are physically and emotionally challenged. With this transition, La Grange evolved into a more traditional nonprofit human service organization and lost most of its feminist roots. Carla developed La Grange into a more efficient and organized service provider, and increased community awareness by training and soliciting help from the local hospital staff and the police force. Although the training of advocates may have lagged from the dynamic feminist approach used by Shannon White, training of hospital staff and members of the police force grew rapidly. The board changed from a group of women in the helping professions to a group of more traditional citizens that represented the community, with backgrounds in finance, marketing, mental health, and law enforcement. The new board was able to maximize fundraising and networking for the organization.

Under Carla's administration, the staff of La Grange grew in size and the organization became more formalized. The number of Spanish-speaking advocates also increased to reflect the large Spanish-speaking population in the area. Other management positions were created to formalize the organization's structure and to coordinate resources, ideas, and make decisions. Because of the expanded staff, Carla had less direct contact with the clients than did the former executive directors. This was probably helpful because it allowed her more time to work on grants (she was an excellent grant writer), and she had an abrasive personality. She formalized the relationship between La Grange and the local hospital through a grant she wrote creating a specialized training project to certify nurses as SANEs. The grant expanded training of new and existing SANEs to include the use of specialized forensic evidence equipment, medications given to clients, and provided for physical space in the local hospital. In order to continue the services to victims and their families, La Grange must maintain strong and appropriate leadership. The organizational chart for La Grange (see Figure 14.7) displays the relationship between Carla Melendrez, the executive director of La Grange, and the other managers and groups in the organization, each needing a distinct type of leadership.

The board of directors is composed of volunteers in the community who donate their time, energy, and resources to aid the cause of assisting victims. They are active in community involvement and educating the

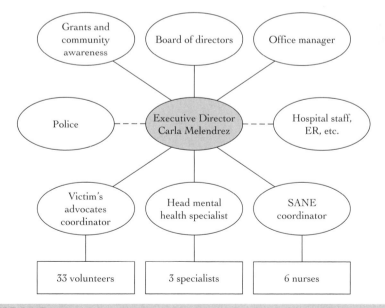

⊪ **FIGURE 14-7** La Grange organizational structure

SOURCE: This case was initially prepared by Jennette Fisher.

public about La Grange. They help represent the center and network for the center, and are involved with the director in planning and decision making. The office manager and staff are extremely important in maintaining the orderly operation of the center to assure that clients are served in an orderly manner. They also maintain client records to assure that needed services and follow-up are provided. The hospital staff and police force are not a part of La Grange, but they provide essential resources and information to help serve the clients. All must work together to help the assault victim with minimal confusion and conflict. The SANEs are essential to the operation of La Grange because they provide medications and needed treatment, as well as gather evidence regarding the assault. The mental health specialists provide follow-up on clients, which is essential for the healing process and recovery. The initial intervention takes place through the victim's advocates, who are volunteers from the community.

When working with a board, especially one for a nonprofit organization, it is essential to involve the members in making final decisions, requesting ideas and suggestions, and allowing all of the voices to be heard. This type of leadership encompasses feelings of involvement and influence, commitment to the goals at hand, and satisfaction with the decision-making process. If Carla

used an inappropriate style for the board, the whole reason for maintaining a board would be shattered. There is a shared leadership between the board and Carla. The board has some jurisdiction over community involvement and educating the public. They also help with the planning and decision making, although they have no contact with clients or with any of the services that are in direct contact with the clients. The board serves as a tool to incorporate the ideas, knowledge, and skills of its members and to use these skills to promote the agency. Representing and networking in the community are key aspects of the job of board members, as well as shared decision making. It is important to note that the members of the board volunteer their time, energy, and resources to aid in the cause of assisting victims. ■

DISCUSSION QUESTIONS

1. Describe the leadership behaviors necessary and appropriate for a director in dealing with each of the following: the board of directors, the office staff, the police, the hospital staff, the SANEs, the mental health specialists, and the volunteer victims' advocates.

2. How does leading a nonprofit organization differ from leading other organizations? What effect does this have on an executive director in this organization?

ENDNOTES ▐ ▐ ▐ ▐ ▐ ▐ ▐

1. Hersey, P., and Blanchard, K. H. (1984). *Management of Organizational Behavior: Utilizing Human Resources,* 4th ed. Englewood Cliffs, NJ: Prentice Hall; Marcic, D. and Seltzer, J. (1995). *Organizational Behavior: Experiences and Cases.* Cincinnati, OH: Southwestern College Publishing; and Vecchio, R. P. (1997). Situational leadership theory: An examination of a prescriptive theory. In R. P. Vecchio (Ed.), *Leadership: Understanding*

the *Dynamics of Power and Influence in Organizations.* Notre Dame, IN: University of Notre Dame Press, 318–333.

2. Lau, J. B., and Jelinek, M. (1984). *Behavior in Organizations: An Experiential Approach.* Homewood, IL: Irwin.

3. Blake, R. R., and Mouton, J. S. (1983). *Consultation: A Handbook for Industrial and Organizational Development.* Reading, MA: Addison-Wesley, 564–565; and Costley, D., Santana-Melgoza, C., and Todd, R.

(1994). *Human Relations in Organizations,* 5th ed. St. Paul, MN: West.

4. Bass, B. M. (1997). Does the transactional-transformational leadership paradigm transcend organizational and national boundaries? *American Psychologist,* 52, 130–139; and Bass, B. M. (1997). From transactional leadership to transformational leadership: Learning to share the vision. In R. P. Vecchio (Ed.), *Leadership: Understanding the Dynamics of Power and Influence in Organizations.* Notre Dame, IN: University of Notre Dame Press, 318–333.

5. Daft, R. L. (1999). *Leadership: Theory and Practice.* New York: Dryden.

6. Hollander, E. P. (1978). *Leadership Dynamics: A Practical Guide to Effective Relationships.* New York: Free Press; Hollander, E. P. (1993). Legitimacy, power, and influence: A perspective on relational features of leadership. In M. M. Chemers and R. Ayman (Eds.), *Leadership Theory and Research: Perspectives and Directions.* New York: Academic Press; and Jacobs, T. O. (1970). *Leadership and Exchange in Formal Organizations.* Alexandria, VA: Human Resources Research Organization.

7. Daft. *Leadership: Theory and Practice.*

8. Dubrin, A. J. (2004). *Leadership: Research Findings, Practice, and Skills,* 4th ed. New York: Houghton Mifflin.

9. Daft. *Leadership: Theory and Practice.*

10. Sergiovani, T. J. (1992). *Moral Leadership: Getting to the Heart of School Improvement.* San Francisco: Jossey-Bass.

11. Dorfman, P. W. (2004). International and cross-cultural leadership research. In B. J. Punnett and O. Shenker (Eds.), *Handbook for International Management Research,* 2nd ed. 265–355. Ann Arbor, MI: University of Michigan Press.

12. Haire, M., Ghiselli, E. E., and Porter, L. (1966). *Managerial Thinking: An International Study.* New York: Wiley.

13. Steers, R. M., Shinn, Y. K., and Ungson, G. R. (1989). *The Chaebol: Korea's New Industrial Might.* New York: Harper.

14. Dorfman, P. W., Howell, J. P., Hibino, S., Lee, J. K., Tate, U., and Bautista, A. (1977).

Leadership in western and Asian countries: Commonalities and differences in effective leadership processes across cultures. *Leadership Quarterly,* 8(3), 233–274.

15. Scandura, T. A., Von Glinow, M. A., and Lowe, K. B. (1999). When east meets west: Leadership "best practices" in the United States and the Middle East. In W. Mobley, M. J. Gessner, and V. Arnold (Eds.), *Advances in Global Leadership,* Vol. 1. Stamford, CT: JAI Press, 235–248.

16. Dorfman, Howell, Hibino, Lee, Tate, and Bautista. Leadership in western and Asian countries: Commonalities and differences in effective leadership processes across cultures.

17. Podsakoff, P. M., Dorfman, P. W., Howell, J. P., and Todor, W. D. (1986). Leader reward and punishment behaviors: A preliminary test of a culture-free style of leadership effectiveness. *Advances in International Comparative Management,* 2, 95–138.

18. House, R. J., Wright, N. S., and Aditya, R. N. (1997). Cross-cultural research on organizational leadership: A critical analysis and a proposed theory. In P. C. Earley and M. Erez (Eds.), *New Perspectives in International Industrial/Organizational Psychology.* San Francisco: The New Lexington Press, 535–625.

19. Bass, B. M. (1997). Does the transactional-transformational leadership paradigm transcend organizational and national boundaries? *American Psychologist,* 52(2), 130–139.

20. Howell, J. P., Bowen, D. E., Dorfman, P. W., Kerr, S., and Podsakoff, P. M. (1990). Substitutes for leadership: Effective alternatives for ineffective leadership. *Organizational Dynamics,* 19, 21–38.

21. Podsakoff, P. M., MacKenzie, S. B., and Bommer, W. H. (1996). Meta-analysis of the relationships between Kerr and Jermier's substitutes for leadership and employee attitudes, role perceptions and performance. *Journal of Applied Psychology,* 8(4), 380–399.

Name Index

Subject Index